CONTEMPORARY AMERICAN CINEMA

Contemporary American Cinema is the first comprehensive introduction to American cinema since 1960. The book is unique in its treatment of Hollywood, alternative and non-mainstream cinema. Critical essays from leading film scholars are supplemented by boxed profiles of key directors, producers and actors; key films and key genres; and statistics from the cinema industry.

Illustrated in colour and black and white with film stills, posters and production images, the book has two tables of contents allowing students to use the book chronologically, decade-by-decade, or by subject. Designed especially for courses in cinema studies and film studies, cultural studies and American studies, *Contemporary American Cinema* features a glossary of key terms, fully referenced resources and suggestions for further reading, questions for class discussion, and a comprehensive filmography.

Individual chapters include:

- The decline of the studio system
- The rise of American New Wave cinema
- The history of the blockbuster
- The parallel histories of independent and underground film
- Black cinema from blaxploitation to the 1990s
- Changing audiences
- The effects of new technology
- Women in US cinema
- Comprehensive overview of US documentary from 1960 to the present

Linda Ruth Williams is Senior Lecturer in Film Studies in the English Department at the University of Southampton. Her previous publications include *The Erotic Thriller in Contemporary Cinema* (2005), *Critical Desire* (1995) and *Sex in the Head: Visions of Femininity and Film in D.H. Lawrence* (1993).

Michael Hammond is Senior Lecturer in Film Studies in the English Department at the University of Southampton. His previous books include *The Big Show: British Cinema Culture in the Great War* (2005) and *Contemporary Television Series* (2005).

Contributors: Michele Aaron, Christine Cornea, Sheldon Hall, Michael Hammond, Helen Hanson, Jim Hillier, Susan Jeffords, Jonathan Kahana, Mark Kermode, Geoff King, Barbara Klinger, Peter Krämer, Steve Neale, Kim Newman, Michael O'Pray, Carl Plantinga, Stephen Prince, Eithne Quinn, James Russell, Jeffrey Sconce, Mark Shiel, Peter Stanfield, Yvonne Tasker, Linda Ruth Williams, Brian Winston, Patricia Zimmermann.

CONTEMPORARY AMERICAN CINEMA

edited by

Linda Ruth Williams and Michael Hammond

The **McGraw·Hill** Companies

London Boston Burr Ridge, IL Dubuque, IA Madison, WI New York San Francisco St. Louis Bangkok Bogotá Caracas Kuala Lumpur Lisbon Madrid Mexico City Milan Montreal New Delhi Santiago Seoul Singapore Sydney Taipei Toronto

Open University Press
McGraw-Hill Education
McGraw-Hill House
Shoppenhangers Road
Maidenhead
Berkshire
England
SL6 2QL

email: enquiries@openup.co.uk
world wide web: www.openup.co.uk

and Two Penn Plaza, New York, NY 10121-2289, USA

First published 2006

A catalogue record of this book is available from the British Library

ISBN 10: 0335 21831 8 (pb) 0335 21832 6 (hb)
ISBN 13: 9 780 335 218 318 (pb) 9 780 335 218 325 (hb)

Library of Congress Cataloging-in-Publication Data
CIP data applied for

Typeset by YHT Ltd
Printed in Great Britain by Bell and Bain Ltd, Glasgow

for
Alex and Sarah Hammond
and Georgia and Gabriel Williams

CONTENTS

The 1970s

The 1980s

The 1990s and Beyond

1980s

Genres and Movements

Science Fiction and Fantasy
– Kim Newman

MTV
– Mark Kermode

Key Films

Heaven's Gate
– Mark Kermode

Do the Right Thing
– Michael Hammond

Back to the Future
– Michael Hammond

Desperately Seeking Susan
– Helen Hanson

Key Players

Simpson and Bruckheimer
– Mark Kermode

Tim Burton
– Michael Hammond

Miramax
– Mark Kermode

Arnold Schwarzenegger
– Christine Cornea

Barbra Streisand
– Michele Aaron

Sigourney Weaver
– Linda Ruth Williams

1990s and beyond

Genres and Movements

Hong Kong in Hollywood
– Mark Kermode

Sequels, Series and Spin-offs
– Kim Newman

Neo-*Noir* and Erotic Thrillers
– Linda Ruth Williams

Key Films

Titanic
– Michael Hammond

Toy Story
– Linda Ruth Williams

The Silence of the Lambs
– Yvonne Tasker

Unforgiven
– Michael Hammond

Key Players

The Agent
– Michael Hammond

Tom Hanks
– Michael Hammond

The Hughes Brothers
– Mark Kermode

John Singleton
– Michael Hammond

Jodie Foster
– Linda Ruth Williams

Kathryn Bigelow
– Yvonne Tasker

Quentin Tarantino
– Mark Kermode

NOTES ON CONTRIBUTORS

Michele Aaron lectures in the Department of American and Canadian Studies at the University of Birmingham, UK. She is the author of *Spectatorship: The Power of Looking On* (2006), and editor of *The Body's Perilous Pleasures* (1999) and *New Queer Cinema: A Critical Reader* (2004), as well as articles on queer film and television, Jewishness and gender.

Christine Cornea is a Lecturer in the Film and Television Studies Department at the University of East Anglia, UK. Her publications include essays on the cyborg for *Blackwell's Companion to Science Fiction* and on David Cronenberg for *Velvet Light Trap*. Her book on the history of science fiction cinema is forthcoming with Edinburgh University Press.

Sheldon Hall lectures in film history, theory and criticism at Sheffield Hallam University, UK. He is the author of *Zulu: With Some Guts Behind It* (2005). Among the other books to which he has contributed are *The Movie Book of the Western*, *The British Cinema Book* (second edition), *British Historical Cinema*, *Genre and Contemporary Hollywood*, *The Cinema of John Carpenter: The Technique of Terror*, *Unexplored Hitchcock*, *Journeys of Desire: European Actors in Hollywood* and the BFI *Reference Guide to British and Irish Film Directors*. He is now co-writing, with Steve Neale, *Spectacles, Epics and Blockbusters*.

Michael Hammond lectures in Film in the English Department at the University of Southampton. He is the author of *The Big Show: British Cinema Culture in the Great War* (2006) and is co-editor with Lucy Mazdon of *The Contemporary Television Series* (2005). He is presently working on a new monograph entitled *The After-image of the Great War in Hollywood Cinema, 1919–1939*.

Helen Hanson is a Lecturer in Film in the School of English, University of Exeter, UK. Her research interests include gender and genre, particularly in the Classical Hollywood Cinema, and the technologies, practices and aesthetics of sound production in the studio era. Her publications include *Hollywood's Gothic Heroines* (I. B. Tauris, forthcoming), and essays on sound effects (for *Sound Journal*), sound in *film noir* (for *The Cambridge Companion to Film Music*) and contemporary versions of the Gothic Woman's film (for *Gothic Studies*).

Jim Hillier is a Senior Lecturer in Film Studies in the Department of Film, Theatre and Television, University of Reading, UK. He is the author of *The New Hollywood* (1993), co-author of *The Film Studies Dictionary* (2001), editor of *American Independent Cinéma* (2001) and *Cahiers du Cinéma Vols 1 and 2* (1985 and 1986), and co-editor, with Peter Wollen, of *Howard Hawks: American Artist* (1996).

Susan Jeffords is Professor of Women's Studies and English Studies at the University of Washington, where she is currently serving as Dean of Social Sciences. She is the author of *The Remasculinization of America: Gender and the Vietnam War* (1989), *Hard Bodies: Hollywood Masculinity in the Reagan Era* (1994), and is co-editor, with Lauren Rabinovitz, of *Seeing through the Media: The Persian Gulf War* (1994). She is currently working on a book exploring narratives about terrorism.

Jonathan Kahana teaches in the Department of Cinema Studies at New York University. His writing on documentary has appeared in *Afterimage*, *Film Quarterly*, and *Social Text*. He is completing a book on the public spheres of American documentary.

Film critic **Mark Kermode** writes and broadcasts widely on film and cultural issues on UK radio and television, and has made numerous documentaries on film subjects, including *The Fear of God: 25 Years of The Exorcist*, *On the Edge of Blade Runner*, *Alien: Evolution*, and *Shawshank: The Redeeming Feature*. He is resident film critic for BBC Radio Five, writes regularly for *The Observer*, and is contributing editor to the British Film Institute journal *Sight and Sound*. He is the author of *The Exorcist* (BFI Modern Classics, 1997) and *The Shawshank Redemption* (BFI Modern Classics, 2003).

Geoff King is a Reader in Film and TV Studies at Brunel University, UK. He is the author of books including *Spectacular Narratives: Hollywood in the Age of the Blockbuster* (2000), *New Hollywood Cinema: An Introduction* (2002), *Film Comedy* (2002) and *American Independent Cinema* (2005).

Barbara Klinger is Associate Professor and Director of Film and Media in the Department of Communication and Culture at Indiana University, USA. She is the author of *Melodrama and Meaning: History, Culture, and the Films of Douglas Sirk* (1994) and *Beyond the Multiplex: Cinema, New Technologies, and the Home* (forthcoming 2006).

Peter Krämer teaches Film Studies at the University of East Anglia, UK. He has published essays on American film and media history, and on the relationship between Hollywood and Europe, in *Screen*, *The Velvet Light Trap*, *Theatre History Studies*, *History Today*, *Film Studies*, *Scope*, *Sowi: Das Journal für Geschichte, Politik, Wirtschaft und Kultur*, *The Historical Journal of Film, Radio and Television*, and numerous edited collections. He is the author of *The New Hollywood: From Bonnie and Clyde to Star Wars* (2005), and the co-editor of *Screen Acting* (1999) and *The Silent Cinema Reader* (2004). He also co-wrote a book for children entitled *American Film: An A-Z Guide* (2003).

Steve Neale is Professor of Film Studies in the School of English at Exeter University, UK. He is the author of *Genre and Hollywood* (2000), co-author of *Popular Film and Television Comedy* (1990), editor of *Genre and Contemporary Hollywood* (2001) and co-editor of *Contemporary Hollywood Cinema* (1998). He is currently writing *Spectacles, Epics and Blockbusters*, co-authored with Sheldon Hall.

Kim Newman is a novelist, critic and broadcaster. His fiction works include *Anno Dracula*, *Life's Lottery* and *The Man from the Diogenes Club* under his own name and *The Vampire Genevieve* and *Orgy of the Blood Parasites* as Jack Yeovil. His non-fiction books include *Nightmare Movies*, *Horror: 100 Best Books*, *Millennium Movies*, and the BFI Classics studies of *Cat People* and *Doctor Who*, as well as *The BFI Companion to Horror* (as editor). He is a contributing editor to *Sight and Sound* and *Empire*. His short story 'Week Woman' was adapted for the TV series *The Hunger* and he has directed and written a tiny short film, *Missing Girl*.

Michael O'Pray is Professor of Film in the School of Architecture and Visual Arts, University of East London, UK. He has published widely on the avant-garde film, including, as author, *The Avant-Garde Film: Forms, Themes and Passions* (2003). He has also edited *Andy Warhol: Film Factory* (1989), *The British Avant-Garde Film 1926–1995: An Anthology of Writings* (1996) and, with Jayne Pilling, *Inside the Pleasure Dome: The Films of Kenneth Anger* (1990). Other publications include *Derek Jarman: Dreams of England* (1996) and *Film, Form and Phantasy: Adrian Stokes and Film Aesthetics* (2004).

Carl Plantinga is Professor of Film Studies at Calvin College, USA. He has published widely on documentary theory and history, and on film and affective response; among his books is *Rhetoric and Representation in Nonfiction Film* (1997).

Stephen Prince is Professor of Communication at Virginia Tech, USA, and President of the Society for Cinema Studies. In addition to many articles and essays, his books include *Movies and Meaning: An Introduction to Film* (2004), *Classical Film Violence: Designing and Regulating Brutality in Hollywood Cinema, 1930–1968* (2003), *A New Pot of Gold: Hollywood Under the Electronic Rainbow* (2000), *Sam Peckinpah's The Wild Bunch* (1999), *The Warrior's Camera: The Cinema of Akira Kurosawa* (1999; Chinese-language edition 1995), *Savage Cinema: Sam Peckinpah and the Rise of Ultraviolent Movies* (1998), and

Visions of Empire: Political Imagery in Contemporary American Film (1992). He was the book review editor for *Film Quarterly* for eleven years, and he has recorded numerous audio commentaries on film DVDs.

Eithne Quinn is a Lecturer in American Studies in the School of Arts, Histories and Cultures at the University of Manchester, UK. She is the author of *Nuthin' but a 'G' Thang: The Culture and Commerce of Gangsta Rap* (2005).

James Russell teaches film studies at the University of East Anglia, UK. His research deals with the interaction of commercial and creative agendas in Hollywood's production strategies since the 1950s, and he recently completed a PhD thesis examining the revival of historical epics in the 1990s.

Jeffrey Sconce is an Associate Professor in the Screen Cultures programme at Northwestern University, Illinois. He is the author of *Haunted Media: Electronic Presence from Telegraphy to Television* (2000), as well as numerous articles on film, television, and popular culture.

Mark Shiel is a Lecturer in Film Studies, and Director of the MA and PhD programmes in Film Studies at King's College, University of London, where he specializes in American cinema, especially in relation to urbanism and politics, and in Italian cinema, especially neorealism. He is a graduate of Trinity College Dublin and completed his PhD at the British Film Institute/Birkbeck College, University of London. He is the author of *Italian Neorealism: Reconstructing the Cinematic City* (2005) and co-editor of, and contributor to, *Cinema and the City: Film and Urban Societies in a Global Context* (2001) and *Screening the City* (2003). He is currently working on a second monograph, *The Real Los Angeles: Hollywood, Cinema, and the City of Angels*, to be published in 2008.

Peter Stanfield lectures in Film Studies at the University of Kent at Canterbury. His primary area of interest is film genres and cycles in American cinema. He has published two books on the Western: *Hollywood, Westerns and the 1930s: The Lost Trail* (2001) and *Horse Opera: The Strange History of the Singing Cowboy* (2002). His latest book is *Body and Soul: Jazz and Blues in American Film, 1927–63* (2005), and he is the co-editor of *Mob Culture: Hidden Histories of the American Gangster Film* (2005).

Yvonne Tasker is Professor of Film and Television Studies at the University of East Anglia, UK. She has published widely on questions of gender, sexuality and popular culture, including *Spectacular Bodies: Gender, Genre and the Action Cinema* (1993) and *Working Girls: Gender and Sexuality in Popular Cinema* (1998). Most recently she has co-edited, with Diane Negra, a forthcoming anthology entitled *Interrogating Postfeminism: Gender and the Politics of Popular Culture*.

Linda Ruth Williams is the author of four books, including *The Erotic Thriller in Contemporary Cinema* (2005), and numerous articles on contemporary US and UK cinema, twentieth-century literature, censorship, feminism and sexuality. She teaches film at Southampton University, UK, and regularly writes for the British Film Institute magazine *Sight and Sound*.

Professor Brian Winston is a Pro-Vice Chancellor at the University of Lincoln, UK. An active journalist, documentary filmmaker and writer, he worked as a producer/director at Granada Television and BBC TV in the 1960s and 1970s. In 1985, he won a US prime time Emmy for documentary scriptwriting (for WNET, New York). He regularly speaks at international documentary film festivals and continues to file journalism and broadcast, primarily for BBC Radio 4. He has served as a governor of the British Film Institute and sits on the boards of the Sheffield International Documentary Festival, the Grierson Trust, the *British Journalism Review* and Journalism Studies. His 11th book, *Lies, Damn Lies and Documentaries*, was published in October 2000. His 9th, *Media Technology and Society*, was voted the best book of 1998 by the American Association for History and Computing. His latest (and 12th), *Messages: Free Expression, Media and the West*, was published in November 2005.

Patricia R. Zimmermann is Professor of Cinema and Photography in the Roy H. Park School of Communications at Ithaca College, Ithaca, New York. She is the author of *Reel Families: A Social History of Amateur Film*, *States of Emergency: Documentaries, War, Democracies*, and co-editor of *Mining the Home Movie: Excavations in Histories and Memories*. She is also co-director of the Finger Lakes Environmental Film Festival, and serves on the boards of International Film Seminars (the Flaherty Film Seminars), *The Moving Image: The Journal of the Association of Moving Image Archivists*, and Northeast Historic Film.

EDITORS' ACKNOWLEDGEMENTS

The editors would like to thank the staff at the Open University Press/McGraw-Hill for all their support in the preparation of this book. They would also like to thank the contributors for their sterling work, and continuing enthusiasm as this large-scale work took shape. Thanks also to Ingrid Stigsdotter and Sarah Hammond for their work on the bibliography and filmography. Finally, huge thanks go to Mark Kermode and Mary Hammond for their support and encouragement throughout.

A NOTE ON BOX OFFICE FIGURES 1960–2004

This book includes some basic box office figures for the period 1960–2004. *Variety* Top Rental Films are listed annually in the Anniversary Edition. The list is compiled of figures for domestic (US-Canada) rental revenues accruing to the distributors. All films earning at least $1,000,000 domestically during the calendar year reported are included. The statement adjacent to the 1961 roundup explains this:

> The figures below are *Variety*'s roundup of rental revenues for the year just ending. They are figures for domestic (US-Canada) markets only. The key definition in the annual compilation is rentals – the money which accrues to the producer of the film as his share. This is the barometer of trade health – viz, the continuing flow of risk capital – distinct from the actual total grosses of the playoff in theatres, part of which is retained as the exhibition share. (*Variety*, Jan. 10, 1961)

Figures for films released up to 1967 included a column of 'revenue anticipated' for rental grosses, but this column was dropped from the Anniversary Edition of *Variety* from 1968 (Jan. 3) onwards. This edition included the following explanation:

> The earlier system of carrying a column of "revenue anticipated" has been abandoned for two reasons: (1) many companies declined to take an educated guess as to the eventual revenue of some films (of the 84 films listed for 1966, 33 had "undetermined" estimates), (2) too frequently estimates provided by film companies have been unrealistic. (*Variety*, Jan. 3, 1968, 23)

All box office statistics and details of award winners for this book have been compiled by Helen Hanson.

INTRODUCTION
The whats, whys and hows of this book

We have organized this book so that it will work for a range of different readers and their research requirements. We wanted to commission a set of essays that would present a cutting-edge overview of ways of looking at American cinema since the 1960s and would combine established models with new ways of thinking through histories and debates. We approached some of the best film writers and academics in the world for pieces anchored in their specialist interests, asking them to update established work to account for recent research. The result was a series of first-class essays written in lucid prose, which combined a good overview of the primary terrain with some acute critical questions. In this sense, the book stands as a collection of important new essays and shorter pieces on the history of US cinema since 1960. We hope that if you are already an established scholar in any of the fields we cover in this book, you will find in these essays some fresh thinking and provocative ways of approaching your area of interest.

We also wanted to commission a book that has an active role in pedagogic debates. We believe very strongly that the best research must have a place in students' lives and scholars' writing. This book presents that research in a number of ways, and we hope that the lively presentation and verbal accessibility that characterize our collection will aid its journey into the classroom. Firstly, and most obviously, we have organized this material chronologically. Decades are, of course, an arbitrary and often misleading means of dividing up movements and histories, but Western media culture still persists in thinking in ten-year blocks, so – perhaps if only for reasons of editorial sanity – we saw this as a clear, if flawed, framework. However, all frameworks must be ready to be twisted out of shape. Ours are broken open at a number of points: an essay that we might have placed in one particular decade's section might also contain material pertinent to an adjacent period. In fact, we actively encouraged this "bleeding" of issues across decade boundaries. Steve Neale's essay, for instance, could have been placed in the 1970s section, raising questions, as it does, about the accuracy of the critical construction of the "Hollywood Renaissance" as an all-too-narrow "window" of challenging films and visionary auteurs during the late 1960s and early 1970s. Filmmakers do not obey the strictures of ten-year boxes, and neither did our writers.

We also wanted the book to offer information in a variety of formats to suit different needs. The longer essays will give more detailed insights into historical, theoretical and critical issues; they have the space to make more extensive connections between ideas, films, filmmakers and movements. These work as part of the temporal and historical picture that each section provides, but they also work generically: Brian Winston's essay on documentary in the 1960s provides a view of US filmmaking in this period which augments Mark Sheil's account of the US New Wave and Michael O'Pray's reading of alternative cinemas in the period. Conjoined with Jonathan Kahana's, or Carl Plantinga's, or Patricia Zimmermann's essays, Winston's also contributes to a strand running throughout this book on documentary from the 1960s to the present. Sheldon Hall's work on the rise of the blockbuster complements Neale's piece on the New Hollywood and Geoff King's essay on recent blockbusters, and Barbara Klinger's study of home viewing extends the scope of Stephen Prince's account of changes in 1980s exhibition technology and industry climate; the crucial impact of video and DVD is also discussed in our introductions to the 1980s and 1990s sections.

Alongside these substantial essays are a rich range of shorter format pieces, some on genres and movements, some on key film texts, some on key players. These complement and supplement the longer essays, providing pithier delivery of important information and insights into how histories of debates have shaped reception and readings of important figures and films. Inevitably our choices are not going to be everyone's, and there will be some omissions here. We have included pieces that fill significant "gaps" – important subjects not covered in the longer essays, or material that worked best presented in this less discursive format. We based many of our choices on texts and movements that work well in the classroom, and with which we know students the world over are engaging. These short-format pieces are one way of providing a starting point for more detailed work, supplemented by our suggestions for further reading and key questions for discussion. If you are interested in researching the development of the blockbuster, for instance, you might start with Mark Sheil's essay on the US New Wave in the 1970s, or Stephen Prince's account of cinema in the age of Reagan, or Geoff King's essay on big budget spectacles from the 1990s onwards, augmented by our sidebars on Steven Spielberg, disaster films, *The Sound of Music*, *Star Wars*, *Back to the Future*, Arnold Schwarzenegger and *Titanic*. Or if you are working on developments in the industrial organization of US cinema, you might start with James Russell's essay on changes to the studio system in the 1960s or Jim Hillier's work on the rise of independent cinema, but you might also consult the shorter pieces on *Heaven's Gate* and United Artists, Miramax, Twentieth Century Fox in the 1960s, or the role of the agent. Equally, projects on women's role in American cinema might be informed by discussions such as the essay on women's cinema and the women's movement, as well as on *Desperately Seeking Susan*, on Jodie Foster, Kathryn Bigelow, or Sigourney Weaver. In this way we hope to present a constellation of connected material and ideas that can support both cross-generic and more broadly historical research projects.

The authors of each area in this book also draw upon diverse and at times competing methods and approaches. While Stephen Prince, Steve Neale, Sheldon Hall and James Russell depend on histories of the industrial infrastructure, Barbara

Klinger and Brian Winston (among others) emphasize in various ways the impact of technology, both aesthetically and culturally. Sheldon Hall and Peter Krämer look to histories of Twentieth Century Fox and Disney respectively, and Susan Jeffords outlines the ideological function of Hollywood films about Vietnam to make broader observations about the role Hollywood has played in the construction of national identity. These and other parallel and conflicting arguments, we felt, were a necessary ingredient in a book about such a large swathe of American film history. They should provide the student with examples and valuable pointers to the study of American cinema and to the rich and lively field of film studies generally.

Finally, we have called this book *Contemporary American Cinema*, yet we start in 1960 and cover over four decades. It may be fairly asked how such a wide span of time can accurately be called "contemporary". In part, this references the widely held, but also widely contested notion that contemporary cinema begins in 1960 with the demise of the studio system and the apparent change in the look, the themes, the development of new genres, and the "New Hollywood" movements that resulted. Embedded in these essays are attempts to explain these changes and shifts in a way that requires a longer view. Some of our authors address this issue explicitly with reference to arguments of "postclassical" style as markedly distinct from the Classical Hollywood. It has been convincingly argued here and elsewhere that whereas Hollywood's studio system as it was structured in the period 1917–60 radically altered during this "New Hollywood" phase, much remained intact (see Bordwell et al. 1985). As Kristin Thompson points out of the 1970s, "Anyone who believes that mainstream Hollywood films went into eclipse during this period would do well to peruse Eddie Dorman Kay's *Box Office Champs*" (Thompson 1999: 5). However, American cinema is more than Hollywood. Our object here is to present the reader with a range of soundings from this considerable period of US film history, providing the coordinates of a national cinema that extends far beyond mainstream studio and "poststudio" multiplex culture. It demonstrates what was most dominant in film culture during this period, while also exploring the forms of US cinema that have continued to resist Hollywood's dream.

References

Bordwell, D., Staiger, J. and Thompson, K. (1985) *The Classical Hollywood Cinema: Film Style and Mode of Production to 1960*. London: Routledge and Kegan Paul.

Thompson, K. (1999) *Storytelling in the New Hollywood: Understanding Classical Narrative Technique*. Cambridge, MA: Harvard University Press.

the 60s
SIXTIES

INTRODUCTION

Walking down the main street of any large to medium-sized city in the United States during 1963 you would have encountered at least one ornate film theatre. And by the look of the place you could have been forgiven for thinking that the film theatre as a modern place of relaxation and entertainment had seen better days. It would have been an older building, dating from the early twentieth century: the backlit marquees with their interchangeable lettering slightly shabby; the poster frames, with their hinged glass fronts, would be worn and probably painted with the gold and glitter of years past. The smell that would have greeted you in the foyer would have been a mixture of popcorn, stale cola-soaked and candy-stained carpet, and of course the ubiquitous smell of years of cigarette smoke. Depending on your point of view this was either an unfortunate and distinctly less preferable alternative to the television at home or the place of unqualified romance.

The films on offer there may also have been a clue to the state of the Hollywood film industry at the time. Due to the effects of the 1948 Paramount Decree by the US Supreme Court, which required the major studios to divorce their interests in their exhibition holdings, the studios had been forced throughout the 1950s to rethink their strategies for bringing audiences to cinemas and for profiting in other ways. Apart from the realization of the value of their back catalogue through selling broadcast rights to the newly established television networks, the exhibition

of films had begun to shift in terms of both the method and type of film screened.

Peter Lev has pointed to four strategies that were adopted by the industry: "the road-show, the traditional first run, the art movie, and the drive-in movie" (Lev 2003: 216).

The film you may have encountered in that urban theatre in 1963 could have been the road-show of Twentieth Century Fox's infamous *Cleopatra*. The historic box-office failure of this film was actually offset by an exhibition strategy known as "road-showing", which aimed to create a sense of the film as a "special event" in order to attract advance rental fees from exhibitors. It was this technique of exhibition that, as Sheldon Hall demonstrates in this section, actually contributed to the restabilization of the studio following the studio's overproduction in the late 1950s.

You might have encountered the joint British/US production of *Tom Jones*, which was an example of a "runaway production" – industry slang for a production undertaken outside the United States to circumvent the high cost of producing films in Hollywood due primarily to union wage demands. If the cinema was smaller, you might have seen a subtitled version of Godard's *Vivre sa vie*, released in the United States as *My Life to Live* by Union Film Distributors Inc.

Many independent urban exhibitors found niche markets for foreign films with students during the late 1950s and early 1960s, a phenomenon that has been generally recognized as a factor in the development of the "Hollywood Renaissance" of the late 1960s and early 1970s. This may have been an influence on young filmmakers such as Martin Scorsese or Kathryn Bigelow, and also a factor in building an audience for a more downbeat and reflective cinema style, which, as Mark Shiel outlines, seems to have enabled certain American fiction films to recognize and illustrate the deeper social and political conflicts at play in the United States in the latter half of the 1960s.

The new audience

These developments in exhibition can be seen as being a necessary part of the seismic changes that the Hollywood industry underwent during the decade of the 1960s. They were also responses to the longer-term effects of the problems Hollywood had been encountering since the late 1940s. Audience figures had been dropping from 1946, the banner year of film attendance of 90 million per week, to a low in 1960 of 40 million per week. One of the most important factors in this decline was undoubtedly the effect that the advent of television had on viewing habits. But this is not the complete story because audience figures were already falling before the majority of Americans owned televisions, which did not occur until the mid-1950s (Lev 2003: 8). The more plausible explanation is the migration of primarily white middle-class families from the urban areas to the suburbs. In 1940, 15 per cent of the US population lived in the suburbs whereas 32.5 per cent lived in metropolitan areas. By 1960, while the figure for metropolitan areas remained virtually the same at 32.3 per cent, those living in the suburbs had doubled to 30.9 per cent. Throughout the 1960s that figure increased to 37.6 per cent whereas the metropolitan areas decreased to

31.4 per cent. This was part of a half-century trend that by 2000, saw 50 per cent of the entire US population living in the suburbs (Sterling and Haight 1978, cited in Lev 2003: 8).

By and large, much of the migration to the suburbs in the 1940s and 1950s was made up of the growing middle class. These post-war couples were the parents of the unexpected population bubble known as the baby boom, or those born between 1946 and 1964. From the late 1940s this trend was the most significant demographic consideration for the Hollywood industry and was characterized by an increasing recognition by the industry of the teenager as the most habitual viewer. Although this remained the case at the beginning of the 1960s, the major studios were not structured in ways that could fully take advantage of it. This move away from urban centres and also from the smaller towns changed the way in which audiences viewed films.

As mentioned above, the urban centres adopted very diverse approaches to this situation, from road-showing big-budget prestige productions to screening European imports of "art" cinema. However, the story of the Hollywood industry's troubles and ultimate salvation is the story of finding ways of making films accessible to the suburbs.

The rise of drive-in theatres was in part a response to the shift to the suburbs and to the growing market of young audiences in the suburbs more generally. The growth of drive-ins from the 1940s and particularly in the 1950s partially offset the decrease in traditional picture theatres. (Lev 2003: 304). The majority of drive-ins were located outside urban centres and between, or at least near, the newly established suburban communities. Families could attend without the need to pay for babysitters and in many ways the drive-in anticipated the more private viewing afforded by television. Nevertheless the drive-in phenomenon signalled the change in post-war viewing habits – a move away from the large urban-centred deluxe movie house and towards the suburban and primarily young audience. However, the drive-in was merely a phase. For various reasons the drive-in would ultimately prove to be unreliable, and it was not until the advent of the multiplex shopping-centre cinemas, starting in the mid-1960s, that access to the suburban youth market was fully realized.

With the shifts in viewing practices, and the attempts by exhibitors to address them, came industry strategies to deal with the changes through production. One well-documented approach in the 1950s was the use of wide-screen technologies to differentiate the theatrical experience from that of the television. However, by the late 1950s studios had begun using television and its demand for product as a means of income both by selling their back catalogues from the 1930s and 1940s to networks (ABC, CBS and NBC) and by making programmes for television. While this was not undertaken by all the studios at the same time, as each studio dealt with its own move in this direction based on its ability to do so, by 1960, virtually all of the studios were involved in production for television (Balio 1990; Anderson 1994; Monaco 2001). It is clear, however, that the industry had not fully embraced television as an "income stream" in the early part of the decade as anxiety about the impact that television would have on the theatrical release business was still palpable. Among the concerns was the already considerable damage that television was perceived to have done to traditional viewing practices nationwide. Further, as Paul Monaco (2001: 17) points out, there was the fear that

the glamour of the big screen and its attendant star system would be diminished by the screening of feature films on the small television screen in the everyday environment of the home. These fears were largely unrealized and by the late 1960s the studios had grown to depend on the selling of their back catalogues to broadcast television.

In fact it is arguable that the star system became a central factor in keeping Hollywood afloat during the 1960s. For example, Elizabeth Taylor and Richard Burton's affair during the making of *Cleopatra* kept the tabloids busy throughout the year running up to the films release, which was, of course, considerable publicity for the film, albeit not as controlled as it might have been during the studio era. More important for the business, however, is the fact that the older means of controlling stars and their images that studios had employed during the 1930s and 1940s had shifted with the collapse of the studio system generally in the 1950s. In reality, the star as producer and the commensurate rise of the agent as dealmaker worked in tandem with the broader shift that the studios made toward financing film packages on a film-by-film basis, backed up by their distribution networks.

The regulation of film content also underwent considerable change in the 1960s. The Production Code, set up in 1930, had been a system that allowed the major studios to successfully avoid state censorship. The system, by which all the studios had agreed to abide, was generally that scripts were submitted for vetting by the Production Code Administration (PCA) before shooting to avoid unnecessary production expense of cutting scenes deemed unacceptable, or likely to be censored by any of the state boards and other censorship bodies. Once approved by the

PCA, the film went into production. This process was not without its conflicts and the history of the PCA's relationship with particular studio bosses, scriptwriters and directors is an entertaining one. Most of this discussion centred around the depiction of sexual relationships and the seal of approval was generally determined by whether there was either a complete disavowal of such relationships in the film or they resulted in some form of punishment or retribution for the characters who transgressed.

By the late 1950s, however, broad shifts in public attitudes towards sex had become evident. The Kinsey reports of 1948 and 1953 ran directly counter to the assumptions about sexual behaviour that had underpinned the Production Code since its inception. As a result of this shift in attitudes, films dealing more-or-less directly with themes of sexual behaviour and sexuality were gaining the seal of approval. Barbara Klinger, in her study of the advertising practices for melodramas with adult themes in the 1940s and 1950s, has noted: "the industry typically defined the adult film through a double language that emphasized its social significance to justify titillating indulgence in the spectacles provided by psychological torment, drugs, sex and murder" (1994: 37–8). Klinger has pointed out that this was partly a response to the threat of television through offering treatment of adult themes. Elia Kazan's *Splendor in the Grass* (1960), starring Natalie Wood and Warren Beatty, dealt directly with the sexual frustration of a young couple and the damage that resulted in their abstinence. An even stronger indication of the way that the "adult theme" began to become explicit for the now teenage baby boomers was the role of Sandra Dee in three films, Delmer Daves' *A Summer Place* (1959), Douglas Sirk's *Imitation of Life* (1959), and

Paul Wendkos's *Gidget* (1959). Sandra Dee played an impossibly innocent teenager confronted with her own burgeoning desires and those of adults, and in the case of *Imitation of Life*, there was a sophisticated depiction of the emotional devastation caused by issue of race in the United States. All of these films were safely within the moral parameters of the Code, but their representation of adult themes and particularly premarital sex marked out a clear shift in the attitudes of audiences.

By the mid-1960s many films, particularly European cinema, were being released without the seal of approval, and ultimately the Production Code was rendered obsolete. Jack Valenti, former aide to President Lyndon Johnson, was appointed head of the Motion Picture Association of America in 1966 and in November 1968 instigated the MPAA Ratings system. Films were rated "G" for general audiences, "M" for mature audiences, "R" for audiences over the age of 17 only, and "X" for adults only. The ratings system was effectively a means by which the industry was able to accommodate the shifting social landscape that had already been recognized by the appearance of films such as *Who's Afraid of Virginia Woolf?* (Mike Nichols, 1966) and *Bonnie and Clyde* (Arthur Penn, 1967, Fig. 2 (*see plate section*)).

Package unit system and runaway production

The move to film-by-film financing, known as "the package unit system" was one of the most important shifts in production practices, and the one that is indicative of the collapse of the studio system in the 1950s. By 1960, the major Hollywood film companies had gradually downscaled their production facilities and had moved into financing single film projects and concentrating on distribution. Janet Staiger describes the package unit system as having arisen with the independent production ventures of the 1930s, such as those by David O. Selznick or Charles Chaplin, and being characterized by neither owning nor being owned by a distribution organization (Staiger 1985: 330). The package unit system "was a short film-by-film arrangement … [where] a producer organized a film project: he or she secured financing and combined the necessary laborers … and the means of production" (Staiger 1985: 330). In the 1960s these packages were put together often by already existing stars and directors of the classical period and by newly established stars such as Paul Newman and Warren Beatty. This type of production also worked hand-in-hand with the phenomenon of "runaway productions", which had become a prominent means of production in the 1950s while creating considerable conflict with the unions in Southern California. As Steve Neale points out in his chapter in this section, this also had an impact on the developing notion in film criticism of the "auteur" or "authored film". As Neale demonstrates, many of the "auteurs" (Hawks, Hitchcock, Fuller) identified both by the *Cahiers du Cinéma* critics, such as François Truffaut, and by the American critic Andrew Sarris, had developed roles as producers and had benefited from the package unit system in terms of artistic control.

Blockbuster mentality

With production costs rising, the production of films decreased through the 1950s and 1960s. The studios had begun to concentrate their investment into fewer but more expensive prestige productions. James Russell points out that, like the package unit system, this was rooted in the independent productions of legendary producers like Selznick and Walter Wanger in the 1930s and 1940s. The benefit for studios was that they no longer held long-term contracts with talent and instead began to concentrate more and more on the prestige production as an event and on the technique of road-showing. The first half of the 1960s saw some significant successes with films such as *The Sound of Music* (1965) and *Lawrence of Arabia* (1962) as well as the high profile failure of *Cleopatra* (1963). However, in most histories of the period the blockbuster is cited as the main ingredient in the financial crisis that the studios found themselves in by the late 1960s. It is also the ruins from which the "radical" auteur-driven, youth-oriented cinema, often termed the Hollywood Renaissance, emerged. Steve Neale suggests provocatively that it is important to recognize that the story of the failure of the traditional family-oriented and middle-brow blockbuster in the second half of the 1960s countered by the more downbeat, youth-oriented and challenging films such as *Easy Rider* and *Bonnie and Clyde* is more complicated. Successful family-oriented films such as *The Love Bug*, *Fiddler on the Roof* and *Hello Dolly!* (Fig. 3 (*see plate section*)) were all made in the second half of the 1960s and were as profitable as films such as *Midnight Cowboy* (1969) and *Easy Rider*, both associated with the radicalization of Hollywood. Regardless of the success of either style of filmmaking at the time, neither was able to pull the studios out of financial crisis. By the late 1960s every major studio apart from Disney and Twentieth Century Fox had been bought up by larger corporate conglomerations. Paramount was bought by Gulf & Western and MGM by Kirk Kerkorian, a hotel and airlines magnate, under whose control MGM stopped producing films. The result of these conglomerations, apart from MGM, was that the studios were now part of larger financial concerns and were able to continue financing and distributing films. In any case the irony is that the blockbuster approach eventually became the *modus operandi* of the studios from 1975 and still holds today, although this was largely made possible by significant changes in the way films were viewed on television and in the new suburb-based shopping-centre multiplexes.

The Hollywood Renaissance and the malling of cinema

Neale's prudent questioning of the now traditional and somewhat romantic view of the Hollywood Renaissance draws a distinction between that group of films and the blockbusters of *Jaws* (1975) and *Star Wars* (1977), which are emblems of "The New Hollywood". This approach offers a helpful way of looking at the interconnections between the studios, independent producers and the development of the youth audience. For Neale, the Hollywood Renaissance is a critical construction that does not completely bear out the history told by the most profitable film lists for the last years of the decade. It is important to add to that the fact that the audience and the various modes of exhibition had changed by the late 1960s. As we have already seen, there were two significant shifts in the viewing habits of audiences. The first was the advent of television and the second was represented by the rise of the drive-in. By the late 1960s, television was having great success broadcasting previously released "road-shown" films and the studios had grown to depend on

this revenue stream considerably. On the other hand the drive-in had, by the mid to late 1960s, peaked in its attractions for audiences, and particularly the family audience. The experience of a drive-in was always second rate at best and dependent on the weather. However, there were other attractions for the youth market in the drive-in experience, as the name "passion pits" suggests, and in the relative freedom that the drive-in afforded. This was often reflected in the type of films screened. American International Pictures (AIP) founded by Samuel Z. Arkoff and Ben Nicholson in the 1950s actively courted this market. While not exclusively screened in drive-ins, these films, with their use of sensationalist and often provocative titles such as *Runaway Girls* (1956), *Premature Burial* (1962) and *The Ghost in the Invisible Bikini* (1966) had, by the mid-1960s, combined mild titillation with politics in motorcycle films such as *The Wild Angels* (1966). It also perfectly suited the mildly carnivalesque atmosphere of the drive-in on a weekend. As the majors wrestled with chasing markets in the suburbs with little but the drive-ins on offer as anything approximating the older conception of the "viewing habit", smaller independents such as AIP were producing films for these markets and also importing low-budget European horror and "art" films. Given the kind of programming available in drive-ins and the type of viewing contexts, which were less restrictive than either the enclosed cinema or certainly the living room with the television set, it is not too fanciful to suggest that this was as significant an audience for canonical "Renaissance" films such as *Bonnie and Clyde* and *Easy Rider* as were the urban audiences in the specialist theatres. In any case, the more efficient means of capturing the family market that was now in the suburbs would not become fully available until the early 1970s.

The "exploitation" cinema of AIP and their best-known director and producer, Roger Corman, had depended upon a form of "saturation releasing", which meant that they booked their films into as many theatres as possible. This technique would later be adopted by the major studios and remains a central strategy. However, in the 1960s, with the demise of the large urban theatre, this was not possible and studios were generally reluctant to give drive-ins first-run films, although this had significant exceptions in the case of the larger drive-in circuits. With the exclusive road-show mentality of the majors in the 1960s, few in the industry could see the advantage of saturation releasing. Further, the multiplex "shopping-centre" cinema had not really taken hold and the proliferation of shopping malls had not become a reality. The multiplex did, however, have its beginnings in the mid-1960s and as the decade wore on, many drive-in sites were transformed into shopping malls with cinemas at the centre (Paul 2002: 282).

Non-fiction film

There was, however, little chance of seeing any of the documentaries that were being made during the early 1960s in cinemas. Much of the work that ultimately resulted in "direct cinema" was undertaken by filmmakers such as Don A. Pennebaker and the Maysles brothers for television. As Brian Winston outlines in this section, the development of direct cinema came from an initial loss of sponsorship for documentary work after the Second World War. Ironically, perhaps, the development of documentary in the United States in the 1960s arose from the US federal government's requirement that television licence holders should provide a news service. That, coupled with the development of a viable portable sync-sound recording system, allowed filmmakers to film actual events rather than rely on the older "reconstruction" method. This gave rise to both the edited construction of filmed events and to the debate, and a set of parameters defining what documentary and specifically "direct cinema" was. Winston shows that the development of this style led to questions of editing for conflict arose where networks required drama and in many cases imposed mediating voice-overs. The development of the direct cinema style, with its attendant code of not intervening in the event being filmed, Winston argues, was an important development in documentary that led in a number of different productive directions. Not the least of these was the financially lucrative "rockumentary", first with Don Pennebaker's *Don't Look Back*, and its ultimate realizations with the theatrically released *Monterey Pop* (1970) and the Maysles brothers' *Gimme Shelter*. Documentary style in this area had found a voice and an audience by the late 1960s, in part due to the shifting terrain of exhibition.

The development of mainly urban theatres as the venues for showing European art cinema and other offbeat and specialist programmes helped to benefit not only the documentary film but also the burgeoning avant-garde cinema. If documentary had trouble with sponsorship during the 1950s, the avant-garde movement was even more "underground" as financing for films was virtually non-existent. Filmmakers such as Jonas Mekas screened his films in various types of venues from coffee houses to art house cinemas. Mainly based in the counter-culture communities of New York and San Francisco, much of this work was self-funded. By mid-decade, funding grants from arts programmes such as the newly formed National Endowment of the Arts in 1966 and the Ford Foundation became available. Michael O'Pray demonstrates the range of issues from concerns with aesthetic form to political issues, ranging from personal and gender politics to the more high-profile issues of race and violence and domestic and foreign American government policy.

The 1960s offered the mainstream Hollywood industry almost insurmountable challenges. The combination of the end of the studio system with the wider sense of social and political dissent and breakdown, a classical style of filmmaking that began to be both contested by young filmmakers and audiences alike, the rise of counter-cinema in both the avant-garde and documentary, both often aimed directly at Hollywood, gave and continue to give a sense of violent change and at times dissolution. The longer historical view demonstrates that, despite these apparent ruptures, the Hollywood industry ultimately not only survived but incorporated aesthetic innovation and reorganized its industry infrastructure to accommodate and profit from the social upheaval in such a way as to inculcate cinema as an indelible factor in the texture of late twentieth-century existence, and to saturate that experience, whether it be in the domestic or public space. A central factor in this, as outlined in this introduction, was the shifting nature of exhibition and reception.

This began with the example of a main street urban cinema in 1963. Consider now that same street in 1970. You might have your impressions of a dying film industry confirmed, or perhaps you might be delighted at the possiblity of seeing non-Hollywood and independent productions such as *Woodstock* (1970). However, a trip to the suburbs would offer a different view. Depending on your point of view, you would find either the greenshoots or the ominous dark clouds of the new Hollywood in the multiplexes and the new shopping malls. The chapters that follow provide a detailed sense of how that happened by offering accounts of the history of the various areas of production, and provide examples of the conflicting approaches used to both account for and explain developments in American cinema in the 1960s and the implications that they held for the future.

References

Anderson, C. (1994) *Hollywood TV: The Studio System in the Fifties*. Austin: University of Texas Press.

Balio, T. (1990) *Hollywood in the Age of Television*. Boston: Unwin Hyman.

Hobbs, F. and Stoops, N. (2002) *Demographic Trends in the Twentieth Century*. Washington, DC: US Government Printing Office.

Klinger, B. (1994) *Melodrama and Meaning: History, Culture, and the Films of Douglas Sirk*. Bloomington: Indiana University Press.

Lev, P. (2003) *Transforming the Screen: 1950–1959*, vol. 7 of *History of the American Cinema*. New York: Charles Scribner's Sons.

Monaco, P. (2001) *The Sixties: 1960–1969*, vol. 8 of *History of the American Cinema*. New York: Charles Scribner's Sons.

Paul, W. (2002) The K-Mart audience at the mall movies, in G.A. Waller (ed.) *Movie-Going America*. Oxford: Blackwell.

Staiger, J. (1985) The package unit system, in D. Bordwell, J. Staiger and K. Thompson (eds) *The Classical Hollywood Cinema: Film Style and Mode of Production to 1960*. London: Routledge and Kegan Paul.

Sterling, C.R. and Haight, T.R. (1978) *The Mass Media: Aspen International Guide to Communication Industry Trends*. New York: Praeger.

1

AMERICAN CINEMA, 1965–70

Mark Shiel

THE YEARS FROM 1965 to 1970 were an exceptionally intense period of change in American cinema, during which the old studio system, now commonly referred to as "Classical Hollywood", was finally swept away by a tide of social and industrial changes whose combined power was arguably the most traumatic experience that Hollywood had ever encountered. The period saw profound developments in American cinema with regard to its thematic content, formal procedures, and industrial organization, which were driven by the most divisive moment of social and political unrest in American history since the Great Depression of the 1930s (Jowett 1976: 393–427; Schindler 1996; Biskind 1999; Monaco 2003).

The Vietnam War intensified and produced a broad-based popular movement of anti-war resistance (Matusow 1984; Farber 1994). As the focus of racial tensions nationally shifted from the rural south to the urban centres of the Northeast, Midwest and West Coast, the liberal politics of the Civil Rights era gave way to the increasingly assertive Left-leaning politics of Black Power. Many of the nation's most inspiring leaders, such as Malcolm X, Martin Luther King, and Robert Kennedy were assassinated. Many American youth became increasingly sceptical of, if not hostile

towards, the spiritual emptiness and moral corruption of consumer capitalism and the hypocrisy of conventional party politics, epitomized by the presidential administrations of Lyndon B. Johnson and, from the beginning of 1969, Richard M. Nixon. Youth disaffection found expression in the political organizing of the New Left and in the hippie escapism of the counter-culture. Out of this experimental new social formation arose influential new ways of thinking about capitalism, government and corporate power, and also about gender and sexuality through the rise of feminism and the gay liberation movement, and about the natural environment through the rise of the ecology movement.

The dominant way of thinking about what happened to American cinema in these years has been to consider Hollywood cinema as generally resistant to the massive social and political changes of the day, only acknowledging them reluctantly and indirectly, or opportunistically and with a strong dose of cynicism, while other forms of filmmaking outside Hollywood addressed them more directly – for example, low-budget "exploitation" cinema, documentary and experimental film. As Peter Biskind has observed, the Hollywood establishment did not enthusiastically welcome the "creeping Leftism" that had characterized the most innovative cinema of the early 1960s in films such as *Spartacus* (1960), *Splendor in the Grass* (1961), *The Birdman of Alcatraz* (1962), *To Kill a Mockingbird* (1963), *Failsafe* (1964), or *The Pawnbroker* (1965) (Biskind 1983). The second half of the decade, however, saw the successful, although short-lived, infiltration of Hollywood by many of the radical social and political agendas of the era – youth counter-culture, the anti-war movement, environmentalism, black nationalism, and feminism – and by the formal and thematic concerns and filmmaking practices of non-Hollywood film cultures.

As Robert Ray has explained, in the late-1960s Hollywood cinema became more and more obviously split between polarized "Left" and "Right" cycles of films and between "Left" and "Right" filmmaking communities, though with Hollywood's Left-liberal tendencies holding the upper hand, at least in the public mind (Ray 1985: 296–324). Thus, for example, the social reformism of the Civil Rights era and the Great Society of President Lyndon B. Johnson were expressed in new representations of previously underrepresented or misrepresented social groups, particularly African Americans, in studies of white racism such as *Guess Who's Coming to Dinner* (1967) and *In the Heat of the Night* (1967), both starring Sidney Poitier, himself a new type of African-American film star for the new era. But, as Al Auster and Leonard Quart have pointed out, relatively mild liberal critiques such as these, essentially middle-class melodramas reorganized around the theme of racial integration, were hopelessly insufficient responses to the realities of late-1960s race relations, which between 1965 and 1967 degraded into open warfare on the streets of cities across America from Baltimore to Los Angeles (Auster and Quart 1984). Black political dissent made

virtually no appearance on American cinema screens in the period, while the larger crisis of American inner cities found expression only rarely – for example, in the hugely successful mix of road movie and study of urban poverty in New York achieved by John Schlesinger in *Midnight Cowboy* (1969).

Indeed, David James has convincingly argued that in the late 1960s Hollywood was, in large part, ideologically unable to deal directly with many of the most urgent social issues of the era and responded to these critical problems only sporadically (James 1989: 174). Melodramas such as *The Sandpiper* (1965) and *Barefoot in the Park* (1967), and even *The Graduate* (1967), couched their treatments of youth non-conformism in terms of gentle social satire and a mild impatience with the conformist pressures of middle-class domesticity. Later, more overtly counter-cultural films such as *Head* (1968) and *I Love You, Alice B. Toklas* (1968) treated the idea of youth revolution largely as zany comedy rather than serious politics. Direct representations of the war in Vietnam were almost entirely absent, except in occasional apologias for the war such as *The Green Berets* (1968), starring John Wayne. Even films such as Mike Nichols' *Catch-22* (1970) and Robert Altman's *M*A*S*H* (1970), which provided biting blackly comical critiques of the military and militarism clearly aimed at US policy in Southeast Asia, played their dramas out not in Vietnam but allegorically – in the former, against the backdrop of the US Air Force campaign in the Pacific during World War II, and in the latter within the confines of a US Army hospital during the Korean War.

However, the anti-authoritarianism of the era did find powerful, undisguised expression in those narratives of urban-to-rural escape associated with the genre of the "road movie", which carried a distinctive symbolic power in films such as *Alice's Restaurant* (1969) and *Easy Rider* (1969). The road movie, emerging as arguably the most characteristic genre of the period in the national controversy surrounding the 1967 release of Arthur Penn's *Bonnie and Clyde* (Fig. 2 (*see plate section*)), manifested a tendency towards a politicized form of pastoral escapism, which, according to its enthusiasts, testified to the mass revulsion with mainstream society and Establishment values felt by the majority of American youth, or, according to its critics, romanticized, ill-defined, nonconformist hippie sentiment without offering any productive analysis of America's urgent social problems and political corruption (Klinger 1997; Leong et al. 1997).

Continued on page 18

The Road Movie

The American road movie, by most critics' estimation, has received its most complete expression in the post-1960 Hollywood cinema. While the genre has examples from the classical period, with Frank Capra's *It Happened One Night* (1934) and John Ford's *The Grapes of Wrath* (1940) most often cited, it is not until the late 1960s with *Bonnie and Clyde* (1967) and *Easy Rider* (1969) that the road becomes a forceful metaphor for a crisis-ridden America. This potential in the road movie "American style" has inspired European filmmakers from Godard (*À Bout de Souffle* [Breathless], 1960 and *Weekend*, 1967) to Wim Wenders (*Der Amerikanische Freund* [*An American Friend*], 1977, and *Paris Texas*, 1984).

Operating in the space between the utopic comforts, or dystopic confinements, of family, home, employment or responsibility, and the promise of freedom represented by the journey on America's highways, the road movie format offered the potential for the kind of existential ambiguity characteristic of the European art film tradition that had such an influence on directors such as Penn and Hopper and the "Hollywood Renaissance" generally. The road movie format is not so much a set of generic conventions as a formal structure that fulfils the classic requirement of character motivation and cause–effect relations through the journey itself. Characters who embark on the journey are acted upon by events along the road. The unexpected and unexplained acts that happen on the road are motivated by the fact that the protagonists are outside of their ordinary sphere of existence. In the process, the characters, and by implication the viewers, find themselves to be "other", the road making them marginal to the places they encounter and, in many films, to the nation itself. Whether it's the bored Bonnie Parker whose life becomes more eventful with each robbery or gunfight or Thelma and Louise who simply seek time out from their humdrum lives, choices are forced upon them by the stops they make along the road and the illusion of the road as a means of controlling fate and a route to freedom is exposed. On a formal level the visual iconography of the road as framed through the windscreen and the rearview mirror provides potential for reflexive musings on the nature of cinema as well as on the peripatetic and diasporic nature of American culture. While this irony may not always be recognized by the characters, its potential for both reflection and comment on the subjective condition of the nation has proved irresistible for filmmakers in the last thirty years of the twentieth century.

The road movie post-1950 has a number of important pre-conditions. Barbara Klinger references these in her discussion of *Easy Rider* as:

the apotheosis of the car, motorcycle and highway cultures that had escalated since the 1950s thanks to factors as various as the National Highway Act of 1956, which created a gigantic system of interstate highways, Beat writer Jack Kerouac's *On the Road* (1957), which deified the experience of cross-country travel by freewheeling male individuals as

Sissy Spacek and Martin Sheen in *Badlands*

an antidote to bourgeois complacency, and the highly publicized presence of the Hell's Angels, the pack of renegade "chopper" riders who were a source of public fear and fascination by the 1960s. (Klinger 1997: 180)

In addition to these factors lies the longer tradition of the journey in literature and myth. These range from Moses wandering in the desert or *The Odyssey* to its central place in American literature exemplified by Mark Twain's *Huckleberry Finn* or Herman Melville's *Moby Dick*. The nature of the American experience as one of escape, migration and rootlessness continues in twentieth-century examples such John Steinbeck's *The Grapes of Wrath* and Henry Miller's non-fiction *The Air Conditioned Nightmare* (1947), a work which "forcefully conveys the spirit of frustrated meandering that precedes and informs the road movie" (Laderman 2002: 9). Alongside these were the popular fiction trends such as the moralizing teen fiction of the 1950s dealing with "hot rod" culture such as *Hot Rod* by Henry Gregor Felson (1950), and later road-crime novels such as *The Getaway* (1959) by Jim Thompson and Truman Capote's "non-fiction novel" *In Cold Blood* (1965). All of these incorporate in various ways the combination of the car, the road and the journey as a source of thrill and sensation and as an antidote to the ennui of the repressive culture of the suburbs and small towns and the encroaching impact of consumerism.

The road movie's ascension as a production cycle occurred in the late 1960s and continued into the 1970s with films such as *Thunderbolt and Lightfoot* (Michael Cimino, 1974), *Scarecrow* (Jerry Schatzberg, 1973), *Two Lane Blacktop* (Monte Hellman, 1971) or *Badlands* (Terence Malick, 1973), each of these depicting in some way protagonists on the margins of society who set out on the road. From the outset, with *Bonnie and Clyde*, tensions concerning sexual politics were intertwined with the anti-hero on the road motif. *Bonnie and Clyde*'s script famously shifted the relationship from a three-way bi-sexual interaction between Clyde, Bonnie and C.W. Moss to a Freudian displacement of guns for male potency and a heterosexual denouement. Clyde finally consummates his relationship with Bonnie at the end of the film just prior to their violent deaths. While this is not a main theme in *Easy Rider*, Billy and Wyatt are still the main couple who share the film's most intimate moments. This general trend developed into the buddy movie, which knowingly or not, drew attention to the erotic homosocial tensions at play in male–male relationships, heightened by the road movie's alternation between the wide open spaces of the landscape and the enclosed space of the car. A consistent script solution to this has been the addition of a third person, usually a woman, as a means of releasing these tensions. "Since so many road movies are same-sex buddy films, the emphasis is usually on how a single female gets to be passed between the hands of two men within the terms of an erotic triangle" (Stringer 1997: 172). Another resolution in the "buddy" road films of this period is either the incapacity of one or both characters, or death. As Robin Wood suggests, "The male relationship must never be consummated (indeed, must not be able to be consummated), and death is the most effective impediment." For Wood, the "buddy movie', which overlaps with the road movie, sets out ideological contradictions that cannot be positively resolved (Wood 1986: 229).

The late 1970s saw a retrenchment from the more contemplative and complex thematic of road "buddy movies" and towards the foregrounding of action through spectacular car chases and accidents. Many of these such as the *Smokey and the Bandit* series (1977, 1980, 1985), and *Cannonball* (1976), *Cannonball Run* (1980) and *Cannonball Run II* (1983) moved the focus away from the philosophical musings afforded by the anti-hero on the road and picked up on the already existing trend of including car chases as a means of attracting audiences. This had been a staple of the crime film since the success of *Bullitt* (1971) and *The French Connection* (1971) (Romao, 2004: 131). In fact, an early example of the road movie which focuses on the spectacle of the car chase and derives from it Hitchcockian levels of suspense is Spielberg's *Duel* (1971), making a metaphor of a demon truck as the antagonist in the internal conflict of the central character with his own masculinity. The lone male in *Duel* references masculinity in crisis and effectively avoids the tensions of male–male relationships that Wood attributes to the buddy films and road movies of the early 1970s. The car chase films of the late 1970s and early 1980s avoid it all together, and while the term "road movie" can loosely be attributed to these, the format remained primarily dormant until the mid to late 1980s.

Ina Rae Hark notes that the mid-1980s saw a return of the buddy-road format but with a revised set of thematic concerns. She labels these "odd couple" or "anti-buddy" narratives and sees them as fellow travellers with a trend in popular culture which expressed a "discomfort with the excesses of 1980s economic practices and the yuppie lifestyle they [Reagan's first term 1980-84] spawned". Citing *Rain Man* (1987), *Midnight Run* (1988) and *Planes, Trains and Automobiles* (1987), she sees these films as attempted yuppie critiques with the "odd couple" consisting of a "high flyer" who is "battling a deadline for some highly personal goal" and a "neurotic" who is "as deficient in capitalist/masculinist qualities as the high flyer is in excess of them" (Cohan and Hark 1997: 204–5). These films, Hark argues, adopt a strategy of critiquing capitalist values through comedy but at the same time demonstrate "a growing incompatibility between the reintegrative goals of road comedy and the dismantling of hegemonic masculinity" (Cohan and Hark 1997: 226).

The male–male heterosexual road movie partly gave way in the 1990s to films which utilized the format to explicitly address themes of sexuality and gender. *Thelma and Louise* (1991), the Australian-made *Priscilla, Queen of the Desert* (1994) and *To Wong Foo, Thanks for Everything! Julie Newmar* (1995) made use of the possibilities for outlining the plight and concerns of the outsider that the road movie offers, and through focusing on heterosexual women or homosexual and trans-sexual men, revived the genre. *Thelma and Louise* did respectable box-office, grossing over $50 million worldwide, having cost only around $16 million to produce. However, its impact was widely felt and sparked considerable debate in the popular US press and even a cover issue of *Time Magazine* (24 June 1991). *Variety* described it with a reference to the attractions of the road movie format as "Despite some delectably funny scenes between the sexes, Ridley Scott's pic isn't about women vs men. It's about freedom, like any good road picture. In that sense, and in many others, it's a classic" (*Variety* 1991). Echoing Robin Wood's observations of death or incapacitation as the narrative solution to male–male relationships in the early to mid-1970s buddy-road movie, Cathy Griggers notes that *Thelma and Louise*'s freeze frame ending as they plunge into the Grand Canyon is only one, albeit dominant, reading of the film. She offers a counter-reading which "refuses the containment strategies of straight femininity's narrative" and suggests that the crucial insight of the film lies in its depiction of the "social-process of becoming a lesbian" (Griggers 1993: 134). Central to this reading is the "road-narrative structure", its "movement" and the format's function of "exposing the subcultural underside of everyday life" (Griggers 1993: 130). While the gender and sexual politics had shifted ground in this revitalization of the genre, the structure worked as it had in previous controversial road movies.

A second trend in the 1990s also dispensed with the male buddy theme and instead offered highly stylized treatments of heterosexual couples such as the Quentin Tarantino-scripted *Natural Born Killers* (Oliver Stone, 1994) and David Lynch's *Wild at Heart* (1991). In both cases the in-built potential for satire and irony of the road movie structure was combined with post-modern pastiche. Lynch's film utilizes the road as a reflective device to string together by turns romantic, violent, comedic and surreal scenes in depicting a romantic couple in an upside-down world. Stone's film of the violent rampages of a fictitious heterosexual couple takes the road format as a means of structuring a more conventional social satire and commentary.

While these alterations and revivals in the road movie format have been the subject of considerable academic attention as well as popular debate, the road format has also been co-opted across more established genres such as horror and comedy. In *The Texas Chain Saw Massacre* (Tobe Hooper, 1974) the protagonists start out on the road and finish with the "final girl" being rescued by a trucker, the road here is salvation. Conversely in films such as *The Hitcher* (Robert Harmon, 1986), Kathryn Bigelow's vampire/western/road movie *Near Dark* (1987) or the Francis Ford Coppola-produced *Jeepers Creepers* I and II (Victor Salva, 2001, 2003), the road is the domain of the monstrous outsider. More recently the road movie format has been adopted as part of the college gross-out comedy trend in *Road Trip* (Todd Phillips, 2000). These later uses of the journey across the highways of the US do not always explicitly utilize the potential for social commentary and contemplation about the state of the nation, but rather parody the earlier films' encounter with the American hinterland. Nevertheless the automobile, the landscape and the strip of highway that disappears over the horizon framed by the windshield have continued to offer essential ingredients for rendering the American experience as rootless, wandering and redolent with endless promise. Depending on the perspective, in contemporary American cinema, an American on the road is either chosen or doomed, or both.

References

Cohan, S. and Hark, I.R. (eds) (1997) *The Road Movie Book*. London and New York: Routledge.

Griggers, C., (1993) *Thelma and Louise* and the cultural generation of the new butch-femme, in Jim Collins, Hilary Radner and Ava Preacher Collins (eds), *Film Theory Goes to the Movies*, London and New York: Routledge.

Klinger, B. (1997) The road to dystopia: landscaping the nation in *Easy Rider*, in S. Cohan and I.R. Hark (eds) *The Road Movie Book*. London and New York: Routledge, pp. 179–203.

Laderman, D. (2002) *Driving Visions: Exploring the Road Movie*. Austin: University of Texas Press.

Romao, T. (2004) "Guns and gas": investigating the 1970s car chase film, in Y. Tasker (ed.) *Action and Adventure Cinema*. London: Routledge.

Stringer, J. (1997) Exposing intimacy in Russ Meyer's *Motorpsycho!* and *Faster Pussycat! Kill! Kill!* In S. Cohan and I.R. Hark (eds) *The Road Movie Book*. London and New York: Routledge.

Variety (1991) Thelma and Louise http://www.variety.com/review/ VE1117795590?categoryID=31&cs=1 (accessed Dec. 17, 2005), posted, Jan 1, 1991.

Wood, R. (1986) *Hollywood from Vietnam to Reagan*. New York: Columbia University Press.

Michael Hammond

Continued from page 14

Only a minority of films made any attempt to represent the politics of the New Left in any direct manner, usually in terms of increasing social and political polarization and violence in everyday American life, and with varying degrees of commercial and critical success, from Brian De Palma's first feature film *Greetings* (1968), through Haskell Wexler's *Medium Cool* (1969), and Michelangelo Antonioni's *Zabriskie Point* (1970), and now less remembered films such as *Getting Straight* (1970), *Hi, Mom!* (1970), and *The Strawberry Statement* (1970) (Sklar 1988).

These films clearly demonstrated that American society and politics were marked by an exceptional degree of hostility and bitterness as the end of the decade approached. This was also manifest in the clear opposition evident between liberal and conservative representations of law and order and policing in American cinema of the period: in the liberal camp, in such critiques of authoritarian law enforcement as *The Chase* (1966), *In the Heat of the Night* (1967), *Cool Hand Luke* (1967), *In Cold Blood* (1967), and *The Detective* (1968); and, in the conservative camp, in films such as *Bullitt* (1968), *Coogan's Bluff* (1968), and *Madigan* (1968) whose celebration of the figure of the tough cop was energized by the strong priority given to the issue of law and order by the Republican presidential candidacy of Richard Nixon in the election year of 1968 (Reiner 1981).

On the other hand, one of the most immediately apparent areas of social change came in the widespread liberalization of social values – particularly with regard to sexual attitudes and sexual behaviour – fuelled by a burgeoning youth population, many of whom saw themselves as increasingly at odds with the established social, political, and economic order. The increasing prevalence of the values of the so-called "permissive society" ushered in

Bob and Carol and Ted and Alice: Paul Mazursky's critique of bourgeois domesticity

by the sexual revolution of the 1960s achieved concrete expression in the breakdown of the systems of censorship that had prevailed in Classical Hollywood since the 1930s, especially with the replacement of the Production Code Administration (often referred to as the "Hays Code") by the more flexible, more tolerant MPAA ratings system – based upon the certificates G, PG, R and X – which testified to a greater openness in American society of the late 1960s to frank portraits of American life, especially in the loosening of restrictions on the depiction of sex, violence, and "social problems" such as drug use (Ayer et al. 1982; Randall 1985).

However, if this loosening of restrictions was positive in allowing more natural representations of nudity and sex – especially in films that attempted some critique of bourgeois domesticity and heterosexual monogamy such as *Bob and Carol and Ted and Alice* (1969), *Five Easy Pieces* (1970), and *Carnal Knowledge* (1971) – it also appeared to many commentators at the time to merely extend the essentially patriarchal politics of American cinema into new degrees of misogyny (Trecker 1972). In her book *Popcorn Venus*, published in 1973, Marjorie Rosen noted with concern that while superficially progressive films such as *Easy Rider*, *Midnight Cowboy*, *Getting Straight*, and *The Strawberry Statement* took advantage of the new artistic licence available in the representation of sex, female roles in these films were either "nonexistent, purely sexual, or purely for laughs" to a greater degree than had even been the case in the classical period when Hollywood's sexual objectification of women had been at least partially balanced by such women-oriented genres as the melodrama (Rosen 1973: 341). What Rosen termed the "exorcism of women from major movies" was balanced only occasionally by filmmakers for whom the woman's point of view was a subject worthy of attention in its own right – as, for example, in the work of the independent filmmaker John Cassavetes in *Faces* (1968), *Husbands* (1970), and *A Woman Under the Influence* (1974).

For better or for worse, however, intense debates on cinema in the period from 1965–70 on such issues as law and order, censorship and freedom of expression, and sexuality and gender, were at least proof positive of the tremendous topicality that the medium of film seemed to hold, and the sense of social and political urgency that seemed to inform the production and reception of so much film culture in the period. Not only did this new topicality receive expression in the popular press – for example, in regular features and special issues in *Newsweek, Time, The Saturday Review*, and *Atlantic Monthly*, as well as in the regular columns of such celebrated reviewers as Pauline Kael and Stanley Kauffmann – but the new topicality of film as a medium and its reinvigorated popularity with youth also led to its growth as a widespread pursuit in film schools and universities across the country, by virtue of which film carried a new intellectual, artistic, and political legitimacy, articulated by such film journals as *Cineaste*, established in 1967 (*Saturday Review* 1969; Wakefield 1969; *Newsweek* 1970; Trilling 1970; Kael 1973; Kauffmann 1975).

Outside of the Hollywood mainstream, and in competition with it, it was the thriving sector of the so-called "exploitation" picture, which most blatantly capitalized on this new topicality of cinema. Producing low-budget films especially for youth audiences, such independent production/distribution companies as American International Pictures, and particular directors such as Roger Corman, had long pushed the boundaries of acceptable representation, and deliberately traded on notoriety and controversy in a way generally avoided by Hollywood, with such sci-fi classics as *The Day the World Ended* (1956), horror film milestones such as *The Little Shop of Horrors* (1960), and light-hearted teen romances such as *Beach Party* (1963) (Levy 1967; Diehl 1970; Ottoson 1985; Schaefer 1999). But in the second half of the 1960s, Corman and other "exploitation" filmmakers such as Richard Rush increasingly turned to making films on contemporary issues such as hippies, Hell's Angels, and drug use, which were largely sympathetic to the counter-culture and which often included elements of visual experimentation with the psychedelic imagery and music of the day. Films such as *The Trip* (1967), *Hell's Angels on Wheels* (1967), *The Savage Seven* (1968), *Psych-Out* (1968), *Wild in the Streets* (1968), *Rebel Rousers* (1967, released 1970), and *Gas-s-s-s* (1970) presented the hippie counter-culture in sympathetic, though usually tongue-in-cheek, terms, which negotiated a fine line between the profit-motives of the low-budget film industry and the desire for meaningful social comment which seemed appropriate to the times (Shiel 2003). The exploitation sector, and Roger Corman, in particular, would prove decisive in helping to launch the careers of many important film actors, cinematographers and directors of the 1960s and later decades, including Peter Fonda, Bruce Dern, Ellen Burstyn, Haskell Wexler, Monte Hellman, Peter Bogdanovich, and Francis Ford Coppola.

Further away again from the Hollywood

Continued on page 22

In 1960, Roger Corman was known as a director/producer with then-disreputable, now-estimable credits in drive-in double bill genres like science fiction (*It Conquered the World*, 1956), juvenile delinquency (*Sorority Girl*, 1957) and horror (*The Undead*, 1959) – mostly under the aegis of exploitation outfit American International Pictures (AIP). Having delivered a couple of quality items, notably the kookily weird *A Bucket of Blood* (1959) and its cult-in-the-making instant remake *The Little Shop of Horrors* (1960), Corman persuaded his AIP bosses James H. Nicholson and Samuel Z. Arkoff to back the ambitious *The Fall of the House of Usher* (1960), an American gothic in widescreen colour with a literary source and a horror star (Vincent Price). The film was successful enough to launch a Poe–Corman–Price franchise that ran until the very intriguing *Masque of the Red Death* (1964) and *The Tomb of Ligeia* (1964) and to give Corman the clout to experiment with a socially-conscious art film (*The Intruder*, 1961), more intellectual s-f (*X – The Man with X-Ray Eyes*, 1963) and a few A-like action pictures (*The Secret Invasion*, 1964). Thanks to the Poe films, which ranged from horror (*The Premature Burial*, 1962; *The Haunted Palace*, 1963) to humour (*The Raven*, 1963), Corman was established as a director. For AIP, he essayed key late 1960s youth exploitation films (*The Wild Angels*, 1966, *The Trip*, 1967) that returned to the social concerns of *The Intruder* but avoided that film's commercial failure by cashing in on headlines about bike gangs and drugs. His first notable major studio credit was *The St Valentine's Day Massacre* (1967), which perhaps prompted AIP to give him the spirited *Bloody Mama* (1968) – but dissatisfaction with AIP over their handling of the satire *Gas-s-s-s!* (1970) and United Artists over *Von Richtofen and Brown* (1971) led him to abandon direction (until the blip of *Frankenstein Unbound*, 1989) to concentrate on mini-moguldom. Half-out from the aegis of

Roger Corman directing Bruce Dern in *The Trip*

AIP, Corman had founded FilmGroup in the late 1950s and had always produced films by other directors, frequently encouraging young, interesting (cheap) talent like Francis Ford Coppola (*Dementia 13*, 1962), Monte Hellman (*The Shooting*, 1965), Peter Bogdanovich (*Targets*, 1967), Jack Nicholson (screenwriter of *The Trip*) and Martin Scorsese (*Boxcar Bertha*, 1972). In 1970, Corman declared independence from AIP and founded New World Pictures, which made or distributed films for drive-ins. He also distributed films by Fellini, Bergman and Kurosawa (Betz 2003: 217–18), but the business of New World was shot-in-the-Philippines women-in-prison movies (*The Big Doll House*, 1971), contemporary horror (*The Velvet Vampire*, 1971), biker action (*Angels Hard as They Come*, 1972), socially-engaged sexploitation (*The Student Nurses*, 1970), blaxploitation (*TNT Jackson*, 1974), and car crash/rural crime (*The Great Texas Dynamite Chase*, 1977). Corman, writes Cook, "scoured the Los Angeles film schools for local talent" (1998: 14), nurturing directors like Jonathan Demme (*Caged Heat*, 1974), Paul Bartel (*Death Race 2000*, 1975) and Joe Dante (*Piranha*, 1978), plus future directors John Sayles and James Cameron (writer and an effects man on *Battle Beyond the Stars*, 1981). Many of these films have now acquired revered cult status (see Rayner 2000, for a discussion of this phenomenon). New World earned a justifiable reputation for delivering pictures a little better than they needed to be, often with socially-conscious themes that expanded the audience to bring in college kids.

Corman sold New World in the early 1980s, as video was replacing the drive-in as a market, but established Concorde, then New Horizons. He remains in business, albeit with a certain reduction of ambition – he continues to turn out direct-to-video franchises (the erotic thriller *Body Chemistry* and sci-fi/horror *Carnosaur* series), and has produced a glut of features for TV. His story is inimitably told in his autobiography (Corman with Jerome 1998), which also serves as a lively account of the world of fringe and independent off-Hollywood low budget production.

References

Betz, M. (2003) Art, exploitation, underground, in Mark Jancovich, Antonio Lázaro Reboll, Julian Stringer and Andy Willis (eds) *Defining Cult Movies: The Cultural Politics of Oppositional Tastes*. Manchester: Manchester University Press, pp. 202–22.

Cook, D.A. (1998) Auteur cinema and the "film generation" in 1970s Hollywood, in Jon Lewis (ed.) *The New American Cinema*, Durham, NC: Duke University Press, pp. 11–37.

Corman, R. with J. Jerome (1998) *How I Made a Hundred Movies in Hollywood and Never Lost a Dime*. New York: Da Capo Press.

Rayner, J. (2000) The cult film, Roger Corman and *The Cars That Ate Paris*, in Xavier Mendik and Graeme Harper (eds) *Unruly Pleasures: The Cult Film and its Critics*. Guildford: FAB Press, pp. 223–33.

Kim Newman

Continued from page 20
mainstream, however, given the political radicalism and social turmoil of the era, many filmmakers and audiences questioned much more deeply the usefulness of narrative cinema as a form of alternative or resistant practice, preferring to develop a film culture that was not compromised by the profit motives of either Hollywood or the exploitation sector. Primarily non-narrative forms of alternative film culture – especially documentary and experimental film – experienced a tremendous

flourishing of popularity, exposure, and creativity in the second half of the 1960s.

In the area of documentary film, the Direct Cinema movement which had emerged in the early 1960s with socially and politically oriented studies such as *Primary* (1960), continued to attract attention in the emergent form of the rock music-oriented documentary, or "rockumentary" which was the most high-profile development in documentary film in the period (Barnouw 1993). In *Don't Look Back* (1967), *Monterey Pop* (1968), *Woodstock* (1970), and *Gimme Shelter* (1970), filmmakers blended social commentary and popular music to critical and commercial success. The brothers David and Albert Maysles, meanwhile, shared the fascination with pop culture celebrity characteristic of the rockumentary in their playful study of the screen icon *Meet Marlon Brando* (1966), but also tended towards a much more austere aesthetic in their examination of the lives of door-to-door Bible salesmen in the American Midwest in *Salesman* (1969). Further again in the direction of social critique, Fred Wiseman's series of powerful films – *Titicut Follies* (1967), *High School* (1969), *Law and Order* (1969), and *Basic Training* (1971) – used documentary for the analysis of institutional authority in the cases of the mental hospital, the high school, the police force, and the US Army boot camp, respectively. Meanwhile, those subjects left largely unaddressed by Hollywood, such as the injustice of the war in Vietnam, fuelled the peculiarly political anti-war documentary filmmaking of individuals such as Emile de Antonio in *In the Year of the Pig* (1969) – a provocative assemblage of footage, interviews, and statistics that deconstructed the official propaganda of the war while viewing the ordinary soldier as a mere pawn – and underground filmmaking collectives such as

Newsreel whose *Columbia Revolt* (1968) and *San Francisco State: On Strike* (1969) sympathetically documented the campaigns of students and activists against the war on university campuses nationwide (Waugh 1985; James 1989: 166–76, 195–236).

Using film in a less overtly political, but no less provocative manner, experimental filmmakers from Andy Warhol in New York to Kenneth Anger in Los Angeles articulated the creativity and excesses of the counter-culture of the period in low-budget films in which narrative was non-existent or relatively unimportant. Warhol's *Chelsea Girls* (1966), dominated by psychedelia and the music of The Velvet Underground, provided an intimate portrait of the relatively bizarre daily lives of the artists, musicians, models, and groupies who frequented The Factory, Warhol's legendary art studio-cum-business headquarters in Lower Manhattan. Produced by Warhol but written and directed by Paul Morrissey, the loosely plotted *Flesh* (1968) and *Trash* (1970) continued the subject but with a particular turn towards the explicit and the outrageous in scenes of cross-dressing, heroin addiction, masturbation, and full-frontal nudity, in a trilogy of films completed by *Heat* in 1973. Kenneth Anger's films such as *Kustom Kar Kommandos* (1966), *Invocation of My Demon Brother* (1969), and *Lucifer Rising* (1973) merged a counter-cultural anti-aesthetic creativity with the expression of a distinctively gay male sexuality, through disturbing montages of provocative imagery from Hell's Angels to Nazi swastikas and icons of Christ (Rowe 1982; Smith 1986; Yacowar 1993). In common with Morrissey's work, Anger's films stood in defiance of the repression of homosexuality that continued in most American cinema even as the gay movement exploded with new confidence in the late

1960s, especially in major cities such as New York and San Francisco.

In the border area between film and contemporary art, meanwhile, some of the most dynamic work of the period emanated from filmmakers who dispensed entirely with any sense of narrative or easily intelligible representation, tending instead towards an abstract form of meditation on film. Pop artist Bruce Conner's *Report* (1967) comprised a thought-provoking 13-minute montage of TV images of the assassination of President John F. Kennedy interspersed with seemingly random segments of found footage from TV commercials, old war movies, and newsreels (Conner 1999). In *Fuses* (1967), Carolee Schneeman, the celebrated feminist performance artist, presented scenes of love making that she and her male partner performed for the camera in a semi-abstract exploration and celebration of the human body and heterosexual intercourse as a subject in its own right. Conner and Schneeman anticipated the increasing prominence that the medium of film would gain in contemporary art generally in subsequent decades.

Many of the formal innovations characteristic of US experimental film of the period managed to infiltrate Hollywood, though belatedly and in relatively diluted form. Indeed, many of the formal conventions and procedures of classical Hollywood with regard to cinematography, *mise en scène*, editing, performance, and sound came under attack during the period from three key directions: not only from the experimental tendencies of US underground filmmakers such as Warhol, Morrissey, and Conner, but also from the indigenous US low-budget "exploitation" film sector and, perhaps most notably, from the modernist aesthetics of European art cinema, whose popularity in the US was at an all-time high, as demonstrated by the success of films by Michelangelo Antonioni, Bernardo Bertolucci, Jean-Luc Godard, François Truffaut, and Ingmar Bergman (Lev 1993).

Now a popular cultural legend in its own right, the hugely successful and critically applauded *Easy Rider* (1969) arguably did more than any other single film to combine these various influences in order to destabilize classical Hollywood's old formal conventions. Its narrative consisted entirely of a rather loose episodic odyssey across America by two cocaine-dealing bikers, which presented, according to one critic, Penelope Gilliatt in the *New Yorker*, "ninety-four minutes of what it is like to swing, to watch, to be fond, to hold opinions, and to get killed in America at this moment" (Gilliatt 1969). *Easy Rider* constructed its linear road movie narrative through an emotive combination of romantic pastoral landscapes of the American West, non-continuity editing inspired by the innovative jump-cutting technique of French New Wave director Jean-Luc Godard, and visually disturbing montages of semi-abstract images of death indebted to the experimentation of Bruce Conner. While *Easy Rider* shared the combination of romanticism and unstable narrative form with other celebrated films of the era such as *Bonnie and Clyde* (1967), *The Wild Bunch* (1969), and *Midnight Cowboy* (1969), in its engagement with contemporary rural American landscapes *Easy Rider* exemplified a distinct tendency toward location filming in much cinema of the period, in which the so-called "dream factory" of the Hollywood studio was abandoned for artistic and ideological reasons.

The rejection of the studio was, in large part, facilitated by a series of fortuitous developments in the area of film technology. One of the most important of these was undoubtedly the popularization of 16 mm film, a vastly simpler, cheaper, and more portable system than the standard 35 mm of commercial narrative filmmaking; and the favoured system of most documentary film-makers as well as many underground film-makers. It also appealed in so far as the relatively imperfect quality of the finished product, with regard to sound and image, coincided perfectly with the ideological desire of many filmmakers to stand apart from or challenge Hollywood through deliberately low production values. The popularization and credibility of 16 mm led, in the late 1960s, to a brief flourishing of the alternative format in Hollywood cinema itself – for example, in the extended 16 mm sequences included in *Easy Rider* and *Medium Cool* (Salt 1992: 255–7).

In an analogous fashion, in 35 mm cine-matography, film stock, cameras, lighting, and production equipment generally developed to allow filmmakers to achieve a greater degree of mobility and flexibility than had generally been previously possible, and at generally lower cost than in the past (Salt 1992: 255–7). For example, lighter, more portable cameras became more widely available; new colour film stocks were produced that allowed for richer colour and higher definition, especially in the filming of night scenes shot with available light; lighting units became increasingly lightweight, and more naturalistic lighting methods were imported to American film-making under the influence of French New Wave cinematographers such as the celebrated Raoul Coutard; and sound recording equip-ment became increasingly sophisticated and fine tuned especially for location filming. Individual developments also contributed to the sometimes idiosyncratic visual aesthetics of the period – for example, the first 35 mm fisheye lenses in 1965, used to suggest the disorientation of LSD in *Easy Rider*, and 70 mm split-screen projection, used to great effect in *The Thomas Crown Affair* (1968) and *Woodstock* (1970). By the end of the decade the tendency towards location filming was increasingly answered by custom-built mobile film production units that afforded new levels of technological sophistication and comfort to large casts and crews on location (*Newsweek* 1970: 49).

All of these developments testified to the fundamental reworking of the visual and aural form of American cinema in the mid- to late-1960s. At the deeper level of narrative form, however, perhaps even more fundamental changes were taking place that would have longer impact than the relatively short-lived vogues of 1960s visual style – particularly in the upheaval of the genre system of classical Hollywood, and the subversion of the cultu-rally and socially affirmative function performed by genre films for preceding generations of American filmmakers and filmgoers (Ryan and Kellner 1988: 76–105; Neale 2000: 226–9). If state-of-the-nation epics like *Bonnie and Clyde* and *Easy Rider* earned new respectability and significance for the road movie as a genre in its own right, cementing their catastrophic prognoses on the future of American society through the symbolic bloody deaths of their heroes, their reworking of American cultural mythology was only the most high-profile and shocking demonstration of a large process of generic revision, a general characteristic of much post-Second World War American cinema but one that moved into high gear in the late 1960s.

Of course, the old genre staples of Holly-wood cinema had not died out by the late 1960s. Indeed, any history of American cinema of the period must recognize that despite the thematic and formal innovation that grabbed most of the headlines, behind the counter-cultural exploration and political agitation of much cinema, formally and thematically conservative films continued to achieve success. Hollywood continued to produce successful and generally well-received melodramas such as *Hotel* (1966) and *Love Story* (1970), romantic comedies such as *Do Not Disturb* (1965), historical extravaganzas such as *Doctor Zhivago* (1965) and *Ryan's*

Daughter (1970), and literary adaptations such as *The Prime of Miss Jean Brodie* (1969), *Goodbye Mr Chips* (1969), and *Hello Dolly!* (1969, Fig. 3 (*see plate section*)). It brought the quintessentially conservative and escapist form of the musical to new levels of spectacle and big-budget expenditure in films such as *The Sound of Music* (1965), *Chitty Chitty Bang Bang* (1968), and *Paint Your Wagon* (1969),

Continued on page 28

The Sound of Music

The Sound of Music (1965) was based on Richard Rodgers' and Oscar Hammerstein II's long-running 1959 stage show, itself an adaptation of the biography of Maria von Trapp, a former nun who, with her husband and seven stepchildren, had fled Nazi-controlled Austria and become successful singers in the United States. The film version was produced and directed by Robert Wise and written by Ernest Lehman, both of whom had performed similar duties on the multi-Oscar-winning *West Side Story* (1961). As Maria, Wise cast English-born West End and Broadway star Julie Andrews after seeing a preview of her film debut, Walt Disney's *Mary Poppins* (1964). Unlike an earlier German-made version of the story, released in the US as *The Trapp Family* (1960), *The Sound of Music* is set entirely in Austria; its first two-thirds are mainly concerned with the budding romance between Maria, the Trapp children's governess,

The Sound of Music

and the starchy Captain von Trapp (Christopher Plummer), while the latter portion shows the newly formed family's escape from the Nazis who would have the Captain serve in the German Navy.

The film was Twentieth Century Fox's fifth Rodgers and Hammerstein musical in under a decade, following *Carousel* (1956), *The King and I* (1956), *South Pacific* (1958) and *State Fair* (1962). With location filming in Austria in Todd-AO 70 mm, it was also, at a negative cost of $8.2 million, the most expensive film the studio had made since *Cleopatra* (1963). Reviews were decidedly mixed but by the end of 1970, it had returned world rentals of $121.5 million, sufficient to make it the highest grossing film released by any studio to that date. $72 million of this total came from the US domestic market, giving the film first place on *Variety*'s All-Time Champs chart from 1966 to 1969, until a reissue of MGM's *Gone With the Wind* (1939) briefly returned that film to the top of the US box-office listings in 1970.

The Sound of Music also broke the industry record for overseas grosses, previously held by MGM's *Ben-Hur* (1959), while still in the early stages of its road-show phase, playing only two performances a day. In some territories the film was road-shown for three or four years before general release. In Britain it opened in March 1965 and remained in continuous circulation until 1969. By December 1965, when it had been shown in only seventeen pre-release engagements in London and the key cities, it had grossed £1,925,869 from 6,926,825 admissions (*Kine. Weekly*, 16 December 1965: 151). A year later it had broken *South Pacific*'s record of £2,300,000, which had been amassed over seven years of release, for the highest gross received by any film shown in Britain, with an estimated 21 million admissions to date (Livingstone 1966: 9). These road-show engagements in many cases ran for years. At the Dominion Theatre, the film's West End premiere venue, it ran continuously for three years and three months, from 29 March 1965 until 29 June 1968. Many local exhibition records were also broken in provincial cities. In Newcastle, for example, the film ran at the Queen's cinema for 140 weeks from April 1965 to December 1967. As a result, it was named by *Kine. Weekly* top UK money-maker of the year for four years in succession, from 1965 to 1968.

Numerous commentators have sought to explain the film's success, often with an air of bafflement (see, for example, Barthel 1966 and Shipman 1966). Undoubtedly the emotional gratification involved in a story of a lively woman discovering her vocation in life, of a broken family being reconstituted, its father rejuvenated and reformed by love, and of goodness defeating the ultimate evil of fascism, had something to do with it. So too, perhaps, did the splendours of location shooting and the sentimental beauties of Rodgers and Hammerstein's music. The anachronism of the film's existence amid the swinging cynicism of the 1960s, its appeal to a neglected older demographic and its residual attraction for other age groups, must also be taken into account. Fox's head of UK distribution, Percy Livingstone, described the film as "a vital development in cinema-going", having appeal "on the widest possible front, suitable for all the family, young and old, highbrows and lowbrows ... it has the ability to give great joy to all who see it ... It is unique in the extent to which all these qualities combine to make the perfect commercial movie" (Livingstone 1966: 9). But however one tries to explain the *why* of the film's success, the *how* is much easier to demonstrate.

Fox's marketing campaign positioned the film skilfully to take full advantage of its all-classes family appeal. The company chose not to compete with its own *Cleopatra* release campaign, or with Warner Bros.' campaign for its rival musical, *My Fair Lady* (1964), by overpricing tickets. Instead, though seat prices remained high by comparison with standard general releases, as was normal for road-show presentations, they were adjusted to the potential spending power of family audiences. Theatres in the US typically charged a top price of $3.75 for evening performances and $2.50 for midweek matinees, by comparison with *Cleopatra*'s record price scale of $5.50 to $4.50 (Barthel 1966).

Audiences responded with multiple visits. The studio discovered that three or more visits per person were not unusual, and unearthed a number of "freak" cases of individuals seeing the film many times over, even every week or every day (more recently, the film has acquired a cult status courtesy of sing-along audience participation screenings, which viewers often attend costumed as nuns or Nazis). According to Percy Livingstone (1966), "All the evidence seems to show that possibly only seven million people, or even less, [had] yet seen the film [in the UK], but they average three or more visits each." He cited some patrons known to have seen the film over fifty times. Partly as a consequence, admission figures for the film's metropolitan first runs in many cases exceeded the cities' population, sometimes by as much as 300 per cent. Over two dozen cities in the US experienced this massively disproportionate attendance. Fox rewarded theatres reaching such a volume of business with a "Certificate of Merit" (Zanuck 1966: 7). Many of the cinemas exhibiting the film were leased by Fox on a "four-wall let" basis, meaning that for an agreed fee the distributor took over the management of the theatre for the duration of the run, paying its running costs and keeping a larger than usual portion of the box-office take. This in itself ensured that Fox benefited more from the film's long runs than theatre owners.

Though *The Sound of Music* brought Fox enormous profits and industry prestige, it was ultimately responsible for the company's (and other studios') disastrous commitment to both big-budget family musicals and the road-show exhibition policy in the latter half of the decade. Darryl F. Zanuck himself subsequently admitted that the film's success "had been a mixed blessing, in that it had led the studio to follow up with more high-cost musicals, which had disappointed to say the least" (*Kine. Weekly*, 5 September 1970: 5).

References

Anon. (1965) *Sound of Music* set to become all-time winner, *Kine. Weekly*, 16 December.
Anon. (1970) Zanuck on cassettes: "4–5 years after theatres", *Kine. Weekly*, 5 September.
Barthel, J. (1966) Biggest money-making movie of all time – how come?, *The New York Times*, 20 November.
Livingstone, P. (1966) "Dim little flick" becomes a world-beater, *Kine. Weekly*, 17 December.
Shipman, D. (1966) The all-conquering governess, *Films and Filming*, August.
Zanuck, D.F. (1966) World markets justify the big risk, *Kine. Weekly* Supplement, 29 September 1970.

Sheldon Hall

Continued from page 26
and it extended traditional male-heroic action genres such as the war movie in similar ways, albeit sometimes with an edgier violence than before, in *The Dirty Dozen* (1967), *Ice Station Zebra* (1968), *Where Eagles Dare* (1968), *Patton* (1970), and *Tora! Tora! Tora!* (1970).

The persistence of these genres even in this period of massive social and political turbulence, however, does not, as some commentators have suggested, invalidate the idea of a radical challenge to Hollywood in the late 1960s (Bordwell and Staiger 1985; Krämer 1998). Rather it belies the deep division that permeated American film culture, which Thomas Schatz has described in terms of "the period's schizophrenic alternation between a developing irony and a reactionary nostalgia" (1983: 261). Nowhere was this schizophrenia more evident than in the Western genre, one of the fundamental pillars of the old Hollywood establishment and, indeed, of American culture as a whole in the twentieth century, which mutated in multiple ways through the late 1960s before petering out some time in the middle of the next decade.

In 1950, there had been 135 feature-length Westerns made in the United States; by 1956 that number had already fallen to 78; from 1965 to 1975, however, only 200 Westerns were made in total, or an average of less than 20 per year (Marsden and Nachbar 1987: 1269). Challenged especially by the encroachment of TV Western serials, big screen Westerns became less numerous and less thematically coherent, though no less visually grandiose. If films such as *The Misfits* (1961), *Lonely Are the Brave* (1962), *The Man Who Shot Liberty Valance* (1962), *Ride the High Country* (1962), and *Hud* (1963) were increasingly sceptical of the received myths of the American West in the early 1960s, by the latter years of the decade, revision of the Western catered to audiences who were fundamentally disillusioned with the masculinist, racist and materialist values that seemed to underpin the genre in its heyday. Westerns as diverse as *Cat Ballou* (1965), *The Wild Bunch* (1969), *Butch Cassidy and the Sundance Kid* (1969), and *The Ballad of Cable Hogue* (1970) effected change in the most fundamental symbolic and iconic vocabulary of the Hollywood cinema, repositioning the heroic rural vision of the Western as something flawed, weak, and hopelessly obsolete. Meanwhile, alongside such so-called "elegiac" Westerns, other less fond representations revealed the supposed "settlement" and "civilizing" of the

American West and its indigenous peoples in the nineteenth century as, in fact, a process of military conquest, cultural imperialism, and environmental destruction. If films such as John Ritt's *Hombre* (1967) questioned the supposed moral goodness of white American settlers by reversing the essential narrative elements of John Ford's classic Western *Stagecoach* (1939), by 1970, with films such as *Little Big Man* (1970), *Soldier Blue* (1970), *A Man Called Horse* (1970), and *Tell Them Willie Boy Is Here* (1970), many Westerns were underpinned by a sense of outrage at the bloody decimation of Native American tribes and tribal ways of life which the settling of the West entailed, especially as perpetrated by the US Army.

Undoubtedly, the strongest "outside" influence on this sea change in the symbolic meaning of the Western in the period was the 1967 US release to tremendous acclaim of the "spaghetti Western" trilogy of Italian director Sergio Leone – *A Fistful of Dollars* (1964), *For a Few Dollars More* (1965), and *The Good, the Bad, and the Ugly* (1966) – all starring Clint Eastwood as the anti-hero, the Man with No Name (Wagstaff 1992; Bondanella 1995). The success of these semi-parodic, semi-operatic westerns in the US market, especially with counter-cultural youth hungry for anti-establishment heroes, altered forever the visual and mythological landscape of the Western genre. Though occasional old-fashioned, reactionary Westerns such as *True Grit* (1969), starring John Wayne, did appear, as Don Graham observes, most American Westerns subsequently showed the Italian influence in their "violence, irony, and self-reflexive commentary on the genre" (Graham 1987: 1259). This is certainly true of the two most important directors working in the Western genre in the late 1960s and in the following decade – Clint Eastwood, in *Hang 'em High* (1967), *The Beguiled* (1970), and *Two Mules for Sister Sara* (1971), and Sam Peckinpah, in *The Wild Bunch* (1969) and *The Ballad of Cable Hogue* (1970). Their various films are united in presenting the American West as an unforgivingly violent arena of self-interested materialistic conflict in which moral propriety is hypocrisy and social order is always collapsing back into anarchy and wilderness.

Despite the interesting innovation of such directors as Eastwood and Peckinpah, the Western was clearly on the wane at the end of the 1960s. Where the genre had been a mainstay of Hollywood cinema for generations, from 1965 to 1970, only two Westerns made it into *Variety*'s annual list of the top fifty box-office grossing films of the year – one being *True Grit* (1969), the other the lighthearted elegy *Butch Cassidy and the Sundance Kid* (1969), which successfully brought the historical revision and self-conscious visual style of the genre firmly into the mainstream (Marsden and Nachbar 1987: 1269–70). Moreover, as Tom Engelhardt has demonstrated, this waning was clearly a consequence of the denting of national ideological self-confidence that characterized the Vietnam era (Engelhardt 1995). The rise of the R-rating and Hollywood's shift of attention from family cinema-going to the interests of disaffected youth audiences further tended to marginalize the Western while genres such as the road movie reworked many of the moral and narrative structures, and much of the visual iconography, of the Western in contemporary settings.

Meanwhile, with their distinctive ability to address the cultural concerns of late twentieth-century audiences in an increasingly urbanized, technological world, the science fiction and horror genres achieved new levels of popularity and respectability, beginning to emerge from the confines of the B-movie and low-budget sectors to the mainstream, which they would firmly occupy in the 1970s. In science fiction, for example, *Planet of the Apes* (1967) topically combined its post-apocalyptic allegory of Black Power with an appeal to popular anxieties over nuclear war and environmental destruction, while Stanley Kubrick's *2001: A Space Odyssey* (1968) completely redefined the standards of the science fiction film in its tremendously lavish and detailed twenty-first-century settings, in its extravagant budget, and in its thematic focus on the dehumanization of society by advanced technology (Greene 1996; Kolker 1988: 114–34). Focusing on dehumanization in a different way, horror films spoke with particular resonance to the rapidly changing social and sexual values of the era: in Roman Polanski's *Rosemary's Baby* (1968), through an exploration of the theme of demonic possession and Satanism set in the superficially comfortable and affluent surroundings of New York's Upper West Side; or in *Night of the Living Dead* (1968), which depicted in gory realist detail the largely unsuccessful efforts of a typical Middle American family to escape a cannibalistic horde of undead zombies recently returned to life in rural Pennsylvania.

The comprehensive reworking of genre that took place in Hollywood cinema in the second half of the 1960s, indicative as it was of a larger breakdown in the thematic and formal standards of American cinema in the period, and of the changing character and tastes of American cinema audiences, went hand-in-hand with a real crisis in the economic fortunes of the Hollywood film industry. Although the United States experienced an economic boom in the 1960s, with

Continued on page 33

Night of the Living Dead

George A. Romero's *Night of the Living Dead* (1968) is, along with *Frankenstein* (1931) and *Psycho* (1960), one of the three most important and influential horror movies of all time. Made by a small group of enthusiasts who had been toiling in a Pittsburgh ad agency, it is a low-budget, black and white picture, loosely inspired by Richard Matheson's novel *I Am Legend* (1953), in which mysterious radiation causes the recently-dead to rise and attack the living, consumed with a desire to eat human flesh. A small group of survivors hole up in a farmhouse, riven with internal conflicts and convincingly panicked by the situation, while the authorities deploy posses of gun-happy hunters to eradicate the menace – the Vietnam-era punchline being that these sharp-shooters not only polish off the zombies but kill the sole survivor, a resourceful black man (Duane Jones), among the humans in the farmhouse. Along the way, many screen taboos are smashed and conventions overturned – family members literally consume each other, heroic actions and romantic love are useless under the siege of the living dead and human entrails and insides are pawed and chewed by the creatures. For Prawer, Romero's "turn of the screw reminds us of a possibility which has been of the greatest importance in the history of the cinematic tale of terror" (1980: 69), that "the harm the living can do matches and even outstrips that of the pathetic clawing corpses to which the title of his film refers" (1980: 68).

   A definite break with the gothic, detached, supernatural style of previous horror movies, *Night of the Living Dead* broke ground which would be ploughed by such other horror filmmakers as Wes Craven (*The Last House on the Left*, 1971; *The Hills Have Eyes*, 1978), Tobe Hooper (*The Texas Chain Saw Massacre*, 1974), David Cronenberg (*Shivers*, 1975; *Rabid*, 1978) and Larry Cohen (*It's Alive*, 1975). Romero then, at least at first, moved away from genre – his second film was an almost-unseen contemporary romantic comedy *There's*

Always Vanilla (1972). But he edged back with *Jack's Wife* (1973), a drama about a suburban wife who finds empowerment through witchcraft, and delivered the first of his revisions of *Night* in *the Crazies* (1973), a cynical action movie about a bioweapons-related outbreak of madness and murder. After *Martin* (1978), a powerful rethink of the vampire theme set in the depressed lower regions of Pittsburgh, Romero finally delivered an official sequel to *Night* in *Dawn of the Dead* (1978), a colourful, satirical effort mostly set in a vast shopping mall where survivors recreate a consumerist utopia while the zombies and other violent factions press against the plate-glass doors. "Like *Night of the Dead* and *Day of the Dead*," writes Williams, "*Dawn of the Dead* contrasts individuals with the mindless crowd surrounding them, whether living or dead" (2003: 87). Memorable as much for effects man Tom Savini's gruesome gags (a forehead sliced by a helicopter blade like a breakfast egg) as its suspense or social comment, *Dawn* was a commercial hit but has proved a hard act to follow.

Romero's next film, *Knightriders* (1980), about a bike gang who adopt medieval armour for jousts, is an interesting attempt to develop the themes of the *Living Dead* movies by suggesting a possible alternative society to the modern world so comprehensively trashed by flesh-eating zombies and rampant materialism. Then he joined with Stephen King to produce the horror comic entertainment *Creepshow* (1982), which yielded a sequel and loose TV spin-offs in the anthology programmes *Tales from the Darkside* and *Monsters* (for which Romero occasionally scripted), and delivered the third and (to date) last of the *Living Dead* series, *Day of the Dead* (1985), a despairing work set mostly in an underground military bunker in a world overrun by the dead where society has vanished entirely. A challenging, serious work (with still more Savini gruesomeness), *Day of the Dead* was somewhat overwhelmed by the many zombie movies that had proliferated in the wake of Romero's earlier films. An Italian co-production backed by Dario Argento, it was relased in Italy as *Zombi*, prompting the opportunist Lucio Fulci to make *Zombi 2* (1979), a luridly mindless (if vaguely endearing) excuse for shark-vs-zombie fights and slow eyeball-gouges, while a novel by *Night of the Living Dead* co-writer John Russo was adapted by Dan O'Bannon into *Return of the Living Dead* (1985), an effective but jokey skit on the whole flesh-eating zombie sub-genre ("more brains!"). In the end, even Romero contributed to this reflexivity by scripting a remake of *Night of the Living Dead* (1990) directed by Savini, which effectively sprung a few new surprises within the old framework but was inarguably an "ordinary" horror film. That said, it approached its original with more respect than the copyright-holders who arranged that *Night of the Living Dead* be first colourized and then re-scored, re-edited and padded (with atrocious new footage directed by Russo) as a 1998 "30th anniversary edition".

From the mid-1980s, Romero found it harder and harder to get films made, and increasingly drew on adaptations of other writers' works. *Monkey Shines* (1988), from a novel by Michael Stewart, is an unsettling drama about the symbiosis between a paraplegic (Jason Beghe) and a trained capuchin monkey; "The Facts in the Case of Mr Valdemar", in the portmanteau film *Two Evil Eyes* (1990) is an EC Comics-style Edgar Allan Poe adaptation eclipsed by its co-feature, Dario Argento's flamboyant take on "The Black Cat"; and *The Dark Half* (1993), from Stephen King's novel, is a spirited *doppelgänger* tale about a novelist (Timothy Hutton) haunted by his murderous pseudonym, which suffers from the contrivances inherent in the material. After a lengthy hiatus, in which he busied himself with music videos and eventually-unproduced projects (like a much-mooted *Mummy* remake squashed to make way for Stepher Sommers' version in 1999), Romero ventured away from his home town for the first time to make a film in Toronto, *Bruiser* (2000), a small-scale "worm turns" melodrama about a put-upon yuppie (Jason Flemyng) who becomes an insane avenger having woken up one day to find a mask stuck permanently to his face. Romero changed the face of horror, enabling a whole new wave of the 1970s, but too many of his admirers were only interested in the gore sequences of his films while he thought of himself as a social and political commentator. Academic discussion has focused on the latter, invested as it is in finding the complexity which Romero hopes he has put in his texts. Rodowick sees "the best work of George Romero" as exploring "a gap, an internal dislocation in which a particularly repressive ideology may be read within the textual system of the film" (1984: 329–30), though Boss argues that "it is difficult to integrate readings of political progressivity with the fantasies of physical degredation and vulnerability" (1986: 18). Romero's imitators, however (like Sam Raimi in *The Evil Dead*, 1983, or Peter Jackson in *Braindead*, 1988) – were more likely to play for slapstick humour than provocative satire. In 2005, he took the franchise one step further, developing its political topicality with *Land of the Dead*, which explores a US class system in which wealthy tower block residents are besieged by a mass of disenfranchised homeless and zombies. Nevertheless, his body of work remains impressive if, like so many bodies in his films, frustratingly incomplete.

References

Boss, P. (1986) Vile bodies and bad medicine, *Screen* 27, Jan./Feb. 1986, pp. 14–24.
Prawer, S.S. (1980) *Caligari's Children: The Film as Tale of Terror*. New York: Da Capo Press.
Rodowick, D.N. (1984) The enemy within: the economy of violence in *The Hills Have Eyes*, in Barry Keith Grant (ed.) *Planks of Reason: Essays on the Horror Film*. Metuchen, NJ and London: The Scarecrow Press, pp. 321–30.
Williams, T. (2003) *The Cinema of George A. Romero: Knight of the Living Dead*. London: Wallflower Press.

Kim Newman

Continued from page 30

unemployment falling 50 per cent from 1960 to 3.5 per cent in 1969, and an average annual growth in GNP of 4.8 per cent throughout the decade, Hollywood's economic fortunes more or less steadily worsened until, by 1970, some commentators were seriously contemplating that the whole system would collapse (James 1989: 4). Attendances at US cinemas had been steadily falling since soon after the end of the Second World War, from an average weekly attendance of 100 million in 1946 to 46 million in 1955, to the relatively tiny figure of 15 million in 1969. Feature film production in the United States, in line with this, had fallen from an average of roughly 500 films per year in the 1930s to 383 in 1950, 254 in 1955, and only 100 in 1969. Box office receipts of the US film industry also plummeted, from a total of $1.8 billion in 1946 to $900 million in 1962 and $350 million in 1970 (Balio 1985: 401–2; Ayer et al. 1982: 220–1).

As Hollywood's traditional family audiences deserted it, the single greatest demographic change that the industry finally had to face in the second half of the 1960s was the decisive rise of youth audiences – that is, those in the 16–25 age bracket – who, by the mid-1960s, constituted 60–80 per cent of the American cinema audience (*Saturday Review* 1969: 7; *Newsweek* 1970: 42; Research Department of Security Pacific National Bank 1974). The burgeoning of the so-called "baby boomers" generation was, of course, one of the most important social developments of the decade, but it was a development with which the Hollywood studios largely failed to come to terms until it began to produce unashamedly youth-oriented hits such as *The Graduate* and *Bonnie and Clyde* in 1967 (Gitlin 1987; Doherty 1988: 233–4). With such films, Hollywood began a difficult process of adjustment to new market realities, to which the low-budget "exploitation" sector had long been well attuned, and which would have profound ramifications by the end of the decade and in subsequent years not only for the type of films the Hollywood industry produced, but also for the way in which the industry was financed, and for the types of creative and managerial personnel who would run it.

That said, conservative cinema persisted: even in 1968, the high point of the social and political unrest of the entire era, the nominations for Academy Awards did not exactly reflect the cultural changes that were sweeping the nation. *Oliver!* (1968), the blockbuster musical adaptation of Charles Dickens' novel, beat off competition for Best Picture from William Wyler's musical romance *Funny Girl* (1968), the historical drama set in medieval England, *The Lion in Winter* (1968), the gentle melodrama about a middle-aged spinster in rural Connecticut, *Rachel, Rachel* (1968), and Italian director Franco Zeffirelli's naïve and stylized dramatization of Shakespeare's *Romeo and Juliet* (1968).

Faced with the creative and ideological stasis that many audiences saw in such films, it is hardly surprising that Hollywood's financial difficulties were compounded by a small but significant loss of market share in the United States to European films on the art house circuit, in colleges, and in film festivals. Having grown in importance since the late

1950s, European filmmakers had their most successful box-office year in the United States in 1966 as Hollywood's traditional dominance in the domestic American and world markets was challenged, particularly by France, Britain, and Italy (Ayer et al. 1982: 223). From 1958 to 1968, the number of foreign films in distribution in the United States actually exceeded the number of American films on release, while, by 1966, 50 per cent of US films were actually "runaway productions" – that is, American-financed but produced almost entirely on location outside the United States (Ayer et al. 1982: 224; Guback 1985).

As widespread acclaim was achieved by European art cinema masterpieces such as *The Battle of Algiers* (1965), *Darling* (1965), *Blow Up* (1966), *A Man and a Woman* (1966), *Baisers volés* (1968), *Z* (1969), *Ma nuit chez Maud* (1969), and *Tristana* (1970), particular European auteurs, including Truffaut, Godard, Rohmer, Fellini, Antonioni, and Bergman, were celebrated in the United States as part of a pan-European New Wave which an emerging generation of American filmmakers such as Martin Scorsese, Robert Altman, Francis Ford Coppola, and Brian De Palma, began to emulate in the late 1960s with early features such as *Who's That Knocking at My Door?* (1968), *M*A*S*H* (1970), *The Rain People* (1969), and *Greetings* (1968). But this American New Wave would not really come to fruition until the following decade – in the late 1960s, the emergence of such new American directors was not enough in itself to offset Hollywood's tremendous economic woes. These came to a head in the period 1969–71 when falling rates of production, falling audiences, and falling revenues were compounded by rapid rises in the cost of film production (particularly in print costs and in marketing), and by a sudden collapse in revenues from the resale of feature films to TV upon which all studios had come to strongly rely since the late 1950s (Balio 1985: 438–9; 1990: 181). These developments further squeezed or wiped out the profits of the major studios, prompting an actual shrinking in the studio system. One commentator, Stephen Farber, announced in 1969:

> [The studios] know that they're on the edge of an unprecedented financial disaster. Many have stopped shooting altogether for a period of months. The Paramount lot is to be sold, and MGM and Twentieth Century Fox are talking of doing the same. Agencies are desperate – even many of their major stars cannot find work. The boom town is close to becoming a ghost town again. (Farber 1969)

As a consequence, the most important new development in film economics at the end of the 1960s lay in Hollywood's belated attempt to learn from the successful strategies of the "exploitation" sector, which had long relied on self-consciously low budgets, relatively low production values, and other cost-effective tactics such as filming on location in order to avoid studio overheads. Although in the period 1965–70, Hollywood continued to produce occasional mega-budget epics such as *Doctor Zhivago* (1965) and *Airport* (1970), for a time at the end of the 1960s the Hollywood studios looked for salvation from their economic nosedive to low-budget, youth-oriented features such as the films of the independent production company BBS, including *Head* (1968), *Easy Rider* (1969), *Five Easy Pieces* (1970), *Drive, He Said* (1971), *A Safe Place* (1971), *The Last Picture Show* (1971), and *The King of Marvin Gardens* (1972) (Cohen 1973). The relationship between BBS and Columbia Pictures epitomized the new partnership that the studios sought to forge with independent production companies, in which the studios increasingly repositioned themselves as film distributors and financiers rather than as the makers of films they had been in previous decades.

In keeping with the independent tendencies of the "exploitation" sector, this new partnership also saw an opening up of authorial control by the Hollywood studios to give producers and directors more control of both the artistic vision and the day-to-day financing and management of their motion pictures. This new filmmaking environment appealed to the new generation of creative personnel who emerged in Hollywood cinema in the late 1960s, many of whom had spent at least some of their early careers in the "exploitation" sector: Brian De Palma, Francis Ford Coppola, Bob Rafelson, Monte Hellman, Henry Jaglom, Peter Bogdanovich, Jack Nicholson, Dennis Hopper, and Peter Fonda; cinematographers such as Laszlo Kovacs and Vilmos Zsigmond; and actors such as Bruce Dern, Dean Stockwell, and Karen Black. Moreover, as BBS successes such as *Easy Rider* and *Five Easy Pieces* demonstrated, the new creative freedom tended to foster exactly the kind of contemporary social relevance in films that Hollywood needed if it was to keep youth audiences interested.

The role of non-producer distributor, which all of the studios eventually came to adopt, was pioneered by United Artists, which found that in the increasingly difficult economic environment of the 1960s the arrangement provided a newly attractive approach, allowing it to limit its liabilities in a volatile market. Not owning any large studio premises of its own, United Artists was known for the unusual degree of autonomy it allowed producers and directors once the essential ingredients of a production deal had been agreed, and for the attractive profit-sharing arrangements it offered to producers, who were permitted to give their own name as the first major credit on a film rather than that of the studio as had been the tradition previously (Balio 1990: 165–84).

By 1966, 30 per cent of US films were independently produced outside of the Hollywood "big five" studios and by 1967 this had risen to 51 per cent (Ayer et al. 1982: 223–4). In stark contrast to the Hollywood heyday from the 1920s to the 1950s, when 80 per cent of American feature films were produced in Hollywood, by 1966, 80 per cent of American feature films were made outside of the Hollywood studio system. The gradual transformation of the major studios from production houses to financing and distribution operations, although never total, was the most long-lasting manifestation of the changed economic climate that dominated Hollywood in the late 1960s, and an essential foundation of Hollywood's recovery in the following decade.

But the transformation was only part of an even larger process in which Hollywood became engulfed in the period 1965–70 and which continues to this day. In 1966, Jack L. Warner, the last remaining of the original Warners who had established Warner Bros in 1918, retired. Warner Bros was bought by the TV distribution company Seven Arts Ltd, before being taken over, in turn, along with the Reprise and Atlantic record labels, by the Kinney National Services corporation in 1969, whose businesses included not only motion pictures but also car rental, undertaking, and real estate (Gustafson 1985: 577). Thus, Warner Bros was incorporated as just one arm of a much larger diversified conglomerate, in a

wave of corporate takeovers and mergers that had already seen Music Corporation of America take over Universal in 1962, and which would be followed by the takeover of Paramount by the agribusiness and natural resources giant Gulf & Western in 1966, of United Artists by the financial services corporation Transamerica in 1967, and of MGM by the leisure industry tycoon Kirk Kerkorian in 1970 (Wasko 1982: 179). These corporate takeovers mirrored the emergence of a new generation of creative personnel in Hollywood cinema with a turnover in management personnel within the industry that affected even the few studios that were not taken over in this period but diversified themselves into other business sectors – as, for example, at Twentieth Century Fox where Darryl F. Zanuck, who had run the company since the mid-1930s was removed in 1969 and replaced as chairman by financial manager Dennis Stanfill, who put the company through a strict regime of cutbacks and austerities that lasted well into the mid-1970s (Gussow 1970; Balio 1985: 443–7).

This emergent corporate reality in Hollywood at the end of the 1960s allowed the studios greater flexibility in a difficult business environment – as, for example, in the relationship between Warner Bros/Seven Arts and Francis Ford Coppola's Zoetrope Studios, established in 1969. It also facilitated the development of new "synergies" between motion pictures and other forms of entertainment – for example, in the rise of the soundtrack album, epitomized by the simultaneous release by Warner Bros Pictures of the film of the legendary rock concert *Woodstock* (1970) and, by Warner Bros Records of the *Woodstock* double LP (Gustafson 1985: 577–81). Moreover, as the studios achieved new flexibility and developed new business opportunities in the new corporate environment, the larger world in which the Hollywood film industry operated became a global one to a greater extent than ever before. Hollywood became increasingly dependent upon overseas markets such that where, prior to the Second World War, Hollywood derived approximately two-thirds of its revenue from the United States and approximately one-third from the rest of the world, by the end of the 1960s, that proportion had shifted to fifty-fifty (Balio 1985: 408). The appointment of Jack Valenti in 1966 as director of the Motion Picture Association of America signalled a recognition of this new global reality within the industry, as Valenti would take a proactive and high-profile approach to the promotion of Hollywood cinema in world markets. As Tino Balio has demonstrated, these world markets would prove increasingly important to Hollywood in the following decade as it emerged from the social and economic turbulence of the 1960s with renewed force and renewed popular appeal, especially in the second half of the 1970s on the back of the blockbuster successes of Steven Spielberg and George Lucas.

While the strength of Hollywood's eventual economic recovery in the latter 1970s may be undeniable, that economic recovery and the relatively conservative artistic and ideological tendencies that accompanied it were not necessarily beneficial to the quality or social value of the cinema it produced and often involved a conscientious attempt to roll back many of the social and cultural changes that had made the late 1960s a truly distinctive period.

References

Auster, A. and Quart, L. (1984) American cinema of the sixties, *Cineaste*, 13(2): 4–12.

Ayer, D., Bates, R.E. and Herman, P.J. (1982) Self-censorship in the movie industry: a historical perspective on law and social change, in G. Kindem (ed.) *The American Movie Industry: The Business of Motion Pictures*. Carbondale: Southern Illinois University Press, pp. 215–50.

Balio, T. (ed.) (1985) *The American Film Industry*. Madison: University of Wisconsin Press.

Balio, T. (ed.) (1990) *Hollywood in the Age of Television*. Boston: Unwin Hyman.

Barnouw, E. (1983) *Documentary: A History of the Non-fiction Film*. New York: Oxford University Press.

Biskind, P. (1983) *Seeing Is Believing: How Hollywood Taught Us to Stop Worrying and Love the '50s*. London: Pluto Press.

Biskind, P. (1999) *Easy Riders, Raging Bulls*. New York: Simon and Schuster.

Bondanella, P. (1995) *Italian Cinema: From Neorealism to the Present*. New York: Continuum.

Bordwell, D. and Staiger, J. (1985) Since 1960: the persistence of a mode of film practice, in D. Bordwell, J. Staiger and K. Thompson (eds) *The Classical Hollywood Cinema: Film Style and Mode of Production to 1960*. London: Routledge.

Cohen, M.S. (1973) The corporate style of BBS: seven intricate pieces, *Take One*, 3(12): 19–22.

Conner, B. (1999) *2000BC: The Bruce Conner Story, Part 2*. Minneapolis: Walker Art Center.

Diehl, D. (1970) The Simenon of cinema, *Show*, 1(5): 26–30, 86–7.

Doherty, T. (1988) *Teenagers and Teenpics: The Juvenilization of American Movies in the 1950s*. Boston: Unwin Hyman.

Engelhardt, T. (1995) *The End of Victory Culture: Cold War America and the Disillusioning of a Generation*. New York: Basic Books.

Erlick, A. (1970) Which way is up? *International Motion Picture Exhibitor*, 20 (May): 1.

Farber, D. (ed.) (1994) *The Sixties: From Memory to History*. Chapel Hill: University of North Carolina Press.

Farber, S. (1969) End of the road? *Film Quarterly*, 23(3): 3–16.

Gilliatt, P. (1969) The current cinema: into the eye of the storm, *New Yorker*, 19 July.

Gitlin, T. (1987) *The Sixties: Years of Hope, Days of Rage*. New York: Bantam.

Graham, D. (1987) Western movies since 1960, in J.G. Taylor et al. (eds) *A Literary History of the American West*. Fort Worth: Texas Christian University Press, pp. 1256–61.

Greene, E. (1996) *Planet of the Apes as American Myth: Race and Politics in the Films and Television Series*. Jefferson, NC: McFarland and Co.

Guback, T. (1985) Hollywood's international market, in T. Balio (ed.) *The American Film Industry*. Madison: University of Wisconsin Press.

Gussow, M. (1970) Studio system passé – Film forges ahead, *New York Times*, 27 May.

Gustafson, R. (1985) "What's happening to our pix biz?" From Warner Bros. to Warner Communications, Inc., in T. Balio (ed.), *The American Film Industry*. Madison: University of Wisconsin Press.

James, D. (1989) *Allegories of Cinema: American Film in the Sixties*. Princeton, NJ: Princeton University Press.

Jowett, G. (1976) *Film: The Democratic Art*. New York: Little, Brown and Co.

Kael, P. (1973) *Deeper Into Movies*. London: Calder and Boyars.

Kauffmann, S. (1975) *Living Images*. New York: Harper and Row.

Klinger, B. (1997) The road to dystopia: landscaping the nation in *Easy Rider*, in S. Cohan and I.R. Hark (eds) *The Road Movie Book*. London: Routledge.

Kolker, R. (1988) *A Cinema of Loneliness*, 2nd edn. New York: Oxford University Press.

Krämer, P. (1998) Post-classical Hollywood, in J. Hill and P. Church (eds) *The Oxford Guide to Film Studies*. Oxford: Oxford University Press, pp. 289–309.

Leong, I., Sell, M. and Thomas, K. (1997) Mad love, mobile homes, and dysfunctional dicks: on the road with *Bonnie and Clyde*, in S. Cohan and I.R. Hark (eds) *The Road Movie Book*. London and New York: Routledge.

Lev, P. (1993) *The Euro-American Cinema*. Austin: University of Texas Press.

Levy, A. (1967) Will big budgets spoil Roger Corman? *Status/Diplomat*, March, pp. 46–52.

Marsden, M.T. and Nachbar, J. (1987) The modern popular Western: radio, television, film, and print, in J.G. Taylor et al. (eds) *A Literary History of the American West*. Fort Worth: Texas Christian University Press.

Matusow, A.J. (1984) *The Unravelling of America: A History of Liberalism in the 1960s*. New York: Harper and Row.

Monaco, P. (2003) *The Sixties, 1960–1969*, vol. 8 of *History of American Cinema*. Berkeley: University of California Press.

Neale, S. (2000) *Genre and Hollywood*. London and New York: Routledge.

Newsweek (1970) The new movies, 76(7): 42–54.

Ottoson, R.L. (1985) *AIP: A Filmography*. New York: Garland Publishing Inc.

Randall, R.S. (1985) Censorship from *The Miracle* to *Deep Throat*, in T. Balio (ed.) *The American Film Industry*. Madison: University of Wisconsin Press.

Ray, R.B. (1985) *A Certain Tendency of the Hollywood Cinema, 1930–1980*. Princeton, NJ: Princeton University Press.

Reiner, R. (1981) Keystone to Kojak: the Hollywood cop, in P. Davies and B. Neve (eds) *Cinema, Politics, and Society in America*. Manchester: Manchester University Press.

Research Department of Security Pacific National Bank (1974) The motion picture industry in California: a special report, *Journal of the Producers' Guild of America*, March, p. 7.

Rosen, M. (1973) *Popcorn Venus: Women, Movies and the American Dream*. New York: Coward, McCann and Geoghegan.

Rowe, C. (1982) Myth and symbolism in the work of Kenneth Anger, in *The Baudelairean Cinema: A Trend within the American Avant-garde*. Ann Arbor, MI: UMI Research Press.

Ryan, D. and Kellner, J. (1988) *Camera Politica: The Politics and Ideology of Contemporary Hollywood Film*. Bloomington: Indiana University Press.

Salt, B. (1992) *Film Style and Technology: History and Analysis*. London: Starword Books.

Saturday Review (1969) The art that matters: a look at today's film scene by the under-thirties, 52 (27 December): 7–21.

Schaefer, E. (1999) *Bold!, Daring!, Shocking!, True!, A History of Exploitation Film, 1919–59*. Durham, NC: Duke University Press.

Schatz, T. (1983) *Old Hollywood/New Hollywood: Ritual, Art and Industry*. Ann Arbor, MI: UMI Research Press.

Schindler, C. (1996) *Hollywood in Crisis: Cinema and American Society, 1929–1939*. London: Routledge.

Shiel, M. (2003) Why call them "cult movies"? American independent filmmaking and the counter-culture in the 1960s, *Scope Online Journal of Film Studies*, Institute of Film Studies, University of Nottingham, May, www.nottingham.ac.uk/film/journal/index.htm.

Sklar, R. (1988) When looks could kill: American cinema of the sixties, *Cineaste*, 16(1–2): 50–3.

Smith, P.S. (1986) *Andy Warhol's Art and Films*. Ann Arbor, MI: UMI Research Press.

Taylor, J.G., Lyon, T.J., Day, G.F., Haslam, G.W., Maguire, J.H. and Pilkington, W.T. (eds) (1987) *A Literary History of the American West*. Fort Worth: Texas Christian University Press.

Trecker, J.L. (1972) Sex, marriage, and the movies, *Take One*, 3(5): 12–15.

Trilling, D. (1970) *Easy Rider* and its critics, *Atlantic Monthly*, 226(3): 90–5.

Wagstaff, C. (1992) A forkful of Westerns: industry, audiences, and the Italian Western, in R. Dyer and G. Vincendeau (eds) *Popular European Cinema*. London: Routledge.

Wakefield, D. (1969) The war at home, *Atlantic Monthly*, 224(4): 119–24.

Wasko, J. (1982) *Movies and Money: Financing the American Film Industry*. Norwood, NJ: Ablex Publ. Corp.

Waugh, T. (1985) Beyond *vérité*: Emile de Antonio and the New Documentary of the 1970s, in B. Nichols (ed.) *Movies and Methods*, vol. 2. Berkeley: University of California Press.

Yacowar, M. (1993) *The Films of Paul Morrissey*. Cambridge: Cambridge University Press.

DEBTS, DISASTERS AND MEGA-MUSICALS: THE DECLINE OF THE STUDIO SYSTEM

James Russell

Twentieth Century Fox's *Cleopatra*

IN MGM'S 1959 release *Ben-Hur*, the title character famously participates in a lengthy and gruelling chariot race. For over 20 minutes of screen time, Ben-Hur (Charlton Heston) risks life and limb to defeat his arch rival, the Roman Messala (Stephen Boyd). At the climax Ben-Hur triumphs, but Messala pays for failure with his life, when he is crushed beneath the wheels of his rival's chariot. The critic Michael Wood has argued that in this spectacular sequence Hollywood celebrates itself, lauding the expense that the American movie industry of the late 1950s and early 1960s could lavish on mere entertainments, and stressing the power of both film and filmmakers. As Wood (1975: 173) puts it, "the hero of *Ben-Hur* is not Ben-Hur, who only won the chariot race, but William Wyler, the director, the man responsible for providing the chariot race for us". One could add that the chariot race also provides a very effective allegory for the position occupied by MGM, the studio that released *Ben-Hur*, as the 1960s began.

Over the course of the 1960s, all the major Hollywood studios were engaged in a high stakes competition where success meant survival, and failure meant death. MGM was jockeying for the lead in 1959, and with the release of *Ben-Hur*, the studio leapt ahead of the pack. The film had cost a reported $15 million to produce, but brought in rentals of $36.7 million, making it, for a time, the highest grossing movie ever released (Finler 2003: 154). However, the race continued, and as the 1960s wore on, MGM began to flag. By 1969 the studio had fallen by the wayside, mortally injured. The fate of MGM, which had dominated Hollywood since the 1920s, was sealed when it was purchased by the entrepreneur Kirk Kerkorian and stripped down into its component assets.[1] This chapter explains how this situation came about, and looks at what happened to all the major studios in the 1960s. The American movie industry had been forced to adapt in the early 1950s, partly as a result of the so-called "Paramount Decrees", partly by the widespread adoption of television, but mainly by changes in audience attendance habits. As the theatrical market declined in importance, new markets opened up, but new strategies were required to cope in this changing marketplace. In the 1960s, these strategies were tested to their limit, and Hollywood, as we understand it today, was forged.

The studio system in transition

What was the studio system in its heyday? By the 1930s, the production, distribution and exhibition of movies in America had come to be dominated by eight companies: Loews (MGM), RKO, Twentieth Century Fox, Warner Brothers, Paramount (known as the "big five" primarily because they owned movie theatre chains as well as production and funding facilities) and United Artists, Columbia and Universal (known as the "little three" because they were, to varying degrees, producers and distributors, and none owned a substantial exhibition network). Between them these companies functioned as "a cartel of movie factories that turned out a feature every week for a hundred million moviegoers", in the words of Thomas Schatz (1988: 4). Although all of the studios were unique to some degree, and broader differences in attitude and operation distinguished the big five from the little three, three general characteristics mark out the practices of the studio system as a unified period in the history of American movie making.

Firstly, the industry at this time was defined by vertical integration. The big five owned resources and the means of manufacture (the studios of Hollywood, and the filmmakers and stars who worked there), networks of distribution (which delivered the product into movie theatres across the world) and the premises of consumption (movie theatres). Although the little three were not integrated in this way, and independents existed in every sector, vertical integration defined the business practices of the industry as whole. The big five had long-standing reciprocal arrangements to exhibit each other's movies in their theatres, and had established similar relationships with the little three. Although the majors could not be said to control the majority of movie theatres in the United States, they owned enough of the most profitable "first run" chains, where movies received their initial releases, to control the market. Secondly, contracting practices tied stars and workers to particular studios for long periods of time. Hence it was possible for MGM to possess "more stars than there are in Heaven", as the studio's tagline put it. Furthermore, the studios' resources were organized to facilitate the speedy production of movies. Technicians and stars could move rapidly from one project to the next, sometimes on the same day. Thirdly, these companies were not owned by larger conglomerates. Although some had interests in music or publishing, moviemaking was their primary concern.

Although the majors absolutely dominated the movie industry at this time, they coexisted with numerous independent producers, distributors and exhibitors. At the time "independent" principally meant "not one of the majors", but there were gradations of independence. An "independent" movie could be produced without any studio input at all, but, more often than not, movies were labelled "independent" if they were overseen by someone who was not tied to a long-term contract with one of the majors – such as the producer David O. Selznick, or the director Alfred Hitchcock. Their films were still funded and distributed by the majors, but they were produced away from the studio assembly line. United Artists was founded as a distributor of such "independent" movies, but among the other majors, assisting independent production was a relatively marginal practice. The independent sector was small, but it could exist because demand for product was so relentless.

In their heyday the studios produced movies for a huge and voracious audience. Between 1930 and 1946 the average number of movie tickets sold per week in the United States never dropped below 50 million.[2] Often sales far exceeded this, and between 1943 and 1946, over 80 million tickets were sold on average every week. According to the US Census Bureau (2000) the population of the United States was 132.2 million in 1940. Even taking into account the fact many attended the movies several times a week, movie going was habit for a huge percentage of Americans at this time. In 1943, over a quarter of the average American's recreational expenditure went on going to the movies (Finler 2003: 376). However, when the war ended, cinema-going patterns changed in an unprecedented fashion. Average weekly attendance dropped from 82 million in 1946 to 42 million in 1953. This pattern continued throughout the 1960s. In 1961, average weekly attendance was 30 million and it dropped continually until it reached a low of 16 million in 1971 (Finler 2003: 379). Put simply, movies became a marginal part of American cultural and commercial life, as Robert Sklar (1999) has shown. Although many audiences had stopped going to cinemas entirely, the major problem was that many more had stopped going with any degree of regularity. At exactly the same time as the effects of this shift were beginning to appear, the majors were forced to change the ways that they operated by the US government's successful prosecution of Paramount Pictures in a landmark antitrust suit.

The "Paramount Decrees", as they are sometimes known, were designed to open up the film market to independent competitors. Consequently, the vertically integrated majors were instructed to separate their exhibition interests from their other activities, either by a process of divestiture (selling these divisions to independent companies), or divorcement (entirely dividing their corporate structure, thus rendering one wing independent from the others). Furthermore, all of the majors, including Columbia, United Artists and Universal, were required to adopt new methods of licensing movies for exhibition in theatres. Prior negotiating, which was perceived as unfair, was outlawed.[3] These new rules required the majors to change their operation at a time when revenues from movie exhibition in America were becoming uncertain. Arguably, the changes that were forced on the industry benefited the majors in the long run, because they shifted responsibility for coping with declining audiences onto the newly minted exhibition sector. The new modes of operation that appeared in the 1950s and 1960s were calculated to maintain the pre-eminence of the majors, and stimulate demand for their product, in ways that severely limited the power of theatre chains.

The road-show era

The main shift that occurred in the 1950s and 1960s was a decrease in the number of films produced for cinemas by the majors. In 1941, the majors had released a total of 379 movies (Finler 2003: 364–5). In 1963, the majors released 142 movies (Finler 2003: 366–7). Reducing supply helped stimulate demand among theatre owners who needed the product. The majors were then able to negotiate favourable rental fees from the exhibition sector.[4] Furthermore, the outstanding hits of the late 1940s seemed to have suggested that a tighter concentration of resources on fewer, larger productions might work in the changed marketplace. Two prestigious 1946 films, *Duel in the Sun* and *The Best Years of Our Lives*, produced independently but distributed by the

Selznick Releasing Organization and United Artists respectively, had each grossed around $10 million – far more than any single release since *Gone With the Wind* (another highly budgeted independent production).[5] In 1949, Cecil B. De Mille's *Samson and Delilah* achieved a similar degree of success for MGM, earning over $9 million in a year when no other release exceeded $5 million in revenues (Finler 2003: 357).

These were all "road-show" releases – which means that they were initially exhibited at a handful of extremely prestigious city centre theatres, with substantially increased ticket prices, and other trappings of the legitimate theatre such as bookable seats, intermissions and overtures.[6] Although such movies would eventually appear in the more usual first and second-run theatre circuits, the road-show release could run for years in the same theatre, attracting increased custom on the basis of increased prestige. The majors often received a greater percentage of the ticket price in road-show theatre than in subsequent-run circuits (Hall 2002: 14). Road-showing had been employed occasionally for decades, as Sheldon Hall (2000) has shown, but in the 1950s the majors increasingly began to favour expensive road-shows, which cost more than ordinary productions, but which were also capable of generating far higher returns. With the release of *This is Cinerama* in 1952 and *The Robe* in 1953, the road-show phenomenon became inextricably linked to innovative widescreen and big-screen technologies such as Cinema-Scope, Todd-AO and Cinerama.[7]

Just as the size of the movie screen increased, so did the potential revenue that any one movie could generate. Throughout the 1950s and 1960s historical epics and prestige musicals consistently earned rentals that were virtually unheard of in the studio era. As

Richard Maltby (1998: 31) has observed, "Before 1960 only twenty movies had grossed over $10 million in the domestic market; by 1970, more than 80 had." In fact, *Ben-Hur* earned $36.7 million in the United States, *The Ten Commandments* (1956) $34.2 million, *Around the World in 80 Days* (1956) $22 million, *Doctor Zhivago* (1965) $43 million and *The Sound of Music* (1965) a staggering $77 million (Finler 2003: 358). As well as being expensive and spectacular, these films were often international in terms of their appeal and their production. As budgets had risen, overseas development and filming, sometimes known as "runaway" production, had begun to make sense (Monaco 2001: 11–15). Not only was it cheaper to film in Europe, or even the Middle East, than in Los Angeles, but international productions were more easily marketable to an international audience, which was growing considerably in the aftermath of the Second World War, at exactly the same time as the American audience diminished. As Tino Balio (1985: 408) has observed, "In 1949, 19 American-interest features were made abroad; in 1969, 183."

For a variety of reasons, then, the majors increasingly focused their movie production budgets on a handful of prestige releases, unlike the diverse and ever changing range of cinematic entertainment offered before 1948. As Peter Krämer (2005: Chapter 1) has shown, this new approach appealed to audiences who rarely visited the cinema. The roadshow trend was a calculated attempt to attract occasional viewers, often families and older people, who had abandoned cinema going as regular activity, but might be attracted back to theatres by something spectacular, edifying and prestigious – the "must-see" movie of the year. Although smaller productions remained a constituent part of the studios' output, scale

and spectacle began to predominate, and the blockbuster approach that characterizes cinema today took shape. However, the films themselves were not a new phenomenon – large-scale hits had appeared in Hollywood's past, but had usually originated outside the studio system. In fact, just as blockbusters began to predominate, so did the independent production methods that had previously been associated with them.

In the past, some of Hollywood's biggest hits had been produced by visionary independents who relied on the majors for funding and distribution, but who organized and oversaw their own productions. A case in point is David O. Selznick, who produced *Gone With the Wind* for MGM. Selznick had previously worked as a production chief at RKO and MGM, but when he went independent, he was able to transcend the mass production ethos of the studios and focus all of his attention on occasional prestige releases. Selznick produced a string of mega-hits, such as *A Star is Born* (1937) and *The Prisoner of Zenda* (1937), which ensured that the major studios were invariably willing to distribute his productions. When such investments paid off, they did so in unprecedented fashion. Even today *Gone With the Wind* remains the highest grossing film ever released if figures are adjusted for inflation. Other successful independent producers operating in the studio era included Walter Wanger, Samuel Goldwyn and Darryl F. Zanuck (at least until his independent Twentieth Century productions merged with Fox studios in 1935). Goldwyn and other independents such as Walt Disney, Selznick and the British mogul Alexander Korda had found a home at United Artists, the studio founded as a distributor of independent movies.

Throughout the 1950s and 1960s, this model of independent production became the norm. As Balio (1976: 237) has observed, United Artists offered a template for survival in a post-antitrust industry. Rather than maintaining the unwieldy assembly line structure of the studio era, the majors recognized that movie production could be more efficient if staff, resources and capital were assembled as they were needed for individual productions, what Janet Staiger (in Bordwell et al. 1985: 330) has called the "package unit system". It was no longer necessary to produce movies for theatrical release at a pre-1948 level, and so movies were increasingly packaged as one-off events, and production resources were rented on an *ad hoc* basis. In this climate, the power of individual stars, producers and directors increased, but not as much as the power of agents. The long-term contracting practices of the studio era disappeared. Stars, directors and studio producers all began founding their own production companies, and increasingly the talent agencies who represented these people held all of the resources needed to make movies happen. Perhaps the most compelling proof of the

Continued on page 50

Twentieth Century Fox in the 1960s

The early 1960s saw the fortunes of Twentieth Century-Fox at their lowest ebb, and the company in the weakest financial position of any Hollywood studio at that time. Under Buddy Adler, who had succeeded Darryl F. Zanuck as executive in charge of production in 1956, the studio had been over-extending itself by producing too many films, most of them loss-makers, at a time when its rivals were reducing their output to suit a shrinking market. Fox's release programme for 1958, for example, totalled forty-two pictures, with the Todd-AO musical *South Pacific* (1958) the only major success. Adler died in 1960, but his short-lived successors, Robert Goldstein, former head of Fox's European operations, and Peter Levathes, head of its TV division, proved even less reliable in their commercial judgement, initiating such large-budget flops as *The Story of Ruth* (1960), *Tender is the Night* (1960) and *Hemingway's Adventures of a Young Man* (1962).

As a result, Fox suffered corporate losses of $2.9 million in 1960, $22.5 million in 1961 and $39.8 million in 1962, the largest for any company in Hollywood history to that date. In 1961, it cut back drastically on production, promising "fewer but better" pictures.[1] Having released thirty-five films that year, the studio handled only twenty-five in 1962 and eighteen in 1963. Following a revolt of shareholders against Fox president Spyros P. Skouras's perceived mismanagement, Darryl Zanuck returned to take charge of the company in 1962. Having himself taken over as president, Zanuck appointed his son Richard vice-president in charge of production and conducted a comprehensive review and rationalization of its operations, going so far as to shut down all production for a period of eight months while the value of its existing commitments and future prospects was assessed, and to sell off part of the studio lot as real estate. During this time, Zanuck's independent production *The Longest Day* (1962) – the story of D-Day, filmed at a total cost of over $10 million, which Fox had partially bankrolled – provided the studio with virtually its only substantial theatrical revenue, ultimately grossing $30 million worldwide.

Another Fox blockbuster, begun in 1960 but not actually completed and released until 1963, became the most expensive movie of its era. *Cleopatra* suffered escalating production problems and ballooning costs which ultimately may have reached $44 million. Although it has the reputation of a box-office disaster, and was certainly a drain on the studio's finances during its three years of production, the film's road-show release pattern actually helped Fox to restabilize. Theatres playing the film charged the highest ticket prices in exhibition history, remitting a substantial portion of their anticipated ticket sales to Fox as an advance and an equally large proportion of the actual gross as a distribution fee. With top tickets set at $5.50 (as compared to a previous high of $4.80 and a more usual road-show seat price of $3.50), the film thus amassed up to $15 million in advance rentals and guarantees even before its June 1963 premiere, making it one of the ten highest grossing pictures in US box-office history before ever having been exhibited.[2] Though the premiere run at New York's Rivoli Theatre lasted seventy-five weeks (due to the theatre having committed itself to a specified length of run), ticket sales were substantially lower than anticipated and the theatre owners sued Fox for supplying it with "an inferior attraction". Nonetheless, according to executive vice president Seymour Poe, "handling *Cleopatra* as a 'road-show', earned [the studio] millions more than it might otherwise".[3]

Buoyed by the grosses earned by both *Cleopatra* and *The Longest Day* through their specialized distribution strategies, Fox subsequently dubbed itself "the road-show company".[4] In the 1965 and 1966 seasons it released no fewer than six road-show pictures, produced at a combined cost of $55 million. All six were filmed overseas and the first to open became the biggest hit of the decade: *The Sound of Music* (1965). Of the remaining five, only *Those Magnificent Men in Their Flying Machines* (1965) and *The Blue Max* (1966) were profitable from theatrical release alone. *The Agony and the Ecstasy* (1965), *The Bible – in the Beginning . . .* (1966) and *The Sand Pebbles* (1966) all recorded losses, though the latter two at least still did good business, earning the studio substantial distribution fees.

Fox seemed to sit comfortably for most of the remaining decade, with annual corporate profits rising steadily from $9.1 million in 1963 to $15.4 million in 1967, and dropping only slightly to $15 million in 1968. Yet revenues from theatrical distribution alone would not have been sufficient to keep it in the black for this period. In each year, with the sole exception of 1965, its annual release slate actually made a loss. Of a total of 123 films Fox released between 1964 and 1970, only thirty-seven went into profit, the majority of these only just breaking even; altogether, the loss on production over these years totalled $161.3 million.[5] The single profitable year was due almost entirely to *The Sound of Music*, which accounted for nearly half of all theatrical revenues received from 1965 releases. More reliable as a source of income were three other areas of activity: television production, which helped pay off a great deal of the studio's overheads; various subsidiary divisions, such as De Luxe Color laboratories, music publishing and overseas exhibition interests; and, most importantly, sales of theatrical films to the US television networks.[6] In 1966, Fox made a deal with ABC for the lease of seventeen pictures which brought the studio $19.5 million, including $5 million for *Cleopatra* (the largest amount yet paid for a single feature, which brought the film into the black).[7] As a result, Fox could claim the highest annual income in its history for 1966, with film rentals totalling $217,364,000, an increase of 40.8 per cent over the previous year.[8]

For later seasons, Fox tried deliberately to repeat the success of *The Sound of Music*. Lacking another Rodgers and Hammerstein property of comparable quality or appeal, Fox commissioned three high-budget musicals. *Doctor Dolittle* (1967), *Star!* (1968) and *Hello, Dolly!* (1969) were respectively, an adaptation of a children's classic with an original score, a showbiz biopic built around a collection of nostalgic hit songs, and a theatrical smash hit still running on Broadway. They were produced and released on an annual basis between 1967 and 1969, so as not to compete with one another in the road-show marketplace (where *The Sound of Music* was still playing out its lengthy engagements). All three were shot in Todd-AO 70 mm, all exceeded their initial budgets to cost between $14 million and $25 million each, and none returned a profit.

The studio's more successful pictures of the second half of the decade were made for the

Robert Altman's *M*A*S*H*, a Vietnam film disguised as a Korean War film, helped to keep Fox afloat

general release market on comparatively modest (though still substantial) budgets, notably *Von Ryan's Express* (1965), *Our Man Flint* (1966), *Valley of the Dolls* (1967), *Planet of the Apes* (1968) and *Butch Cassidy and the Sundance Kid* (1969). An early 1970 release, grossing $31.2 million worldwide by the end of the year, pointed the way forward. *M*A*S*H* (1970) made an almost 500 per cent profit on a budget of $6.5 million, dollar for dollar a greater success than *The Sound of Music*. Appealing largely to the college-educated youth market, which musicals typically bypassed, the anti-war satire also outgrossed Fox's final two road-shows, *Patton* (1970) and *Tora! Tora! Tora!* (1970), both war pictures whose costs (respectively, $12.6 and $25.5 million) far exceeded those of Robert Altman's film.

In 1969, Richard Zanuck hired a team of consultants from the Stanford Research Institute to assess and advise on the company's financial position and its cost-effectiveness. The conclusions it reached were devastating, pointing to Fox's complete non-viability as a profit-making entity.[9] The company declared corporate losses of $27.5 million in 1969 and a massive $76.4 million in 1970, the largest any of the Hollywood majors suffered in those crisis years. Between 1969 and 1971 Fox was forced to conduct a radical review of its operations, especially its film production programme, to arrive at a more realistic accommodation to the changing marketplace. This included reducing both the maximum amount to be spent on individual films (henceforward ranging from an average of $1.5 million to $3 million, with an absolute ceiling of $5 million), as well as the total number of films produced annually. Several road-shows planned for production in 1970–71 were cancelled. Lower estimates of income from film sales to TV networks, which had receded drastically after the mid-1960s boom, were also built into budget planning, and the company substantially expanded its non-film activities, especially investments in real estate, with half the studio lot being sold off or leased for construction. To emphasize its diversification, the company dropped the word "film" from its corporate name, Twentieth Century-Fox Film Corporation; a few years later, it also dropped the hyphen.

Senior personnel were also shaken up in the corporate restructuring. In 1969, Darryl Zanuck had assumed the role of chairman and chief executive officer, with Richard promoted to studio president and the latter's producing partner David Brown made head of production. This arrangement did not remain in place for long. Richard Zanuck resigned at the end of 1970, as did his father early in 1971 to become "Chairman Emeritus" of the board of directors (in effect a nebulous post). His former position was filled by Dennis C. Stanfill, whom Richard had initially hired as the company's financial officer.[10] As both chairman of the board and president, with Gordon Stulberg as head of production, Stanfill masterminded the "reorientation" of Fox and its eventual return to a profitable basis in 1974 (when Stulberg resigned and Stanfill took over his post, too, until 1976). Thereafter, Darryl Zanuck effectively retired from the industry, while Richard went into independent production with David Brown; together they made many successful films, including two of the biggest hits of the following decade: *The Sting* (1973) and *Jaws* (1975), both for Universal.

Notes

1   "Change in policy decided on at Fox", *New York Times*, 8 May 1961.
2   See, for example, *The Daily Cinema*, 21 January 1963, p. 1; "*Cleo*'s 13 million dollar advance", *Kine. Weekly*, 4 April 1963, p. 13; "£300,000 advance sets a new pattern for *Cleo*'s release", *Kine. Weekly*, 30 May 1963, p. 86; *Variety Film Reviews*, 19 June 1963. These sources disagree on how much money was paid in advance to Fox, and therefore whether it was placed seventh or ninth in the all-time box-office listings.
3   Milton Esterow, "*Cleopatra* termed 'success'", *New York Times*, 27 March 1964; see also Vincent Canby, "Costly *Cleopatra* is nearing its break-even point", *New York Times*, 25 March 1966.
4   "Fox to make six road show films", *Kine. Weekly*, 17 October 1963, p. 10; "World-wide advertising campaign for Fox's road show films", *Kine. Weekly*, 14 January 1965, p. 6.
5   For details of costs and revenues for all Fox releases from 1964–70, see Stephen Silverman, *The Fox That Got Away: The Last Days of the Zanuck Dynasty at Twentieth Century-Fox* (Secaucus, NJ: Lyle Stuart, 1988), pp. 323–9.
6   See "20th-Fox's record 6-month profit; cost cut outpaces income drop", *Variety*, 4 September 1968, pp. 3 and 24.
7   "Fox roadshows in $20m Fox US TV deal", *Kine. Weekly*, 6 October 1966, p. 5.
8   "Fox income reaches all-time high", *Kine. Weekly*, 1 April 1967.
9   On the SRI's research and resultant report, see Silverman, 1988, pp. 163–6, 177–289.
10   See, for instance, "20th Century-Fox shake-up prepares for expansion", *Kine. Weekly*, 6 September 1970, pp. 3, 9; Leonard Sloane: "A new Zanuck looks at a new century", *New York Times*, 19 October 1969; "20th-Fox losses, but profits soon", *Kine. Weekly*, 19 September 1970, p. 7; "Richard Zanuck and David Brown out of Fox", *Kine. Weekly*, 2 January 1971, p. 3; "Fox forecasts profit in first quarter", *Kine. Weekly*, 20 March 1971, p. 7; "Zanuck quits the chair at Fox", *Kine. Weekly*, 22 May 1971, p. 3; "It was our Battle of Britain", *Kine. Weekly*, 3 July 1971, pp. 5, 25.

Sheldon Hall

Continued from page 46

power of agents in the industry came in 1962 when Lew Wasserman's talent agency MCA (Music Corporation of America) completed its takeover of Universal Studios.[8] For the first time (but not the last), an agent assumed the position of a movie mogul. Like the other studio heads at the beginning of the 1960s, Wasserman doggedly pursued the road-show trend. Expensive epics and musicals made up more and more of the studio's theatrical output, but in the 1960s the perils of this approach began to show.

Studio production in the 1960s

Twentieth Century Fox had always been at the forefront of the road-show trend. Under production chief Darryl F. Zanuck the studio had concentrated resources on glossy, prestigious dramas and epics like *The Robe* (1953), *Prince Valiant* (1954), *The Egyptian* (1954), and *South Pacific* (1958). It was also studio policy to encourage production in the new CinemaScope system, and even after Darryl F. Zanuck left in 1956 (to become an independent producer) Fox continued to employ a high expense, prestige formula for its major releases. However, as the 1960s began, fault lines in the studio's stability were beginning to show. Although Fox had recorded a profit throughout the 1950s, the studio made a loss of almost $15 million in 1960 (Finler 2003: 124). Over the next two years these losses increased dramatically. In 1961, Fox reported an annual loss of $22.5 million, and in 1962 losses were $39.8 million (Finler 2003: 124). Had it not been for the sale of Fox's Los Angeles backlot to real estate developers in 1961, the losses would have been far greater (Monaco 2001: 35).

The main problem seems to have been the

troubled production of the studio's most ambitious film to date, *Cleopatra* (1963), produced by the independent Walter Wanger. The star, Elizabeth Taylor, had suffered a string of illnesses, delaying production, the original director, Rouben Mamoulian, had to be replaced halfway through filming by Joseph L. Mankiewitz, and at one point the entire production was moved from America to Italy. Throughout this time the film generated a welter of controversy as Elizabeth Taylor and co-star Richard Burton embarked on a very public extramarital affair. Reports about Burton and Taylor could not help but also note the increasingly chaotic nature of the production. Paul Monaco (2001: 36) has argued that, in this context, *Cleopatra* offers a good example of the ways that the studio system was fragmenting. According to Monaco, lines of control had been weakened by the shift to package unit production. However, in 1962, the board of directors at Fox responded to the *Cleopatra* crisis by rehiring the one man who had maintained control of the studio through some very difficult times – Darryl F. Zanuck.

Zanuck oversaw the completion of *Cleopatra*, albeit at a cost of over $40 million, and the film went on to gross $26 million in rentals (Finler 2003: 123). By the standards of previous blockbusters this was an above average return, but, of course, it meant that the film did not break even at the box office. Furthermore, revenues from *Cleopatra* were generated over the course of several years, as was the case with all road-shows. Nevertheless, with *Cleopatra* finished, Fox's finances improved between 1963 and 1968 (Finler 2003: 124). Zanuck instigated a series of smaller productions, which helped the company stay in the black, but he also continued the blockbuster trend by initiating the mega-musical *The Sound of Music*. Released in 1965, this proved to be Fox's biggest hit to date, and was by far and away the highest grossing film of the decade. At Fox, and across Hollywood, the film's success seemed to prove that road-shows were entering a new era of increased popularity. In the same year, MGM achieved similar heights of success with *Doctor Zhivago* (which took rentals of $43 million). These two films were taken to be representative but, in fact, they were highly exceptional. Already, throughout the early part of the decade almost all of the majors had seen at least one potential blockbuster run into trouble.

United Artists had lost money on *Solomon and Sheba* in 1959, *The Alamo* in 1960, and the studio had its single biggest flop of the era in 1965 with *The Greatest Story Ever Told*. Hits like *Exodus* (1963), *West Side Story* (1961, Fig. 4 (*see plate section*)), *It's a Mad, Mad, Mad, Mad World* (1963) and smaller-scale runaway productions with British involvement, such as the James Bond films and *Tom Jones* (1963) helped keep the studio relatively stable throughout the early 1960s, although United Artists still recorded a loss in 1963, as revenues were sucked up by the $20 million production of *The Greatest Story Ever Told*. Meanwhile Warner Brothers had become wary of the blockbuster trend after all their putative road-show epics (*The Silver Chalice* in 1954, *Helen of Troy* and *The Land of the Pharaohs* in 1955) had failed to turn a profit. Nevertheless, the studio still reported its most significant annual loss in 1963, as it struggled to fund another mega-musical, *My Fair Lady*. Although this film achieved considerable critical acclaim, like so many movies at the time it failed to break even when it was released in 1964.[9] Until that point, the studios that managed to avoid annual losses were, in fact, those who had

focused on more modest productions – notably Universal and Columbia.

Nevertheless, the twin successes of *The Sound of Music* and *Doctor Zhivago* prompted a serious case of hubris across the industry. Fox put three more mega-musicals into production, *Doctor Doolittle* (1967), *Star!* (1968) and *Hello Dolly!* (1969, Fig. 3 (*see plate section*)). The studio also released the biblical epic *The Bible: In the Beginning* (1966) and the war epic *Tora! Tora! Tora!* (1970). All lost millions. Pauline Kael's (1970: 74) review of *Tora! Tora! Tora!* ran "One merely dozes, knowing that *Tora! Tora! Tora!* is one of the last of its kind; the only question is whether it will sink the oft bombed Twentieth Century Fox." Throughout this period, Fox's slightly more modest productions, like *Planet of the Apes* (1967) and *Valley of the Dolls* (1967) had kept the studio in the black. Although these were often budgeted at above average levels, they were not as exorbitantly expensive as the road-show epics and mega-musicals of the period. By 1970, even hits like *M*A*S*H* and *Butch Cassidy and the Sundance Kid* could not stop the studio recording a loss of over $100 million (see Monaco 2001: 37 and Finler 2003: 124).

Similarly, United Artists lost money on *Chitty Chitty Bang Bang* (1968), *The Private Life of Sherlock Holmes* (1970) and *The Battle of Britain* (1969) – all British co-productions. The commercial failure of these films, which had been developed and filmed in the United Kingdom but funded and distributed by United Artists, prompted the studio to reduce investment in runaways. In the early 1960s Paramount had endured the failure of two epics from independent producer Samuel Bronston, *The Fall of the Roman Empire* and *Circus World* (both 1964), but the studio still initiated production of *Darling Lili* and *Paint Your Wagon* (both 1970), a pair of highly expensive prestige musicals that failed to recoup anywhere near their budgets at the box office. Warner Brothers, meanwhile, saw their adaptation of the stage hit *Camelot* (1967) lose money. However, the performance of Columbia studios throughout the 1960s offers an interesting counterpoint to the trials endured by the other majors.

In 1962, Columbia released the critically and commercially successful *Lawrence of Arabia* – a project with strong international connections from independent producer Sam Spiegel. In 1966, the studio had a major hit with *A Man for All Seasons* – yet another critically acclaimed historical epic with strong British connections. Then in 1968 the studio released two hugely successful mega-musicals, *Oliver!* and *Funny Girl* (the latter directed by William Wyler, who had also directed *Ben-Hur*). While the other studios were floundering, Columbia oversaw a string of extremely popular mainstream hits, often in exactly the same genres as the other majors' notable flops. The success of Columbia's epics and megamusicals indicates that audiences were *not* tired of prestige pictures (just as the success of *Doctor Zhivago* seemed to hint at the longevity of epics). Rather, the late 1960s was a period of massive overproduction at the prestige end of the movie business.[10] The majors had hit upon road-shows as a way attracting occasional viewers back to cinemas. As screens began to fill with expensive, prestigious, spectacular product, the audience became increasingly thinly spread, as Peter Krämer has demonstrated. Krämer's work (2005: Chapter 1) indicates that throughout the 1950s and 1960s, regular and occasional viewers had often united to see the big movie hit of the year. However, as a glut of mega-musicals and epics appeared in the late 1960s, and American audiences continued to decrease, it became less

and less likely that a sufficient majority of these movies could dominate in the way that *Ben-Hur* had. In fact, when one or two outstanding hits did appear, as with Columbia's releases, it sent the other majors spiralling into crisis.

Nevertheless, most of the majors survived the 1960s, and as Sheldon Hall will document later in this volume, the blockbuster trend continued. While studio productions came to seem increasingly perilous, stability came as the studios were bought up by larger conglomerates, with diversified interests, and also from closer involvement with television. In fact, television is the key to understanding the fortunes of all the major studios since the 1950s.

The value of the studios

The Hollywood majors had always been interested in television, but the antitrust action of the late 1940s had prohibited them from establishing television networks. With the majors excluded from the market, television broadcasting instead developed out of the pre-existing radio networks. Within a few years it came to operate in a similar manner, and was dominated by the same companies. Initially most primetime programming was broadcast live, much like radio. However, television demanded high volumes of visual entertainment and, as a result, the form quickly came to offer audiences exactly what cinemas had offered in the pre-war period – an ever changing schedule of filmed entertainment products, from news, through one-off dramas, to narrative serials. As movie production and movie audiences declined in the 1950s, the majors set about establishing themselves as the prime providers of filmed entertainment to the

Continued on page 56

The classic Hollywood musical was born out of a studio system that could support the casting of large chorus numbers, highly trained star performers and lavish settings. As a staple genre of Hollywood's "golden years", it is not surprising that the decline of the classic musical film coincided with the gradual break-up of the studio system and the later birth of a "post-classical" or "new" Hollywood in the 1960s. Following the Paramount court case in 1948 and the ensuing divorcement of the studios from the major theatrical exhibition outlets, in the 1950s and 1960s the studios faced new threats in their struggle to retain dominance. The advent of television and a growing trend toward suburban living meant that film attendance dropped off markedly during this period. In a last-ditch attempt to draw audiences, some studios chose to concentrate production on a relatively small number of big, "A" pictures designed to appeal to a family audience. So, relying heavily on proven Broadway hit shows or cutting-edge, spectacular effects, a few musical "A" films, like *My Fair Lady* (dir: George Cukor, 1964), *Mary Poppins* (dir: Robert Stevenson, 1964) and *The Sound of Music* (dir: Robert Wise, 1965), succeeded in drawing the crowds and generating good financial returns from both a home and overseas market.

Alongside these family musicals, the industry was also producing films aimed specifically at a new generation of high-spending, rock "n" roll-loving, teenagers. Somewhat reluctantly, studios had begun to cater for this market in the 1950s, although featured teens, in films like MGM's *Blackboard Jungle* (dir: Richard Brooks, 1955), were often represented as juvenile delinquents and rock "n" roll as the music that fuelled their anti-social behaviour. But, studio tactics altered when Elvis Presley signed a seven-year movie contract with Paramount Pictures. Presley went on to star in 33 films, 27 of which were released between the years of 1960–69. These comparatively low-budget star vehicles generally followed a narrative formula in which a misunderstood youth (Presley) would become integrated into society through his music and the love of a good woman. Although Elvis' rock musicals marked the industry's acceptance of a shift in musical tastes and markets for the genre, they also retained conventions common to the classic musical. For example, Elvis invariably performed his songs to a diegetic audience, his musical numbers typically functioned to draw people together, and there was usually a correspondence between the eventual success of "the show" and the happy resolution of the heterosexual romance. In this way, as Ben Thompson comments, Elvis' "primal raunch" was thereby "sanitised into social responsibility" (Thompson 1995: 34).

In the late 1960s and 1970s, the scramble to re-define the Hollywood product and appeal to a younger, now cine-literate, audience led to a period of greater experimentation that allowed for a more self-conscious and critical cinema. Following this trend, mainstream musical films, such as those starring Barbra Streisand, were critically reflexive and frequently interrogated the romantic underpinnings of the classic genre. For instance, while the diegetic audience was still present in the Streisand films, she also became known for her sung soliloquies, in films like *On a Clear Day You Can See Forever* (dir: Vincente Minnelli, 1970) and the later *Yentl* (dir: Barbra Streisand, 1983). These "private" moments typically involved an outpouring of the character's inner turmoil as worked through in song.

The director and choreographer, Bob Fosse, was also a central figure in the development of the musical at this time. Following *Sweet Charity* (1968) with *Cabaret* (1972) and *All That Jazz* (1979), his musicals were set against a decidedly dystopian backdrop, ironically drawing attention to the gap between a "utopian sensibility"[1] to be found in the musical numbers and the harsh reality of the world in which a, strangely naïve, central performer was placed. For instance, the relentlessly vivacious, eponymous heroine (Shirley MacLaine) of *Sweet Charity* is introduced to the audience in a series of shots in which she is shown singing, dancing and

Joel Grey and friend in *Cabaret*

expressing the joys of romantic desire. As the number progresses it becomes apparent that her somewhat taciturn love object is not the man she thinks he is and the sequence comes to an abrupt finish when he steals her money and throws her into a nearby river. However, Fosse's quasi-Brechtian style is probably best represented in *Cabaret* in which the exuberance of musical numbers is set against the rise of fascism in Germany. During one particular scene the protagonists travel into the German countryside, stopping at a Beer Keller for refreshment, where a young boy spontaneously bursts into song, seemingly in tribute to the idyllic pastoral setting. The haunting melody and the purity of his voice seem calculated to enthral the film's audience as it does the diegetic audience in the scene. But, as the gathered crowd in the Keller join in, the darker side of community values is made manifest when the song transforms into a fascist anthem. The film audience is therefore uncomfortably implicated in the politics of the diegetic audience; nationalistic "politics is articulated as the phenomenon of spectators being willing to join in the show" (Mizejewski 1992: 176).[2]

Toward the end of the 1970s, "new Hollywood" entered a second phase, largely signalled by the emergence of the blockbuster film. Released in the same year as *Star Wars* (dir: George Lucas, 1977), Thomas Schatz sees *Saturday Night Fever* (dir: John Badham, 1977) as a significant and symptomatic film of this period, indicating the "multimedia potential of movie hits" and launching the trend for what he calls "music movies" in the 1980s (Schatz 1993: 22). In his use of the term "music movies", Schatz is obviously referring to the increasing deployment of pop music soundtracks in a variety of genre films in the 1980s. Nevertheless, even though the generic boundaries of the musical became less stable during this period, *Fever* can be located within the genre because of its use of diegetic music alongside the centrality of the disco-dance numbers in the film and the now familiar narrative strategy that separates and parallels diegetic "show space" with harsh reality. *Fever* remains a provocative film that deals with serious issues like rape, suicide and racial discrimination. In this sense, this "rite of passage" musical drama bears a resemblance to the often hard-hitting and more subversive films that were common to the experimental Hollywood of the earlier 1970s. But *Fever* also pre-figures a cycle of rather more conservative "teen musicals" that include films like *Grease* (dir: Randal Kleiser, 1978), *Grease 2* (dir: Patricia Birch, 1982), *Flashdance* (dir: Adrian Lyne, 1983), *Footloose* (dir: Herbert Ross, 1984) and *Dirty Dancing* (dir: Emile Ardolino, 1987). Rather than deconstructing the genre or providing a critical perspective, as Jane Feuer puts it, "the teen musicals of the 1980s represent(ed) a 'reconstruction' ... of the conventions of the classic musical" (1993: 130). As if to indicate a return to classic form, a number of these films were nostalgically set in the 1950s and they were generally organized around the kind of dual-focus structure that Rick Altman recognized as central to classic Hollywood musicals.[3] This structure was frequently based upon a gendered divide and involved comparative, parallel scenes designed to mark out specifically masculine and feminine spheres. A clear example of this can be found during the musical number "Summer Nights" in *Grease*, when the leading couple, Danny (John Travolta) and Sandy (Olivia Newton-John), recount the tale of their romance to their friends. The sequence repeatedly cross-cuts between Sandy, singing to her female friends in the school café, and Danny, singing to his all-male gang on the benches of the school athletics field. This dual-focus structure goes on to dominate the film, until its closing moments, when the romantic leads are able to overcome their differences.

This brief trajectory of the mainstream Hollywood musical brings us to the 1990s and beyond. Although the number of Hollywood musicals released between 1960 and 1990 does not measure up to the hundreds produced in the classic period, the genre does appear to have survived. However, apart from the occasional translation to screen of stage show musicals (e.g. *Evita* [dir: Alan Parker, 1996], *Chicago* [dir: Rob Marshall, 2002]) and re-visiting of teen musical (e.g. *8 Mile* [dir: Curtis Hanson, 2002]), Hollywood has all but deserted the genre since the 1980s.[4] Perhaps more interesting developments within the genre can now be witnessed as emanating from outside of the Hollywood machine. For example, in *Everybody Says I Love You* (1996) Woody Allen uses the genre for deeply ironic purpose, exposing the idealistic and illusory nature of romantic love alongside his deconstruction of the genre's codes and conventions. Baz Luhrmann's camp and excessive *Moulin Rouge* (2001) pays homage to the gay male following that the Hollywood musical has attracted, and Kenneth Branagh's combination of the "low art" Hollywood musical with the "high art" Shakespeare play becomes central to his project to make this quintessentially English poet more accessible to an international film audience. Given its studio heritage, paradoxically, the Hollywood musical continues to survive in the hands of a small number of auteur directors who re-visit and re-shape the genre to their own purpose.

Notes

1 See Richard Dyer, "Entertainment and utopia", *Only Entertainment* (London and New York: Routledge, 1992), pp. 17–34, for a discussion of this in relation to the musical.
2 Here Mizejewski is primarily talking about the Broadway, stage version of *Cabaret*, but her comments are also relevant to the film.
3 See Altman's discussion of "The American Film Musical as Dual-Focus Narrative", in Altman (1998: 16–27).
4 For the sake of expediency, I have chosen not to include the numerous cartoon musicals that span both the classic and post-classic periods in Hollywood. It would also be interesting to consider the parameters of the Bollywood musical in relation to classical Hollywood and new Hollywood versions of the form.

References

Altman, R. (1998) The American film musical as dual-focus narrative, *The American Film Musical* Bloomington: Indiana University Press, pp. 16–27.
Feuer, J. (1993) *The Hollywood Musical* London: The Macmillan Press Ltd.
Mizejewski, L. (1992) *Divine Decadence: Fascism, Female Spectacle and the Makings of Sally Bowles*. Princeton, NJ: Princeton University Press.
Schatz, T. (1993) The new Hollywood, in Jim Collins et al. (eds), *Film Theory Goes to the Movies*. New York and London: Routledge.
Thompson, B. (1995) Pop and film: the charisma crossover, in J. Romney and A. Wootton (eds), *Celluloid Jukebox: Popular Music and the Movies since the 1950s*. London: BFI Publishing, pp. 32–41.

Christine Cornea

Continued from page 52

television networks. Live broadcasting was increasingly supplemented by prerecorded shows, produced at first by a series of innovative independents such as Desi Arnaz and Lucille Ball's Desilu, and then by many of the major Hollywood studios.

Columbia led the way for the majors, when in 1949 the studio converted its "Screen Gems" department from producing movie shorts into a putative television production operation. Not only did Columbia start selling pre-existing material to the networks, they also set about recording shows specifically for television broadcast. In 1954, Columbia provided ABC with the first prerecorded episodic TV drama, *The Adventures of Rin Tin*

Tin. Meanwhile, other producers were following Columbia's lead. Disney's *Disneyland* show premiered on ABC in 1954 and Warner Brothers' *Cheyenne* appeared on ABC the following year.[11] At around the same time the majors also began leasing their libraries of films to the networks. They had previously resisted doing this because the networks had been unable to pay what the majors considered reasonable licensing fees. This changed in 1955 when RKO sold its film library to a programming syndicate for $15 million. Shortly afterwards Warner Brothers followed suit, selling a select package of movies for $21 million. Balio (1985: 135) has reported that by 1958 around 3700 features had been sold or leased for an estimated $220 million.

Even when the ailing RKO studios eventually collapsed in 1958, its fate was closely linked to the emergent form. RKO's holdings were purchased by Desilu to provide production facilities for their roster of shows, including the hugely popular *I Love Lucy*. Historian Christopher Anderson (1994: 5) has noted that the significance of television production grew throughout the 1950s until, at one point in January 1959, Warner Brothers was not actively shooting a single theatrical release, but was filming eight different series that made up almost a third of ABC's weekly output. In licensing fees alone, these series generated over $30 million per year.

These were fundamental changes in the nature of the movie business. Firstly, the major's film libraries became increasingly valuable assets. Television functioned as a new, "ancillary" market, where films had a second opportunity for recoupment. When ABC paid Columbia $2 million for the rights to screen *Bridge on the River Kwai* (1957) in 1965, it was becoming apparent that television licensing fees could supplement box office income. The enormous ratings achieved when *Bridge on the River Kwai* was screening on 12 September 1966 (with 60 million sets apparently tuned in) also proved that major cinematic hits could go on to become hits in other markets (Balio 1985: 435). Today, the film libraries owned by the majors are the main asset against which they borrow money to fund film production, as Martin Dale (1997: 25) has demonstrated. Secondly, all the resources that the majors had owned during the studio system could be turned over to television production. If anything, the "always on", competitive nature of network broadcasting actually demanded more product than the majors had produced during the studio era. The production strategies that defined theatrical releases in the 1960s must be understood in the context of a burgeoning television market. After 1948, mass movie production, which had previously generated a huge number of "B" movies, newsreels, shorts, and filmed entertainment of other sorts, was transformed into television production. Cinemas became the province of higher budget, more spectacular movies, not to compete with television, but to ensure a differentiation between the majors' two main areas of business.[12]

However, the 1960s remained a period of profound instability because the majors were still learning to meet the requirements of these two different markets for filmed entertainment. Although television offered stable profits, these were significantly smaller than revenues generated by the theatrical sector, and the cinematic failures of the 1960s had a profoundly destabilizing effect. The annual losses reported by the studios at this time could not be denied. The overproduction of blockbusters had forced many of the majors into debt, causing their share value to decline, and thus opening them up to the prospect of corporate takeovers. As noted, in 1959, the talent agency MCA began purchasing shares in Universal, and their takeover was completed in 1962. A series of mergers and takeovers followed, as other studios were bought out by larger conglomerates. Paramount was purchased by Gulf & Western (which had interests in diverse range of activities including automobile manufacture, zinc mining and real estate) in 1966, United Artists by the financial services conglomerate Transamerica in 1967, Warner Brothers merged with television producers Seven Arts in 1967, and was then taken over by Kinney National Services (initially a real estate conglomerate) in 1969. Only Columbia and Fox remained independent at the time. MGM suffered the most ignominious fate of all. The ailing company was purchased by Kirk Kerkorian in 1969, who ceased production of movies and TV shows, sold the film library and began to focus on the company's hotel and casino interests, specifically the MGM Grand in Las Vegas. This round of takeovers was possible because the studios' share value had declined to the point where it no longer reflected the actual value of the assets, such as film libraries and real estate holdings in Los Angeles, and because the losses in the film sector masked healthy profits from television production.

The sudden predominance of conglomerates at the top end of the industry added a further level of stability to the studios' operations. For the controlling conglomerate, losses in the movie sector could theoretically be absorbed by profits in other sectors. Furthermore, although studios sometimes made considerable annual losses, especially in the 1960s, profitable years generally predominated and in the long term, moviemaking remained a relatively profitable business, even if individual pictures failed to recoup for many years, while television only added potential areas for recoupment. Finally, the glamorous allure of filmmaking for Wall Street investors also should not be under-estimated.[13] For all of these new owners, the fiscal year 1969/1970 was punishing, as the consequences of high budget overproduction were played out, but at the end of the decade the industry appeared to have weathered the storm. Although many structural changes had occurred, the majors that survived the 1960s entered the 1970s in the form they still occupy today.

Conclusion

Today, movies remain at the heart of Hollywood's business, although they only constitute a small amount of the majors' actual product when compared to television production. The pre-1948 studio system may have declined but in the 1960s it was replaced by a system that was both different and the same. The majors still existed, and still made movies, but the processes involved were irrevocably altered. By the end of the decade none of the majors were vertically integrated; movies were produced according to an *ad hoc*, package unit system; business was split between television and movie sectors, which required different operational practices; products in both markets were usually independently packaged and produced; and most of the majors were owned by larger conglomerates. Relatively marginal practices, such as independent production, had become the norm, and the majors themselves were no longer production plants, but had become financier-distributors of filmed entertainment for cinemas and television. While television production grew, movie output never returned to pre-1948 levels. Statistics quoted by Finler (2003: 366) show that in 1970 the majors released 153 movies between them, and in recent years their output stabilized at an average of just over 100 movies released per annum (although more continue to come from independent distributors). Moviemaking remained central to the majors' operation, but the widespread failure of road-show epics and mega-musicals in the late 1960s forced the majors to seriously consider the nature of their production schedules for the next few years. In the process, opportunities arose for more marginal and challenging films to enter the mainstream.

Notes

1 For a more comprehensive overview of MGM's collapse, see Bart (1990).

2 All figures relating to attendance in this paragraph are from Finler (2003: 378), unless otherwise stated.

3 For a full list of the requirements of the consent decrees, see Conant (1978: 98–9).

4 Rentals are the percentage of the box office gross that goes back to the distributor (usually around 50 per cent of the total box office gross). Unless otherwise stated, all figures in this chapter refer to rentals.

5 The attempt to distribute *Duel in the Sun* independently was a stark demonstration of why the majors remained major. Despite the film's massive rentals, the cost of distributing one film alone ruined Selznick (see Thomson 1992).

6 For more details on the history of road-showing, see Hall (2002: 12–15).

7 A comprehensive overview of the widescreen technologies that emerged at this time, and the impact they had on the viewing experience, can be found in Belton (1992).

8 In fact, MCA had already moved into television production, and purchased the studio because it needed a base to run these operations. In accordance with anti-trust regulations, the talent agency segment of MCA was sold off but, in reality, this had already become a marginal part of Wasserman's business empire. See Gomery (1998, 2005) and Bruck (2003).

9 *My Fair Lady* cost $17 million and made $12 million in rentals (Finler 2003: 298).

10 This point has been made in considerably more detail by Maltby (1998), Hall (2000) and Krämer (2005).

11 Anderson (1994: 133–90) has argued that Disney, more than any other single studio, recognized and exploited the potential of TV, in both marketing and exhibiting their productions.

12 Other accounts which provide a more comprehensive weight of evidence supporting this argument are Maltby (1998) and Krämer (2005).

13 In particular, the maverick entrepreneur Charles S. Bluhdorn, whose Gulf & Western corporation came to control Paramount Studios, was apparently attracted by the opportunity to mix with Hollywood stars and engage in the high-stakes fiscal competition that was Hollywood filmmaking (Dick 2001). A sensational but nevertheless illuminating account of Bluhdorn's reign at Paramount can also be found in Evans (1994).

References

As well as works cited in the text, I have also included some key studies of events and institutions that readers may find instructive.

Anderson, C. (1994) *Hollywood TV: The Studio System in the Fifties*. Austin: University of Texas Press.

Balio, T. (1976) *United Artists: The Company Built by the Stars*. Madison: University of Wisconsin Press.

Balio, T. (1985) Retrenchment, reappraisal and reorganisation, 1948–, in T. Balio (ed.) *The American Movie Industry*, rev. edn. Madison: University of Wisconsin Press.

Balio, T. (ed.) (1990) *Hollywood in the Age of Television*. Boston: Unwin Hyman.

Bart, P. (1990) *Fade Out: The Calamitous Final Days of MGM*. New York: William Morrow.

Belton, J. (1992) *Widescreen Cinema*. Cambridge, MA: Harvard University Press.

Bordwell, D., Staiger, J. and Thompson, K. (1985) *The Classical Hollywood Cinema: Film Style and Mode of Production to 1960*. London: Routledge.

Bruck, C. (2003) *When Hollywood Had a King: The Reign of Lew Wasserman, Who Leveraged Talent into Power and Influence*. New York: Random House.

Conant, M. (1978) *Antitrust in the Motion Picture Industry*. New York: Arno.

Custen, G.F. (1997) *Twentieth Century's Fox: Darryl F. Zanuck and the Culture of Hollywood*. New York: Basic Books.

Dale, M. (1997) *The Movie Game: The Film Business in Britain, Europe and America*. London: Cassell.

DeVany, A. (2004) *Hollywood Economics: How Extreme Uncertainty Shapes the Film Industry*. New York: Routledge.

Dick, B.F. (ed.) (1992) *Columbia Pictures: Portrait of a Studio*. Lexington: University Press of Kentucky.

Dick, B.F. (1997) *City of Dreams: The Making and Remaking of Universal Pictures*. Lexington: University Press of Kentucky.

Dick, B.F. (2001) *Engulfed: The Death of Paramount Pictures and the Birth of Corporate Hollywood*. Lexington: University Press of Kentucky.

Evans, R. (1994) *The Kid Stays in the Picture*. New York: Hyperion.

Finler, J.W. (2003) *The Hollywood Story*. 3rd edn. London: Wallflower.

Gomery, D. (1998) Hollywood corporate business practice and periodising contemporary film history, in S. Neale and M. Smith (eds) *Contemporary Hollywood Cinema*. London: BFI.

Gomery, D. (2005) *The Hollywood Studio System: A History*, rev. edn. London: BFI.

Hall, S. (2000) Hard ticket giants: Hollywood blockbusters in the widescreen era, Unpublished PhD thesis, University of East Anglia.

Hall, S. (2002) Tall revenue features: the genealogy of the modern blockbuster, in S. Neale (ed.) *Genre and Contemporary Hollywood*. London: BFI.

Hoberman, J. (2003) *The Dream Life: Movies, Media and the Mythology of the Sixties*. New York: New Press.

Jowett, G. (1976) *Film: The Democratic Art*. Boston: Little Brown.

Kael, P. (1970) Review of *Tora! Tora! Tora!*, *New Yorker*, 3 October.

Krämer, P. (1997) The lure of the big picture: film, television and Hollywood, in J. Hill and M. McLoone (eds) *Big Picture, Small Screen: The Relations Between Film and Television*. Luton: John Libbey.

Krämer, P. (1998) Post-Classical Hollywood, in J. Hill and P.C. Gibson, *The Oxford Guide to Film Studies*. Oxford: Oxford University Press.

Krämer, P. (2005) *The New Hollywood: From Bonnie and Clyde to Star Wars*. London: Wallflower.

Lev, P. (2003) *Transforming the Screen, 1950–1959*. New York: Charles Scribner's Sons.

Maltby, R. (1998) "Nobody knows everything": post classical histriographies and consolidated entertainment, in S. Neale and

60   Contemporary American Cinema

M. Smith (1998) *Contemporary Hollywood Cinema*. New York: Routledge.

Monaco, P. (2001) *The Sixties: 1960–1969*. New York: Charles Scribner's Sons.

Schatz, T. (1988) *The Genius of the System: Hollywood Filmmaking in the Studio Era*. New York: Pantheon.

Sklar, R. (1999) "The lost audience": 1950s spectatorship and historical reception studies, in M. Stokes and R. Maltby (eds) *Identifying Hollywood's Audiences: Cultural Identity and the Movies*. London: BFI.

Thomson, D. (1992) *Showman: The Life of David O. Selznick*. New York: Knopf.

United States Census Bureau (2000) *Statistical Abstract of the United States*. www.census.gov (accessed 1 Aug. 2005).

Wood, M. (1975) *America in the Movies, or, "Santa Maria, It Had Slipped My Mind!"* London: Secker and Warburg.

3 AMERICAN UNDERGROUND CINEMA OF THE 1960s

Michael O'Pray

THE AMERICAN UNDERGROUND film of the 1960s occupies a mythical place in the history of cinema. Well outside the Hollywood dream machine, it nevertheless experienced enormous public visibility that was unique in the history of cinema, appearing in newspapers, glossy magazines and the mass media. Films that had been seen by only a handful of people became sensationalist fodder for the international press. Low budgets, technically primitive techniques and either banal or sexually explicit content became cool, fashionable and equally derided. It also attracted more writing at the time than any other historical moment of the *film avant-garde*.[1] In many ways it also became and remains the model for a kind of cinema that has never gone away but rather in recent years has burgeoned once more to occupy a central place in the art world, something it failed to do in the 1960s and 1970s. Though primarily, and importantly, based in New York, underground film was not restricted to what was at the time the international centre of the *avant garde* in the visual arts. For example, important contributions were made on the American West Coast around San Francisco, the location of the immediate postwar *avant garde* film.

As A.L. Rees points out, the "underground" movement was an international phenomenon that included the French *lettristes* and *situationistes* and the Viennese Action Group of the 1950s.[2] Nevertheless it is now identified with certain kinds of American *avant garde* film of the 1960s and its importance and influence cannot be overestimated. It has a mythical reputation yet it was short-lived. In his critical study of the period, James argues that the underground film movement enjoyed success roughly between 1959 and 1966, giving way, as we shall see, to a more conceptual minimalist *avant garde* aesthetic heralded by the arrival of Michael Snow's classic film *Wavelength* in 1967, which interestingly remains an underground film and a reminder of how such categorizing is always somewhat rough-and-ready.[3] In fact, American *avant garde* cinema during this decade was marked by a plethora of styles and approaches. Heterogeneity reigned.

The terms "underground" and "*avant garde*" are both pertinent to the cinema that burgeoned in the 1960s in America. What is meant by these categories? The term "underground film" was first used by the critic and painter Manny Farber in the context of discussing what he saw as a kind of anti-artiness in particular male action films of the 1940s. Its adaptation by the alternative cinema of the 1960s followed on from nomenclatures like "New American cinema" and "poetic film". Interestingly, when Sitney wrote his classic *Visionary Film* in the 1970s he referred to the "American avant-garde film" in its subtitle, suggesting rightly that the underground is a form or *kind* of *avant garde* film of the post-war American cinema. But the term "*avant garde*" itself is still contested.[4] By and large, "*avant garde* film" has come to be associated with either a no-budget filmmaking, radical in form and content and directly connected, as we shall discuss later, with similar movements in the other arts, or with the historical moments of the 1920s in Europe or 1960s and 1970s in America and Europe.

Renan defines underground films as primarily involving the filmmaker's own personal expression, as "dissenting" in form or content and finally as being made for very little money.[5] Rees suggests that the different components of the American underground film were unified by their investigation of the film medium itself. For James the underground cinema embraced a "utopian aestheticism" with a limited capacity to respond to the urgent political situation that developed in the 1960s.[6] More popular perceptions link it with the so-called sexual "revolution" of the 1960s and there is little doubt that its most public and notorious examples (as we shall see in Jack Smith and Andy Warhol's work) involved representations of what was perceived as outrageous sexual behaviour, but it was also seen as extraordinarily banal and boring. Warhol's reputation, totally off the mark, was

identified with the pedestrian images of the Empire State Building and a man asleep. The filmic equivalent of Carl Andre's infamous sculpture comprised of ordinary bricks.

Outside these misinformed views and prejudices, we can understand American underground cinema as being the result of two broad and often intertwining impulses.[7] One emanated from the art scene largely sited in New York at the time that was attempting to redefine various art practices, from dance and music through to painting and film, in ways that dealt with their basic form or forms and as such comprised an *avant garde*.[8] The other was a response to the society and culture of the times and was inspired by critique, a desire to shock and a social utopianism albeit often disguised in what seemed like the self-indulgence of drugs, sexual experimentation and anarchic life styles that owed much to the Beats. Underground cinema understood itself as repressed and forced to operate beneath the dominant culture except that it enjoyed a fashionable status among the intellectual and the artistic elite of New York.

Part of the American underground's lasting impact is this all-encompassing creative dualism. In the undergound cinema a burgeoning alternative to Hollywood became culturally significant and came to have an influence on the studio system itself that had reached a creative impasse in the 1960s. It was marked by a realism in its attempt to represent in an almost improvisational form what had not been previously depicted in cinema.

The underground cinema comprised a distinct set of elements, namely the films of individual artist filmmakers; new forms of organization in terms of how films were made, distributed and exhibited; a new discourse of critical writing and, not least, an audience who found in the films some sort of expression of their own sensibilities and views. The Vietnam War, national civil unrest, especially over race and institutional radicalism in the form of the counter-culture, were influential aspects of the decade, and although not always visible in the *avant garde* in New York, did create an urgent sense of new beginnings (James 1989).

However, the underground film emerges before the 1960s in the New York bohemianism of beat poets and the theatre work of Jack Smith.[9] The Beats was essentially a literary movement comprising figures like Jack Kerouac, Ken Kesey, Allen Ginsberg, Gregory Corso and in the background William S. Burroughs. The Beat generation, as it came to be called, formed a broader base of intellectuals and artists from the world of painting and music, especially jazz but also folk, associated with Left-wing politics in America at the time. The bohemian beat movement's position in the margins of the American mainstream was to foster ideas and forms of life that would become intrinsic to the 1960s, although realigned to popular culture with the underground's references to B movies, drag performance and its fascination, especially in Warhol's case, with fashion, pop music and celebrities.

Avant garde film activity had subsided after the West Coast explosion in the immediate post-war years.[10] Maya Deren's film production slowed down to barely nothing in the 1950s while Anger had moved to France in 1950. Brakhage, for much of the 1950s, was a fairly isolated figure who was also by choice geographically isolated too. Subscribing to a Romantic aesthetic of imagination and setting the individual against the hegemony of state culture, Brakhage had been associated with the Black Mountain college and especially the American modernist poets influenced by Pound, particularly Charles Olsen, Robert

Duncan, Robert Creeley and Louis Zukofsky. Brakhage's importance in the present context is his development of a personal "home movie" aesthetic that flowed into the Beats and the underground and Warhol especially. But in many ways the underground cinema was a reaction to Brakhage's lyrical abstractionist cinema though there is a sumptious visual quality to *Flaming Creatures* and a stunning use of colour and superimposition in Ron Rice's *Chumlum* (1964). Equally elements of the Beats and the undergound are present in Brakhage's work as he addressed domestic life, sex and alternative life styles.[11]

A key film marking the beginnings of the underground cinema is Alfred Leslie and Robert Frank's *Pull My Daisy* (1959). The film is an amiable, freewheeling, slightly arch homage to the everyday life of urban American cosmopolitan bohemian intellectuals. It depicts a kind of "family" of kindred spirits that includes the beat poets Allen Ginsberg and Gregory Corso and is narrated by the leading figure of the Beats, Jack Kerouac. This "family" was to be given a perverse form in Warhol's own "family" films made in The Factory in the 1960s where an intellectual marginalization and isolation were replaced by one of sexuality and drug abuse. In this way *Pull My Daisy* not only introduces the mundanity of subject matter – almost a diary or home movie – that was to characterize underground cinema but also a simplicity of form, a move away from the lyrical craftsmanship of filmmakers like Brakhage, one of the few *avant garde* filmmakers active in the 1950s.

Pull My Daisy's references are largely literary and musical (jazz). The rhythms of poetry merge with those of jazz and to this extent the film jostles for a place in high culture as jazz had been steadily adopted by white artists and intellectuals since the late 1940s. It is now known that the poetry scene in New York, which often merged with the folk music scene, was more influential (on Warhol, for example) than was previously thought.[12] For example, Mekas uses the expression "poetic cinema" (as did Deren before him) to describe the burgeoning underground cinema before the latter terminology was adopted. In contrast, Anger's *Scorpio Rising* and even Snow's *Wavelength* were to feature pop music even though Snow was a jazz musician. Warhol also produced and filmed the Velvet Underground.

In the late 1950s, filmmaker Ken Jacobs collaborated with Jack Smith to make what was eventually to be the classic film *Blonde Cobra* (1959–63), an episodic, ruptured and manic display of Smith's camp performance as an ennui-ridden drag queen. It is one of the founding films of underground cinema. Unlike *Pull My Daisy*, *Blonde Cobra* constructs a world of sexual deviation that is sited primarily in the imagination and not in a downtown apartment. Its delirious and ironic theatricality finds no comfort in any notion of community except a negative one of exclusion. While *Pull My Daisy* is commitment to social and personal relationships, *Blonde Cobra* reveals an isolation and subjectivism of mental fragility and cultural dementia as it reworks the low cultural form of the drag artist.

Blonde Cobra's subversive strategy was to be fully accomplished in Smith's own classic underground film, *Flaming Creatures* (1963), made some years later but released in the same year as *Blonde Cobra*. *Flaming Creatures* met both critical acclaim and public approbation being confiscated by the police who raided theatres where it was showing. Featuring Smith's friends from the New York demimonde, the film mines American popular culture, from B movies to lipstick ads using a

semi-mythic structure and a polysexuality that affronted the mores of the mainstream. No doubt its nudity and sexual "deviancy" attracted the law and turned it into a *cause célèbre* with which Smith to his discomfort was forever identified. Its use of ready-made "personalities" like Mario Montez and its chaotic anti-art aesthetic influenced Warhol's approach to film.

What perhaps conjoins these three films is their emphasis on ways of living, or lifestyles. Alternatives are being suggested here, emanating from the underbelly of American society. Poets, gays, drag artists – New York bohemia meets the culture of the streets, a culture rarely represented in American arts at the time and lacking a political or social programme, unlike its European Leftist counterpart of the late 1960s and 1970s. However, there is an implicit and sometimes explicit notion of community in the films – all portray groups of people defined and drawn together by attitudes and values that find no real place in mainstream American culture.

The underground cinema was consolidated by other films made in a similar vein, especially Jacobs's *Little Stabs at Happiness* (1959–63 and also "starring" Smith) and Ron Rice's *The Queen of Sheba Meets the Atom Man* (1963), which emphasized improvised performance (especially in the latter film by Taylor Mead who was later to be used by Warhol), and subcultural lifestyles as Jacobs's film in the footsteps of *Pull My Daisy* depicts a bohemianism that is not rooted in jazz and poetry but in the everyday of children's street games.

A defining feature of *Blonde Cobra*, Smith's and Warhol's films generally, and other films of the period is that of the body and performance. In such films, the body and performance are key elements that were only to occupy centre stage much later in the 1980s and 1990s. For the underground cinema, personal expression went beyond that of the filmmaker to the performers themselves. Figures like Edie Sedgwick and Ondine were not actors in a narrative but essentially playing themselves, often in improvised scenarios. A form of narcissism and what Stephen Koch calls "a cool" gaze at the camera replaced the psycho-dramas of the *avant garde* tradition of Brakhage, Deren and Anger. A realist tone dominated in which authenticity was key. When Warhol used Ronald Tavel's "scripts" for his sound cinema after 1964, he was drawing on the strategies of the Theatre of the Ridiculous (practised also by Smith) in which notions of proper "acting" and plot were constantly undermined.

To some extent this explains the resurgence of Warhol's reputation and a belated revival of interest in Smith after his death from AIDS in 1989. It needs to be said that it is no accident that both Smith and Warhol were gay.[13] Another film of classic underground propor-tions was made by another gay filmmaker, Kenneth Anger, in the 1960s, *Scorpio Rising* (1963), which likewise focuses on a subcultural group, namely bike boys, to examine American mores and to celebrate the accoutrements of popular culture (Suarez 1996). Anger's return to America after a long sojourn in Europe (Paris and London) resulted in a film that was to influence the mainstream. With its pop music soundtrack and candid treatment of drugs, sex, subcultural fashions and moral codes, it opened the door to such 1970s films as Scorsese's *Mean Streets*.

The most elusive figure in terms of cate-gories was Warhol. His influence was immense and at least two-pronged. On the one hand, in the early black-and-white films often using a static camera, a single take and a slowed-down projection speed, he founded the structural film as Sitney understood it and as the European, especially British, *avant garde* understood it too, despite the earlier work of Kren and Kubelka. This formal purity with what seemed throwaway subject matter seemed to be the filmic equivalent of the minimalist painting and sculpture movement burgeoning in America in the 1960s. It was the integrity of reel time with real time, the homogeneity of space unsullied by editing and the total lack of narrative or at least the reduction of representation to simple acts (a man eating a mushroom) or events (night passing over the Empire State Building) that seemed very much at odds with the new underground movies full of personalities, fractured editing and handheld camera. The second significant influence was that Warhol, within a few years and with the acquisition of sound, was to make classic "underground" films. Using a memorable group of performers who improvised for camera (for example, Edie Sedgwick in *Beauty No 2*, Ondine in *The Chelsea Girls* (1966), Mario Montez, in *Camp*) or "acted" their way through Ronny Tavel's "ridiculous" scripts (*Vinyl*, *Kitchen*), Warhol was to drag the underground into the public eye with his keen eye for publicity as eye-catching iconic work and his *reductio ad absurdum* of cinema itself.

As mentioned, the underground was not restricted to New York. The West Coast nurtured filmmakers who made an important contribution to the movement. After all, San Francisco and its environs had been a Beats haven and had a long bohemian tradition. Ron Rice and Taylor Mead under the influence of *Pull My Daisy* made the Beat film *The Flower Thief* there in 1960. On a broader front, the underground film was also furthered by Bruce Baillie whose lyricism and colour experiments were grounded in the world outside. In his

Contemporary American Cinema

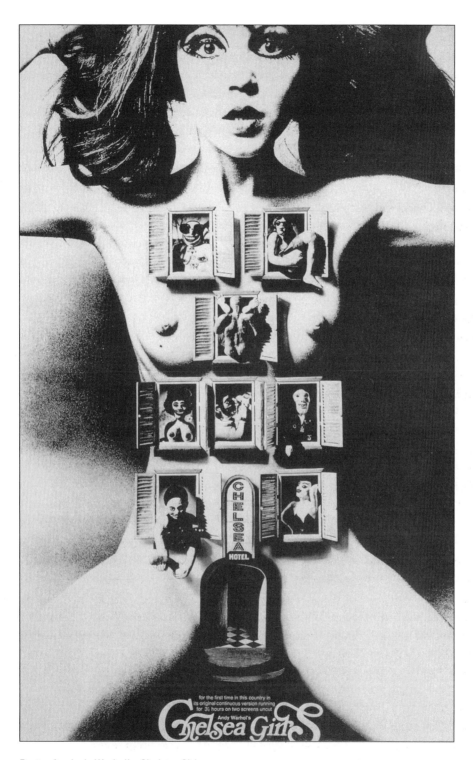

Poster for Andy Warhol's *Chelsea Girls*

later work, especially *Mass for the Dakota Sioux* (1963–4), he engaged with social issues concerning the American Native Indians. Similarly, performance artist Carolee Schneeman's *Fuses* (1964–7) took explicit lovemaking as its subject matter. With its layered optical printing effects it seemed to be more part of the "free love" hippy lifestyle. Another major influence on the mainstream was Bruce Conner who founded the Canyon Film in San Francisco in 1962. Connor made a series of found-footage films that pillaged educational film, documentaries, ads and B movies from the 1950s to construct a more radical critique of America (James 1989). Conner, like Anger, used montage and music as a formal means of portraying an America that many found alienating and disturbing. In his found-footage film *Report* (1967) he manipulated film documentation of the Kennedy assassination both to reconstruct and deconstruct the latter event and American consumerist society as it infiltrated the mass media. In a similar vein, in *Marilyn Times Five* he put a Marilyn Monroe soundtrack over what purported to be a Monroe stag movie to dwell on issues of sexual commodification and exploitation and mortality itself. Conner's hard-edged intelligence and wit cuts through some of the underground's narcissism and its tendency towards infantilism.

We need to be reminded at this point that originally the relationship, at least critically, between the New American Cinema and the underground film was intertwined. Cassavetes's feature-length art-movie *Shadows* (1959) tackled race and the nuances of bohemian relationships in the world of contemporary jazz in ways that placed it at the radical edge of American cinema and can be seen as more related to *Pull My Daisy* in its conservative form and social motives than to the formal experimentations of Warhol and Smith. In contrast, Robert Nelson's *Oh Dem Water Melons* (1965) was to take a more humorous and confrontational position on race.

Alongside this underground movement but only really flowering in the late 1960s was one that owed more to the *avant garde* scene in New York in the 1960s and was inspired by a minimalist aesthetic found in dance, painting, sculpture, music and a burgeoning performance art scene (Wollen 1989; Barnes 1993). This featured a stripped-down aesthetic that revealed an awareness of film as a material apparatus and expressed a strong interest in structure. With its abstractionist leanings it emphasized form and process rather than content. Warhol typically straddles the two and Ken Jacobs was one of the few underground filmmakers to make the transition to the new aesthetic. Pointedly, it was P. Adams Sitney who introduced the notion of structural film in the late 1960s. He recognized that the underground cinema had given way to a quite different film tendency personified, for him, by the work of Ernie Gehr, George Landow, Paul Sharits, Tony Conrad, Joyce Wieland, Hollis Frampton and Michael Snow.[14] This was a radical shift in priorities towards a modernist concern with the materiality of the medium and its overall integrity as an art object. The social and picaresque qualities of the underground aesthetic were upturned by one in which subject matter was largely irrelevant but ultimately necessary in terms of the photographic reproduction of reality that was retained as a fundamental aspect of the film, thus avoiding by and large any collapse into abstraction (though many came near – Snow in *Back and Forth* (1969), for example, and Sharits more generally). The structural tendency was much more associated with the art world than the underground, and to that extent falls under the rubric of *avant garde*. Later, in the early 1970s, the influential art magazine *Artforum* under Annette Michelson's editorship was to support and develop this film modernism, accruing theoretical writings in a way that the underground failed to do.

A key structural filmmaker was the Canadian artist Michael Snow, who had been a practising jazz musician and sculptor in New York since the 1950s. Snow was more aligned to the gallery and art world. The 1960s heralded an upsurge in abstract formalist work without precedence since the 1920s in Europe. Linked to Snow were Sharits, Jacobs and Frampton and of course the Warhol of the early black-and-white, slowed-down, single-take based films like *Eat* (1963), *Henry Geldzahler* (1963–5), *Kiss* (1963) and the quintessential minimalist study, *Empire* (1963) (O'Pray 1989; Koch 1991). For Snow, Frampton, George Landow and others, film was not essentially a means of subverting sexual and social mores through performance, camp and high stylization but an art form that required formal experimentation in order to articulate its own language so to speak. In other words, Snow and others were keen to reoccupy the high ground, returning the medium to the high culture already occupied by fellow artists like Robert Morris, Carl Andre and Frank Stella.

Snow's *Wavelength* was another iconic film of the 1960s and the ultimate "structural underground" film, although it lacked most of the characteristics set out by Sitney who had early Warhol as a model (Sitney 1979; O'Pray 1982–3). *Wavelength* was a remarkable fusion of underground and *avant garde* characteristics in its poetic shape fashioned by a long but dislocated zoom across a loft space that incorporated a narrative obliquity (furniture movers, a dead man prompting a phone call

and the Beatles' *Strawberry Fields*) as well as an almost psychedelic use of colour. Using colour filters and a rising sine wave, it has a magisterial quality evoking ontological questions about the nature of film, photography and reality itself as it comes to settle in intense close-up on the photograph of sea waves. Its punning and poetic sense has come to the fore with the passage of time. Its so-called structural affinities seem now less important. In many ways it has a good underground pedigree with its almost psychedelic pop-art optical effects and documentary flavour infringed by a touch of narrative. With respect to the latter, *Wavelength* can be seen as a distant relative of the spatio-temporal experiments of Antonioni's 1960s films such as *Blow Up* (1965) with its manic pursuit of the "mysteries" of the photograph. But in most ways Snow is more typical of the *avant garde* tendency in American film experimentation. His cultural framework owes as much to the fine arts and music (especially modern jazz) as it does to film. In a series of hard-edged films like *Back and Forth* (1968–9), *One Second in Montreal* (1969) he explored, but always with precision and a formal complexity, the parameters of cinema in terms of its material properties (zooms, pans, back and front projection, stasis) but never neglecting the power of the image.

In many ways more intellectual in his approach, Frampton embarked on a series of experiments but truly found his place in the canon with *Zorns Lemma* (1970) which matches *Wavelength* in its formal structure. The film is fused with a poetics of mystery and American pastoralism particularly in its memorable final long-held image of figures walking in the distance through a snowy landscape towards a forest. Frampton was associated with the rising generation of minimalist artists like Robert Morris, Richard

Serra and Carl Andre.[15] For Frampton structures were also systems that used linguistic and visual puns that had a playful element. In Frampton's *Nostalgia* (1971), photographs are slowly burnt on a stove, obliterating their image, and a verbal account of them occurs after they are no longer readable. Hence the audience is always listening to the description of a preceding photograph while watching another photograph. Frampton's exploration of memory, language and the relationship between the aural and visual tracks in film placed him firmly outside the largely modernist work of many of his contemporaries. His theoretical writings also placed him at the intellectual edge of *avant garde* thinking about not only film but also photography.

Central to the American underground were institutional innovations that owed something to the old problem of film as a high capital-investment medium (cameras, printers, processors, and so forth) and more, perhaps, to the climate of self-help that was part of the bohemian/hippy ethos. Jonas Mekas and others established the Filmmakers Cooperative in New York. The Filmmakers' Cinematheque was founded to provide a dedicated venue for *avant garde* film, but coffee house, college film societies and makeshift locations were common. The New York film cooperative was to be the model for a swathe of film coops throughout Europe in the 1960s. They helped to spread the cost of equipment and made access to it more economically reasonable. As a democratically organized structure, run mainly by filmmakers, the New York coop provided artists with both control and, importantly, a sense of cultural identity. It also organized distribution of the films, thus providing a centralized means of disseminating the films and making them available to exhibitors and, not least, providing some financial remuneration and organization. It also, inevitably and more controversially, became very influential as an aesthetic and ideological power base, a problem perhaps for the older generation of filmmakers, and especially for the rugged individualism of Brakhage.

Equally important was the role of the journal *Film Culture*, founded by Mekas in 1955. Under his editorship it moved away from being a supporter of art in film to being a partisan mouthpiece for the underground cinema by the early 1960s. Mekas eventually embraced a dual support of Hollywood and underground movies, jettisoning "art" films, especially American ones, to the ashcan.[16] More important in terms of raising the profile of underground cinema with the wider public was Mekas's column in *Village Voice*[17] in which he sustained a steady stream of celebratory writing about this new cinema and invective at the Establishment. In his writing for both publications Mekas elaborated a Romanticist conception of the underground film as a dissenting movement promulgating a way of life as much as a particular aesthetic. For Mekas, underground cinema was a preserver of humanist values against the corruption of modern-day governments who "are encroaching upon [man's] personal being with the huge machinery of bureaucracy, war and mass communication".[18]

If the myth of underground cinema remains alive, there is little doubt that research into it has fallen behind in recent years. Its complexity and hybridity, forever crossing over art forms, have not been surpassed even in contemporary postmodern art that in many ways reworks its strategies and "coolness". What this more contemporary scene cannot retrieve is the underground cinema's exuberance in the 1960s in its own new-found freedom. The shift to structural modernist *avant garde* renders the decade an almost comprehensive expression of *avant-garde* impulses going back on the one hand to Dada and Futurism and on the other to Soviet Constructivism and early abstractionism. Its potency and interest lie in this almost monolithic embrace of these two great tendencies in twentieth-century art. At the same time, the lags, overlaps and hybrid forms that characterize many art movements, resisting all attempts at art historical categorization, are very present in the American *avant garde* of the 1960s, rendering it a rich and complex field of filmmaking.

Notes

1   For example Battcock (1967), Renan (1967), Youngblood (1970), Mekas (1972), Tyler (1974), Koch (1991).
2   See Rees (2001: 62–4).
3   See James (1992: 94).
4   The other common term is "experimental film". For a discussion of these terms, see the introduction to O'Pray (2003).
5   Renan (1967: 17). For a fuller discussion, see James (1992: 94–100).
6   James (1992: 164).
7   Kelman made a similar distinction at the time in his "Anticipations of the light", in Battcock (1967).
8   On the cultural background, see Wollen in O'Pray (1989) and Barnes (1993).
9   On the Beats and film, see Sergeant (1997).
10   See Sitney (1971).
11   See James (1989: 29–57).
12   See Wolf (1997).
13   See Suarez (1996) and Grundmann (2003).
14   Sitney's essay "Structural film" was published in 1969 in *Film Culture* no 47.

It was and remains a much disputed term especially in the European *avant garde* camp. See Le Grice (1976); Gidal (1977).
15   On the art scene context of Snow in the 1960s, see Rees (2001).
16   See James (1989: 102–4).
17   See Mekas (1972).
18   Mekas (1972: 14).

References

Barnes, S. (1993) *Greenwich Village 1963: Avant-garde Performance and the Effervescent Body*. London: Duke University Press.

Battcock, G. (ed.) (1967) *The New American Cinema: A Critical Anthology*. New York: Dutton.

Farber, M. (1971) *Negative Space*. New York: Praeger.

Gidal, P. (1977) *Structural Film Anthology*. London: BFI.

Grundmann, R. (2003) *Andy Warhol's Blow Job*. Philadelphia: Temple University Press.

Hanhardt, J. (1976) The medium viewed: the American avant-garde film, in *A History of the American Avant-garde Cinema*. New York: American Film Association.

Hoberman, J. (2001) *On Jack Smith's Flaming Creatures and Other Secret Flix of Cinemaroc*. New York: Granary Books.

Horak, J.C. (ed.) (1995) *Lovers of Cinema: The First American Film Avant-Garde 1919–1945*. London: University of Wisconsin.

James, D.E. (1989) *Allegories of Cinema: American Film in the 1960s*. Princeton, NJ: Princeton University Press.

James D.E. (ed.) (1992) *To Free the Cinema: Jonas Mekas and the New York Underground.* Princeton, NJ: Princeton University Press.

Koch, S. (1991) *Stargazer: Andy Warhol's World and His Films*, rev. edn. New York: Marion Boyars.

Leffingwell E., Kismaric, E.C. and Heiferman, M. (eds) (1997) *Jack Smith: Flaming Creatures: His Amazing Life and Times.* London: Serpent's Tail.

Le Grice, M. (1976) *Abstract Film and Beyond.* London: Studio Vista.

MacDonald, S. (2002) *Cinema 16: Documents Toward a History of the Film Society.* Philadelphia, PA: Temple University Press.

Mekas, J. (1972) *Movie Journal: The Rise of the American Cinema 1959–1971.* New York: Collier Books.

Michelson, A. (1966) The radical inspiration, in P.A. Sitney (ed.) *Film Culture: An Anthology.* London: Secker and Warburg.

Michelson, A. (1976) Toward Snow, in P. Gidal (ed.) *Structural Film Anthology.* London: BFI.

O'Pray, M. (1982–3) Framing Snow, in *Afterimage*, 11, Winter.

O'Pray, M. (ed.) (1989) *Andy Warhol: Film Factory.* London: BFI.

O'Pray, M. (2003) *Avant-Garde Film: Forms, Themes and Passions.* London: Wallflower Press.

Rees, A.L. (1999) *A History of Experimental Film and Video.* London: BFI.

Rees, A.L. (2001) Working both sides of the street: film and art in Michael Snow, in (catalogue) *Michael Snow: Almost Cover to Cover.* Bristol: Black Dog Publishing.

Renan, S. (1967) *The Underground Film: An Introduction to Its Development in America.* London: Studio Vista.

Sergeant, J. (ed.) (1997) *Naked Lens: Beat Cinema.* London: Creation Books.

Sitney, P.A. (1971) *Film Culture: An Anthology.* London: Secker and Warburg.

Sitney, P.A. (1979, 2000) *Visionary Film: The American Avant-Garde 1943–1978.* London: Oxford University Press.

Suarez, J. (1996) *Bike Boys, Drag Queens and Superstars: Avant-Garde, Mass Culture, and Gay Identities in the 1960s Underground Cinema.* Bloomington: Indiana University Press.

Tyler, P. (1974) *Underground Film: A Critical Inquiry.* Harmondsworth: Penguin Books.

Waugh, T. (1996), Cockteaser, in J. Doyle, J. Flatley, and J.E. Munoz (eds) *Pop Out Queer Warhol.* London: Duke University Press.

Wolf, R. (1997) *Andy Warhol, Poetry, and Gossip in the 1960s.* London: University of Chicago Press.

Wollen, P. (1989a) The two avant-gardes, in M. O'Pray (ed.) *Andy Warhol: Film Factory.* London: BFI.

Wollen, P. (1989b) Raiding the ice box, in M. O'Pray (ed.) *Andy Warhol: Film Factory.* London: BFI.

Youngblood, G. (1970) *Expanded Cinema.* New York: Dutton.

NORTH AMERICAN DOCUMENTARY IN THE 1960s

Brian Winston

IF YOU WANT to understand the charismatic force of John F. Kennedy, few more vivid impressions of this can be found than those in *Primary* (1960). Indeed, *Primary* makes a compelling case as to the overwhelming power of the documentary to record the nuances of the human condition that are not easily conveyed by other means – the young girls running towards JFK as if he were Elvis; the adoration of the crowd at a political meeting; Jackie's nervous finger twisting, behind her back, as she addresses the throng; Kennedy pacing his hotel suite waiting for the results of the Democratic Party primary in Wisconsin, the election that is the subject of the film and which he won, confirming the viability of his run for the Democratic candidacy, and then the presidency.

Such an intimate picture of a campaign was to become a cliché of election coverage in the West but in 1960 to be this close, this observant, was breathtaking, unprecedented. Things today taken for granted – Kennedy's opponent Hubert Humphrey chatting casually in sync in the back of car, for example – had simply never been seen before – not without elaborate feature camera-rigs on the outside of the vehicle. It is hard to convey the sense of excitement, of liberation these long handheld available light and sound shots had, especially for younger documentary filmmakers in North America and Britain. *Primary* was, in a real sense, revolutionary. It marked the start of an almost complete and comparatively rapid change in mainstream documentary film style in the United States, a mainstream that was already largely to be seen solely on television. From 1960 to the present, well into the era of digital image gathering, this observational mode has dominated factual filmmaking practice. For the public it appears to have defined what documentary is, casting doubt on the legitimacy of the older forms of reconstruction, poetry, personal impression, political polemic and the rest. *Primary* is the template for all subsequent mainstream Anglophone documentary.

Of course, it did not spring from nowhere. Throughout the post-Second World War period, there had been a growing sense of confusion and lack of purpose in the documentary world. One problem was sponsorship; a second, sound.

The first generation of documentary film-makers in the United States and Canada was supported, as elsewhere, by the government or official bodies of one sort or another. After the war, as that source of funding began to dry up, the documentarists were increasingly forced to rely on what had been a secondary source of funds, more purely commercial sponsorship. The results were dire: "Anyone looking at a representative sampling of American documentaries produced in the late 1940s and early 1950s would be forced to conclude that few of us who made them were either socially bold or artistically innovative" (Stoney 1978: 15).

This opinion is compelling not least because it comes from one of the most experienced documentarists working during this period, George Stoney. His sponsored film about midwifery, *All My Babies* (1953), was actually a training piece but won international prizes. Nevertheless, upon reflection he wrote in the 1980s:

> I blush to think of all the agitprop dramas I "re-enacted" myself back in the late forties and fifties. Then, most of us were filming real people and situations and basing our plots on real events; but our "messages" (and there was always a message) were being determined by our sponsors. We were working in a tradition of documentary set by John Grierson's English and Canadian units which few of us questioned at the time. Today, most of those documentaries are considered stylistically archaic. (Stoney 1983/4: 10)

Given that the filmmakers, almost without exception, had emerged from a world of progressive American politics and had high creative ambition, this reality drove an increasingly impassioned debate about documentary's future.

Yet even more vexed than the controls of the few corporations who were prepared to use film for PR purposes was the issue of sync sound shooting. If sync was required, then all pretence at observation needed to be abandoned. The technology of the optical sound and silent-running (blimped) 35 mm film cameras was so overwhelmingly bulky that it killed all spontaneity. This is not to be wondered at because the equipment had been designed essentially for studio use; but the effects on the documentary were profound as Ricky Leacock recalled from his experience working with Robert Flaherty in 1946/8 on *Louisiana Story* (made for Esso):

> When we were using the small [noisy, unblimped] cameras [to shoot silent footage], we had tremendous flexibility, we could do anything we wanted, and get a wonderful sense of cinema. The moment we had to shoot dialogue, lip-sync – everything had to be tied down, the whole nature of the film changed. The whole thing seemed to stop. We had heavy disk recorders, and the camera that instead of weighing six pounds, weighed 200, a sort of monster. As a result of this, the whole nature of what we were doing changed. We would no longer watch things as they developed. We had to impose ourselves to such an extent upon everything that happened before us, that everything sort of died. (Bachman 1961: 19)

The need for sync sound, from the 1930s on, necessitated ever more extensive reconstructions or reenactments for the camera. It was no longer merely a question of asking subjects to repeat actions, normal practice even when shooting silent material. Now it became an elaborate process of researching situations (including noting dialogue) and re-enacting them so they could be shot like a feature film as, after all, the equipment demanded. By 1948, a documentary was being defined as:

all methods of recording on celluloid any aspect of reality either by factual shooting or by sincere and justifiable reconstruction, so as to appeal either to reason or emotion, for the purpose of stimulating the desire for, and the widening of human knowledge and understanding, and of truthfully posing problems and their solutions in the spheres of economics, culture and human relations. (Barsam 1973: 1)

Clearly, the way had been lost. It was not just that this high-minded rhetoric was designed to justify films such as *Louisiana Story*, a highly romanticized picture of the beneficence of big oil – not many "truthfully posing problems" there. It was also that "sincere and justifiable reconstruction" had come to include not only scenes previously witnessed by the documentarist, the subject or another observer. It was also deemed to include material that had no prior witness but that *could* or *might* have happened. At this point, it is only the absence of professional actors that distinguishes the documentary from fiction.

For the next generation – that is for Leacock and his peers – the problem of reconstruction was a major difficulty. Leacock was increasingly frustrated, feeling that documentary, in its essence, ought to mean that "the story, the situation is more important than our presence" as filmmakers (Labarthe and Marcorelles 1963: 26). This was to become a dictum: "Let the event be more important than the filming." Reconstruction or reenactment, however "sincere", could never be a legitimate proceeding. It could certainly not be "justified" by the need for sync sound recording; and if the equipment was driving that need, then the equipment would have to be changed. The entire agenda of documentary film concerns was transformed. It was no longer about such issues as:

- the inevitability of manipulation (always involved in any photographic process);
- people performing for the camera;
- the exploitation of the people involved in front of the lens and other ethical questions;
- the distortions involved in editing material in the name of the need to tell stories, one way or another, without which the attention of an audience would wander;
- the perhaps improper influence of sponsors, producers or television organizations.

Now all these issues took second place to only one topic:

- can we find equipment which would let us film without the intervention necessary if we continue to use the cameras and sound recorders we have borrowed from the feature film studio stage?

This was an entirely acceptable refocusing as far as Leacock was concerned. He had trained as a physicist and was well aware of the advances in film technology then *en train* because of the rise of TV news.[1] In the 1950s, his attention was increasingly on 16 mm film.

The Federal Communications Commission required the burgeoning number of US television licence holders to provide a news service and 16 mm, which had been introduced as an amateur stock in 1923 and used professionally only as a distribution gauge during the Second World War, came into its own as the most economic way of filming the news. Arnold & Richter, who had introduced a massively successful 35 mm reflex newsreel camera in Germany just before the war, the Arriflex,[2] now downsized it to 16 mm (the ST) and saw it become the industry norm, an effective professional electric-driven alternative to the 16 mm clockwork Bell Howell Filmo and the Paillard Bolex, both originally designed for amateur use. The Arri ST was expected to be tripod-mounted but handholding for combat coverage during the war had become a feature of news and documentary so it and its rivals were increasingly carried and operated without "legs". But they were unblimped – noisy – unsuitable for sync shooting even if a sound recording system was to hand – and TV news needed sync (Winston 1996: 75).

The answer was provided by a small camera manufacturer, Walter Bach. He produced the Auricon Cine-Voice, a smaller version of his typically square, self-blimped 35 mm studio camera, with miniature valves, which, prior to the widespread introduction of the transistor, were being used by the military. These enabled him to build an optical sound recording system into the camera and still keep it small; not so small as to be easily useable without a tripod but vastly less bulky than the rig Leacock had first encountered in the 1940s. At the end of 1955, Bach introduced the Auricon Filmagnetic, a variation that used 16 mm film with a magnetic sound recording strip replacing one set of sprockets. At about the same time, the Americans were made aware of advances in editing developed by Südwestfunk-Fernsehen, the TV station in Baden-Baden. The Germans had been transferring their sound tracks, recorded on the Filmagnetics' audio strip, to 16 mm sprocketed magnetic film facilitating cutting on specially built "flat-bed" Steenbeck editing tables (Winston 1996: 78ff, 83).

The year before the announcement of the Auricon, Leacock was already endeavouring to handhold a 35 mm camera to shoot unrehearsed sync. In 1954, he photographed for Willard van Dyke, one of America's most famous documentary pioneers, a fairly straightforward television film about the last travelling rural showman and his "tent show", *Toby and the Tall Corn*. News apart, the early 1950s were a time when television's voracious appetite for material embraced the older documentary community and gave it the first glimmers of a way out of the commercial sponsorship dead end in which it found itself. CBS had transferred its most successful radio documentary series to television in 1951. *See It Now*, with veteran reporter Edward R. Murrow, was to become a benchmark for the new medium's authority, power and influence. For example, its searing indictment of the demagogic red-baiting Senator Joe McCarthy, in an edition in Spring 1954, is credited with contributing much to his fall from power. *Victory at Sea*, Henry Salamon's masterly archival documentary series (with music by Richard Rogers) used the Second World War naval film archive to create a massive critical and popular success for NBC in 1952. But such early programming did nothing to alter the established vocabulary of documentary filmmaking. It did not even rush to use the new 16 mm news equipment, preferring to rely on old-fashioned 35 mm. Leacock was therefore before his time in struggling to film handheld sync for a couple of sequences in *Toby*. The significance of his boldness was noticed. Van Dyke described the result of these few shots as "a breath of fresh air for the documentary" (Jaffe 1965: 43); and one member of the television audience, a young *Life* reporter on leave doing a course at Harvard, Robert Drew, immediately rushed to New York to find out who was responsible for the film.

Drew was interested in reviving his company's filmmaking activities after the death of its prestigious newsreel series *March of Time* in 1951 (O'Connell 1992: 32ff). It was to take Drew and Leacock the rest of the 1950s to get to *Primary* and the fulfilment of the promise raised by the brief sequences in *Toby*. Using Time-Life Broadcasting funds, they commissioned a brilliant camera engineer in New York, Mitch Bogdanovitch, to recast an Auricon Filmagnetic in lighter aluminium to facilitate handholding. It was not more ergonomic but the camera's 26 lbs were much reduced. They also worked out how to use the new high-fidelity battery-driven audiotape recorders from France (the Perfectone, marketed in 1959) and Switzerland (the Nagra, on the market a year later) rather than the more basic commag (combined magnetic) recording head Bach had built into the camera. This involved keeping the two machines in sync at first by transmitting a pulse down a physical wire and, later, via a wireless transmission from the camera to the tape recorder (Winston 1996: 84–5).

Drew and Leacock were not alone in seeking the conflicting goals of liberation from the tripod and, at the same time, sync. There were other filmmakers in Leacock's circle, Donn Pennebaker and Al Maysles, as well as some Canadians. At the National Film Board of Canada there had been a structured exploration of the possibilities of 16 mm separate magnetic sound and some films had been made with the new equipment, notably the short *Les Raquetteurs* (*Snowshoes*), shot in 1958 by Michel Brault.[3] When Drew and the others arrived in Minneapolis to film *Primary* they were joined, surprisingly, by another NFBC cameraman with handholding sync experience, Terry Macartney-Filgate.

For Drew, *Primary* represented something of a grail:

We were getting the real stuff, on the move, for the very first time, maybe in history, in sync sound ... Kennedy walks back out, gets in the car and drives off – it's *all on film and tape, continuously!* When we got back in the car, Leacock and I looked at each other, and this was it! This was our dream – the first time ever. (O'Connell 1992: 65; emphasis in the original)[4]

The film was transmitted by the Time-Life station in Minneapolis and a few other independents. The next Time-Life assignment, *On the Pole*, a study of an Indy 500 racing driver, was screened by CBS. The third, *Yanqui No!*, was a study of anti-USA sentiment in Latin America and it was commissioned by ABC, then the struggling third network looking for a news documentary presence to match the prestige of its rivals who were screening well-regarded series. *CBS Reports*, for example, ran a study of migrant workers, *Harvest of Shame*, in November 1960, which caused an uproar. The ABC anthology title was *Close-Up* and Drew Associates, as they now were, made a number of films for Time-Life Broadcasting, which were sold to the network and sponsored by Bell & Howell, a firm happy to be associated with cutting-edge filmmaking.

Drew's background in news magazines' photo-essays and the journalistic predilections of the network commissioners established that the first strength of the new style was its ability to provide dramatic contextual stories featuring a strong central conflict. In 1961, these included a searing study of America's persistent racism in the face of school integration (*The Children Were Watching*) and the bitter basketball rivalry of two high schools (*Mooney v. Fowle*). The following year saw the drama of a death-row prisoner suing for clemency (*The Chair*) and the tensions of a Broadway opening night (*Jane*) with Jane Fonda's first (and last) attempt at live New York theatre. Sometimes faulty journalistic judgement led the team[5] astray, as in *Nehru* (1962) where they went looking for the supposed excitements of an election (shades of *Primary*) but found instead a foregone landslide. This search for conflicts, though, provided Drew Associates with situations of such compelling importance to the participants that the event could indeed be "more important than the filming".

The experience of these early films led to the elaboration of a dogma:

- the filmmakers, having arranged for their presence, should then say nothing further to the subjects of the film, certainly never ask them to repeat actions or do anything for the camera, least of all interviews;
- the filmmakers should never use artificial lights but rely on the increasing sensitivity of film stocks, further enhanced by forced development;[6]
- they should never add sound – neither effects, nor music nor, most importantly, "voice-of-God" commentary.

Of course, they immediately cheated. They filmed subjects being interviewed by the media. They allowed diegetic music and, in the earliest phase, were still on occasion using one portable battery light (a Sun-Gun), often mounted on the top of the camera, its bulky battery being another box to hang from the shoulder of the operator. Above all, their editors, notably Patricia Jaffe and Charlotte Zwerin, manipulated the footage in order to release the meaning of their long shots and create the necessary stories audiences expected from a narrative. They were also forced to compromise as the networks insisted on commentary.

Nevertheless, Drew's (and the networks') need for dramatic conflict sustained direct cinema's belief in the possibility of minimal manipulations. So central was this that one early scholar of the breakthrough, Steve Mamber, thought that "crisis structure" was essential to direct cinema (Mamber 1974: 115ff). But this was not the case. Of course, audiences expected, as ever, to be told engrossing stories – and these filmmakers, especially the women who developed the editing techniques to mould the long takes, became ever more effective at doing this.[7] But as the decade progressed and the original group broke up to pursue more independent productions, other less fraught topics were found. For example, in 1963, the year Leacock and Pennebaker left Drew to establish their own production company, Leacock made a film for ABC about the impact on a small town, Aberdeen, South Dakota, of the birth of quintuplets (*Happy Mother's Day*). More important than the (comic) crisis media attention caused in the community is the way Leacock manages to document his rapport with the mother, Mrs Fisher, creating a sort of conspiracy of the two of them against the insanity swirling all around. This makes the film (especially in his version, rather than the transmitted ABC one with its condescending commentary) exceptional – unthinkable in terms of the traditional style. *Happy Mother's Day* was a precursor to what was to become a theme, the exploration of private lives at a new level of intimacy, which achieved its first formative expression at the end of the decade in Canadian Allen King's *A Married Couple* (1969). King and his crew rigged up practically every room in the home of Antoinette and Billy Edwards to facilitate filming a contemporary marital relationship – the sort of subject traditional documentary could not hope to get close to – only to find they were in fact

A homesick Bob Dylan in Donn Pennebaker's *Don't Look Back*

documenting a marriage breakdown that culminated in divorce.

In the hands of a Leacock, a humanist whose interest in his fellow creatures is without limit, direct cinema probing has often resulted in sympathetic portraits – even of such unlikely figures as police chiefs at a convention (*Chiefs*, 1969). Having been completely delighted with the film, the policemen were horrified when they realized audiences were appalled by their behaviour, for instance salivating over weapons systems on display at the meeting; but that was not Leacock's fault. In other hands, say, Al Maysles', the camera has been merciless. For instance, in *Salesman* (1968), an independently made 90-minute feature cut for theatrical release by Zwerin, the inadequacies of the central figure are as ruthlessly exploited by the filmmakers (Al and his

brother Dave on sound) as are Willy Lomax's in Arthur Miller's fictional *Death of a Salesman*.[8]

The new intimacy also allowed the exploration of the private spaces behind public facades. In 1962, for the National Film Board, Roman Kroiter and Wolf Koenig made *Lonely Boy*, an intimate study of pop star Paul Anka where, among the traditional interviews and performance footage, was also material shot, rather as with Kennedy in his hotel room in *Primary*, in the star's dressing room. Two years later, in *What's Happening: The Beatles in America*, the Maysles obtained similar footage, but far more entertaining because the Beatles were a lot wittier and more interesting than Anka.[9] Donn Pennebaker built on this beginning and in *Don't Look Back* (1967)

Continued on page 83

The marriage between pop music and movies dates back to 1955, when director Richard Brooks laid Bill Haley's *Rock Around the Clock* over the opening credits of *Blackboard Jungle*. A controversial *cause célèbre*, the film's incendiary power was attributed by many to its theme song, which, according to Matthews (1994: 132), was usually accompanied in UK screenings by the "sound of teds slashing cinema seats" (1994: 132). The ensuing publicity benefited both the record and film: the disc, which had flopped in 1954, promptly topped the Billboard charts, while *Blackboard Jungle* defined a new money-spinning template for "youthsploitation" movies. As David Rubel (1994: 41) observes, "Watching *Blackboard Jungle*, you get the feeling that when the schlockmeisters in Hollywood saw this film for the first time, they shot right up out of their seats and shouted, 'Yes! That's it!'."

In the fifty years since *Blackboard Jungle*, cinema's so-called "celluloid jukebox" has continued to flourish and mutate, ranging from movies with prominent pop soundtracks –

Poster for *Woodstock*

Contemporary American Cinema

Dennis Hopper's *Easy Rider* (1968); George Lucas's *American Graffiti* (1973); Adrian Lyne's *Flashdance* (1983); Martin Scorsese's *Casino* (1995); The Hughes Brothers' *Dead Presidents* (1995) and so forth – through pop biopics, transposing the successful format of *The Glenn Miller Story* (1953) to pop hits like *The Buddy Holly Story* (1978) and *The Doors* (1991), to big screen documentaries and concert films. The latter genre reached its apotheosis in the double-whammy of *Woodstock* and *Gimme Shelter* (both 1970), which jointly represented the light and dark side of the 1960s. Building upon the conflicted intimacy of D.A. Pennebaker's Bob Dylan documentary *Don't Look Back* (1967), later cannibalized for Scorsese's TV production *No Direction Home* (2005), and the political posturing of Jean-Luc Godard's *Sympathy for the Devil* (1968), these two masterpieces were as interested in the audience as the bands, blending social observation with musical performances to stunning effect. The Maysles brothers' *Gimme Shelter* is a particularly savage document, climaxing in the onscreen stabbing of Meredith Hunter by Hell's Angels, who were allegedly enlisted to police the gig, and whose violence seems completely incomprehensible to the naïve Stones. As rock biographer Philip Norman has observed, it is to the band's credit that they allowed a film which portrayed them in such a negative light to be released at all – such a release would be inconceivable in today's rigorously controlled marketplace.

Few subsequent festival films or rock documentaries have matched the candour of *Gimme Shelter*. For all its lavish conceptual set pieces, *The Song Remains the Same* (1976) tells us little about Led Zeppelin, comprising live footage from three nights of the band's 1973 US tour interspersed with bland travelogue montages, "at ease" footage, and fantasy sequences. Even Scorsese's acclaimed document of The Band's swansong *The Last Waltz* (1978) is perhaps best remembered by some as the film which inspired the rock parody *This is Spinal Tap* (1984), as a baseball-capped Marty awkwardly shoots the breeze with band members. Penelope Spheeris' *The Decline of Western Civilization Part II: The Metal Years* (1988) redressed the cosy balance somewhat, exploring the excessive lifestyles and retrograde "philosophies" of Kiss, Aerosmith, and Ozzy Osbourne with a refreshing frankness, and paving the way for more recent "rockumentaries" like *Metallica: Some Kind of Monster* (2004), which finds the bickering band performing onscreen psychotherapy. The justifiable mocking of the "rockumentary" format would continue in Tamra Davis' *CB4* (1993) and Rusty Cundieff's *Fear of a Black Hat* (1994), both of which took *Spinal Tap*-style swipes at the world of rap.

In his influential essay "Access All Areas", Jonathan Romney (1995: 83) astutely observes that

> "Backstage" is the most potent of all concepts designed to separate performer and fan. It is a space of privacy, a world behind the curtain in which the *real being*, the ineffable precious essence of the performer's self, supposedly lies shielded from sight ... The audience is not normally permitted behind the sacred veil, but it is a convention of the music documentary to include scenes which take us backstage and offer us tantalising glimpses of the reality behind the show.

Yet, as is amply demonstrated in Alex Keshishian's titillatingly entitled *In Bed with Madonna* (1991), a.k.a. *Madonna: Truth or Dare*, the antics of today's media-savvy entertainers "caught on camera" backstage are as much of a performance as their onstage routines – it is the appearance, rather than the reality, of intimacy that has latterly replaced the insights of *Don't Look Back* and *Gimme Shelter*. In this marketplace, fictional films such as *Almost Famous* (2000), drawn from director Cameron Crowe's experiences as a young journalist for *Rolling Stone* magazine, perhaps offer more honest backstage insights than their supposedly factual counterparts.

Away from the concert stage, and unburdened by the promise of "truthfulness", pop movies have a long history of simply serving as substitutes for live performances. The infamous Elvis movie catalogue, from *Love Me Tender* (1956) to *The Trouble with Girls* (1969), discounting the more adventurous *Change of Habit* (1969), functioned largely as an alternative to concerts, complementing television appearances to alleviate the need for Presley to embark upon world tours. Although the Beatles' movies (*A Hard Day's Night*, 1964; *Help*, 1965; *Yellow Submarine*, 1968; *Let it Be*, 1970) were more formally inventive, blending surreal slapstick, animation, and documentary, they still substantially fulfilled the remit of pop fans denied access to concerts. Despite being eclipsed by the rise of television, the "performance platform" movie genre nevertheless continued in the 1970s, with tacky fare like the UK production *Never Too Young to Rock* (1975) limply reviving the bandwagon jamboree of Frank Tashlin's epochal *The Girl Can't Help It* (1956). In the 1980s, multimedia artist Prince starred in three movies – *Purple Rain* (1984), *Under the Cherry Moon* (1986) and *Sign 'o' the Times* (1987) – all (in varying degrees) featuring performance numbers. The latter, along with *U2: Rattle and Hum*, signalled a return to popularity of the "concert-film-rockumentary", albeit bereft of the genre's former cutting edges.

More intriguing have been the conceptual hybrids that have attempted to meld the mediums of music and movies to create new forms of "performance". In the late 1960s and early 1970s, several counter-culture filmmakers teamed up with rock musicians to produce edgy dramatic features. Stories of Kenneth Anger's fiery collaborations with rock musicians on his occult-inflected shorts are legend, although films such as *Invocation of My Demon Brother* (1969) and *Lucifer Rising* (1972) remained underground. More significant were those movies (more often produced in Europe than America), which, although experimental, still made a mark upon the mainstream. In 1967, for example, Rolling Stones founder Brian Jones famously provided music for Volker Schlöndorff's *Degree of Murder* (1967), while Mick Jagger starred in Nicolas Roeg and Donald Cammell's extraordinary *Performance* (1970), a milestone of British cinema. Michaelangelo Antonioni enlisted Page and Beck's Yardbirds to trash a nightclub to the strains of "Stroll On" in the enigmatic *Blow Up* (1966), while the soundtrack sleeve notes to his *Zabriskie Point* (1970) famously declared that "Contemporary music doesn't merely tell a story or set a mood; it *is* the story. It *is* the mood" (Kermode 1995: 12). This was certainly true of Barbet Schroeder's *La Vallée/The Valley (Obscured by Clouds)* (1972), a tale of paradise lost and found for which Pink Floyd provided the perfect aural accompaniment. Floyd's *Live at Pompeii* (1972) is a rare example of a genuinely intriguing live performance piece, set in a bizarre location with no diegetic audience, and *Pink Floyd: The Wall* (1982) ranks alongside *Tommy* (1975) as one of the most successful screen renderings of a rock opera. David Bowie perfected his androgynous alien stage persona in Roeg's *The Man Who Fell to Earth* (1976), before forging an erratic screen career in movies as diverse as *Merry Christmas Mr Lawrence* (1983) and *The Last Temptation of Christ* (1988), while Art Garfunkel earned critical plaudits for roles in *Catch-22* (1970) and *Carnal Knowledge* (1971), and explored the limits of taboo screen sex (implied necrophilia) in *Bad Timing* (1980). More recently, Courtney Love confounded her critics with a flawless starring role in *The People Vs Larry Flynt* (1996). Rappers such as Ice T, Ice Cube, and Snoop Dogg, all of whom were once charged with corrupting America's youth, have become mainstream movie stars thanks to roles in innocuous action-comedies like *Starsky and Hutch* (2004) and *XXX2: The Next Level* (2005) (Ice Cube has also branched out into writing, production and direction).

Despite the corporate mentality of much contemporary pop cinema, there are suggestions that alternative collaborations are still possible. In the field of "rockumentary" Ondi Timoner's *DiG!* (2004) dubbed "a real life *Spinal Tap*", offered an intimate portrait of the longstanding rivalry between The Dandy Warhols and The Brian Jonestown Massacre, culled from hundreds of hours of digital video footage, much of which had clearly been unobtrusively filmed. Meanwhile, the intercutting of handheld concert footage (Black Rebel Motorcycle Club, Franz Ferdinand, Primal Scream, The Dandy Warhols) with scenes of hardcore sex in Michael Winterbottom's headline-making *9 Songs* perhaps proves that the limits of the pop movie performance have yet to be breached.

References

Kermode, M. (1995) Twisting the knife, in J. Romney and A. Wootton (eds) *Celluloid Jukebox: Pop Music and the Movies since the 50s*. London: BFI Publishing, pp. 8–19.

Matthews, T.D. (1994) *Censored*. London: Chatto and Windus.

Romney, J. (1995) Access all areas: the real space of rock documentary, in J. Romney and A. Wootton (eds) *Celluloid Jukebox: Pop Music and the Movies since the 50s*. London: BFI Publishing, pp. 82–93.

Rubel, D. (1994) Blackboard Jungle, in M. Crenshaw (ed.) *Hollywood Rock*. London: Plexus, p. 41.

Mark Kermode

Continued from page 79
presented a behind-the-scenes picture of Bob Dylan's first triumphant British tour – the real template for the rockumentary, which did more than simply film dressing-room cavortings. Dylan's unwarranted rock-star contempt for many of those he encounters is well captured as is the strength of his concert performances.

Direct cinema also permitted the careful exploration of institutional life at a new level of insightfulness, the master of which has been Frederick Wiseman. Wiseman's long march through American institutions began with a study of a prison for the criminally insane, *Titicut Follies*, 1968, shot for him by an experienced ethnographic filmmaker, John Marshall,[10] and recorded and edited by himself. At this time he was still a law professor in Boston and the film was produced, he said, to show his pupils what the dark side

of the criminal justice system looked like; but he premiered it in a New York City art cinema before he used it in any classroom. A public television station in New York, WNET, quickly reached an agreement with him to provide a feature-length film a year, often on the basis of only the most minimal of pitches. Before the decade turned, Wiseman had produced, with cameraman Richard Leiterman, a study of a Philadelphia High School (*High School*, 1968) and of the police in Kansas City (*Law and Order*, 1969) with Bill Brayne who was to be his cameraman for the eight films shot during the 1970s. With Wiseman's œuvre, now numbering over 30 titles, direct cinema came of age.

This revolution, though, had its critics. For one thing, the traditional documentary community, now largely working for the television industry, was hard pressed to match the skill and stamina of direct cinema camera operators. They took refuge in a dismissive rhetoric, suggesting the new-style films consisted of nothing but shaky camerawork and inaudible sound. A more justified professional complaint was that the films merely presented surfaces and were less illuminating than their makers claimed, and it must be admitted that following people around with a camera can yield an awful lot of footage of the backs of their necks. But it was jealousy and conservatism that motivated most of such criticism.

As late as 1964, some network documentaries were still being shot on 35 mm. Eventually 16 mm did take over completely, albeit without the full panoply of direct cinema dogma being deployed; and, on occasion, journalistic documentaries of considerable significance were transmitted. For example, in 1968, Charles Kurault reported in traditional style for *CBS Reports* on *Hunger in America*. Over the opening shot of a malnourished premature baby in an incubator, he voiced: "This is an American: watch him die." The film (upon which Hilary Rodham worked as an intern) was instrumental in helping Congress establish the food stamps programme. By then mainstream camera operators had worked out how to shoot like Leacock or Pennebaker but the excessive ratios required by "pure" direct cinema shooting (often as high as 60:1 when traditionally 4:1 was considered reasonable) meant that costs were prohibitive. The end result of the direct cinema revolution, as far as network news documentary was concerned, was merely to add long hand-held takes over which to voice commentaries to the traditional mix of reporter-to-camera and interviews, shot on the tripod with lights if necessary.[11] Only a very few filmmakers, notably Wiseman with his sweetheart WNET relationship, were allowed the ratios required by the direct cinema dogma.

A more important attack on the direct cinema practitioners was brought about by their own rhetoric. They were utterly dismissive of the past: "In my opinion, [older] documentary films in general, with very few exceptions, are fake", asserted Drew (Bachman 1961: 17). He claimed that his colleagues were very different: "the filmmakers' personality is in no way directly involved in the action" (Bachman 1961: 14). The Maysles said that they "were trying to find out what's going on. We capture what takes place"; nothing more (Haleff 1964: 23). Pennebaker held that: "It's possible to go to a situation and simply film what you see there, what happens there, what goes on ..." (Levin 1971: 235). "We were simply observers", claimed Leacock (Mamber 1974: 197); "often we discover a new sort of drama that we were not really aware of when we shot it". Much was made of this: "The filmmakers didn't even know what the girl was saying until later; someone just held a microphone up and afterwards they found a prayer had been recorded" (Mamber 1974: 83). The subjects being filmed, absorbed by their various "crises", were of course, equally unaware: "I [Leacock] retired into the corner and got lost sitting in a big comfortable armchair with the camera on my lap. I am quite sure [JKF] hadn't the foggiest notion I was filming" (Mamber 1974: 83).

Critics were at first convinced: "With this equipment [direct cinema practitioners] can approximate quite closely the flexibility of the human senses" (Graham 1964: 34). The films, thought Louis Marcorelles, give "a sensation of life, of being present at a real event" (1963: 16). "It is life observed by the camera rather than, as is the case with most documentaries, life recreated for it" (Taylor 1971: 401). It was but a small step for these claims, grounded in what Mamber called "an ethic of nonintervention" (1974: 145) to be elaborated into a claim of objectivity. Leacock made much of his background as a scientist: "The physicist is a very objective fellow" (Blue 1965: 16). Wiseman claimed that when watching his films, "you have to make your own mind up about what you think ... You are not being spoon-fed or told what to think about this or that" (Halberstadt 1976: 301). But soon, these presumptions were being roundly attacked and as Noel Carroll was to note:

> Critics and viewers turned the polemics of direct cinema against direct cinema. A predictable *tu quoque* would note all the ways that direct cinema was inextricably involved with interpreting its materials. Direct cinema opened a can of worms and then got eaten by them. (Carroll 1983: 6)

Firstly, one could not be sure that the event, however momentous, was always more important than the filming. Molly Haskell (1971: 475), for example, felt that the cameras impelled Billy and Antoinette Edwards in *A Married Couple* into a "showdown". Secondly, there were inevitable partialities to be unearthed in what had been filmed (in however a non-interventionist style) and what had been omitted in the final cut. Wiseman repeatedly found himself in trouble because of this – concentrating on the most violent and disturbed prisoners in *Titicut Follies* at the expense of coverage of the major part of the institution; filming in the worst classrooms and highlighting disciplinary problems in *High School* while ignoring the honours students and so on. Critics have even found unevenness in the coverage of Kennedy (enthusiastic rallies) and Humphrey (thinly attended meetings with bored farmers). These attacks are in one sense unfair because the film is the film and what happens, happens for whatever reason. But in another sense, the constant strident claims by the filmmakers of non-intervention; the assertion that evidence was being presented in a new way for audiences to make up their own minds; the comparative silence as to the importance of editing – all these made the direct cinema practitioners vulnerable. They were like politicians playing the family values card but being caught in sexually compromising positions.

Take nonintervention: the filmmakers might seek to be as inconspicuous as possible while filming but their very unobtrusiveness created new and disturbing levels of intimacy, sometimes bordering on voyeurism. *Titicut Follies*, for example, was virtually banned for decades because Wiseman had failed to obtain releases from the men he mercilessly exposed on the screen. (These inmates, of course, being mentally ill by definition, could not give their consent anyway.) Filmmakers increasingly resorted to well-worn journalistic shibboleths to justify their intrusions. They claimed to be giving people a voice or speaking truth to power and, when all else failed, they fell back on the legalism of the release form. Under the probing direct cinema lens, the question of informed consent, and its abuse in their hands, became an issue for the first time.

Or take editing. Films were extremely carefully crafted out of the long takes. All had closures even when "the event" had none. Logical progressions and illuminating juxtapositions (not necessarily, or even often, reflecting the order in which the material was shot), made the films hang together as coherent, compelling narratives, for all the talk at the time and later of "mosaics" (Mamber 1974: 4; Nichols 1981: 201). Nevertheless Al Maysles once went so far as to claim properly shot material of suitable events needed no editing. Leacock dismissed this as a piece of

Al's frippery by simply pointing out that his brother Dave did the editing (Levin 1971: 204); but this was no joke. Downplaying the editing process was no accident; nor was it merely a reflection of 1960s sexism because editing rooms were dominated by women. It was important to ignore the centrality of editing because it so obviously played against the rhetoric of happenstance and nonintervention during filming. This was especially so given the enormous ratios that were being reduced to manageable length. The problem was that the refocused agenda of the late 1950s entirely concentrated on the filmic event; it ignored all the other ways in which documentarists brought their sensibilities to bear on the materials they shot. It was fine to make a big deal out of nonintervention and eschewing commentary but audiences could be, and were, as influenced by subtle editing as by voice-of-God narration; and one is seldom unaware of the personal, and indeed often the political, position of the direct cinema documentarists for all the strident claims of being mere unbiased observers.

Faced with these quickly changing attitudes among the informed, the filmmakers soon began to back off. In 1965, Leacock might have claimed to be an objective physicist but he also acknowledged that such a fellow "was very selective". As befits a Boston law professor, Wiseman elaborated the most effective, if convoluted, counter-rhetoric: "I don't know how to make an objective film. I think my films are a fair reflection of the experience of making them" (Levin 1971: 322). No more talk of evidence, of the audience as a species of jury; Wiseman is just trying to capture the truth of his own experience. For him, far from being direct cinema's *raison d'être*, objectivity was "a real phoney baloney argument" (McWilliams 1970: 22); "a lot of nonsense"

(Rosenthal 1971: 70); "a lot of bullshit" (Levin 1971: 321). Nevertheless, he wants to have his cake and eat it. Dismissing objectivity allows him to position himself as an auteur as much as any art-house movie director;[12] but he, and all the other documentarists working in direct cinema or *vérité* mode, also still wanted to lay claim to be evidencing the real. Hence the black-and-white images (for the longest time), extremely mobile cameras, raw location sound, available light (often more like available shadow), long takes; these all feed the audience's assumptions about the nature of the authentic realist image.

Despite the contradictions and confusions; despite exacerbated ethical difficulties; and despite the mainstream's inability to fund direct cinema at the levels its dogma required, the style – as *vérité* – came to enjoy a complete triumph. What now constitutes the documentary in the public mind is what Drew and the others said constituted it in the 1960s. It was not until the late 1980s that the first chinks really started to appear. In 1988, Erroll Morris, a filmmaker who had been building a reputation for quirky, off-beat humorous documentaries in the standard mode, produced *The Thin Blue Line*, a miscarriage-of-justice documentary. He shot it on 35 mm as if it were a noir thriller, thereby not only attracting enough attention to the predicament of wrongfully imprisoned Randall Adams but also demonstrating that older documentary styles might still have some vitality.[13] In 1989, a radical print journalist released a film about the plight of his hometown, Flint, Michigan, destroyed by General Motors moving production "off-shore". In *Roger and Me*, Michael Moore chose to express his anger through satire and by putting himself in the frame, *cinéma vérité* style. The film was an unexpected hit on mall screens all over

America and another blow against direct cinema was struck.

Despite an increasing willingness among documentarists to look for ways old and new that are different, direct cinema/*vérité*'s hold remains very strong over most mainstream documentary production, for all that is now electronic rather than photographic. Moreover, in the first decade of the new century, with new levels of manipulation in "simulated documentaries" such as *Wife Swap*, the essential elements of the direct cinema style are all more or less still in place. Indeed, such programmes, which present totally artificial situations dreamed up by television producers but then filmed in the dominant observational style, completely rely for their "authenticity" on the body of techniques and rules the Americans laid down nearly half a century ago. The era of direct cinema that began in 1960 is by no means over.

Notes

1 He was to have a lifelong obsession with the moving image technology. In his eighties, as the millennium turned, he was still at work using the smallest possible hi-res DVD cameras.

2 Arriflex was awarded an Oscar in 1967.

3 Brault was to shoot much of the other seminal documentary made in 1960, *Chronique d'un été* in Paris for Edgar Morin and Jean Rouch exactly because he had the rare experience of shooting handheld sync. The terms *cinéma vérité* and direct cinema (or *cinéma direct* in French) were used very interchangeably at the time but it is logical to reserve *cinéma vérité* for the reflexive use of the equipment in the tradition of *Chronique* and term direct cinema for the more observational North American style.

4 Audiences and critics were so impressed that they saw sync when there was none. Take *Primary*'s most famous moment: the original direct cinema "follow the subject" shot – a 75-second take of Kennedy making his way through an adoring crowd. At the end of this shot as he reaches the podium, there is a fleeting glimpse of Leacock with the Auricon – the only sync camera at the location. This shot, taken by Al Maysles, was made with a standard silent Arriflex ST (with a 5.7 mm wide-angle lens, also brand new at that time), and the random sound picked up quite independently.

5 The auteurist concept of a single director did not apply. The style forced the cameramen, primarily Leacock, Pennebaker and Al Maysles, into fulfilling the traditional functions of the director as well. They were, in fact, "filmmakers", although their credits were only as "photographers". Drew was the executive producer. Noninterventionism and continuous-take shooting dissolved the meaning of traditional credits and left a legacy of considerable ill feeling, between Drew and Leacock especially, which persists.

6 Although the networks were by now transmitting in colour, colour film stocks were too slow to be used without elaborate lighting, which the direct cinema practitioners were eager to avoid. Indeed, they used forced development of black-and-white to push sensitivity from the standard 160ASA rating to 1000ASA, thereby increasing exponentially the graininess of the images they captured. But this, and black-and-white, merely reinforced the authenticity of the material. Graininess and the legacy of wartime hand-held combat footage were earnests of the

noninterventional, observational quality of the films.

7   Specially designed equipment was now being brought to market – notably an ergonomic French camera, the Éclair, which sat comfortably on the shoulder with its viewfinder in place before the eye. Brault used a prototype to shoot part of the first *cinéma vérité* film in Paris in 1960s (*Chronique*) but it was not marketed in North America until 1963. That same year Nagra produced a special version of its tape recorder for film use where the second stereo recording track was adapted to receive the pulse transmitted by the camera. Two years later, Arriflex unveiled the self-blimped Arri 16 BL, less radical, more traditional and more reliable than the Éclair. Specially designed self-blimped cameras and a Nagra tape-recorders kept in sync by wireless crystal control were to be the standard news and documentary rig in the West for the next 30 years until it was slowly replaced by video cameras (Winston 1996: 84–5).

8   In old age Al Maysles (his brother died in 1987) has taken to insisting that the clue to his cinema is his sensitivity to his fellows but this is simply not on view in his masterworks such as *Salesman* or *Grey Gardens* (1976), which equally unkindly and unsympathetically probes the lives of two extremely eccentric, reclusive distant relatives of the Kennedys.

9   The footage was shot for Granada TV in the UK under the direction of Dick Fontaine who had hired the Maysles as his crew. His version was transmitted on UK TV as *Yeah! Yeah! Yeah!* but the Maysles, astutely, asked for and obtained US rights to the material, foregoing the production fee they had agreed.

10 Ethnographic filmmakers had also a pressing need to give their subjects a voice. This had been a main driver for Jean Rouch's work at Le Musée de l'Homme in Paris in the late 1950s but American anthropologists were slow to follow. It was not until 1970 that Robert Gardner, who was in charge of John Marshall's extensive archive of K!ung material at Harvard, made the first ethnographic film in the direct cinema style. Using an established documentarist, Hillary Harris, he produced *The Nuer*, an extremely pictorialist study of Nilotic herdsmen in the Upper Nile basin in Ethiopia; but they did speak (with subtitles).

11 In Britain, this bastardization became known as "verite".

12 For example he has always asserted his copyright with a positively Disneylike tenacity.

13 Adams was released the following year.

References

Bachman, G. (1961) The frontiers of realist cinema: the work of Ricky Leacock, *Film Culture*, 19–23 (Summer).

Barsam, R. (1973) *Non-Fiction Film*. New York: E.P. Dutton.

Blue, J. (1965) One man's truth: an interview with Richard Leacock, *Film Comment*, 3(2).

Carroll, N. (1983) From real to reel: entangled in the nonfiction film, *Philosophical Exchange*. Brockport, NY: SUNY Brockport.

Graham, P. (1964) Cinéma-vérité in France, *Film Quarterly*, Summer.

Halberstadt, I. (1976) Interview with Fred Wiseman, in R. Barsam (ed.) *Non-Fiction*

Film: Theory and Criticism. New York: E.P. Dutton.

Haleff, M. (1964) The Maysles Brothers and "direct cinema", *Film Comment*, 2(2).

Haskell, M. (1971) Three documentaries, in L. Jacobs (ed.) *The Documentary Tradition: From Nanook to Woodstock*. New York: Hopkinson and Blake.

Jaffe, P. (1965) Editing cinema vérité, *Film Comment*, 3(3).

Labarthe, A. and Marcorelles, L. (1963) Entretien avec Robert Drew et Richard Leacock, *Cahiers du Cinéma*, 24(140).

Levin, G.R. (1971) *Documentary Explorations*. Garden City, NY: Anchor Press.

Mamber, S. (1974) *Cinéma Vérité in America*. Cambridge, MA: MIT Press.

Marcorelles, L. (1963) L'expérience Leacock, *Cahiers du Cinéma*, 22(144).

McWilliams, D. (1970) Frederick Wiseman, *Film Quarterly*, 24(1).

Nichols, B. (1981) *Ideology and the Image*. Bloomington: University of Indiana Press.

O'Connell, P.J. (1992) *Robert Drew and the Development of Cinema Vérité in America*. Carbondale, IL: Southern Illinois University Press.

Rosenthal, A. (1971) *The New Documentary in Action*. Berkeley: University of California Press.

Stoney, G. (1978) "We've never had it so good!": observations on the American social documentary, *Sightlines*, Fall.

Stoney, G. (1983/4) The future of documentary, *Sightlines*, Fall/Winter.

Taylor, C. (1971) Focus on Al Maysles, in L. Jacobs (ed.) *The Documentary Tradition: From Nanook to Woodstock*. New York: Hopkinson and Blake.

Winston, B. (1996) *Technologies of Seeing: Photography, Cinematography and Television*. London: BFI.

5

"THE LAST GOOD TIME WE EVER HAD?" REVISING THE HOLLYWOOD RENAISSANCE

Steve Neale

Disney's family hit, *101 Dalmatians*.

IN AN ARTICLE entitled "'The Last Good Time We Ever Had': Remembering the New Hollywood Cinema", Noel King writes that "As we move into the twenty-first century ... we are invited to remember the period of New Hollywood Cinema, as a brief moment of aesthetic adventure that happened between the mid-1960s and the mid to late 1970s and then vanished" (King 2004: 19–20). Acknowledging that "any notion of a 'New Hollywood' will always be a discursive construction", he notes, nevertheless, that "one strong strand of criticism", a strand with which he clearly agrees, sees "New Hollywood" as a brief window of opportunity when an adventurous new cinema emerged, linking the traditions of classical Hollywood genre filmmaking with the stylistic innovations of European art cinema. This concept of "the new" is predicated on a new audience demographic making its aesthetic preferences felt by opting for a new kind of cinema, alliteratively described by Andrew Sarris as a cinema of "alienation, anomie, anarchy and absurdism" (King 2004: 20).

As is now well documented, there are at least two New Hollywoods in recent accounts of Hollywood's history. The first corresponds to Noel King's description and is often also called the "Hollywood Renaissance". The second is generally exemplified by *Jaws* (1975) and *Star Wars* (1977), films whose alleged status as aesthetically conservative corporate blockbusters is said to have inaugurated an altogether different era in Hollywood's history (Schatz 1993; Krämer 1998; King 2002). For the sake of clarity, I will use the terms "Hollywood Renaissance" when referring to the former and "New Hollywood" when referring to the latter. In doing so, though, my aim is to endorse neither these terms nor the critical preferences that guide their

deployment. On the contrary, while focusing in particular on the Hollywood Renaissance, I want to highlight the extent to which they produce a partial and misleading picture of the American film industry, its output and its audiences in the 1960s and early 1970s. In doing so, I also want to highlight the extent to which they are governed by a set of founding oppositions: between commerce and art on the one hand; and between the capitalist nature of the American film industry and radical political ideologies on the other. For proponents like Noel King, the miracle of the Hollywood Renaissance was that it appeared to dissolve or override these oppositions. Aesthetic experimentation, generic revisionism, European-style auterism and an anti-establishment ethos were all for a while underwritten by market demographics and audience taste, contemporary social and political events, a new generation of Hollywood executives, and the abandonment of the Production Code. The extent to which this was actually the case, the extent to which, in particular, audiences actually or solely endorsed the films associated with the Hollywood Renaissance is one of the topics pursued in this essay. Another is the assumption that auterism is a single, uncontentious concept, and that corporate support for auterism and "an adventurous new cinema" was itself a new thing. Yet another is the assumption that it was the films of the Hollywood Renaissance that first marked a break with "classical" aesthetic and ideological values.

It is worth pointing out, first of all, that the version of auterism celebrated by the proponents of the Hollywood Renaissance is indeed only one version. It is often suggested that the auterism of *Cahiers du Cinéma*, Andrew Sarris and *Movie* influenced college-educated filmmakers and the baby-boom audience alike in the 1960s and early 1970s, and that the collapse of the old-style studio system of production paved the way for unprecedented directorial freedoms. David A. Cook, for instance, writes as follows:

> the baby-boomers – often styled as the "film generation" – were drawn toward the kind of film the *Cahiers* critics had been writing about … films that were visually arresting, thematically challenging, and stylistically individualized by their makers. Because this audience was large and was projected to grow for at least another five years, the studios briefly – and somewhat desperately – turned the reins over to auteur directors who might strike a responsive chord in the "youth market". (Cook 2000: 69)

However, this is to muddy the chronological waters, to conflate distinct notions of auteurism, and to ignore differences in critical taste. Among other things, *Cahiers*, Sarris and *Movie* were advocates of hitherto undervalued Hollywood directors like Alfred Hitchcock, Howard Hawks, Otto Preminger, Anthony Mann, Sam Fuller, Nicholas Ray and Vincente Minnelli. Most of these directors were of an older generation than those associated with the birth of the Hollywood Renaissance – Arthur Penn, Mike Nichols, Robert Altman, John Boorman, John Schlesinger and Dennis Hopper – and all directed films valued by *Cahiers*, Sarris and *Movie* in the 1960s: films such as *The Birds* (1963), *Marnie* (1964), *Hatari!* (1962), *El Dorado* (1967), *The Cardinal* (1963), *Exodus* (1964), *El Cid* (1961), *The Fall of the Roman Empire* (1964), *Shock Corridor* (1963), *The Naked Kiss* (1965), *The Savage Innocents* (1960), *55 Days at Peking* (1964), *Home from the Hill* (1960), *Two Weeks in Another Town* (1962) and *The Four Horsemen of the Apocalypse* (1962). These were all early-to-mid rather than late 1960s films. And although Robin Wood of *Movie* wrote a book on Arthur Penn as well as books on Hitchcock and Hawks, *Movie* and Sarris were often sceptical as to the artistic talents of those who directed the first wave of Renaissance films. In his book on *The American Cinema*, Sarris placed Arthur Penn in the category of "Expressive Esoterica", arguing that *Bonnie and Clyde* (1967) "still seems excessively Europeanized for what it is supposed to be" (Sarris 1968: 136). John Schlesinger he placed in the category of "Strained Seriousness". And Mike Nichols and John Boorman he placed in the category of "Oddities, One-Shots and Newcomers", thus reflecting the fact that although Sarris had been writing film criticism since the 1950s, *The American Cinema* itself was initially published in 1968, too early to evaluate the later work of a number of initial Renaissance directors and too late to influence their cultural formation.

Partly for this reason, it is more generally argued that the directors valued by *Cahiers*, Sarris and *Movie* had most impact not on the first wave of Renaissance directors, but on younger Movie Brats like Martin Scorsese, Brian De Palma, Steven Spielberg and Francis Ford Coppola. Penn and his contemporaries, most of whom began their directorial careers in film or television in the 1950s and early 1960s, were much more influenced not by older Hollywood directors and the critical culture that valued their work, but by ideas of film art associated with European directors like Ingmar Bergman, Roberto Rossellini, Frederico Fellini, Michelangelo Antonioni, Jean-Luc Godard and François Truffaut. While *Cahiers*, Sarris and *Movie* valued at least some of the work of these directors too, different versions of auteurism, different

Continued on page 96

Anthony Perkins in *Psycho*

One of the most famous and notorious horror films in American film history, Alfred
Hitchcock's *Psycho* (1960) originally began as a low-budget project based on Robert Bloch's
1959 pulp novel *Psycho* which used the grisly case of serial killer Ed Gein as its starting point.
Bloch's novel explored the idea of uncovering a shocking underside to the apparently normal.
The dreary banality of the Bates Motel is revealed to be the location of unspeakable horror,
the agent of which is the quiet and unassuming Norman Bates. This aspect of the novel
appealed to Hitchcock's sense of the macabre, and the powerful way in which he put this on
the screen remains one of the most compelling and unsettling aspects of the film.

   Psycho marks an important moment Hitchcock's career. Since 1953 he had been loosely
attached to Paramount Studios, enjoying a good deal of autonomy over his film projects.
During the 1950s he produced a string of high-budget technicolor suspense-thrillers, such as
Dial M for Murder (1954), *Rear Window* (1954), *To Catch a Thief* (1955), *The Trouble with Harry*
(1955), *The Man Who Knew Too Much* (1956), *Vertigo* (1958) and *North by Northwest* (1959).
With their mix of glamour and crime these films have popularly come to stand for Hitchcock's
"style". However, despite their enduring critical popularity, and familiarity from television

re-runs, in their contemporary moment they garnered mixed box-office success and critical responses. While Hitchcock was indisputably a very successful figure by the late 1950s, there was pressure on him to remain innovative and to continue to surprise the public (Rebello 1998: 16–17). He was interested in the box-office figures of low-budget horror films being turned out in the mid-1950s, and had been impressed by the gritty and gripping style of Henri George Clouzot's French thriller *Les Diaboliques* (1954) which created a stir internationally (Rebello 1998: 21–2). In addition, his role as the figurehead of the television series *Alfred Hitchcock Presents* (1955–62) allowed Hitchcock an insight into the disciplines demanded by television production, i.e. a rapid turnover of stories, and low-budget (but effective) production values. Thus, in selecting *Psycho* as a project to follow *North by Northwest*'s polish and prestige, Hitchcock's move towards a more realist aesthetic represents a break in style. *Psycho* represented an opportunity for Hitchcock to experiment with shocking narrative material which frankly presented sex and violence, while the film's low budget ($806,947) meant minimal studio interference (Rebello 1998: 156).

Despite its low production budget, considerable time and care were spent on the publicity and promotion surrounding *Psycho*'s release. Posters of a semi-clad Janet Leigh promised explicit sexual content, and advertisements asked cinemagoers not to reveal the plot and warned them that admission after the film had started would be refused. The restrictions on cinemagoers was a daring strategy for audiences who were accustomed to dropping in and out of cinemas at any point during the movie. However, Hitchcock insisted that cinema exhibitors should stick to his policy, effectively "disciplining" both cinema exhibitors and audiences in the way that *Psycho* should be screened and seen, and "fundamentally alter[ing] viewing habits" (Williams 2000: 351). Hitchcock himself also appeared in trailers for *Psycho*, including one in which he takes the audiences on a tour of the Bates Motel, hinting at the murderous surprises the film has in store. His direct address to camera reprised his droll role on his television series *Alfred Hitchcock Presents*, and is evidence of his familiarity with audiences, Hitchcock as household name, and his public profile as the "Master of Suspense". *Psycho* opened in thousands of cinemas across America and within weeks of its release it had become an event. Newspapers reported on the uproar that it was creating, and audiences both screamed and laughed their way through the film, and queued around the block for the potent combination of fear and thrills that *Psycho* offered.

Thus *Psycho* was emphatically a huge popular phenomenon on its release, but it has also come to be seen as a "watershed" film in film criticism. The narrative structure of the film, its spectacular montage of sexualized violence, and its foregrounding of psychology as a theme have all been given attention by critics deploying a range of historical and theoretical approaches. The death of the main protagonist, Marion Crane (Janet Leigh), a third of the way into the film, has been understood as an instance of a radical departure from the classical structure of Hollywood narrative, which devastates audience expectations of story progression and leaves them with no central figure to identify with. Raymond Bellour calls this a "structural perversion" (1986: 313) while Robin Wood writes "we are left shocked, with nothing to cling to, the apparent centre of the film entirely dissolved" (1989: 146). Richard Maltby suggests the film can be seen as reinscribing the "safe" relation of audience to classical narrative, and inaugurating the new narrative modes of post-classical cinema: "from [*Psycho*] on ... we look on the screen more warily, in the knowledge that our comforting ability to predict what will happen in a space or a story can be arbitrarily violated" (1995: 218–19). Feminist film criticism has found Hitchcock's work to be fertile ground for analysis, and *Psycho* is a rich text, particularly in relation to psychoanalytic theories of spectatorship and representation. Linda Williams (1983) sees the film as articulating the problematics of woman's relation to the look, presenting the female body as both highly sexualized (Marion) and monstrous and castrating (Marion and Mother). She suggests that *Psycho* innovates the "psychopathic horror" formula that became widely imitated within the horror genre. Rather differently inflected feminist readings are produced by Tania Modleski (1988) and Carol Clover (1992). Modleski draws on Julia Kristeva's work on abjection in order to trace the "threat of annihilation" as embodied by a "devouring, voracious mother" as central in much of Hitchcock's work (1988: 107). She argues that Hitchcock's films express a "profound ambivalence about femininity" through the way that they both seek to "destroy *and* preserve" it (1988: 112). Modleski suggests that *Psycho* is "paradigmatic" of this problematic relation to femininity, a film where "men's fears become women's fate" (1988: 107). Clover sees *Psycho* as a generically influential film, "the appointed ancestor of the slasher film" (1992: 23), particularly in its "sexualisation of motive and action", and the figure of the killer "propelled by psychosexual fury, more particularly a male in gender distress . . . [T]he progeny of Norman Bates stalk the genre up to the present day" (1992: 27). In her reading of *Psycho*, and of the slasher genre more widely, Clover also highlights an ambivalence around gender, but her focus is on the shakiness of masculinity as a construction rather than on the plight of the female character at the hands of the male killer or through the eyes of the male director, and male spectator position. She suggests that *Psycho* paves the way for a genre in which young male audiences might identify both sadistically, with the killer, and masochistically, with the female victim-hero or "final girl" who suffers but survives to the end of the narrative.

Clover's work illustrates *Psycho*'s generic heritage, but it is also a film which has been unusually enduring, and highly fertile in the film texts and art works that it has influenced. It has been appropriated, adapted, echoed and paid homage to in numerous films, particularly in works such *Dressed to Kill* (Brian De Palma, 1980) and Gus Van Sant's remake *Psycho* (1998). Its wider cultural influence is evident in works such as Gordon Burn's video installation "24 Hour Psycho", a work which resides outside the cinema, but which reminds us of *Psycho*'s powerful evocation of dark emotions and desires.

References

Bellour, R. (1986) Psychosis, neurosis, perversion, *Camera Obscura*, no. 3–4 (1979), reprinted in M. Deutelbaum and L. Poague (eds) *A Hitchcock Reader*, Aimes: Iowa State University Press.

Chion, M. (1999) *The Voice in the Cinema*. ed. and trans. C. Gorbman, New York: Columbia University Press.

Christie, I. and Dodd, P. (1996) *Spellbound: Art and Film*. London: Hayward Gallery and BFI Publishing.

Clover, C. (1992) *Men, Women and Chain Saws: Gender in the Modern Horror Film*. London: BFI Publishing.

Durgnat, R. (2002) *A Long Hard Look at "Psycho"*. London: BFI Publishing.

Maltby, R. (1995) *Hollywood Cinema*. Oxford: Blackwell.

Modleski, T. (1988) *The Women Who Knew Too Much: Alfred Hitchcock and Feminist Theory*. New York and London: Routledge.

Rebello, S. (1998) *Alfred Hitchcock and the Making of Psycho*. London: Marion Boyars.

Rothman, W. (1982) *Hitchcock: The Murderous Gaze*. Cambridge, MA: Harvard University Press.

Spoto, D. (1982) *The Life of Alfred Hitchcock: The Dark Side of Genius*. London: Collins.

Weis, E. (1982) *The Silent Scream: Alfred Hitchcock's Sound Track*. London and Toronto: Associated University Presses.

Williams, L. (1983) When the woman looks, in M.A. Doane, P. Mellencamp and L. Williams (eds) *Re-Vision: Essays in Feminist Film Criticism*. Frederick, MD: University Publications of America.

Williams, L. (1994) Learning to scream, *Sight and Sound*, December, 14–17.

Williams, L. (2000) Discipline and fun: *Psycho* and postmodern cinema, in C. Gledhill and L. Williams (eds) *Reinventing Film Studies*. London: Arnold, pp. 351–78.

Wood, R. (1989) *Hitchcock's Films Revisited*. New York: Columbia University Press.

Helen Hanson

Psycho

Continued from page 92

attitudes to Hollywood, and different ideas as to which films "were visually arresting, thematically challenging, and stylistically individualized" were at stake here as well.

As Derek Nystrom (2004: 19–31) has stressed, versions of auteurism that entail notions of directorial autonomy were and are a matter of contractual agreements, union rules and professional status as well as a matter of individualized styles. David A. Cook (2000: 69) quotes Arthur Penn as arguing that in the late 1960s, "What was happening was that enormous power had devolved upon the directors because the studio system had kind of collapsed". However, the studio system had collapsed by the end of the 1950s. By that time nearly all of the older directors favoured by *Cahiers*, Sarris and *Movie* had achieved a degree of autonomy by becoming producers as well as directors, by becoming partners in production companies, and by employing agents to secure artistically and economically advantageous contractual rights. United Artists had adopted a policy of funding and distributing films made by independent directors and producers as early as 1952. It was joined during the course of the decade by Warner Bros, Paramount and Columbia (Maltby 2003: 23–32, 201–10). "By 1960", as Paul Monaco (2001: 24) points out,

> the movie industry was well on its way toward a model of production in which practically each new movie was put together, packaged, and financed individually, with distribution arranged through one of Hollywood's major companies.

Using Nystrom's article as a basis, it could be argued that the late 1960s are marked by the struggles of Movie Brats like De Palma and Coppola for a place in the new order of the kind already achieved not just by Preminger and Hitchcock, nor even just by Penn, Nichols and Schlesinger, but by directors like Blake Edwards and Norman Jewison too. Edwards and Jewison both directed box-office hits in the 1960s and early 1970s, films such as *A Shot in the Dark* (1964), *The Great Race* (1965), *In the Heat of the Night* (1967) and *Fiddler on the Roof* (1971). For Renaissance proponents, however, the key year is not 1960 but 1967, the key directors are not Edwards and Jewison, but Nichols and Penn, the key box-office hits are not *The Great Race, A Shot in the Dark* or *Fiddler on the Roof*, but *Bonnie and Clyde* and *The Graduate*.

Together *The Graduate* and *Bonnie and Clyde* earned over $66 million in the United States and Canada alone in 1967 and 1968.[1] In combining stylistic innovations from Europe with American subject matter, in adopting an iconoclastic attitude to prevailing social and cinematic conventions, in exploiting the suspension of the Production Code in their depictions of violence, nudity and sex, in featuring new young performers like Faye Dunaway and Dustin Hoffman, and in appealing to what was characterized as a new, youthful, cine-literate audience, they were said to mark the beginnings of what *Time* magazine in December 1967 first called a "renaissance" in American film (Krämer 1998: 297).

I will return to the characteristics of these and other Renaissance films in a moment. What is important to stress at this point is that they were perceived by contemporary commentators and by later historians alike as fundamentally different not just from previous Hollywood films, but from previous box-office hits. In 1964, the biggest box-office hits included *My Fair Lady* and *The Carpetbaggers*;

Continued on page 99

Warren Beatty

Warren Beatty's career spans old Hollywood and New Hollywood, and has survived into the age of new media. The pretty boy of 1960s cinema, Beatty's star image as a handsome young lead who became a respected actor-producer-director in the 1970s, 1980s and beyond has flourished, undiminished by his Left-wing politics and his celebrity image as a womanizing playboy. But his successes look even more contradictory on closer inspection. He had been performing since 1959 (his first film was Elia Kazan's *Splendor in the Grass*, 1961), but his most significant early role came with *Bonnie and Clyde* (1967, directed by Arthur Penn, who had also directed Beatty in *Mickey One* (1965), a paranoid, proto-*noir*), which confirmed his position as a baby-boom generation player. Beatty produced as well as starred in this moment-defining film ("few films have been better produced", David Thomson (2004: 61) has said). As performed by glamorous couple Beatty (as Clyde) and Faye Dunaway (as Bonnie), alongside Gene Hackman, Estelle Parsons and Michael J. Pollard as their cronies, the 1930s Barrow Gang became popular heroes, refashioned with semi-mythical status in road-movie format for the 1960s. Furthermore, Beatty's public image as prime heterosexual specimen was not tarnished by the ambivalent sexuality of the role.

This ability to take chances with roles and survive in Hollywood characterized his later work, although his output is not prolific. He has performed in some of the most innovative films of new Hollywood, including Robert Altman's revisionist Western *McCabe and Mrs Miller* (1971) and Alan J. Pakula's paean to paranoia, *The Parallax View* (1974). Beatty's screen style, however – despite the glamour and political conviction of the star's non-fictional performances – projects a less than assured masculinity: "the Beatty hero seems fundamentally awkward", writes Dana Polan (2001: 147), "unable to perform even ordinary activities with skill or efficiency ... all of Beatty's 1990s films give great prominence to scenes of frantic scrambling. "John Belton (1994: 105) calls Beatty an anti-star, the "by-product of a 1960s counterculture" whose celebrity is qualified. Undoubtedly he could have flourished as a producer, producing ten films, including all four of his directorial outings – *Reds* (1981), *Dick Tracy* (1990), *Bulworth* (1998), and, co-directed with Buck Henry, *Heaven Can Wait* (1978). The star was also both lead performer and producer for Hal Ashby's "sophisticated blend of sex farce and political satire" (Cook 2000: 112) *Shampoo*, which he also co-wrote with Robert Towne. Surprisingly for a relatively counter-culturally inflected movie (set at the moment of Nixon's presidential election but released after his disgrace), *Shampoo* was "the third highest earner in a year of megahits" (Cook 2000: 113).

Warren Beatty directs, produces, co-writes, stars in the Oscar-winning epic biopic, *Reds*

However, Beatty's most significant all-round success is *Reds*, which he directed, produced, wrote and starred in – perhaps unlikely subject-matter for an Oscar-winning mainstream title (it won three Oscars and a Golden Globe). On a vast romantic-epic canvas, it tells the story of Marxist John Reed, author of the Russian Revolution account *Ten Days that Shook the World*, and the only American to be buried in the Kremlin. Ryan and Kellner (1990: 266) call Beatty one of the few US filmmakers to criticize capitalism; perhaps he is the only one to have done so from inside New Hollywood – as Roger Ebert (1981) wryly notes in his review of the film, "maybe only Beatty could have raised $35 million to make a movie about a man who hated millionaires". Beatty's sleight of hand was to produce a character-focused romantic period piece that casts audience-friendly Diane Keaton as Reed's lover Louise Bryant, alongside a wealth of other sympathetic faces smoothing along the process of identification with nontraditional US heroes (Jack Nicholson as playwright Eugene O'Neill, Maureen Stapleton as anarchist Emma Goldman, Paul Sorvino as founder of the American Communist Party Louis Fraina, Gene Hackman as editor Pete van Wherry). But *Reds* was also innovative in its use of real survivors of the historical events described in the dramatic sequences, who speak directly to camera, providing an "authentic" documentary-style political commentary as they interrupt the action at key moments. More than an appreciative account of one thread of Left-wing political history in the US, this use of real-life witnesses could be the film's most subversive move. Ryan and Kellner (1990: 276) argue that it "demythologizes history ... plac[ing the characters] closer to the people in the audience ... When history is made to seem less mythic and more 'real,' it seems more like something anyone could step into and change."

Set against the lighter movies in which he was also involved during the 1980s and 1990s, *Reds* only underlines the contradictions of this politically and artistically serious man. As

Heaven Can Wait (which Beatty co-wrote with Elaine May, a remake of the 1941 fantasy *Here Comes Mr Jordan*) showed in 1978, the politically committed actor-producer-director has throughout his career also been willing to lend his talents to upmarket entertainment fare. He followed *Reds* with *Ishtar*, one of the most cataclysmic box-office failures of the 1980s, a comedy starring Beatty and Dustin Hoffman, which effectively ended Elaine May's directing career. Then came portraits of all-American hero/villains, the big-screen rendition of comic-book character *Dick Tracy* (1990) and the biopic of the founder of Las Vegas Bugsy Segal (*Bugsy*, 1991), as well as a walk-on appearance in then-lover Madonna's backstage documentary *Truth or Dare* (a.k.a. *In Bed with Madonna*, 1991). But Beatty has also continued to play politics in his movies, if not in real life – rumours that he was going to stand for president on a Democratic ticket were quickly quelled by the star in 2000 (Polan 2001: 141). Had he done so, it would have constituted a curious instance of life following art, for just two years earlier Beatty had produced, directed and starred in *Bulworth* (1998), a hilarious skit on political campaigning and US race relations. Perhaps more than any secure statement of political assuredness, *Bulworth*, in all its shambolic refusal to tow a line, embodies what Hollywood films do best when approaching political subjects: it critiques, satirizes, reveals contradictions, but it refuses to proselytize. For Polan (2001: 148) "The confusions here are the unavoidable conditions not only of a man and his cinema but of a whole way of conceiving politics and change at the end of the twentieth century."

References

Belton, J. (1994) *American Cinema/American Culture*. Maidenhead: McGraw-Hill.

Cook, D.A. (2000) *Lost Illusions: American Cinema in the Shadow of Watergate and Vietnam, 1970–1979*. Berkeley, CA: University of California Press.

Ebert, R. (1981) Reds, in *Chicago Sun-Times*, 1 January, archived at http://rogerebert.suntimes.com/.

Polan, D. (2001) The confusions of Warren Beatty, in J. Lewis (ed.) *The End of Cinema As We Know It: American Film in the Nineties*. New York: New York University Press.

Ryan, M. and Kellner, D. (1990) *Camera Politica: The Politics and Ideology of Contemporary Hollywood Film*. Bloomington and Indianapolis: Indiana University Press.

Thomson, D. (2004) *The New Biographical Dictionary of Film*. London: Little, Brown.

Linda Ruth Williams

Continued from page 97

in 1965, they included *The Sound of Music* and *Doctor Zhivago*; and in 1966, they had included *Hawaii* and *The Bible in the Beginning* . . . These were not viewed as innovative films with youth appeal or even (with the possible exception of *My Fair Lady*) as big-budget vehicles for those established Hollywood auteurs favoured by *Cahiers*, Sarris and *Movie*. Instead they were seen as family or adult-oriented blockbusters of one kind or another, road-shown "event" films with middlebrow values and specific appeal, in most cases, to women. By contrast, and in the wake of the success of *Bonnie and Clyde* and *The Graduate*, the biggest box-office hits of 1969 included *Midnight Cowboy* and *Easy Rider* and the biggest box-office hits of 1970, *Woodstock*, *Little Big Man* and *M*A*S*H*, all of them films with counter-cultural youth appeal, and all of them central to Renaissance mythology. Moreover, as if to confirm the nature of the

Revising the Hollywood Renaissance

changes that had taken place, such late 1960s blockbusters as *Star!* (1968), *Hello, Dolly!* (1969), *Paint Your Wagon* (1969) and *Ryan's Daughter* (1970) all, as Renaissance historians have gleefully stressed, lost large sums of money (Schatz 1993: 14; Cook 2000: 9, 71; Monaco 2001: 37).

However, the picture is more complicated than this. Although they made losses, *Hello, Dolly!* and *Paint Your Wagon* both earned over $14 million at the domestic box office and featured in annual lists of box-office hits. If highly profitable films such as *Thoroughly Modern Millie* (1967), *Camelot* (1967), *Funny Girl* (1968), *Oliver!* (1968), *Fiddler on the Roof, Jesus Christ Superstar* (1973), *That's Entertainment* (1974) and *Funny Lady* (1975) are also taken into account, it is clear that big-budget road-shown musicals, whether aimed at families, married women or adults in general, were popular at the box office throughout the 1960s and early 1970s. The same could be said of road-shown war films. In the wake of the success of *The Longest Day* (1962), films such as *The Dirty Dozen* (1967), *Where Eagles Dare* (1969), *Patton* (1970), *Tora! Tora! Tora!* (1970) and *Midway* (1976), all appealing principally, at least on the face of it, to older as well as younger men, performed well at the box office too. Other musicals, particularly those aimed at children, were popular as well as children's films in general. From *One Hundred and One Dalmatians, The Absent-Minded Professor* and *The Parent Trap* in 1961, through *The Sword in the Stone* and *Son of Flubber* in 1963, *Mary Poppins* in 1964 (Fig. 1 (*see plate section*)), *That Darn Cat* in 1965, *The Jungle Book* in 1967, *The Love Bug* in 1969, *The Aristocats* in 1970, *Bedknobs and Broomsticks* in 1971 and *Robin Hood* in 1973, Disney, in particular, produced a string of box-office hits (Krämer 2002: 188–9). In addition,

it is worth noting that *Gone with the Wind* (1939), with its appeal to older audiences, earned over $23 million on its re-release in 1968, and that Renaissance films like *Zabriskie Point* (1970) and *Medium Cool* (1970) earned far less money at the box office than *Paint Your Wagon* or *Tora! Tora! Tora!*.

Two points are worth making here. The first centres on the film industry and its policies; the second on issues of critical taste. Annual production of a handful of big-budget blockbusters, most of them road-shown, had been established in the 1950s as a means of catering to family and adult audiences who only occasionally went to the cinema. Road-showing, in particular, made both the films and the occasions special, justifying the higher prices paid by patrons to see these films and enabling the studios to garner additional income. This policy continued into the 1960s, as films like these proved particularly profitable. Meanwhile, as Richard Maltby has pointed out, revenues from the screening of films on television increased substantially: "The average price for two showings of a feature rose from $150,000 in 1961 to $400,000 in 1965 and $800,000 in 1968, when the networks were scheduling movies every night of the week" (Maltby 2003: 174). Prices were even higher for road-shown productions. ABC paid Columbia $2 million for *The Bridge on the River Kwai* (1957) in 1966 and Twentieth Century Fox $5 million for *Cleopatra* (1963) the following year (Balio 1990: 38). Given the success of films such as *The Longest Day, My Fair Lady, Doctor Zhivago* and *The Sound of Music* in the cinema in the early-to-mid-1960s, given the familial and middlebrow-adult orientation of these films and of television programming, and given the prospective revenues from television networks,

Continued on page 103

Mike Nichols' *The Graduate* (1967) was both a small film and a huge hit. With an estimated budget of $3 million, it became one of the biggest earners of the late 1960s; Schatz (1993: 15) cites it as making $43 million, ahead of both *Bonnie and Clyde* and *2001: A Space Odyssey*. It won Nichols the Best Director Oscar, and garnered six other Academy nominations, as well as Golden Globe and BAFTA wins among other international awards, and helped to establish the film company that financed it, Avco Embassy, as a mini-major (Cook 2000: 10, 324-5). It is a rather slight tale of a young man, Benjamin Braddock (Dustin Hoffman), who returns to his suburban home after graduation and, while avoiding making any decision about his career, becomes sexually involved with Mrs Robinson (Anne Bancroft), one of his parents' friends, before falling in love with her daughter Elaine (Katharine Ross). Benjamin is apathetic, almost catatonic, and unable to act positively, but the relationship with Elaine, and his growing disaffection regarding his parents' lifestyle, awaken a more decisive self. As the film proceeds, he becomes less polite, more alienated but also more passionate, and what seems like a coming-of-age drama also insinuates itself as something of a coming-to-political-consciousness drama. It has been read as a powerful critique of the American Dream, for the new youth audiences of the 1960s; Kolker (2000: 350) calls it a "hymn to the passive side of the rebellion of the sixties". One turning point comes when Benjamin's landlord (played by radical filmmaker Paul Mazursky) calls him an "outside agitator", an act of othering that, ironically, agitates him into becoming even more of an outsider. As he says to Elaine when they visit a hamburger joint: "It's like I've been playing some kind of game but the rules don't make any sense to me – they're being made up by all the wrong people. Maybe no-one makes them up – they seem to have made themselves up." The Robinson parents try to break up the relationship, but Benjamin pursues Elaine to Berkeley, only to be rejected. In a now iconic and much-parodied final sequence, Benjamin storms the church where Elaine is marrying another man, and whisks her off (after barring the church door with a wooden cross) to (perhaps) a different future. For King (2002: 18) Benjamin's is "a gradual emancipation", though whether the couple are free as they flee on the bus is open to question.

These are the bare narrative bones of a film that has become something of an American national treasure. *The Graduate* is a rich object of analysis, approachable through various interpretative modes (textual, reception, historical) but it is best understood through a combination of all of these. It is undoubtedly a lively text, funny and multilayered, the product of Buck Henry and Calder Willingham's screenplay (based on a novel by Charles Webb), Mike Nichols' experience in comedy (he was formerly one of a pioneering comic duo, with Elaine May), and pitch-perfect tragicomic performances, particularly from Hoffman, Bancroft and William Daniels as Benjamin's father. It also richly rewards different interpretative frameworks – psychoanalytic (the Oedipal resonances of Benjamin having sex with a mother figure – and the film was received as shockingly explicit on this issue), gender analysis (the film's wry framing of family life and career opportunities), and genre. This last issue is perhaps one of the trickiest frameworks for understanding this curiously unplaceable movie – not quite a comedy, unlike any other mainstream drama of the time, it might best be described as a "youth film", and was clearly marketed as such (one trailer for it opens with an image of Benjamin at Berkeley looking despondent, overshadowed by a US flag). Cook (2000: 99) calls it "the prototypical youth-cult movie". It also is an interesting text for historical reception analysis, because on its original release it was squarely aimed at a youth audience looking for plots and images appropriate to their experience in 1960s protest movements (anti-Vietnam, student revolts, the civil rights movement and the women's movement). The dark or difficult, dissenting or unresolved film narratives this audience turned into hits were not, however, only the stuff of art houses, but could be seen in mainstream American cinemas. This makes *The Graduate* a particularly interesting object for film historians, telling as it does a specific story about the shifts in Hollywood production and audiences in this period. It has been read as typical of those edgy late 1960s box office successes which were directed by a new wave of US auteurs spearheading the so-called Hollywood Renaissance. In this context Nichols is seen as one of a new pantheon of directorial talents, which also includes his close contemporaries Robert Altman, Dennis Hopper, Peter Bogdanovich and Arthur Penn, all directors of films that have come to constitute a canon of important late 1960s/early 1970s cinema (*M*A*S*H*, *Easy Rider*, *Targets*, *Bonnie and Clyde* respectively). Clearly there are problems with the idea that these were *the* most significant films of their moment, and with the model of these directors forming an exclusive pantheon of (white, male) American talent – problems associated with the wider notion of auteurism and, as Steve Neale argues elsewhere in this book, with the idea that counter-cultural cinema dominated the US box office in the 1960s.

Nevertheless, *The Graduate* was indisputably a huge financial success, attaining a visual and narrative edginess while never alienating its financiers. In its gentle, box-office-friendly deployment of soft *avant garde* techniques, it bears out a certain Hollywood Renaissance "look" and attitude to counter-cultural subjects. Although comic in tone, it uses nonclassical techniques which make it sometimes difficult to watch and which disrupt subjective codes – questions concerning who our hero is and how he should behave. Hollywood Renaissance directors were often read as being stylistically influenced by the European New Wave, as is borne out by Roger Ebert's review of the film when it came out, in which he argued that it was "inspired by the free spirit which the young British directors have brought into their movies" (Ebert 1967). Sequences in the film such as Benjamin's birthday party, when he emerges from the house in a diver's suit to applause from his parent's awful friends, demonstrate Nichols' sometimes bizarre stylings. The scene cuts between Ben's muffled, rather surreal, aural and visual experience from inside the suit, locking us into his subjective view through distorting modes of representation (the faces of his onlookers seen obscurely through the facemask, the sound of his breathing overwhelming all else), and the suburbanite's external view of him. He dives into the swimming pool and would rather stand on the bottom than engage in social intercourse. Elsewhere Nichols makes liberal use of decentred compositions and asymmetrical framing, losing human figures in a wider canvas and refusing to prioritize their identities by fixing them centrestage. Scenes are also edited in a way which disrupts a linear sense of space and time; for Ryan and Kellner (1988: 21), the film's critique of bourgeois society is "executed through its editing. Nonrealist transitions permit Ben to walk out of one space (his parent's outdoor pool) and into another quite different one (the hotel room where he carries on his affair), thus establishing contiguous links that suggest the interchangeability of upper-class luxury and cynical adultery." Sound is also used innovatively, highlighting the visuals or blanking out competing sounds – we are prevented from hearing key information at times (private conversations between Ben and Elaine, for instance). Nichols also uses overlapping dialogue, sometimes questioning the distinction between scenes taking place in different locations and on different days. *The Graduate*'s seminal pop soundtrack by Simon and Garfunkel also seems to speak to its moment in a "*Zeitgeist*" fashion, though filmically there is no necessary correlation between score and action (the song "Mrs Robinson" is the only one that actually has any diegetic connection to the film).

The Graduate has remained popular with more recent viewers, so analysis of its significance for audiences and critics in the 1970s, 1980s and 1990s (especially as this cherished object of US popular culture comes to be released on video and DVD) is a potentially rewarding area of enquiry. Interest was heightened in the late 1990s when a play by Terry Johnson based on the film was staged both in London's West End and on Broadway, part of a curious recent trend for basing theatrical productions on successful movies (*The Lion King*, *Mary Poppins*, *The Producers*). The role of Mrs Robinson (much coveted by mature actresses) was performed by Kathleen Turner in both London and New York, and by Amanda Donohoe and Jerry Hall in London, with Alicia Silverstone and Jason Biggs playing Elaine and Benjamin on Broadway. The sequel scurrilously pitched in Robert Altman's *The Player* (1992) has never come to pass but *The Graduate* also inspired Rob Reiner's 2005 spin-off movie *Rumour Has It ...* , about a family that believes it was the real-life inspiration for the central story of *The Graduate* (Benjamin's cross-generational affair with Mrs Robinson). The final question the film asks is just how post-suburban Benjamin and Elaine's lives will be. Benjamin has, after all, replied to Elaine's question, "Why don't you just drag me off if you want to marry me so much?" with "I might just do that – after we get the blood tests." The final tableau on the bus suggests that the couple will inevitably take their place in the same old family structure and will probably turn out just like their parents. Mike Nichols, on the other hand, graduated to a hugely successful career in mainstream Hollywood, director of titles such as *Catch-22* (1970), *Carnal Knowledge* (1971), *Silkwood* (1983), *Working Girl* (1988), *Postcards from the Edge* (1990) and *Primary Colors* (1998), and working hard well into his seventies.

References

Cook, D.A. (2000) *Lost Illusions: American Cinema in the Shadow of Watergate and Vietnam, 1970–1979*. Berkeley: University of California Press.

Ebert, R. (1967) "The Graduate", review, *Chicago Sun-Times*, 26 December, archived at http://rogerebert.suntimes.com/.

King, G. (2002) *New Hollywood Cinema: An Introduction*. London: I.B. Taurus.

Kolker, R. (2000) *A Cinema of Loneliness: Penn, Stone, Kubrick, Scorsese, Spielberg, Altman*. Oxford: Oxford University Press.

Ryan, M. and Kellner, D. (1988) *Camera Politica: The Politics and Ideology of Contemporary Hollywood Film*. Bloomington and Indianapolis: Indiana University Press.

Schatz, T. (1993) The new Hollywood, in J. Collins, H. Radner and A. Preacher Collins (eds) *Film Theory Goes to the Movies*. New York: Routledge, pp. 8–36.

Linda Ruth Williams

Continued from page 100

it is hardly surprising that companies like Twentieth Century Fox, Columbia and Paramount continued to invest heavily in films like this. Moreover, as if further to confirm their acumen, overexpenditure on *Cleopatra, The Greatest Story Ever Told* (1965) and *The Fall of the Roman Empire* had already prompted these and other major companies to concentrate on big-budget war films and musicals rather than epics set in the Ancient world. What happened, however, was that, enticed by the prospect of income from television, new companies like CBS, ABC and National General entered the field. These companies increased the supply of films and bid aggressively for talent and properties, contributing to the escalation of budgets to a level insupportable by theatrical demand. At the same time the networks, having acquired enough product

Revising the Hollywood Renaissance   103

to meet their needs for four seasons, suddenly stopped buying movies in 1968, leaving the theatrical market oversupplied with product. Bankers estimated that the industry was spending approximately twice as much on production as the market could return, and the major companies registered corporate losses of $200 million in 1969 (Maltby 2003: 175).

It was thus not the inherent unpopularity of big-budget war films and musicals, nor the sudden loss of family and adult audiences, nor the conservative tastes of aging executives that prompted these losses, but the fact that an important income stream was suddenly denied to big-budget productions, that "too many movies were competing for the box-office dollar" alone, and that "income was, as a result, spread more thinly" (Maltby 2003: 175). The ensuing crisis affected Renaissance films as well as blockbusters, but to a lesser degree, and for the most part because, with the marginal exception of *Little Big Man*, Renaissance films were all low-to-medium budget productions. This is a key point. It reflects the long-standing budgetary status of youth-oriented movies and artistically inclined American movies alike since the Second World War. The industry as a whole had known perfectly well that young people in their teens and early twenties comprised the bulk of regular moviegoers. That is why most major companies made films with what they adjudged to be youth appeal in the 1950s and early 1960s. It also had known that there was a small but growing audience for European art films and for artistically ambitious Hollywood fare. That is why companies like United Artists, MGM and Universal invested in the distribution and production, often overseas, of films directed by the likes of Antonioni, Bergman, Fellini and Truffaut in the 1950s and 1960s, and why films like *Twelve Angry Men* (1957), *Cat on a*

Hot Tin Roof (1958), *The Hustler* (1961), *The Miracle Worker* (1962), *Lolita* (1962), *The Pawnbroker* (1965), *Mickey One* 1965) and *Whose Afraid of Virginia Woolf?* (1966) were made in increasing numbers (Balio 1987: 226–32, 276–82; Lev 1993: 24–5). However, it had known, as well, that middlebrow blockbusters were the films that tended to make the most money. The huge profits made by *Bonnie and Clyde*, *The Graduate*, *Easy Rider* and *Midnight Cowboy* were clearly exceptional. They indeed signalled the growing importance of the baby-boom audience in the late 1960s. But they were not, as we have seen, the only films to sell tickets at the box office. In terms of profit-ability, at least two of Disney's films, *The Love Bug* and *The Aristocats*, were every bit as noteworthy as *Midnight Cowboy* and *Easy Rider*. Like *The Sound of Music*, *Hello, Dolly!*, *Fiddler on the Roof* and *Tora! Tora! Tora!*, they have never been regarded, though, as worthy of critical attention. The same could be said, at the opposite end of the cultural spectrum, of *Deep Throat* (1972) and *The Devil in Miss Jones* (1973), box-office hits that followed in the wake of European imports such as *I Am Curious: Yellow* (1969) and *Sexual Freedom in Denmark* (1972), and which were as much a product of the abandonment of the Production Code as *Midnight Cowboy*, *A Clockwork Orange* (1971) and *Last Tango in Paris* (1973) (Lewis 2000: 143–229).

Disney was one of only two major companies to emerge unscathed from the crisis and from the wave of conglomerate takeovers that marked the late 1960s and early 1970s. The other was MCA-Universal, the company that pioneered (or rather revived) the disaster film as a cut-price format for the family- and adult-oriented road-shown blockbuster with *Airport* (1970).[2] *Airport* made more money at the box office in the 1970s than *M*A*S*H*, *Little Big*

Man or *Woodstock*, paving the way for *The Poseidon Adventure* (1972), *The Towering Inferno* (1974), *Earthquake* (1974) and subsequent films in the *Airport* series. The only film that made more money that year was *Love Story*. *Love Story* was produced by Robert Evans, one of the new young executives at Paramount. As the producer of *Rosemary's Baby* (1968), *Chinatown* (1974) and *The Godfather* (1972), Evans is often celebrated as a quintessential Renaissance executive. But although *Love Story* centred on youthful characters, involved generational conflict, celebrated mildly unconventional behaviour and featured loosely integrated montage sequences and passages of play, it is not usually regarded as a Renaissance film. The same could be said of *Butch Cassidy and the Sundance Kid*, a film that focused on outlaws, which also celebrated unconventional behaviour, which also featured loosely integrated montage sequences and passages of play, and which topped the box-office charts in 1969. *Butch Cassidy and the Sundance Kid* was directed by George Roy Hill for Twentieth Century Fox. Hill had already had a hit in 1967 with *Thoroughly Modern Millie* and was to have another with *The Sting* in 1973. These, though, are not the films Noel King has in mind when he writes of the "adventurous new cinema" endorsed by the "new demographic".

Aside from the films already mentioned, the Hollywood Renaissance is generally exemplified by movies such as *Alice's Restaurant* (1969), *The Wild Bunch* (1969), *Five Easy Pieces* (1970), *Two-Lane Blacktop* (1971), *The King of Marvin Gardens* (1972), *Deliverance* (1972), *Images* (1972), *The Long Goodbye* (1973), *The Last Detail* (1973), *Bring Me the Head of Alfredo Garcia* (1974), *The Parallax View* (1974), *California Split* (1974), *Thieves Like Us* (1974), *Nashville* (1975), *The*

Conversation (1976), *Night Moves* (1976) and *Buffalo Bill and the Indians* (1976). In what remains the best account of these and other late 1960s and early 1970s films, Thomas Elsaesser underlines the extent to which they break with classical narrative and classical ideological conventions. The "classical narrative", he writes:

> was essentially based on a dramaturgy of intrigue and strongly accentuated plot, which managed to transform spatial and temporal sequence into consequence, a continuum of cause and effect ... Out of conflict, contradiction and contingency the narrative generated order, linearity and articulated energy. Obviously, at a deeper level, such a practice implied an ideology – of progress, of forging in the shape of the plot the outlines of a cultural message ... Ideological critics have ... detected in the classical cinema a fundamentally affirmative attitude to the world it depicts, a kind of a-priori optimism located in the very structure of the narrative about the usefulness of purposive action. Contradictions were resolved and obstacles overcome by having them played out in dramatic-dynamic terms or by personal initiative: whatever the problem, one can *do* something about it. (Elsaesser 1975: 13–14)

By contrast, in a period in which television has "left ideologically less representative groups in the cinemas", and in which "independent producers and directors are now ... under pressure to adequate their films to the ideological assumptions of prospective audiences", "it is not surprising to find films reflect stances of dissent among minority groups".

Compared with the 40s and 50s, the commercial cinema has such a tenuous hold over its audiences that it is in practice forced to seek them out, capture them either by an intensity of emotional involvement that is unavailable to television – a dramaturgy of suspense, spectacle and violence – or by anticipation of favoured emotional anti-stances, such as cynicism, or the detached cool of a certain *machismo*. Cop-thrillers or disaster-movies cater for the first type, road-movies with rebels as heroes are a useful outlet for the second. (Elsaesser 1975: 14)

While cop thrillers like *Dirty Harry* (1971) and *Death Wish* (1974) are built around char-acters "so purposive and determined, so firm and single-minded" that "they appear powered by the purely negative energy of resentment, frustration, and ... petty-bourgeois spite", the protagonists of *They Shoot Horses, Don't They?* (1969), *The Mean Machine* (1974) and the road films convey an "almost physical sense of inconsequential action, of pointlessness and uselessness, a radical scepticism, in short, about the American virtues of ambition, vision, drive" (Elsaesser 1975: 15). Either way, the classical "affirmative-consequential model of narrative" is rejected, replaced, or put under strain from within (Elsaesser 1975: 14).

Elsaesser's account remains exemplary in many ways, not least because, although it tends, like many later accounts, to construct binary oppositions rather than kaleidoscopic patterns,[3] it seeks to take account of a number of genres and trends. (The only major trend Elsaesser does not refer to is blaxploitation, a vehicle for rather differently motivated forms of resentment and frustration.) I would want, however, to underline the points I have made already about the continued appeal of family-, female- or adult-oriented films with classical ideological and narrative values throughout the late 1960s and early 1970s: the Disney films, the musicals, the war films, road-shown

adventure films like *Papillon* (1973) and John Wayne Westerns like *True Grit* (1969), *Chisum* (1970), *Big Jake* (1971), *Rooster Cogburn* (1975) and *The Shootist* (1976), as well as disaster films. I would want to point, too, to the appeal throughout the 1960s and 1970s of the James Bond films. In spite (or perhaps because) of their tongue-in-cheek tone, the Bond films clearly allied the values of "suspense, spectacle and violence" both to "the detached cool of a certain *machismo*" *and* to "affirmative-consequential" classical values. Although technically British, their high-profile presence in the United States needs to be acknowledged more often than it usually is in accounts of the period.

On the other hand, I would want to underline the extent to which the undermining of classical conventions began earlier on. In *The Classical Hollywood Cinema*, Bordwell, Staiger and Thompson suggest, albeit tenta-tively, that "the force of the classical norm was reduced" by 1960 (Bordwell et al. 1985: 10 and Krämer 1998: 291–5).[4] In this context, and aside from genuinely independent films such as *Shadows* (1959), I would point to Richard Maltby's discussion of *Psycho* (1960) as a film that breaches fundamental classical conven-tions by creating what he calls "unsafe space" (Maltby 2003: 353–7) and to Paul Monaco's (2001: 2) argument that *Psycho* helped create a new "cinema of sensation" in contrast to "the cinema of sentiment" that had constituted the aesthetic core of classic Hollywood from the late 1920s through the 1950s. I would point, as well, to the refusal of *Anatomy of a Murder* (1959) to resolve what Oscar Gould (1969: 5) has called the "incredible ambiguities" in those events in the film we never witness, and to *Shock Corridor*, *The Naked Kiss* and *The Chase* (1966) as films that, while "consequential" in structure, can hardly be said to be "affirmative". None of these films appear to be influenced by European art cinema, and none of them possessed obvious youth appeal. While the films themselves are hardly unknown, they were part of a heterogeneous mix of films, styles, genres and audiences whose dimensions in the 1960s and 1970s were probably as wide as they had ever been, but whose diversity has all too often been unexplored in Renaissance-oriented accounts of the period.

Notes

1   Unless otherwise noted, box-office and other figures cited from this point on are derived from Pirie (1981), Finler (1988), Brown (1995), and annual and revised lists published in *Variety*.

2   Big-budget disaster films such as *The Hurricane* (1937) and *In Old Chicago* (1938) had been a small but significant element in Hollywood's output in the late 1930s. *Airport* and later disaster movies were big-budget films too, but they were nowhere as expensive as *Paint Your Wagon*, *Hello Dolly!*, *Ryan's Daughter*, and *Tora! Tora! Tora!*.

3   This tendency can be found in books as diverse as Ray (1985), Biskind (1999) and Cook (2000).

4   As Peter Krämer points out, the 1950s and early 1960s witnessed a number of pronouncements to the effect that Classical Hollywood was dead and that a New Hollywood was either in place or was on its way.

References

Balio, T. (1987) *United Artists: The Company that Changed the Film Industry*. Madison: University of Wisconsin Press.

Balio, T. (1990) Introduction to Part 1, in Balio, T. (ed.) *Hollywood in the Age of Television*. Boston: Unwin Hyman.

Biskind, P. (1999) *Easy Riders, Raging Bulls: How the Sex-Drugs-and-Rock 'N Roll Generation Saved Hollywood*. New York: Touchstone.

Bordwell, D, Staiger, J. and Thompson, K. (1985) *The Classical Hollywood Cinema: Film Style and Mode of Production to 1960*. London: Routledge and Kegan Paul.

Brown, G. (1995) *Movie Time*. New York: Macmillan.

Cook, D.A. (2000) *Lost Illusions: American Cinema in the Shadow of Watergate and Vietnam, 1970–1979*. New York: Scribner's.

Elsaesser, T. (1975) The pathos of failure: American films in the 70s, *Monogram*, no. 6 (October): 13–19.

Finler, J. (1988) *The Hollywood Story*. London: Octopus.

Gould, O. (1969) "*Anatomy of a Murder*", *Brighton Film Review*, 15 (December): 5.

King, G. (2002) *New Hollywood Cinema: An Introduction*. London: I.B. Tauris.

King, N. (2004) "The last good time we ever had": remembering the New Hollywood cinema, in T. Elsaesser, A. Horwath and N. King (eds) *The Last Great American: New Hollywood Cinema in the 1970s*. Amsterdam: Amsterdam University Press.

Krämer, P. (1998) Post-Classical Hollywood, in J. Hill and P.C. Gibson (eds) *The Oxford Guide to Film Studies*. Oxford: Oxford University Press.

Krämer, P. (2002) "The best Disney films Disney never made": children's films and the family audience in American cinema since the 1960s, in S. Neale (ed.) *Genre and Contemporary Hollywood*. London: BFI.

Lev, P. (1993) *The Euro-American Cinema*. Austin: University of Texas Press.

Lev, P. (2003) *The Fifties: Transforming the Screen, 1950–1959*. New York: Scribner's.

Lewis, J. (2000) *Hollywood v. Hard Core: How the Struggle over Censorship Saved the Modern Film Industry*. New York: New York University Press.

Maltby, R. (2003) *Hollywood Cinema*. Oxford: Blackwell.

Monaco, P. (2001) *The Sixties: 1960–1969*. New York: Scribner's.

Nystrom, D. (2004) Hard hats and movie brats: auteurism and the class politics of the New Hollywood, *Cinema Journal*, 363: 18–41.

Pirie, D. (ed.) (1981) *Anatomy of the Movies*. London: Winward.

Ray, R.B. (1985) *A Certain Tendency of the Hollywood Cinema, 1930–1980*. Princeton, NJ: Princeton University Press.

Sarris, A. (1968) *The American Cinema: Directors and Directions, 1929–1968*. New York: Dutton.

Schatz, T. (1993) The new Hollywood, in J. Collins, H. Radner and A. Preacher Collins (eds) *Film Theory Goes to the Movies*. New York: Routledge.

Box Office Figures, 1960s	1960–69		Rentals to date for year just ending
	1960	Ben-Hur	$17,300,000
	1961	Guns of Navarone	$8,600,000
	1962	West Side Story	$11,000,000
	1963	How the West Was Won	$8,000,000
	1964	The Carpetbaggers	$13,000,000
	1965	Mary Poppins	$28,500,000
	1966	Thunderball	$26,000,000
	1967	The Dirty Dozen	$18,200,000
	1968	The Graduate	$39,000,000
	1969	The Love Bug	$17,000,000

1960

Academy Awards of Motion Pictures Arts and Sciences
Best picture: *The Apartment* – Billy Wilder
Best director: Billy Wilder – *The Apartment*
Best actor in a leading role: Burt Lancaster – *Elmer Gantry*
Best actor in a supporting role: Peter Ustinov – *Spartacus*
Best actress in a leading role: Elizabeth Taylor – *Butterfield 8*
Best actress in a supporting role: Shirley Jones – *Elmer Gantry*
Cannes International Film Festival
Palme d'Or: *La Dolce Vita* – Federico Fellini
Venice International Film Festival
Golden Lion: *Le passage du Rhin* – André Cayatte

1961

Academy Awards of Motion Pictures Arts and Sciences
Best picture: *West Side Story* – Robert Wise
Best director: Robert Wise, Jerome Robbins – *West Side Story*
Best actor in a leading role: Maximilian Schell – *Judgement at Nuremberg*
Best actor in a supporting role: George Shakiris – *West Side Story*
Best actress in a leading role: Sophia Loren – *Two Women*
Best actress in a supporting role: Rita Moreno – *West Side Story*
Cannes International Film Festival
Palme d'Or: *Une Aussi Longue Absence* – Henri Colpi and *Viridiana* – Luis Buñuel
Venice International Film Festival
Golden Lion: *L'année dernière à Marienbad* – Alain Resnais

1962

Academy Awards of Motion Pictures Arts and Sciences
Best picture: *Lawrence of Arabia* – Sam Spiegel
Best director: David Lean – *Lawrence of Arabia*
Best actor in a leading role: Gregory Peck – *To Kill a Mockingbird*
Best actor in a supporting role: Ed Begley – *Sweet Bird of Youth*
Best actress in a leading role: Anne Bancroft – *The Miracle Worker*
Best actress in a supporting role: Patty Duke – *The Miracle Worker*
Cannes International Film Festival
Palme d'Or: *O Pagador de Promessas* – Anselmo Duarte
Venice International Film Festival
Golden Lion: *Ivanovo Detstvo* – Andrej Tarkovskij and *Cronaca Familiare* – Valerio Zurlini

1963

Academy Awards of Motion Pictures Arts and Sciences
Best picture: *Tom Jones* – Tony Richardson
Best director: Tony Richardson – *Tom Jones*
Best actor in a leading role: Sidney Poitier – *Lilies of the Field*
Best actor in a supporting role: Melvyn Douglas – *Hud*

Best actress in a leading role: Patricia Neal – *Hud*
Best actress in a supporting role: Margaret Rutherford – *The V.I.P.s*
Cannes International Film Festival
Palme d'Or: *Il Gattopardo* – Luchino Visconti
Venice International Film Festival
Golden Lion: *Le Mani sulla Città* – Francesco Rosi

1964

Academy Awards of Motion Pictures Arts and Sciences
Best picture: *My Fair Lady* – Jack L. Warner
Best director: George Cukor – *My Fair Lady*
Best actor in a leading role: Rex Harrison – *My Fair Lady*
Best actor in a supporting role: Peter Ustinov – *Topkapi*
Best actress in a leading role: Julie Andrews – *Mary Poppins*
Best actress in a supporting role: Lila Kedrova – *Zorba the Greek*
Cannes International Film Festival
Grand Prix International du Festival: *Les Parapluies du Cherbourg* – Jacques Demy
Venice International Film Festival
Golden Lion: *Deserto Rosso* – Michelangelo Antonioni

1965

Academy Awards of Motion Pictures Arts and Sciences
Best picture: *The Sound of Music* – Robert Wise
Best director: Robert Wise – *The Sound of Music*
Best actor in a leading role: Lee Marvin – *Cat Ballou*
Best actor in a supporting role: Martin Balsam – *A Thousand Clowns*
Best actress in a leading role: Julie Christie – *Darling*
Best actress in a supporting role: Shelley Winters – *A Patch of Blue*
Cannes International Film Festival
Grand Prix International du Festival: *The Knack ... And How to Get It* – Richard Lester
Venice International Film Festival
Golden Lion: *Vaghe stelle dell'Orsa* – Luchino Visconti

1966

Academy Awards of Motion Pictures Arts and Sciences
Best picture: *A Man for All Seasons* – Fred Zinnemann
Best director: Fred Zinnemann – *A Man for All Seasons*
Best actor in a leading role: Paul Schofield – *A Man for All Seasons*
Best actor in a supporting role: Walter Matthau – *The Fortune Cookie*
Best actress in a leading role: Elizabeth Taylor – *Who's Afraid of Virginia Woolf?*
Best actress in a supporting role: Sandy Dennis – *Who's Afraid of Virginia Woolf?*
Cannes International Film Festival
Grand Prix du XXème Anniversaire du Festival International du Film: *Un Homme et Une Femme* – Claude Lelouch and *Signore e Signori* by Pietro Germi
Venice International Film Festival
Golden Lion: *La battaglia di Algeri* – Gillo Pontecorvo

1967

Academy Awards of Motion Pictures Arts and Sciences
Best picture: *In the Heat of the Night* – Walter Mirisch
Best director: Mike Nichols – *The Graduate*
Best actor in a leading role: Rod Steiger – *In the Heat of the Night*
Best actor in a supporting role: George Kennedy – *Cool Hand Luke*
Best actress in a leading role: Katharine Hepburn – *Guess Who's Coming to Dinner*
Best actress in a supporting role: Estelle Parsons – *Bonnie and Clyde*
Cannes International Film Festival
Grand Prix International du Festival: *Blow Up* – Michelangelo Antonioni
Venice International Film Festival
Golden Lion: *Belle de jour* – Luis Buñuel

1968

Academy Awards of Motion Pictures Arts and Sciences
Best picture: *Oliver!* – John Woolf
Best director: Carol Reed – *Oliver!*
Best actor in a leading role: Cliff Robertson – *Charly*
Best actor in a supporting role: Jack Albertson – *The Subject Was Roses*
Best actress in a leading role: Katharine Hepburn – *The Lion in Winter* and Barbra Streisand – *Funny Girl*
Best actress in a supporting role: Ruth Gordon – *Rosemary's Baby*
Cannes International Film Festival – the 1968 festival was interrupted due to political events
Venice International Film Festival
Golden Lion: *Die Artisten in der Zirkuskuppel: ratlos* – Alexander Kluge

1969

Academy Awards of Motion Pictures Arts and Sciences
Best picture: *Midnight Cowboy* – Jerome Hellman
Best director: John Schlesinger – *Midnight Cowboy*
Best actor in a leading role: John Wayne – *True Grit*
Best actor in a supporting role: Gig Young – *They Shoot Horses, Don't They?*
Best actress in a leading role: Maggie Smith – *The Prime of Miss Jean Brodie*
Best actress in a supporting role: Goldie Hawn – *Cactus Flower*
Cannes International Film Festival
Grand Prix International du Festival: *If* – Lindsay Anderson
Venice International Film Festival – no Golden Lions were awarded at the Venice Festival between 1968 and 1979.

SUGGESTED FURTHER READING

Bordwell, D., Staiger, J. and Thompson, K. (1985). *The Classical Hollywood Cinema: Film Style and Mode of Production to 1960.* London: Routledge.

Cohan, S. and Hark, I.R. (eds) (1997) *The Road Movie Book.* London: Routledge.

Farber, D. (ed.) (1994) *The Sixties: From Memory to History.* Chapel Hill: University of North Carolina Press.

Gomery, D. (2005) *The Hollywood Studio System: A History.* London: BFI.

Hanhardt, J. (1976) *A History of the American Avant-Garde Cinema.* New York: American Film Association.

Jacobs, L. (ed.) (1971) *The Documentary Tradition: From Nanook to Woodstock.* New York: Hopkinson and Blake.

James, D. (1989) *Allegories of Cinema: American Film in the Sixties.* Princeton, NJ: Princeton University Press.

James, D. (ed.). (1992) *To Free the Cinema: Jonas Mekas and the New York Underground.* Princeton, NJ: Princeton University Press.

Krämer, P. (2005) *The New Hollywood: From Bonnie and Clyde to Star Wars.* London: Wallflower.

Monaco, P. (2003) *The Sixties, 1960–1969,* vol. 8 of *History of the American Cinema.* Berkeley and London: University of California Press.

O'Pray, M. (ed.) (1989) *Andy Warhol: Film Factory.* London: BFI.

O'Pray, M. (2003) *Avant-Garde Film: Forms, Themes and Passions.* London: Wallflower Press.

Romney, J. and Wooton, A. (eds) (1995) *Celluloid Jukebox: Popular Music and the Movies Since the 50s.* London: BFI.

Sayre, N. (1996) *Sixties Going on Seventies,* New Brunswick, NJ: Rutgers University Press.

QUESTIONS FOR DISCUSSION

This section contains brief background notes which are designed to guide students to some of the main issues that have been raised by the various articles here on the 1960s. These are followed by some sample essay questions which both students and tutors may find useful in guiding class discussion as well as setting exercises.

Background Notes

The 1960s and the early part of the 1970s saw changes in the American film industry that included the end of the studio production system and an extended period of reorganization which affected every aspect of the industry. While the Hollywood studios continued to produce big-budget films and genre pictures, a burgeoning underground cinema was developing in New York and San Francisco. Documentary film, which had grown out of newsreel and television reportage, began to find small but significant audiences in urban-centred art-house cinemas. Hollywood producers and financiers also found that a more challenging content and style appealed to the teenage and early twenties age group, at first with student audiences in art-house cinemas and then more widely by the end of the decade. The 1960s was also a period of considerable social change with the Civil Rights movement, the momentum of second-wave feminism, gay rights, continued suburbanization and the war in Vietnam having a profound impact on the way Americans thought and felt about their own history, their way of life and their future. These significant and, in many ways, unquantifiable factors cannot be ignored in any consideration of the history of film in the USA. The significant social changes generally and the aesthetic developments in filmmaking were not unrelated. In fact, in Hollywood as well as in documentary filmmaking, much of the challenging content of films centred around the contentious issues of race, "the generation gap", politics and student unrest.

Questions

The following questions have been devised to help guide further research and thinking about this period.

1 One of the most widely discussed aspects of this period has been the rise of the "auteur" or, in Steve Neale's terms, the Hollywood Renaissance. Discuss the work of one director working in the late 1960s/early 1970s who exemplifies the term "Hollywood Renaissance" (e.g. Mike Nichols, Arthur Penn, Robert Altman).

You might also want to discuss filmmakers who were controversial at the time such as Don Siegel, Sam Peckinpah or William Friedkin. As a reference point, consider the 1960s work of a director whose career was established in the classical period (e.g. Robert Wise, Alfred Hitchcock, John Ford).

2 Exhibition practices changed considerably in the 1960s. The drive-ins which had been shifting their emphasis from targeting family audiences to catering to a youth audience, were often a place where "exploitation films" were screened. Further, young student audiences had been a profitable market in urban centres for art-house cinemas where foreign-language films as well as retrospectives were popular. Discuss the importance of youth audiences and the influences of both exploitation cinema and art-house fare in relation to the following films: *Easy Rider, The Graduate, Bonnie and Clyde, Midnight Cowboy, Alice's Restaurant, M*A*S*H*.

3 You might also consider the merits of reading two of these films as examples of a filmmaking which differs from that of the studio-made big budget feature. For example Chris Hugo wrote: "In general, the most frequent narrative strategy in *Easy Rider* could be summarised in terms of simply reversing the conventions of classic Hollywood practice from positive to negative" (Chris Hugo, "*Easy Rider* and Hollywood in the 70s". *Movie*, 31/32, Winter, 1986, p. 71). Does such a narrative construction constitute a departure from the classical style? What might be the implications of the use of formal techniques that come from non-narrative forms of filmmaking or from documentary techniques such as *direct cinema* in commercial films attributed to the "Hollywood Renaissance"?

4 Television became an important source of revenue for the studios in the late 1950s. A productive line of inquiry would be to consider the results of the developments in the relationship between television and cinema during this period. These could be in terms of how the studios reorganized their production and distribution practices. Follow a case study of the fortunes of one studio that went through significant changes in the 1960s and 1970s and the role of television in that history.

5 Steve Neale writes: "There are at least two New Hollywoods in recent accounts of Hollywood history." He suggests that in some accounts of this period, attention to the "maverick directors" has been at the expense of recognizing films such as *The Love Bug* or *The Sound of Music*, which enjoyed top box office. Discuss the differences between these Hollywoods of the 1960s.

6 One of the most important factors on the content of films after 1966 was the creation of the ratings system by the MPAA. Discuss the impact of changes in film classification on US cinema from the late 1960s onwards.

7 Although the studio-based system of film production declined in the 1960s, technological innovations continued and in many ways accelerated the move away from studio production to location shooting, for example. The arrival of hand-held sync-sound cameras in documentary had an effect on feature film production, filming in colour became dominant in features as did the use of zoom lenses. Considering these and other developments, discuss the changes in production technology as they are evident in one or two films.

the 70s

SEVENTIES

INTRODUCTION

If the seismic shifts of the previous decade had produced a very different profile of Hollywood and its products, the 1970s proved to be even more eventful, both in terms of how the US film industry was organized, and in terms of the kinds of films it produced. It has been argued that the 1970s was the most dynamic decade in post-war cinema, at both high- and low-budget ends of production, and because of massive shifts in technological possibilities. For many, the release of *Jaws* in 1975 constitutes the true birth of New Hollywood. A huge film in so many ways, not least its box office receipts, *Jaws* has been credited with inventing the concept of the summer blockbuster, the must-see "event" movie cut to the measure of the big screen, a sure-fire draw that would take families away from their TV sets. Along with *Star Wars* two years later, the rollercoaster-ride aesthetics and massive returns at the box office signalled a change of heart on the part of Hollywood and a fresh awareness that film could draw audiences back into the theatres if its scale of spectacle were huge enough, and if it piled on enough hype around the edges of the film itself. Mark Sheil and Sheldon Hall in this section, and Stephen Prince, Peter Krämer and Geoff King in subsequent sections, trace one history of this form. Readers new to this area could also productively consult the excellent overviews provided by Ryan and Kellner (1988), Corrigan (1991) and Cook (2000).

Many popular histories define the word "blockbuster" as invented by the huge 1970s products which both preceded and took their cue from *Jaws*.[1] Of course, there have always been big movies, from the epics of Cecil B. De Mille in the 1920s to the "sand and sandals" epics of the 1950s (some also by De Mille), to *The Sound of Music* itself. What differentiates blockbusters from the 1970s onwards is their role in the increased specialization of Hollywood product – from expensive "A" features seen as one element in a diverse portfolio of studio products across which financial risk could be spread (Maltby 1995: 74), to mega-blockbusters as a studio's primary product. But *Jaws* did not invent the blockbuster, although its success did much to convince the industry that intense investment in fewer products, which were guaranteed crowd pleasers, was the shape of the future. Predating its success, as Hall points out in his essay below, was the massive box-office draws of *The Godfather* (the biggest film of 1972) and *The Exorcist* (the biggest film of 1974, Fig. 5 (*see plate section*)), which are also significant for what they tell us of the changing face of the auteur in the 1970s. A further mid-decade draw was disaster movie monsters such as *The Poseidon Adventure* and *Earthquake* discussed below by Helen Hanson, who quotes Larry Gross as writing "While Hollywood was at its post-war artiest, with people named Robert Altman, Hal Ashby and Bob Rafelson getting the majority of critical ink, Irwin Allen was busy making shitloads of money with *The Poseidon Adventure* and *The Towering Inferno*" (Gross 2000). All very true, up to a point. But it is also true that this was the era in which Europhile auteurs of the so-called US Renaissance turned to the mass market. While Ashby was making quirky proto-indie works and political satires like *Harold and Maude* and *Shampoo*, William Friedkin – a Francophile maverick if ever there was one – turned to the mainstream in the most spectacular way. Peter Biskind's *Easy Riders, Raging Bulls*[2] cites his comments following a Damascene moment after meeting classical Hollywood director Howard Hawks: "What we were doing wasn't making fucking films to hang in the Louvre," he says; "We were making films to entertain people and if they didn't do that first they didn't fulfil their primary purpose" (Biskind 1998: 203–4). (Friedkin has also famously said, "When I see a film *by* someone rather than *for* someone I smell art.") *The Godfather* must also be read as a cross-over work, marketed and historicized as part-auteur vision, part-mainstream saga (its generational narrative, luscious cinematography, and ambivalently all-American message make it as much family-movie-for-adults as exercise in neoviolence). It is also significant for its role in the rejuvenation of a genre as old (and adaptable) as Hollywood itself: the gangster film, just one of the genres like the musical (*Cabaret*, *Grease*, Fig. 8 (*see plate section*)), or the thriller (*Chinatown*, *Play Misty For Me*), to find a new form in 1970s New Hollywood. Like *Jaws* and *The Exorcist*, *The Godfather* also had its feet firmly in that most popular of cultural locations, the airport bookstore, as (like a number of the decade's most successful films) an adaptation of a worldwide bestseller. This, then, is also the period in which another trend of the moment developed, the tendency for revered auteurs – those whose reputations were established in smaller-scale, counter-cultural, perhaps European-influenced art-works – to become actively assimilated into the mainstream.

However, while many histories of the 1970s deal with the films themselves (particularly when written by those who grew up on these movies), studio and industry changes in the decade can be seen as a far more significant way of signalling difference from past modes of production. Cook (2000: 1) cites the decade as one in which the US film industry changed more than at any other time, with the possible exception of the coming of sound. Significant shifts include the escalation in the costs of film production, inflating, as Cook (2000: 2) reports, "from $2 million in 1972 to nearly $10 million in 1979", which may not seem like much to twenty-first-century filmgoers used to products, like *Titanic*, which cost near to $200 million, but was unprecedented at the time – "an increase of 450 percent in less than seven years" (Cook 2000: 2). Also for the first time, "the cost of promoting a film actually exceeded the cost of producing it" (Cook 2000: 2), as advertising campaigns budgets rocketed. From this period onwards films need increasingly to be seen as part of a wider range of related products. Following the buy-outs of most of the major studios during the 1960s and early 1970s, filmmaking was seen as only one strand in a conglomerate's portfolio of potentially synergistic activities, with movies being ultimately owned by the same conglomerate that produced accompanying music soundtracks, books, toys and other merchandise. The 1970s became the decade in which franchise filmmaking began to take hold, especially following the phenomenal success of *Star Wars* in 1977. As Peter Krämer argues in his later chapter on Disney and Family Entertainment, during the 1970s, child and family audiences began to take a central place in the target demographic, not just as viewers, but as potential purchasers of a wide range of movie-related products, and *Star Wars* was the primary turning point for this development, practically inventing the concept of the family adventure movie which also provided young consumers with ample shopping opportunities.

But 1975 is not just cited as a watershed year because of its shark. It also saw Sony launch Betamax onto the market, the first home video viewing and recording system, signalling the beginning of a shift in the way that producers distribute and market their products, as well as the way that viewers consume them. Betamax was followed in 1976 by Matsushita's launch of VHS (Video Home System), and after a protracted battle between the two forms (and despite Betamax being considered by many to be technically superior to VHS), VHS became, and has remained, internationally the dominant video playback system for home viewing. Only in the early twenty-first century did DVD (digital versatile disc, sometime called digital video disk) begin to take over the market, as Barbara Klinger discusses later. Video, initially conceived of as a new way of releasing films for home viewers to purchase, soon emerged as a lucrative rental market: consumers wanted to watch movies in the home as they had in the theatres, for one night only, and so the first video rental houses were born in the late 1970s – an event that changed the face of the film distribution industry as well as the high street, even as old-style independent cinemas were closing just down the road.

But for many, including the authors of a number of the chapters in this section, the decade's significance lies in the forms which its films took, the stories they told. The so-called US Renaissance of edgy, often inconclusive or downright bleak auteur works, is frequently discussed as flowering in the window of opportunity between the rise of movies such as *Bonnie and Clyde* and *Easy Rider* from the late 1960s to the development of the blockbuster

proper in the mid-1970s. Many of the most significant titles of this moment are discussed by Mark Sheil both above and below (readers of the previous section will also note Steve Neale's challenge to the Hollywood Renaissance model). Films as diverse as *Harold and Maude*, *McCabe and Mrs Miller* and *Five Easy Pieces* are characterized by what we might call textual failure if judged by the standards of old Hollywood narrative and characterization, depicting, in Murray Smith's (1998: 10) definition: "uncertain, counter-cultural and marginal protagonists, whose goals were often relatively ill-defined and ultimately unattained, in contrast to the heroic and typically successful figures around which classical films revolved".

The pleasures of these films may seem masochistic, lacking narrative closure, let alone happy endings, asking us to identify with central characters who are bizarre or even downright dislikable, pushing the permissive envelope of acceptable action and spectacle towards violence and sexual challenge. For Robin Wood (1986: 58), *Looking for Mr Goodbar*, Richard Brooks' (1977) film detailing the perils and pleasures of promiscuity, is supremely unreadable, entirely failing to resolve or recognize "its contradictions". Like *Cruising* and *Taxi Driver*, to which Wood compares *Goodbar*, the film is all the more interesting because of its "incoherence". "Failure", then, is precisely what makes texts of this period so alluring, imbued with an invitation to decode and a challenge to conventional personal and political practices – especially given that they appeared not only on marginalized art-screens but squarely in the heart of the mainstream.

The challenges of such movies from this period are often bookended or contextualized by critics in terms of significant contemporary events. Robin Wood's 1970s is the stretch "from Vietnam to Reagan"; for David Cook the decade's landmarks are the Watergate scandal and the inconclusive conclusion to the Vietnam War. But this is also a decade in which the embryonic protest movements of the 1960s found a stronger voice in Hollywood, through mainstream movements such as blaxploitation, discussed below by Eithne Quinn and Peter Krämer, and the occasional mainstream nod to feminism (*Alice Doesn't Live Here Anymore*; *Coming Home*). There was also some limited opportunity for counter-cultural figures such as Melvin van Peebles or Jane Fonda to state their position and still make successful movies. This should not be overstressed, however; as essays in the 1980s and 1990s sections of this book attest, it was some time after the civil rights and second-wave feminist movements began to find a more public voice in the 1960s that women and African-Americans gained a more powerful voice in US cinema. The 1970s may have produced some stunningly unconventional Hollywood movies but they were generally still made by, and starred, white American men. This may, of course, account for the paranoia of some of the decade's films – paranoia rather than protest being one of its watchwords, with titles such as *The Conversation* and *All the President's Men* exploring suspicion of established authority structures, and films as diverse as *Deliverance* and *The Deer Hunter* suggesting a pervasive sense of "masculinity in crisis" against a Vietnam, or Vietnam-comes-home, backdrop.

Perhaps, then, it is surprising that by the 1970s these issues are not confined to fringe counter-cultural cinema but are also manifest in popular contexts. We might be able to see *Deliverance* (the third most successful film of 1973) as part of the same wave of filmmaking that spawned *Bonnie and Clyde* and others – undecidable and ambiguous, drawing political issues such as ecology and the destruction of the American wilderness, others-within-America, and the Vietnam War, onto its canvas. It was also directed by a European auteur (John Boorman), who stages a series of acute conflicts between self and other, savage and civilized, conscious and unconscious, masculine and feminine, for mainstream screens. It would, of course, be possible to cast one's eye down a list of the decade's most successful releases and surmise almost anything from them – from *Woodstock* to *Love Story*, from *The French Connection* to *Fiddler on the Roof*, from *Rollerball* to *Annie Hall*, from *Saturday Night Fever* to *Superman*. A number of these titles evidence the "mainstreamization" of the counter-culture, an assimilation (and taming) by the industry of oppositional forces, which is certainly one useful way of understanding some of the currents running through 1970s cinema. But others are simply good old-fashioned entertainment movies of the kind that Hollywood had refined in the 1920s and 1930s, and are – for all their sporadic formal innovativeness – still comprehensible in terms of the dominant template of Hollywood form established during the classical studio period, and detailed so exhaustively in Bordwell, Staiger and Thompson's (1988) definitive account. A number prefigure the increasingly Right-wing jingoism that was to characterize many mainstream films of the next decade and beyond, as both Stephen Prince and Susan Jeffords discuss in the next section – for every *Coming Home* (one of the first home-front Vietnam films, as much about America in crisis refracted through a crisis in masculinity) there is a *Rocky* (a white male fantasy of individualist success, which arguably gave birth to the

Fig. 1: *Mary Poppins*.

New technologies and
neo-families: *Mary Poppins* and
Bonnie and Clyde.

Fig. 2: *Bonnie and Clyde*.

Fig. 3 (above): *Hello Dolly!*

Fig. 4 (left): *West Side Story*.

Hits and misses: one of the paradoxes of 1960s studio production is the different fates related genre products met at the box office — *West Side Story* helped to keep United Artists afloat.

Fig. 5 (left): *The Exorcist.*

Fig. 6 (below): *The Godfather Part II.*

Icons and auteurs:
Friedkin's *The Exorcist*, Coppola's
The Godfather Part II, Lucas's
American Graffiti.

Fig. 7 (left): *American Graffiti.*

Fig. 8: *Grease*.

Fig. 9: *Alien*.

Fig. 10: *Sleeper*.

muscular masculinity of some 1980s and 1990s cinema). For Ryan and Kellner (1988) the latter is symptomatic of a turning of the tide, when the "critical, satiric, pessimistic vision" of the 1970s up to 1976 loses ground, and cinema takes on an ever more conservative mode. By the mid-decade "Criticism gives way increasingly to ideology" (Ryan and Kellner 1988: 86).

Yet this pre- and post-1977 division of the decade's films into radical or reactionary is misleading. Perhaps most interesting is the way in which a number of movies from the period can be read as *both* ambivalent works of undecidability – protest films, even – *and* as mainstream entertainment movies. Perhaps this is what continues to be so alluring about the period for film critics; the texts are just so *resonant*. *The Exorcist* has been read as both a meditation on the potency of youth protest (the possessed little girl Regan as emblematic of her gender and age group) and a celebration of reactionary controlling forces (the triumph of the priesthood as substitute father figures). *Alien* (Fig. 9 (*see plate section*)) has been read as an exploration of sexual anxiety, a platform for (what Carol J. Clover calls) the "final girl". Yet there is no doubt that it succeeded on mainstream screens partly because it is also a skilful popcorn monster movie. *One Flew Over the Cuckoo's Nest* can be read – as it is by Mark Sheil below – as "either as a comic and sentimental liberal humanist parable on the dangers of conformism or as an allegorical indictment of the essential injustice and inequality of American society and its institutions". Winning five Oscars, the biggest grossing film of 1976 (therefore pitched right between the unambiguous schlock thrills of *Jaws* and *Star Wars*), this was nevertheless a film inflected with the concerns of the art-house, surviving release into the mainstream with its anti-establishment credentials intact. Based on a

cult novel by counter-culture icon Ken Kesey, produced by left-liberal rookie producer Michael Douglas, it also starred the wild man of Hollywood, Jack Nicholson. Nicholson himself had not by then taken on the mantle of grand master of the "A" list, and was still partially identified by his work with Roger Corman, his role in *Easy Rider*, and his dalliance with European cinema (Antonioni's *Professione: reporter* in Europe, but also Polanski's *Chinatown* at home).

If studio movies were learning how to be all things to all audiences at this point, they were also to some extent imperializing the product of different cinemas. *Jaws* is the most prominent example of another trend in the history of mainstream Hollywood, which makes plain its intimate relationship to fringe or "off-Hollywood". Some of the decade's most successful titles (and, indeed, those of the 1980s and 1990s) are prime blockbuster examples of newly reinflected genres such as science fiction (*Superman*, *Star Wars*, *The Empire Strikes Back*). What we might think of as "1970s genres" are reincarnations of established genres with long histories both inside and beyond US cinema, which were always hybrid and fluid in their form, such as the gangster movie, the war film, and horror. Yet what we might call the neo-genre films of the 1970s also rely heavily on cheaper versions of themselves which garnered little of the fame and fortune of the decade's biggest titles. Hollywood is adept at plagiarizing, and, indeed, cannibalizing, both itself and its children. In particular, the relationship between mainstream "A" feature movies and "B" movies is rife with theft of ideas, personnel, and genre templates. Independent director and producer Roger Corman, discussed earlier by both Kim Newman and Mark Sheil, has argued that by the 1970s *Jaws* and its ilk were stealing the stock-in-trade of low budget genre filmmakers like himself, by showing that what were once the cheap-and-cheerful degraded genres of the exploitation fringes could be spruced up by a large budget and some big stars to become big releases:

> The major challenge has been finding new markets and recouping costs while the majors have dominated the exploitation genres with budgets ten times higher than ours. . . . [I]t was Vincent Canby of *The New York Times* who once wrote, "What is *Jaws* but a big-budget Roger Corman movie?" But when the Spielbergs and the Lucases make technically exquisite genre films, they cut deeply into the box-office appeal of our kind of picture. (Corman 1998: xi)[3]

A number of titles from this period thus need to be seen as merely the most expensive versions of a wider range of similar, cheaper movies, which may indeed have invented the ideas subsequently traded by the blockbusters. This is a model of "trickle up" influence, from "low"/fringe products to the "high"/mainstream fare, which is propounded by Carol J. Clover in her book on horror cinema since the 1970s and by Linda Ruth Williams in her (2005) book on erotic thrillers. *Men, Women and Chain Saws* articulates the relationship between anodyne mainstream products fit for a mass audience and exploitation fringes as a relationship between avowed conscious experience and the disavowed repressed. Exploitation cinema, Clover writes, is what mainstream cinema has repressed. And, like the relationship between the repressed and the consciously avowed in psychic life, whereby consciousness depends upon that which it has repressed for its sense of self-identity, mainstream cinema needs the repressed world of exploitation to define itself. The US cinema of the 1970s sustains all of these differences, between high and low, art-house and studio products, continuing the process of "mainstreamization" that had begun in the 1960s whereby the search for an audience caused producers to look to fringe subjects for their mass-market product. Films marked by sometimes contradictory qualities often turned out to be the period's most successful titles. Though Corman's lament addresses the increasing tendency of the studio-based industry to homogenize and specialize investment in bigger winning products, this is only part of the story of 1970s cinema. The essays in this section, which include discussions of developing threads in documentary and independently produced US cinema as well as mainstream fiction films, seek to account for the productive contradictions and differences that make up this rich moment, or series of moments, in US film history.

Notes

1   *Jaws* was in any case a rather surprising start to what has become a release schedule regular – the summer-release family film – given its adult/horror movie content.

2   A text quoted by a number of contributors to this book, which does constitute a lively way in to the period. However, it paints its film history with very broad brushstrokes and should be read with a critical eye.

3   See also Neale (2003: 52–3) for a discussion of this.

References

Biskind, P. (1998) *Easy Riders, Raging Bulls*. London: Bloomsbury.

Bordwell, D., Staiger, J. and Thompson, K. (1988) *The Classical Hollywood Cinema: Film Style and Mode of Production to 1960*. London: Routledge.

Clover, C.J. (1992) *Men, Women and Chain Saws: Gender in the Modern Horror Film*. London: BFI.

Cook, D.A. (2000) *Lost Illusions: American Cinema in the Shadow of Watergate and Vietnam, 1970–1979*. Berkeley: University of California Press.

Corman, R. with Jerome, J. (1998) *How I Made a Hundred Movies in Hollywood and Never Lost a Dime*. New York: Da Capo Press.

Corrigan, T. (1991) *A Cinema Without Walls: Movies and Culture After Vietnam*. New Brunswick, NJ: Rutgers.

Gross, L. (2000) Big and loud, in J. Arroyo (ed.) *Action/Spectacle: A Sight and Sound Reader*. London: BFI.

Maltby, R. (1995) *Hollywood Cinema*. Oxford: Blackwell.

Neale, S. (2003) Hollywood blockbusters' historical dimensions, in J. Stringer (ed.) *Movie Blockbusters*. London: Routledge.

Ryan, M. and Kellner, D. (1988) *Camera Politica: The Politics and Ideology of Contemporary Hollywood Film*. Bloomington: Indiana University Press.

Smith, M. (1998) Theses on the philosophy of Hollywood history, in S. Neale and M. Smith (eds) *Contemporary Hollywood Cinema*. London: Routledge.

Williams, L.R. (2005) *The Erotic Thriller in Contemporary Cinema*. Edinburgh: Edinburgh University Press.

Wood, R. (1986) The incoherent text: narrative in the 70s, in R. Wood (ed.) *Hollywood from Vietnam to Reagan*. New York: Columbia University Press.

AMERICAN CINEMA, 1970–75

Mark Shiel

THE 1970S HAS often been characterized as little more than the aftermath of the 1960s. It has been presented as a decade in which social and political turbulence subsided, overtaken by a widespread popular yearning for stability and traditional values after the revolutionary energy and creativity that had rocked American society in the previous ten years (Miller 1999: 13–64; Lev 2000: xv–xxii). This attitude certainly informed early 1970s movies such as the coming-of-age stories *The Last Picture Show* (Bogdanovich, 1971) and *American Graffiti* (Lucas, 1973), as well as postmodern pastiches of classical genre films such as *The Sting* (1972) and *The Way We Were* (1973), reworkings of the 1930s gangster film and 1940s wartime romance, respectively. The nostalgia that underpinned these films was symptomatic of what Marshall Berman has described as the dual economic and emotional recession of the period 1970–5 (Berman 1993: 330). Indeed, it would intensify as the decade wore on, ultimately leading to the conservative reaction of science fiction and fantasy films such as *Star Wars* (1977) and *Close Encounters of the Third Kind* (1977) later in the decade and in the Reagan era of the 1980s (Wood 1986: 162–88; Ryan and Kellner 1988: 217–65).

However, conservative reaction against what many perceived as the "excesses" of the 1960s can only be a small fraction of any explanation of American cinema in the period 1970–5. For the Hollywood film industry, the coming of the 1970s, far from auguring a return to order and stability, meant only an intensification of the urgent economic crisis that had dogged the industry in the 1960s. Falling cinema attendances and box-office revenues were increasingly compounded by spiralling inflation in the costs of film production and in the national economy at large. As the US economy strained under the dual pressures of massive federal expenditure on the continuing war in Vietnam, and on social programmes and law and order at home, 1971 saw the first overall US trade deficit since 1893. The three years 1969–71, in particular, constituted a critical transitional moment in the economic fortunes and the organizational structure of the Hollywood film industry during which all of the studios were burdened by unprecedented debts, some almost to the point of collapse (Balio 1990: 259–62). Twentieth Century Fox, for example, made a loss of $77 million for 1969–70 despite such big box-office successes as *Butch Cassidy and the Sundance Kid* (1969) and *M*A*S*H.* (1970). MGM was sold to Kirk Kerkorian in 1970 with $141 million debts, becoming part

Continued on page 126

Alan Arkin's career in the early 1960s and early 1970s indicates, in ways that perhaps Dustin Hoffman, Jack Nicholson or Bruce Dern more famously have indicated, the rise of the ironic and dilemma-ridden male protagonist. Balanced against more traditionally handsome male stars such as Warren Beatty, who managed to portray a psychopathic and sexually ambivalent Clyde Barrow in *Bonnie and Clyde* (Arthur Penn, 1967) and still be beautiful, Arkin's visage and mannerisms set him out as the character-actor-as-star and unlikely hero. This was most manifest in his portrayal of the justifiably paranoid Yossarian in Mike Nichols' version of Joseph Heller's *Catch-22* (1970) but also in his range as an actor and his work as a director. In his first film role Arkin was nominated for an Academy Award for his comic portrayal of a Russian submariner in *The Russians Are Coming! The Russians Are Coming!* (Norman Jewison, 1966). Starting in the Second City comedy group, he moved quickly to a successful theatrical debut on Broadway in Carl Reiner's Tony Award-winning comedy *Enter Laughing* (1963) and then more success later in *Luv* (1964). He followed up his film debut with a disturbing portrayal of a manipulative and murderous villain terrorizing a blind Audrey Hepburn in *Wait Until Dark* (Terence Young, 1967) and his poignant turn as the deaf mute in

Alan Arkin in *Catch-22*

The Heart is a Lonely Hunter (Robert Ellis Miller, 1968). His appearance in edgy roles such as that in *Catch-22* and as the Puerto Rican immigrant in *Popi* (Arthur Hiller, 1969), who works out a scheme for getting his two sons out of the ghetto, indicate a propensity to direct his considerable comic talent to more satiric ends, an everyman figure pushed to extremes. These early roles were supplemented by forays into directing, the most notable being the film adaptation of Jules Pfeiffer's *Little Murders* (1971).

Arkin's star persona as offbeat but sophisticated was the result of his range as an actor. His earlier film characters' mixture of cynicism and helplessness served to invest his image with a gravitas that resonated in his lighter characterizations such as that in *Freebie and the Bean* (Richard Rush, 1974) and *Rafferty and the Gold Dust Twins* (Dick Richards, 1975). Arkin's persona was often given the added frisson of cutting against the mainstream Hollywood as in this description of him in a 1975 *Guardian* article that surrounded the release of his role as Sigmund Freud in *The Seven Percent Solution* (Herbert Ross, 1976): "Arkin seems to get all the character leads that are maybe just outside Dustin Hoffman's range ... People who like 'serious' films tend to mention Arkin when they moan about the superficiality of American films, the kind he isn't in" (Shrink proof 1975). His association with the Hollywood Renaissance and European art cinema influences was a critical part of Arkin's early career, particularly in the early 1970s – he starred in Vittorio de Sica's *Woman Times Seven* (1967). With the rejuvenation of the industry mainstream in the late 1970s and 1980s Arkin's character roles became less high profile although as an actor he was no less prolific and his legacy lies in his vivid renditions of the comic and alienated character central to the sensibilities found in contemporary American "independent" films such as those of Hal Hartley or Jim Jarmusch.

Reference

Shrink proof *The Guardian*, 28 December 1975.

Michael Hammond

Continued from page 124
of Kerkorian's diversified operations (which also included tourism and leisure industries in the MGM Hotel in Las Vegas) (Eames 1982: 347; Wasko 1982: 175; Balio 1985: 408). MGM withdrew from distributing its own films in 1973 – instead joining the new distribution joint-venture, Cinema International Corporation (CIC), which had been founded by Universal and Paramount in 1970 – and it merged defensively with United Artists to form MGM-UA in 1974. Meanwhile, having reported losses of $28 million for 1971, Columbia Pictures had run up total debts of $227 million by 1973, reporting $50 million losses in that year and imposing austerity measures in response such as a $3 million per picture budget limit, which would remain in force through much of the rest of the decade (Wasko 1982: 190). Faced with harsh business conditions, every studio attempted a new fiscal responsibility as a means of self-preservation. Defensive measures, meanwhile, were matched by a proactive reconfiguration of the Hollywood studio system as a whole. This reconfiguration was greater than any seen since the Paramount anti-trust decision of 1948.

Tino Balio, Janet Wasko, Thomas Guback and others have written extensively about this reconfiguration, which gathered pace during the recession of the early 1970s, arguing persuasively that in this period the studios moved from their former role as producers and distributors of motion pictures to a new role as financier-distributors of independently produced motion pictures. In this new relationship, as Guback has explained, corporate banks acted to a new degree as "silent partners" to the Hollywood studios, tying the fortunes of the movie business even more closely than ever before to the fortunes of American corporate capitalism (Guback 1982: xv). Although Fox and Columbia avoided actual corporate take-over until the 1980s (unlike Warner Bros, Paramount, Universal, and United Artists who had been taken over during the 1960s), the general trend throughout Hollywood saw all studios either incorporated within or trans-forming themselves into large diversified corporations for whom cinema was but one activity among many – alongside television, recorded music, entertainment, and tourism (the latter particularly in the case of Disney). Indeed, as Robert Gustafson has explained with regard to the difficult position of Warner Bros Pictures within Warner Communications Incorporated, for some of these corporations the business of motion pictures would be far from the most profitable sector of their overall activities (Gustafson 1985). In due course, with films such as *Star Wars*, *Close Encounters of the Third Kind*, and *E.T.* (1982), the later 1970s and 1980s would see the perfection of new strategies, such as movie-related merchandising aimed at children, designed precisely to capitalize upon this newly diver-sified corporate-cultural environment. But in the few years prior to 1975 such developments were on the horizon only.

Instead, Hollywood was busy learning the lessons of the 1969–71 recession. For the most part under new corporate management, the studios were finally convinced that, in contrast to the mass production principles of earlier decades, there was a limit to the number of releases with which the market could cope in any given year. Overall output of feature films was cut by 50 per cent from 1969 to just over 100 in 1977 (Balio 1985: 439–41). A consen-sus emerged that, in future, the bulk of revenue in any given year would be driven by only a handful of very big pictures or "block-busters" rather than by a balanced spread of high- and low-budget productions as in former times. In the emergent genre of the "disaster movie", for example, blockbusters such as *Airport* (1970), *The Poseidon Adventure* (1972), *The Towering Inferno* (1974), and *Earthquake* (1975), combined big budgets – $12.5 million for *The Towering Inferno*, $7.5 million for *Earthquake* – with star-studded casts, straightforward characterization, a lack of visual or thematic complexity, and essen-tially old-fashioned narratives of epic danger and adventure (Phillips 1982). Even Francis Ford Coppola's lavish mega-hit *The Godfather* (1972) appeared to integrate the youth-oriented, politically and formally self-conscious New American Cinema of the 1960s quite comfortably with the big business model of the Hollywood blockbuster. But more than any of these, the release of Steven Spielberg's *Jaws* (1975) quickly came to epitomize the new blockbuster approach, with the film's release preceded by a long lead-in period during which saturation publicity (especially television advertising driven by simple visual imagery, memorable catchphrases, and an easily recog-nizable signature tune) built up public antici-pation for the widespread simultaneous release of the film on hundreds of cinema screens nationwide, now a standard process known as

Continued on page 131

Taking a look at the cycle of disaster movies which flourished in the Hollywood of the early to mid-1970s allows a consideration of a number of key issues relating to both shifting genre styles within the Hollywood film industry and to the critical trends that shape the ways in which film histories are understood. Disaster movies enjoyed huge commercial success in the first half of the 1970s, with *Airport* (1970) and *The Poseidon Adventure* (1972) both topping *Variety*'s annual rentals chart for their year of release. *The Towering Inferno* (1974) came second only to *Jaws* (1975), a film that has now become synonymous with the term "blockbuster"; and *Airport '75* (1974), *Earthquake* (1974), and *Airport '77* (1977) all performed sufficiently well to put them within the top 25 films of their respective years. Despite this commercial success, critical histories of New Hollywood have often tended to elide this group of films. Critically derided as "schlock" (Biskind 1998: 16), they are often perceived as centring on narratively predictable scenarios, peopled with two-dimensional characters and marked by ideological conservatism (Ryan and Kellner 1988: 52; Keane 2001: 1–2). However, it is important to try to account for the success of these movies and to consider their particular historical and industrial moment. Critical histories have preferred to think about the ways that films like *Bonnie and Clyde* (1967) or *Easy Rider* (1969) represented a break with "old" Hollywood norms, offering an American art cinema, often speaking to a youth audience, before the return of blockbusting family entertainment films in the mid-1970s with *Jaws* (1975) and *Star Wars* (1977). The popular success of disaster movies in the early 1970s modifies this picture of film history, showing that while the stylistic breaks with "old" Hollywood were important, disaster movies represented a mode of filmmaking that not only showed the continuity of a commercially successful mainstream but prepared the way for the coming of high concept "event" cinema. Andrew Sarris rather ruefully observes that "the battle was lost when Hollywood realized in 1970 that there was still a huge middle-American audience for *Airport*" (Sarris, in Cook and Bernink 1999: 102). Larry Gross is less pessimistic, analysing disaster movies' development of a highly successful narrative structure:

> While Hollywood was at its post-war artiest, with people named Robert Altman, Hal Ashby and Bob Rafelson getting the majority of critical ink, Irwin Allen was busy making shitloads of money with *The Poseidon Adventure* and *The Towering Inferno* ... gut-churning jeopardy fuelled every minute of their narrative structure ... they were films utterly involved in the romance of spectacular technology. They were films as engineering problems, something that men like James Cameron and John McTiernan have shown enormous interest in. (Gross 1995, in Arroyo 2000: 5)

Disaster movies have a generic heritage in the action-adventure tradition which has been a part of Hollywood's production since the 1910s (Neale 2000: 55). They feature star performances and high production values, both in their luxurious settings and their deployment of effects, to produce spectacular and delightedly wanton destructions of those settings. These standard elements of Hollywood practice were recombined and given a novel twist as they were put to the service of a plot predominantly focused on a disaster situation. They have large, all-star casts of characters whose stories become interwoven, and the character relationships and conflicts are put into play by the disaster situation. Locations such as a snowbound airport (*Airport*), an upturned ship (*The Poseidon Adventure*), a burning tower block (*The Towering Inferno*) all function to isolate the characters from the outside world, and narratives focus on the need of these characters to form a group in order to survive: "no help can be expected from outside. Further, the threatened characters are jammed together, without escape, without relief from each other" (Yacowar 1986: 226). From the group a (white male) leader often emerges, and must "demonstrate his fitness to lead"

The Towering Inferno

(Roddick 1980: 256) but the variety of the group remains important and the focus is on how the leader understands and motivates the different members of the group. The disaster situation also creates an immovable deadline for the group: the airport's runway must be cleared for a plane, damaged by a hijacker, to land; water is rising inside the ship; fire is taking hold of the building. These deadlines create interest by putting pressure on the group dynamic – the audience can speculate as to the sagacity of the group's decisions because the wrong choice may mean death. Throughout the trials the films repeatedly draw attention to the ways in which the different characters deal with the disaster. This "human interest" aspect of disaster movie narration has been heavily criticized as reducing characters to archetypes, however, it is in the vignette structure that moments of humorous and poignant performance come across most strongly. In *Airport* an accomplished elderly con-woman Ada Quonsett (Helen Hayes) provides comic diversion through the trouble that she causes Transglobal Airlines, eluding airport security and boarding the ill-fated flight to Rome that is to be hijacked. Her skill in performance, however, is put to the good of the group as she helps stewardess Gwen (Jacqueline Bissett) attempt to seize the hijacker's briefcase. In *The Poseidon Adventure* the matronly Belle Rosen (Shelley Winters) is desperate to prove herself helpful rather than burdensome to the small group of survivors who are trying to make their way up to the engine room of the SS *Poseidon*. Deploying her skills in swimming underwater she saves Scott, the leader of the group, who has become trapped, but her exertion brings on a fatal heart attack. Belle's death is often cited as a camp disaster movie moment but it also tells poignantly of the desire to do something for the good of the group through the sincerity of Winter's performance. *The Towering Inferno* includes a touching "twilight romance" between a con-man, Harlee Claiborne (Fred Astaire) and an art teacher, Lisolette (Jennifer Jones) (Dyer 1978: 30; Keane 2001: 46). The developing romance is cut short by Lisolette's death and the impact of the disaster is brought home in one of the final scenes of the film, which shows Harlee searching, in vain, for Lisolette among the survivors.

The ideological conservatism for which disaster movies have been criticized is often attributed to the ways in which they portray their post-disaster worlds. Roddick argues that disaster movies have to negotiate a careful line between the (potential) hubris of modernity and the ideal of progress to both show the benefits (and dangers) of technological progress. This is focused on the figure of the hero, a man who understands and can use technology but who also displays old American puritan values of strength and common-sense humanity. Thus technology *per se* is not represented as dangerous, but only becomes so if it falls into the wrong hands (Roddick 1980: 257). The same kind of balance is evident in a "negotiation" in which the corporatism of modern America escapes criticism by the way that the films focus only on the "particular" examples of bad practice or management rather than critiquing the "general" larger system. Thus *Airport* can end with one of its pilots saluting "Mr Boeing" for his great designs; while the film shows that to run an airport safely and efficiently takes a team of "heroes". In *The Towering Inferno* the architect, Doug, is less to blame for the inherent dangers of his building than Duncan Enterprises, who departed from his plans, to build it on the cheap. Disaster movies have also been criticized as shifting attention away from any complexities that their situations raise. Peter Lev argues that this is a way in which the films deal with their contemporary moment:

Overall, the disaster movie of the early 1970s is a way to displace contemporary problems into simple, physical confrontations – for example, man versus shark, or airline crew versus hole in the tail section. These confrontations are generally resolved via old-fashioned virtues: hard work, individual initiative, group cooperation. The disaster movie is thus a conservative response which "solves" the 1970s malaise by drastically simplifying and reframing it. (Lev 2000: 49)

The disaster cycle peaked in popularity in 1974, with *The Towering Inferno* and *Earthquake*, and although the *Airport* series had some limited success with *Airport '77* (1977) and *Concorde: Airport '79* (1979), the cycle overall declined into the late 1970s. The tightly defined generic formula had run its course and had no room for development; "any more disaster would make them ludicrous fantasies, any more character would make them completely different" (Keane 2001: 49). The cycle was also very effectively spoofed in *The Big Bus* (1976) and *Airplane* (1980), perhaps showing audiences how familiar the formula had become. Despite its brief flourish and then decline, the disaster cycle can be seen as "transitional" (Keane 2001: 49), bridging a gap between the "alternative", more independent mode of production of the late 1960s and the blockbusters of the mid-1970s. In addressing a mixed-age audience and maintaining a formula of big budgets (big stars and spectacle) to big returns, the disaster cycle contained the beginnings of industrial and stylistic strategies that would become key to Hollywood's next phase of development.

References

Biskind, P. (1998) *Easy Riders, Raging Bulls: How the Sex 'n' Drugs 'n' Rock 'n' Roll Generation Saved Hollywood*. London: Bloomsbury.

Cook, P. and Bernink, M. (eds) (1999) *The Cinema Book*, 2nd edn. London: BFI.

Dyer, R. (1978) American cinema in the '70s: *The Towering Inferno, Movie*, 21: 30–3.

Gross, L. (1995) Big and loud, *Sight and Sound*, (August), reprinted in J. Arroyo (ed.) (2000) *Action/Spectacle: A Sight and Sound Reader*. London: BFI.

Keane, S. (2001) *Disaster Movies: Cinema of Catastrophe*. London: Wallflower Press.

Keyser, L. (1981) *Hollywood in the Seventies*. New York: A S Barnes/Tantivy Press.

Lev, P. (2000) *American Films of the '70s: Conflicting Visions*. Austin: University of Texas Press.

Neale, S. (2000) *Genre and Hollywood*. London and New York: Routledge.

Roddick, N. (1980) Only the stars survive: disaster movies in the seventies, in D. Bradby, L. James and B. Sharratt (eds) *Performance and Politics in Popular Drama: Aspects of Popular Entertainment in Theatre, Film and Television 1800–1976*. Cambridge: Cambridge University Press.

Ryan, M. and Kellner, D. (1988) *Camera Politica: The Politics and Ideology of Contemporary Hollywood Film*. Bloomington: Indiana University Press.

Sarris, A. (1978) After *The Graduate, American Film*, 3(9): 32–7.

Sontag, S. (2001) The imagination of disaster, in *Against Interpretation and Other Essays*. London: Vintage.

Yacowar, M. (1986) The bug in the rug: notes on the disaster genre, in B.K. Grant (ed.) *Film Genre Reader*. Austin: University of Texas Press.

Helen Hanson

Continued from page 127
"saturation booking" (Wyatt 1994: 113–17; Wyatt 1998).

Therefore, the tendency to low budgets and low production values that briefly flourished in Hollywood in the tough business climate of the late 1960s and early 1970s was an important but short-lived phenomenon. If low budgets and self-consciously low production values were a hallmark of the idealistic artistic and counter-cultural rebellion of independent filmmakers, the corporate environment of American cinema that consolidated through the 1970s forged an accommodation in relations between the studios and independent producers. Beginning with *Easy Rider* at the end of the 1960s, Columbia had pioneered a productive new type of hands-off relationship with one such independent production company, BBS, headed by Bob Rafelson and Bert Schneider, which led to a series of timely, youth-oriented films such as *Five Easy Pieces* (1970), *The Last Picture Show* (1971), *Drive, He Said* (1971), and *The King of Marvin Gardens* (1972). At the same time, Warner Bros established a relationship with the new independent production company and film studio American Zoetrope. Founded in 1969 by the 30-year-old emergent talent Francis Ford Coppola, American Zoetrope followed the road-movie character study of a disaffected Long Island housewife, *The Rain People* (1969), with George Lucas's first feature, the science fiction film *THX1138* (1971), and

Coppola's own *The Conversation* (1974), a conspiracy thriller revolving around the gradual mental breakdown of its protagonist Harry Caul (Gene Hackman) (Sweeney 1970).

But if the critical reputation of many BBS and Zoetrope films of the period 1970–75 is undoubtedly high, the commercial fortunes of many of their films were mixed or poor, despite their appeal to counter-cultural youth audiences. In 1974, BBS produced its final film, *Hearts and Minds*, Peter Davis' documentary about the attitudes of opponents of the Vietnam War while, after *The Conversation*, Zoetrope did not have another significant success until *The Black Stallion* and *Apocalypse Now*, both in 1979.

In the long term, therefore, at least in terms of economic and industrial trends, perhaps the most important new production company to emerge in the period was Malpaso Pictures, established by Clint Eastwood in 1971, which would maintain a troubled though profitable producer–distributor relationship with Universal Pictures from 1971 to 1975, and subsequently, after 1975, with Warner Bros. Still operating successfully to this day, Malpaso has long outlived BBS and has achieved more consistent commercial success than Zoetrope, beginning in the period 1971 to 1975 with a series of moderately successful Westerns such as *The Beguiled* (1971), *Joe Kidd* (1972), and *High Plains Drifter* (1972), and controversial but widely popular thrillers such as *Play Misty for Me* (1971), *Dirty Harry* (1971), and *Magnum Force* (1973). Malpaso also produced more idiosyncratic, youth-oriented films such as *Breezy* (1973), about a romance between a middle-aged businessman and a hippie teenage girl, and Michael Cimino's directorial debut *Thunderbolt and Lightfoot* (1974, with United Artists), a bank-heist road movie that investigated father–son type inter-

generational tensions in the relationship between the two lead characters, played by Eastwood and Jeff Bridges. In general, however, the company's perpetuation of the Western genre coupled with its expansion of the archetypal, super-masculine tough cop hero tended to identify Malpaso and Clint Eastwood in the public mind with Right-wing reactionary politics in the first half of the 1970s. By extension, the company's success and gradual ascendancy through the decade appeared to many to signal the end of the counter-culture and of cinema sympathetic to the counter-culture in Hollywood (Agan 1975; Gallafent 1994).

In every case, however, whatever the politics of the particular films produced, the new relationship between distributors and producers in the period 1970–75 fundamentally altered the notion of independent production in American cinema. All film production, even in Hollywood, became "independent" by definition, such that it was no longer clearly meaningful to speak of it as "independent", at least in any artistic or ideological sense. As Tino Balio states, reviewing the situation from the 1960s to the 1980s:

independent production has become assimilated by the majors as an alternative to the studio system of production. The term "independent" no longer has meaning in this new context and is best used to describe the producer of documentaries, experimental films, and low-budget features that are handled outside the channels of mainstream Hollywood. (1990: 11)

But even for these sectors, the period 1970–75 was one of decline rather than expansion relative to the intensity of production and innovation in American cinema outside Hollywood, which had characterized the

1960s. In the exploitation film sector, one of the most important engines of creativity in the 1960s, the by-now-legendary Roger Corman, left his long-time employer American International Pictures in 1970, viewing it as having become too mainstream, and founded instead his own production company, New World Pictures, in 1971. He also withdrew entirely from directing after his *Von Richtofen and Brown* (1971) was recut against his wishes by United Artists. New World continued exploitation formulae, producing sensationalist low-budget successes such as the "women-in-prison" film *Women in Cages* (1971), the *Bonnie and Clyde* comic parody *Big Bad Mama* (1974), and the futuristic *Death Race 2000* (1975), the latter returning $4 million on a typical Corman budget of $300,000. Although Corman's exploitation films did not continue the social and political topicality that had characterized much exploitation filmmaking of the 1960s, Corman did continue exploitation cinema's important role in fostering new talent by producing early features by some of the most important names of the 1970s and 1980s, including Martin Scorsese's *Boxcar Bertha* (1972), Jonathan Demme's *Caged Heat* (1974), and Joe Dante's *Hollywood Boulevard* (1976). Corman and New World also balanced exploitation production with a relatively small but important role in the distribution of high prestige European art cinema in the first half of the 1970s, including Ingmar Bergman's commercially successful *Cries and Whispers*, which won the Academy Award for Best Cinematography in 1974, as well as important features by other key European directors such as Federico Fellini's *Amarcord* (1973) and François Truffaut's *The Story of Adèle H* (1975).

Throughout the period, Corman largely managed to avoid the extreme economic turbulence that characterized the first half of

the 1970s for the Hollywood majors. In 1974, the *Journal of the Producers' Guild of America* continued to report on the hard times being experienced by the Hollywood industry – unprecedented economic volatility, an increasing concentration of financial risk on a dwindling number of releases, an unprecedented lack of available capital for investment, chronic unemployment, and, for exhibitors, the widespread closure of non-viable film theatres in cities and towns across the United States. Occasional successes such as Bergman's *Cries and Whispers* notwithstanding, art-house cinemas, in particular, struggled with the gradual slowdown of European art cinema in the first half of the 1970s. A minority, rather than facing closure, switched to the increasingly prominent softcore and hardcore pornographic film sector. This was a different form of exploitation cinema, which emerged to much public controversy and significant profits after the 1968 replacement of the Production Code by the MPAA Ratings System ushered in a new realism and frankness in adult subject matter in both Hollywood and exploitation motion pictures (Sklar 1975: 296–300). With regard to the depiction of sex, the line between mainstream and exploitation cinema was blurred, for example, by the release by Twentieth Century Fox of Russ Meyers' X-rated *Beyond the Valley of the Dolls* (1970), while the more plainly hardcore *Deep Throat* (1973) set records by taking in $4 million in its first year of release and the French release *Emmanuelle* (1974) achieved significant success in the United States with its blend of softcore pornography and pastiche of European art cinema style.

In retrospect, this blurring of the lines between exploitation cinema, pornography, and European art cinema, which accelerated in

Continued on page 138

Thanks to the gothic revival spearheaded in the late 1950s by Hammer Films, which broke the American science fiction/monster movie trend of the 1950s, horror in the early 1960s had an English accent, even when made in America (or Italy). *Psycho*, the most significant horror film of 1960, an apparent alternative to Hammer, came from expatriate Englishman Alfred Hitchcock and straddles the soulless new (American?) world of the shower stalls of the Bates Motel and the fetid old (European?) world of the old dark house up on the hill. Meanwhile, Roger Corman began a series with *The Fall of the House of Usher* (1960), creating an American gothic answer to Hammer, drawing on established Hollywood genre stars (first Vincent Price, later Boris Karloff, Basil Rathbone and Peter Lorre) and taking his inspiration from home-grown horror "name" Edgar Allan Poe.

The success of *Psycho* influenced films from William Castle (*Homicidal*, 1960) and Robert Aldrich (*Whatever Happened to Baby Jane?*, 1962) and even odd efforts like Herk Harvey's *Carnival of Souls* (1964) and Peter Bogdanovich's *Targets* (1968), encouraging filmmakers to explore contemporary America for its gothic shadowy corners. "American culture at large has become suffused with Gothic assumptions, with Gothic characters and plots," argues Mark Edmundson (1997: xii), reading gothic horror conventions into a wide spectrum of cultural artefacts. However, in 1968, Roman Polanski's *Rosemary's Baby* and George Romero's *Night of the Living Dead* opened up new avenues for American genre horror. Polanski's take on Ira Levin's novel stands at the head of a stream of big-budget horrors, often drawn from best-selling novels and promoted as "mainstream" cinema, and is significant for raising Stephen King to a best-seller superstardom unattainable by such niche-market pulp forerunners as H.P. Lovecraft, Robert Bloch and Richard Matheson. In this tradition are William Friedkin's *The Exorcist* (1973), Steven Spielberg's *Jaws* (1975), Richard Donner's *The Omen* (1976), Brian De Palma's *Carrie* (1976) and Stanley Kubrick's *The Shining* (1980), and (by association with the science fiction and action blockbuster genres) such horror-in-disguise items as Ridley Scott's *Alien* (1979), John Carpenter's *The Thing* (1982) and David Fincher's *Se7en* (1995). These films fulfil the commercial ambitions of all genre film makers, in that their primary audiences are people who wouldn't consider paying to see a horror movie.

George Romero followed his breakthrough debut with interesting and influential sequels *Dawn of the Dead* (1979) and *Day of the Dead* (1985), and also managed a remarkable vampire variant in *Martin* (1978). He brought horror to the heartland and encouraged a 1970s generation of hand-to-mouth auteurs. Wes Craven (*The Last House on the Left*, 1972; *The Hills Have Eyes*, 1978), Canadian David Cronenberg (*Shivers*, 1976), John Carpenter (*Halloween*, 1978), Tobe Hooper (*The Texas Chain Saw Massacre*, 1974) and Larry Cohen (*It's Alive*, 1975) emerged from the underground with a ferocious attitude but one-upped 1960s gore-slashers like H.G. Lewis (*Blood Feast*, 1962) by combining accomplished filmmaking skills and a seriousness of purpose with a willingness to indulge in violent or sexual extremes. The politenesses of traditional gothic are torn apart by Romero's ravening ghouls, Hooper's chainsaw family and Cronenberg's sex slugs, mounting what seems like a concerted attack on such institutions as the American family, the Vietnam-Watergate era US government and the conservative definition of what exactly constitutes a monster. Writing in the 1980s, Robin Wood argued that horror was "an alternative definition of those 'good old values' that the Reagan administration and 80s Hollywood cinema are trying to convince us are still capable of reaffirmation" (Wood 1986: 87). Horror, for Wood, rethinks the concepts of both America and its families.

Carpenter's *Halloween*, a "fun" scare movie on the model of William Castle's gimmick pictures, inhabits the same terrain as early Romero and Craven but abjures their intensely

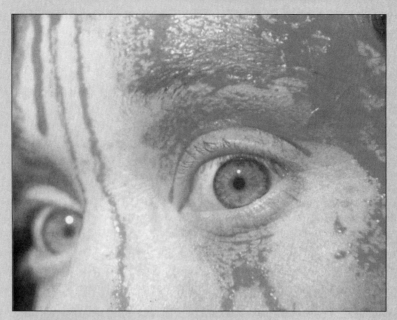

Sissy Spacek as *Carrie*

motivated brutalities in favour of a dark fairytale rollercoaster. It presents an apotheosis of the hand-through-the-window knee-jerk shock while at the same time reviving for the 1970s perhaps the oldest of all film formulae – the woman-in-peril thriller – as baby-sitter Jamie Lee Curtis fends off a masked, unstoppable bogey man. Hundreds of calendar-tied *Halloween* imitations, from *Friday the 13th* (1980) onwards, intensify the brutalities albeit without the motivation, creating a Christians-to-the-lions cinema many die-hard defenders of horror have found hard to cope with. Bruce Kawin defends "good horror" cinema against "bad horror cinema", the latter presenting "a spectacle for the simple purpose of causing pain in the viewer's imagination – not just scaring the hell out of us ... but attacking and brutalizing us on a deeper level" (Kawin 1986: 241). There has also been a rich history of critical debate around the woman-in-peril figure, fuelled by a feminism that has on the one hand lamented female victimage, while on the other challenging the notion of the genre as a male preserve. Carol J. Clover (1992) focuses on figures such as the Curtis character in *Halloween* (and her cinematic sisters) as more heroic "final girls", whereas Rhona J. Berenstein (1996: 201) reads the genre as partly driven by its attacking leading ladies, oscillating "between convention and transgression", and engaging in numerous "gender-bending forays".

In the 1980s, much critical attention was paid to the so-called "splatter movie" (and its close cousin, "body horror"), concentrating on the objectification (and dissection) of women (but not only women), the manipulation of the audience's identification with killer and victim via devices like the subjective camera, and the rising prominence of special effects. This allowed figures such as make-up maestro Tom Savini to be seen as stars in their own right. That achievements in effects make-up can prompt directions in genre film is demonstrated by the early 1980s revival of the werewolf film, not because the *Zeitgeist* was attuned to lycanthropy but because Rob Bottin and Rick Baker had developed new and amazing methods of transformation for Joe Dante's *The Howling* (1981) and John Landis's *An American*

Werewolf in London (1981). Splatter cinema also became overtly comedic around this time. William Paul (among others) has explored the crossovers between comedy and horror, particularly since the 1970s, arguing that:

> Gross-out, whether comedy or horror, is based on ambivalence because gross-out explicitly acknowledges the attractive in the repellent, the beautiful in the ugly. As it is a mode moving in two directions at once, the horror films may invoke comedy, while the comedies may take on suddenly nightmarish imagery. (Paul 1994: 419)

Pinedo addresses this indulgence in spectacle in another way. "Unlike classical horror films, which tell and imply but show very little of the destruction wrought upon the human body", she writes, "the postmodern horror film is obsessed with the wet death, intent on imaging the mutilation and destruction of the body" (1997: 51). This is contemporary cinema "deliberately seeking viewers' visceral intolerance" (Wu 2003: 88–90). This practice of rendering the inside explicitly visible is explored by a number of writers on body horror in general and David Cronenberg in particular (see, for example, Williams 1999).

In the 1980s and 1990s, horror lost its way, with the auteur-stars of the 1970s suffering career reversals (Romero) or drastic declines (Hooper). Like David Lynch (*Eraserhead*, 1978; *Blue Velvet*, 1986) and the Coen Brothers (*Blood Simple*, 1984; *Barton Fink*, 1991), David Cronenberg made a niche for himself with films not strictly classifiable as horror but which still inform and are shaped by the genre proper (*Videodrome*, 1983; *The Fly*, 1986; *Dead Ringers*, 1988; *Crash*, 1996). Only Craven, with *A Nightmare on Elm Street* (1984) and *Scream* (1996) achieved a continuing career and a developing identity, albeit at the cost of a see-sawing of ambition and achievement as remarkable work (*The People Under the Stairs*, 1991) alternated with hackery (*Shocker*, 1989). Sam Raimi's *The Evil Dead* (1982), a development of the Romero–Craven mode of substituting slapstick for social content, founded a 1980s horror style, inspiring the farcical *grand guignol* work of entertainers such as Stuart Gordon (*Re-Animator*, 1986), the bottom-feeding of production house Troma (*The Toxic Avenger*, 1985), and dozens of low-budget direct-to-video filmmakers. Raimi and Gordon have found it as difficult as Carpenter or Hooper to sustain careers within the genre.

Hollywood also indulged in a brief, overblown gothic revival in the form of Francis Ford Coppola's *Dracula* (1992) and Neil Jordan's *Interview with a Vampire* (1994), which reincarnate the screen's oldest fiend for a mass audience as a sympathetic, tragi-romantic figure – prefigured by *House of Dark Shadows* (1970) and *Blacula* (1972) – whose supernatural attributes are as much superpowers like Superman's as they are manifestations of an infernal curse. Aside from a few AIDS references and some homoerotic undercurrents, 1990s Hollywood gothics are largely backward-looking, not merely resurrecting old horrors for a new generation but evoking the history of genre as if it were a dead art form. More provocative vampire variants came from Kathryn Bigelow (*Near Dark*, 1986), Abel Ferrara (*The Addiction*) and Larry Fessenden (*Habit*, 1997). Meanwhile, horror has taken other directions. The byway of *Psycho* and *Halloween*, which elevated the modern figure of the serial murderer to the pantheon of movie monsters, re-emerged with a vengeance in influential adaptations from the novels of Thomas Harris: Michael Mann's *Manhunter* (1986), Jonathan Demme's *The Silence of the Lambs* (1991), Ridley Scott's *Hannibal* (2001) and Brett Ratner's *Red Dragon* (2002, revisiting the same source as *Manhunter*). These movies revolve around the figure of Hannibal Lecter (played by both Brian Cox and Anthony Hopkins), a genius serial killer who works most of his evil from behind bars like Dr. Mabuse, and who is contrasted not only with the FBI psycho-specialists with whom he jousts verbally (played by both William Petersen and Jodie Foster) but with less articulate, less controlled mutilation murderers (Tom Noonan, Ted Levene). Yvonne Tasker (2002: 88) reads *Silence* as a Bluebeard story that also "offers up monsters, desires and actions that seem inexplicable". Though John McNaughton's *Henry . . . Portrait of a Serial Killer* (1988) is authentic horror *vérité* about a low-rent mass murderer, the cinema has preferred to conjure up more flamboyant fiends along the lines of Lecter: from the supernatural Freddie Krueger of the *Elm Street* series and the body-hopping demon of *Fallen* (1997) to such demented artists of flesh and blood as Terry O'Quinn in Joseph Ruben's *The Stepfather* (1986) and Kevin Spacey in *Se7en*.

The significant name of the late 1990s was Kevin Williamson, screenwriter of *Scream*, *I Know What You Did Last Summer* (1997) and *The Faculty* (1998), and director of *Teaching Mrs Tingle* (1999). These tap into the enormous audience for "young adult" horror novels and rejuvenate the tired stalker movie with knowing irony (albeit in a less interesting way than *Wes Craven's New Nightmare*). However, like the backward-looking gothics, they insist on treating horror as a solved puzzle that can only be picked apart and reassembled. In foregrounding an awareness among their characters that they are trapped in a horror movie, these films establish an ironic distance from the conventions they milk shamelessly and entertainingly, but at the expense of anything like subtext. The drives and desires that animate even lesser early Wes Craven movies (*Deadly Blessing*, 1981) are absent, except in a form so diluted as to count as one more inclusion of an obligatory horror movie element along the lines of the clever jokes on hoary devices like the last-moment-return-from-the-dead-for-one-more-shock. That this attitude could extend from the slasher film to more supernatural horror is demonstrated by the spin-off TV series *Buffy the Vampire Slayer*, and action-horror hybrids like David S. Goyer's *Blade* (1998) and Stephen Sommers's *The Mummy* (1999). Nevertheless, the project of the horror film remains alive and vital, and the twin successes of *The Blair Witch Project* (1999) and *The Sixth Sense* (1999) suggest a renaissance for the Val Lewton style of "suggestive" supernatural cinema. As society becomes more complex and contradictory, so do the fears that the genre must engage with. As a genre it also becomes increasingly difficult to pigeon-hole: "the further away from . . . default horrors we travel, the more blurred distinctions become, and horror becomes less like a discrete genre than an effect which can be deployed within any number of settings or narrative patterns" (Newman 1996: 11). While there are still any number of direct-to-video rehashes of old ideas (the ten-film *Witchcraft* series or the *Howling* sequels have thrived purely on VHS or DVD rentals), good work has still been possible and, indeed, necessary.

References

Berenstein, R.J. (1996) *Attack of the Leading Ladies: Gender, Sexuality, and Spectatorship in Classic Horror Cinema*. New York: Columbia University Press.

Clover, C.J. (1992) *Men, Women and Chain Saws: Gender in the Modern Horror Film*. London: BFI.

Edmundson, M. (1997) *Nightmare on Main Street: Angels, Sadomasochism, and the Culture of Gothic*. Cambridge, MA: Harvard University Press.

Kawin, B.F. (1986) Children of the light, in B.K. Grant (ed.) *Film Genre Reader*. Austin, TX: University of Texas Press, pp. 236–57.

Newman, K. (1996) Introduction, in K. Newman (ed.) *The BFI Companion to Horror*. London: BFI Publications, pp. 11–16.

Paul, W. (1994) *Laughing Screaming: Modern Hollywood Horror and Comedy*. New York: Columbia University Press.

Pinedo, I.C. (1997) *Recreational Terror: Women and the Pleasures of Horror Film Viewing*. New York: State University of New York Press.

Tasker, Y. (2002) *The Silence of the Lambs*, BFI Modern Classics. London: BFI.

Williams, L.R. (1999) The inside-out of masculinity: David Cronenberg's visceral pleasures, in M. Aaron (ed.) *The Body's Perilous Pleasures: Dangerous Desire and Contemporary Culture*. Edinburgh: Edinburgh University Press, pp. 30–48.

Wood, R. (1986) *Hollywood from Vietnam to Reagan*. New York: Columbia University Press.

Wu, H.H. (2003) Trading in horror, cult and matricide: Peter Jackson's phenomenal bad taste and New Zealand fantasies of inter/national cinematic success, in M. Jancovich, A.L. Reboll, J. Stringer and A. Wallis (eds) *Defining Cult Movies: The Cultural Politics of Oppositional Taste*. Manchester: Manchester University Press, pp. 84–108.

Kim Newman

Continued from page 133

US film culture in the first half of the 1970s, has led some commentators to identify the period as a heyday of so-called "trash cinema" in which an increasingly segmented cinema marketplace catered to a plethora of sensationalist minority tastes, which defined themselves against the Hollywood mainstream (Sconce 1993; Hawkins 2000). But a far more meaningful oppositional film culture continued to exist elsewhere outside Hollywood in the form of American political film which in the first half of the 1970s was forced to operate in an increasingly hostile political climate. As David Farber has explained, the early 1970s were marked, on the one hand, by the persistence of many of the liberal and Leftist social and political agendas of the 1960s and, on the other, by Right-wing reaction from the so-called "Silent Majority" of conservative Americans celebrated by President Richard Nixon (Farber 1994: 291–316). The naïve idealism that had accompanied the sexual revolution of the 1960s dissipated; the Nixon administration intensified its war efforts in Southeast Asia through the saturation bombing of Vietnam and Cambodia; recession and the Nixon administration curtailed spending on social programmes and poverty; American cities witnessed some of the largest ever anti-war demonstrations before the US withdrawal from Vietnam in 1973; and tensions between radical groups and the state degraded into gun battles between police and the Black Panther Party or into terrorist attacks by splinter groups such as The Weathermen.

The activities of the various seminal agit-prop Newsreel film collectives, which had first emerged in the 1960s, responded powerfully to this continuing social and political turbulence as, for example, in Newsreel's account of the protest activities of anti-war Vietnam veterans, *Only the Beginning* (1971). The Newsreel collectives continued the dynamic American tradition of documentary filmmaking with moving critiques of institutional power and injustice – as, for example, in Third World Newsreel's *Teach Our Children* (1973), an account of the 1971 prisoner uprising at Attica in which 31 inmates were shot dead by guards, and *In the Event Anyone Disappears* (1974), a study of living conditions for prisoners in New

Jersey maximum security jails. Newsreel collectives also sought to develop practical programmes to increase participation in film-making by women and people of colour, and to develop alternative film and video distribution networks for their films on gender and race issues such as San Francisco Newsreel's *The Women's Film* (1971), on the women's liberation movement of the early 1970s, and Third World Newsreel's *El Pueblo Se Levanta* (1971), a study of the hardships faced by inner-city Puerto Rican immigrant communities.

Political critique of a less direct form also found its way into Hollywood cinema to a greater extent even than it had in the 1960s, as the critical and questioning function that American cinema had developed in that decade became increasingly mainstream. This was evident in the work of already established directors such as Arthur Penn and Robert Altman, and in the celebrated generation of young film auteurs who had come of age in the 1960s but whose careers matured artistically and expanded commercially in the 1970s – for example, Martin Scorsese, Francis Ford Coppola, Brian De Palma, and Michael Cimino. These so-called "movie brats" were responsible for a renaissance in the formal and thematic creativity of Hollywood cinema that was much celebrated in the 1970s and which has been studied extensively since by film scholars such as David Cook and Robert Kolker (Monaco 1979; Pye and Myles 1979; Cook 1998; Kolker 2000). They benefited from a new degree of autonomy and authority accorded to the film director by the major studios for whom, following the popularization in the US of auteurist approaches to cinema, the film director now possessed not

Continued on page 144

Though auteur theory has a history almost as long as cinema, its most prominent manifestation is post-Second World War, with the philosophy of cinematic authorship spearheaded by the French journal *Cahiers du cinéma* and its co-founder, André Bazin. In particular, François Truffaut's 1954 essay "Une certaine tendance du cinéma" became the manifesto of auteur theory, and of French New Wave filmmaking in general, validating the view that the director is the primary producer of the meaning of a film. This has been taken up as a model akin to literary notions of the author as controller of a written text's meaning (the filmmaking process lending itself to conveying the director's ideas, as a novel might convey those of its author). *Cahiers* critics looked to the way in which a director ideally deploys elements of *mise en scène* to convey his uniquely cinematic vision, identifying key themes and motifs repeated across his corpus which bear out a developing but singular vision. The movement was also polemically engaged in valorizing a canon of US directors (Alfred Hitchcock, Howard Hawks, John Ford) at the expense of older school French filmmakers (whom the New Wave was in the business of deposing). It reassessed the prevailing view by suggesting that these revered directors working in Hollywood's studio system should be seen more as artists than hacks, challenging the model of popular cinema as "only entertainment", and breaking down distinctions between art cinema and mainstream movies. As Helen Stoddart writes,

> A true auteur, it was argued, was distinguished by the presence in each film, above and beyond generic variations, of a distinctive personality, expressed as a world-view or vision, which would thereby constitute a trace or "personal stamp" of the director's presence in the film and therefore within their œuvre. (1995: 40)

The impact of this view in the United States. was felt initially through the work of *Village Voice* writer Andrew Sarris (the term "auteur theory" was originally his, first described in a 1962 essay). Sarris's 1968 text *The American Cinema: Directors and Directions 1929–1968* was little short of an extended and value-led separation of auteur sheep from studio-hack goats, including discussion of dozens of US directors, pigeon-holed via types, categories and styles, building up into a canon of "great men" – greatness being an index of how successfully an individual could transcend the constraints of the studio system. Sarris's project is comparable to that of F.R. Leavis's "great tradition" model of literary assessment propounded in the journal *Scrutiny* in the 1930s, and may therefore be seen as symptomatic of a new discipline (in this case, film studies) developing models that would shore it up as a legitimate area of intellectual enquiry. Sarris's individualist view of the history of a cinema constructed through judgements on key directors also seemed to have augmented the reception of *The American Cinema* itself. As Kent Jones put it in his amusing survey of Sarris's impact, in a 2005 issue of *Film Comment*, "*The American Cinema* has the monumentally timeless authority of an originary text – it does not appear to have been written as much as handed down from above and received by mankind" (Jones 2005). (Jones also reports that a friend of his once complained, "I can't get those fucking categories out of my head").

This crucial text could not have impacted on US cinema at a better time. The late 1960s – as the essays in the 1960s section of this book evidence – was precisely when a range of hip young directors were thought to be "saving" Hollywood from disaster. Sarris's subjects are primarily classical-era directors, and his project is to some extent retrospective; in the 1962 essay he promoted auteur theory as a critical model with real potential for reassessing US film history (1970; see Staiger (2003) for a critical discussion of Sarris and other approaches). If Sarris's work was primarily historical, the French auteurists had built a manifesto for new forms of filmmaking, and arguably both of these impulses worked together to influence the work of contemporary filmmakers as well as inflecting their reception. Sarris's work was primarily instrumental in revising views of US cinema: "For the hard-core auteurists," he wrote in his 2003 overview of the theories he drew upon and influenced, "the hitherto despised Hollywood movies could be judged as high art" (Sarris 2003: 28). This "highbrowing" of popular cinema was also aided by the self-proclaimed Francophilia of key directors, who were drawing upon the styles of the European New Wave even as they were validated by the theories of the *Cahiers* group. The script of *Bonnie and Clyde* had, of course, originally been offered to Truffaut; Bogdanovich's directing career was preceded by critical work on the *Cahiers* movement, and Scorsese claims active allegiance with European auteurs. "What Godard was showing was new ways to use images to tell a story, new ways to shoot, to cut," he told Peter Biskind (1998: 228). Friedkin – himself a passionate Europhile – recalls that early in his career Coppola "bought a new lightweight Arriflex, said, 'Look at this, this is what Godard uses and this is how we're all gonna make films someday, and all this big shit is gonna disappear and we're gonna be free to tell our stories in the street'" (Biskind 1998: 150). As a model and a manifesto, auteurism was, then, highly opportune, providing a framework for understanding the impact of ambitious young helmsmen like Stanley Kubrick, Bob Rafelson or Arthur Penn, which matched the individualism of the *Zeitgeist*, just as European auteurs were providing a toolkit for alternative filmmaking styles in the mainstream. Yet the mission of exposing the cracks in the American dream and championing political causes did not contradict the prevailing individualism of the counter-culture; those who hailed New Wave directors as their cinematic champions also happened to be heavily invested in myths of the free-speaking sovereign self. Thus a pantheon of directors was promoted as the voice of New America in a way that was as American as apple pie. Diane Jacobs, author of one of the first retrospectives of the early decade, writes glowingly of "a conglomeration of talent descending upon Hollywood and insisting on having a say in the future of movies. As [director Paul] Mazursky pointed out, for the first time American directors were making 'personal' films that were packaged as such" (1977: 14).

Auteurism is therefore not just an abstraction of film theory. It had real impact on how film, via arguments that served to deify a select group of in-touch "geniuses", came to be seen as the most socially relevant art-form at a time of social unrest. Of course, important factors in the construction and reconstruction of the film industry also served to promote and empower the figures most associated with this moment. Changes in studio hegemony enabled the making of Hopper's *Easy Rider*, Penn's *Bonnie and Clyde* or Altman's *M*A*S*H*, and changes in audience demographic made them hits. That their success was more readily accounted for via a philosophy of singular auteurial genius is entirely in keeping with the individualism of the moment. It is hardly surprising that the "greats" of American cinema who were popularly valorized after Sarris's 1968 cut-off point continued to be generally white and male. Only by the late 1980s, when some small change could be discerned, did women and black filmmakers begin to find their feet as fully paid-up auteurs in any significant numbers – ironically at a time when the critical establishment had become most suspicious of auteurism in general (how galling must it be, as a member of a minority group, to achieve auteur status only when it has become critically unfashionable). The Hollywood Renaissance of the late 1960s and early 1970s was then so called not just because it constituted a "renewal" but because it concentrated on a small cluster of "genius" figures. It is hard to think of US cinema between 1968 and 1975 without having as your landmarks figures like Francis Ford Coppola, Peter Bogdanovich and Hal Ashby. Robert Kolker, in *A Cinema of Loneliness*, his seminal study of five such figures (Arthur Penn, Stanley Kubrick, Martin Scorsese, Steven Spielberg, Robert Altman; Oliver Stone was added for the third edition in 2000) has "independence" as its watchword, valuing "the ability of these filmmakers to function more independently than those who came before them" (Kolker 2000: x, from "Preface to the First Edition").

So how has auteurism impacted on our view of 1970s (and subsequent) cinema? As the recent output of enthusiastic new histories of the period evidence, this is widely seen as a golden age of US cinema. Diane Jacobs (1977: 11) quotes Orson Welles's summation of a period when political chaos was matched by artistic energy: "Rome might be burning, but Nero's orchestras were fiddling *beautifully*." Film histories of the 1970s have, up until very recently, recorded cinematic achievement via an illustrious roll-call of sometimes maverick individuals who have since graduated into blockbuster-era royalty ("maverick" was a term that found some currency in descriptions of indie auteurs in the late 1980s and 1990s). Jacobs's book is one such list: the cover of the 1977 edition reads *Hollywood Renaissance: Altman Cassavetes Coppola Mazursky Scorsese and Others*, all in the same bold red and blue typeface. Along with Woody Allen, Martin Scorsese is often read as a New York auteur, as well as – latterly – a Hollywood hired hand, but 1970s and 1980s film criticism (and Scorsese himself, in texts such as *Scorsese on Scorsese*) saw his "vision" as bound to a number of repeated concerns, on the model of consistency propounded in Gelmis's seminal text of auteurism from this period, *The Film Director as Superstar*. Here Bernardo Bertolucci, in interview, propounds the idea that "If we ... put the films [of any single director] all together we will have the figure of one man, of an auteur, the life of an auteur ... But the film is one film" (Gelmis 1970: 171). An auteurist analysis of Scorsese's "one film" (comprising the 42 films and shorter works he has directed) would then read him as consistently returning to a dialectic of street violence and spiritual redemption, often augmented by biographical resonances. He peppers his movies with pop scores, and returns to rock music as one of the baby-boom generation's common experiential pillars (he edited *Woodstock*, 1970, and *Elvis on Tour*, 1972; he directed *The Last Waltz*, 1978, executive produced Allison Anders' sublime fictional rock biopic *Grace of my Heart*, 1996, and has most recently been responsible for the epic account of Bob Dylan's early career, *No Direction Home*). Scorsese's *œuvre* has also generated a veritable flood of critical studies (see Friedman 1997, Dougan 1997, and Grist 2000, for instance). Yet this profile – consistent themes developed across the decades, some of which speak to his generation and his personal history – must be tempered by another influencing factor, which is that he cut his directorial teeth under the mentorship of a highly controlling producer. As with a number of New Wave figures, Scorsese worked for Roger Corman, who was both a ''B'' movie mogul and a promoter of individual vision and talent. Francis Ford Coppola was also nurtured by Corman, and although he has latterly focused more on production and development than on directing, he was a central figure of the 1970s New Wave. But Coppola's auteur identity is also rather contradictory. He is certainly not a typical New Wave counter-cultural champion, making small films that double as political critiques (like, for instance, the Hal Ashby of *Harold and Maude*, 1971, and *The Last Detail*, 1973, or the Terrence Malick of *Badlands*, 1973, and *Days of Heaven*, 1978). Rather, an auteur analysis of his career would frame him as an auteur-as-mogul, creating tragi-operatic, broad canvas and large budget movies which have entertained as well as provoked huge audiences globally (*The Godfather*, 1972, *The Godfather Part 2*, 1974, *Apocalypse Now*, 1980, *The Cotton Club*, 1984, *Dracula*, 1992). Whereas the career trajectory of other New-Wave directors has been from edgy counter-cinema to mainstream assimilation (Friedkin's move from *The People Versus Paul Crump*, 1962, to *The Exorcist*, 1973, for instance, or Spielberg's move from *Duel*, 1971, to *Jaws*, 1975), Coppola also continued to work on smaller-scale projects (*The Rain People*, 1969; *The Conversation*, 1974; *Rumble Fish*, 1983; *The Outsiders*, 1983), suggesting an auteur with parallel career trajectories in both blockbuster and smaller-scale, sometimes more personal, filmmaking. Revisionist auteur histories of 1970s US cinema would also do well to supplement lists of the usual suspects with the few women and black filmmakers who were working in Hollywood at this time (Elaine May, Gordon Parks), and the many more who were working off-Hollywood and in independent production (Stephanie Rothman, Melvin van Peebles). And, as a number of recent nostalgic DVD documentaries have shown, this was also a period in which the producer as auteur re-emerged in a new form; that of the powerfully independent (sometimes glamorously dissolute) dealmaker – see discussion, for instance, of BBS Productions and of Robert Evans in *A Decade Under the Influence* (Ted Demme, Jerry Kupfer and Richard LaGravenese, 2003), and *The Kid Stays in the Picture* (Nanette Burstein, 2002). This is terrain that is also entertainingly discussed by Biskind (1998).

In film studies more recently, post-auteur theories such as structuralism, psychoanalysis and reception theory have tempered or challenged the power of the auteur with reference to other factors important in producing meaning, such as the spectator, the audience, the collaborative nature of production, or language itself. Hollywood has always found the ''name above the title'' to be a useful marketing device. By the 1980s and 1990s this practice, along with wider strategies for using name directors as promotional devices, became more prevalent. The commodities of name-brand auteurs may be more appropriately understood as the product of genre or other industrial structures rather than the emanations of genius, but once an individualist filmmaking identity has been established, it seals the manner in which a corpus of films are read and received. As Williams (2005: 396) argues:

The most prominent name directors working in Hollywood since the 1980s operate in a positive feedback-loop of auteurial self-regard: statements such as De Palma's "One is a director because one wants to be the master" ... have been fed through into the system of reception. PR bodies have used these (like the promise of generic repetition) to promote a guaranteed, standardised product (Kubrick's control is so strong that you can be sure his next film will live up to his last), which has then been rewarded when reviewers have constructed their reading of a film wholly within the context of a pre-existing directorial profile.

Directorial profile can also be amplified by other industry factors – trading on the intersection of a saleable genre and a prominent directorial brand, for instance, can be highly lucrative. Genre formula films can benefit from association with an auteur name (James Cameron or Kathryn Bigelow and action cinema, for instance); a director can ride on a marketable genre trend, or work with it over a range of films so that – as in the case of De Palma – genre is incorporated into a directorial trademark (his association with stylish thriller/slasher horror cinema, for instance). In this new, post-*Cahiers* vision of the "unauthorized auteur" (in Dudley Andrew's words), the director is transformed from "an individual with a vision or even a programme" into "a dispersed, multi-masked, or empty name bearing a possibly bogus collateral in the international market of images, a market that increasingly trades in 'futures'" (Andrew 1993: 81). But auteurs now also figure centrally within celebrity culture. To quote Timothy Corrigan (1998: 38–9): "if auteurism – as a description of movies being the artistic expression of a director – is still very much alive today, the artistic expression of contemporary directors is fully bound up with the celebrity industry of Hollywood." Might we now be better off reading the auteur within the frame of theories of stardom, since directors (such as Quentin Tarantino or Guy Richie) are now almost as central to celebrity culture as are their stars and their celebrity, in turn, is essential to the promotion of their movies?

Critics have been as quick to point out problems with auteur theory as they have been ready to embrace it. As Corrigan argues (1998: 40): "[A]uteurs and theories and practices of auteurism have never been a consistent or stable way of talking about movies. ... [F]rom its inception, auteurism has been bound up with changes in industrial desires, technological opportunities, and marketing strategies." For Richard Maltby (1995: 33): "The multiple logics and intentions that continue to impinge on the process of production ensure that authorship remains an inadequate explanation of how movies work." Andrew points out that even André Bazin's championing of the auteur was uniquely situated within a complex understanding of the interconnectedness of cinematic processes, which undermine classic auteurism's image of author as God: "The author may have been primary for him", writes Andrew (1993: 78), "but only as a tortion in the knot of technology, film language, genre, cultural precedent, and so forth, a knot that has in the past decades grown increasingly tangled." The tension and interplay between presumed auteurial vision and other forces have been the subject of a number of studies. Auteurism's place as an important influence upon developments in film history in the late 1960s and early 1970s is rather more certain than its sovereignty in film theory today.

References

Andrew, D. (1993) The unauthorized auteur today, in J. Collins, H. Radner and A. Preacher Collins (eds) *Film Theory Goes to the Movies*. New York: Routledge.
Biskind, P. (1998) *Easy Riders, Raging Bulls: How the Sex 'n' Drugs 'n' Rock 'n' Roll Generation Saved Hollywood*. London: Bloomsbury.

Corrigan, T. (1998) Auteurs and the New Hollywood, in J. Lewis (ed.) *The New American Cinema*. Durham, NC: Duke University Press.

Dougan, A. (1997) *Martin Scorsese*. London: Orion.

Friedman, L. (1997) *The Cinema of Martin Scorsese*. London: Roundhouse Publishing.

Gelmis, J. (1970) *The Film Director as Superstar*. Harmondsworth: Penguin.

Grist, L. (2000) *The Films of Martin Scorsese, 1963-1977: Authorship and Context*. Basingstoke: Palgrave Macmillan.

Jacobs, D. (1977) *Hollywood Renaissance: Altman Cassavetes Coppola Mazursky Scorsese and Others*. South Brunswick: A.S. Barnes and Co.

Jones, K. (2005) Hail the conquering hero, *Film Comment*, (May/June), archived at http://www.filmlinc.com/fcm/5-6-2005/Sarris.htm.

Kolker, R. (2000) *A Cinema of Loneliness: Penn, Stone, Kubrick, Scorsese, Spielberg, Altman*. Oxford: Oxford University Press.

Maltby, R. (1995) *Hollywood Cinema: An Introduction*. Oxford: Blackwell.

Nyce, B. (2004) *Scorsese Up Close: A Study of the Films*. London: Scarecrow Press.

Sarris, A. (1962/3) Notes on the *auteur theory* in 1962, *Film Culture*, 27 (winter): 1–8, reprinted in P. Adams Sotney (ed.) *Film Culture Reader*. New York: Praeger.

Sarris, A. (2003) The auteur theory revisited, in V. Wright Wexman (ed.) *Film and Authorship*. New Brunswick, NJ: Rutgers University Press.

Staiger, J. (2003) Authorship approaches, in D.A. Gerstner and J. Staiger (eds) *Authorship and Film*. New York: Routledge.

Stoddart, H. (1995) Auteurism and film authorship, in J. Hollows and M. Jancovich (eds) *Approaches to Popular Film*. Manchester: Manchester University Press.

Williams, L.R. (2005) *The Erotic Thriller in Contemporary Cinema*. Edinburgh: Edinburgh University Press.

Linda Ruth Williams

Continued from page 139

only a greater degree of intellectual and artistic weight but also important box-office drawing power. These directors, and others such as Terrence Malick, self-consciously imported into Hollywood much of the visual style, narrative complexity, and thematic ambiguity of European art cinema, often combined with the working methods of exploitation cinema (where many of them had started out), in a range of highly celebrated films including Penn's *Night Moves* (1975), Altman's *The Long Goodbye* (1973), Scorsese's *Mean Streets* (1973), Coppola's *The Godfather* (1972), De Palma's *Sisters* (1973), Malick's *Badlands* (1973), and Cimino's *Thunderbolt and Lightfoot* (1974) (Kolker 2000: 6–7). All of these were united to one degree or another by visual experimentation in the use of locations and sets, in cinematography, lighting and editing, and often in the innovative use of sound. Many, such as *Nashville* (Altman, 1975) or *Shampoo* (Ashby, 1975), were coloured by a sense of what Peter Lev has called the emotional or moral "exhaustion" characteristic of the era (Lev 2000: xix). Many centred on directionless antiheroes, and were structured around loose narratives whose endings were unsettlingly bleak or simply indecipherable as, for example, in the prominent wave of neo-noir private eye remakes that marked the early 1970s, from Altman's *The*

Long Goodbye (1973), to Polanski's *Chinatown* (1974) and Penn's *Night Moves* (1975).

Such films articulated a sophisticated existentialist anti-authoritarianism, which was matched in more directly political form by the distinctive conspiracy thrillers of the period – Coppola's *The Conversation* (1974), Pollack's *Three Days of the Condor* (1975) and, especially, Alan J. Pakula's trilogy *Klute* (1971), *The Parallax View* (1974), and *All the President's Men* (1976). These addressed the profound alienation from and distrust of both government and big business that became endemic for many Americans as the Watergate scandal revealed corruption, criminal activity, and abuses of power at the heart of President Richard Nixon's administration in Washington, DC (White 1975). Disillusionment with conventional politics was also expressed in biting satires such as Michael Ritchie's *The Candidate* (1972), starring Robert Redford as a disillusioned young senator on the make who is swept to electoral victory by his cynical media handlers and the superficial rhetoric of the campaign trail.

Of course, as the vogue for revised *films noirs* and conspiracy thrillers suggests, Hollywood film genres remained unstable and rapidly mutating in the first half of the 1970s. The era ultimately witnessed the emergence to new mainstream prominence of genres such as the science fiction and horror film, as well as new exploitation film genres such as the martial arts movie, which elevated Bruce Lee to stardom in films such as *Fists of Fury* (1971), *The Way of the Dragon* (1972), and *Enter the Dragon* (1973). This process of generic revision had been proceeding with particular intensity since the mid-1960s – for example, through Westerns such as *Cat Ballou* (1965), *Hombre* (1967), and *The Wild Bunch* (1969), whose revision of the traditional Western was now

extended by firmly counter-cultural westerns such as Altman's *McCabe and Mrs Miller* (1971), Fonda's *The Hired Hand* (1971), and Hopper's highly experimental *The Last Movie* (1971).

Although occasional conservative Westerns such as John Wayne's *The Cowboys* (1972) did appear, the traditional Western had effectively become a thing of the past, traditional myths of the heroic white settlement of the American West now powerfully discredited by exposés of the officially sanctioned oppression and extermination of Native Americans by settlers and the US Army on the frontier in such films as *Little Big Man* (1970), *Soldier Blue* (1970), and *Ulzana's Raid* (1972), which inevitably elicited parallels between nineteenth-century American history and the ongoing war in Vietnam. In Altman's *McCabe and Mrs Miller* (1972), and Pollack's *Jeremiah Johnson* (1973), as well as in the simultaneously brutal and romantic Westerns of Sam Peckinpah such as *Junior Bonner* (1972) and *Pat Garrett and Billy the Kid* (1973), many Westerns, even as the genre was in steep decline, achieved unprecedented degrees of visual spectacle and majesty in their representation of the wilderness landscape of the West, in a trend capped in 1980 by Michael Cimino's *Heaven's Gate*. Clint Eastwood's *High Plains Drifter* (1972), on the other hand, presented the West as a godforsaken landscape in which one small town, isolated amidst endless barren plains, is defended by a supernatural gunfighter who, in a psychopathic reprise of the classic *High Noon* (1952), defends the undeserving and corrupt people of the town from a band of brutal killers, burning the town to ashes in a Dante-like inferno before vanishing eerily into the horizon leaving only death and destruction in his wake.

Despite the frequently high artistic

Clint Eastwood in *Dirty Harry*: the neo-violence of Hollywood's counter-revolution

accomplishment of many Westerns in the period from 1970 to 1975, however, no Western ever made it into *Variety*'s list of the top 50 films in any given year (Marsden and Nachbar 1987: 1269–70). In 1974, Mel Brooks' comic Western *Blazing Saddles* (1974) seemed to complete the debunking of the mythology of the Hollywood Western in its parodic portrait of the cattle town of Rock Ridge and its white racist, homophobic inhabitants, saved from land speculators by a black sheriff – a case of generic revision along racial lines matched in the horror film by *Blacula* (1972) and in comedy by *Car Wash* (1975) (Lipsitz 1998). After *Blazing Saddles* and a small number of other notable Westerns of the mid-1970s, such as *The Outlaw Josey Wales* (1976) and *The Missouri Breaks* (1976), the Western would effectively die out on the big screen except for occasional revivals such as

Eastwood's *Pale Rider* (1985) and *Unforgiven* (1990) and Kevin Costner's *Dances with Wolves* (1990).

Much of the mythology of the Western, however, found new expression in the form of the police thriller, which, through the so-called "supercop" characters of Popeye Doyle in *The French Connection* (1971) and *The French Connection II* (1975), and Harry Cala-han in *Dirty Harry* (1971) and *Magnum Force* (1973), became a prominent and controversial vehicle of conservative or Right-wing thinking on crime, law enforcement, poverty, race, gender, and the contemporary American city. The cop protagonists of these films were portrayed as hardened professionals, engaged in a constant battle with lone psychos and organized crime in cities, which, the films suggested, had been wrecked by the lawlessness and immorality of 1960s liberalism and were in need of authoritative law enforcement. For Douglas Ryan and James Kellner, the emergence of new authoritarian motifs in these films and in vigilante revenge thrillers such as *Death Wish* (1973) effected a "Hollywood counter-revolution" against the social and political progressivism that underpinned American cinema of the 1960s but very much in line with the counter-revolution in American politics of the Nixon administration and the Silent Majority (Ryan and Kellner 1988: 37).

Indeed, many film critics and social commentators at the time lamented what they saw as the rise of a new type of extremely dehumanizing cinematic violence: for the critic Pauline Kael in *The New Yorker*, for example, violence in 1970s films such as *Dirty Harry* (1971), *A Clockwork Orange* (1971), *Straw Dogs* (1971), *Deliverance* (1972), *Death Wish* (1974), and *Bring Me the Head of Alfredo Garcia* (1974) did not carry the critical or poetic meaning it had carried in 1960s films such as *Bonnie and Clyde* (1967), *The Wild Bunch* (1969), or *Easy Rider* (1969). On the contrary, it seemed evidence only of increasing cynicism and negativity in American society and culture as the 1960s receded into history (Costello 1972; Goodwin 1972; Kael 1972a).

However, conservative films such as *Dirty Harry* were importantly countered by liberal thrillers that doubled as realist exposés of police corruption and police brutality such as Sidney Lumet's gritty *Serpico* (1973) and *Dog Day Afternoon* (1975), both starring Al Pacino. These and other contemporary social portraits such as *Joe* (1970), *Five Easy Pieces* (1971), and *The Last Detail* (1973), often focused partly or wholly on the American working-class rather than on the middle-class subjects often favoured by Hollywood. Moreover, they did so without endorsing the idealism of the

American Dream, which had generally accompanied representations of labour and the self-made man in classical Hollywood films such as *The Grapes of Wrath* (1940) or *On the Waterfront* (1953) and which continued to underpin the ideology of the Nixon presidency and the Silent Majority.

This characteristic interest in working-class urban milieux also intersected with a rise in portraits of particular racial and ethnic communities in the 1970s. So-called "blaxploitation" movies such as *Shaft* (1971), *Superfly* (1972), and *Cleopatra Jones* (1973) merged the low budget approach of exploitation cinema with a focus on inner-city African Americans, crime, poverty, drugs, and sex to produce a cinematic style, at once realist and tremendously stylized, which wavered between a serious interest in the politics of Black Power – most powerfully articulated in *Sweet Sweetback's Baad Asssss Song* (1971) and *The Spook Who Sat By the Door* (1973) – and a sensationalist sexualized stereotyping of black men and women that threatened merely to reproduce rather than challenge the racism to which African Americans had long been subject in Hollywood cinema (James 1989: 177–95; Ryan and Kellner 1988: 31–3, 121–8). Meanwhile, white working-class ethnic identity proliferated in a wide variety of films from studies of Italian-America such as Coppola's mafia epic *The Godfather* (1972) and Scorsese's intimate study of small-time hoodlums in New York's Little Italy, *Mean Streets* (1973), to John G. Avilsden's romantic boxing drama *Rocky* (1976), and Michael Cimino's study of Polish-American Vietnam veterans in small-town Pennsylvania, *The Deer Hunter* (1977).

Such representations as these challenged the traditional priority given by Hollywood cinema to images of the middle class and to

Continued on page 149

Peckinpah's battles with the studio bosses over the final cut of his films, which he always lost, have garnered him an unshakeable aura of a maverick filmmaker with an authentic vision too real for the undiscerning second-rate movie moguls. Like his outlaw heroes, Peckinpah was fighting a bureaucratic system that first stymied and then destroyed the individual. Yet since his death in December 1984 at the age of 59, Hollywood studios have worked hard to recuperate Peckinpah as one of America's great filmmakers, releasing "definitive director's cut" versions of *The Wild Bunch* (1969), *Pat Garrett and Billy the Kid* (1973), and *Major Dundee* (1965). These three films were thrown out in truncated form on their initial releases, and alongside *Straw Dogs* (1971), form the core of the *œuvre* on which Peckinpah's reputation stands: violent, sentimental, misogynistic, *cinematic* ruminations on America's and Americans' tortured past and present.

The romantic view of the artist that Peckinpah's army of hagiographers hold has tended to cast him as an American visionary on a par with such giants of literature as Herman Melville and Ernest Hemingway, or the filmmakers John Ford and John Huston. Though some of his more whimsical forays such as *Ride the High Country* (1962), *The Ballad of Cable Hogue* (1970), and *Junior Bonner* (1972), alongside his Western masterpieces, share a common sentimentality through a fixation on the wounded individual and male camaraderie with Hemingway, Peckinpah is better understood as belonging to the less esteemed tradition of post-war pulp stylists. Like Philip K. Dick in his science fiction musings, Luke Short in his Western writings, and Jim Thompson in his crime stories, Peckinpah understood and respected generic convention. For all the truth that the stories of the artist at odds with the system holds, it should also be remembered that Peckinpah made films that had real clout at the box office, even if they had few artistic qualities: *The Getaway* (1972), *The Killer Elite* (1975), *Cross of Iron* (1977), *Convoy* (1978). Peckinpah's peers are Don Siegel, Samuel Fuller, Robert Aldrich, and Anthony Mann – art brut stylists and pulp modernists. These are filmmakers who understood how to tell stories visually, and who peopled their films with heroes who have a severely restricted understanding of their inconsequential role within a fragmented and alienating modern world.

Peckinpah's pulp modernism is best revealed in *Bring Me the Head of Alfredo Garcia* (1974) that the director described as "the story of a man caught up in the brutality of the world around him, who loses all sense of morality with one act of violence begetting another, until there is no return to respectability, only retribution. The lasting theme of the film is that such acts only end in disaster for those involved" (Prince 1998). The reviewer for *The Wall Street Journal* did not share such a lofty appreciation of the film which he thought so "grotesque in its basic conception, so sadistic in its imagery, so irrational in its plotting, so obscene in its effect, and so incompetent in its cinematic realization that the only kind of analysis it really invites is psychoanalysis" (quoted by Prince 1998). "The first time I saw him he was dead," says Benny (Warren Oates) of Alfredo Garcia. In true pulp style Benny is soon doubling for the corpse of Alfredo as he heads ever deeper into the madness of contemporary America. In the age of the DVD, Peckinpah's status as a maverick American filmmaker ensures his commercial appeal, but I doubt his particular vision is any more palatable today with studio executives than it was in the 1970s.

References

Prince, S. (1998) *Savage Cinema: Sam Peckinpah and the Rise of Ultraviolent Movies.* London: Athlone Press.

Peter Stanfield

Continued from page 147

middle-class audiences to a degree unknown since the brief heyday of the Prohibition-era gangster in early 1930s films such as *The Public Enemy* (1931). That most middle class of Hollywood genres, the family melodrama, which had been such a staple for Hollywood from the 1940s to the mid-1960s in films from *The Best Years of Our Lives* (1946) to *Rebel Without a Cause* (1955) and *The Graduate* (1967), fell into decline. It was maintained in the early 1970s only by such wry psychological studies of middle-class angst as Neil Simon's *The Out-of-Towners* (1970), *Plaza Suite* (1971), and *The Prisoner of Second Avenue* (1972), until a rejuvenation of the genre in the early 1980s in *Ordinary People* (1980) and *Terms of Endearment* (1983).

As studies by Thomas Elssaesser and others have authoritatively shown, the melodrama had been one of the most important genres in which Hollywood filmmakers after the Second World War had explored issues of gender and sexuality in modern America (Elsaesser 1985). But for many commentators, the period 1970–75 saw a serious degeneration in relations between men and women on American cinema screens, which contrasted worryingly with the positive strides then being made by women in American society at large thanks to the rise of feminism. In 1973, while mainstream magazines like *Harper's* published feature articles lamenting the demise of traditional heterosexual romance in the movies, Marjorie Rosen, in *Popcorn Venus*, one of the earliest books of feminist film criticism, suggested that a clear polarization had taken place in female character types in American cinema of the early 1970s between the worldly-wise political attitude and sexual assertiveness represented by Jane Fonda in *Klute* (1971) and the naïve and passive femininity of Ali McGraw in *Love Story* (1970) (Denby 1973; Rosen 1973). In this atmosphere of crudely polarized sexual stereotyping, images of women as victims of gratuitous physical and sexual violence appeared to many to be proliferating in films such as Sam Peckinpah's *Straw Dogs* (1971), and Clint Eastwood's *Play Misty for Me* (1971).

Such films as these became focal points of heated public debate about issues of screen morality because of their provocative mix of violence and sex. Peckinpah's R-rated *Straw Dogs* recounted the traumatic experiences of a young American mathematician and his wife who move to a small English town to get away from the violence of modern America only to find themselves subject to increasingly serious harassment by the locals: when the young woman, played by Susan George, is raped in their home, her mild-mannered husband, played by Dustin Hoffmann, erupts in an orgy of vengeful violence. In general terms, critic David Denby, writing in *Atlantic Monthly*, admired Peckinpah's abilities as a director, but abhorred the film's uncompromising suggestion that civilization is underpinned by innate human barbarity (Denby 1972); Jay Cocks, in *Time* magazine, was horrified by Peckinpah's creation in the film of "a self-contained universe of indifferent terrors" (Cocks 1971). But Pauline Kael more specifically accused the film of complicity in a disturbing "sexual fascism" within American culture in what she saw as the film's suggestion "that women really want the rough stuff, that deep down they're little beasts asking to be made submissive" (Kael 1972b; Rosen 1973: 337–41). For Kael, Peckinpah's graphic rape scene exemplified the brutalization of women in the movies and the nihilistic super-masculine violence in American cinema of the day, which appeared to want to reverse the achievements of feminism while endorsing the sexual revolution of the 1960s only in so far as greater freedom in the cinematic representation of sex worked in favour of the gratification of male audiences. In contrast, the following year, Kael enthusiastically praised the no less controversial but more philosophically and psychologically complex study of sex and violence in Bernardo Bertolucci's Franco-Italian production *Last Tango in Paris* (1972), starring Marlon Brando and Maria Schneider, which achieved significant critical and commercial success in the United States.

In any event, films such as *Straw Dogs* and *Last Tango in Paris* testified to the massively changed sexual culture in which American cinema operated in the first half of the 1970s, and public debate about such films carried a strong sense of the 1960s as a watershed that separated America from its past, for better or worse. This sense of dislocation informed nostalgic portraits of adolescence before the sexual revolution in Peter Bogdanovich's *The Last Picture Show* (1971) and George Lucas's second feature *American Graffiti* (1973, Fig. 7 (*see plate section*)) – set in 1951 and 1962, respectively – and would eventually lead to the naïve nostalgia of *Grease* (1978, Fig. 8 (*see plate section*)). It also informed Hal Ashby's retrospective commentary in *Shampoo* (1975) on the short-sighted and spiritually empty promiscuity of the 1960s counter-culture through the figure of Hollywood hairdresser-playboy George Round, played by Warren Beatty. Meanwhile, in a manner of speaking, Woody Allen built an entire career in the early 1970s by making comedy out of the sexual neuroses of the American male in an openly promiscuous society in films like *Everything You Always Wanted to Know About Sex* (1972) – a theme that he had made his own in *What's New Pussycat?* (1965) and which neatly tied in with his light-hearted examination of other aspects of the 1960s counter-culture such as political revolution in *Bananas* (1971) and environmentalism in *Sleeper* (1973, Fig. 10 (*see plate section*)).

It is not to deny the quality of such films of the first half of the 1970s to recognize that they did demonstrate the beginning of a fundamental shift in the cultural, political, and cinematic landscape of the United States. As Fredric Jameson has convincingly argued in his essay "Periodizing the 60s", the 1960s as an era ended not with the official beginning of a new decade in 1970 but, later, in 1972, 1973, or 1974, as the United States withdrew from Vietnam, the Nixon era passed into history, the mass protest movements that had raged around issues of war, race, and gender for at least a decade dissolved, and both the United States and the global economy were gripped by recession (Jameson 1988: 183). These conditions would become increasingly apparent in American cinema after 1973 when a marked change of tone emerged even in the genre that in the 1960s had been most firmly stamped with counter-cultural credentials – the road movie. The tone of counter-cultural defiance which had underpinned *Easy Rider* and other biker movies in the late 1960s was at first continued in the early 1970s by the rebellious escapism of *The Getaway* (1971), *Two-Lane Blacktop* (1971), and *Vanishing Point* (1971); but it was then increasingly supplanted by a tone of reconciliation in road movies such as *Electra Glide in Blue* (1973) and *Thunderbolt and Lightfoot* (1974), both of which characterized the by-now conventional deaths of their protagonists not as a sign of revolutionary counter-cultural defiance in the face of an unjust America but as the tragic outcome of needless social conflict in a fundamentally good society.

This mood of reflection continued implicitly

Mainstream counter-culture: *One Flew Over the Cuckoo's Nest.*

in Milos Forman's hugely acclaimed *One Flew Over the Cuckoo's Nest* (1975), which addressed similar anti-establishment concerns to those of the road movie but within the very confined institutional setting of a mental hospital. In a firmly mainstream success that won five Academy Awards, including Best Picture, the film toned down the disturbing content of the 1962 book by counter-cultural icon Ken Kesey, upon which the screenplay was based, so that its study of institutional cruelty and the inmate's desire for escape could be read either as a comic and sentimental liberal humanist parable on the dangers of conformism or as an allegorical indictment of the essential injustice and inequality of American society and its institutions (not just hospitals, but the educational system, the military, the police, or government). But the latter reading was only barely permitted by the film: the film's popularization of Kesey's counter-cultural values in the American cinematic mainstream came at the price of a dilution of their original radical import. This is a compromise for which we should not fault the film too harshly today, however: in the mid-1970s the human scale, challenging moral themes, and anti-generic qualities of films such as *One Flew Over the Cuckoo's Nest* were increasingly threatened by a newly dominant approach to filmmaking, which would fuel the economic recovery of Hollywood cinema, its distinctive political turn to the Right, and its return to classical form and convention in the late 1970s.

The most explicit formulation of this turn, of course, appeared in the early 1970s in the overtly reactionary politics of supercop films such as *Dirty Harry*. But a conservative turn was also evident in the success of lavish period costume dramas such as the 1920s Chicago gangster pastiche *The Sting* (1973), the 1930s upper-class Agatha Christie whodunnit *Murder on the Orient Express* (1974), and the 1940s romance *The Way We Were* (1973). In their preference for studio sets over location filming, these films suggested a return to the escapism of classical Hollywood in reaction to the tendency in much 1960s cinema to use filming on location in everyday American settings, both urban and rural, as a means of rejecting the Hollywood studio system of production and strengthening the contemporary social and political relevance of films in general. Elsewhere, as Robin Wood has explained, in the rise of disaster movies such as *The Poseidon Adventure* (1972), *The Towering Inferno* (1974), and *Earthquake* (1975), Hollywood relied in a similar way upon escapist heroic dramas, which, despite their spectacular catastrophic scenes of the destruction of ships, buildings, and cities, and despite their occasional gentle critique of the arrogance of American big business, ultimately emphasized the importance of the survival of the status quo, especially of the resilience of the individual and the nuclear family (Wood 1986: 28).

The importance of preserving a specifically masculine individualism and patriarchy, meanwhile, is identified by Ryan and Kellner as a key characteristic of many horror films of the early 1970s, such as William Friedkin's *The Exorcist* (1973, Fig. 5 (*see plate section*)) and Brian De Palma's *Sisters* (1973) (Ryan and Kellner 1988: 168–93). For Ryan and Kellner, although the period saw the horror film genre move away from its "B" movie and exploitation

cinema roots towards a new auteurist artistic credibility and commercial importance, it did so as a prominent part of the neo-conservative reaction against the 1960s which increasingly informed Hollywood cinema as the 1970s wore on. The narratives of the demonic possession and exorcism of a young girl in *The Exorcist* and of the psychosexual malfunction and murder of a young woman by her Siamese twin in *Sisters* continue the denigration of women, of feminism, and of sexual liberation that characterized vigilante thrillers like *Dirty Harry* and *Straw Dogs*. They carry the similarly unhealthy message that the proper response to social anxiety and the destabilization of the status quo is the reassertion of male authority, especially through repressive violence.

However, it is the ambivalence of the horror film in the first half of the 1970s, rather than its inevitable conservatism, upon which Robin Wood's somewhat different reading of the genre rests. For Wood, although *The Exorcist* does hide a reactionary message behind its stylistic sophistication, *Sisters* stands as "one of the great American films of the 70s" (Wood 1986: 151). Pointing out that it was an independent production of American International Pictures where *The Exorcist* was a Warner Bros release, Wood sees *Sisters* as a powerful mix of art cinema and Alfred Hitchcock in its visual style and narrative structure. He also reads it as a continuation of the radical political spirit of the 1960s in popular cinema through a genuinely subversive deconstruction and rejection of patriarchy and an anarchic celebration of unrepressed female sexuality. *Sisters*, therefore, like the equally celebrated and notorious *The Texas Chain Saw Massacre* of the following year, continues an important independent tradition of establishment critique in horror cinema of which Ryan and Kellner are dismissive.

Indeed, the ideological tendency of that other key genre to emerge into the mainstream in the 1970s – the science fiction film – is similarly ambivalent and debatable at least, again, in the first half of the decade. Following on the defining moment of *2001: A Space Odyssey* (1968), sci-fi became increasingly prevalent in American cinema through such films as George Lucas's directorial debut *THX1138* (1971), Douglas Trumbull's *Silent Running* (1972), and John Carpenter's *Dark Star* (1974). These, alongside the earliest screen successes of sci-fi writer-director Michael Crichton such as *The Andromeda Strain* (Wise, 1971, based on Crichton's novel) and *Westworld* (Crichton, 1973), ensured not only the numerical proliferation of science fiction films but the increasing commercial centrality of the genre within American cinema as a whole. Broadly speaking, all these films articulated a concern with the dangers posed to human society by excessive technological experimentation and/or its control by corrupt government or big business. But there were important differences. In *Silent Running*, for example, the use of hippie iconography and folk music in the representation of the destruction of the natural environment (plants, trees, animals) by commercialized science clearly allied that film to the ecological values of the 1960s counter-culture. However, Lucas's narrative in *THX1138* of the ultimately successful escape of one man from an inhuman techno-totalitarian future society could be read in terms of a Left-wing critique of the machine and consumer society harking back to the counter-cultural values of the 1960s or in terms of a Right-wing, romantic libertarianism, which would achieve dominance during the era of President Ronald Reagan in the 1980s.

Though it would be wrong to identify *THX1138* as simply Right-wing, the conservative reading of *THX1138* certainly seems to fit more neatly, in retrospect, with Lucas's subsequent direction of *American Graffiti* (1973) and *Star Wars* (1977), both of which are identified by numerous critics, including Wood, Ryan and Kellner, and Kolker, with the increasing conservatism and artistic decline of American cinema in the latter half of the 1970s and into the 1980s. Indeed, focusing especially on their shared fascination with what he sees as facile visual spectacle and big budget extravagance, Wood goes so far as to lump Spielberg and Lucas together under the one derogatory heading – "the Spielberg-Lucas syndrome". Wood uses the term as a convenient shorthand for everything that went wrong with American cinema after 1975 in contrast to the creativity and progressive politics of American cinema of the previous decade-and-a-half (Wood 1986: 162). Following Wood's logic, one would have to read Steven Spielberg's early features, *Duel* (TV, 1971) and *The Sugarland Express* (1974), despite the fact that they are road movies, as conservative reworkings of that distinctively counter-cultural genre which had achieved such powerful expression in *Easy Rider* (1969) but which Spielberg refocused away from renegade, drug-dealing bikers onto the domestic figures of a middle-class, suburban family man (in *Duel*) and a young mother seeking to be reunited with her child (in *The Sugarland Express*).

Here, as with *THX1138*, it is important not to oversimplify: Spielberg's *The Sugarland Express* and *Jaws* (1975), and also his later *Close Encounters of the Third Kind* (1977), do contain a very dilute residue of the anti-authoritarian conspiracy thinking characteristic of much Left-leaning cinema of the period: for example, in the blaming of the carnage in *Jaws* on the greed, hypocrisy and officialdom of the Mayor of Amityville who insists against all the evidence that there is no threat to swimmers from sharks and that the town's beaches should be kept open for the sake of the summer tourist trade. But, as Kolker has shown, this weak anti-authoritarian motif in *Jaws* does nothing to undermine the film's ultimate reassertion of conservative middle-class values, the priority of the nuclear family and of patriarchal authority, all of which are actually vested in the film not in the Mayor, who is really a comic buffoon, but in Chief Brody whose heroism stems not only from his final single-handed killing of the shark but from his clearly defined status as a father and a husband (Kolker 2000: 290–305).

For Kolker, then, Spielberg's cinema, like that of Lucas, epitomizes the tendency of much Hollywood cinema of the later 1970s towards a backward-looking "politics of recuperation", which, far from precluding innovation in visual spectacle and technical wizardry – *Close Encounters* and *Star Wars* clearly demonstrate innovation in those areas – depends upon the visual and technical aspects of cinema, and an old-fashioned conception of its magical effects on the viewer, to suppress deeper meaning, ambiguity, bitter conflict, and unresolvable mystery in order to replace them with a conservative and childlike morality of good versus evil (Kolker 2000: 237–40). This particular cocktail of film form and politics constitutes nothing less than an outright revocation of the most interesting aspects of American cinema of the preceding ten years – of the most artistically and politically complex filmmakers working within Hollywood such as Penn, Altman, and Scorsese, to say nothing of experimental and political agitprop film outside Hollywood. This sea change in film culture has led some to describe the displacement of the latter "modernist" cinema by the

rejuvenated "classical" cinema of Spielberg and Lucas by reference to the notion of a new "postmodern" film culture that is still with us today. Indeed, the early 1970s is commonly identified in a range of other areas of culture and society as the moment in which "postmodernism" can be said to have "begun", so to speak, and a case can be made for identifying 1975 as the key moment in American cinema history in which the decisive shift took place not only because of the emergence of key epoch-defining feature films – such as *One Flew Over the Cuckoo's Nest* and *Jaws* – which seemed to mark the end of one era and the beginning of another (Shiel 2003; see also Harvey 1990; Jameson 1993).

For 1975 is also widely agreed to be the year in which, largely thanks to the new formulae perfected in *Jaws*, Hollywood cinema was able to emerge from the long period of internal instability that had caused particular difficulties for it since the early 1960s such that it was once again a "strong and profitable" cinema, which has been in an aggressively expansionist mode more or less constantly ever since (Wasko 1982: 149; Maltby 1998). This recovery would establish Hollywood in the aggressively competitive position it has occupied for the past three decades, based upon a number of key realizations within the industry itself. 1975 was the single most successful box-office year in the United States since 1963, with an all-time box-office record of $2 billion being set. *Jaws* became the biggest ever box-office success in Hollywood history, and was joined in that year by the huge successes of *Earthquake*, *The Towering Inferno*, *The Godfather II*, and *Murder on the Orient Express*. Some studios continued to experience problems with debt in the later 1970s, but 1975 became the single most profitable year ever for MGM, Universal managed to contain its long-standing financial problems thanks to the success of *Jaws*, and Disney also cleared $100 million of debt in that year (Wasko 1982: 174–9). Put simply, Hollywood had become accustomed to the new routine of making fewer films for a smaller total audience, but bigger pictures and for a larger audience per picture than ever before. This new routine would underpin its economic success for a whole generation to come, although it could do nothing to guarantee the artistic or intellectual value of the films produced. Increasingly after 1975, and certainly in the 1980s, some audiences would look to the then-emergent "indie" film phenomenon – for example, David Lynch's *Eraserhead* (1977) or John Sayles' *The Return of the Secaucus Seven* (1980) – for relief from an increasingly monotonous Hollywood.

References

Agan, P. (1975) *Clint Eastwood: The Man Behind the Myth*. New York: Pyramid Books.

Balio, Tino (ed.) (1985) *The American Film Industry*. Madison: University of Wisconsin Press.

Balio, T. (1990) *Hollywood in the Age of Television*. Boston: Unwin Hyman.

Berman, M. (1993) *All That is Solid Melts Into Air: The Experience of Modernity*. New York: Verso.

Cocks, J. (1971) Peckinpah: primitive horror, *Time*, 98(20 December): 85–7.

Cook, D.A. (1998) Auteur cinema and the "Film Generation" in 1970s Hollywood, in J. Lewis (ed.) *The New American Cinema*. Durham, NC: Duke University Press.

Costello, D.P. (1972) From counter-culture to anti-culture, *Commonweal*, 46(16): 383–6.

Denby, D. (1972) Violence enshrined, *Atlantic Monthly*, 229 (April): 118–22.

Denby, D. (1973) Men without women, women without men, *Harper's*, 247 (September): 51–4.

Eames, J.D. (1982) *The MGM Story*. London: Octopus Books.

Elsaesser, T. (1985) Tales of sound and fury: observations on the family melodrama, in B. Nichols (ed.) *Movies and Methods*, vol. II. Berkeley: University of California Press.

Farber, D. (1994) The silent majority, in D. Farber (ed.) *The Sixties: From Memory to History*. Chapel Hill: University of North Carolina Press.

Gallafent, E. (1994) *Clint Eastwood: Actor and Director*. London: Studio Vista.

Goodwin, M. (1972) Tooling up for Armageddon, *Take One*, 3(4): 6–7.

Guback, T. (1982) Foreword, in J. Wasko, *Movies and Money: Financing the American Film Industry*. Norwood, NJ: Ablex.

Gustafson, R. (1985) "What's happening to our pix biz?": from Warner Bros. to Warner Communications, Inc., in T. Balio (ed.) *The American Film Industry*. Madison: University of Wisconsin Press.

Harvey, D. (1990) *The Condition of Postmodernity: An Enquiry into the Origins of Cultural Change*. New Malden, MA and Oxford: Blackwell.

Hawkins, J. (2000) *Cutting Edge: Art-horror and the Horrific Avant-garde*. Minneapolis: University of Minnesota Press.

James, D. (1989) *Allegories of Cinema: American Film in the Sixties*. Princeton, NJ: Princeton University Press.

Jameson, F. (1988) Periodizing the 60s, in S. Sayres, A. Stephanson, S. Aronowitz and F. Jameson (eds) *The 60s Without Apology*. Minneapolis: University of Minnesota Press.

Jameson, F. (1993) *Postmodernism, or the Cultural Logic of Late Capitalism*. New York: Verso.

Kael, P. (1972a) Saint cop, *New Yorker*, 15 January. (Kael's film reviews from this period are collected in *Deeper into Movies*, Boston: Atlantic, Little, Brown, 1973.)

Kael, P. (1972b) *New Yorker*, 47 (29 January): 83.

Kolker, R.P. (2000) *A Cinema of Loneliness: Penn, Stone, Kubrick, Scorsese, Spielberg, Altman*. New York and Oxford: Oxford University Press. (The chapter on Spielberg in the 1988 and 2000 editions replaced a chapter on Coppola in the original 1980 edition.)

Lev, P. (2000) *American Films of the '70s: Conflicting Visions*. Austin: University of Texas Press.

Lipsitz, G. (1998) Genre anxiety and racial representation in 1970s cinema, in N. Browne (ed.) *Refiguring American Film Genres*. Berkeley and London: University of California Press.

Maltby, R. (1998) "Nobody knows everything": post-classical historiographies and consolidated entertainment, in S. Neale and M. Smith (eds) *Contemporary Hollywood Cinema*. New York: Routledge.

Marsden, M.T. and Nachbar, J. (1987) The modern popular Western: radio, television, film, and print, in Western Literature Association, *A Literary History of the American West*. Fort Worth: Texas Christian University Press.

Miller, S.P. (1999) *The Seventies Now*. Durham, NC: Duke University Press.

Monaco, J. (1979) *American Film Now: The People, the Power, the Money, the Movies*. New York: New American Library.

Phillips, J.D. (1982) Film conglomerate blockbusters: international appeal and product homogenization, in G. Kindem (ed.) *The American Movie Industry: The Business of Motion Pictures*. Edwardsville: Southern Illinois University Press.

Pye, M. and Myles, L. (1979) *The Movie Brats: How the Film Generation Took Over Hollywood*. New York: Holt, Rinehart and Winston.

Rosen, M. (1973) *Popcorn Venus: Women, Movies and the American Dream*. New York: Coward, McCann and Geoghegan.

Ryan, D. and Kellner, J. (1988) *Camera Politica: The Politics and Ideology of Contemporary Hollywood Film*. Bloomington: Indiana University Press.

Sconce, J. (1993) Spectacles of death: identification, reflexivity, and contemporary horror, in J. Collins, H. Radner and A. Preacher Collins (eds) *Film Theory Goes to the Movies*. New York: Routledge.

Shiel, M. (2003) A nostalgia for modernity: New York, Los Angeles, and American Cinema in the 1970s, in M. Shiel and T. Fitzmaurice (eds) *Screening the City*. London: Verso.

Sklar, R. (1975) *Movie-Made America: A Cultural History of American Movies*. New York: Chappell and Co.

Sweeney, L. (1970) The movie business is alive and well and living in San Francisco, *Show*, 1(4): 34–7, 82.

Wasko, J. (1982) *Movies and Money: Financing the American Film Industry*. Norwood, NJ: Ablex.

White, T.H. (1975) *Breach of Faith: The Fall of Richard Nixon*. New York: Atheneum.

Wood, R. (1986) *Hollywood from Vietnam to Reagan*. New York: Columbia University Press.

Wyatt, J. (1994) *High Concept: Movies and Marketing in Hollywood*. Austin: University of Texas Press.

Wyatt, J. (1998) Marketing/distribution innovations, in J. Lewis (ed.) *The New American Cinema*. Durham, NC: Duke University Press.

Taxi Driver

One of the landmarks of 1970s cinema, *Taxi Driver* is the brilliant but disturbing progeny of some then up-and-coming, now established, industry talents. Directed by Martin Scorsese, produced for Columbia by Michael and Julia Phillips, written by Paul Schrader, starring Robert de Niro, Harvey Keitel, and Jodie Foster, with cinematography by celebrated D.P. Michael Chapman, it also boasted a remarkable score by legendary Hollywood composer Bernard Herrmann, who completed it only hours before he died. Scorsese had been directing and editing since the early 1960s, and had made an impact with *Mean Streets* (1973) and *Alice Doesn't Live Here Anymore* (1974). The Phillipses came to it fresh from their success on the mainstream hit *The Sting* (1973), and Herrmann had, of course, composed a range of celebrated scores including those for *Citizen Kane*, *Vertigo* and *Psycho*. Other cast and crew members were, however, relatively unknown. For all its counter-cultural edginess of form and subject matter, *Taxi Driver* served to promote the careers of each of its central figures with audiences far wider than those to which they had hitherto had any currency. This is remarkable, considering the film's sheer disturbing strangeness, with a central character performing his story like a man visiting not just the hell of New York but the hell of his own mind, as he externalizes his own bitter psychosis, finally letting rip in the film's culminating scene of savage violence.

Taxi Driver is the disturbing story of Vietnam veteran Travis Bickle (De Niro) who returns to New York, darkly figured as the "excremental city", to deploy Robin Wood's term. The film's plot is fairly sparse and, typical of Scorsese's wider œuvre, is character-driven rather than plot-driven, developing his interest in damaged male psyches. Bickle (termed "God's lonely man" in Schrader's original script), finds work as a taxi driver, becoming increasingly horrified by the scenes of exploitation and decadence he witnesses as he cruises around the city at night. Scenes in his apartment show him honing himself into an armed vigilante fit to defeat the enemy. After a failed romance with a glamorous political campaign worker (Cybill Shepherd) and a failed assassination attempt upon her employer Senator Palantine (Leonard Harris), Bickle sets about trying to save child-prostitute Iris (Jodie Foster). It is Iris's pimp (Keitel), plus sundry johns, whom Bickle attacks in the showdown. For an epilogue Scorsese's camera picks out some laudatory newspaper cuttings proclaiming Bickle not as dangerous psycho but as urban hero.

Jodie Foster in *Taxi Driver*

Travis Bickle is therefore an unsettling anti-hero figure, his moral stance qualified not only by the unnerving brutality of his retribution, but by the ambiguous qualities of the targets of his horror and sympathy. As played by a 12-year-old Foster, Iris is cool and as streetwise as Bickle, and seems to love her pimp, who in turn is sensitive to her, even if he is positioned as monstrous by other aspects of the film. And while the visual rhetoric of *Taxi Driver* forces us to follow Bickle's journey, identification with his character as hero – despite those closing news headlines – constantly wrongfoots the viewer looking for an anchor in the process of understanding the protagonist. Even Chapman's camera seems not to trust its primary object of focus, nor even – at times – to be particularly interested in him, and takes full advantage of a widescreen format to isolate its subject on a broad canvas. Here Scorsese engages in some peculiarly anti-Hollywood techniques of the kind that had, during the 1960s and early 1970s, caused so-called "Hollywood Renaissance" directors to be compared to the European new wave. Kolker (2000: 217) reads *Taxi Driver* as "an extension of *Mean Streets*", and like its predecessor (shot by Kent Wakeford), *Taxi Driver*'s jittery camera movements underline both the restless tensions of its urban milieu, and of its unsettled hero. At one point, when Bickle is making a phone call, the camera simply wanders off, looking around, showing us anything but him – walls, doors, an empty corridor, with Bickle's voice audibly desperate. For Robin Wood, this is part of *Taxi Driver*'s central failure at establishing "a consistent, and adequately rigorous, attitude to the protagonist" (1986: 53). The famous scene in which Bickle practises his quick-draw firearms skills with himself in the mirror ("You talking to me? There ain't nobody else here", he says to his reflection) is a masterpiece of paranoia, performance, and subjective-splitting, and one of several scenes in Scorsese's films in which men play out their problematic relationships with the image. Think of Jake La Motta's "I could have been a contender" speech at the end of *Raging Bull* (1980) – this is De Niro doing La Motta doing Brando – or Rupert Pupkin's stand-up comedy performance delivered to a still photograph of an audience that has been pasted onto his bedroom wall in *King of Comedy* (1983). When Travis addresses himself, it is hard to tell who is the "I" and who is the "you". If he is both, where are these beings positioned? Are they there, or aren't they? For Amy Taubin (1999: 19) the answer lies in the eye of the beholder: "Travis is largely a cipher that each viewer decodes with her or his own desire."

This is all in keeping with Scorsese's more generalized fascination with the foibles of contemporary masculinity, and with men's relationship to masochism and failure, beautifully borne out in *Raging Bull* and frequently played out by his muse of urban male neurosis, Robert de Niro, who has featured in eight Scorsese films. For Amy Taubin (1999: 17) "*Taxi Driver* is steeped in failure – the US failure in Vietnam, the failure of the 60s counterculture, and, most unnervingly, at least to 49 per cent of the population, the failure of masculinity itself." This failure is also frequently writ large on the damaged male body. As Bickle works out we see a scar on his shoulder, and the film's violence is lavishly aestheticized (comparisons can also be made with the fleshly damage and liberally disseminated bodily fluids of the fight sequences of *Raging Bull*, as well as man-on-man violence, often carried out to the accompaniment of sublime classical music or energizing pop soundtracks, in *Mean Streets*, *Goodfellas* and *Casino*).

There is also the question of how to place *Taxi Driver* generically. Ryan and Kellner (1988: 87–9) read it as an anti-liberal social problem film. Robin Wood reads it as warped homage to two classical Hollywood genres, both undergoing radical revisions in the period since 1960s. For Wood, it is both a horror film, featuring Bickle as psychopath-monster, and a Western, featuring him as gunfighter-hero. Both Taubin and Wood read it as a post-Vietnam reworking of *The Searchers*, with Sport as the Indian Scar who snatches the white girl as his squaw, and Bickle as John Wayne's Ethan, racist and heroic by turns. To Travis, 1970s street culture is what Native American Indian culture is to Ethan. *Taxi Driver* has also been widely read as an embryonic form of neo-*noir*, refitting the *noir*ish city of nightmares with the contemporary props of the counter-culture. For Cynthia Fuchs (1991: 34) *Taxi Driver* is "noir meets Nam"; its "revisionary use of film noir stylistics (such as shadows, neon, and the voice-over narration) and thematic concerns (the duplicitous woman, the inadvertent hero, the confusion of a world out of balance) complement its Vietnam context". The extreme imagery also posed a challenge for classifiers; as Cook (2000: 146) reports, "*Taxi Driver* pushed the R-rating envelope just about as far as it would go, suggesting that a limit of tolerance had been reached for CARA and audiences alike." Acutely aware of the cinematic history which frames his films, none of this is lost on Scorsese. He is resolutely the filmmaker's filmmaker, a cinephile who has become "the self-appointed guardian of American cinema history" (Larke 2002: 289); (see also *A Personal Journey with Martin Scorsese through American Movies*, Scorsese and Wilson, 1997). The *noir* stylings are a consciously knowing nod to a film tradition he grew up on and loves. Yet film history is only one of *Taxi Driver*'s historical coordinates. It is also a "returning veteran" movie, of which there were a number from the mid-1970s onwards (*Coming Home*, *The Deer Hunter* and, later *Born on the Fourth of July*). However, the "othering" demarcation between home/foreign upon which returning vet stories rest is problematized in *Taxi Driver*, which reads New York itself as a battle zone. Made in the wake of the US retreat from Saigon, it focuses on "the war at home"; Bickle, indeed, declares war *on* home. He is, then, not so much a returning vet as a soldier continuing his campaign on a different front, a place where "all the animals come out at night". It is consequently often hard to tell unequivocally who's on which side: "Sport and Travis will meet at this self-reflexive crossroads-as-mirror", writes Fuchs (1991: 46). This is a place "where the cowboys look like Indians, where Americans were killing themselves as well as others in Vietnam, where difference is made similarity". This is a place where moral distinctions begin to collapse, and not only does the image of the enemy become unclear, the image of the self becomes deeply unsettling.

References

Cook, D.A. (2000) *Lost Illusions: American Cinema in the Shadow of Watergate and Vietnam, 1970–1979* Berkeley. University of California Press.

Fuchs, C.J. (1991) "All the animals come out at night": Vietnam meets *noir* in *Taxi Driver*, in M. Anderegg (ed.) *Inventing Vietnam: The War in Film and Television*. Philadelphia, PA: Temple University Press.

Kolker, R. (2000) *A Cinema of Loneliness: Penn, Stone, Kubrick, Scorsese, Spielberg, Altman*. Oxford: Oxford University Press.

Larke, G.S. (2002) Martin Scorsese: movies and religion, in Y. Tasker (ed.) *Fifty Contemporary Filmmakers*. London: Routledge, pp. 289–96.

Ryan, M. and Kellner, D. (1988) *Camera Politica: The Politics and Ideology of Contemporary Hollywood Film*. Bloomington: Indiana University Press.

Scorsese, M. and Wilson, M. (1997) *A Personal Journey with Martin Scorsese through American Movies*. London: Faber.

Taubin, A. (1999) God's lonely man, *Sight and Sound*, 4(9): 17–19.

Wood, R. (1986) *Hollywood from Vietnam to Reagan*. New York: Columbia University Press.

Linda Ruth Williams

In the full beam of America's increasingly bright media spotlight, Jane Fonda has graduated from sex kitten to radical activist to *grande dame*. Daughter of a legendary showbiz dynasty (socialite Frances Seymour Brokaw and cinema icon Henry Fonda), her biography charts the achievements of a woman born into old Hollywood who then helped to shape New Hollywood's presentation of women and its approach to social issues. But it is also the story of the radical transformations in US culture and counter-culture from the 1950s to the present – few female performers are as identified with their troubled times as is Fonda. Her star identity is then constructed as much by what is known of her public campaigning and private life as it is by her complex cinematic performances. This is a central contradiction in how she is publicly conceived – an independent feminist radical who is nevertheless framed by the coordinates of her relationships with others (father Henry, brother Peter Fonda, niece Bridget Fonda, as well as her various husbands – director Roger Vadim, activist Tom Hayden, and CNN mogul Ted Turner); "Jane Fonda's relationship to men has been a central theme around which her image has been organised at certain times" (Perkins 1991: 238).

Her passage into movies seems in retrospect effortless but Fonda became interested in acting fairly late in her young adulthood, taking private classes with Lee Strasberg (Fonda 2005: 112–25). She made her movie debut in 1960 with *Tall Story*, distinguished herself in Elliot Silverstein's *Cat Ballou* (1965) and Arthur Penn's *The Chase* (1966), became a fully paid-up 1960s icon in the title role of *Barbarella* (1968), directed by her then-husband Roger Vadim. But Fonda came of age with a series of films that established her as a serious, skilled performer, marked by often politically questioning roles: *They Shoot Horses, Don't They?* (1969), *Klute* (1971), *A Doll's House* (1973), *Julia* (1977), *Coming Home* (1978), *The China Syndrome* (1979), *The Electric Horseman* (1979), *Nine to Five* (1980) and *On Golden Pond* (1981).

Reception of these movies, and of Fonda's wider public profile, was profoundly inflected by her support, from the late 1960s onwards, for political activities such as the Black Panther movement and anti-Vietnam War protests, garnering her the nickname "Hanoi Jane" following her meeting with the Vietcong in North Vietnam in 1972; see Hershberger (2005) and Holzer and Holzer (2002) for detailed discussions of this chapter of Fonda's life. She also, arguably due to her feminism, had "trouble with the male left, who attacked her for different reasons than those for which the mainstream was attacking her" (Perkins 1991: 244); Perkins cites as evidence Jean-Luc Godard and Jean Pierre Gorin's critical documentary *Letter to Jane* (1972), made after she had featured in the former's 1972 film *Tout Va Bien*. Richard Dyer reads her as an ambiguous all-American heroine: "Fonda-as-star-as-revolutionary dramatises the problem of what role privileged white people can have in the struggles of under-privileged non-whites" (Dyer 1998: 78). Thus Fonda was attacked as too left-wing for the right-wing establishment, and either not left-wing enough, or else too feminist, for the male left. It is testament to her power in Hollywood, as well as – of course – her talent, that "Hanoi Jane" could continue making films at all. She won her first Oscar, for *Klute*, in the midst of the most antagonistic press coverage. This is the film that perhaps has most significance for feminist critics (two key essays on it by Gledhill, reassessing both feminism and genre, formed the opening and closing statements for the influential 1978 collection *Women in Film Noir*). It is also easy to forget that the home front saga, *Coming Home*, for which she won her second Oscar, was produced by Fonda's company IPC, named after the Indochinese Peace Campaign which she helped to organize. David Thomson (himself something of an opinionist) has called her "the fiercest opinionist in American show business" (Thomson 2004: 299); it has been said that she views "every one of her roles in broader sociological terms" (Abramowitz 2000: 129).

Jane Fonda with Donald Sutherland in *Klute*

Though she is adept at comedy when she gets a chance, her signature style is that of the brainy, often uptight woman, sometimes struggling to find hope in difficult contemporary circumstances, sometimes succeeding in securing justice or at least revealing how the personal is the political (her films often chart the radicalization or enlightenment of initially naïve characters). But equally influential on her star image have been her pioneering exercise videos and recordings in the 1970s and 1980s; *Jane Fonda's Workout* (1982) is one of the most successful fitness artefacts ever and she capitalized on this with a series of videos and publications on exercise and health, and, latterly, empowerment and ageing. Her 2005 autobiography, *My Life So Far*, details her anguished relationship with her father, with whom she starred in *On Golden Pond* (sometimes read as a semi-biographical film), and her lifelong battle with eating disorders. After a lengthy semi-retirement from the screen, she returned in barnstorming form as the appallingly badly behaved mother-in-law of *Monster-in-Law* (2005). The image of a troubled, talented, thinking woman that emerges from these texts makes Fonda a compelling, if contradictory, icon of late twentieth-century US cinema.

References

Abramowitz, R. (2000) *Is That a Gun in Your Pocket? Women's Experience of Power in Hollywood*. New York: Random House.

Dyer, R. (1998) *Stars*, new edition. London: BFI.

Fonda, J. (2005) *My Life So Far*. London: Ebury Press.

Gledhill, C. (1978) *Klute* 1: a contemporary film noir and feminist criticism, and *Klute* 2: feminism and *Klute*, both in E.A. Kaplan (ed.) *Women and Film Noir*. London: BFI.

Hershberger, M. (2005) *Jane Fonda's War: A Political Biography of an Antiwar Icon*. New York: The New Press.

Holzer, H.M. and Holzer, E. (2002) *Aid and Comfort: Jane Fonda in North Vietnam*. New York: McFarland.

Perkins, T. (1991) The politics of ''Jane Fonda'', in C. Gledhill (ed.) *Stardom: Industry of Desire*. London: Routledge.

Thomson, D. (2004) Jane Fonda, in *The New Biographical Dictionary of Film*, 4th edn. London: Little, Brown.

Linda Ruth Williams

BLOCKBUSTERS IN THE 1970s

Sheldon Hall

Production, distribution and exhibition

The virtual collapse of Hollywood in the fiscal crisis of 1969–71 resulted in a period of drastic reorganization by the studios. The capping of budgets by almost all the companies and the reduction of output overall resulted in an initial retreat from production of the large-scale spectaculars and big-budget blockbusters that had characterized the preceding two decades.

In addition to a general fall in the cost of the average picture, this retrenchment was most evident in the fall in costs for the industry's front-rank releases. The most expensive pictures of 1969 and 1970 – Twentieth Century Fox's *Hello, Dolly!* (1969) and *Tora! Tora! Tora!* (1970), both of which had entered production before the crisis was apparent – cost over $25 million apiece, more than any previous Hollywood film with the exception of Fox's *Cleopatra* (1963). By contrast, the most expensive pictures of 1972, Paramount's *The Godfather* and Warner Bros' *The Cowboys*, each cost just over $6 million. Between 1971 and 1975 inclusive, only ten Hollywood pictures cost $10 million or more, and, with the possible exception of Disney's *Bedknobs and Broomsticks* (1971), none cost more than $15 million (*Variety*, 20 January 1988: 64).

However, this period of relative parsimony did not last for long. As the decade progressed, the cost of the average studio picture rose steadily, with a particular leap occurring between 1977 and 1978 – significantly, following the release of Fox's *Star Wars* (1977), which itself cost $11 million. Between 1976 and 1980 inclusive, at least 23 pictures cost $20 million or more, with another ten costing between $14 million and $19 million. *King Kong* (Paramount/Universal, 1976), *A Bridge Too Far* (United Artists, 1977), *The Wiz* (Universal, 1978) and *1941* (Universal, 1979) each cost around $25 million; *Apocalypse Now* (UA, 1979), *Moonraker* (UA, 1979), *The Blues Brothers* (Universal, 1980) and *The Empire Strikes Back* (Fox, 1980) each cost around $30 million; *Heaven's Gate* (UA, 1980, Fig. 12 (*see plate section*)) and *Raise the Titanic* (ITC, 1980) both cost $36 million, *Star Trek – The Motion Picture* (Paramount, 1979) cost $42 million, and *Superman* (Warner, 1978) and *Superman II* (Warner, 1980) each around $55 million.

The resumption of the studios' interest in blockbusters was partly caused by the structural organization of the industry following the effective collapse in the 1960s of the traditional studio system. The purchase by multinational conglomerates of several of the major corporations from the early 1960s onwards, the subsequent diversification of the remainder into various non-film activities, and ultimately the restructuring in the 1970s of all the studios into media entertainment conglomerates provided not only a safety net for a large investment (losses in theatrical film divisions could be offset by the profitability of other areas) but an incentive: the popular success of a blockbuster could be "spun off" into the ancillary markets (such as toys, games, book and music publishing, television and video) in which the studios also had an interest. They therefore represented, and continue to represent, "a safe risk": the higher the stakes, the greater are both the safeguards and the potential rewards (Wyatt 1994: 77–81). The latter were vividly demonstrated by the unprecedented grosses achieved by a number of pictures in the 1970s, which resulted in the industry record for the highest domestic grosses being broken four times throughout the decade: in turn by *The Godfather, The Exorcist* (Warner, 1973, Fig. 5 (*see plate section*)), *Jaws* (Universal, 1975) and *Star Wars*. The safeguards against failure, and the means of attaining the rewards, lay in the methods used in distribution.

Blockbusters offered the kind of prime product needed to entice exhibitors to offer competitive bids against one another for the right to play the picture (effectively a resumption of the practice of "blind bidding" previously outlawed by anti-trust legislation in the 1940s), to guarantee it extended playing time (exhibition contracts often specified a minimum length of run), and to pay advances on anticipated box-office receipts. Exhibitors' advance payments and guarantees allowed the studios to begin paying off their production loans some time before the pictures opened (and in many cases before the films had even

been completed). The banks themselves could be persuaded of the safety of their capital investment if the blockbusters seemed guaranteed of success (such ventures seeming more assured of an audience than most lower-cost pictures). The steep rental terms demanded for them, combined with the non-returnable advances, gave the distributors the upper hand and helped insure them against losses even if the box office ultimately proved disappointing.

The promise of a blockbuster also permitted distributors to exact a larger than usual proportion of the box-office gross from exhibitors. By the early 1960s in the United States this had typically reached 90/10 for road-shows: that is, up to 90 per cent of receipts after deduction of the "house nut" (theatre operating expenses) were to be remitted to the distributor. While this situation may seem extortionate (and must have done to many exhibitors), it was usually applicable only to the very early stages of a run; thereafter, a "sliding scale" took over, with rentals reducing in increments over the weeks or months of the run, though usually with a minimum percentage of the gross specified as a "floor". Although initially reserved only for key theatres in New York and Los Angeles, especially for road-shows, the 90/10 arrangement eventually became standard for national first-run exhibition of most pictures (Balio 1987: 208).[1]

With deals such as these, the studios were able to cushion themselves against the possibility of box-office failure and to reduce their exposure in the event of a flop. Only when the product delivered proved unsaleable to exhibitors and public alike did a complete disaster result, as happened with United Artists' *Heaven's Gate*. In this case, the film's critical and commercial reception was so poor that it was withdrawn from its New York premiere

Continued on page 169

Steven Spielberg and E.T.

In recent years it has become increasingly difficult to summarize Steven Spielberg's work as a director, writer, producer, entrepreneur, mentor and patron.[1] He has been involved in too many projects to count, among them dozens of movies and also numerous television series ranging from *Amazing Stories* (1985–97) and the animated *Animaniacs* (1993–98) to the top-rated episodic drama *ER* (1994–) and the high profile mini-series *Band of Brothers* (2001) and *Taken* (2002). Today Spielberg is best known for the movies he has directed since 1974; for founding the production house Amblin Entertainment in 1984 and the multibillion-dollar major studio Dream Works SKG in 1994; and for his support of various Jewish history projects, most notably the Survivors of the Shoah Visual History Foundation, which he launched in 1994.

Unlike some of his contemporaries, such as Francis Ford Coppola and George Lucas, Spielberg has always worked with, rather than against, the major Hollywood studios. Starting out as an amateur filmmaker in his teens, he first worked as a contract director for Universal's television department from 1968 and then made the transition to theatrical features with *The Sugarland Express* (again Universal) in 1974. Following the enormous success of *Jaws*, Spielberg gained an exceptionally high degree of control over the films he made. However, while he was given story or script credits for several of his early features, after *E.T.* he preferred to work with other people's material in his features (the only exception being *A.I.*). Starting in 1977, Spielberg made films for all the majors, and early on he formed particularly close relationships with two industry leaders – Universal's Sidney Sheinberg in the 1970s and soon afterwards Steve Ross at Warner Bros. With Sheinberg and Ross as his mentors, Spielberg was able to set up his own companies and in turn to support many young filmmakers. Chief among them were Robert Zemeckis (whose script for *1941* Spielberg filmed in 1979 and whose early directorial efforts he produced) and Chris Columbus (who wrote the scripts for two early Amblin productions, *Gremlins* and *The Goonies*).

Of the 50 all-time top grossing films in the United States as of May 2003, Spielberg has directed seven (*E.T.* at number 3, *Jurassic Park* at number 6, *Jaws* at number 21, *Raiders of the Lost Ark* at number 26, *The Lost World* at number 32, *Saving Private Ryan* at number 38, *Indiana Jones and the Last Crusade* at number 49) and produced another three (*Men in Black*, 1997, *Twister*, 1996, and *Back to the Future*, 1985); the Dream Works production *Shrek* (2001) also made it onto the list.[2] In addition to *Back to the Future*, another six films in the top 50 were directed by Spielberg's protégés Zemeckis and Columbus, most of them – notably *Forrest Gump* (1994) and the first two *Harry Potter* films (2001 and 2002) – with a distinctly Spielbergian flavour.

At the heart of Spielberg's filmmaking are his overwhelming desire and exceptional ability to move audiences (that is, to provide them with sensual thrills and emotional stimulation). He focuses strongly on families both on and off screen, telling stories about problem-ridden relationships between parents and children to multigenerational audiences. He is driven by a belief in cinema's potential to engage people with important developments in American and indeed world history, to offer models of moral behaviour, and even its ability to provide spiritual comfort. His mastery of extended yet unflaggingly suspenseful chase sequences was already fully developed in his made-for-TV movie *Duel*, and it later shaped the second half of *Jaws* as well as, for example, large parts of the *Indiana Jones* and *Jurassic Park* films. Awe-inspiring spectacle, which overwhelms characters on the screen as much as the people in front of it, can be found in many Spielberg films, beginning with the climactic sequence of *Close Encounters of the Third Kind*. While Spielberg's initial attempts at slapstick and romantic comedy (*1941* and *Always*) were commercial and critical flops, his ability to move mass audiences to tears was in evidence in films ranging from *E.T.* to *The Color Purple* and *Schindler's List*.

The most intense sadness in Spielberg's films is often associated with the separation of people, both young and old, from their parents or parental substitutes (like E.T., or Captain John Miller in *Saving Private Ryan*). Indeed, many of his films – starting with his first theatrical feature – revolve around incomplete, dysfunctional or disintegrating families and around weak, absent, abusive or irresponsible fathers and father figures. The films often trace the attempts of children and women to come to terms with the damage the fathers have done (as, for example, in *E.T.*, *The Color Purple* and *Indiana Jones and the Last Crusade*), or the attempts of paternal figures to redeem themselves (as, for example, in *Jaws*, *Hook*, *Jurassic Park*, *Schindler's List* and *Minority Report*). In several instances, the films end by emphasizing the primacy of the mother–child bond, as in *E.T.*, *The Color Purple* and, most strikingly, *A.I.* Arguably, Spielberg's focus on problematic father figures and disintegrating families is typical of the baby-boom generation to which he belongs. Born in 1946, Spielberg had first-hand experience of the dramatic rise in the divorce rate when his parents split up in 1965 and again when his own first marriage with Amy Irving failed in 1989. Like the majority of baby boomers, he became a parent in the 1980s, eventually forming a large family with

Steven Spielberg

second wife Kate Capshaw, which included his own offspring as well as a stepchild and adopted children. Thus, Spielberg's biography – as well as his filmic output – is in line with his generation's move away from the traditional family towards other familial configurations.

Furthermore, Spielberg shares some of the political concerns of the baby-boom generation. While apparently disconnected from the Civil Rights movement during his youth in the 1960s, he later used his clout as a commercial filmmaker to make a black-cast historical woman's picture based on Alice Walker's Pulitzer Prize-winning novel *The Color Purple* and to launch his Dream Works studio with the slavery epic *Amistad*. His concern for black history was probably connected with the rediscovery of his own ethnicity (again in line with broader trends among baby boomers in the 1970s and 1980s), which culminated in the production of the Holocaust drama *Schindler's List*. The spiritual dimension of this film, and of other Spielberg films ranging from *Close Encounters* and *Raiders of the Lost Ark* to *The Color Purple* and *Always*, corresponds to a wider return to religious traditions among baby boomers since the 1970s. Finally, already during his teens, Spielberg took the Second World War as the single most important historical reference point for his films. From the Indianapolis speech in *Jaws*, the comedy of *1941* and the prewar Nazi capers of *Raiders of the Lost Ark* to the in-depth exploration of the wartime experiences of civilians and combat soldiers in *Empire of the Sun* and *Saving Private Ryan*, Spielberg persistently returns – as do many baby boomers – to the historical event that had shaped his parents' generation.

It is also his fellow baby boomers who have constituted a substantial portion of the American cinema audience since the 1960s. Together with his talents as a filmmaker and his ability to cooperate with the major studios, this generational sense has enabled him to make a number of crucial interventions into the development of the American entertainment industry. For instance, in 1975, *Jaws* became the model for the contemporary "summer movie": a big-budget youth-oriented rollercoaster ride given a wide release supported by television advertising.[3] Together with the *Star Wars* trilogy, many of the films Spielberg directed and produced between 1977 and 1985 helped to return family entertainment (rather than youth entertainment) to the centre of Hollywood's output, where it has remained ever since.[4] The success of Spielberg's animated production (*An American Tail*, 1986) and (*Who Framed Roger Rabbit?*, 1988) contributed to the revitalization of Disney's animation division and an overall increase in animated features across the industry in the 1990s. His heavy investment in epic films about nineteenth- and twentieth-century history from 1985 onwards, in particular the commercial and critical success of *Schindler's List* and *Saving Private Ryan* (for both of which he received Best Director Oscars), was a crucial factor in relaunching the historical epic as an important Hollywood genre. Spielberg's influence can be felt everywhere in contemporary Hollywood: in serious explorations of religion, history and science such as *Contact* (1997); in *Titanic* (1997) and other modern epics; in Disney and Pixar's computer-animated superhits; in blockbuster adaptations of children's literature; and, more generally, in the abundance of thrilling summer movies.

Notes

1   For a more extensive summary, see my Steven Spielberg in Tasker (2002: 319–28). The best biographical study is McBride (1997). A wide range of interviews are reprinted in Friedman and Notbohm (2000). A review of early writing on Spielberg can be found in Gordon (1989). Analyses of a range of Spielberg films are contained in Silet (2002).

2   "The Top Grossing Moves of All Time at the USA Box Office", *Internet Movie Database*, http://us.imdb.com/Charts/usatopmovies, accessed May 2003.

3   See Schatz (1993: 8–36).
4   See Chapter 12 in this book.

References

Friedman, L.D. and Notbohm, B. (eds) (2000) *Steven Spielberg: Interviews*. Jackson: University Press of Mississippi.

Gordon, A. (1989) Science-fiction and fantasy film criticism: the case of Lucas and Spielberg, *Journal of the Fantastic in the Arts*, 2(2): 81–94.

Krämer, P. (2002) Steven Spielberg, in Y. Tasker (ed.) *Fifty Contemporary Filmmakers*. London: Routledge.

McBride, J. (1997) *Steven Spielberg: A Biography*. London: Faber and Faber.

Schatz, T. (1993) The new Hollywood, in J. Collins, H. Radner and A. Preacher Collins (eds) *Film Theory Goes to the Movies*. New York: Routledge, pp. 8–36.

Silet, C.L.P. (ed.) (2002) *The Films of Steven Spielberg*. London: Scarecrow Press.

Peter Krämer

Continued from page 165

engagement within a week of opening to be re-edited, and when it re-emerged six months later few takers could be found among wary exhibitors, resulting in a loss of $44 million. As a consequence, United Artists' corporate owners, Transamerica, sold the cash-strapped company to MGM, in the first instance since RKO's liquidation in the late 1950s of a major studio going under (although United Artists still exists today as a production subsidiary of MGM, and both are now owned, along with Columbia-TriStar, by the Sony Corporation of Japan).

Though many of the late 1970s big-budget pictures were in some ways comparable in scale to their late 1960s counterparts, the methods of distributing and marketing them were quite different. The tried and tested road-show method of slow, staggered release and exclusive, two-shows-a-day exhibition at raised prices had largely been discredited by the crisis of 1969–71, which was often blamed on the excessive number of road-shows competing for a limited market. Although there were still a few remaining in the early 1970s – *Nicholas and Alexandra* and *Fiddler on the Roof* (both 1971), for example, were road-shown in the traditional manner – by 1976 road-shows had become scarce enough for *Variety* to refer in passing, in its year-end box-office survey, to "road-show type films (remember them?)" (Frederick 1976: 18). Instead, new distribution and exhibition patterns came to prominence, and with them different patterns of commercial performance and different generic cycles from those which had characterized Hollywood heretofore.

The new era of blockbuster distribution was inaugurated by the wide, "saturation" releases of *The Godfather*, which opened concurrently in five New York theatres and 350 nationwide, and *Jaws*, which opened on 464 domestic screens, accompanied by a massive nationwide print and television advertising campaign. Both these films became, in succession, the most commercially successful yet released, ultimately grossing $80.3 million and $129.5 million, respectively, in the domestic market. Before *The Godfather* and *Jaws* this

Table 7.1 Total number of engagements of *Star Wars* (Fox, 1977) in the first 11 weeks of its initial US release.

Weekend	Date	Engagements
Opening day	25 May	32
1	27 May	43
2	3 June	45
3	10 June	48
4	17 June	157
5	24 June	360
6	1 July	496
7	8 July	577
8	15 July	628
9	22 July	811
10	29 July	956
11	5 August	1,044

(Source: Coate 2003)

sort of policy had been associated with low-grade exploitation pictures, which stood to benefit from a "hit-and-run" strategy: it had been pioneered on a regional basis by David O. Selznick for his "sex Western" *Duel in the Sun* (1946), and on a national basis by Joseph E. Levine for the low-budget Italian imports *Hercules* (Warner, 1958) and *Hercules Unchained* (Warner, 1959). However, it was the 1970s blockbusters that set the pattern for the future in being high-prestige, major-studio releases (Wyatt 1998: 78–9; Hall 2002).

Saturation release on a blockbuster scale incurs massive costs in prints and publicity, including television advertising (in which Levine had also been a pioneer). Successive films have raised the stakes by increasing the number of screens on which they are released, rising from the 900 prints on which *King Kong* was released a year after *Jaws* to the more than 3000 prints used for 1990s blockbusters like Spielberg's *Jurassic Park* (Universal, 1993). There are, of course, partial exceptions to this pattern. *Star Wars* opened in the United States in only 32 engagements, as according to some reports, exhibitors could not initially be convinced of its box-office potential; others suggest that this limited "platform" release was a deliberate marketing strategy by Fox. Nonetheless, the film proved an instant success, grossing $2.1 million in its first four days, thus ensuring far wider subsequent distribution, with over 1000 engagements by the eleventh week of its initial release and over 1750 for its 1978 reissue (Coate 2003; see Table 7.1).

Such saturation coverage is made possible by the increased number of screens brought about by the rise of the multiplex theatre. The late 1960s and 1970s saw a cinema-building boom in America, with the number of indoor cinema screens in America increasing from around 10,000 in 1975 to 22,750 by 1990 (Schatz 1993: 20). The vast majority of these were in multiplexes constructed inside shopping malls or in out-of-town leisure parks. With a dozen or more screens available under a single roof, a blockbuster may now open on as many screens as the distributor and exhibitors see fit.

Generic cycles and production trends

One conspicuous feature of *Variety*'s annual box-office charts from 1970 onwards was their domination in each year by one or two films, which showed a clear lead over all other releases. For example, in 1970 Universal's *Airport* earned nearly $10 million more than its nearest rival, Fox's *M*A*S*H*; the following year, Paramount's *Love Story* (which opened at Christmas 1970) earned over $20 million more than Fox's *The French Connection*; and in 1972, Paramount's *The Godfather* earned more than twice as much (some $80 million in total) as United Artist's *Fiddler on the Roof*. This phenomenon led to the increasing interest of the major studios in developing "tentpoles": films that, by virtue of their stand-alone popularity, or their potential as a "franchise" (a picture defined by its ability to generate various spinoffs such as sequels and merchandising opportunities), could be capable of propping up the entire studio's operations for a season or more, wiping out its losses on lesser pictures and in effect subsidizing riskier ventures. Conversely, nine out of ten releases could be expected to earn no more than break-even profits, or to lose money.

Such franchises occasionally arose out of a "sleeper" (surprise hit) which exceeded all expectations, most notably in the case of *Star Wars*. Increasingly, however, tentpoles were planned, carefully nurtured and developed from initial concept to fully realized package. Paramount's *Love Story* and *The Godfather* represent seminal early instances of such a process, as the company, through its corporate owner Gulf & Western's publishing subsidiary Simon & Schuster, published and marketed the novels on which the films were based (*Love Story* was actually Erich Segal's novelization of his screenplay, but it was published before the film's release precisely to stimulate advance interest in it) and then precisely targeted the films' promotional campaigns at the books' readers.

Adaptations of, and tie-ins with, bestselling novels were key features of blockbusters in the first half of the 1970s. Virtually all the highest grossing films of the year for every year between 1970 and 1976, including *Airport*, *Love Story*, *The Godfather*, *The Poseidon Adventure* (Fox, 1972), *The Exorcist*, *The Towering Inferno* (Fox/Warner, 1974), *Jaws* and *One Flew Over the Cuckoo's Nest* (United Artists, 1975), were adapted from popular novels (*The Towering Inferno* was actually adapted from two). This pattern began to change significantly in the later 1970s, after which a more likely tie-in source for a blockbuster hit was a comic-strip (*Superman*), a television series (*Star Trek – The Motion Picture*) or, most commonly, another film.

Sequels were not unknown in Classical Hollywood, but they tended to be rare among prestige pictures: in the 1930s and 1940s the series film was most likely to be a "B" picture. The 1960s saw the first sequel/series franchise of the modern era in the James Bond films, which began in 1962 and have continued until (at the time of writing) 2006. *Planet of the Apes* (Fox, 1968) led to another four feature films, a live-action and an animated TV series between 1970 and 1976, but the theatrical sequels were made on progressively smaller budgets to successively smaller box-office returns. From about 1974 onwards, the studios began to treat sequels as major events in their own right, in many cases costing more than their originals:

Continued on page 174

Spanning four decades, from 1977 to 2005, George Lucas's six-part *Star Wars* saga has become the most profitable screen franchise of all time. Originally conceived as a mid-priced sci-fi romp, tailor-made for cinematic audiences, this big-screen spectacle broke video and DVD records, wooing new generations of home viewers who would subsequently put its belated trio of prequels at the top of the box office. More than just an example of emergent blockbuster cinema, *Star Wars* and its sequels/prequels serve as a perfect paradigm for the synergistic relationship between film, video, and ancillary marketing.

Set "Long ago, in a galaxy far far away", the *Star Wars* cycle follows the oedipal inter-family fortunes of Luke Skywalker and his nemesis Darth Vader, an imperial warmonger who is revealed (in *The Empire Strikes Back*, 1980) to be Luke's father. A quest to rescue Princess Leia (Luke's long-lost sister) and aid her rebel comrades in their struggle against the Empire leads the young Jedi Knight on a voyage of spiritual discovery, guided by the twin forces of Obi-Wan Kenobi and the gremlin-like Yoda, to a final restoration of cosmic "balance" in "The Force" (*The Return of the Jedi*, 1983). The later trio of prequels covers the transformation of the young innocent Anakin Skywalker (*The Phantom Menace*, 1999) through his Jedi training (*Attack of the Clones*, 2002) and eventual conversion to "The Dark Side" (*Revenge of the Sith*, 2005), mirroring the Republic's corrupt mutation into an Empire as Anakin becomes Darth Vader.

Taking his inspiration from a blend of fairytale myths and the literary traditions of Joseph Campbell and Carlos Castenada, Lucas strove in *Star Wars* (1977) for a nostalgic recreation of the cliffhanger suspense and knockabout action of Saturday morning sci-fi serials. Having cut his auteur-teeth on the esoteric sci-fi film *THX1138* (1970), Lucas devoted a significant part of *Star Wars'* comparatively moderate budget to the creation of spectacular interstellar dogfights, aided by John Dykstra's pioneering computerized motion-control systems for Industrial Light and Magic. A groundbreaking (and Oscar-winning) Dolby stereo soundtrack

Star Wars: Surprise hit becomes global franchise

also upped the sensory ante, paving the way for Lucasfilms' THX trademarked sound systems, which guaranteed the highest level of theatrical sound reproduction. (Twenty years later, the prequels would test the boundaries of digital visual technology and virtual computer-generated environs.)

The original *Star Wars* was finished for around $12 million, and "neither Lucasfilm nor Fox expected to earn back more than about twice that in domestic rentals, because of the traditionally hard-sell market for science fiction" (Cook 2000: 139). Yet by November 1977, *Star Wars* had eclipsed *Jaws* as the highest grossing film ever made, a phenomenon that redefined the accounting parameters of the blockbuster movie. According to Tim Corrigan, Lucas's space fantasy played a key role in the industry's belief that "a movie could attract audiences through the excess of its investment in capital, technology, and any other assets that carry the glow of extremity". Its unprecedented box-office success encouraged conglomerates to "pursue the *Star Wars* figures; $27 million invested in 1977 ... returning well over $500 million by 1980, for a 1,855 percent profit in three years" (Corrigan 1991: 20). Lucas, meanwhile, wisely retained both sequel and merchandising rights, the latter of which soon outstripped the profits of the film itself, approaching the billion-dollar mark by the decade's end (Cook 2000: 140).

Exactly what audiences saw in *Star Wars* and its spin-offs, which included two best-forgotten TV "Ewok" adventures, *Caravan of Courage* (1984) and *Battle for Endor* (1985), remains a source of heated debate. In their influential work *Camera Politica*, Ryan and Kellner argue that *Star Wars* (a.k.a. *Episode IV*) offered "A New Hope" for white middle-class Americans alarmed by the changes of mid-1970s society. "The rhetoric of the film," they write:

> promotes individualism against the state, nature against technology, authenticity against artifice, faith and feeling against science and rationality, agrarian values against urban modernity, etc. ... The film thus displays the ingredients of the dominant American conservative ideology that makes US culture so resistant to urban-based rational socialist ideals. (Ryan and Kellner 1988: 229–30)

Addressing the fans whose devotion to the *Star Wars* franchise has partly defined the series' cultural status, Matt Hills (2003: 118) concludes that the apparently contradictory phenomenon of

> [the] cult blockbuster does not represent a phantom menace, that of the loss of all cultural hierarchies and forms of cultural status. Instead, it offers a new hope: that established patterns of cultural status can be, and have been, reconfigured via the situated agency of fans, theorists, producers, marketers and journalists.

As for Lucas, he could be found, while promoting *Revenge of the Sith* at the Cannes Film Festival in May 1998, apparently endorsing a reading of the *Star Wars* saga as an unfolding metaphor for American politics from Vietnam to Iraq.

Significantly, the only common critical consensus on the *Star Wars* cycle is that, despite twice being Oscar-nominated as Best Director, Lucas remains essentially a producer. Having previously scored a popular hit with *American Graffiti* (1973), he handed directorial chores on the two *Star Wars* sequels over to Irvin Kershner and Richard Marquand respectively, with winning results. Throughout the 1980s, he supplemented the success of his *Star Wars* output by co-producing Steven Spielberg's *Indiana Jones* movies, which rapidly became the second most successful film franchise of all time, giving Lucas a credit on five out of ten of the decade's highest earning films. With his financial autonomy unassailable, and the multiple merchandising rights to the *Star Wars* series secured, Lucas's uncertain return to the directorial chair to helm *Episodes I–III* seemed more an act of vanity than creativity. While history may remember him as one of the era's definitive movie moguls, Lucas's aspiration to become a respected auteur remains perhaps his greatest fantasy.

References

Cook, D.A. (2000) *Lost Illusions: American Cinema in the Shadow of Watergate and Vietnam, 1970–1979*. Berkeley: University of California Press.
Corrigan, T. (1991) *A Cinema Without Walls: Movies and Culture After Vietnam*. New Brunswick: Rutgers University Press.
Hills, M. (2003) *Star Wars* in fandom, film theory, and the museum, in J. Stringer (ed.) *Movie Blockbusters*. London: Routledge, pp. 178–89.
Ryan, M. and Kellner, D. (1988) *Camera Politica: The Politics and Ideology of Contemporary Hollywood Film*. Bloomington: Indiana University Press.

Mark Kermode

Continued from page 171

examples include *The Godfather, Part II* (Paramount, 1974), which cost $15 million compared to *The Godfather*'s $6.2 million (and earned less than half as much), and *Jaws 2* (Universal, 1978), which cost $20 million compared to *Jaws*' $12 million. Of the 55 films listed in Table 7.2 as the highest grossing films for each of their respective years between 1970 and 1980, 23 resulted in one or more sequels, and a further six are themselves sequels.

The success of certain films also resulted in numerous short-term cycles of generically similar but narratively unrelated pictures. Thus, as well as inspiring direct sequels, *The French Connection* and *Dirty Harry* (Warner, 1971) led to a spate of violent "dirty cop" films; in addition to its two sequels, *The Godfather* produced a cycle of gangster sagas; *The Last Picture Show* (Columbia, 1971), *Summer of '42* (Warner, 1971) and *American Graffiti* (Universal, 1973, Fig. 7 (*see plate section*)) prompted a number of nostalgic high-school comedies and dramas, to which *National Lampoon's Animal House* (Universal, 1978) and its progeny added gross-out humour; *Enter the Dragon* (Warner, 1973) heralded the popularity in the West of the martial arts action thriller; *The Exorcist, The Omen* (Fox, 1976) and the enormously profitable independent release *Halloween* (Compass International, 1978) all led to cycles of horror films in their various subgenres.

Commercially perhaps the most significant blockbuster genres to come to prominence in the 1970s were the disaster film and science fiction. *Airport* was not the first disaster film: a cycle of costume dramas centred on natural disasters had been made in the late 1930s, including *San Francisco* (MGM, 1936), *The Hurricane* (United Artists, 1937), *In Old Chicago* (Fox, 1937) and *The Rains Came* (Fox, 1939); a similar period adventure, *Krakatoa, East of Java* (Cinerama, 1969), had been a recent flop, and there was a brief cycle of airborne suspense thrillers in the 1950s, including *No Highway in the Sky* (Fox, 1951) and *The High and the Mighty* (Warner, 1954).

But *Airport*'s combination of lavish production values, all-star cast, modern technology and basis in a best-selling novel combined to earn it a domestic gross of $45.22 million, resulting in three direct sequels throughout the decade: *Airport 1975* (1974), *Airport '77* (1977) and *Airport '79: The Concorde* (1979), all released by Universal. The success of *The Poseidon Adventure* (Fox, 1972), which earned $42 million, led its producer Irwin Allen to commit himself exclusively to the production of disaster movies for both cinema and television. He scored the genre's biggest hit with *The Towering Inferno* (jointly financed by Fox and Warners), which grossed $48.65 million, but a series of flops at the end of the decade – *The Swarm* (Warner, 1978), *Beyond the Poseidon Adventure* (Fox, 1979), and *When Time Ran Out ...* (Warner, 1980) – effectively killed the genre as well as Allen's career.

These films hark back to Classical Hollywood in their rosters of star names and their all-classes appeal, even while they draw upon the audience's willingness to see those stars – many of them survivors of the studio system, such as *Airport*'s Burt Lancaster and Dean Martin, *The Towering Inferno*'s William Holden and Fred Astaire, and the ubiquitous Charlton Heston, star of *Skyjacked* (MGM, 1972), *Earthquake* (Universal, 1974) and *Airport 1975*, among others – caught up in scenes of violence and destruction made palatable for family viewing. It could be argued that *Jaws*, with its scenes of mass panic, also belongs with the disaster genre, though it is equally indebted to the horror film, the sea adventure and the post-Watergate conspiracy thriller.

Science fiction had traditionally been seen as a genre whose appeal was confined largely to child and teenage audiences, hence such films tended to be produced on low budgets by the smaller studios (notably Universal) and independents (such as Roger Corman and American International Pictures) for the exploitation market. Prestige science fiction items, such as *20,000 Leagues Under the Sea* (Disney, 1954) and *Forbidden Planet* (MGM, 1956), were exceptions to the rule. Two 1968 hits, MGM's *2001: A Space Odyssey* and Fox's *Planet of the Apes* – which cost $11 million and $5.5 million, respectively, and earned $26.32 million and $15 million – demonstrated that the genre could be attractive to both a mass audience and to "serious", mainstream filmmakers. However, it was the runaway success of *Star Wars* and *Close Encounters of the Third Kind* (Columbia, 1977) that persuaded the major studios that science fiction could generate massive profits, and which led to its large-scale revival from the late 1970s onwards, including such pictures as *The Black Hole* (Disney, 1979), *Star Trek – The Motion Picture* and its various follow-ups, the James Bond fantasy *Moonraker*, and the TV spin-offs *Battlestar Galactica* (Universal, 1978) and *Buck Rogers in the 25th Century* (Universal, 1979).

Both the disaster and science fiction (or science fantasy) booms partly depended on the development and availability of state-of-the-art technologies to render their spectacle suitably overwhelming. The disaster films largely relied upon traditional techniques such as large-scale modelwork, matte paintings and tricks of perspective, but *Earthquake* served as the showcase for a short-lived sound system, Sensurround, which used "subaudible sound to create vibrations that made the audience feel the effects of earthquakes, explosions, crashes, and the like" (Carr and Hayes 1988: 249–50). It was used for only four more pictures: *King Kong* (for overseas release only), *Midway* (Universal, 1976), *Rollercoaster* (Universal, 1977) and *Battlestar Galactica*, but another

Table 7.2 Annual top five box-office hits, United States and Canada, 1970–80. Note: Figures indicate distributor gross, i.e. rentals, not box-office gross. All figures are in millions of dollars. Note that the year under which the film is listed is usually the one in which it did the bulk of its box-office business rather than the calendar year in which it opened (where different, this is indicated in brackets); an exception is made in the case of *Billy Jack*, most of whose final gross was earned on its 1973 reissue but which is listed under its initial release year, 1971. Initial gross is the figure carried by *Variety* for the first year in which the film appears in its annual box-office chart; final gross is the cumulative amount taken by the film to date in the domestic theatrical market. In some cases the latter is larger than the former, indicating the continuance of the theatrical run and in some cases the revenue earned by reissues (including revenue earned by the special editions of *Star Wars, Close Encounters of the Third Kind* and *The Empire Strikes Back*). In some cases the final gross is smaller than the initial gross, indicating a recalculation by *Variety* of the film's ultimate theatrical revenue.

Year	Film (studio)	Initial gross	Final gross
1970	*Airport* (Universal)	37.65	45.2
	M*A*S*H (Fox)	22.0	36.7
	Patton (Fox)	21.0	28.1
	Woodstock (Warner)	13.5	16.4
	Hello, Dolly! (Fox, 1969)	13.0	15.2
1971	*Love Story* (Paramount, 1970)	50.0	48.7
	Billy Jack (Warner; reissued 1973)	4.0	32.5
	The Aristocats (Disney, 1970)	10.1	26.46
	The French Connection (Fox)	6.1	26.3
	Summer of '42 (Warner)	14.0	20.5
1972	*The Godfather* (Paramount)	81.5	80.3
	Fiddler on the Roof (United Artists, 1971)	25.1	38.3
	What's Up, Doc? (Warner)	17.0	28.0
	Cabaret (Allied Artists/Cinerama)	10.885	20.25
	Diamonds Are Forever (United Artists, 1971)	21.0	19.73
1973	*American Graffiti* (Universal)	10.3	55.1
	The Poseidon Adventure (Fox, 1972)	40.0	42.0
	Deliverance (Warner, 1972)	3.0	22.6
	The Way We Were (Columbia)	10.0	22.46
	Jeremiah Johnson (Warner, 1972)	8.35	21.9
1974	*The Exorcist* (Warner, 1973)	66.3	89.0
	The Sting (Universal, 1973)	68.45	78.2
	Blazing Saddles (Warner)	16.5	47.8
	Earthquake (Universal)	7.9	35.85
	The Trial of Billy Jack (Warner)	15.00	31.1

Table 7.2 *continued*

Year	Film (studio)	Initial gross	Final gross
1975	*Jaws* (Universal)	102.65	129.5
	The Towering Inferno (Fox/Warner, 1974)	55.0	48.8
	Young Frankenstein (Fox, 1974)	30.0	38.82
	The Rocky Horror Picture Show (Fox)	3.5	35.0
	The Godfather, Part II (Paramount, 1974)	28.9	30.67
1976	*One Flew Over the Cuckoo's Nest* (United Artists, 1975)	56.5	59.94
	All the President's Men (Warner)	29.0	30.0
	The Omen (Fox)	27.851	28.54
	The Bad News Bears (Paramount)	22.266	24.89
	Dog Day Afternoon (Warner, 1975)	19.8	22.5
1977	*Star Wars* (Fox)	127.0	270.92
	Rocky (United Artists, 1976)	54.0	56.52
	Smokey and the Bandit (Universal)	39.774	58.95
	A Star is Born (Warner)	37.1	37.1
	King Kong (Paramount/Universal, 1976)	35.851	36.91
1978	*Grease* (Paramount)	83.091	96.3
	Close Encounters of the Third Kind (Columbia, 1977)	23.0	82.75
	Saturday Night Fever (Paramount, 1977)	71.463	74.1
	National Lampoon's Animal House (Universal)	52.368	70.83
	Jaws 2 (Universal)	49.299	50.43
1979	*Superman* (Warner, 1978)	81.0	82.8
	Star Trek – The Motion Picture (Paramount)	35.0	56.0
	Every Which Way But Loose (Warner, 1978)	48.0	51.9
	Rocky II (UA)	43.049	42.17
	Alien (Fox)	40.086	40.3
1980	*The Empire Strikes Back* (Fox)	120.0	173.8
	Kramer vs. Kramer (Columbia, 1979)	60.528	59.99
	The Jerk (Universal, 1979)	43.0	42.99
	Airplane (Paramount)	38.0	40.6
	Smokey and the Bandit II (Universal)	37.6	38.9

(Source: *Variety*)

sound system proved to be a key factor in the success of *Star Wars*. In 1975 Dolby Laboratories had introduced optical stereo soundtracks for 35 mm prints, and Dolby noise reduction had been used in the sound recording of various films since 1971. But *Star Wars* was the first film to be widely exhibited in the optical stereo process, its success in early engagements persuading many subsequent exhibitors to install the system. Both *Star Wars* and *Close Encounters of the Third Kind* were also made available in a limited number of 70 mm blow-up prints with superior, multi-channel magnetic tracks encoded with Dolby noise reduction, and this in turn stimulated the release of increasing numbers of 70 mm prints for blockbusters throughout the next 15 years, before the introduction of digital sound made magnetic tracks, and with them 70 mm, redundant. In numerical terms, the late 1970s and 1980s were "the real boom time for 70mm, with the number of 70mm theatres actually growing, particularly in America, rising from only a few key cities to almost 1500 during the 80s" (Lobban 1995).[2] *Star Wars* also pioneered the use of computerized motion-control cameras for its numerous effects shots; such technological spectacle was a feature of most other science fiction and fantasy pictures.

While these genres prospered, others slipped into comparative redundancy as changes in public tastes became apparent along with the demographic composition of audiences: as much as 73 per cent of tickets sold in 1973 were to people aged between 12 and 29 (American Film Institute report, cited in Hugo 1980–1: 47). The Western, for example, achieved only four major box-office hits in the 1970s: *Little Big Man* (National General, 1970), *Jeremiah Johnson* (1972), *The Outlaw Josey Wales* (1976) – respectively, vehicles for Dustin Hoffman, Robert Redford and Clint

Eastwood, among the decade's most potent male stars – and Mel Brooks' spoof *Blazing Saddles* (1974); the very existence of the latter seemed to Pauline Kael to call the genre's continued relevance into question. The fall in numbers of Westerns throughout the decade (fewer than sixty American Westerns were made between 1970 and 1979) and the disastrous failure of *Heaven's Gate* in 1980 effectively spelled the end of the genre as a major commercial force, despite subsequent isolated successes such as *Dances with Wolves* (Orion, 1990) and *Unforgiven* (Warners, 1992).

The musical has often been blamed for the studios' disastrous performance in the late 1960s, but unlike the Western it managed to reinvent itself, for a time at least, in the 1970s. Despite the success early in the decade of *Fiddler on the Roof*, further adaptations from Broadway shows, such as *Man of La Mancha* (United Artists, 1972), *1776* (Columbia, 1972), *Lost Horizon* (Columbia, 1973), *Mame* (Warner, 1974), *A Little Night Music* (New World, 1977) and *Hair* (United Artists, 1979), were expensive flops. However, other musical films were more successful in gauging the temper of the times and adapting themselves to the new market. Thus *Cabaret* (Allied Artists/Cinerama, 1972), *The Rocky Horror Picture Show* (Fox, 1975), *Saturday Night Fever* (Paramount, 1977) and *Grease* (Paramount, 1978) all pitched at either the "adult" or the youth market rather than the amorphous family audience at which *The Sound of Music* (Fox, 1965) and its imitators had been aimed – number among the decade's major hits. On the strength of *Funny Lady* (Columbia, 1975), the sequel to *Funny Girl* (Columbia, 1968), and the rock-music remake of *A Star is Born* (Warner, 1976), as well as various non-musical vehicles, Barbra Streisand became the single most important female star of the 1970s,

Count Basie makes a surprise cameo in Mel Brooks' spoof Western *Blazing Saddles*

testifying to the continuing significance of the musical despite the erosion of its traditional audience.

Blockbuster aesthetics

If I were asked to pick a single emblematic moment of 1970s cinema – an image that might serve as a symbol of the post-classical reconfiguration of Hollywood and a portent of the cinema soon to come about – I should have no hesitation in nominating the blowing up of the shark at the end of *Jaws*. Its only possible rival – the blowing up of the Death Star at the end of *Star Wars* – seems to me as much a derivative of this moment as its equivalent. The explosion signifies not just the triumph of spectacle and special effects, or the transcendent victory of the patriarchal male hero, but the intensification of emotional manipulation and the satisfaction of desire at a level that approaches the sexual. So exhilarating are both these moments that audiences in theatres invariably let out a cheer, broke into applause or rose to their feet at the delivery of a climax in such gratifyingly orgasmic form. It would not, I think, be an exaggeration to say that all Hollywood blockbusters since have sought to reproduce those moments and the feelings provoked by them, to the extent that whole movies have seemed to be constructed around a succession of climaxes.

Spectacle is not, of course, new or exclusive to post-1970s Hollywood: it was the commodity on which most 1950s and 1960s road-shows based their appeal, and its centrality to commercial entertainment extends back not just to the silent era but to the Victorian popular theatre and beyond. Nonetheless, the *type* of spectacle primarily associated with "new" Hollywood – both technological and emotive, "sophisticated" in its formal construction and primal in its mode of address – found its definitive form in these two films. It is a form that resists interrogation, but demands repetition: not just the replay of these moments or the revisiting of these particular films – a mega-hit is produced by repeat visits more than by any other factor – but its replication in other movies. The phenomenal success of *Jaws* and *Star Wars* determined the course, not just of the blockbuster, but of Hollywood cinema as a whole in the subsequent decades.

By contrast, the form of cinema that has *not* prevailed is represented by certain other huge hits of the 1970s, and by certain hugely expensive flops that effectively ruled out the continuance, in the commercial mainstream, of that critical, questioning, subversive attitude celebrated by critics as the hallmark of the early part of the decade. Among the films listed in Table 7.2, *M*A*S*H*, *Deliverance* (Warner, 1972), *One Flew Over the Cuckoo's Nest*, *Dog Day Afternoon* (Warner, 1975) and *All the President's Men* (Warner, 1976) have few equivalents in Hollywood after the 1970s. Indeed, the presence of the last three among the top five US box-office hits of 1976 seems like a last hurrah for the socially critical, stylistically adventurous cinema soon to be displaced by the ideologically and formally conservative work of Steven Spielberg, George Lucas, and their successors and imitators.

Part of the responsibility for this sea change can be attributed to the concurrent box office failure – relative to cost and expectations or absolute – of a number of pictures, all directed by "movie brat" auteurs, which also aspired to blockbuster status but which were largely rejected by both audiences and critics. They include Martin Scorsese's *New York, New York* (United Artists, 1977), William Friedkin's *Sorcerer* (UK: *Wages of Fear*, Paramount/ Universal, 1977) and *The Brink's Job* (Universal, 1978), Francis Ford Coppola's *Apocalypse Now* and *One from the Heart* (Columbia, 1982), Michael Cimino's *Heaven's Gate*, Milos Forman's *Ragtime* (Paramount, 1981) and even Spielberg's own *1941* (Universal, 1979). This is a mixed bunch, and one would not necessarily want to claim for them the status of neglected masterpieces. Yet what their collective failure produced was not a reaction against the principle of big-budget genre movies – as had been the case at the beginning of the 1970s, with the phasing out of road-shows – but against that of uncontrolled directorial talent. Henceforth it would be the fiscally irresponsible filmmaker who had to be reined in, rather than the reckless executive policy.

Notes

1 For further details of 90/10 deals, see Beaupré (1986: 196–201).
2 Of all the 1970s blockbusters, only *Airport* was actually photographed in a wide gauge (Todd-AO 65 mm) process rather than being printed up from 35 mm. The industry's economy measures after 1970 ruled out wide-gauge photography, which has since been used for only a half-dozen full-length features, though it has often been used for special effects sequences.

References

Anon. (1988) 1956–1987 Big-buck scorecard, *Variety*, 20 January: 64.

Balio, T. (1987) *United Artists: The Company That Changed the Film Industry*. Madison: University of Wisconsin Press.

Beaupré, L. (1986) How to distribute a film, in P. Kerr (ed.) *The Hollywood Film Industry*. London: Routledge and Kegan Paul/BFI.

Carr, R.E. and Hayes, R.M. (1988) *Wide Screen Movies: A History and Filmography of Wide-Gauge Filmmaking*. Jefferson, North Carolina, and London: McFarland.

Coate, M. (2003) *The Original First-Week Engagements of* Star Wars. http://www.in70mm.com/news/2003/star_ wars/star_wars_1977.htm#Trivia%20 (U.S.%20and%20Canada%20release (accessed 24 June 2003).

Frederick, R.B. (1976) Terror-joy of *Jaws*: $102,650,000, *Variety*, 7 January: 18.

Hall, S. (2002) Tall revenue features: the genealogy of the modern blockbuster, in S. Neale (ed.) *Genre and Contemporary Hollywood*. London: BFI.

Hugo, C. (1980–1) American cinema in the '70s: the economic background, *Movie*, 27/28 (Winter/Spring): 47.

Lobban, G. (1995) Coming in 70 mm: is there a future for 70mm theatrical prints? *Cinema Technology*, (April): 40–6.

Schatz, T. (1993) The new Hollywood, in J. Collins, H. Radner, and A.P. Collins (eds) *Film Theory Goes to the Movies*. New York and London: Routledge.

Wyatt, J. (1994), *High Concept: Movies and Marketing in Hollywood*. Austin: University of Texas Press.

Wyatt, J. (1998) From roadshowing to saturation release, in J. Lewis (ed.) *The New Hollywood*. Durham, NC: Duke University Press.

William Friedkin

One of Hollywood's true mavericks, William Friedkin has filled the screen with some of the darkest images in mainstream cinema, provoking applause and outrage in equal measure. A leading figure in the emergence of New Hollywood cinema, Friedkin combined a background in American TV and documentary filmmaking with an admiration for the aesthetics of the European *nouvelle vague*. Just as his most fantastical dramas are tinged with *vérité* realism, so his early documentaries often played like works of high drama. Although *The People Versus Paul Crump* (1962) was famously pulled from broadcast, biographer Nat Segaloff (1990: 33–7) suggests that it was influential in saving the convict from the electric chair. A fascination with the bonding rituals of police work fostered in *The Thin Blue Line* (1966, not to be confused with Errol Morris' 1988 film of the same name), fed into the breakthrough thriller *The French Connection* (1971), for which Friedkin won a Best Director Oscar. Shot with an "induced documentary" style, the film cross-fertilized a real-life crime narrative with elliptical, *avant garde* editing, laying a new template for edgy 1970s thrillers. Its celebrated car chase became a generic high water mark, which the director would revisit and redefine in *To Live and Die in L.A.* (1985) and *Jade* (1995).

Friedkin's most infamous work, *The Exorcist* (1973), from the best-selling novel by William Peter Blatty, was an unparalleled supernatural shocker which "bore as little resemblance to

William Friedkin directs Ellen Burstyn on the set of *The Exorcist*

the gothic horror chillers of the 60s as Nixon did to JFK" (Kermode 1997: 9). Nominated for ten Oscars, the film (which had initially appalled studio executives) became a prototype blockbuster hit, the extraordinary success of which Cook (1998: 22) describes as changing "the ways in which movies would be cost-projected and marketed". In the area of sinister eroticism, Friedkin also pushed the boundaries of mainstream acceptability with *Cruising* (1980), a tale of a cop going undercover in New York's gay S&M clubs, which is characterized by Williams (2005: 80) as instrumental in solidifying the "erotic thriller" genre that flourished in the 1980s and 1990s. Friedkin would subsequently reexamine the genre in *Jade* (from *Basic Instinct* writer Joe Eszterhas) and *Bug* (2006), adapted from the controversial play by Tracy Letts.

Throughout his career, Friedkin's relationship with the press and public has been volatile. *Sorcerer* (1977), a remake of Clouzot's *The Wages of Fear* (1953), was panned by critics and overlooked by audiences; other notable failures include the *Strangelove*-like satire *Deal of the Century* (1983) and the Brother's Grimm-style horror romp *The Guardian* (1990). Yet despite being dismissed by Thomson as a "jumped up TV director" and "chronic sensationalist" (2004: 316), Friedkin has continued to reinvent both himself and his career. The military actioner-cum-courtroom-drama *Rules of Engagement* (2000) put him back at the top of the US box-office, while *The Hunted* (2003) displayed an edgy flair for physicality uncommon in mainstream American cinema. Having learned his trade in television, Friedkin has continued to work on the small screen, directing episodes of *The Twilight Zone* and *Tales from the Crypt*, and helming an award-winning remake of *Twelve Angry Men* (1997). He has also directed several stage plays and operas, the latter becoming his particular forte.

References

Clagett, T.D. (1990) *William Friedkin: Films of Aberration, Obsession and Reality*. North Carolina: McFarland.

Cook, D. (1998) Auteur cinema and the "film generation" in 1970s Hollywood, in J. Lewis (ed.) *The New American Cinema*. Durham, NC: Duke University Press, pp. 11–37.

Kermode, M. (1997) *The Exorcist*. London: BFI.

Segaloff, N. (1990) *Hurricane Billy: The Stormy Life and Films of William Friedkin*. New York: William Morrow & Co.

Thomson, D. (2004) *The New Biographical Dictionary of Film*. London: Little Brown.

Williams, L.R. (2005) *The Erotic Thriller in Contemporary Cinema*. Edinburgh: Edinburgh University Press.

Mark Kermode

BLAXPLOITATION

Eithne Quinn and Peter Krämer

IN HIS GROUNDBREAKING study of 1970s American cinema, James Monaco (1979: 187) declared:

> [t]he birth of the Black film of the late sixties and early seventies – with Blacks, by Blacks, and for Blacks; written, directed, and acted by Blacks (and sometimes even produced and financed by Blacks) – was the major success of the Hollywood Renaissance of 1968–1970

and Black film's "virtual disappearance" by mid-decade the "greatest failure of the American film business". At the commercial and, some would argue, cultural centre of this black film wave was the "blaxploitation" (or black action) cycle. From 1970 to 1975, over 100 films were released (the number varies depending on the parameters used) that featured mainly black casts performing action-adventure narratives in the ghetto. These low-budget action films, some of which were written and directed by African Americans, catered primarily to black urban, working-class audiences – filmgoers who had previously been neglected by Hollywood and who demonstrated a vast appetite for dramas about black private eyes, vigilante heroes, cops, gangsters, drug dealers, and so on, getting even with the system and sometimes also "getting over" (making big money). As we shall see, the term "blaxploitation" is charged and contentious, embracing a set of films with very different meanings, messages, and production contexts. Nonetheless, taken together, this cycle held an immense cultural and commercial significance that outran its short shelf-life by some distance.

Blaxploitation departed dramatically from the race images and themes that scaled the box-office charts in the late 1960s. After all, one of the highest grossing films of the 1967–9 period was the re-release of *Gone with the Wind* (1967/68, earning $29 million in rentals), in which the most prominent black character is the subservient "mammy", played by Hattie McDaniel (Steinberg 1982: 25). Moreover, Sidney Poitier became the first black performer to be voted by theatre owners onto the top ten list of Hollywood's biggest stars, after starring in three hit movies released in 1967 (Steinberg 1982: 60). His major-league success sent an important signal to Hollywood about the commercial potential of black personnel. In his 1967 hit *In the Heat of the Night* (a white-directed film targeting primarily a white liberal audience), Poitier plays an assertive black detective in a role that somewhat foreshadows blaxploitation heroes. However, Poitier's assimilationist roles in films like *Guess Who's Coming to Dinner* (1967 – another of the period's top-grossing films, with rentals of $25 million) and *To Sir with Love* (1967), were widely seen as sexless, non-threatening (for white audiences), and even subservient (to the interests of white society) (for an influential critique, see Neal 1969: 13, 18; figures from Steinberg 1982: 25). So how can we account for the emergence of blaxploitation's gritty ghetto narratives in the context of a film culture characterized by *Gone with the Wind*'s nostalgic images of old-South race relations and Poitier's integrationist screen persona?

Of all film production trends, perhaps none has been more directly shaped by social and political forces than black action films. The late 1960s was a period of social turbulence in America. The major civil rights gains of the mid-1960s (the Civil Rights and Voting Rights Acts) worked to improve the prospects for some black people, but urban neighbourhoods with large black populations actually started losing ground in the late 1960s, creating a sense of frustration and disillusion. Riots erupted in major cities, as protest strategies shifted away from liberal integrationism and towards the militancy of the Black Power youth (see Carson 1981; Van Deburg 1992, 1997; Winant 2001: 147–76). With this mood of insurgency came a proud new attitude towards blackness, as black culture scholar S. Craig Watkins (1998: 94) describes: "The new assertive political posturing also gave birth to new style politics (the Afro) and conceptions of self ('black is beautiful') that began to transform the social production of black popular and expressive cultures." Black moviegoers were ready to see screen portrayals that reflected these new sensibilities and Hollywood, once it grasped the market potential, quickly responded.

While blacks made up about 11 per cent of the American population in 1967, the film industry's leading trade paper *Variety* estimated that they bought about a third of all tickets in first-run, urban theatres (Beaupré 1967: 3). Added to this, Hollywood had been under increasing pressure from civil rights organizations to improve the quantity and quality of its representations of African Americans, and to employ more blacks both in front of and behind the camera (see Leab

1976: 233; Guerrero 1993: 84–5). Thus both commercial imperatives and the threat of legal action and boycotts pushed Hollywood towards black subject-matter, the employment of more black personnel, and the recognition of the specific expectations of African-American audiences. Residential and demographic shifts – the youthfulness of the "baby boom" populace and the "white-flight" exodus to the suburbs – coalesced to generate new industry interest in young black urban filmgoers (see Stanfield 2004).

The result of these social and industrial developments was a string of highly profitable black movies (on the emergence of blaxploitation film, see Bogle 1973: Chapter 8; Leab 1976: Chapter 10; Guerrero 1993: Chapter 3; Van Deburg 1997: Chapter 4; Cook 2000: 259–66). As film scholar Rick Altman (1999) and others demonstrate, film genres and cycles have no stable or singular point of origin, and blaxploitation is no exception. Early indicators include sport star Jim Brown's butch performance in *The Dirty Dozen* (1967), which was foregrounded in publicity for the film, and the extraordinary success of Poitier (to which blaxploitation was both response and rebuttal). However, three fairly diverse, black-directed films launched the black action movie cycle. First came *Cotton Comes to Harlem* (1970, United Artists), Ossie Davis' adaptation of black crime writer Chester Himes' novel about two tough black detectives, which became the first-ever black-directed film produced by a major studio to turn a significant profit (earning $5.1 million in rentals, off a budget of $1.2 million) (Leab 1976: 241; Cohn 1993: C76). The film first presented many of blaxploitation's recurring themes: the colourful ghetto setting; the unabashed black styles, sensibilities, and humour (crystallized in

Continued on page 188

The stand-up comedy film has been a minor, although at times lucrative genre since 1979. Bill Sargent is generally credited with creating the first example of the genre with his production of *Richard Pryor Live in Concert* in that year. Sargent had formed Electronovision in the early 1960s to produce videotaped performances for release in movie theatres. His first release was Richard Burton's *Hamlet* which was a taped dress rehearsal at the Lunt-Fontanne theatre in New York in 1964. He tapped into the youth market in that same year when he produced *The T.A.M.I. Show* (Teenage Awards Music International) which was the first filmed rock concert with performances from James Brown, Chuck Berry, Marvin Gaye, the Beach Boys and the Rolling Stones. Sargent had considerable success with these ventures and also can be credited with recognizing the potential of the large-scale charity rock concert prior to *Live Aid* (1985) and *Live 8* (2005) in his plans to stage a "Stop the War" benefit concert with Warren Beatty which never came to fruition due to pressure from the Nixon Administration. Sargent's recognition of the potential to exploit links between the music industry and the film industry in this way led to the filming of Richard Pryor's live show over two nights at the Long Beach Terrace Theatre. Pryor himself returned to stand-up in the late 1970s after writing and starring in films which had followed the enormous success in record sales of his Grammy award-winning albums of his live act: *That Nigger's Crazy* (1974) and *Bicentennial Nigger* (1976).

Stand-up comedy records by artists such as Bob Newhart and Bill Cosby had been rivalling popular music in sales since the early 1960s. Comedy records had been available since the 1920s (Kennedy 1994: 35) and had been a ready and relatively cheap source of income for small record companies as there was little involved in terms of recording expenses. In the 1950s Redd Foxx, whose dirty joke routines were well established on the "chitlin" circuit of nightclubs catering to black audiences, produced a number of "party records" which were highly successful, although Foxx saw very little of the profits. His comedy was both explicit and had political "edge", dealing with issues of race and appealing at first to a predominantly black audience. By contrast, Newhart and Cosby were able to attract major record label support with comedy that did not depend on profanity, although Cosby's comedy brought the culture of black humour to the attention of mainstream white audiences. With the advent of the ratings system in the late 1960s and the turn to more socially relevant sit-coms like the Norman Lear productions of *All in the Family* (1971–79) and *Sanford and Son* (1972–77), comedians such as Foxx with *Sanford and Son* and the young Richard Pryor as an actor and writer were able to move into film and television. By the time of the release of *That Nigger's Crazy* in 1974 Pryor was able to bring the astute, often tragic and yet hilarious narrative-based humour he had developed in comedy clubs to a wide audience base that crossed racial boundaries.

Richard Pryor Live in Concert begins with an aerial shot of the Long Beach Terrace Theatre where the concert was recorded. The film is simply directed by Jeff Margolis who later handled events such as the Academy Awards and Country Music Awards. This type of direction cuts in when the comedy depends on Pryor's facial expressions and out in order to capture the expertly executed body mime as Pryor imitates John Wayne's walk, Muhammad Ali's backward boxing style, a white sax player whose body is rigid compared with his fellow black musicians, and an old-style boxer being kicked in the testicles by a street fighter who knows kung fu. Pryor's use of characters begins immediately, as he has obviously arrived on stage earlier than the audience expects. The camera cuts to a shot of the audience rushing back to their seats as he heckles them imitating black and white voices and immediately establishes that this routine will centre on the experience of African Americans. He will use no restraint in the expressive use of the expletive language where "motherfucker" is as much a rhythmic cadence as a term of abuse. His ability to bring characters to life depends on his verbal and physical comedy which provides depth to his performance and lends detail to his already widely known act on recorded albums. The situations he describes are laced with a pathos and reinforced by a wavering quality in his voice which underscores his vulnerability even as he describes the real-life situations he has experienced, from shooting the tyres of his own car the previous New Year's Eve to the beatings he received from his brutal father. This fine balance between comedy and tragedy is perhaps no more relevant than in his description of the activities of the Long Beach Police department:

> Police got a choke hold they use out here, man, they choke niggahs to death … That means you'll be dead when they through. Did you know that? Niggahs going "Yeah, we know", white folks going "No, I had no idea." Yeah, two grab your legs, one grabs your neck, it snaps, "Oh shit, he broke, we broke a nigger. Can we break a nigger? Is it OK? Let's check the manual. Yep, page 8, you can break a nigger."

The truth of this situation was borne out two years later when black high school football star Ron Settles was arrested and later found "hanged" in his cell at the Signal Hills Police Department in Long Beach. A coroner later testified that he had been the victim of the choke hold that Pryor had joked (and warned) about. No police officers were charged.

Richard Pryor Live in Concert was released in theatres in 1979 and made $32 million and was producer Bill Sargent's biggest film hit. Arguably the film appealed to the youth market and was an example of an independent release through Sargent and David Permut's company Special Events Entertainment. It drew upon the already established concert film that was a staple of art-house cinemas throughout the late 1960s and early 1970s. It also brought the profit potential of the stand-up comedy film to the attention of the majors, and the genre was kick-started and flourished throughout the 1980s and 1990s and into the twenty-first century. Pryor did two follow-up films; *Live on the Sunset Strip* (1982), which brought in $36 million, and *Here and Now* (1985), which made a relatively modest $16 million. The genre either launched or sustained the careers not only of younger black comedians such as Eddie Murphy or later Martin Lawrence but also became the template for the comedy concert film and the flourishing of comedy-only channels on cable and satellite. In 2004, according to *Variety*, the genre seemed to be waning primarily due to the fact that the taboo subject matter of comedians like Pryor, or later Bill Hicks, had become more accessible with the expansion of cable channels. Another reason given was that, at the present time, $38 million profit on a $3 million investment is no longer as attractive as blockbuster profits are to the majors and, perhaps more importantly, it's easy to say no to a comedy project by claiming it's not funny (McNary 2004). The stand-up film's demise may be premature as such proclamations usually are, but *Richard Pryor Live In Concert* ushered in and set the standard for the genre in terms of form and style and in its potential for appealing to young audiences regardless of race. Through his insistence on a political agenda Pryor outlined the effects of racism and the experience of African Americans through humour and pathos. He achieved this through his refusal to turn away from difficult and forbidden subject matter and in doing that Pryor helped to redraw the boundaries of film comedy.

References

Friedman, L.D. (1991) *Unspeakable Images: Ethnicity and the American Cinema*. Urbana: University of Illinois Press.

Gray, H. (1995) *Watching Race: Television and the Struggle for "Blackness."* Minneapolis: University of Minnesota Press.

Kennedy, R. (1994) *Jelly Roll, Bix and Hoagy: Gennett Records and the Birth of Recorded Jazz*, Bloomington: Indiana University Press.

MacDonald, J.F. (1993) *Blacks and White TV: Afro-Americans in Television Since 1948.* Chicago: Nelson-Hall.

McNary, D. (2004) Comics no longer king: cable bulldozes once lucrative stand-up genre, Jan. 4, http://www.variety.com/index.asp?

Michael Hammond

Continued from page 185

the scene-stealing performance of stand-up comedian Redd Foxx); the proud and effective detectives mediating between black and white worlds; the charismatic black hustler (played by acclaimed actor Calvin Lockhart); the, by turns, vindictive, corrupt, and comic white characters; and the pointed social commentary. Pressure had been exerted by the studio to downplay the film's black themes in an effort to attract white patrons. However, this film's success, recouped from an overwhelmingly black audience, showed that, as Daniel Leab (1976: Chapter 10) put it in his book chapter title, "black is boxoffice".

Then came *Sweet Sweetback's Baadasssss Song* the following year, a stark portrayal of a hip black sex worker who challenges the system and wins. This X-rated film, directed by Melvin van Peebles, was a mixture of experimental and independently produced cinema, pornography, political essay and crime thriller, featuring sex, fights, and an extended chase after Sweetback attacks two police officers to defend a young black militant (see Cripps 1990; Guerrero 1993: 86–91). At the film's end, Sweetback evades punishment, with the closing caution: "A BAADASSSSS NIGGER IS COMING BACK TO COLLECT SOME DUES" – an ending that thrilled many black viewers long accustomed

to narrative closures that see unruly black protagonists coming to no good. The movie earned $4.1 million in rentals and, because it was cheaply made, most of this was profit. *Sweetback* became a lightning rod for debate about shifting black sensibilities, its cultural meanings and political messages hotly debated in the black community and beyond (see Cripps 1990; Hartmann 1994). Huey Newton (1971: A–L), leader of the Black Panther Party, hailed it as "the first truly revolutionary Black film". James Monaco (1979: 201) captures something of the movie's event status in the black power years: "the film succeeds as a *cri de cœur*, an announcement that black militancy has reached your neighbourhood movie screen and that things will never be the same". However, many other critics – black, white, feminist, leftist, conservative – criticized the film (see especially Bennett 1971).

The second big black hit of 1971 was *Shaft*, a studio picture directed by Gordon Parks Sr., about a stylish black private-eye. It was among the twenty highest grossing films of the year with rentals of $6.1 million, and was accompanied by an award-winning, best-selling soundtrack (Cook 2000: 498). While *Shaft* (adapted from a white-authored detective novel) was far less experimental and political than *Sweetback*, it did feature black militants and talk of urban riots as well as a considerable amount of sex and violence. Like *Cotton Comes to Harlem*, the success of *Sweetback* and *Shaft* was mainly due to their popularity with black audiences, especially black urban youth. Sex, action, fashion, music, and storylines about beating "whitey" (as in the climactic battle with the mafia goons in *Shaft* – a film that elsewhere does, however, show cooperation between the black hero and the white police) were identified as the key ingredients for success with young black movie audiences. When these assumptions were confirmed by the box-office performance of *Super Fly* (1972) – a film about a drug dealer making one last big deal before he gets out of the business – the floodgates opened. Both Hollywood studios and independent production companies made large numbers of black-oriented films. It is estimated that between 1969 and 1971, the annual output of black-oriented films rose from six to 18; from 1972 to 1974, the output rose to 25–50 films per year (with 1973 as the peak year) (Cook 2000: 261, 263).

Black exploitation film

The term "blaxploitation" was coined in the summer of 1972, following the release of *Super Fly*. Black activist Junius Griffin, the former leader of the Hollywood branch of the National Association for the Advancement of Colored People (NAACP), was quoted in *Variety* using the term and it quickly caught on ("NAACP blast super nigger trend", 16 August 1972, cited in Martinez et al. 1998: 54). This neologism – an elision of black and exploitation – was very charged indeed, invoking both industry and racial meanings. The industry term "exploitation", in usage since the 1950s, referred to films that, as film scholar Thomas Doherty (1988: 8) describes,

are "*triply* exploitative": they exploit sensational happenings "for story value", notoriety "for publicity value", and audiences "for box office value" (see also Schaefer 1999). Most of these black crime films possessed all these attributes. First, they qualified as exploitation because they had low, substandard budgets, ranging in most cases from $250,000 to $1 million (in 1971, the average cost for a major studio release was $1.75 million and in 1974 $2.5 million) (Steinberg 1982: 50). Next, these films followed the exploitation logic by cashing in on topical issues and controversial trends, thus enabling sensational promotion. Many blaxploitation films, for instance, portrayed the timely figure of the black militant, capitalizing on the political energies of the period; they folded in fads like the kung fu craze (*Black Belt Jones*, 1974; *Dolemite*, 1975); and they fetishized the underground economy of pimping (*The Mack*, 1973; *Willie Dynamite*, 1974), and drug dealing (*Super Fly*, *Black Caesar*, 1973). Furthermore, like other exploitation fare, these black movies included explicit and stimulating subject matter. Witness blaxploitation's inter-racial sex scenes; its objectification of the female and black male body; its brutal and comic violence and fast-paced action scenes; and its glamorous criminal activity. Finally, black action films catered to young black cinemagoers, thus following the exploitation tactic of targeting a niche market.

The turn of the 1970s was a "golden age" of exploitation cinema, extending well beyond the confines of black-oriented production. Cultural change and social ferment gave rise to Supreme Court rulings that relaxed the definitions of obscenity and, in the case of the film industry, the dropping of the strict Production Code in the late 1960s, opening the way for more explicit screen depictions of sex and violence (see Lewis 2000). As a consequence,

Poster for *Sweet Sweetback's Baadasssss Song*

mainstream filmmaking increasingly foregrounded exploitational elements. But this did not dampen demand for more full-blooded exploitation cycles: kung fu sagas, horror shockers, and, most plentiful of all, pornographic pictures. If exploitation elements were thus so widely deployed in this period, it raises the question of why black commentators were so deeply concerned about the import of black action films. When Griffin coined the term "blaxploitation", its industry meanings were clearly overlaid with racial meanings. It was not simply understood as exploitation cinema with a "racial twist". Instead, as Watkins (1998: 172) points out, "the association of the term *exploitation* with African Americans conjures up ideas of unfair, even racist, treatment". "Blaxploitation", remarks film scholar Ed Guerrero (1993: 69), "might as easily and accurately describe the cruel injustice of slavery or, for that matter, much of the historical sojourn of black folk in America." African Americans have faced an extraordinary history of race-based labour exploitation, as Guerrero suggests, and the charged term "blaxploitation" brought to mind long-standing and continuing racial experiences and injustices in times of new black self-awareness and pride.

The black critics who condemned these films as being racially exploitative did have a compelling point. First and foremost, though most of the creative energy and cultural labour came from blacks, the profits mostly ended up in white pockets (an age-old story in the US cultural industries). Two studies capture this racialized political economy: "Black films, white profits", by Reneé Ward (1976), and *Black Film/White Money* by Jesse Rhines (1996: Chapter 4). Indeed, these white profits helped secure certain major and independent film companies through hard times when they were threatened with bankruptcy, including

MGM (which produced *Shaft* and *Shaft's Big Score* in 1972) and Cinemation (distributor of *Sweetback*). This inequitable state of affairs reflects the fact that black people (like women) were locked out of senior executive positions in Hollywood, owned a tiny proportion of movie theatres, and represented very few of the shareholders profiting from this film boom.

And if white executives and producers profited from these films, they also largely controlled the thematic and narrative course of this wave of cheaply made films. There is no question that blacks directed most of the aesthetically and politically significant (as well as most commercially successful) films in the cycle. Whites, however, directed and produced the vast majority of blaxploitation films, and, as the cycle developed, churned out films with increasingly stereotypical characterizations and formulaic plot lines, with portrayals of sexualized and racialized violence that were prurient and outlandish. There were "racial exceptions", for instance, white director Larry Cohen's excellent *Black Caesar* (1973). But for the most part, the distance between black creative personnel projecting images that freely satirized and sent up ghetto life for a black audience (even if these were also partly subject to external control) and white-devised stereotypical portrayals of blacks (that had long been a mainstay of Hollywood movies) was very considerable. The sudden demise of black-oriented filmmaking after 1974 crystallized the sense of disempowerment and resentment for many black personnel, when falling profits (probably due to excessive repetition and overfamiliarity with cheaply made blaxploitation formulas), campaigning pressure, and above all changing industry policies left black actors and directors out of work. The withdrawal of the major studios from blaxploitation production in 1975 was partly due to the fact that they had realized that they could reach black audiences through their blockbusters. Once industry sources had noted that both *The Godfather* (1972) and *The Exorcist* (1973, Fig. 5 (*see plate section*)) were extremely popular with black audiences, Hollywood had responded by co-starring well-known black performers in several of its biggest productions to appeal specifically to blacks (see Krämer 2005). *Earthquake* (1974), for example, featured Richard Roundtree, and *The Towering Inferno* (1974) O.J. Simpson.

Shifting our focus from the politics of production to questions of audience raises further charges of exploitation. These films provoked controversy in the black community about their potentially harmful effect on the self-image and behaviour of black youth. Reflecting the polemical charge of these discussions, Conrad Smith (1972), Western Regional Director of the Congress of Racial Equality (CORE), charged that the films have a "devastating and all encompassing impact on the life values, posterity and concepts of all black individuals". Psychologist Alvin Poussaint (1974) concurred with Griffin in his article subtitled "Cheap thrills that degrade blacks". Growing concern about the potentially disempowering influence of these superheroic portrayals on black youth was encapsulated by Clayton Riley's influential *New York Times* article (1972: 22), "Shaft can do everything, I can do nothing." For many commentators, it was not simply that these film heroes were bad role models, but that blaxploitation symbolized the abrupt and ignoble end of the integrationist dream of Civil Rights and the attendant "respectable" portrayals of Sidney Poitier. As Ed Guerrero persuasively outlines in his illuminating chapter on blaxploitation film, these critics were engaged in an intensely felt debate – heavily freighted with generational, racial, and class concerns – about the politics of black representation.

Of all blaxploitation films, *Super Fly* both generated the most controversy (provoking the launch of the Coalition Against Blaxploitation) and enjoyed the greatest hold over the black youth imagination. In his semi-autobiographical book on black film, critic Nelson George (1994: 54) states that "*Super Fly*'s cocaine dealer was a more romantic, conflicted figure whose slang and clothes cut deeper than *Shaft* into the black community's psyche." In his best-selling autobiography, black journalist Nathan McCall (1995: 102) describes how *Super Fly* influenced his own decision, as a young man, to start dealing drugs, observing that, "perhaps for the first time in this country's history, young blacks were searching on a large scale for alternatives to the white mainstream. One option, glamorized by *Super Fly*, was the drug trade, the black urban answer to capitalism." While integrationist voices were lambasting such movies for romanticizing criminal occupations and leading black youth (like McCall) astray, radical commentators lamented their containment of political energies. It must be remembered that this was a period of grassroots mobilization, when Marxist and black nationalist critiques of race and class exploitation were widely and intensely debated. In this context, blaxploitation films (after the contested radicalism of *Sweetback*), with their glamorization of lumpen lifestyles and trivializing portrayals of black militants, were seen as powerful tools of demobilization. Again, *Super Fly* is considered one of the most egregious: when the cocaine-dealing hero, Priest, has a standoff with black radicals, he emerges as the rhetorical victor and they run scared. Numerous scholarly articles have appeared, stressing the depoliticizing impulse of blaxploitation (see Washington and Berlowitz 1975; James 1987; Davis 1998; Lyne 2000). Black Marxist scholar Cedric Robinson (1998), for instance, recently published "Blaxploitation and the misrepresentation of liberation", stressing the political significance of blaxploitation in light of the decline in black protest culture and rise of individualism in the post-civil rights period.

Reconsidering blaxploitation

However pointed and persuasive the critiques levelled against blaxploitation, the representational politics of this movie cycle remain highly complex and contradictory. One danger of emphasizing the racially exploitative features of the genre is that one ends up reproducing a narrative of black disempowerment, of young black people as "culture dupes" (to use Stuart Hall's 1981 phrase). In fact, black people, as crafters and consumers of this production trend were, in many important ways, very active agents. Although white executives, producers, and other personnel were involved in and profited most from of these films, blaxploitation did create considerable employment opportunities for African Americans, and in a considerable number of cases the film's content and style were largely controlled by black personnel (on the extent of black agency in blaxploitation, see Reid 1988; Rhines 1996, Chapter 4; Lott 1998). An acknowledgement of black agency underwrites many of the critical reinterpretations of the genre.

Some critics have examined the style politics of blaxploitation's flamboyant clothing, hairstyles, language, accessories, and so on. These key components of the genre's iconography, critics argue, serve to communicate a repudiation of the conservative styles and respectable mores of both middle America and the black bourgeoisie. By celebrating marginal identities and underground activities, founded on a sense of social exclusion, the style politics of figures like the black "pusher man" and pimp hold charged class and race meanings (and pleasures) (see Mercer 1994; Bruzzi 1997; Quinn 2001; Neal 2002). Equally, the gender and sexual politics of these movies have come under critical scrutiny. Blaxploitation films were products of the "sexual revolution", with their explicit portrayals of nudity and sex. Most of the films present women in passive and sexually objectified roles or as untrustworthy and manipulative, in both cases giving powerful illustration of the black feminist edict that black women are doubly oppressed – by race and by gender (see Davis 1983; hooks 1990; Hill-Collins 1991). However, blaxploitation superheroines did emerge, notably Pam Grier in *Coffy* (1973, "the baddest one-chick hit-squad that ever hit town!" according to the poster's tagline) and *Foxy Brown* (1974), and Tamara Dobson in *Cleopatra Jones* (1973). These women portrayed active, sexualized, and victorious "black mamas", in roles that have been sharply debated. Recent critics have stressed the feminist potential, sexual transgression, and gendered ambivalence of blaxploitation heroines (and indeed, in some cases, heroes) (see Brody 1999; Hankin 2002; Wlodarz 2004).

While these scholars focus on gender transgression, others have explored *genre* transgression. Many blaxploitation films were genre remakes (*Black Caesar* reworked the gangster classic *Little Caesar*, 1931; *Blackenstein*, 1973 and *Dr. Black, Mr. Hyde*, 1976 remade classic horror stories, and so on). Recent scholarly articles have appeared, exploring the interesting racial implications of reworking genre films from a black perspective, and, inversely, the genre implications of tracing race over established Hollywood stories. Harry Benshoff (2000: 37), for instance, has explored how blaxploitation horror films "reappropriated the mainstream cinema's monstrous figures for black goals, turning vampires, Frankenstein monsters, and transformation monsters into agents of black pride and black power". *Blacula* (1972) has provoked the most critical interest, offering, according to Benshoff (2000) and Leerom Medovoi (1998), a powerful, if ambivalent, racial critique, in which the "normal" racist society is cast as monstrous and the monstrous avenger as heroic, his actions justified by the cruelty of racial oppression (see also Lipsitz 1998).

While these critical departures focus on stylistic, thematic, and narrative features, it must be stressed that the representational politics of blaxploitation extend beyond film content to encompass the high-profile black personnel involved in these projects. Some of the most successful and critically acclaimed black musicians of the day (indeed, perhaps of all time) – Curtis Mayfield, Bobby Womack, James Brown, Isaac Hayes – produced chart-topping, highly acclaimed soundtracks. These soul and funk stars, some of whom made cameo appearances, were key components of the films' success, capturing the exciting mood of the times and also often commenting, through the music, on narrative developments. For instance, the Curtis Mayfield tracks "Freddy's Dead" and "Pusherman" from *Super Fly* provide ethical counterpoints to the hero's glamorously individualist stance. As Greil Marcus (1977: 97) argues, the "songs were not background, but criticism".

Equally, scholarly accounts often neglect the extratextual significance of black filmmakers, who, like the soul stars, themselves served as

symbols of the cycle's brand of black empowerment. Importantly, those who first fashioned blaxploitation were highly esteemed black cultural professionals and communitarians. Before making *Cotton Comes to Harlem*, Ossie Davis was an acclaimed actor and theatre director, as well as a prominent socialist and civil rights activist who gave the memorable eulogy at Malcolm X's funeral. Gordon Parks Sr. was an acclaimed *Life* photographer, novelist, and filmmaker, before he set his sights on *Shaft*. Melvin van Peebles was a bilingual writer and award-winning young filmmaker prior to *Sweetback*. In all three cases, aesthetic and cultural range extended well beyond the criminal yarns of black action films (for informative accounts of these black directors, see Patterson 1975; Monaco 1979; Donalson 2003).

Indeed, in some cases the movie narratives themselves worked as self-conscious allegories of black financial control and artistic prowess. Van Peebles understood that the image and fact of black creative self-determination were extremely important in these times of black cultural awakening. It could be argued that the success of *Sweetback* rested as much on his own publicity image as fêted and picaresque cultural producer as it did on the film itself. Van Peebles not only wrote, directed, and starred in the movie, but also controlled its advertising and marketing, driven by his status as extraordinarily resourceful and self-determined black cultural entrepreneur. The book he published about the film's making consolidated his image of macho self-reliance (Van Peebles 1996). Through his one-man marketing campaign, he drew attention to the parallels between his own status as "baadasssss" filmmaker and Sweetback's sexual and racial prowess in the film. Sweetback's sex hustles, which allow him to thwart the authorities *and* regular sexual conventions, paralleled the business "hustles" surrounding the movie's production and distribution, and its independent, "X-rated" status (for instance, he publicized the fact that he had pretended to make a porno film to avoid the unions and save money). Journalists picked up on the parallels, as one *New York Times* title put it: "The baadasssss success of Melvin van Peebles" (Gussow 1972).

Thus, the polar logic of "Shaft can do everything, I can do nothing" is interrupted by the wider sense of dawning black creativity and control surrounding these films. The tendency towards polemical critique also tends to overemphasize blaxploitation's role at the expense of other strands of early 1970s black-oriented filmmaking. Certainly, an extraordinary number of cheap black crime flicks were churned out during the period. But when James Monaco described the "birth of black film" (quoted at the beginning of this piece), he had in mind many different kinds of cinema. This period saw a mushrooming of independent and experimental black filmmaking, as well as more upmarket, black-themed films. For example, the bio-pic *Lady Sings the Blues* and the historical drama *Sounder* were both in the top ten films of 1972, appealing to older blacks as well as whites (Cook 2000: 498).

Nevertheless, early 1970s black-oriented filmmaking does tend to be subsumed under the banner of blaxploitation, not least because this cycle has proved to be very influential for the film industry and indeed for mainstream culturemaking since. Some of blaxploitation's waning energies were diverted in the mid-1970s into black caper-comedies (which, ironically, reprised the spirit of the first blaxploitation film, *Cotton Comes to Harlem*). Along with black-directed hits like *Let's Do It Again* (1975, directed by Sidney Poitier) and *Car Wash* (1976), the astonishing success of the Western spoof *Blazing Saddles* (1974, earning rentals of $48 million), with its interracial action-comedy team of Cleavon Little and Gene Wilder, offered the major studios a highly effective model for appealing to both black and white audiences, a model that would turn first Richard Pryor (co-writer of *Blazing Saddles*) and then Eddie Murphy into Hollywood superstars (Cook 2000; see Krämer 2005). We can also see blaxploitation's legacy in the ghetto action films made by young black directors like John Singleton and Allen and Albert Hughes (see, above all, Watkins 1998); in the crime-caper movies of Quentin Tarantino (see Martinez et al. 1998), and in a string of recent neo-blaxploitation spoofs and remakes. Darius James' recent journalistic account (1995) of the cycle gives a lively indication of its continuing relevance to African-American culture. More generally, blaxploitation's rich afterlife persists in the hip-hop styles and sounds that have recently taken the mainstream by storm (see Boyd 1997; Neal 2002; Quinn 2005).

References

Altman, R. (1999) *Film/Genre*. London: BFI.

Beaupré, L. (1967) One-third film public: negro; Columbia and UA pitch for biz, *Variety*, 29 November.

Bennett, L. (1971) The emancipation orgasm: Sweetback in wonderland, *Ebony*, 26 (September): 106–16.

Benshoff, H. (2000) Blaxploitation horror films: generic reappropriation or reinscription? *Cinema Journal*, 39(2): 31–50.

Bogle, D. (1973) *Toms, Coons, Mulattoes, Mammies, and Bucks: An Interpretive History of*

Blacks in American Films. New York: Bantam Books.

Boyd, T. (1997) *Am I Black Enough for You? Popular Culture from the 'Hood and Beyond.* Bloomington: Indiana University Press.

Brody, J.D. (1999) The returns of Cleopatra Jones, *Signs*, 28(1): 91–121.

Bruzzi, S. (1997) *Undressing Cinema: Clothing and Identity in the Movies.* London: Routledge.

Carson, C. (1981) *In Struggle: SNCC and the Black Awakening of the 1960s.* Cambridge, MA: Harvard University Press.

Cohn, L. (1993) All-time film rental champs, *Variety*, 10 May.

Cook, D. (2000) *Lost Illusions: American Cinema in the Shadow of Watergate and Vietnam, 1970–1979.* New York: Scribner's.

Cripps, T. (1990) Sweet Sweetback's Baadasssss Song and the changing politics of genre film, in P. Lehman (ed.) *Close Viewings: An Anthology of New Film Criticism.* Tallahassee: Florida State University Press.

Davis, A. (1983) *Women, Race, Class.* New York: Vintage.

Davis, A. (1998) Afro images: politics, fashion, and nostalgia, in M. Guillory and R. Green (eds) *Soul: Black Power, Politics, and Pleasure.* New York: New York University Press.

Doherty, T. (1988) *Teenagers and Teenpics: The Juvenilization of American Movies in the 1950s.* Boston: Unwin and Hyman.

Donalson, M. (2003) *Black Directors in Hollywood.* Austin: University of Texas Press.

George, N. (1994) *Blackface: Reflections on African-Americans and the Movies.* New York: HarperCollins.

Guerrero, E. (1993) *Framing Blackness: The African American Image in Film.* Philadelphia, PA: Temple University Press.

Gussow, M. (1972) The baadasssss success of Melvin van Peebles, *New York Times*, 20 August.

Hall, S. (1981) Notes on deconstructing "the popular", in R. Samuel (ed.) *People's History and Socialist Theory.* London: Routledge and Kegan Paul.

Hankin, K. (2002) *The Girls in the Black Room: Looking at the Lesbian Bar.* Minneapolis: University of Minnesota Press.

Hartmann, J. (1994) The trope of blaxploitation in critical responses to *Sweetback, Film History*, 6: 382–404.

Hill-Collins, P. (1991) *Black Feminist Thought: Knowledge, Consciousness, and the Politics of Empowerment.* New York: Routledge.

hooks, b. (1990) *Yearning: Race, Gender, and Cultural Politics.* Boston: South End Press.

James, D. (1987) Chained to devilpictures: cinema and black liberation in the sixties, in M. Davis, M. Marable, F. Pfeil and M. Sprinkler (eds) *The Year Left 2: An American Socialist Yearbook.* London: Verso.

James, D. (1995) *That's Blaxploitation: Roots of the Baadasssss 'Tude.* New York: St. Martin's Press.

Krämer, P. (2005) *The New Hollywood: From Bonnie and Clyde to Star Wars.* London: Wallflower Press.

Leab, D. (1976) *From Sambo to Superspade: The Black Experience in Motion Pictures.* Boston: Houghton Mifflin.

Lewis, J. (2000) *Hollywood V. Hardcore: How the Struggle over Censorship Created the Modern Film Industry*. New York: New York University Press.

Lipsitz, G. (1998) Genre anxiety and racial representation in 1970s cinema, in N. Browne (ed.) *Refiguring American Film Genres, History, and Theory*. Berkeley: University of California Press.

Lott, T. (1998) Hollywood and independent black cinema, in S. Neale and M. Smith (eds) *Contemporary Hollywood Cinema*. London: Routledge.

Lyne, W. (2000) No accident: from black power to black box office, *African American Review*, 34(1): 39–59.

Marcus, G. (1977) *Mystery Train: Images of America in the Rock'N'Roll Music*. New York: Omnibus Press.

Martinez G., Martinez, D. and Chavez, A. (eds) (1998) *What It Is … What It Was! The Black Film Explosion of the '70s in Words and Pictures*. New York: Hyperion.

McCall, N. (1995) *Makes Me Wanna Holler: A Young Black Man in America*. New York: Vintage.

Medovoi, L. (1998) Theorizing historicity, or the many meanings of *Blacula*, *Screen*, 39(1): 1–21.

Mercer, K. (1994) *Welcome to the Jungle: New Positions in Black Cultural Studies*. New York: Routledge.

Monaco, J. (1979) *American Film Now*. New York: Plume.

Neal, L. (1969) Beware of the tar baby, *New York Times*, 3 August.

Neal, M.A. (2002) *Soul Babies: Black Popular Culture and the Post-soul Aesthetic*. New York: Routledge.

Newton, H. (1971) He won't bleed me: a revolutionary analysis of "Sweet Sweetback's Baadasssss Song", *Black Panther* 6, 19 June: A–L.

Patterson, L. (1975) *Black Films and Filmmakers*. New York: Dodd, Mead and Co.

Poussaint, A. (1974) Blaxploitation movies: cheap thrills that degrade blacks, *Psychology Today* 7 (February): 22–31.

Quinn, E. (2001) " 'Pimpin' ain't easy": work, play, and "lifestylization" of the black pimp figure in early 1970s America, in B. Ward (ed.) *Media, Culture and the Modern American Freedom Struggle*. Gainesville: University Press of Florida.

Quinn, E. (2005) *Nuthin' but a "G" Thang: The Culture and Commerce of Gangsta Rap*. New York: Columbia University Press.

Reid, M. (1988) The black action film: the end of the patiently enduring black hero, *Film History*, 2(1): 23–36.

Rhines, J. (1996) *Black Film/White Money*. New Brunswick, NJ: Rutgers University Press.

Riley, C. (1972) Shaft can do everything, I can do nothing, *New York Times*, 14 August.

Robinson, C. (1998) Blaxploitation and the misrepresentation of liberation, *Race and Class*, 40(1): 1–12.

Schaefer, E. (1999) *Bold! Daring! Shocking! True! A History of Exploitation Films, 1919–59*. Durham, NC: Duke University Press.

Smith, C. (1972) Fight "black exploitation" in pix, *Variety*, 16 August.

Stanfield, P. (2004) Walking the streets: black gangsters and the "abandoned city" in the 1970s blaxploitation cycle, in L. Grieveson, E. Sonnet, and P. Stanfield (eds) *Mob Culture: Essays on the American Gangster Film*. New Brunswick, NJ: Rutgers University Press.

Steinberg, C. (1982) *Reel Facts: The Movie Book of Records*. New York: Vintage.

Van Deburg, W. (1992) *New Day in Babylon: The Black Power Movement and American Culture, 1965–1975*. Chicago: University of Chicago Press.

Van Deburg, W. (1997) *Black Camelot: African-American Culture Heroes in Their Times, 1960–1980*. Chicago: University of Chicago Press.

Van Peebles, M. (1996) *The Making of Sweet Sweetback's Baadasssss Song*. Edinburgh: Payback Press.

Ward, R. (1976) Black films, white profits, *Black Scholar*, 7(8): 13–24.

Washington, M. and Berlowitz, M. (1975) Swat "Superfly": blaxploitation films and high school youth, *Jump Cut* (Fall): 23–4.

Watkins, S.C. (1998) *Representing: Hip Hop Culture and the Production of Black Cinema*. Chicago: University of Chicago Press.

Winant, H. (2001) *The World is a Ghetto: Race and Democracy since World War II*. New York: Basic Books.

Wlodarz, J. (2004) Beyond the black macho: queer blaxploitation, *Velvet Light Trap*, 53 (Spring): 10–25.

THE 1970s AND AMERICAN DOCUMENTARY

Jonathan Kahana

AS IS OFTEN the case when film historians try to characterize a period in documentary film-making, the following historical account places greater emphasis on the culture of independent cinema than it does on other kinds of nonfiction film, like network television, or government agencies. This is in part because fewer of the films made for these venues are available for us to watch or study today, but perhaps also because these significant areas of nonfiction film practice have, in recent decades, been somewhat resistant to radical change. For example, network television, which had been one of the most important sponsors of new filmmakers in the early 1960s, was practically barred to independents by the end of the decade. With a few notable exceptions – including the controversial CBS Reports exposé *The Selling of the Pentagon* (Peter Davis, 1971), PBS's landmark experiment in domestic *cinéma vérité* (the term "reality TV" was not yet in use), *An American Family* (Craig Gilbert, 1973), and the networks' brief flirtation with the experimental video projects discussed below – television continued to rely on the tried-and-true styles

of documentary that persist to this day. But even restricting the field to the world of the documentary independent, the task of identifying unique and significant features of American documentary cinema in the 1970s has posed a challenge for film historians, who tend to disagree about whether the decade was a period of innovation or one of retrenchment (Rothman 2000).

This problem derives from history itself. At the level of social and political life, the 1970s were experienced, especially in the first half of the decade, as the aftershock of the tumultuous 1960s. Some veterans of the period's cultural wars liked to say that the decade didn't really begin until the "Summer of Love" of 1967 or the widespread anti-war and anti-establishment protests of 1968, and didn't end until 1973, the year in which President Richard Nixon resigned, the democratically elected Chilean leader Salvador Allende was assassinated in a CIA-sponsored military coup, and the US military presence in Southeast Asia began finally to end. In her account of the 1972 Republican presidential nominating convention, journalist Nora Sayre captured this feeling that the times were out of joint:

> Inside the Hall there were the realities of the Seventies, which culminated in a warmth-binge: Nixon shaking hands with a rapturous line-up while the lights gleamed on Agnew's forehead. What went on outside was back in the Sixties: a suppressed memory of bad days that were over. (Sayre 1996: 299)

But Nixon's very presence on the stage of national politics – poised, in Sayre's depiction, to defeat the Democratic anti-war candidate, George McGovern, by a landslide – was itself uncanny. In 1968, Nixon had returned from the political graveyard to which his party had consigned him after his 1960 loss to John F. Kennedy. Nixon's loss to Kennedy had been ascribed by many, including media guru Marshall McLuhan, to his performance in his televised debates with Kennedy, especially the infamous first debate, during which Nixon sweated visibly and, because of a poor choice of wardrobe, faded into the back of the set. For the 1968 campaign, Nixon hired a team of media experts to revamp his image, including the filmmaker Eugene Jones, whose *cinéma vérité* film *A Face of War* (1968) documented three months he and a small crew spent with a single company of Marines in Vietnam in 1966. Jones contributed to a media campaign designed to make Nixon into a trustworthy and straight-shooting voice of reason who would bring the country back from the brink of anarchy. These handlers used the very qualities of television that had been Nixon's enemies in 1960 – its immediacy and spontaneity – which made his resurgence all the more remarkable.

Mirroring this effort to undo the public's memory of Nixon, the 1970s was a period of retrospection and revision in American documentary. In contrast with the most important documentary form of the previous decade, *cinéma vérité*, which maintained an intense focus on the present, filmmakers of the 1970s tended to innovate around issues of history, either in technique or theme, or both. More and more, documentary filmmakers were relying on the methods of the historian, including interviews and the use of archives, both official and folkloric, to tell their stories. Similarly, the focus of many films was the past. This could be the biographical past of individuals, as in the personal portrait films that flourished in the period. Some of these were works of love and admiration, like Emile de Antonio's study of the liberal Democratic Senator Eugene McCarthy, *America is Hard to See* (1970), Judy Collins and Jill Godmilow's appreciation of the first female orchestra conductor in America, *Antonia: A Portrait of the Woman* (1974), and Ross McElwee's homage to his high-school teacher and friend, *Charleen* (1978). Others might be critical of their subjects, like de Antonio's vitriolic portrait of Nixon, *Millhouse: A White Comedy* (1971), or bemused studies of eccentrics, like Albert and David Maysles's *Grey Gardens* (1975), and Errol Morris's *Gates of Heaven* (1978). But history could also take the form of the collective past of social groups and social movements, as was the case in a spate of films examining the origins and traditions of the American Left, including *Union Maids* (James Klein and Julia Reichert, 1976), *With Babies and Banners* (Lorraine Gray, 1978), and *The Wobblies* (Stuart Bird and Deborah Shaffer, 1979). (One of the period's most challenging documentaries, Jon Jost's sprawling political home movie, *Speaking Directly* (1973), attempted to fuse the two kinds of portrait by treating the filmmaker's own life, including his difficult relationships with family and friends, into a microcosm of the nation and imperial aspirations.) Even films concerned with the present-day left, Like *Hearts and Minds* (Peter Davis, 1974), *Underground* (Emile de Antonio, 1976), and *Harlan County, USA* (Barbara Kopple, 1976), could have a recollective air. By the end of the 1970s, the mood of American social documentary was decidedly reflective, and even, it seemed, a little nostalgic for the prominent, even urgent role documentary had played in culture and politics at other moments in its history.

The renewal of interest in folklore among social documentarians, like the films about southern culture produced by the Kentucky-based Appalshop collective, the Center for Southern Folklore, and Les Blank, was itself a throwback to the 1930s, when the politics of social documentary oriented it towards manual and agricultural work and the culture of the "folks" who performed it. Notwithstanding their interest in folkways, some of these projects made use of especially progressive new technologies, like small-format video and public-access cable television, which addressed tiny, "narrowcast" audiences. Two such examples were Media Bus, a video collective made of artists who had left New York City for the placid environs of rural Lanesville, New York, and Johnson City, Tennessee's Broad-side Television, the brainchild of Ted Carpenter, a disciple of the legendary nonfiction filmmaker and teacher George Stoney, whose Alternate Media Center at New York University was the birthplace of many of the decade's most interesting experiments in democratic video and television.

These developments prompted Bill Nichols, the author of a mid-decade study of the most radical documentary organization of its period, The Newsreel (1967–early 1970s), to wonder at the beginning of the 1980s whether documentary had "lost its voice" as a result of its turn towards introspection, personal history, and the standpoint of the individual (Nichols 1980). The attention given to the unique experience of individuals in such films reflected a wider change in the focus and the conduct of anti-establishment politics in the decade. Turning from the Vietnam War and the "military-industrial complex" that waged it, activists began to concentrate on the politics of group identity. Their challenges to middle-American values and social structures took various forms, each generating its own repertoire of documentary, including a revitalized feminist movement (*The Woman's Film*, Women's Caucus of San Francisco Newsreel, 1971; *Janie's Janie*, Geri Ashur and Peter Barton, 1971; *Healthcaring: From Our End of the Speculum*, Denise Bostrom and Jane Warrenbrand, 1976) and many variations on the civil rights movement of the 1960s, including a militant continuation of the struggle for African-American social equality (*Finally Got the News*, Stewart Bird, Rene Lichtman, and Peter Gessner in Association with the League of Revolutionary Black Workers, 1970; *The Murder of Fred Hampton*, Mike Gray Associates, 1971), movements for the sexual liberation and civil rights of gay people (*Some of Your Best Friends*, Kenneth Robinson, 1971; *Word Is Out*, Mariposa Film Group, 1977), and the organization of groups celebrating the cultures of those visible minorities most subject to discrimination, such as Asian-Americans (*I Told You So*, Alan Kondo, 1973; *From Spikes to Spindles*, Christine Choy, 1976), Puerto Ricans (*Break and Enter*, New York Newsreel, 1970; *El Pueblo Se Levanta*, New York Newsreel, 1971), and Chicanos (*The Other Side*, Danny Lyon, 1979). Although films made by and for social minorities were unlikely to draw the sizeable audiences of films that addressed the broader constituencies of "youth" (like Michael Wadleigh's 1970 concert documentary, *Woodstock*) or the working class (like Kopple's Oscar-winning *Harlan County, USA.*), important changes in the ways that film could be circulated and shown inspired many of these groups to take up documentary film (and, on a much smaller scale, video) to articulate their cause and spread their messages. These included the flowering of numerous small, independent distribution organizations, many of them artist-run collectives, specializing in work by and about women and other economic or social minorities: notable examples include New Day Films, established in 1971, Women Make Movies (1972), and two offshoots of The Newsreel, Third World Newsreel (1973), based in New York, and California Newsreel (1975); all are still in operation.

If the films distributed by these upstart companies are relatively unknown today, even among students of American film history, the issues they raised and the style in which they raised them are still relevant. Indeed, many of the techniques that filmmakers use today originate in this period. In the next section of this chapter, we look more closely at a group of groundbreaking films and the artistic and social problems they addressed. Common to all of these films is formal innovation: some made use of a new form of recording – videotape – while others pursued new uses of documentary sound.

Video tactics: Portapak politics

In the early years of the 1960s, documentary filmmakers benefited from the Kennedy Administration's liberalizing policies. Political and cultural pressure placed on the major television networks to better serve the public interest created openings in the mainstream for social documentary. One result was a spate of films produced in the relatively new format of portable synch-sound 16 mm: the new freedom of movement and expression this equipment offered the filmmaker mirrored, implicitly, the freedoms promised by Kennedy's "New Frontier" policies. This happy coincidence of ideology and technology helped documentary cinema promote popular trust and involvement in government, making political processes seem real to ordinary citizens.

But with the assassination of Kennedy in 1963, the subsequent escalation of US aggression in Southeast Asia, and the election of Nixon, a law-and-order president intent on fanning the flames of economic and racial division and deeply suspicious of the public media, which he tried in various ways to undermine, the government became something of an enemy for documentary filmmakers. Just as with the election of Kennedy and the establishment of the liberal attitudes of Kennedy's "New Frontier", this ideological shift coincided with a fortuitous technological development: the introduction to the US market of cheap, portable video recording equipment. Like the developments in documentary sound discussed above, video brought changes to documentary that changed permanently its aesthetics and its practices.

In 1967, Sony unveiled a lightweight video camera/recorder combination known as the Portapak. Because the Portapak sold for around $1500, and because it used 1/2-inch tape, rather than the larger professional formats, ran under battery power, and weighed less than 20 pounds, the Portapak helped make video available to non-industrial and non-professional applications. Some of the first users were artists and activists experimenting with the medium in the representation of politics, as a way of competing with the commercial news organizations. One of the first of these experiments was a pair of hour-long programmes about the Democratic and Republican National Conventions of 1972, *The World's Largest TV Studio* and *Four More Years*. The programmes were produced by Top Value Television, a collaboration between a number of grassroots video production organizations. As its acronym suggested, TVTV aimed to cover the conventions in a way that would mirror the commercial networks' coverage. In doing so, it would draw attention to the excesses and redundancies of media spectacle. At the same time, the rough, loose style of the TVTV tapes would make an argument for decentralized, independent electronic journalism as a tool for alternative politics: one that might replace film as a medium of social change.

In *Guerrilla Television* (1971), his seminal handbook of the independent video movement, Michael Shamberg, a central figure in TVTV, called film an "evolutionary link between print and videotape" (Shamberg 1971: 7). Film was too much like print to survive the accelerated pace of media evolution, Shamberg argued. The expense and difficulty of its use had prevented it from truly democratizing communication. With the term *feedback*, Shamberg named both the technical capacity of video to produce an image at the same time that the image was being recorded and the democratizing potential of the new medium.

When TVTV went to Miami for the 1972 conventions with their Portapaks, they found an equally narcissistic and insular process in both camps. With a small amount of funding from a number of cable systems and a loose commitment from these systems to broadcast their tapes, TVTV managed to secure one of the non-network press passes to the convention floors (Boyle 1997: 36–8).[1] Their appearance and their equipment set them apart from the network crews, alternately drawing suspicious and admiring glances. (In *Four More Years*, Nixon's daughters Tricia and Julie pause in their movement along a receiving line to exclaim "Cute!" and "Incredible!" when they see one of the TVTV cameras.) Although at 28 members and several cameras, TVTV was a large operation by the standards of independent documentary, it was dwarfed by the 400- and 500-person armies of the network organizations. Governed neither by a primetime broadcast slot nor by professional codes of craft, TVTV was free to capture impressions that had been "neglected, rejected and missing from media coverage to date", and to do so in ways that drew attention to the expense, the hierarchical division of labour, and the false sense of urgency that determined the look and pace of network news coverage (Boyle 1997: 39).

Nixon's incumbency meant that the Republican Convention provided less dramatic intrigue. Nixon barely appears in *Four More Years*, showing up in only two brief shots. Instead, TVTV occupies itself with an investigation of the media that made Nixon seem so palatable to the "silent majority" of voters he claimed to represent. The news media come under special scrutiny, and the tape consistently returns to the question of how documentary form supports the journalist doctrine of objectivity. In its use of low-resolution half-inch video, long takes, and jarring editorial juxtapositions, the tape offers a subtle, equivocal response to Walter Cronkite's suggestion, during an interview with TVTV, that democracy was sustained by the consumption of many different news sources, and that the task of the professional journalist, in a crowded marketplace of information, was to provide a clear picture of events. The blurry pictures recorded by the Portapak only underscored the necessity of *interpreting* the documentary image. Although the TVTV tapes share with *Primary* (Robert Drew Associates, 1960), their *cinéma vérité* ancestor, a fascination with the improvisatory possibility of portable recording technologies, they are at pains to point out that the documentary camera was not a window on the truth, or at least not a very clean window.

This point is made consistently in the last part of the tape, as the antagonism between the protesters, particularly the Vietnam Veterans Against the War, and the Republican delegates moves to the foreground. On the last night of the convention, a large crowd of VVAW protesters threatened to force their way into the convention to disrupt Nixon's nomination (and keep Nixon out of primetime television). Making use of footage captured by TVTV's roving crews, *Four More Years* moves back and forth between the inside and the outside of the convention. After observing a passionate but ineffective attempt by protesters to make themselves heard from the back of the hall, the tape ends in ambiguity. Viewers are left with the image of the vacant media areas of the convention, the futile shouts of the veterans ringing in their ears.

Sound tactics: noise, the interview, and the underground

The various forms of sound that were important to radical politics in the 1960s and 1970s – music, speech, and noise – were equally important to the development of a new documentary aesthetics. In the self-conception of the New Left, sound had an important symbolic and organizational function: making

noise was a fundamental goal of the Left opposition and its public spheres. They were equally significant to the organization and the self-image of the New Left itself. The challenge that radical filmmakers set themselves was to document these outbreaks of political passion without turning them into spectacle, drained of their infectious energy. The audiospheres of revolutionary politics would provide documentary with new models of what, exactly, the political event could be.

The methods and concerns of European and North American *cinéma vérité* documentary had promised a method of social commentary in cinema that would be freed from the imperious voiceover exposition of classical documentary. Radical documentarists saw that *cinéma vérité*, especially as it was practised in the United States, was in this way no more "free" than its predecessors, and that it lent itself just as readily to an affirmation of the American way of life in both its individualist and corporatist aspects. Filmmakers who had cut their teeth in the civil rights and anti-war movements aimed to give voice to those marginalized social or political constituencies whose struggles were too local or too global to be considered "American" in the terms established by the national media. This project implied a self-aware method of media production that reflected the economic, technical, and organizational problems of film as a medium. Fidelity was the principle of this filmmaking: to put it simply, the less sophisticated the technology of representation, the higher the fidelity to the Movement (*Cineaste* 1972: 14–20). Thus, yelling, immoderate proclamations, ear-splitting rock music, electronic feedback, bad singing, untranslatable speeches and songs, accented English, and all manner of "wild" sounds became the aural icons of revolutionary cinema.

The work of The Newsreel, the Left documentary collective founded in 1967, followed this principle (Renov 1987; Nichols 1972, 1983). Newsreel (the definite article is usually dropped when critics write about the group) thought of itself as a news service, and it still intended to cover events. In their earliest formulations of the organization's goals, the founders of Newsreel didn't hesitate to describe their methods in conventionally journalistic terms: they still intended to "cover", to "show", and to "provide information" (Mekas 1972: 306). Forced by limited means and an ambitious production schedule to work simply, early Newsreel productions make the *absence* of polish and sophistication into a formal and political strategy. "Our films remind some people of battle footage", remarked founding member Robert Kramer:

> grainy, camera weaving around trying to get the material, and still not get beaten/trapped. Well, we, and many others, are at war. We not only document that war, but try to find ways to bring that war to places which have managed so far to buy themselves isolation from it. (Kramer 1968–9: 44)

In this spirit, a film like Newsreel's *People's War* (1969) wasn't only an opportunity to show viewers outside North Vietnam a sympathetic picture of popular resistance to the American invasion: it was also a way to "bring the war home", to use a phrase seen in anti-war flyers and posters of the time. Combining handheld-camera images shot by Newsreel cameramen inside North Vietnam and footage supplied by the North Vietnamese Army and the National Liberation Front in a rapid, patchwork montage, *People's War* presents an image of the conflict that was partial, in both senses of the word. By incorporating images produced on the other side of the conflict (some of which are accompanied by commentary, songs, or synchronous-sound dialogue in Vietnamese that the filmmakers leave untranslated), the filmmakers reinforce the point they make in the visual montage: that there was no such thing as an objective position on the war from which it might be viewed simply as an international crisis. To represent the war in the comprehensive, authoritative manner of the establishment news media was to presume that communications technologies and networks could still be ideologically neutral. For the radical Left, this was an impossible position.

A number of filmmakers took their oppositional politics in a different direction, turning instead toward the method of oral history to challenge the status quo. In some works of Left documentary that followed, the interview – whether staged directly for the filmmaker or shot in a public setting of testimony and confession – became, like the use of noise and non-synchronous sound in the Newsreel films, a way for these films to contest the self-evidence of the documentary image. Two of the most significant examples of this tactic were *Interviews with My Lai Veterans* (1970), a 22-minute compilation of interviews with five soldiers who participated in the infamous March 1968 massacre, and *Winter Soldier* (1971), a film of one of the public hearings staged in 1970 and 1971 by Vietnam Veterans Against the War (VVAW) and produced in collaboration with the veterans. In these films, the physical presence of the Vietnam veteran's intact body was betrayed by the shocking and traumatic nature of his testimony.

Winter Soldier documents the hearings held in Detroit at the end of January 1971 by VVAW, an event that was organized to generate national publicity for VVAW's "winter soldier" campaign to make public veterans' eyewitness accounts of military atrocities. When the March 1968 atrocities committed by US military personnel in the village of My Lai were made public in the fall of 1969, VVAW decided to hold its own hearings, to demonstrate that the torture and killing of prisoners and civilians and the wanton destruction of property, were hardly unusual practices for the military, and were in fact sanctioned at the highest levels of authority. The veterans' collaboration with the Winterfilm collective, a group of Left filmmakers based in New York City, was intended to spread the veterans' testimony even further, following the path laid by *Interviews with My Lai Veterans*, a short, Oscar-winning documentary on the same theme from the previous year. In his *Village Voice* review of *Winter Soldier*, alternative film critic and exhibitor Amos Vogel insists that there is "simply no substitute for seeing the faces of the men as they testify, their strain, tears, hesitations, and artless innocence", all of which serve as "inexorable guarantors of veracity, none available from a reading of the testimony" (Vogel 1972: 73). These images of the pain of testimony counterbalance the colour photographs and footage scattered throughout the film, images of American and South Vietnamese soldiers abuse prisoners and civilians. Some of the visible images that shock Vogel show soldiers gaily posing with suffering or dead bodies; they are, presumably, snapshots made as gruesome prizes, just as American soldiers cut ears from the dead at My Lai and elsewhere.

The filmmaker of the period most committed to the interview as a political tactic, however, was Emile de Antonio. Refined in films like *Point of Order* (1963), *Rush To Judgment* (1966), *In the Year of the Pig* (1969) and *Millhouse* (1971), de Antonio's method pitted interview subjects against each other, and against the commonsense evidence of official history found in newsreels and other mainstream sources of political information. In *Underground* (1976) de Antonio abandoned any impression of balance in his interviews, joining the fugitives of the Weather Underground at a secret location to talk with them on film about their revolutionary beliefs. In its politics, *Underground* complemented *Winter Soldier*: the object of both films was to bring voices of resistance out of hiding.

The film was shot over three days in the spring of 1975 but not released until May of the following year, a delay aggravated by a highly public federal government campaign to seize the footage and suppress the film (Biskind, 1975a, 1975b; Biskind and Weiss 1975; Hess 1975).[2] De Antonio became interested in making the film after reading *Prairie Fire*, a 150-page tract that the Weather Underground published in 1974, advocating collaboration among radical groups (Dorhn et al. 1974). The film endorses this strategy in its cinematic methods. To establish historical context, de Antonio and his brilliant editor, Mary Lampson, borrow heavily from the work of other filmmakers. To tell the group's own story, however, de Antonio staged an unusual group interview in a safe house used by the fugitives. He and cinematographer Haskell Wexler employ a number of devices to deface or, as de Antonio puts it, "sanitize" the image of the fugitives, including shooting them through a gauzy curtain and silhouetting them (Biskind 1975a: 26; Kifner 1977: 12).[3] One of these set-ups had Wexler shooting into a mirror, so that all the members of the production were gathered together in a single shot. Subverting the traditional conception of action in political documentary, *Underground* becomes a film of people listening to each other think about history. Wexler's subtle images and Lampson's clever editing challenge the audience to notice the resemblance between the discussion on screen and its own act of listening. They encourage us to think of dialogue as a stage in the process of social change.

Remainders of utopia: prison and documentary

If the underground was one place where Left utopias could still be conceived, prison was another. The experience of prisoners became a useful, if unexpected, political allegory for those on the Left in search of hope, especially after a number of spectacular instances of rebellion in state prisons in California, New York, and the Midwest. The most resonant of these was the inmate revolt in September 1971 at Attica State Prison in upstate New York. In the subsequent attempt by state authorities to put down the four-day rebellion, thirty-nine prisoners and guards were killed by police forces. A number of documentary and feature films about the event were produced in its wake. In their creative manipulation of sound and its relation to image, two of these films – Cinda Firestone's *Attica* (1973) and *Teach Our Children* (1973), the first film by the breakaway "Third-world" faction of New York Newsreel (directed by the uncredited pair Christine Choy and Susan Robeson, granddaughter of civil-rights hero Paul Robeson) – follow the path of the period's most inventive filmmakers.

Cinda Firestone's 1973 film *Attica* is based in interviews with subjects who fail in important ways to appear on screen. A protégé of Emile de Antonio, Firestone was working for the Liberation News Service when she began work on a pamphlet about the Attica prison rebellion. As she gathered more information,

the project grew into a short and then a feature-length film. *Attica* borrows its editing pattern from the films of de Antonio, like *In the Year of the Pig* (1969), where a dialogue is fabricated from interviews and archival footage between opposing points of view. Like de Antonio, Firestone argues against the revelation of truth in the *cinéma vérité* manner, where intense looking leads to discovery; instead, *Attica* suggests, knowledge is grounded in contestation and contradiction. Encouraged to come to his or her own conclusions, the viewer is in a position to honour the prisoners' revolutionary and fatal demands: that is, not only to better understand the tragedy, but to testify as well to the violent power of misrepresentation in the mainstream media on vulnerable minorities. It is in Firestone's presentation of interviews with the prisoners still behind bars, including the leaders of the rebellion, that this is most clear.

State regulations limiting the access of the media to prison meant that Firestone was forced to use still photographs of the prisoners to illustrate the audiotaped interviews with those members of the rebellion who were still serving sentences. Firestone arranges the photographs in series that partially animate them, keying the expressions on the faces to the rhythms of the prisoners' voices. This disjunction between sound and image has the effect of sympathy: the film's degraded capacity to adequately represent the prisoners reminds us that prison impedes movement. These reconstructed interviews serve as a cinematic approximation of prison, the mark of an experience the film wants us to share with the prisoners.

A different but no less sonoric approach is taken by *Teach Our Children*, released the same year as *Attica*, but much less well known or studied. The soundtrack of *Teach Our Children* establishes a dialogic and polyphonic space, one that acts as a counterpoint to the monolithic "America" referred to in the film's images, some of which depict the country's political and economic leaders in crude parodies. After an excerpt from a recording of the demands of the Attica prisoners, which ends abruptly, an instrumental tune with a Latin beat comes up under the images, which shifts shortly into a soul groove; these sound cues signal the filmmakers' intent to turn the issue of prison into an explicitly racial and ethnic one. Accompanying the sounds and following the quotation from Malcolm X are a series of brief documentary images of black and Latino city-dwellers, most of whom are smiling, laughing, and moving in a playful and unselfconscious way. Among these portraits is one of a group of children in a vacant lot, whom we see over and over during the film. The juxtaposition of sounds with each other and with the images, which draws attention to the editing, suggests an alternate view of the social world of American cities: against the homogenous social body achieved by the segregation of the poor and visible minorities in places like prisons, the viewer of this film is invited to imagine a heterogeneous space.

The rest of the film elaborates the themes presented in the first several shots in this pre-title sequence, and goes on to establish the parallel legacies of oppression and revolution: on the one hand, that of the oppressive conditions at Attica and in American prisons in general, the American class system, and American imperialism going back to the slave trade; and on the other hand, that connecting the Attica rebellion to the emergence of American social movements based on racial and ethnic identity, and anti-colonialist or anti-imperialist insurgency in the Third World. The film uses no voiceover narration, so these connections are implied only by the juxtaposition or intercutting of shots or sequences.

Underscoring these connections between what goes on inside prison and what goes on outside are a number of moments where the film seems to address the viewer directly. For instance, the familiar footage immediately following the film's title in which Elliot (L. D.) Barkley, one of the leaders of the Attica uprising, makes a statement for the press, in which Barkley calls all those watching "to assist us in putting an end to this situation that threatens the lives of not only us but of each and every one of you as well". If it is somewhat ironic that Barkley, who was slain during the siege by state forces, is seen and heard to call for direct action in support of the uprising through clips from television news, this irony is not lost on the makers of *Teach Our Children*: over and over, the film makes clear that we have seen and heard a great deal of the material of which *Teach Our Children* is composed, and gives the argument that America is another name for prison its resonance.

Indeed, *Teach Our Children* seems to project with great prescience the anxiety about actuality that documentary evinces today. The ambivalence with which one must approach the analysis of this powerful little film is familiar to the viewer of the postmodern documentary, which replaces sober truth claims with parody and sarcasm. Mixing the experimental and documentary forms with progressive thought, *Teach Our Children* joins other radical documentary of its period in proposing alternatives to the despair of the Left in the 1970s. If the social change these films envisioned did not, by and large, come to pass, they remain, nonetheless, important reminders of the ways that documentary itself changed during the decade.

Notes

1 Boyle's book provides a thorough account of TVTV and its contemporaries.
2 For accounts of FBI harassment of the filmmakers and the abortive Federal Grand Jury proceedings against the film, see Biskind (1975a, 1975b), Biskind and Weiss (1975) and Hess (1975).
3 De Antonio is quoted in Biskind (1975a). The term has an unfortunate resonance with the criticism Dohrn and others directed at the film after its release, accusing de Antonio and some members of Weather of seeking to "sanitize the image of the organization".

References

Biskind, P. (1975a) Subpoenaed over a movie on radicals, *The New York Times*, 5 June.

Biskind, P. (1975b) Does the US have the right to subpoena a film in progress?, *The New York Times*, 22 June.

Biskind, P. and Weiss, M.N. (1975) The Weather Underground: take one, *Rolling Stone*, 6 November.

Boyle, D. (1997) *Subject to Change: Guerrilla Television Revisited*. New York: OUP.

Cineaste, (1972) Radical American film? A questionnaire, *Cineaste*, 5(4): 14–20.

Dohrn, B., Ayers, B., Jones, J. and Sojourn, C. (1974) *Prairie Fire: The Politics of Revolutionary Anti-Imperialism*. New York: Communications Co.

Hess, J. (1975) Feds harass film crew, *Jump Cut*, 7 (August–September): 23–5.

Kifner, J. (1977) Weather Underground splits up over plan to come into the open, *The New York Times*, 18 January.

Kramer, R. (1968–9) Newsreel, *Film Quarterly*, 20(2): 44.

Mekas, J. (1972) *Movie Journal: The Rise of the New American Cinema, 1959–71*. New York: Macmillan.

Nichols, B. (1972) Newsreel: film and revolution. Master's thesis, University of California, Los Angeles.

Nichols, B. (1980) *Newsreel: Documentary Filmmaking on the American Left*. New York: Arno Press.

Nichols, B. (1983) The voice of documentary, *Film Quarterly* 36(3): 17–30.

Renov, M. (1987) Newsreel old and new – towards an historical profile, *Film Quarterly*, 41(1).

Rothman, W. (2000) Looking back and turning inward: American documentary films of the seventies, in D.A. Cook (ed.) *Lost Illusions: American Cinema in the Shadow of Watergate and Vietnam, 1970–1979*, vol. 9. New York: Charles Scribner's Sons.

Sayre, N. (1996) *Sixties Going on Seventies*. New Brunswick, NJ: Rutgers University Press.

Shamberg, M. and Raindance Corporation (1971) Meta-manual, in *Guerrilla Television*. New York: Holt, Rinehart and Winston.

Vogel, A. (1972) [untitled review], *The Village Voice*, 3 February: 73.

"The term 'cult' movie", writes David Hughes "is as overused and misapplied as the term 'genius', but *Eraserhead* (1977) defines the former term as surely as it defines its auteur as the latter" (2001: 32). This is indeed correct. Best described as "A dream of dark and troubling things", David Lynch's feature debut infamously became a quintessential midnight movie hit in the US, before slowly spreading its diseased spell around the globe. A surreal nightmare about a terrified man who finds himself in sole charge of a monstrous child, *Eraserhead* boasted extraordinary monochrome visuals (courtesy of cinematographers Frederick Elmes and Herbert Cardwell), a hair-raising performance from John (Jack) Nance, and a disorientatingly powerful soundtrack cooked up by Lynch and his long-time aural collaborator Alan Splet. Conjuring a Kafka-esque vision of an industrial wasteland beset by guilt, anguish, and madness inspired by Lynch's time in Philadelphia ("It's my *Philadelphia Story*," he told Chris Rodley, "It just doesn't have Jimmy Stewart in it!" (Rodley 1997: 56]), the film suggested art-house influences ranging from Lang through Buñuel to Cocteau, only some of which Lynch acknowledges. Yet for all its *avant garde* credentials "the film's pervasive uncanniness" as Schneider (2004:16) astutely notes "is most fruitfully explained, though never explained away, when situated within the context of the horror genre and its established traditions". It was this element of horror that attracted the cult film fans who first put *Eraserhead* on the map, despite a wildly dismissive (and with hindsight extremely foolish) panning in the industry bible *Variety*, which labelled it "a sickening bad-taste exercise" (Elley 1992: 208).

Eraserhead

Having cut his teeth on art installations and short film projects (*Six Figures Getting Sick*, 1967; *The Alphabet*; 1968; *The Grandmother*, 1970), Lynch, who by then was at the American Film Institute's Center of Advanced Film Studies, was offered $50,000 by Fox to transform his *Gardenback* script into a low-budget monster movie. After struggling with the project, he instead set about making *Eraserhead* with $10,000 funding earmarked for a six-week shoot. Work began in May 1972, but the original tight schedule promptly unravelled into a four-year odyssey, postproduction not being completed until April 1976, and the final recut stretching into 1977. During the course of the film's protracted gestation and birth, Lynch wrestled with marriage, divorce and fatherhood, supported himself with a paper round, and fuelled his soul with sugary milk shakes from the local Bob's Big Boy Diner. During one hiatus, he completed the short film *The Amputee* (1974), images from which would later be echoed in his daughter Jennifer's feature *Boxing Helena* (1993). Indeed, Jennifer, who was born with club feet, has been quoted as saying that *Eraserhead* "without a doubt . . . was inspired by my conception and birth, because David in no uncertain terms did not want a family. It was not his idea to get married, nor was it his idea to have children. But . . . it happened" (Woods 1997: 35). While accepting that "Obviously, since a person is alive and they're noticing things around them, ideas are going to come", David Lynch insists that literal interpretations of *Eraserhead* are "ridiculous" (Rodley 1997: 78).

Exactly what *Eraserhead* is about remains a mystery, though it is loosely the story of Henry (Nance) finding himself in the sole care of a mutant child which he appears to have fathered. Most interpretations are sensibly general, such as Andrew's (1998: 44) reading that "Clearly, the movie is a phantasmagoric meditation, loosely disguised as a kind of horror movie, on problems associated with marriage, parenting, and the whole cycle of sex and birth, love and death." Lynch himself has proven consistently unwilling to explain *Eraserhead*, becoming particularly evasive on the subject of the creation of the "baby" (some reports suggest that it is an animated bovine foetus), confessing only to having examined the insides of a cat ('the membranes, the hair, the skin") (Rodley 1997: 78). It is known that Lynch began practising transcendental meditation (TM) during the film's strange gestation, and has continued the practice throughout his feature film career, eventually establishing a centre for the promotion of TM and its healing powers. Several talismanic tropes, which recur throughout his work, are cemented in *Eraserhead*, in particular the arcing electrical imagery and ambient industrial soundscapes, which became a trademark. (Lynch currently mixes his films on a custom-built console, the foundations of which contain some of the ashes of Alan Splet.) The haunting Lady in the Radiator (played by Laurel Near) seems to be a clear precusor of the Man from Another Place in *Twin Peaks*, and Lynch himself has noted that "The floor pattern in Henry's apartment lobby is the same as the floor in the Red Room in *Twin Peaks*" (Rodley 1997: 64). Catherine Coulson, who worked as an assistant director and camera operator on *Eraserhead*, and was to have appeared in a cut scene, reports that Lynch first came up with her *Twin Peaks* Log Lady character during the extended shoot, while Lynch's longstanding relationship with Coulson's husband Jack Nance (who also appeared in *Dune*, *Blue Velvet*, *Wild at Heart*, *Twin Peaks* and *Lost Highway*) was sealed on *Eraserhead*.

Originally screened for the American Film Institute (and subsequently at the Filmex festival) at a length of around 100 minutes, *Eraserhead* was recut to a trimmer 89 minutes, losing three or four scenes, the absence of which has generated much interest among fans, if not Lynch himself. Reportedly one of Stanley Kubrick's favourite films, *Eraserhead* served as an extraordinary calling card for Lynch, who was subsequently enlisted by Mel Brooks to helm *The Elephant Man* (1980) with which it shares a uniquely hellish vision of industrial existence. After the mainstream failure of *Dune* (1984), Lynch secured his position as America's favourite surrealist director with the nightmare-behind-the-smile terrors of *Blue Velvet* (1986). Several Oscar nominations and prestigious international awards have helped him maintain his position at the apex of the arthouse *and* the multiplex, despite the violent rejection of *Twin Peaks: Fire Walk with Me*, which remains his most underestimated feature. Reflecting upon *Eraserhead* from the vantage point of his later success, Lynch admitted that he had viewed a print of it several years after its completion and felt, on that particular day, that "It's a perfect film" (Rodley 1997: 86).

References

Andrew, G. (1998) *Stranger Than Paradise: Maverick Film-Makers in Recent American Cinema*. London: Prion.

Elley, R. (ed.) (1992) *Variety Movie Guide*. London: Reed.

Hughes, D. (2001) *The Complete Lynch*. London: Virgin.

Nochimson, M.P. (1997) *The Passion of David Lynch*. Austin: University of Texas Press.

Rodley, C. (ed.) (1997) *Lynch on Lynch*. London: Faber and Faber.

Schneider, S.J. (2004) The essential evil in/of *Eraserhead* (or, Lynch to the contrary), in E. Sheen and A. Davison (eds) *The Cinema of David Lynch: American Dreams, Nightmare Visions*. London: Wallflower Press, pp. 5–18.

Woods, P. A. (1997) *Weirdsville USA: The Obsessive Universe of David Lynch*. London: Plexus.

Mark Kermode

1970–79	Rentals to date for year just ending
1970 *Airport*	$ 37,650,000
1971 *Love Story*	$ 50,000,000
1972 *The Godfather*	$ 81,500,000
1973 *The Poseidon Adventure*	$ 40,000,000
1974 *The Sting*	$ 88,450,000
1975 *Jaws*	$102,650,000
1976 *One Flew Over the Cuckoo's Nest*	$ 56,500,000
1977 *Star Wars*	$127,000,000
1978 *Grease*	$ 83,091,000
1979 *Superman*	$ 81,000,000

1970

Academy Awards
Best Picture: *Patton* – Frank McCarthy
Best Director: Franklin J. Schaffner – *Patton*
Best Actor in a leading role: George C. Scott – *Patton*
Best Actor in a supporting role: John Mills – *Ryan's Daughter*
Best Actress in a leading role: Glenda Jackson – *Women in Love*
Best Actress in a supporting role: Helen Hayes – *Airport*
Cannes International Film Festival
Grand Prix International du Festival: *M*A*S*H* — Robert Altman

1971

Academy Awards
Best Picture: *The French Connection* – Philip D'Antoni
Best Director: William Friedkin – *The French Connection*
Best Actor in a leading role: Gene Hackman – *The French Connection*
Best Actor in a supporting role: Ben Johnson – *The Last Picture Show*
Best Actress in a leading role: Jane Fonda – *Klute*
Best Actress in a supporting role: Cloris Leachman – *The Last Picture Show*
Cannes International Film Festival
Grand Prix International du Festival: *The Go-Between* — Joseph Losey

1972

Academy Awards
Best Picture: *The Godfather* – Albert S. Ruddy
Best Director: Bob Fosse – *Cabaret*
Best Actor in a leading role: Marlon Brando – *The Godfather*
Best Actor in a supporting role: Joel Grey – *Cabaret*
Best Actress in a leading role: Liza Minnelli – *Cabaret*

Best Actress in a supporting role: Eileen Heckart – *Butterflies Are Free*
Cannes International Film Festival
Grand Prix International du Festival: *Il Caso Matei* – Francesco Rosi and *La Classe Operaia Va in Paradiso* – Elio Petri

1973

Academy Awards
Best Picture: *The Sting* – Tony Bill, Michael Phillips, Julia Phillips
Best Director: George Roy Hill – *The Sting*
Best Actor in a leading role: Jack Lemmon – *Save the Tiger*
Best Actor in a supporting role: John Houseman – *The Paper Chase*
Best Actress in a leading role: Glenda Jackson – *A Touch of Class*
Best Actress in a supporting role: Tatum O'Neal – *Paper Moon*
Cannes International Film Festival
Grand Prix International du Festival: *Scarecrow* — Jerry Schatzberg and *The Hireling* — Alan Bridges

1974

Academy Awards
Best Picture: *The Godfather Part II* – Francis Ford Coppola, Gray Frederickson, Fred Roos
Best Director: Francis Ford Coppola – *The Godfather Part II*
Best Actor in a leading role: Art Carney – *Harry and Tonto*
Best Actor in a supporting role: Robert De Niro – *The Godfather Part II*
Best Actress in a leading role: Ellen Burstyn – *Alice Doesn't Live Here Anymore*
Best Actress in a supporting role: Ingrid Bergman – *Murder on the Orient Express*
Cannes International Film Festival
Grand Prix International du Festival: *The Conversation* – Francis Ford Coppola

1975

Academy Awards
Best Picture: *One Flew Over the Cuckoo's Nest* – Saul Zaentz, Michael Douglas
Best Director: Milos Forman – *One Flew Over the Cuckoo's Nest*
Best Actor in a leading role: Jack Nicholson – *One Flew Over the Cuckoo's Nest*
Best Actor in a supporting role: George Burns – *The Sunshine Boys*
Best Actress in a leading role: Louise Fletcher – *One Flew Over the Cuckoo's Nest*
Best Actress in a supporting role: Lee Grant – *Shampoo*
Cannes International Film Festival
Palme d'Or: *Chronique des Années de Braise* — Mohammed Lakdha-Hamina

1976

Academy Awards
Best Picture: *Rocky* – Irwin Winkler, Robert Chartoff
Best Director: John G. Avildsen – *Rocky*
Best Actor in a leading role: Peter Finch – *Network*
Best Actor in a supporting role: Jason Robards – *All the President's Men*
Best Actress in a leading role: Faye Dunaway – *Network*

Best Actress in a supporting role: Beatrice Straight – *Network*
Cannes International Film Festival
Palme d'Or: *Taxi Driver* – Martin Scorsese

1977

Academy Awards
Best Picture: *Annie Hall* – Charles H. Joffe
Best Director: Woody Allen – *Annie Hall*
Best Actor in a leading role: Richard Dreyfuss – *The Goodbye Girl*
Best Actor in a supporting role: Jason Robards – *Julia*
Best Actress in a leading role: Diane Keaton – *Annie Hall*
Best Actress in a supporting role: Vanessa Redgrave – *Julia*
Cannes International Film Festival
Palme d'Or: *Padre Padrone* – Vittorio Taviani

1978

Academy Awards
Best Picture: *The Deer Hunter* – Barry Spikings, Michael Deeley, Michael Cimino, John Peverall
Best Director: Michael Cimino – *The Deer Hunter*
Best Actor in a leading role: Jon Voight – *Coming Home*
Best Actor in a supporting role: Christopher Walken – *The Deer Hunter*
Best Actress in a leading role: Jane Fonda – *Coming Home*
Best Actress in a supporting role: Maggie Smith – *California Suite*
Cannes International Film Festival
Palme d'Or: *L'Albero degli Zoccoli* — Ermanno Olmi

1979

Academy Awards
Best Picture: *Kramer vs. Kramer* – Stanley R. Jaffe
Best Director: Robert Benton – *Kramer vs. Kramer*
Best Actor in a leading role: Dustin Hoffman – *Kramer vs. Kramer*
Best Actor in a supporting role: Melvyn Douglas – *Being There*
Best Actress in a leading role: Sally Field – *Norma Rae*
Best Actress in a supporting role: Meryl Streep – *Kramer vs. Kramer*
Cannes International Film Festival
Palme d'Or: *Die Blechtrommel* — Völker Schlondorff and *Apocalypse Now* — Francis Ford Coppola

SUGGESTED FURTHER READING

Biskind, P. (1998) *Easy Riders, Raging Bulls: How the Sex 'n' Drugs 'n' Rock 'n' Roll Generation Saved Hollywood*. London: Bloomsbury.

Clover, C. (1992) *Men, Women and Chain Saws: Gender in the Modern Horror Film*. London: BFI.

Cook, D. (1998) Auteur cinema and the "film generation" in 1970s Hollywood, in J. Lewis, (ed.) *The New American Cinema*. Durham, NC: Duke University Press, pp. 11–37.

Cook, D. (2000) *Lost Illusions: American Cinema in the Shadow of Watergate and Vietnam, 1970–1979*, vol. 9 of *History of the American Cinema*. Berkeley and London: University of California Press.

Elsaesser, T., Horwath, A. and King, N. (eds) (2004) *The Last Great American Picture Show: New Hollywood Cinema in the 1970s*. Amsterdam: Amsterdam University Press.

Gilbey, R. (2003) *It Don't Worry Me: Nashville, Jaws, Star Wars and Beyond*. London: Faber & Faber.

Keane, S. (2001) *Disaster Movies: Cinema of Catastrophe*. London: Wallflower Press.

Kolker, R. (2000) *A Cinema of Loneliness: Penn, Stone, Kubrick, Scorsese, Spielberg, Altman*. New York and Oxford: Oxford University Press.

Lev, P. (2000) *American Films of the '70s: Conflicting Visions*. Austin: University of Texas Press.

Paul, S. (1999) *The Seventies Now: Culture as Surveillance*. Durham, NC and London: Duke University Press.

Ryan, D. and Kellner, J. (1988) *Camera Politica: The Politics and Ideology of Contemporary Hollywood Film*. Bloomington: Indiana University Press.

Schatz, T. (1993) The new Hollywood, in J. Collins, H. Radner and A.P. Collins (eds) *Film Theory Goes to the Movies*. New York and London: Routledge.

Wood, R. (1986) *Hollywood from Vietnam to Reagan*. New York: Columbia University Press.

QUESTIONS FOR DISCUSSION

This section contains brief background notes which are designed to guide students to some of the main issues that have been raised by the various articles here on the 1970s. These are followed by some sample essay questions which both students and tutors may find useful in guiding class discussion as well as setting exercises.

Background Notes

The 1970s was the setting for a distinct swing in the direction and fortunes of the Hollywood industry. In the opening years of the decade a considerable amount of Hollywood production followed up on the trend towards a European-influenced style of filmmaking which was more contemplative with less goal-driven and more ambiguously rendered characters and themes. However, alongside this was a reverence for the classical period. Although it was less obvious at the time, this was the direction that became the basis for the "New Hollywood" perhaps best exemplified by the phenomenal success of Steven Spielberg with *Jaws* (1975) and George Lucas with *Star Wars* (1976). Technological innovations, from the motion-control system developed by Lucasfilm for the space battle sequences in *Star Wars* to multi-track "sound designing" Dolby noise reduction, made effects visually more effective and often more cost efficient. These developments helped to aid the rise of the spectacle-based cinema associated with Spielberg and Lucas.

In the mainstream exhibition sector there was a steady move toward the multiplex as shopping malls began to proliferate in the suburban areas. By the decade's end drive-ins had given way to this development although the urban art-house cinema remained vibrant. The development of the saturation release and the recognition of the advantages of the summer release of films aimed at family audiences were central to the New Hollywood signalled by Lucas and Spielberg.

Documentary production at this time had a similar dual direction in that the direct cinema style developed in the 1960s continued to be the method of choice for some documentary filmmakers and for the less adventurous television networks. Alongside that was the development of more experimental styles that questioned objectivity. Further, the 1970s saw an emphasis on the past and a rewriting of history from a number of political perspectives. As Jonathan Kahana discusses above, this was a departure from the "intense focus on the present" of the direct cinema style.

Questions

The following questions have been devised to help guide further research and thinking about this period.

1 The first half of the decade is characterized by some as a rare moment in Hollywood cinema when a politically and artistically challenging cinema was possible. This is mainly associated with the vision of directors like Bob Rafaelson, Melvin Van Peebles, Arthur Penn, Francis Ford Coppola, Martin Scorsese, Robert Altman or Woody Allen. Also these directors, in some way or another, have acknowledged the influence of auteurist critics and filmmakers such as Jean Luc Godard and François Truffaut on their films. Define what is particular and distinct about the style of film-making of a director of your choice from this period, referring closely to at least two films, and to theories of auteurism from the period. As an extension of these references to authorship, discuss filmmaking in the context of the work of a particular producer or production company (e.g. BBS Productions, Robert Evans) or specific documentary filmmakers such as Frederick Wiseman, Emile de Antonio or Jill Godmilow and Judy Collins.

2 The release of *Jaws* in the summer of 1975 in many ways instigated a trend in the release strategies of blockbuster films that continues to the present day. As an exercise which may help to demonstrate this, compare the marketing and reception of a blockbuster from the 1970s with one from the 1990s.

3 The 1970s has been seen as the decade where Hollywood studios recognized the value of the exploitation cinema associated with low-budget companies like American International Pictures of the 1950s and 1960s. Films such as Friedkin's *The Exorcist* (1973) and Spielberg's *Jaws* have been noted as having reworked the sensational horror film of the 1950s. Further, "exploitation" was a term applied to specific audiences as well as films. Melvin Van Peebles' *Sweet Sweetback's Baadasssss Song* (1971) drew the attention of the industry to the profit potential represented by black urban audiences and gave rise to the "blaxploitation" cycle of films. Define the various meanings of "exploitation cinema" with reference to two or three particular films.

4 Following the theme of horror, the 1970s saw the production of at least two highly influential films. *The Exorcist* and *The Texas Chain Saw Massacre* (1974) are noteworthy for the considerable press and public reaction they received as well as initiating the "demonic possession" and the "slasher" cycles respectively. Collect some contemporary reviews or articles reporting the reception of one of these films and try to identify the themes or concerns that are driving their opinions. Alternatively, discuss the way in which any horror film from the 1970s or 1980s dramatizes one of the following: adolescence; bodies; troubled families; and absent fathers.

5 It was also apparent in the 1970s that there was paradoxically a reverence for the Hollywood genres of the 1930s and 1940s as well as a reworking and updating of their themes. Westerns such as *Soldier Blue* (1970) or *Ulzana's Raid* (1972) offered a revisionist approach to the

Western, as did *The Godfather* films (parts I and II, 1972 and 1974). Analyze how one or two films from this period work with the narrative and stylistic conventions of a specific genre which was revisited in this decade.

6   Stars have been an important factor in publicity strategies, hopefully ensuring a film's success throughout the history of Hollywood. In the 1970s a number of factors enhanced this role from the rise of the agent as deal broker in the package unit system to the prevalence of the blockbuster mentality. In each of these cases the star was central; an established star could in itself help to "green-light" a project. Stars in some cases enjoyed unprecedented control over their choice of projects. Trace the construction of one star of your choice from this period, paying attention to the type of roles or character played, any sense of casting against type and the surrounding advertising for the films and their subsequent reviews and feature stories.

7   Given that changes in production technology impacted on filmmaking practices in the 1970s, most obviously with the blockbuster spectacle-based cinema of Lucas and Spielberg, consider how these might have had wider effects on filmmaking generally. For instance, how might small-scale independent production have been affected?

the **80s**

EIGHTIES

INTRODUCTION

The history of Hollywood is certainly not one of unchanging stability in the films, their reception or the formation of the industry. The 1980s are often thought of as the time when Hollywood consolidated its hold on world markets while paradoxically becoming an overtly "nationalistic", reactionary cinema. This view, as this section suggests, is only partly accurate, and demonstrates that when looked at in more detail, the 1980s was a decade of considerable instability, profound change and challenging films.

Perhaps the widely held view of the 1980s as a period of politically retrograde cinema is not surprising given some of the high profile comments at the time from political figures and filmmakers alike. Famously, in June 1985, newly re-elected President Ronald Reagan – in reference to the release of the TWA hostages held by terrorists in Lebanon – stated that he had seen *Rambo* (*First Blood Part II*, George P. Cosmatos, 1985) the night before and that next time "he would know what to do". Less than a year later Oliver Stone in his acceptance speech for winning the Best Picture Oscar for *Platoon*, a morality tale rendered through a "realistic" depiction of the violence of combat during the American war in Vietnam, told his audience "What you're saying is that for the first time you really understood what happened over there, and that it should never happen again." Albeit from different political perspectives, both exhibit hubristic, over-inflated confidence in the ideological project of Hollywood (i.e. that cinema can solve national dilemmas). In any case the perception of the Reagan era remains "Hollywood as politics" and "politics as Hollywood".

It is true that many of the high profile movies of the decade do seem to directly address either the overtly political issues of the day such as *First Blood* (Ted Kotcheff, 1982), *Platoon* (Oliver Stone, 1986), *Rambo: First Blood Part II*, *The Delta Force* (Menahem Golan, 1986), or the more "personal politics" of family, in films like *E.T.* (Steven Spielberg, *1982*), *Back to the Future* (Robert Zemeckis, 1985), and that most lucrative of family romances, the second and third instalments of the Star Wars franchise, *The Empire Strikes Back* (Irvin Kershner, 1980) and *Return of the Jedi* (Richard Marquand, 1983).

However, the decade was anything but stable. It opened with the box office disaster and critical failure of Michael Cimino's *Heaven's Gate* (1980), which caused United Artists' parent company Transamerica to sell its entertainment wing, thus signalling both the end of the period of conglomeration of diverse companies that had begun in the late 1960s, and the demise of industry confidence in the "vision" of the auteur. Big budgets would continue but were more readily attached to tried and true genres such as science fiction and with directors like Spielberg and Lucas, and less often with the downbeat timbre associated with 1970s auteurs such as Robert Altman or Martin Scorsese. As Stephen Prince demonstrates in this section, the 1980s would be marked by the development of "synergy" where the film became part of a larger set of related cultural products such as soundtracks, television spin-offs, video games, toys and books. Further, these "synergistic" practices extended to commercial tie-ins – so much so that Richard Maltby has suggested that this is a marker of the difference between the "classical industry" and the "new" Hollywood:

> Where the classical industry generally declined to permit advertising in its products or its exhibition sites ... [since] 1975, movies have become increasingly commodified, both in themselves as objects forming part of a chain of goods, and as 'multipliers' for the sale of other products. (Maltby 1998: 27)

These developments provided both the setting and the impetus for perhaps the most significant change in the history of Hollywood since the coming of sound, the creation and successful exploitation of a new form of exhibition/site of consumption, home video.

As we have already seen, the film industry had been dependent upon the theatrical release and then sell-through to network television since the late 1950s. The pre-1980s format for releasing a mainstream Hollywood film was the "saturation release" or the "platform release" method. The first method is where the film is released in a large number of theatres nationwide to maximize the effect of the pre-release hype, and to minimize the dependence on "word-of-mouth". This had been an unmitigated success with *Jaws* (1975) and was the industry's preferred method by and large for big-budget features. The platform method was reserved for films that "had solid commercial potential but required a careful build to reach that potential" (Prince 2000: 90). Films such as Woody Allen's *Hannah and Her Sisters* (1986) were given limited release in a few major cities like New York or Los Angeles with the hope of garnering good critical reviews and building an impression of "grassroots" approval and positive "word of mouth". Once the apex of interest in the film had been reached, the broadcasting rights for a limited number of screenings were sold to network television. The 1980s saw this change dramatically: where films would go through a more extended set of release stages or "windows", which helped to maximize the profit of theatrically successful films but perhaps, more importantly, provided a more dependable means for recouping investment for films that had been less successful theatrically. Titles would go to release on home video six months after the theatrical release then on to pay-cable after a further six months. As Prince suggests elsewhere, this pattern by and large exhausted the interest in the film, so television "found that they could pay studios less for their top films, and studios in turn, began exploring alternatives to network television" (2000: 92).

The advantages of video "sell-through" and the development of multiple release windows for the major Hollywood studios were that they were able to spread the risk involved in an environment of ever-escalating costs of production. Paradoxically the industry spent the first part of the decade wrangling in the courts, seeking copyright protection for what was perceived as a potential loss in revenue through pirating and through an uncontrolled video renting industry. However, the longer-term effects of the video market were by the end of the decade the addition of a lucrative income stream in videos sold by the majors directly to the consumer and perhaps, more significantly, the creation of a demand for films that the majors alone were not able to fulfil. Home video was a convenience that at first the industry saw as a threat to theatrical receipts, but which in the end provoked a resurgence in interest in film ultimately worldwide. This demand allowed for the advent of smaller independent companies which, as Stephen Prince points out, "became an enduring part of eighties film culture, offering alternative styles and visions to the more traditional product handled by the majors" (2000: 117).

This same phenomenon provided the impetus for the adult film industry's exponential growth throughout the 1980s as the urban porn theatre of the 1970s gave way to the privacy of home viewing. Video also made the production of hardcore pornography more cost effective, which resulted in an increase in production: in 1982 400 such titles were released in the United States, whereas by 1989 this had increased to 1300 (Prince 2000: 122). Video also meant that films which were either unable to get backing for theatrical distribution or were too "adult" to get an MPAA rating could be released "direct-to-video" as a means of meeting the increased demand for product to be watched in the home. These tended to be genre "exploitation" horror, crime and softcore films. Softcore "erotic thrillers" such as *Body Heat* (Lawrence Kasdan, 1981) or *Body Double* (Brian De Palma, 1984) were feature release films that became the template for direct to video releases of more explicit but still softcore erotic thrillers like *Night Eyes* (Jag Mundhra 1989) in the 1990s (Williams 2005: 267–8).

Video made possible a new access to films and in its turn encouraged a much wider set of "ancillary markets" for the industry than had the older theatrical television pattern. Traditional cinema exhibition in the older version, particularly the art-house and old-style "A" list theatrical releases, had generally been a means by which the event of the film was special, whether it was a road-shown blockbuster or a treasure from the canon of classic cinema. Since the beginning of the film industry audiences had been limited in the access they had to films, often seeing a film only once on its original release. Of course, the arrival of television as a mass-viewing form in the 1940s and 1950s began to challenge this. Television then supplemented urban art centres or art-house theatres. However, by the end of the 1980s, much of the back catalogue of Hollywood cinema, and increasingly European and world cinema, was beginning to become available for the type of viewing on demand and repeated viewing that video made possible. In fact, where the purchase of a theatre ticket gave one the ephemeral pleasure of the film's spectacle and narrative limited to the length of the film's run, video shifted the terms of the exchange so that the film became a tangible object rather than a hoped-for experience.

Throughout this book we have referenced in one way or another the impact of generational trends. The baby boom has continued to be perhaps the most significant of the underlying factors in the developments and shifts in the American film industry since 1960 (Allen 1999). The impact of video gave a considerable impetus to the adult film industry but the major film companies made the much more high profile shift towards attracting the family audience. Here synergistic practices of surrounding family-oriented feature films with related products such as toys, books, or television spin-offs proved remarkably successful. The leaders in this respect were Spielberg and Lucas. Peter Krämer outlines the fact that the model for this practice was Disney who had been working "synergistically" almost from the creation of Mickey Mouse in the 1920s, but certainly since the creation of the Disneyland theme-park in Anaheim, California, in the 1950s. Krämer demonstrates how Disney had actually appealed to baby boomers first in the 1950s and early 1960s and then in the late 1970s and 1980s when this generation moved into parenthood. Paradoxically the majors had spent much of their efforts targeting teenagers and older adults in the late 1960s and 1970s but it was only in the 1980s that they began to take notice of the family audience and, as Krämer shows, structured their corporations in line with the "Disney Model".

The *Indiana Jones* franchise was a product of a combination of Lucasfilm with Paramount. Not only was this an example of how successful the strategy of synergy could be – it also demonstrates the higher profile role that independent filmmakers began to have in the industry. George Lucas is, of course, not associated with the aesthetics of independent filmmaking, which usually run counter to blockbuster sensibilities, despite his early direction of two relatively non-mainstream "American classics" *THX1138* (1971) and *American Graffiti* (1973). However, his working practices and geographical distance from Hollywood in Northern California appear more in line with a strict definition of independence. Jim Hillier outlines these definitions and suggests that the 1980s offered a range of independent films which were not of the contemplative style such as John Sayles' *Return of the Secaucus Seven* (1980) or ironic pastiche (Jim Jarmusch's *Mystery Train* (1989)) or the surrealist fantasy of David Lynch's *Blue Velvet* (1986). In fact, many, perhaps the majority, of independent films were genre pictures such as *Nightmare on Elm Street* (Wes Craven, 1984) or *Dirty Dancing* (Emile Ardolino, 1987).

Despite the range and diversity of films produced in the United States during the 1980s, the extensive reorganization of the industry and, as we have seen, the changes

wrought by new technologies of "delivery", the image of the 1980s as the genesis of a global industry fuelled by ideologically retrograde blockbusters persists. Susan Jeffords offers an insight into those high profile films of the 1980s dealing with the Vietnam War. The spectre of this conflict pervaded American culture in the 1980s, and the association of John Rambo's line in *Rambo: First Blood Part II* "Do we get to win this time?" with Reagan's proclamation that "America is back!" are merely the most obvious examples of a decade where cinema and politics seemed interchangeable. (Reagan's pronouncement sounds for all the world like the exhortation on a cinema poster in the 1940s.) Jeffords provides an incisive analysis of the way that these films depicted the Vietnam veteran as victim of a corrupt bureaucratic government. As she demonstrates, the films offered a revitalizing absolution from earlier depictions of the veteran as deranged and unstable, which hinged on the crises in identity that progressive movements such as feminism and the minority rights posed for a masculinist image of the nation.

Politics and film intertwined, however, in a different way through documentary in the 1980s. Carl Plantinga outlines how the funding for documentaries such as that provided by the National Endowment for the Arts, for example, set up in the 1960s, were the target for funding cuts by Republicans. Documentaries that challenged traditional notions of family, sexuality or drew attention to the neglect of government in responding to the AIDS crisis attracted particular criticism from conservative groups. One of the characteristics of Reagan's "revitalizing" rhetoric in the 1980s conjured a vision of America's past that called up images of the heroic Second World War effort, or the nuclear family nestled in the suburbs of the 1950s. Documentaries such as *The Life and Times of Rosie the Riveter* (Mary Dore, Noel Bruckner, Sam Sills, 1983), like those that exposed the contradictions in conservative myth-making of the present, offered a counternarrative of the past, by focusing on the work of labour unions and Leftist organizations.

Perhaps, given this polarization in political discourse as it found expression in American cinema in the 1980s, it makes sense that some of the most popular films of the period focused on family issues as well as foreign and domestic policy events. Films such as *E.T.*, *Back to the Future* and *Star Wars* set out the narrative conflicts around the reformation of the family, and particularly father–son relationships. It is also the case that these films are by no means simple renderings of those conflicts, and those complexities do in some way reflect their attempt to appeal to a wide political spectrum and age range. Intentionally producing texts that are open to a number of different interpretations is something at which Hollywood has been adept for years. As Richard Maltby points out in relation to *Casablanca* (Michael Curtiz, 1943):

> [it] presents an incomplete narrative requiring of its viewers a good deal of basic work in hypothesis-forming and – testing before the movie's story can be constructed – and importantly, providing considerable autonomy to individual viewers to construct the story as they please – that is, the story which provides each individual viewer with a maximum of pleasure in the text. (Maltby 1996: 449–50)

The difference here may not be one of structure or form but one of historical moment. The family as a concept provided much of the battleground between liberalism and conservatism in the United States in the 1980s. Where *Casablanca*, as Maltby lucidly points out, constructed its indeterminacy around extramarital sex ("Did Rick and Ilsa sleep together?"), an issue that was centre stage in wartime America, *E.T.* offers resolutions to family strife brought about by divorce that can be interpreted from either side of the debate about what constitutes a "normal" family.

Further, the 1980s seem to have once and for all seen the end of the rivalry for audiences with television. Or perhaps, more accurately, what was revealed in this decade were the opportunities that home viewing presented for the film industry. The appearance of the television in films, like that in *Gremlins* (Joe Dante, 1984), where Billy Peltzer's mother is watching Frank Capra's *It's a Wonderful Life* (1946) and peeling onions, illustrates a reflexivity: Hollywood representing its emotional impact, while at the same time offering multiple avenues of interpretation. When Billy asks her why she is crying and she says "sad movie", the film offers not only an embracing of television and a reference to classical Hollywood but also the uncertainty of the cause of the tears. Is it the onions or the story that are making her cry? Hollywood's reformation and revitalization in the 1980s are probably the result of this classical Hollywood strategy. Those strategies, along with the sea changes in its economic structure and technologies, say as much about the 1980s as does its popular characterization as revisionist and reactionary. It is that, but so much more.

References

Allen, R.C. (1999) Home alone together: Hollywood and the family film, in M. Stokes and R. Maltby (eds) *Identifying Hollywood's*

Audiences: Cultural Identity and the Movies. London: BFI.

Maltby, R. (1996) "A brief romantic interlude": Dick and Jane go to 3½ seconds of the Classical Hollywood cinema, in D. Bordwell and N. Carroll (eds) *Post-Theory: Reconstructing Film Studies*. Madison: University of Wisconsin Press.

Maltby, R. (1998) "Nobody knows everything": post-classical historiographies and consolidated entertainment, in S. Neale and M. Smith (eds) *Contemporary Hollywood Cinema*. London: Routledge.

Prince, S. (2000) *A New Pot of Gold: Hollywood Under the Electronic Rainbow*. New York: Charles Scribner's Sons.

Williams, L.R. (2005) *The Erotic Thriller in Contemporary Cinema*. Edinburgh: Edinburgh University Press.

HOLLYWOOD IN THE AGE OF REAGAN

Stephen Prince

Tom Cruise in *Top Gun*

THE 1980S WAS a decade of economic turbulence and of fundamental structural change for the motion picture industry. The major studios were bought by, merged with or otherwise absorbed into multinational communications empires. Rupert Murdoch's Australian-based News Corporation acquired Twentieth Century Fox in 1985. The Coca-Cola Co. bought Columbia Pictures in 1982 and then sold the studio to Japan's Sony Corporation in

1989. Matsushita Co., another Japanese electronics multinational, purchased MCA (which owned Universal Studios) in 1990. Time, the huge publishing empire, purchased Warner Communications Inc. (which owned Warner Bros) in 1989.

With these moves, American film became part of the communications operations of global firms, where it has remained to date. The $800 million box-office that Sony proudly trumpets for *Spider Man* represents a global market, not US earnings alone. In a similar fashion, the huge earnings posted by *Lord of the Rings* and *Harry Potter* only make sense as part of a global marketing blitz. The evolution of American film in the 1980s took it from a pattern of old-line corporate conglomeration to the present oligarchy of global media giants that specialize in the merchandising of information and entertainment, of which film is now but one media operation among many.

As Hollywood film became part of global media operations, the nature of cinema underwent fundamental changes. Theatrical film was displaced as the primary medium in which audiences watched movies, and film as film – on celluloid – declined in favour of emerging new electronic formats. Introduced in the late 1970s, the ancillary market of home video was the most important of these new formats. It was readily embraced by the public and represented a decisive move away from the pre-eminence of theatrical film in favour of home viewing on demand. Although some of the major studios tried to fight the technology of VCRs by seeking to have the home recording of film and television programmes declared illegal (as an infringement of copyright), in fact, all of the majors moved quickly to market their films for sale and rental on videocassette. Even while the suit filed by

Continued on page 234

Science Fiction and Fantasy since 1960

The science fiction cycle of the 1950s began with *Destination Moon* (1950) and *The Thing From Another World* (1951), major studio efforts with a broad appeal and a certain topical seriousness, peaking by the end of the decade, only to mutate over the next 40 years. The likes of George Pal (at Paramount) and Howard Hawks were less typical of the science fiction filmmaker circa 1960 than drive-in independents like American International's Roger Corman or Bert I. Gordon, who were turning out quickie creature features with teen appeal. One effect of this was that even major studio science fiction films were geared to the children's matinee market. Robert Wise's *The Day the Earth Stood Still* (1951) and Irwin Allen's *Voyage to the Bottom of the Sea* (1961), both from Twentieth Century Fox, are markedly different. The 1951 film has its flying saucer and robot, but is a political-religious allegory in documentary-like black and white, whereas the 1961 successor is all about colourful gadgetry and widescreen effects, the trailer promising not only battles with undersea monsters but also pop star Frankie Avalon blowing his trumpet.

The 1950s atomic doom cycle, which had reached its apotheosis in *On the Beach* (1959), continued, but in films that were less likely to be classed as science fiction such as *Dr Strangelove* or *Fail Safe* (both 1964), or even *The Manchurian Candidate* (1961) and the James Bond films. For most of the 1960s, science fiction and fantasy were equivalent genres, best represented by the child-friendly works of special effects master Ray Harryhausen (*Jason and the Argonauts*, 1963; *The First Men in the Moon*, 1964). However, 1950s-style B-pictures continued to appear with some regularity (*The Day Mars Invaded Earth*, 1962, *Destination Inner Space*, 1967) and Corman, while involved with his Vincent Price/Edgar Allan Poe series, turned his hand to one challenging little picture, *X – the Man with X-Ray Eyes* (1963), scripted by Twilight Zone alumnus Charles Beaumont. Then, in 1968, came a clutch of very different, highly significant films: Stanley Kubrick's *2001: A Space Odyssey*, Franklin J. Schaffner's *Planet of the Apes*, Ralph Nelson's *Charly* (a science fiction film that won a best actor Oscar for Cliff Robertson), George A. Romero's *Night of the Living Dead*, and Roger Vadim's *Barbarella*. Though these titles did not exclude the traditional young science fiction audience, they all had a wider appeal, big enough budgets to use major stars and convincing special effects and make-ups, and various stabs at "adult" content – predictive, religious, satrical, psychological, political, violent, sexy; Tarratt (1986: 276) writes that *2001* is "concerned with moral and metaphysical speculation combined with a delight in technical virtuosity for its own sake".

Because the 1968 science fiction films were very different from each other, the movies launched in their wake – which included sequels both to *Planet of the Apes* and *Night of the Living Dead* – came in a variety of mini-cycles. The first half of the 1970s yielded booms in post-apocalypse action in the *Apes* mode (*The Omega Man*, 1971; *A Boy and His Dog*, 1975); arty low-budget dystopias (*Glen and Randa*, 1971; *THX1138*, 1971 – one of Ryan and Kellner's (1988: 245–54) "technophobic" films); near-future hard-boiled misery (*Soylent Green*, 1973; *Rollerball*, 1976); absurdist comedy (*Sleeper*, 1973; *Death Race 2000*, 1975); adaptations of "cult" science fiction novels (*Slaughterhouse Five*, 1972; *The Man Who Fell to Earth*, 1976); and low-budget science fiction/horror with political overtones (*It's Alive*, 1975; *The Hills Have Eyes*, 1978). The arrival of Michael Crichton, first a novelist and then a director, led to challenging entertainments like Robert Wise's *The Andromeda Strain* (1971); Mike Hodges's *The Terminal Man* (1973) and Crichton's own *Westworld* (1973) and *Coma* (1978).

Aside from a couple of Harryhausen *Sinbad* sequels and the odd Disney "family" epic (*Bedknobs and Broomsticks*, 1970), fantasy in this period was in abeyance, perhaps deemed an irrelevance in the committed Vietnam-Watergate era – even the horror films of the period preferred monsters from science or psychology to the traditional supernatural, or took care to set their olde worlde vampires in hip, ultramodern settings (*Count Yorga, Vampire*, 1970). The picture changed with the explosive arrival of George Lucas's *Star Wars* (1977), the most important fantasy film ever made, though marginal as science fiction. Stripped of all the "content" that had marked even such flimsy precursors as *Logan's Run* (1976), *Star Wars* applied the technology of *2001* to the comic-strip vision of *Flash Gordon* (1936). *Star Wars'* unprecedented success meant an end to the likes of *Phase IV* (1975), a killer-ant monster movie that winds up with an idea-bomb about *2001*-style evolution, and a resurgence in child-oriented matinee-style moviemaking. There were instant imitations (*Battlestar Galactica*, 1979; *The Black Hole*, 1979; *Battle Beyond the Stars*, 1980) but the next significant blockbuster was Steven Spielberg's *Close Encounters of the Third Kind* (1978), which is more rooted than *Star Wars* in present-day reality but still expresses a New Age mystic yearning for transcendence rather than any genuine curiosity about the possibilities of life in outer space. Ryan and Kellner (1988: 244) note of this period that "The triumph of conservatism made itself particularly felt in the fantasy genre", though they single out Spielberg as using the form consistently to promote "liberal ideals". Lucas and Spielberg have remained the dominant names in science fiction fantasy cinema, expressing a paradoxical obsession with the technologies (from modelwork to CGI) of filming the imaginably impossible alongside a paranoid distrust of actual science, as represented by the valuing of the Force above technology in the *Star Wars* films or the runaway consequences of genetic engineering in the Crichton-originated *Jurassic Park* cycle.

Ridley Scott's *Alien* (1979), which was developed as a low-budget monster movie but produced as a mainstream post-*Star Wars* blockbuster, reprises an ancient creature-kills-off-the-cast plot in a dirty space freighter, having an impact – and inspiring a series – because of its attempts at "realism" (cynical, nasty characters), its post-*Coma/Halloween* adoption of Sigourney Weaver's character Ripley as the ballsy "final girl" heroine (see Clover 1992, for a discussion of the "final girl"), and extremely imaginative alien design (courtesy of the Swiss surrealist, H.R. Giger). Otherwise, *Star Wars* sent studios looking to their backlists: *Flash Gordon* was inevitably remade in 1980, and other franchises were revived. The *Star Trek* TV series, relaunched in 1979 with Robert Wise's *Star Trek: The Motion Picture*, spawned numerous film sequels and TV spinoffs that continue (see, for instance, *Star Trek: Nemesis*, 2002). *Superman* flew onto the big screen in 1978 and continued through several sequels, perhaps inevitably leading to a similar, big-budget revival of Clark Kent's comic book stablemate, *Batman* (1989), who was also sequelized (see Pearson and Uricchio 1991 for a discussion of the franchise). All these films look like science fiction with their spaceships, aliens and gadgets, but hew closer to the pulp mythic archetypes of comic books, as do the fantastical Lucas–Spielberg *Indiana Jones* films and even the more ambitious likes of John Boorman's *Excalibur* (1981).

Scott followed up *Alien* with *Blade Runner* (1982, Fig. 13 [*see plate section*]), a genuine science fiction film based on a Philip K. Dick novel, which has never been satisfactorily finished (hence the several different release versions) and can't quite contain all its ideas, but still set the standard for depictions of the neo-*noir* near future and post-human robotics (see Bukatman 1997, and Kerman 2003). Again, fantasy was on the rise: Spielberg's *E.T.: The Extra-Terrestrial* (1982), about a magical visitor befriending a child, was the box office hit *Blade Runner* failed to be and also eclipsed John Carpenter's gritty, downbeat remake of *The Thing* (1982). The Scott and Carpenter films have proved lastingly popular and influential, at least among other filmmakers, especially when married to 1980s-style overdrive action by James Cameron in *The Terminator* (1984), a low-budget picture that made the careers of Cameron and star android Arnold Schwarzenegger, opening the way for the likes of Paul Verhoeven's *RoboCop* (1986) and *Total Recall* (1990). Cameron moved to bigger budgeted sequels, *Aliens* (1986) and *Terminator 2: Judgment Day* (1992), as well as *The Abyss* (1989), also getting in early on the millennial and "rubber reality" booms by scripting Kathryn Bigelow's *Strange Days* (1995). There was also room for various returns to the past with updated technical effects and new social contexts, as in David Cronenbrg's remake of *The Fly* (1986) and Tim Burton's remake of *Planet of the Apes* (2001), reprises of the *Invasion of the Body Snatchers* concept by Philip Kaufman (1978) and Abel Ferrara (1993) and (most literally) the time travel fancies of Robert Zemeckis's *Back to the Future* (1985) and Francis Ford Coppola's *Peggy Sue Got Married* (1986).

Jurassic Park (1992), picking up Cameron-sponsored innovations in CGI technology, returned Spielberg to a dominant place in the science fiction pantheon, though his ambitious attempt at a more "serious" effort in taking over Stanley Kubrick's project *A.I. Artificial Intelligence* (2001) showed a fumbling, persistent need to escape from science fiction (robotics) into fantasy (Pinocchio). Tino Balio (2002: 168) notes that, during the 1990s, "the science-fiction trend accounted for five titles in the top twenty", so the genre has continued to produce high box-office returns. One of these was George Lucas's prequel *The Phantom Menace: Star Wars Episode 1* (1999), the first title in the renewed *Star Wars* franchise, which became hugely successful with a new generation of children and young adults. But it was technically and narratively overshadowed by the real cutting-edge science fiction of the late 1990s – the Wachowski Brothers' *The Matrix* (also 1999, spawning two sequels, both in 2003). This harked back to the 1980s literary cyberpunk movement, though it was tricked up with fashionable virtual reality themes, and was multiply influenced – Mellencamp (2001) notes

Robocop: Science fiction as post-human satire

that it "eclectically blends Asian and American film genres (particularly action adventure, sci-fi, Kung Fu/Hong Kong martial arts), live action and animation (Japanese anime, Warner Brothers Cartoons), and other media (comic books, TV, and computer/video games". The *Alien* and *Star Trek* series also continued into the new century, though – as some earlier precedents had shown (*The Right Stuff*, 1983; *Apollo 13*, 1995) – space exploration in the cinema was more likely to click if rooted in history than the future (as in the disappointing Martian cycle of 2000–1: *Red Planet, Mission to Mars, Ghosts of Mars*). Alien invaders, whether arriving *en masse* (*Independence Day*, 1996) or covertly (*The X-Files*, 1998), all tended to play up American patriotic or paranoid neuroses, though Tim Burton's *Mars Attacks!* (1996) managed a comprehensive trashing of the sub-genre and the planet – J. Hoberman (2003: 33) called it a "megamillion-dollar Hollywood blockbuster based on a bunch of 35-year-old bubblegum cards".

Fantasy, still rarely regarded as a genre to itself, struggled awhile as filmmakers tried to do *Star Wars*-type epics with fairytale settings to disappointing results (*The Dark Crystal*, 1983; *Krull*, 1983; *Legend*, 1985; *Labyrinth*, 1986; *Willow*, 1988), but the annual successes of Disney's cartoons since *The Little Mermaid* (1989) eventually made way for such pre-sold, literary-based fantasy blockbusters as the *Harry Potter* franchise (from 2001 onwards) and *The Lord of the Rings* trilogy (2001–3). The near future, it seems, will belong to the wizards.

References

Balio, T. (2002) Hollywood production trends in the era of globalisation, 1990–99, in S. Neale (ed.) *Genre and Contemporary Hollywood*. London: BFI.
Bukatman, S. (1997) *Blade Runner*. London: BFI.

Clover, C.J. (1992) *Men, Women and Chain Saws: Gender in the Modern Horror Film*. London: BFI.

Hoberman, J. (2003) *Mars Attacks!*, in *The Magic Hour: Film at the Fin de Siècle*. Philadelphia, PA: Temple University Press, pp. 33–5.

Kerman, J.B. (ed.) (2003) *Retrofitting Blade Runner: Issues in Ridley Scott's "Blade Runner" and Philip K. Dick's "Do Androids Dream of Electric Sheep?"*. Bowling Green, OH: Bowling Green University Popular Press.

Mellencamp, P. (2001) The zen of masculinity – rituals of heroism in *The Matrix*, in J. Lewis (ed.) *The End of Cinema as We Know it: American Film in the Nineties*. New York: New York University Press, pp. 83–94.

Pearson, R. and Uricchio, W. (1991) *The Many Lives of the Batman: Critical Approaches to a Superhero and His Media*. London: Routledge.

Ryan, M. and Kellner, D. (1988) *Camera Politica: The Politics and Ideology of Contemporary Hollywood Film*. Bloomington; Indiana University Press.

Tarratt, M. (1986) Monsters from the Id, in B.K. Grant (ed.) *Film Genre Reader*. Austin: University of Texas Press, pp. 258–77.

Kim Newman

Continued from page 230

Disney and Universal against Sony and its Betamax videotape recorders was pending, Disney, Universal and the other majors started their own home video subsidiaries and moved aggressively to release films in this medium. Between January 1979 and March 1980, for example, the majors placed 477 films into video release. Public enthusiasm for the format was overwhelming, and by mid-decade revenue from home video was outpacing returns from the box office. More people were watching movies on videocassette than in theatres.

On the one hand, this meant that henceforth the theatrical market would generate a declining share of film revenues and that, for home viewers, cinema was reduced to television. Videotape lacked the contrast, colour saturation and resolution of a properly projected film image, and home television screens became miserable miniaturized versions of big screen theatres showing washed-out videotape versions of movies, many of which were panned and scanned to format widescreen for TV. But the public loved the convenience of home viewing and happily consented to this reduction of cinema to television.

On the other hand, the success of home video saved Hollywood by giving it a vital new revenue stream to offset a rapid rise in production and marketing costs. Furthermore, home video actually strengthened the theatrical market, instead of killing it, as many doomsayers had predicted. By helping to create a huge demand for product – new titles to feed the VCRs in the nation's homes – home video helped fuel a boom at mid-decade in the production and distribution of new films. Because the resources of the majors were already fully committed in the funding of production, independent filmmakers, distributors and production companies largely supplied the boom. The majors, in their turn, picked up for distribution many of these independently financed films. This new influx of talent and organizational infrastructure helped widen the tone and scope of American film in this period. *sex, lies and videotape* (1989), *Blue Velvet* (1986), *Salvador* (1986), *Platoon* (1987), *Mishima* (1985), *She's Gotta Have It* (1986), *River's Edge* (1986), and *84 Charlie MoPic* (1989) were among the many unconventional pictures produced from the new opportunities in funding and distribution that the ancillary success of home video had helped make possible.

The filmmakers who were associated with this boom in independent filmmaking include many who are now major talents in the industry. These include Steven Soderbergh, whose *sex, lies and videotape* presaged the onset of a career whose arc is still rising and that includes *Out of Sight, The Limey, Erin Brockovich* and *Traffic*. Oliver Stone's punchy brand of political filmmaking in *Salvador* and *Platoon* helped launch his career and was made possible by financing from the independent companies Hemdale and Vestron. An emerging new generation of African-American filmmakers was visible in the work of Spike Lee, whose *She's Gotta Have It* found distribution through the independent Island Pictures. Other filmmakers emerging as part of the expanded production and distribution opportunities have remained true to their independent origins by not affiliating with the majors, as Soderbergh and Lee have done. These include John Sayles (*The Return of the Secaucus Seven*, 1980, *Matewan*, 1987) and Jim Jarmusch (*Stranger Than Paradise*, 1984, *Down By Law*, 1986).

The increase in film production stimulated by home video also added value to the nation's movie theatres. As the revenue stream from home video grew, so did the importance of theatrical release, which furnished the launching pad for a film's performance on home video and became the guarantor of a picture's downstream success on home video. This pattern has held constant in the decades since the 1980s. A film that generates a lot of attention theatrically will also be a hit on home video, and pictures that do poorly in theatres can move quickly to home video to start recouping their losses. The success of home video, and other ancillaries like pay cable, created a renewed demand for film product. As an indicator of this new demand, the number of theatre screens around the country dramatically increased, with the biggest yearly jumps since the late 1940s. Moreover, the major studios moved back into exhibition, purchasing theatre chains in recognition of the new vitality of this traditional market segment. These purchases returned the majors to their pre-television origins when they routinely counted theatre ownership as a part of their holdings.

These transformations helped to make the 1980s a period of flux and of some turmoil for the film industry. The flux occurred as the major studios were bought and sold in a corporate feeding frenzy as the global media companies moved in to control Hollywood. The turmoil occurred as theatrical film jostled for dominance with the new electronic delivery systems of home video and cable television. Accordingly, the pictures produced during this era reflect a healthy mix of perspective, style and intended audiences. Filmmaking during the period was decidedly heterogeneous. This is an important point that is often minimized in discussions of the period, which tend to see Hollywood's output as being more uniform. Some filmmaking reflected, often stridently, the bellicose rhetoric of the Reagan Presidency, which revived a new Cold War, focused on the Soviet Union as the locus of evil in the modern world, and engaged in much sabre-rattling. Other films, though, opposed the rightward drift of US foreign policy in these years, while the decade's biggest box-office hits, *E.T.* (1982) and *Return of the Jedi* (1983) among them, stayed outside politics altogether by offering special effects showcases and thrill-ride narratives. At the same time, the new vitality of independent film brought creative and offbeat styles and talents into the mainstream.

The most iconic embodiment of Reaganite America on film was Sylvester Stallone's Rambo character, which appeared in three, increasingly ideological productions during the decade. *First Blood* (1982) introduced the character as a dazed Vietnam veteran wandering through the Pacific Northwest. Harassed by small-town cops, Rambo goes beserk and wages a one-man war against the local constabulary. The film depicts Rambo as a borderline psychopath making war on America, a quality and action ill-suited to political heroism. In the next two films, Rambo's violence is unleashed on America's official enemies, which serves to redeem the character's bloodthirsty nature and to offer the country symbolic military victories over the Vietnamese and the Soviet Union. In *Rambo: First Blood Part II* (1985), he goes to Vietnam to search for MIAs and to make new war on the Vietnamese. The American loss in Vietnam reverberated deeply within 1980s political culture and, for decades, had inhibited the subsequent use of US ground troops in armed conflict. On film, however, Rambo's superhuman warrior abilities offered viewers a symbolic, substitute victory which reversed the military realities of the war. This time around, Rambo, not the Vietnamese, is the skilled jungle fighter, using stealth and low-tech weapons to defeat his enemies, a ploy that turns US military prowess into the foe it was fighting in Vietnam. After walloping the

Vietnamese, he went on, in *Rambo III* (1988), to battle Soviet forces in Afghanistan. More explicitly than in the second film, Rambo is pitched as a "freedom fighter" (the term borrowed from the counter-revolutionary army funded by the CIA in Nicaragua), allied with revolutionaries against an entrenched and oppressive government. The political schizophrenia here is remarkable, and recent events give *Rambo III* an unpleasant resonance its makers cannot have foreseen. The events of September 11 demonstrate one of the results of funnelling arms to radical groups in Afghanistan because they are anti-Soviet and then walking away.

The ideological appeal of the second and third Rambo films is bald and crude, and yet the character came to personify – archetypally, with Stallone's engorged muscles and naked torso entwined with bandoliers – the resurgent military power of the United States. President Reagan publicly invoked Rambo when threatening American military action overseas. And yet Rambo remained a creature of the political imagination – the administration embarked on no major military ventures outside of its secret proxy wars in Central America. In such a context, Rambo was the emblem of a threat, expressing the idea of what America might do militarily if it so chose.

The Rambo films helped to define a cycle of new Cold War filmmaking that depicted the United States as being under threat from the Soviet Union and advocated the need to project American military power overseas. Stallone's *Rocky IV* (1985) sent the boxer to the Soviet Union to battle a robotic Soviet opponent, with the contest depicted in metaphorical terms as a face-off between the rival political systems. The film ends with Stallone literally wrapping himself in the American flag as Rocky's victory inspires the Soviet people to voice their demand for American-style freedom.

While Rambo and Rocky were taking the fight to the Soviet Union, other films depicted traditional nightmares of Soviet expansionism. In *Red Dawn* (1984), the Soviet Union improbably launches an invasion of the United States by way of tiny Cuba, with American military power so humbled by the Vietnam defeat that it cannot defend the homeland. Only a band of high-school students, waging guerilla war and who embody the new generation of the Reagan years, stands up against the Soviets. Directed by John Milius, *Red Dawn* is a comic strip of political paranoia. Elsewhere, in *Invasion USA* (1985), the Soviets recruit bands of Third World terrorists to launch attacks on US soil, and only action film hero Chuck Norris stands ready to stop them.

As these descriptions suggest, the new Cold War films drew comic book portraits of contemporary political tensions. They trafficked in stereotypes and cartoon characters but found a solid audience for the Right-wing fantasies that they depicted. Their paranoid view of the world resonated through a great many of the decade's films – *Top Gun* (1986), *Iron Eagle* (1986), *No Way Out* (1987), *Little Nikita* (1988). Many of these films did quite well at the box office, suggesting perhaps the hold or the appeal that the dominant ideology of Soviet perfidy held in the popular imagination of the period. As exercises in political filmmaking, however, many of these films deal in little more than caricatures. More complex and accomplished political filmmaking was found in films dealing with the Vietnam War and the proxy wars the Administration waged in support of dictatorships in Central America.

Explorations of the Vietnam War – the nature of the conflict and its meaning for America – were a major focus of film in the 1980s. Prior to that decade, American film had dealt with Vietnam in a glancing, offhand manner. But, starting with *The Deer Hunter* (1978) and *Apocalypse Now* (1979), a wave of major productions, lasting throughout the decade, offered a sustained and deeply felt artistic interrogation of that conflict. In contrast to the cardboard fantasy figures in the Rambo films, the portrait of American soldiers that emerged in *Platoon*, *84 Charlie MoPic*, *Hamburger Hill* (1987) and others strove to honour those who served while avoiding the simplistic rah-rah heroics that would falsify the history of a controversial war. In addition to these battlefield films, other pictures – *Gardens of Stone* (1987), *The Hanoi Hilton* (1987), *Bat 21* (1988), *Born on the Fourth of July* (1989), *Good Morning, Vietnam* (1987) – examined politics on the home front, the air war, and the physical and psychological effects of the war on those who fought.

Collectively, these films rehabilitated the cinematic image of the Vietnam veteran, overcoming the legacy of 1970s film where veteran characters served as stock villains. This shift was a major achievement of 1980s film culture, although it accompanied a tendency of the Vietnam films to obfuscate the terms of the conflict by depicting the enemy as little more than a shadowy figure darting through the jungle. Only in *Good Morning, Vietnam* does a Vietnamese soldier voice an articulate opposition to the American presence in Southeast Asia.

In this respect, the Vietnam films differ from Hollywood's productions about the Second World War. Those films depicted the German enemy with some political specificity, with many films even allowing German soldiers to state their political beliefs. Nothing

Continued on page 239

Simpson and Bruckheimer

The rise of producer power in 1980s cinema was typified by Don Simpson and Jerry Bruckheimer, who rivalled Spielberg and Lucas as the most financially successful filmmakers of the decade. Stephen Prince (2000: 208–9) characterizes them as "producer-auteurs", who "imposed a powerful visual and narrative style" on their films in a manner ironically reminiscent of "old Hollywood" stalwarts such as David O. Selznick and Arthur Freed. In stark contrast to the "cult of the director", which flourished in the 1970s, Simpson and Bruckheimer recruited graduates from the advertising and promo industries for whom aesthetics were often more important than content. Directors such as Tony Scott (*Top Gun*, *Beverly Hills Cop II*, *Days of Thunder*, *Crimson Tide*), Adrian Lyne (*Flashdance*) and Michael Bay (*Bad Boys*, *The Rock*) enjoyed huge financial success under the Simpson–Bruckheimer banner despite frequently disparaging and hostile critical reviews.

Describing themselves as the "V & V Twins", Simpson and Bruckheimer divided their working roles between the "verbal" and the "visual", with writer and sometime actor Simpson concentrating on the story while budding photographer-editor Bruckheimer oversaw the films' distinctive look. A reliance upon fast-paced pop-video aesthetics and often heavy-handed record placement helped create a synergetic product that could simultaneously assault both the film and record charts. Several Simpson-Bruckheimer hits boasted pop-chart tie-ins, most notably *Flashdance* (1983, which famously spawned Irene Cara's "Flashdance ... What a Feeling" and Michael Sembello's "Maniac"), *Beverly Hills Cop* (1984, Glenn Frey's "The Heat is On"), *Top Gun* (1986, Berlin's "Take My Breath Away" and Kenny Logins' "Danger Zone"); and latterly *Dangerous Minds* (1995, Coolio's "Gangsta's Paradise"). Multi-million-selling soundtrack albums were also a predictable part of the package. As legendary production designer (and one-time head of production at Paramount) Richard Sylbert said, "All their movies were rock and roll, MTV videos", a sentiment echoed by Fleming (1998: 45) who argues that "Simpson may have been the first producer in Hollywood to understand the power that the nascent MTV would become. He was certainly the first to properly exploit it."

The "high concept" formula of films that could be pitched in less than 25 words (famously parodied in Robert Altman's 1992 *The Player*) is widely attributed to Simpson. As Arroyo (2000: xii) notes: "Though people as diverse as Michael Eisner and Jon Peters claim credit for the idea, the term is popularly associated with Don Simpson [and] co-producer ... Jerry Bruckheimer." In a now infamous internal document from 1980, which laid the template for high-concept cinema, Simpson declared that "The pursuit of money is the only reason to make movies ... but in order to make money, we must always make entertaining movies" (Fleming 1998: 192). To this end, Simpson and Bruckheimer perfected three-act romps with "clean" (uncluttered) narratives in which a heroic (and often blue-collar) figure triumphs over adversity to achieve an orgasmic success characterized by a final triumphant freeze-frame ending.

Although frequently berated for the reactionary politics of their product, Simpson and Bruckheimer helped launch the mainstream cinema careers of several African-American actors by employing them in roles originally written for white stars. Eddie Murphy, Martin Lawrence and Will Smith, for example, received major career boosts through the recasting of key roles in *Beverly Hills Cop* and *Bad Boys* (1995). After a life of drug-fuelled excess, Simpson died of heart failure in January 1996, leaving his former partner to continue the pair's winning formula in popcorn fodder like *Con Air* (1997), *Armageddon* (1998) and *Pearl Harbor* (2001), the latter grossing over $450 million worldwide despite a blizzard of negative reviews, proving once again his former partner's maxim that "We have no obligation to make art."

References

Arroyo, J. (ed.) (2000) *Action/Spectacle Cinema*. London: BFI.
Fleming, C. (1998) *High Concept: Don Simpson and the Hollywood Culture of Excess*. London: Bloomsbury.
Prince, S. (2000) *A New Pot of Gold: Hollywood Under the Electronic Rainbow, 1980–1989*. Berkeley: University of California Press.
Wyatt, J. (1994) *High Concept: Movies and Marketing in Hollywood*. Austin: University of Texas Press.

Mark Kermode

Continued from page 237

comparable exists in the Vietnam films. Vietnamese characters are often wholly absent, except as distant figures in the jungles, and they never give voice to a perspective or history of the war outside the terms of American discourse. This development makes not only for bad politics but for bad filmmaking. Without an articulated political opposition, the stakes in the war cannot be dramatized and typically in these films they are not.

Furthermore, because the films' stories are typically set in the late 1960s, during the high point of American military involvement, they offer a snapshot portrait of a historical event whose duration exceeds the frame boundaries of the snapshot. Without examining the roots of American involvement, which go back to the 1940s, the films necessarily offer limited insight into the causes and origin of the conflict. The films typically omit any depiction of the government and armed forces of South Vietnam, on whose behalf the United States was ostensibly fighting. *Go Tell the Spartans* (1978) was one of the few films to evoke the corrupt and weak nature of political authority in South Vietnam. The films also fail to evoke the political organization and battle strategy of the North Vietnamese army and guerrillas in the South, against whom the United States

was fighting. These failures entail that the Vietnam films have a somewhat solipsistic focus, concentrated on American characters and only there. They are films from which the Vietnamese have been displaced.

The 1980s Vietnam films, therefore, achieve a mixed degree of success. They vividly portray the conditions of jungle warfare and ennoble the figures of American soldiers – once so controversial – but the films are quite limited in the degree of political clarity that they bring to the conflict. In this regard, they reproduce a dominant cultural paradigm about the war, namely that it is an event that eludes understanding. Thus, a contemporary viewer coming to this important 1980s cycle of filmmaking will gain a vivid sense of what it felt like to be in a jungle environment fighting an elusive enemy but will lack a larger context, at least as supplied by the films, for understanding the war as a historical event.

The biggest and longest-range impact of the 1980s Vietnam films, however, lay in the valorizing of the American soldier fighting overseas. In this respect, the films collectively worked to erase the unpleasant aura of American imperialism that clung to the war by narrowing the focus onto the heroism and sacrifice of the American characters in the story. The influence of this ploy has been tremendous and still influences contemporary war films, evident in pictures like *Black Hawk Down* (2001) and *We Were Soldiers* (2002).

This valorizing of the American soldier notwithstanding, the political viewpoint of the Vietnam films is actually rather ambivalent. The war was too wrenching and controversial for the films to offer easy heroics or simple affirmation. The films are haunted by the violence and waste of the American endeavour in Southeast Asia, just as the country itself wrestled with the haunting meanings of the war throughout the 1980s. Fallout from the war's controversy prevented the large-scale mobilization of American troops in overseas ventures during this period, but the Reagan Administration waged a series of secret wars in Central America, propping up a corrupt government and its death squads in El Salvador and funding an opposition army to overthrow a democratically elected government in Nicaragua.

The films about these conflicts offer much sharper and clearer political perspectives than the Vietnam War films. *Missing* (1982), *Under Fire* (1983), *El Norte* (1984), *Latino* (1985), *Salvador* (1986), and *Romero* (1989) are very critical of US support for dictatorship in the region and for the tortures and murders carried out by security forces funded and trained by Washington. Most of these films were independent productions, but two – *Missing* and *Under Fire* – came from major Hollywood studios and featured such prominent stars as Jack Lemmon, Sissy Spacek, Gene Hackman and Nick Nolte. *Missing* examined US support for the bloody military coup against the democratically elected government of Chile, and *Under Fire* presented a positive view of the Sandinista revolution in Nicaragua. *Latino* portrayed the clandestine CIA-supported war against the Sandinistas, and *Salvador* and *Romero* criticized US involvement in El Salvador on behalf of that country's corrupt government and its death squads.

In sharp contrast to the new Cold War films, these pictures criticize the US role in Latin America and question the imperialism by which the US has claimed the prerogatives of deciding which governments stay in power and which fall in the region. Most significantly, the films break with the dominant ideological assumption of the Reagan era, namely, that political unrest in Central America – and, indeed, anywhere in the world – was financed and directed by the Soviet Union as part of its plans for world domination. Instead of this Cold War view, the films show that the region's strife originates in conditions of widespread poverty and that US policy has sided with the landowning elite, not the people.

The co-existence of the Latin American films, alongside the cycles dealing with Vietnam and the new Cold War, shows that 1980s cinema contained a relatively wide range of political expression. This fact becomes more striking when one adds the large number of films, of varying perspectives, dealing with other social and political issues – the farm crisis in the Midwest (*Places in the Heart*, 1984, *Country*, 1984, *The River* (1984)), the "greed is good" ethic spawned by the 1980s economy (*Risky Business*, 1983, *Wall Street*, 1987), urban decay and corporate control of the public sector (*Escape from New York*, 1981, *Blade Runner*, 1982, Fig. 13 (*see plate section*), *Robocop*, 1987, *Total Recall*, 1990), the weakening of the political Left in American society (*Return of the Secaucus Seven*, 1980, *The Big Chill*, 1985, *Daniel*, 1983, *Running on Empty*, 1988), and racial tension and animosity (*Colors*, 1988, *Do the Right Thing*, 1989, Fig. 14 (*see plate section*)).

Popular and critical discussion of American film in the 1980s often construes it in terms of blockbusters and politically conservative films, such as *Rambo*. But the range of political expression during this period is actually considerably wider than this, as the films described above indicate. To be sure, blockbusters were a vital part of the industry and popular culture, and although they were perhaps the most visible industry products during the decade, this visibility has tended to obscure the actual range of filmmaking that prevailed. Many serious filmmakers sustained careers outside the blockbuster format. These included Woody Allen, Oliver Stone, Barry Levinson, Francis Ford Coppola, Martin Scorsese and Spike Lee. Moreover, the major studios funded and distributed many pictures with limited commercial prospects and whose style and sensibility were outside the commercial mainstream. These included *Mishima*, *Kagemusha* (1980, by Japanese director Akira Kurosawa), and *The Last Temptation of Christ* (1988).

But the blockbuster phenomenon was real, and the industry was deeply committed to the format. It had to be. The cost of making and distributing films exploded in the 1980s, rising from $13 million to $32 million. It has continued to escalate even more drastically since then. No film earned back its production cost from the theatrical market; it required the additional revenues from the ancillary markets of home video, cable television and product licensing and merchandising. As the inflationary costs of doing business eroded the industry's financial health, the studios looked to the ancillary markets for their salvation. And the ancillaries performed well – by middecade, as noted, revenues from home video were outpacing those from theatrical box office. But the best return from the ancillaries

occurred when all of these nontheatrical markets worked together, in synergy. Blockbusters provided the means for achieving this. Herein lay their critical importance for the industry, the reason the studios embraced them. *Batman* (1989), for example, could be marketed simultaneously as a movie, a book, a comic book, a soundtrack album, and a diverse array of product lines, including toys and clothing. Since Warner Bros and its parent company controlled all of these distribution venues, all of the associated revenue streams would stay in house. Blockbuster films cost more to make because they had big stars and special effects, but their earnings potential was huge and – of critical importance – it reached beyond the theatrical market and into the ancillaries, where revenue could be generated over a longer time frame than was possible with theatrical.

Just as *Rambo* is identified with a certain stereotyped notion of 1980s cinema and political reaction, the films of Steven Spielberg and George Lucas achieved such high visibility that they have come to embody the identification of New Hollywood with blockbusters. Though Lucas and Spielberg emerged in the 1970s as blockbuster moviemakers, their phenomenon achieved its maturity in the 1980s. The second two installments of Lucas's first *Star Wars* trilogy – *The Empire Strikes Back* (1980) and *Return of the Jedi* (1983) – appeared during these years, and Spielberg contributed his *Raiders of the Lost Ark* trilogy as well as *E.T.: The Extra-Terrestrial* (1982). Each of these pictures was among the highest grossing films in the year it appeared, and nearly all were that year's number one box office attraction.

Because these pictures are fantasy entertainments that go light on complex thematics

Continued on page 244

A Tim Burton film is instantly recognizable – in its way as distinctive as a movie by Hitchcock. Burton plays consistently with a kind of modern Gothic, his films often darkly comic explorations of the everyday made monstrous, the unsettling juxtaposition of suburbia and the surreal. There are unmistakably autobiographical elements in much of his work. Born and raised in Burbank, California, in an ordinary suburb that rubbed shoulders with the fantasyland of Hollywood, Burton confesses to a lonely childhood in which he inhabited a bizarre inner world of his own devising, and left his intolerant parents' home at the age of 12 to live with his grandmother (Charity 1994: 23). His first career was as an animator when, after graduating from the California Institute of the Arts, he was snapped up by Disney. He spent a miserable few years drawing cute creatures for mainstream animated features such as *The Fox and the Hound* (1981) when all he really wanted to do was to draw villains: "The foxes I drew", he later admitted, "looked like roadkill" (Charity 1994: 22). Finally taken off the larger projects due to his unusual penchant for the grotesque, he was given a certain amount of leeway and permitted to work on his own. During this period he produced such quirky shorts as *Vincent* (1982), in which a 7-year-old boy drives his parents crazy dreaming about being a horror icon like Vincent Price, and finally commits suicide; and *Frankenweenie* (1984), in which another strange child reenacts Gothic horror by revivifying his dead dog with electricity. *Frankenweenie* was considered unsuitable for general release but it led to a productive encounter with Paul Reubens (aka Pee-wee Herman) who, on the strength of it, chose Burton to direct his first big feature film. *Pee-wee's Big Adventure* (1985) was a surprise box-office hit, grossing $45 million in America alone, and it enabled Burton to devote his energies to his own increasingly individualistic projects.

Beetle Juice (1988), an uneven but compelling *tour de force*, sends a sweet suburban married couple (played by Geena Davis and Alec Baldwin) into the underworld when they are killed in a car crash. Back from the dead, they witness their beloved old home being redecorated by its hip, bored new owners. Visible only to the new family's lonely Goth daughter (Winona Ryder), the couple are forced to call on the underworld maverick Beetlegeuse (Michael Keaton) for some supernatural help. Physically repellent, sexually transgressive, lewd, rude and loud – everybody's nightmare guest – Beetlegeuse goes about teaching the perfect couple how to be bad enough to frighten away their home's new owners. Typical of a Burton film, though, *Beetle Juice* inverts audience expectations, turning on its head the classic horror device of a "nice" couple threatened by unnatural events. Here, the "nice" couple are themselves unnatural and, as their education under Beetlegeuse continues and we become familiar with their darkly comical world, the film subtly points to where the real horror lies – in the empty lives of a suburban family too desensitized by consumption to be scared.

More playing around with generic conventions followed in Burton's next film, the hugely successful *Batman* (1989). Again casting Michael Keaton, Burton employs his talents as a cartoonist on the strange sets that resemble a modern city far less than they do a zoo enclosure. In Burton's version of the classic cartoon, the caped crusader is only marginally stranger than the citizens he's trying to protect. In a world where people and animals seem to morph into each other, where the interface between the organic and the man-made is blurry at best, civilization becomes relative, and – as a useful and very Burtonesque side-effect – our hero's identity crisis becomes even more complicated. The grotesque melding of humans and animals, villains and heroes, continues and is still more pronounced in Burton's sequel, *Batman Returns* (1992). Burton's next major solo venture, *Edward Scissorhands* (1990) focused more strongly on the theme of sympathy for the outsider. Sensitive, tragic, and perhaps the least comical of his films, *Edward Scissorhands* teamed him for the first time with Johnny Depp, an association that was to prove fruitful and long-standing. Depp

Paul Reubens in *Pee Wee's Big Adventure*

went on to star in several more Burton films – *Ed Wood* (1994), *Sleepy Hollow* (1999), *Charlie and the Chocolate Factory* (2005) and as the lead male voice in the animated feature *Corpse Bride* (2005).

Not all of Burton's films have achieved the cult status of his earlier work. *Ed Wood* (1994) was deemed a failure at the box office, though it received some of the highest critical accolades of his career, whereas *Planet of the Apes* (2001) attracted good audiences even as it was critically panned. But, marked by his cartooning sensibilities and his obsession with the extraordinary in the everyday, Burton's steady output of visually compelling films displays an impressive range as well as a unique, indelible signature. Although he handed direction of *The Nightmare Before Christmas* (1993) out to Henry Selick, the animated project (on which he receives credit for story and characters, alongside titular endorsement) remains distinctively his own. (He also served as producer on Selick's acclaimed adaptation of *James and the Giant Peach*, 1996.) From the recasting of fairytales in the early films of his Disney years like *Hansel and Gretel* (1982), through the sci fi spoof *Mars Attacks!* (1996), to the tender, intricate story of filial relationships in *Big Fish* (2003) (in which – motivated, perhaps, by its director's own maturing world-view – the hero finds out too late that his father was a good man), Burton has provided the film industry with something that often works counter to the mainstream, even as it appeals to vast audiences.

References

Charity, T. (1994) Santa Claws, *Time Out*, (23–30 November): 22–3.
Johnston, S. (1998), Chance of a ghost, *The Independent*, 28 July.

Michael Hammond

Continued from page 241
and generally lack ambiguity or irony, they were roundly dismissed by critics, who worried that the films collectively represented a shift of industry resources, away from serious picture-making and toward a kind of CinemaLite. Taken strictly within the context of 1980s film, this worry was premature. As I indicated, the range of production was really quite diverse. As we begin the new millennium, however, the concern seems more relevant. The industry's economic problems – inflationary costs, high overhead, low returns from most releases – have only worsened, and this has arguably intensified the role played by CinemaLite blockbusters in contemporary film. If the problem existed at a lower level of menace than many critics supposed in the 1980s, today it may represent more of a threat to the cinema's viability as a medium of artistic and cultural expression.

The popular audience in the 1980s loved these pictures, and the robust popularity of science fiction/fantasy made the genre into the industry's showcase for new technological breakthroughs in digital sound editing (*Indiana Jones and the Temple of Doom* (1984, Fig. 11 (*see plate section*))) and digital visual effects (*Star Trek II: The Wrath of Khan* (1982); *The Abyss* (1989)). George Lucas took the lead in applying digital technology to filmmaking, and while this revolution did not happen during the 1980s, Lucas was doing his research, getting proprietary digital image and sound editors on line, and preparing for the next decade when the dinosaurs designed by Industrial Light and Magic for Spielberg's *Jurassic Park* (1993) would usher in the new era of digital.

The popular embrace of Spielberg and Lucas's films – and the work of other filmmakers that they inspired – coupled with the staggering box-office returns from these films unquestionably cemented the vital role of blockbuster filmmaking in industry economics. But, like the ready equation of *Rambo* with 1980s politics, the prominence of the blockbusters can conceal more about 1980s Hollywood than it reveals. It conceals, for example, the expansion in the production and distribution of independent films in this period. Moreover, George Lucas invested some of his *Star Wars* earnings in backing offbeat and unusual pictures by directors outside the blockbuster format. (He also ploughed other earnings into creating Industrial Light and Magic, the industry's premiere visual and audio effects facility, and into the campaign to aggressively move filmmaking into the digital arena. That effort accelerated in the 1990s.)

The 1980s, therefore, are marked by trends that are somewhat contradictory. On the one hand, the shifting economics of the industry legitimized blockbuster production and moved it into the mainstream of popular culture as the industry's most visible product. The prime season for releasing blockbusters is the summer, when big, loud, special-effects-centred films grab headlines, magazine covers, and moviegoing dollars. The industry earns between 30 per cent and 40 per cent of theatrical revenue from the summer season. This legacy from the 1980s thoroughly characterizes contemporary film and shows no sign of going away. On the other hand, the ancillary markets that matured in the 1980s, and that drive blockbuster production, also created an ongoing need for films of all types. This served to broaden the range of films in production. While the news media and many young people were principally focused on blockbusters, offbeat, independent films thrived in the 1980s. This development has not received the attention it warrants in general commentary on the period. 1980s American film will probably be forever identified with *Rambo*, the *Star Wars* franchise and *E.T.*, but this composite portrait is a stereotype. The reality was more complex and variegated.

At base, American film in the 1980s was tremendously vital and versatile in its style and modes of address, as the industry that produced these pictures transformed into a subsidiary of global media enterprises and embraced the shift away from celluloid film to electronic formats and home delivery systems. The extent and importance of these changes deepened and intensified in the next decade, which makes the 1980s the key decade of transition, in which the present contours of American film and the industry first emerge.

The cult of the director, which flourished in American cinema in the late 1960s and early 1970s, ended in 1980 with the disaster of Michael Cimino's *Heaven's Gate*. For Corrigan (1991: 11), "If there is a single movie that, deservedly or not, has come to represent the crisis in contemporary film culture, it is … *Heaven's Gate*", a film that is widely cited as sounding the death knell for United Artists (Fig. 12 [*see plate section*]). Founded in 1919 by Charlie Chaplin, D. W. Griffith, Mary Pickford and Douglas Fairbanks, United Artists released its founders' films alongside the work of such prestigious directors and stars as Buster Keaton, Rudolph Valentino and Gloria Swanson, to both critical and public acclaim. In the mid-1950s it went public, and in 1967 became a subsidiary of the TransAmerica Corporation. Three prestigious Best Picture Oscar wins followed in the 1970s, for *One Flew Over the Cuckoo's Nest* in 1976, *Rocky* in 1977 and *Annie Hall* in 1978. Yet the departure of several key executives and the failure of *Heaven's Gate* jointly brought the company to its knees by the beginning of the 1980s.

Seduced by the reputation of *The Deer Hunter* (1978), United Artists signed Michael Cimino to make a Western, inspired (like 1953's *Shane*) by the Johnson County War of 1892. A triangular love story between Sheriff Jim Averill (Kris Kristofferson), Cattle Growers' regulator Nate Champion (Christopher Walken) and young French-born brothel owner Ella Watson (Isabelle Huppert) provided the scant human interest in a lavish (and inaccurate) political parable, characterized by Philip French as "a radical story directed against the Wasp ascendancy and their plutocratic collaborators who have usurped the law and subverted the democratic system" (2005: 136). Beautifully shot by Vilmos Zsigmond and visually reminiscent of the epic cinema of David Lean, *Heaven's Gate* nevertheless suffered from an often tedious and incoherent narrative, courtesy of Cimino's self-penned script.

Disastrously, United Artists' contract with Cimino left them to shoulder the cost of an increasingly profligate production, with no penalty for the director. The original budget of $7.5 million escalated to a reported $36 million, with Cimino shooting thousands of feet of film (his first cut ran to five-and-a-half hours), none of which studio executives were allowed to view. Having similarly lost control of Coppola's *Apocalypse Now*, United Artists fatally failed to rein in Cimino's expanding epic. For Stephen Prince (2000: 33), "Production of *Heaven's Gate* was a chronicle of studio waste and of failure to control a runaway production" that ultimately marked "the endgame for unrestrained auteurism". This endgame was signalled by a unanimously downbeat press and public response to a movie that Roger Ebert dubbed "The most scandalous cinematic waste I have ever seen", and of which *Variety* (1980–14) observed that "The trade must marvel that directors now have such power that no-one … was able to impose some structure and sense."

Accusations of gross historical distortion were the least of the problems for the film, which

Heaven's Gate and United Artists

was withdrawn and recut without crowd-pleasing success; it bombed at the box office. Blame for its failure was laid at Cimino's feet, but as King (2005: 91) argues:

> Coppola and Cimino were not given freedom on *Apocalypse Now* and *Heaven's Gate* simply because the studio – United Artists in both cases – had ceded control to individual directors. The studio was using the status of their directors as part of its strategy to design and promote prestige blockbuster productions. This backfired, especially in the case of *Heaven's Gate*.

Whatever the reason, the toll upon United Artists' revenues was hefty, prompting TransAmerica's sale of the company to MGM in 1981. "For all intents and purposes," reported *Variety* on 13 January 1982, "United Artists has disappeared as a major, self-contained production and distribution company" (Hollinger 1982: 1). After several ownership changes, MGM/United Artists fell into the hands of Crédit Lyonnais in 1992. A sobering lesson in mismanagement, the *Heaven's Gate* saga was famously documented by United Artists' production executive Steven Bach in his book *Final Cut* (1986), which is hailed by Thomson (2003: 158) as "one of our best pieces of contemporary movie history ... a book one is ready to trust because it never denies the executives' blame or Cimino's creative urge".

References

Bach, R. (1986) *Final Cut: Dreams and Disaster in the Making of Heaven's Gate*. London: Faber & Faber.
Corrigan, T. (1991) *A Cinema Without Walls: Movies and Culture after Vietnam*. New Brunswick, NJ: Rutgers University Press.
Ebert, R. (1980) Heaven's Gate, *Chicago Sun-Times*, 26 November.
French, P. (2005) *Westerns: Aspects of a Movie Genre, and Westerns Revisited*. Manchester: Carcanet.
Hollinger, H. (1982) Production control changes marked 1981, *Variety*, 13 January, 1.
King, G. (2005) *New Hollywood Cinema: An Introduction*. London: I.B. Tauris.
Prince, S. (2000) *A New Pot of Gold: Hollywood Under the Electronic Rainbow, 1980–1989*. Berkeley: University of California Press.
Thomson, D. (2003) *The New Biographical Dictionary of Film*. London: Little, Brown.

Mark Kermode

US INDEPENDENT CINEMA SINCE THE 1980s

Jim Hillier

John Sayles' *Matewan*

"AMERICAN INDEPENDENT CINEMA" (although, given all the problems with the term "American" I prefer to refer to "US independent cinema") has come to have relatively specific and accepted meanings and associations: feature-length, usually – but not always – fictional narrative films made and distributed outside the "normal" financing and distribution channels of the major "studios" and therefore marginal to the mainstream movie industry which accounts for the vast majority of box office revenues in both North America and Europe and large parts of the rest of the world. Very often, this "independent cinema" is seen as a phenomenon, if not exclusively then at least primarily of the 1980s and 1990s. Although the "marginality" of US independent cinema has economic and other industrial causes and effects, it is also seen as arising from the differences that mark the independent product from the mainstream product – often different kinds of stories, sometimes – though not always – slighter and less conventionally "dramatic", less often, if at all, driven by stars, genres or action and special effects, sometimes – though by no means always – working with more daring or controversial subject matter, very often marked by distinctive styles of camerawork or editing or narrative organization, though generally not *so* distinctive that the films would not be largely accessible to audiences used to mainstream product. To a greater or lesser degree, such "independent" films would be aiming at an audience – often defined as a "niche" audience – which crosses over with the audience at which mainstream films are targeted.

Immediately, therefore, we can see how tentative any attempt at definition needs to be, and yet we would probably find a broad consensus on many of the names and titles associated with "US independent cinema".

Some names and titles and (US) distributors in the decade from the mid-1980s to the mid-1990s (taken from Pierson 1996) can put some flesh to these definition bones: Jim Jarmusch and *Stranger Than Paradise* (1984, Goldwyn), *Down by Law* (1986, Island), *Mystery Train* (1989, Orion Classics); Richard Linklater and *Slacker* (1991, Orion Classics); Hal Hartley and *The Unbelievable Truth* (1990, Miramax), *Simple Men* (1992, Fine Line); Stephen Soderbergh and *sex, lies and videotape* (1989, Miramax); David Lynch and *Wild at Heart* (1990, Goldwyn); Gus van Sant and *Drugstore Cowboy* (1989, Avenue), *My Own Private Idaho* (1991, Fine Line); Whit Stillman and *Metropolitan* (1990), *Barcelona* (1994, both Fine Line); Ang Lee and *The Wedding Banquet* (1993), *Eat, Drink, Man, Woman* (1994, both Goldwyn); Wayne Wang and *Dim Sum* (1985, Orion Classics), *Slamdance* (1987, Island); Allison Anders and *Gas Food Lodging* (1992, IRS), *Mi Vida Loca* (1994, Sony Pictures Classics); Maggie Greenwald and *The Kill-Off* (1990, Cabriolet), *The Ballad of Little Jo* (1993, Fine Line); John Sayles and *Matewan* (1987, Cinecom), *City of Hope* (1991, Goldwyn), *Passion Fish* (1992, Miramax); Abel Ferrara and *King of New York* (1990, New Line), *Bad Lieutenant* (1992, Aries); Kevin Smith and *Clerks* (1994, Miramax); John Dahl and *Red Rock West* (1994, Roxie Releasing), *The Last Seduction* (1994, October); Quentin Tarantino and *Reservoir Dogs* (1992), *Pulp Fiction* (1994, both Miramax); Errol Morris and *The Thin Blue Line* (1988, Miramax), *A Brief History of Time* (1992, Triton); Alan Rudolph and *Choose Me* (1984, Island), *Trouble in Mind* (1986, Alive); Lizzie Borden and *Working Girls* (1987, Miramax); Todd Haynes and *Poison* (1991, Zeitgeist) and *Safe* (1995, Sony Pictures Classics); Julie Dash and *Daughters of the Dust* (1992, Kino). A long list, but only a small selection of the films from those years – and the range of "independent" films and their distributors is already very clear.

My own sense of US independent cinema would have to bring in a much wider historical sweep, with these films and filmmakers perhaps forming a sort of centre ground in a continuum that runs from a much earlier period and from frankly experimental *avant garde* work to movies indistinguishable from mainstream studio product. As Matthew Bernstein (1986, 1993) and Kevin Hagopian (1986) have shown, for example, there is a long, honourable history of "independent" films made by major stars like James Cagney and director/producers like Fritz Lang, Walter Wanger and Sam Goldwyn who formed their own production companies and made narrative feature films destined for distribution by the major studios. These were "independent" only in the sense that they might offer Hollywood players a greater degree of freedom in the development of projects (as well as certain tax benefits). After the 1947 Paramount divorcement decrees – designed precisely to encourage independent production and distribution – this became much more common and many stars, among them Burt Lancaster, Kirk Douglas and John Wayne, also established their own production companies to produce movies for distribution by the majors. Alongside them were the independent productions of companies like AIP – American Independent Productions – producing exploitation fare aimed primarily at the youth market (and encouraging filmmakers like Roger Corman to imagine later versions of the same practice with New World Pictures in the 1970s). There were also films made quite outside the Hollywood system but nevertheless by Hollywood filmmakers. Perhaps the best known

Continued on page 251

Do the Right Thing (Fig. 14, *see plate section*), Spike Lee's third film, is both his signature work and arguably the film that marked out the arrival of a New Black Cinema as a movement in mainstream commercial filmmaking. Lee's background as a graduate of New York University's postgraduate film programme, his novel approach to finding finance for his films, and his development of an aesthetic which incorporated formal devices designed to disrupt the "seamlessness" of classical narrative and yet to tell stories which challenge widely held conceptions of issues of race generally and the African-American experience, combined to make him the exemplar of the creative energy embodied by a new generation of young black filmmakers. *Do the Right Thing*, in its production history, its story and execution in style and storytelling, and in its reception, mirrors the narrative's depiction of conflict and demonstrates both the effectiveness and the volatility of the subject matter.

The film is set in Bedford Stuyvesant, a predominantly black area of Brooklyn, and takes place during the hottest day of the summer. It relates the personal desires and motivations of multiple characters to delineate the underlying tensions that culminate in a night of violence. The story takes place primarily on one street corner and in Sal's Famous Pizzeria, owned and operated by Italian American Sal (Danny Aiello) with the help of his two sons Pino (John Turturro) and Vito (Richard Edson), with Mookie (Spike Lee) a local resident doing the deliveries. The film hinges on the experiences of Mookie and his role in the conflict between Sal and his friends Buggin' Out (Giancarlo Esposito) and Radio Raheem (Bill Nunn). Sal's racism is masked by a paternal and self-deluding attitude to his black customers which is borne out in the differences between his two sons. Pino's racism and anger are blatant, he resents having to work in Bed Stuy and his friends at home ridicule him for it. Pino bullies his

Do the Right Thing

brother Vito both physically and emotionally for defending Mookie and resisting his racist attitudes. Buggin' Out becomes incensed that Sal has no pictures of African Americans on his "wall of fame" and provokes Sal. This ultimately leads to a confrontation after they have closed the Pizzeria in which Radio Raheem is killed by the police and Sal's Pizzeria is burned out.

The strength of the film lies in its interweaving of the personal lives of the characters in the community, their thoughts and desires and the build-up to the confrontation. It doesn't limit itself to portraying racial tensions but outlines domestic, economic, historical and cultural issues which gives a deeper sense of the complexity of the texture of living in poor urban communities. The stylistic means by which this is achieved gives the film force. The film at first appears to be elliptical in its structure but two things anchor the narrative: the construction of the space and the interlocking commentary on the action by DJ Mister Señor Love Daddy (Samuel L. Jackson) in the nearby WE-LOVE radio station. Bordwell and Thompson argue that the film fits by and large within the classical cinematic paradigm but with notable exceptions (2003: 423–6). One of these is that the characters' goals are not spelled out as clearly or as early as is often found in the classical form. Mookie's and Sal's desires are similar, Mookie wants to get paid while Sal's goal is to make his business pay. Both of these are not the kind of goals generally associated with the goal-oriented protagonist of the classical narrative. In fact, they owe something to the art cinema tradition in that the characters are plagued by dilemmas. The film also diverts attention from these understated goals as it moves from person to person, group to group in the community. The effect of this is a slow build-up to the violent climax of the film.

There is an overriding sense of ambiguity in the film which is explicitly stated at the end with two quotes appearing on screen, one from Martin Luther King warning against the spiral of chaos that violence brings and one by Malcolm X which argues that violence is justified when in self-defence. However, this is only a culmination of Lee's filmic strategies that are a central structuring mechanism in the film's style. The use of direct address operates not simply as a rupturing device but directly challenges the viewer while offering multiple and conflicting viewpoints. The conflict between Sal and Radio Raheem is undertaken in this way, placing the viewer in between the antagonists. The film breaks out of the diegesis in particular key moments when characters directly address a camera tracking in to them as they elicit a stream of racial abuse. Humorous and disturbing at the same time, this sequence begins with Mookie's rant against Italian Americans, followed by Pino's invective against African Americans and followed by more racial epithets which culminates in Love Daddy's demand that everyone chill. His demand re-establishes the diegesis but not before the viewer has been implicated into this world and into the real issues that they represent. Specific moments of ambiguity occur throughout, for example, when Da Mayor and Mother Sister banter in the early part of the film. Da Mayor is apparently held up by the film for some ridicule as he is a drunk, and the music underscores this through the playing of minstrelsy themes that call up the traditional ways in which African Americans have been treated in the classical Hollywood period. Yet later in the film he rescues a young boy from being run over by a car, and he tries to stop the violence in the pizzeria at the end of the film. Through Da Mayor and Mother Sister, Lee is able to convey a sense of history that is cyclical, doomed to repetition, a sense which permeates the film.

Ambiguity and the refusal to deal in the superficialities of stereotype and simplistic good/ evil paradigms are carried through in less obvious but effective ways. The colour scheme of the set and the treatment it receives from Ernest Dickerson's cinematography elicit a palpable sense of tension without calling on the stock washed-out representations of urban landscapes common in many films and ubiquitous in American media coverage. Lee builds into the *mise-en-scène* direct reference to real historical events, and these too usually signify an ambiguity. A shot of graffiti which states "Tawana told the truth"refers to the Tawana Brawley rape case which remains controversial to the present day, while the graffiti itself echoes the dedication to the family of Michael Stewart, a graffiti artist who was killed by the same police choke hold that takes the life of Radio Raheem in the film. This precedes the section of *Do the Right Thing* where Sal's behaviour towards his sister draws Mookie's suspicions and creates tension between his sister and Sal. This provides another layer of suspicion that underlies the community's attitude to Sal.

Lee's play with ambiguity, his insistent reference to real events, is achieved through his commitment to acting styles which work towards authenticity and his expressive use of cinematic devices. In this he was able to fashion a film that struck a chord with audiences. Paramount, the film's original distributor, had refused to finance the film unless Lee made specific changes to the script, and deemed its potential commercial success too great a risk. They cited the ending as "too volatile and could possibly incite black moviegoers to riot". The script was picked up by Universal for a smaller price than Lee's original $10 million budget but Lee was able to retain "final cut"approval (Watkins 1998: 116–17). *Do the Right Thing* was released in the summer of 1989 and in its 17-week run in the top 20 took over $26 million. Lee's formula of maintaining control at the cost of having to work with smaller than usual budgets worked well and helped him to gain a confidence from the Hollywood industry that, however short-lived, managed to get complex and intelligent films on the screen and in front of paying audiences. "Lee's willingness to use the arena of popular film to explore complex social problems like racism allows him to tap into that stream of moviegoers who prefer films that are more intellectually stimulating and engaging" (Watkins 1988: 122). *Do the Right Thing* established Lee's style as aggressive and challenging, and is marked by a refusal to employ the dominant representations of African Americans, of the condition of urban communities and of ethnicity more broadly. In the process Lee was able to bring to the screen a more nuanced, finely sketched and yet accessible rendering of the multifaceted aspects of cross-cultural tensions and the impact of the imbalance and abuse of cultural, economic and institutional power that plagues the US.

References

Bordwell, D. and Thompson, K. (2003) *Film Art: An Introduction*. London: McGraw-Hill.
Diawara, M. (1993) Black American cinema: the new realism, in M. Diawara (ed.) *Black American Cinema*. London: Routledge, pp. 3–25.
Guerrero, E. (2002) *Do the Right Thing*. BFI Modern Classic, London: BFI.
Watkins, C. (1998) *Representing: Hip Hop Culture and the Production of Black Cinema*. Chicago: University of Chicago Press.

Michael Hammond

Continued from page 249

example is *Salt of the Earth* (1953), financed – partly by trade-union funding – and made independently because it could not be made otherwise: its makers were blacklisted and its subject matter – union militancy, exploitation and racism – was not of a kind likely to find much favour in the political atmosphere of Hollywood in the early 1950s. Even so, *Salt of the Earth* was a narrative feature that its makers would have liked to have the widest possible theatrical distribution, although this was made even more difficult when the film was blacklisted by the projectionists' union. From the 1940s, a very wide range of *avant garde* films began to be made by independent filmmakers like Maya Deren, Kenneth Anger and, a little later, Stan Brakhage, all of whom worked with rather different notions of independence (indeed, Brakhage's touring show was titled "Stan Brakhage: American Independent Filmmaker"). Their films were "independent" in much more obvious ways: they did not seek, or need to seek, finance from the same kinds of sources; they did not take the form of feature-length narrative films and they were not intended for showing in regular theatres. And this is, of course, a tradition and area of independent filmmaking that continue throughout the period since the 1940s and are still vital – see, for example, the work of Su Friedrich, James and Sadie Benning, Leslie Thornton, Peggy Ahwesh, Abigail Child.

"Independence", then, was far from a new idea when John Cassavetes and others started making "independent" films in the late 1950s, but they did seem to be doing something very different. They – Cassavetes at least – based their practice, however, on very old-established ideas about what was wrong with Hollywood (Cassavetes 1959) and in this sense at least they hooked up to some extent with the motives of those stars and others who had tried to work independently in the 1940s and 1950s – and they also, of course, favoured the feature-length narrative film and aspired to theatrical distribution. Cassavetes' *Shadows* was financed and made more in the manner of *Salt of the Earth* than the basically Hollywood "independent" pictures, although for its production methods rather than for its

political sympathies. Cassavetes' dismal experience (as a director, in any case – his experience as an actor reads rather differently) in more mainstream Hollywood production leads directly to his pioneering efforts – along with others associated with the "New American Cinema" group and directors like Shirley Clarke (*The Connection*, 1962, *The Cool World*, 1963, *Portrait of Jason*, 1967; Clarke was also co-founder, with Jonas Mekas, of the New York Filmmakers Cooperative), Michael Roemer (*Nothing But a Man*, 1964), Joseph Strick (*The Savage Eye*, 1959, with Ben Maddow and Sidney Meyers, *The Balcony*, 1963) – to create an independent film practice in the 1960s and 1970s (and we should not forget the more marginal, but no less influential in the longer term, prolific output of Andy Warhol in the 1960s). In some ways, as the 1960s evolved, Cassavetes' efforts, though always interesting, looked less necessary, given other developments in the movie industry. In the heart of Hollywood itself, in the late 1960s and early 1970s, much innovative work was made for and distributed by troubled major studios, which were unsure of what would work for what little was left of the mass audience. As David Thomson put it:

The American movie was doing very well in the late sixties and early seventies. In the gradual breakup (or metamorphosis) of control in the picture business, there were young, willful and maverick directors having their own way and making fresh, dangerous pictures that entertained millions while whispering to them about the true troubled state of the nation: Arthur Penn did *Bonnie and Clyde* and *Little Big Man*; Sam Peckinpah made *The Wild Bunch*; Robert Altman was at his first peak with *M*A*S*H*, *McCabe and Mrs Miller* and *The Long Goodbye*;

Martin Scorsese would soon deliver *Mean Streets*. (1996: 394)

I have suggested elsewhere (Hillier 2001: ix) that the degree of renewal and innovation in narrative filmmaking during this period – in the work of the filmmakers Thomson mentions, but also, for example, Dennis Hopper, Monte Hellman, Bob Rafelson – bears close comparison with the renewal and innovation evident in the "new" American independent cinema of the 1980s and 1990s. Strikingly, Altman was a central figure, and equally at home, in both periods, after a more marginal period in the later 1970s and 1980s.

By 1980, Cassavetes' career as an "independent" filmmaker was largely at an end and we might argue that this then ushers in a new period and one which owes something to his efforts – even if very few of the "independent" films of the 1980s and beyond look or feel much like the work of Cassavetes. Although Cassavetes usually tried to organize the distribution of his films himself, his love–hate relationship with Hollywood meant that he also often flirted with the system. *Minnie and Moskowitz* (1971) was distributed by Universal and *Gloria* (1980, Fig. 15 (*see plate section*)) was distributed by Columbia, although neither enjoyed much commercial success (though this should not surprise us, given that both work with fairly radical subversion of the conventions of the narrative feature). Cassavetes' final properly personal project (leaving aside *Big Trouble* (1985), more of a commission and a favour) was *Love Streams* (1983), and this does bring us more into a 1980s context of independent production. The film was funded and distributed by Cannon, one of several "independent" "mini-studios" of the late 1970s and 1980s. Cannon specialized in lower budget mainstream action films and what its owners

Golan and Globus ("deal-kings of the 1970s") made of *Love Streams* (one of Cassavetes' most meandering and baffling narratives) is anyone's guess.

The point here is that this was a period when, with a relative lack of high-end product coming from the studios, and a new demand from cable companies and a new boom in video rental that the majors were yet to exploit, several distributors like Cannon were active. Vestron, Goldwyn, New Line, New World (Roger Corman's old company, but in a new incarnation), like Cannon, aspired to challenge the majors directly for the mainstream audience in terms of the kinds of films they made and distributed. New Line, of course, gave birth to the *Nightmare on Elm Street* series, from 1984 onwards and had its biggest success with *Teenage Mutant Ninja Turtles* (1990). Vestron achieved its greatest success with *Dirty Dancing* in 1987. In both cases, these were films that relied very little on star value (which helped to make them cheap), went in for relatively conventional approaches to narrative style and content, and targeted a mainstream – essentially youthful – audience with enormous success. Of course, there were many films made in the same vein that were not successful and many which went straight to video, but this was still a period when such "independent" activity was vigorous – to the point where Vestron too engaged, towards the end of its life, in more "prestige" productions like John Huston's James Joyce adaptation *The Dead* (also 1987). Although the situation today is very different and – noticeably – none of the companies mentioned above have survived in their earlier form, we should remember that the majority of "independent" films made today – though barely visible – continue to be of this kind. A relatively random example is the 1998 film *Don't Look*

Down, directed by Larry Shaw, produced by Wes Craven/Maddalena Films in association with Von Zerneck-Sertner Films and presented by VZ/S Productions and Hallmark Entertainment, Inc. This was an anonymous and somewhat creaky genre piece, a horror thriller, with no known stars and only Craven's probably very distant involvement to distinguish it. It was made in Canada, like so much current film production, to take advantage of nonunion pay rates.

In his year-by-year list of "American 'Independent' theatrical releases" John Pierson (1996: 345) places *Dirty Dancing* alongside other 1987 productions such as Lizzie Borden's *Working Girls* (Miramax), Tim Hunter's *River's Edge* (Island) and John Sayles' *Matewan* (Cinecom) and these juxtapositions should remind us, once again, that when we talk about US "independent" cinema we are talking about a continuum which incorporates some very different kinds of product with very different origins and aspirations. Indeed, the only meaningful relationship we might see between *Dirty Dancing* and the other films mentioned here is restricted to their economic-industrial status as distinct from the major studio distributors: *Dirty Dancing* would not fit any of the criteria that this chapter began by suggesting most people would associate with "independent cinema". And this is even more true of a wave of big budget films produced by companies such as Carolco, Castle Rock and Imagine in the late 1980s and early 1990s which also came to be described as "independent", or "neo-independent". This was the case, for example, with a blockbuster like Carolco's *Terminator 2: Judgment Day* (1991), which used studio deals for national and international distribution to secure funding. Clearly, it involves stretching the idea of "independent" a long way to think of such projects as truly independent. If, as Roger Corman put it, "a true independent is a company that can finance, produce and distribute its own films", then such companies are "partial independents, connected in some way to a major studio ... independent producers but not truly independent companies". Or, put more bluntly by Troma's Lloyd Kaufman, "independent no longer means 'independent'. It now means 'appendage'" (quoted in Hillier 2001: xv).

If "independent cinema" is a continuum, then we might see Carolco and Castle Rock, at this time, as in bed with the studios, and companies like Vestron and New Line as competing for much of the same market as the major studios, with product in many cases similar to that of the majors, then further along the continuum we might identify other important independents of the 1980s and early 1990s such as Cinecom, Miramax, Circle, Goldwyn as dabbling on the margins of the majors with product that might be described as more "art cinema" and more like what most people would think of as "American independent cinema". Indeed, such companies should be compared in their strategies with the "classics" divisions formed by several of the majors – United Artists (and then Orion) Classics, Fox Classics and, later, Sony Classics to deal with more marginal material or material they found difficult to deal with. United Artists Classics, for example, recut and retitled Joan Micklin Silver's art-filmish *Chilly Scenes of Winter/Head Over Heels* (1979) in an attempt – never really successful – to find a market for it, as well as, as we have seen, the more obviously "indie" films such as Wang's *Dim Sum* (1985), while Fox Classics released *Paris, Texas* (1984) and later Orion Classics released more obviously experimentally "indie" material such as Jarmusch's *Mystery Train*

(1989) and Linklater's *Slacker* (1991). The range of work involved becomes even wider when we include the more politicized, virtually no budget/no distribution work by filmmakers like Jon Jost with films such as *Last Chants for a Slow Dance* (1977), *Slow Moves* (1983) and *Sure Fire* (1990). Jost himself breaks through into more mainstream indie territory with *All the Vermeers in New York*, 1992, distributed by Strand. There is also the lesser-known work of someone like black filmmaker Charles Burnett whose uncompromising racial vision in *Killer of Sheep* (1977) and *My Brother's Wedding* (1983) are definitely American and definitely independent but somehow off the usual "American independent" map. Burnett, like Jost, also broke through into more mainstream indie territory with pictures like *To Sleep with Anger*, 1990 and *The Glass Shield*, 1995. It is precisely this range, even within the field of narrative fiction feature pictures, which makes talking about "US independent cinema" as a recognizable entity so tricky.

Focusing more centrally on the main events and figures of the "American independent cinema" of the 1980s and 1990s, and into the present, there is probably broad consensus on two "defining moments". The first was the triumph of Soderbergh's *sex, lies and videotape* at the Sundance Film Festival in 1989 and its winning the main prize for best film, the Palme d'Or, at the Cannes Film Festival. The second was the commercial and critical success of Tarantino's *Pulp Fiction* in 1994 (Fig. 19 (*see plate section*)). Writing a year later, Pierson called it "the determining off-Hollywood event of the last year, and probably the last ten years" (Pierson 1996: 332). More recently, Xan Brooks, writing of the "*Pulp Fiction* effect", describes how "on the wider, cultural level, [the film's] critical and commercial success repositioned the goalposts of American

cinema, blurring the boundary between mainstream Hollywood product and the independent fringe" (Brooks 2003: 11). Significantly, Miramax – "the house that Quentin Tarantino built" as Harvey Weinstein put it (Brooks 2003: 11) – was behind the distribution of both films. There can be little doubt about the landmark nature of these two moments, but how did they reflect what was happening in the field of independent American cinema and the relationship of that cinema to cinema in the United States more generally, and how far were they indications of what was to come?

Pierson pointedly refers to the *Pulp Fiction* phenomenon as "off-Hollywood" rather than "independent":

> there are a few problems in using [*Pulp Fiction*] as a bookend for this entire [1984–1994] independent decade. If a film like *Stranger than Paradise* empowered new filmmakers, *Pulp* has almost the opposite effect … Even worse, you have to bend over backward and jump through hoops to define *Pulp Fiction* as independent. Begin with the fact that it stars John Travolta and Bruce Willis. Even without their profit participations, it cost $8 million dollars. It was originally set up at TriStar and, eventually, had a 1,200-print release by Miramax, a division of Disney. (Pierson 1996: 332)

The *Pulp Fiction* story, then, rather than being an astonishing proof of how successful an "independent" film could be, is part of a wider story of the dismantling, or transformation, of the structures of independent production and distribution which characterized the 1980s. The acquisition of Miramax by Disney in 1993, for $60 million, was simply one of the more visible signs of this transformation, and the creation of what Justin Wyatt termed the "curious hybrid, the 'major independent'" (1998: 86–7). In the same year New Line and Fine Line – along with the neo-indie Castle Rock – were taken over by Turner Broadcasting (New Line/Fine Line for $600 million), only for Turner Broadcasting to be itself taken over by Time Warner in 1996. (Time Warner itself, of course, was the result of Time taking over Warner Communications in 1989, while Time Warner in turn later merged with, or was, effectively, taken over by AOL to form AOL Time Warner in 2000; Disney, meanwhile, as well as acquiring Miramax, took over Capital Cities/ABC TV network in 1995.) Miramax, partly because of the degree of freedom of operation that formed part of the takeover deal with Disney, is still routinely referred to as an "independent" – and brothers Bob and Harvey Weinstein have maintained a resolutely high profile rather than disappearing into corporate anonymity. All the same, Miramax's dependent relationship with Disney was (and remains) crucial in terms of funding and distribution. Until *Pulp Fiction* and the Disney relationship, Miramax had been primarily a distributor – had indeed been the distributor of one of the formative films of the US independent wave, *Stranger than Paradise* – and had often courted notoriety and controversy as a means of exploiting its releases (as in the case of, for example, Morris's *The Thin Blue Line*). Now they were to be seen "rescuing" projects from the majors – as well as *Pulp Fiction*, *The English Patient* (Anthony Minghella, 1996) from Fox, *Good Will Hunting* (Gus Van Sant, 1997) from Castle Rock. It is therefore not surprising that Jim Jarmusch was able to accuse them of abandoning low-budget independent films.

In a sense, this exemplifies much of the present confusion about what constitutes an "independent" film, which, in the wake of *Pulp Fiction*, was already seen by Pierson: "One thing is clear: The definition of 'independent' now is much more elusive than a decade ago" (1996: 333). How are we to make any useful sense of the claim by Warren Buckland that "Most contemporary Hollywood films begin as independent productions, while the major studios continue to finance and distribute them" (Buckland 2003: 89)? This seems a gross misuse of the term "independent" in relation to the history of independent film production in the United States during the 1980s and 1990s, but the misuse is, of course, understandable. Similarly, Xan Brooks, having made the point that *Pulp Fiction* had set off a blurring of the boundary between mainstream Hollywood films and independent films, goes on to say that it paved "the way for a rash of other iconoclastic pictures made within the studio system – the likes of *Being John Malkovich*, *Solaris* and *The Royal Tenenbaums*" (2003: 11). Using "studio system" in this way inevitably connotes the old studio system, rather than the much more complex – and elusive – production, financing and distribution arrangements in contemporary US filmmaking. More recently, Ryan Gilbey has argued that

> in the years since *Pulp Fiction* the demarcation between what was formerly known as 'Hollywood' and 'independent' filmmaking has vanished. When *The Royal Tenenbaums*, *Election* and *Being John Malkovich* can be studio-financed, and figure in the Oscar nominations, it's clear that the border isn't even being patrolled any more. (2003a: 9)

Anthony Kaufman talks about Steven Soderbergh in the late 1990s and early 2000s as "an

Continued on page 258

A driving and often controversial force in the rise of "indie" cinema in the 1980s and 1990s, Miramax (and later its genre subsidiary Dimension) became emblematic of the blurred line between "independent" and "studio" production and distribution. Established in 1979 by Bob and Harvey Weinstein (whose parents' names Miriam and Max inspired their moniker), the company proved adept at purchasing and promoting foreign, art-house, and "niche market" pictures. The acquisition of Billie August's *Twist and Shout* (1986) for a reported $50,000, for example, resulted in a $1.5 million return at the North American box office, and other success stories of the mid-1980s included *I've Heard the Mermaids Singing* (1987), *Working Girls* (1987), and *Pelle the Conqueror* (1988), all of which turned a healthy profit for Miramax.

The company's major break came when it picked up Steven Soderbergh's Palme d'Or winner *sex, lies and videotape* (1989). Made for a reported $1.2 million, this went on to gross around $25 million in the United States, a figure that "destroyed the previous benchmark for an art house hit" thanks in large part to characteristically "aggressive marketing by Miramax" (Wyatt 1998: 79). A savvy campaign that smartly repositioned the gender-bending political Brit picture *The Crying Game* (1992) as a cool, sexy thriller with a talking point "secret" paid similar dividends as the film took $62.5 million in America. In 1994, the Miramax-backed Palme d'Or winner *Pulp Fiction* topped the $100 million mark, exemplifying the company's ability to parlay art-house credentials and critical plaudits into cold hard cash. In the wake of the runaway success of *Pulp Fiction*, Harvey Weinstein lovingly dubbed Miramax "the house that Quentin built".

In fact, despite Tarantino's undoubted contribution to Miramax's fortunes, it was Mickey Mouse who actually bankrolled the company, thanks to an acquisition (reported at around $75 million) in 1993. As John Pierson (1996: 332) observes; "you have to bend over backward ... to describe *Pulp Fiction* as independent ... It was originally set up at TriStar and, eventually, had a 1,200-print release by Miramax, a division of Disney." Indeed, the Disney deal effectively transformed Miramax into a mini-major, a company best defined as only "partly independent", in the mould of competitors like Fine Line, Castle Rock, and October (Andrew 1998: 38). With this merger came restriction. While Miramax had made much publicity of its battles with the US ratings board over Peter Greenaway's *The Cook, The Thief, His Wife and Her Lover* (1989) and Almodóvar's *Tie Me Up! Tie Me Down!* (1989), the Disney deal stipulated against the distribution of NC17 material, prompting the establishment of Shining Excalibur Pictures to distance Disney from the Miramax acquisition *Kids* (1995). Stockholder dismay at the parent company's involvement in the distribution of Antonia Bird's *Priest* (1994), a provocative tale of sex and Catholicism, prefigured the selling of the religious farce *Dogma* (1999, from Miramax stalwart Kevin Smith) to Lions Gate. "The moral of all this", wrote Peter Biskind (2005: 346) "is that when studios gobble up indies, it's bad for the kind of freedom prized by these film-makers and distributors. 'Independent' became 'dependent'." Finally in 2005, following Disney's refusal to distribute Michael Moore's Palme d'Or winner *Fahrenheit 9/11*, the Weinsteins sold the Miramax name and back catalogue (approximately 550 movies) for a reported $140 million and, in a new bid for "independence", established The Weinstein Co.

Political scuffles aside, the Disney–Miramax years were extraordinarily successful, with Miramax's tireless PR machine helping to turn *The English Patient* (1996), *Shakespeare in Love* (1998) and *Chicago* (2002) into Best Picture winners at the Oscars. Tales of the Weinsteins' legendary interference with their directors' freedoms (prompting the nickname "Harvey Scissorhands") failed to impact upon the company's success. As film historian David Thomson (2004: 399) concludes, despite the negative publicity and tales of outrageous behaviour "Harvey Weinstein is exactly what the picture business in America now deserves –

a gambler, a hustler, a man of taste, and so riotously confused by his own mixture that he attracts attention ... In a time of great stress, he has made the American independent movie a viable genre."

References

Andrew, G. (1998) *Stranger than Paradise: Maverick Film-makers in Recent American Cinema*. London: Prion.

Biskind, P. (2005) *Down and Dirty Pictures*. London: Bloomsbury.

Pierson, J. (1996) *Spike, Mike, Slackers and Dykes: A Guided Tour Across a Decade of American Independent Cinema*. London: Faber.

Thomson, D. (2004) *The Whole Equation*. London: Little, Brown.

Wyatt, J. (1998) The formation of the "major independent", in S. Neale and M. Smith (eds) *Contemporary Hollywood Cinema*. London: Routledge, pp. 74–90.

Mark Kermode

Continued from page 256
important figurehead of an industry often called Indiewood, a mixture of autonomy and individuality with the Hollywood machine's marketing and star-power" (2002: xvi).

Certainly, these can be taken as plausible characterizations of at least part of the current Hollywood landscape, with movies being distributed by the major studios (either directly or through some subsidiary), which at an earlier historical moment like the late 1980s/early 1990s might have been seen as being very "independent" in spirit and which would have had independent distributors. Of Xan Brooks' examples, Spike Jonze's *Being John Malkovich* (1999) was developed by Polygram, which was then taken over by Universal, who distributed the film, while Wes Anderson's *The Royal Tenenbaums* (2001) was made for Disney's Touchstone and distributed by Disney's Buena Vista. For further examples, *Timecode* (2000) was made by Mike Figgis' own production company, Red Mullet, for Screen Gems, a Columbia/Sony Pictures Entertainment subsidiary, and distributed by Columbia TriStar, while Kimberly Peirce's *Boys Don't Cry* (1999) was made for Fox Searchlight – Fox's "independent" front – and distributed by Fox. In this sense "independent" has become, if you like, more of a marketing label than a definition rooted in a film's conditions of production and distribution.

The processes by which major studios co-opted much of the independent film activity and phenomenon during the 1990s owe as much to the earlier success of Soderbergh's *sex, lies and videotape* as to *Pulp Fiction*. The film's success identified Soderbergh as a kind of figurehead or exemplar of the American independent cinema, and seemed to be a beginning and promise a bright future for independent film. As Pierson argues, in retrospect, that film's success and its effects make it look more like a turning point, or the beginning of the end of American independent film as it looked in the 1980s and Soderbergh himself later recognized, on the negative side, that its success "established an unrealistic benchmark for other films" (quoted in Wyatt 1998: 80). Certainly, as we have noted, by the time of *Pulp Fiction*, some four years later, the landscape for independent cinema already looked very different. Soderbergh's own career since *sex, lies* has been very interesting, of course, and very indicative of some of the changes in the industry and its present state. After making *Kafka* (1991) in Europe, Soderbergh appeared to abandon independent film by making *King of the Hill* (1993) and *The Underneath* (1995) for Universal but, no doubt spurred in part by the experience of making the films and their relative commercial – and critical – failure, Soderbergh then appears to rethink. At this juncture, Soderbergh seems to rediscover his indie roots – or at least give up on the attempt to make studio pictures in a more "indie" way: "I've lost interest in the cinematic baggage you have to use to make a film palatable for a mass audience" (quoted in Johnston 1999: 12). This reads like an almost classic "indie" stance, implying, as it did, a desire to work in a nonmainstream style aimed at a nonmainstream audience (as well as recalling, for example, Cassevetes' attempts after the success of *Shadows* to work within the mainstream industry with *Too Late Blues*, 1961, and *A Child is Waiting*, 1963). Two much more identifiably marginal, off-beat, independent films then followed for Soderbergh: *Gray's Anatomy* and *Schizopolis* (both 1996).

This reversion now looks rather odd in the light of what we know of Soderbergh's career since this moment – back to Universal, and to considerable commercial and critical success with *Out of Sight* (1998), *Erin Brockovich* (2000), *Traffic* (USA Films, part of Universal, 2000) and to Warners for *Ocean's Eleven* (2002) – and his current thinking that he sees no real reason why filmmakers with an art film or independent background cannot work in the mainstream. Indeed, Soderbergh seems to take the very practical and somewhat conservative view that the health of Hollywood depends upon independent talent moving into the mainstream, providing some measure of "independent" qualities can be maintained (Morris 2001: 7). In reality, of course, we know that this is not the whole story, and that *The Limey* (1999) constituted a much more "independent" take on the crime thriller, that the low-budget, digitally shot *Full Frontal* (2002, for Miramax) was considered commercially unviable and critically mauled as self-indulgent and that Soderbergh is still planning *Schizopolis 2*. In effect, Soderbergh has used a commanding position in Hollywood – a position no doubt dependent in the future on continued commercial success – to work with one foot in "Hollywood" and one foot out, prompting questions such as "Is Mr Soderbergh an independent who has infiltrated Hollywood, or was he always a mainstream director in maverick's clothing?" and, indeed, whether Soderbergh is set to dissolve such distinctions for good (Morris 2001: 7). To greater or lesser degrees, Soderbergh has tried to bring an "indie" sensibility to his mainstream projects as well as continue a more obviously independent, low-budget line of work. "The independent movement, or whatever you want to call it, has been swallowed up by the studios; so it seems inevitable that I'd be some sort of hybrid" (Soderbergh, quoted in Kaufman 2002: xvi). As far as Soderbergh is concerned, an account of the films he has directed does not tell the whole story, and Soderbergh has taken his position seriously following *sex, lies* as sort of "godfather" to independent film, producing, for example, *Suture* (Scott McGehee and David Siegel, 1993, for Goldwyn), *The Daytrippers* (Greg Motolla, 1996, for Cinepix) and *Pleasantville* (Gary Ross, 1998, for New Line).

In reality, Soderbergh is not alone in trying to work the system in this way. Mike Figgis, for example, is another director who has for many years tried to work out a "one for them, one for me" policy (Hillier 1993: 173) (as well as working between the United States and the United Kingdom), with large-budget pictures like *Internal Affairs* (1990), *Mr Jones* (1993), *The Browning Version* (1994), *Cold Creek Manor* (2003) alongside more formally adventurous narrative fictions like *Liebestraum* (1991), *Leaving Las Vegas* (1995) and *One Night Stand* (1997) and much smaller-scale, more experimental work like *The Loss of Sexual Innocence*, *Miss Julie* (both 1999), *Timecode* (2000), *Hotel* (2001) and *The Battle of Orgreave* (2001).

Unsurprisingly, Soderbergh also makes very explicit the relationship between 1980s/1990s/ 2000s "independent" cinema and the "New Hollywood" filmmaking of the late 1960s/ 1970s, and has talked many times along the lines of seeing "if we can get back to that period we all liked in American cinema twenty-five years ago" (Kaufman 2002: 134) – Penn, Altman, Rafelson, Hellman and others whose films seem to have been made in somewhat similar conditions of independence/ dependence to those of the 1990s/2000s, with a great deal of creative independence, and room to be adventurous, but nevertheless tied to studio finance and distribution. For Soderbergh that period definitely includes *Jaws*, whose blockbuster success helped to usher in a new period in Hollywood's evolution that in many ways put paid to some of the more adventurous work which he refers to most frequently: "the three films that I kept in mind while making *sex*, *lies* were *The Last Picture Show*, *Five Easy Pieces* and *Carnal Knowledge*. They were all made in 1971 and have a very honest quality, much different than films today [1989]" (Kaufman 2002: 37). Hence also, acknowledging some of the European

influences on that late 1960s/early 1970s US cinema, Soderbergh's expressed sense of needing to get back to "that feeling of the French and British New Wave, and the films of the 60s and 70s, of pushing the language a little bit" (Morris 2001: 7).

Justin Wyatt sees the formation of the "major independents" as "a key shift in the industrial parameters of independent film, studio moviemaking and the New Hollywood":

> The major independents have fragmented the marketplace for independent film further and further – through producing films parallel to the majors and through stressing art house acquisitions which have the potential to cross over to a wider market. While New Line and Miramax have gained financial backing through their affiliations, the remaining unaffiliated companies have experienced greater difficulty in acquiring product at a reasonable price. The net effect is a contraction in the market for independent film, bolstering the status of the majors and major independents, and creating an increasingly competitive market for those smaller companies. (Wyatt 1998: 87)

It is therefore not surprising that the trend for independents to affiliate with majors has continued. Bérénice Reynaud (2003: 54–5) has usefully reported on the lower profile but nonetheless symptomatic evolution of other independents. Good Machine is a New York-based production company founded in 1990 by Ted Hope and James Schamus, probably best known for their production of Ang Lee's 1990s films, the most successful of which was *Crouching Tiger, Hidden Dragon*, distributed by Sony Pictures Classics, although they also made Todd Field's *In the Bedroom* and produced over 100 shorts and features over the decade. No doubt their recent high profile and commercial success prompted interest from Universal, which in 1997 had acquired another important production (and in this case, distribution too) company, October Films. Universal had sold October on to Barry Diller, who renamed it USA Films. In 2001, USA Films was bought back by Universal, which in 2002 bought Good Machine, merged it with USA Films (whose recent releases had included Soderbergh's *Traffic*, the Coens' *The Man Who Wasn't There* and Altman's *Gosford Park*) and renamed it Focus Films, with James Schamus and David Linde (who had come from Miramax in 1997 to head Good Machine International, which now became Focus Films International, partnered with Vivendi Universal's StudioCanal). This convoluted – though not particularly unusual – series of developments then begins to explain how an indie/art movie masquerading as a blockbuster, special effects action picture like Ang Lee's *Hulk* (2003) comes to be made for Universal, with Schamus as co-producer and co-writer and Good Machine as co-production company.

These developments can also take us, as a further example, to the production context of *Far From Heaven* (2003), directed by Todd Haynes, whose earlier work had marked him as one of the most important independent filmmakers. The usual complexities of funding and production apply, but we can identify, among the production companies involved, Focus Features (the Universal company formed from Good Machine and October Films), Section Eight (whose main players are Steven Soderbergh and George Clooney) and Killer Films, headed by Christine Vachon. Vachon was one of the most active independent producers in the 1980s/1990s with films like Haynes' *Poison* (1990) and *Safe* (1995), Tom Kalin's *Swoon* (1992), Rose Troche's *Go Fish* (1994), Larry Clark's *Kids* (1995), Todd

Solondz's *Happiness* (1997), *Storytelling* (2000) and *Boys Don't Cry* to her credit. Along with these, there was funding from French television, TF1 International, probably connected with Vivendi Universal's French roots, and Vulcan Productions, Seattle-based independent production company which, under the earlier name of Clear Blue Sky Productions had made, for example, John Sayles' *Men With Guns* and Julie Taymor's *Titus*.

There is no one tidy end to these ongoing developments, but it is worth trying to conclude with a variety of different perspectives. First, what have been the implications of the changes for current and future "independent" production? The new production/distribution landscape has some benefits for established independent filmmakers – or perhaps we should call them "previously independent filmmakers" or "filmmakers with an independent background" – but it may imply the opposite for new filmmakers. It is in the nature of the system as a whole that there will always be starting-out as well as continuing filmmakers who are either forced to be or choose to be "independent". Various channels exist to encourage such filmmakers, although they are not always as independent as they at first seem. To take some recent and new examples, Rebecca Miller's *Personal Velocity: Three Portraits* (2001) is a low-budget DV feature developed by the Independent Film Channel, made by InDigEnt Productions and benefiting from a prize at Sundance, whose Institute and Festival continue to play an important role in independent filmmaking, although its role has also changed since the early 1990s and now reflects more than it used to the shifting affiliations noted earlier. The Independent Film Channel, an alternative cable company established in 1994, added a theatrical distribution arm in 1997 and has been involved with films like Karyn Kusama's *Girlfight*, Richard Linklater's *Waking Life*, Errol Morris' *Mr Death* and Kimberly Peirce's *Boys Don't Cry*. Next Wave Films offers funds for films to be finished. InDigEnt – self-professedly "inspired by the spirit of Danish collective Dogme 95 and John Cassavetes" (and, significantly, Catherine Hardwicke, director of the controversial *Thirteen* (2003) also cites Cassavetes' *A Woman Under the Influence* and Thomas Vinterberg's *Festen*, as well as *Mean Streets*, as influences) – was founded in 1999 to produce low-budget digi-tally shot features, although it is directed primarily at established filmmakers. Its output also includes Linklater's *Tape* and Ethan Hawke's *Chelsea Walls* (produced by Christine Vachon) (both 2001). This should also serve to remind us about the important role played by new technology and the advent of the digital camera. As Mike Figgis, who has now shot several DV features, has put it:

the truth is that it is no longer that difficult to make a film. One cheap camera and a laptop will get you there ... The biggest challenge now is not shooting the film for a small budget but getting it seen, getting distribution. (2000: 9)

Home Box Office (HBO) has been playing an important, innovative role in US film-making – in the sense that it is prepared to take risks – since its foundation in the early 1980s (see, for example, Hillier 1993: 119). Indeed, it added a separate label, HBO Showcase, in 1986, for its more alternative type of material, which it renamed in 1996 HBONYC to reflect the association of New York City with the "indie" scene, although this has since (1999) been merged back with the original HBO Pictures as HBO Films. Shari Springer Bergman's and Robert Pulcini's

American Splendor won the main Sundance prize in 2003 and might be considered a symptom of the continuing vitality of "inde-pendent cinema", but it was developed for HBO by Ted Hope – earlier one of the founders of Good Machine – and taken up by Fine Line for theatrical distribution. Home Box Office began as part of the Time empire and is now one of AOL Time Warner's companies – as is Fine Line, so it is difficult to think of such a film as "independent" in the sense that one might have done a decade earlier.

Second, we might look at the current situation, in 2003, of Gus Van Sant, one of the earlier pioneers of 1980s/1990s independent cinema. Writing in 2001, I noted that

the career trajectory of Van Sant – from the experimentation of *Mala Noche* (1986) to the relative "realism" of *Drugstore Cowboy* (1989) and the richly convoluted *My Own Private Idaho* (1991) to the mainstream conventionality of *Good Will Hunting* (1997) and the simply puzzling remake of *Psycho* (1998) – seems to tell a story of incorpora-tion into the mainstream, although this is not yet quite clear. (Hillier 2001: xiii)

This incorporation seemed to have become much clearer with *Finding Forrester* (2000) but Van Sant has since staged a stunning return to his "indie" roots with *Gerry* (2001, but not released until 2003) and *Elephant* (2003), which will be viewed as two instances of the continuing health of American independent cinema, or at least of its spirit. Both films are experimental, in different ways. *Gerry*, partially in the form of a road (and offroad) movie, has been called a "self-consciously arthouse project", for which actors Casey Affleck and Matt Damon share writing and editing credits with Van Sant. Affirming the continuing influence of European art cinema on US independent practice, they reportedly "swotted up on the films of Tarkovsky and Chantal Akerman among others", as well as being strongly influenced by Béla Tarr, with "a 'thank you' in the end credits to that Hungarian auteur" (Gilbey 2003b: 50). *Elephant*, which won the Palme d'Or and Best Director prizes at Cannes in 2003 and (like *American Splendor*) was developed at HBO by Ted Hope and taken up for theatrical distribution by Fine Line, was inspired by the Columbine high-school massacre and adopts a complex narrative structure. Jean-Marc Lalanne suggests that these films should be seen as representing a new phase in Van Sant's career, rather than a return to his independent beginnings – Van Sant as "contemporary artist" (following on from the phases as "independent film-maker" and as "studio artisan") because of the strongly formalist, abstract quality of the new works (Lalanne 2003: 52).

While it is reported (Gilbey 2003a: 9) that "Indiewood" figures Soderbergh, Spike Jonze, Alexander Payne and David Fincher are hatching plans to establish a "studio", what, finally, of Jim Jarmusch, regarded by many as *the* central figure in US independent cinema since the 1980s? Jarmusch's *Stranger than Paradise* (1984), surely that cinema's founding work, established a number of the qualities associated with the US independent cinema as a whole – hip, off-beat subject matter and low-key, attenuated narrative and visual style – to the point of epitomizing it to a significant degree. Talking about the film at the time and pointing to more general characteristics of the emerging independent cinema, Jarmusch conceded the European and other influences on the film but at the same time emphasized its American-ness:

I think the film is very American, especially in terms of the characters and the acting styles. Because it takes its formal influences from European or Japanese cinema, people have called it European. It is certainly farther from Hollywood than most American films, but it isn't European. I'm American, it's a story about America. (Linnett 1985: 26)

The international dimension of Jarmusch's work has also been reflected in its co-production and funding arrangements: *Stranger than Paradise* was co-produced by West German television, and Jarmusch has consistently drawn on European co-production funding (including Britain's Channel Four). Since *Mystery Train* (1989) Jarmusch's films have also drawn upon Japanese funding, from JVC Entertainment and *Ghost Dog: Way of the Samurai* (1999) was a US-Japan-France-Germany co-production.

In the processes of co-option of independent cinema by the mainstream industry during the 1990s and 2000s, Jarmusch has remained remarkably consistent in his vision and manner of working – "my films are hand-made in the garage, so it takes me a little while to get them together", as he puts it – and he has appeared to resist or refuse co-option more than anyone else. But, inevitably, he has been affected by the changes in the indie scene: Jarmusch's 1980s films were distributed by companies like Goldwyn, Island and Orion Classics, most of which have gone out of business, and his experience of having *Dead Man* (1995) released by Miramax in its new, post-Disney incarnation was an unhappy one. Jarmusch's "consistency" – remarkable when juxtaposed with the career changes of filmmakers like Van Sant or Soderbergh – has sometimes been read as a lack of progress or development in his work and Jarmusch openly admits to a lack of ambition in the career sense. But his later work – *Dead Man* and *Ghost Dog* – while still very much recognizable from his earlier work, is also very different, not least in its exploration of elements of genre, another mark of the American-ness of the work.

At the start of this chapter, I suggested marginality as a characteristic of the American independent cinema as it emerged in the 1980s. If Jarmusch is "the last of a dying breed, defender of the purist faith", as Andrew Pulver (2000: 6) has put it, then it is surely Jarmusch's relationship to this marginality that makes him so: "I like being in the margins. I'm happy where I exist. The things that inspire me I find in the margins. I'm not consciously trying to be marginal, it's just where I end up and where I live" (Pulver 2000: 7).

References

Bernstein, M. (1986) Fritz Lang Incorporated, *The Velvet Light Trap*, 22: 33–52.

Bernstein, M. (1993) Hollywood's semi-independent production, *Cinema Journal*, 32(2): 41–54.

Brooks, X. (2003) Special relationship: why is Miramax so willing to give Tarantino $55m and carte blanche for his new movie? *Guardian Review*, 18 July.

Buckland, W. (2003) The role of the auteur in the age of the blockbuster, in Julian Stringer (ed.) *Movie Blockbusters*. London: Routledge.

Cassavetes, J. (1959) What's wrong with Hollywood? *Film Culture*, 19: 4–5.

Figgis, M. (2000) Low budget, high fidelity, *Guardian Review*, 25 February.

Gilbey, R. (2003a) Younger and wiser, *Observer Review*, 23 February.

Gilbey, R. (2003b) Gerry, *Sight and Sound*, 13(10): 50–1.

Hagopian, K. (1986) Declarations of independence: a history of Cagney Productions, *The Velvet Light Trap*, 22: 16–32.

Hillier, J. (1993) *The New Hollywood*. London: Studio Vista.

Hillier, J. (2001) *American Independent Cinema*. London: BFI.

Johnston, S. (1999) The flashback kid, in J. Hillier (2001) *American Independent Cinema*. London: BFI.

Kaufman, A. (2002) *Steven Soderbergh: Interviews*. Jackson: University Press of Mississippi.

Lalanne, J-M. (2003) Gus Van Sant: localisation zéro, *Cahiers du Cinéma*, 577, March: 52–3.

Linnett, R. (1985) As American as you are: Jim Jarmusch and *Stranger than Paradise*, *Cineaste*, 14(1): 26–8.

Morris, M. (2001) What a lucky Soderbergh, *Observer Review*, 7 January.

Pierson, J. (1996) *Spike, Mike, Slackers and Dykes: A Guided Tour across a Decade of Independent American Cinema*. London: Faber & Faber.

Pulver, A. (2000) Indie reservation, *Guardian Review*, 31 March.

Reynaud, B. (2003) Les producteurs indépendents en difficulté: stratégies de survie des "indies", *Cahiers du Cinéma*, 577: 54–5.

Thomson, D. (1996) *Rosebud: The Story of Orson Welles*. London: Little, Brown & Co.

Wyatt, J. (1998) The formation of the "major independent": Miramax, New Line and the New Hollywood, in S. Neale and M. Smith (eds), *Contemporary Hollywood Cinema*. London: Routledge.

DISNEY AND FAMILY ENTERTAINMENT

Peter Krämer

WHEN *NATIONAL GEOGRAPHIC* published a profile of the Disney company in 1963, the spotlight was on its award-winning output of nature documentaries and the Disneyland theme park (De Roos 1963). The magazine also recounted the company's history, which began with animated shorts and the creation of Mickey Mouse in the 1920s, embraced merchandising and the production of animated features in the 1930s, branched out into documentaries during the 1940s and diversified into live action features, TV programmes and a theme park in the 1950s. In 1962, the article reported, the company's revenues were $74 million – "more than twenty million dollars from Disneyland alone" – and its profits exceeded $5 million (De Roos 1963). Far from dismissing the company's varied output as kids' stuff, the writer emphasized the educational dimension, for both children and adults, of Disney's documentaries and of Disneyland, noting that "adult guests outnumber children three and a half to one" (De Roos 1963).

At the time, the other major Hollywood studios were also in the business of providing entertainment for both young and old, but they focused almost exclusively on film and television production and were, on the whole, much less successful than Disney. While their revenues tended to exceed those of the Disney company, often by a wide margin, in 1962 and 1963 their profits were mostly lower, with Fox and MGM even making catastrophic losses (Finler 1988: 286–7). What is more, many industry observers claimed that Hollywood increasingly moved away from its traditional aim of providing entertainment suitable for everybody: "Moviemakers tend to think exclusively of teen-agers and older. There remains a neglected body of the American public, about 55,000,000 strong and under 14 years old, for whom pictures are rarely made at all" (Waugh 1962) – except, of course, by Disney.

It is possible to tell the story of American cinema since the 1950s by charting the distance between the activities of the traditional Hollywood studios and the Disney model. In the course of the 1960s and the early 1970s, the other majors moved further and further away from Disney and its emphasis on family entertainment, yet since the mid-1970s they have gradually reconceived their output and reorganized their corporate operations along Disney lines, returning family entertainment to the centre of their transnational multimedia operations. One important factor in this development – but by no means the only one – has been the aging of the huge baby boom generation, that is Americans born between 1946 and 1964, which included those 55 million Americans under the age of 14 in 1962 mentioned above. When the older segment of the baby boom reached its teenage years, the pursuit of family audiences became less attractive for Hollywood, yet when this segment reached parenthood, family entertainment moved centre stage again.

The Disney model

Throughout the 1960s and 1970s, Disney combined the release of feature films with other commercial activities, most notably theme park operations. Whereas in 1962, as noted above, Disneyland accounted for less than a third of the company's overall revenues, in 1971 it was more than half ($78 million out of $175 million) (Anon. 1975). Following the opening of Walt Disney World in Florida in October 1971, the 1972 revenues were even more heavily skewed towards theme park operations, which earned $221 million out of $329 million, that is two-thirds of Disney's total income. The other third came from movie rentals in the United States and abroad ($62 million), the sale of records, books and related media products ($35 million), licensing fees for merchandise based on Disney characters ($9 million) and the domestic and international distribution of TV programmes ($9 million).

It might be said that by the early 1970s Disney had become a theme park operator with a sideline in audiovisual media and merchandising, but this would underestimate the cross-promotional, synergistic relationship between the company's various activities. Licensing of merchandise and television brought in comparatively little money for Disney, yet the licensed products and Disney's TV programmes served as highly effective

advertising for the company's films and theme parks (Anon. 1967). Furthermore, the merchandise, the broadcast of TV programmes and Disney's distribution of feature films, which included regular rereleases of classic Disney films, (re)acquainted audiences with characters and settings that were also featured as attractions in the theme parks, and thus served as an inducement to visit them (this had already been crucial for the marketing of Disneyland in the 1950s – Anderson 1994: Chapter VI).

Disney had set up its own distribution company (Buena Vista) in 1953, usually releasing four new films per year, a figure that temporarily rose to six in the early 1960s (Maltin 1995). These films included nature and animal films (variously situated on the continuum between documentary and fiction); live action comedies, dramas and adventures; and animated features (on average one every three years). All of these films were seen to be eminently suitable for children, but their reviews and box office success indicate that the audience was by no means restricted to youngsters (see the reviews excerpted in Maltin 1995 and in Elley 2000). Indeed, a high proportion of Buena Vista releases (on average two per year between the mid-1950s and early 1970s) made it into *Variety*'s end-of-year lists of the 20 top grossing movies in the United States (Steinberg 1980: 22–6).

Particularly successful years included 1961, when *Variety* listed four Disney films in the top ten, three of which were in the top four. In 1965 *Mary Poppins* (released late in 1964, Fig. 1 (*see plate section*)) was named as the year's top grossing movie, although *The Sound of Music* and *Doctor Zhivago* (both released in 1965) would eventually make more money. Similarly, *The Love Bug* was listed as the top grosser of 1969. Disney's most successful new releases tended to be live action films, which sometimes included animated sequences, as in *Mary Poppins*. However, animated features did particularly well during their regular rereleases. Thus, the high production costs of animated features were justified as long-term investments, which would pay off over decades. Most live action films, on the other hand, were made with modest budgets and could therefore more easily make a profit during their first release.

The most important exceptions to Disney's modest budgeting of live action features were three very expensive musicals: *Mary Poppins*, *The Happiest Millionaire* (1967) and *Bedknobs and Broomsticks* (1971). While *Mary Poppins* was a blockbuster success (with US rentals of $29 million during its initial release, and $9 million during its 1973 rerelease; Steinberg 1980: 25, 27), the other two films were only moderate hits ($5 million and $11 million respectively; Cohn 1993) and, due to their high production costs, made little, if any, profit. This was not a problem for the company because it produced very few of these films and had massive revenues from theme parks as well as a steady income from its other film (re)releases.

The traditional Hollywood studios, however, had depended heavily on such superproductions (widely known as "blockbusters") since the 1950s and, as a consequence of excessive budgets and limited box office returns for many of these films, had faced financial collapse in the late 1950s and early 1960s, and again around 1970 (Schatz 1993: 11–14; Hall 2002: 11–17). Thus, in 1972, Walt Disney Productions had profits of $40 million (Wasko 2001: 31), while Columbia recorded a loss of $3 million in 1972, and the profits of Fox, MGM, United Artists and Warners (ranging from $8 million to $23 mil-

lion) were far from making up for the huge losses these companies had incurred since 1969; even the profits of the financially stable Paramount and Universal ($30 million and $20 million respectively) fell well short of Disney's result (Finler 1988: 286–7).

One key factor in the comparatively poor performance of these studios was their overproduction (up to about 1970) of big budget musicals and historical epics. A second important reason was the fact that large segments of the American population had been alienated from cinemagoing following the release, since the mid-1960s, of large numbers of mostly low to medium budget taboo-breaking films (Krämer 2005: Ch. 2). Indeed, weekly ticket sales reached the all-time low of 16 million in 1971, less than half of what it had been in the late 1950s, and less than a quarter of the wartime peak (Finler 1988: 288). Prominent among those who largely stayed away from cinemas were families, that is young children and their parents jointly enjoying themselves – the very people who generated Disney's huge profits.

The decline of the family audience

Reversing long-term trends in American society, the years following the Second World War saw a significant increase in birth rates, which peaked in 1957 but did not return to wartime levels until the mid-1960s (Klein 2004: 174–7). One consequence of this so-called baby boom was shifts in the age profile of the US population. The share of Americans under 15 grew steadily before peaking in the early 1960s. In 1960, for example, 31 per cent of the total population of 181 million was in this age group (Wattenberg 1976: 10). There is evidence that these children were regular cinemagoers, making up a significant portion of the overall audience. A 1957 survey of cinema audiences found that 31 per cent of all tickets were bought by children under 15; the figure for the youngest group up to the age of 9 was 16 per cent (Jowett 1976: 476). What is more, married adults with children under 15 bought 22 per cent of all tickets, whereas the almost equally large group of adults with no children under 15 only bought 12 per cent (Jowett 1976: 477). Thus, the presence of younger children encouraged parents to go to the movies more often, largely, it would seem, in family groups – whereas older teenagers went with their friends or dates.

Although such audience research also revealed that teenagers and young, childless adults were the most avid cinemagoers (Jowett 1976: 476), the high percentage of tickets sold to baby boom children and their parents encouraged studios to continue catering for a family audience. Nevertheless, as we have seen, already in the early 1960s there were complaints in the press that, with the exception of Disney, Hollywood had begun to neglect young children (Waugh 1962). By the early 1970s, this had become a central concern in debates about Hollywood. A 1970 survey, for example, found that a staggering 68 per cent of respondents were dissatisfied "with available children's fare" (Wolf 1970: 7). Two years later, the headline of an article Jerry Lewis published in *Variety* proclaimed: "Children, too have film rights" (Lewis 1972: 32).

Unfortunately, by the early 1970s, it was no longer possible to measure ticket sales to children with any precision, because by then audience surveys only included persons over 11 (Jowett 1976: 486). Nevertheless there is some statistical evidence for the decline in family viewing. For example, in the early 1970s older people, most of whom were parents, went to

the cinema much less frequently than in the late 1950s. The age group 30–39 is of particular interest, because the children of people in their 30s are likely to be old enough to join their parents for visits to the cinema, but most of them are not yet teenagers who want to go without their parents. In 1957, people aged 30–39 made up 14 per cent of the population and bought 13 per cent of all tickets; by contrast, in 1972, they made up 15 per cent of the population over 11, yet bought only 11 per cent of all tickets purchased by those over 11 (Jowett 1976: 485).

At the same time, the industry's dependence on the youth audience had become more pronounced, so that in 1972 12–29-year-olds bought 73 per cent of all tickets purchased by those over 11 (Jowett 1976: 476, 485). This shift towards teenage and young adult ticket buyers was underpinned by the changing age profile of the American population brought about by the end of the baby boom and the aging of the boomers. The share of the American population younger than 15 decreased from 31 per cent in 1960 to 28 per cent in 1970, while the share of 15–24-year-olds increased from 14 per cent to 18 per cent, adding 12 per cent people to this age group (Wattenberg 1976: 10).

Such demographic shifts influenced Hollywood's production and marketing strategies, but other factors also contributed to the increasing focus of the old studios on youth audiences and their neglect of families. These factors include the disruption of traditional studio hierarchies and practices through corporate reorganization across the 1950s and 1960s, with most of the studios being taken over by other companies; the weakening of the film industry's Production Code in 1966, which until then had aimed to ensure that all films receiving a mainstream release were basically suitable for all audiences, and the Code's replacement by an age-specific ratings system in 1968, which simply abandoned the idea that all films could and should be suitable for everyone, including young children; the rise to the top of new generations of studio executives and filmmakers with a different outlook on the role of cinema in American society, privileging notions of art and social commentary, which led them to embrace the new freedoms of post-Production Code Hollywood; and, last but not least, the liberalization and polarization of American public opinion in the 1960s and early 1970s, which, among other things, made it increasingly difficult to make films that appealed to everybody (Krämer 2005: Chapters 2–3).

For all these reasons, then, the 1960s and early 1970s saw the traditional Hollywood studios – but not Disney – turning away from younger children and their parents, and families staying away from cinemas. Partly as a result of this, most of the studios, as we have seen, had substantial losses between 1969 and 1972, while Disney's profits continued their long-term growth.

The return of the family audience

From 1972 to 1976, the old studios turned profitable again, most notably Paramount (with a profit of $50 million in 1976) and Universal ($100 million) (Finler 1988: 286–7). These profits depended heavily on individual blockbusters, chief among them Universal's *Jaws* (1975), which was the highest grossing film of all time up to this point, earning rentals in excess of $100 million in 1975 and another $16 million during its first rerelease in 1976 (Steinberg 1980: 27–8). By contrast, Disney had no blockbusters, yet still easily outperformed the other majors, except for Universal,

with profits of $62 million in 1975 and $75 million in 1976 (Wasko 2001: 31). As before, two-thirds of Disney's revenues came from the theme parks, and about one-fifth from domestic and foreign film rentals; however, together with international TV sales, film rentals made up two-fifths of Disney's operating income (that is profits before general corporate expenses and taxes are deducted), which was almost as much as the share of the theme parks (Anon. 1975). Films definitely remained crucial for the company's profits.

From 1972 to 1976, Disney continued to place on average two films per year, including both rereleases and new productions, in the annual charts of the 20 top grossing movies (Steinberg 1988: 26–8). These films ranged from live action adventures and comedies to animated features; Disney's most successful of these years was the *Love Bug* sequel *Herbie Rides Again* (1974) with rentals of $17 million (Cohn 1993). Thus Disney's hits were left far behind by the other studios' big successes. What is more, most of these successes (such as *The Godfather*, 1972; *The Exorcist*, 1973, Fig. 5 (*see plate section*); *Blazing Saddles*, 1974 and *One Flew Over the Cuckoo's Nest*, 1975, all with rentals in excess of $45 million) were far from family-friendly, often featuring profanity and graphic depictions of sex or violence as well as dealing with controversial subject matter such as race relations. In many cases, their distance from family entertainment was indicated by their R rating, which required children under 17 to be accompanied by an adult (see http://www.mpaa.org).

However, several of the most expensive and most successful productions were widely received as a return to traditional Hollywood entertainment, suitable for the whole family. These films included *The Poseidon Adventure* (1972, rentals $42 million), *The Sting* (1973,

$78 million), *The Towering Inferno* (1974, $49 million) and *Earthquake* (1974, $36 million) (Krämer 2005: Chapter 2). In addition, in the early to mid-1970s independent distributors such as Pacific International Enterprises (PIE) developed large-scale marketing campaigns for low budget releases to cater for the "great untapped public for family-oriented wilderness films, particularly in small towns and rural regions" (Rose 1982: 54–5). Pacific International Enterprises scored a minor hit with *The Vanishing Wilderness* (1973, rentals $7 million) (Cohn 1993).

This strategy proved so successful that the major studios copied it with rereleases "emphasizing the family/adventure elements" of films with rural or wilderness settings such as *Billy Jack* (1971) and *Jeremiah Johnson* (1972) (Rose 1982: 55). Other family-oriented adventure hits by both major and independent distributors, variously located on the spectrum between fiction and documentary and often modelled on Disney's nature films, included *Brother of the Wind* (1972, $12 million), *The Life and Times of Grizzly Adams* (1975, $22 million), *The Other Side of the Mountain* (1975, $18 million), *The Adventures of the Wilderness Family* (1976, $15 million) and *In Search of Noah's Ark* (1976, $24 million) (Cohn 1993).

Most of these adventure films and all Disney releases were rated G – that is, they were deemed suitable for "general audiences", which was usually taken to mean that they were in fact children's films (Krämer 2002: 191–2). Only a small number of hits were rated G during these years; in addition to Disney films and nature adventures, the annual top ten included only a couple of G-rated slapstick comedies (*What's Up, Doc?* 1972, and *The Return of the Pink Panther*, 1975; see Krämer 2005: Appendix 1). However, as

mentioned above, PG-rated disaster movies such as *The Poseidon Adventure* were also widely understood as family entertainment, as were PG-rated hit comedies such as *The Bad News Bears* (1976) featuring child star Tatum O'Neal.

The success of these various types of family-friendly movies went hand-in-hand with a partial return of the family audience. Thus, in 1976 30–39-year-olds, presumably often going to the cinema with their children, purchased 13 per cent of all tickets bought by persons over 11 – up from 11 per cent in 1972 – while their share of the population over 11 had remained the same as in 1972 (15 per cent) (Gertner 1979: 32A). At the same time, overall attendance levels recovered somewhat from the all-time low of 16 million ticket purchases per week in 1971 to between 18 million and 20 million in the mid-1970s (Finler 1988: 288).

Nevertheless, complaints about Hollywood's neglect of the family audience continued: 76 per cent of respondents in a 1974 survey said that the studios' output of "family pictures" was "not enough" (Anon. 1974). Industry observers also noted that the oldest baby boomers were going to turn 30 in 1976, and that from then on the absolute and relative size of the 30–39 age group in the US population was going to increase substantially, making it attractive again for Hollywood to pursue "a truly mass audience" of children, youth and adults (Murphy 1975: 3). More generally, the 1970s saw the widespread recognition of pre-teen children as a substantial market segment in the American economy, which was targeted by businesses with a wide range of products and services (McNeal 1992: 5–6). This in turn encouraged the film industry to make more of an effort to service children (Harwood 1975).

It is in this context that a number of groundbreaking science fiction/fantasy projects were being developed, each over a period of several years from the mid- to late 1970s. Some of these projects were among the most expensive in Hollywood history, with budgets ranging from $20 million to $40 million (Steinberg 1980: 50–1), and all targeted children in one way or another. *Superman* (1978) and *Superman II* (1981), which had gone into production together, were adapations of a classic comic book. *Star Trek: The Motion Picture* adapted a cult television series and was released with a G rating in 1979. Steven Spielberg took inspiration from classic Disney animation for his follow-up to *Jaws, Close Encounters of the Third Kind* (1977) (McBride 1997: 262). Last but by no means least, George Lucas gradually transformed the script that was to become *Star Wars* (1977) from a story aimed at teenagers to one aimed at the whole family, citing Disney as a model (Krämer 2004: 363–5).

All of these films were tremendous hits, with rentals in excess of $55 million, but it was *Star Wars*, the film with by far the smallest budget in this group ($11 million; Finler 1988: 99), which had by far the biggest success. With unprecedented rentals of $194 million during its initial release and several rereleases by the mid-1980s, *Star Wars* became a turning point in American film history, providing both cinema audiences and Hollywood studios with a model for family entertainment that both parties would persistently pursue from then on (Krämer 2005: Conclusion). Films in this mould – which we can call family adventure movies – aim to address children and their parents as well as teenagers and young adults, typically – but not exclusively – by telling stories about the spectacular, often fantastic adventures of young or youthful, male protagonists and about their familial or quasi-familial relationships, especially with fathers or father substitutes; by evoking entertainment forms associated with childhood (such as fairy tales, ghost stories, movie serials, comic books, rollercoaster rides and other amusement park attractions); and by being released in the run-up to, or during the summer and Christmas holidays (Krämer 1998).

Within a few years, in which the record-breaking success of *Star Wars* was nearly matched by its sequels *The Empire Strikes Back* (1980, with rentals in the 1980s of $142 million) and *Return of the Jedi* (1983, $169 million) and surpassed by Spielberg's *E.T.* (1982, $229 million) (Cohn 1993), family adventure movies dominated the American box office. What is more, the release of these films was tied in with massive sales of merchandise, notably toys, games and other products for children, thus emulating Disney's marketing strategies. Furthermore, the films themselves were widely received by reviewers, and presumably by audiences, as Disneyesque (Krämer 2002: 187). Finally, with films such as the *Superman* and *Star Trek* series, the other major studios made use of the synergies that Disney had long been known for, whereby products released by various divisions of a media company are closely related to, and thus generate business for, each other. Warner Bros adapted *Superman* from the comic book owned by its DC subsidiary, and Paramount adapted *Star Trek* from a show owned by its television division, which in turn used the success of the movies to launch follow-up shows.

In this way the Disney model was increasingly emulated by the other major studios in the late 1970s and early 1980s, and, by and large, their profits kept growing. In 1983, for example, profits ranged from $60 million to $160 million (with only Fox making a loss) (Finler 1988: 286). Somewhat ironically, during the same years, Disney's profits had their first downturn in two decades, declining from a peak of $135 million in 1980 to $93 million in 1983 (Wasko 2001: 31). This decline was partly a result of Disney's attempt to attract the teenage and young adult audience, in addition to their traditional family business. Since the mid-1970s, the company had embarked on several big budget science fiction and fantasy productions starting with *The Black Hole* (1979, Disney's first PG release) which, however, failed to generate blockbuster business (Krämer 2002: 192–3).

A much more successful attempt to broaden the audience base for the company's films was the creation of its Touchstone label, which was launched with *Splash* in 1984 and soon released R-rated movies (Gomery 1994: 79–

80). As a result the company was becoming a little bit more like the other major studios, while they, in turn, were becoming much more like Disney. Indeed, in the course of the 1980s, the traditional Hollywood studios became part of media conglomerates that coordinated the activities of their various divisions (ranging from publishing, music and licensing to video distribution, theme parks, television and cinema chains) so that they all generated business for each other (Schatz 1997).

The dominance of family entertainment

Weekly ticket sales in American cinemas went up from 18–20 million in the mid-1970s to

Continued on page 275

Back to the Future

Robert Zemeckis's 1985 film *Back to the Future* could arguably stand as the representative film of the 1980s. The film was once described by Zemeckis himself as a "comedy-adventure-science-speculation-coming-of-age-rock-and-roll-time travel-period film". In that respect the film followed the trend of genre mixing high-yield blockbusters like *Ghostbusters* and *Gremlins* of the previous year, where comedy, adventure and special effects was the favoured recipe. *Back to the Future* featured a similar thematic and generic blend but added an undertone of nostalgia and sentimentality. This was not new and can be seen as a crucial ingredient in the family adventure film production cycle that marked out the work of Steven Spielberg and George Lucas – not surprisingly as Zemeckis was a Spielberg protégé. In that respect it can be seen as a follow-up to *American Graffiti* (1973), Lucas's more poignant foray into the national memory of the 1950s. Released in the very middle of the 1980s (July 1985), the film managed to bring in most of the high-profile cultural anxieties associated with that decade, ranging from the breakdown of the nuclear family to the acquisition of nuclear material by Middle Eastern-based terrorists. Using a family romance of comic and unsettling proportions combined with a depiction of the 1950s, which provided the centrepiece for its design spectacle, the film resonated with audiences and critics on a number of levels. It was the highest grossing film of the year 1985, inaugurating an explicit connection between a national historical memory that saw the 1960s and 1970s as having wounded the national psyche and the salving ointment of the feel-good ending, and it was endearingly self-aware, referencing film history as much as national history.

The story revolves around the friendship of a teenage everyman, Marty McFly, and an eccentric inventor, 'Doc' Emmett Brown. Doc's invention of a time machine provides an unexpected opportunity for Marty to rearrange the past so that his dysfunctional family, which includes a weak father, an alcoholic mother and two underachieving siblings, can fulfil the promise that "if you put your mind to it, you can accomplish anything". This is a sentiment, associated with the family comedy series of the 1950s such as *Father Knows Best*

Contemporary American Cinema

Christopher Lloyd in *Back to the Future*

(1954–60) and *Leave It to Beaver* (1957–63), which seem to operate with alternating sincerity and irony. The film's comedy centres on Marty's and Doc's incredulity about the shape of both the past of the 1950s and the present of the 1980s but, more particularly, on the explicit reference to the potentially incestuous relationship between Marty and the 1955 version of his mother. Marty's father in the present is, in the parlance of the 1980s, a "wimp". George has never been able to stand up to the high school bully and consequently the house they live in is run down, his mother holds forth with 1950s values on teenage behaviour while topping up her vodka, his brother works in a fast food restaurant and his sister can't get a date. Doc has stolen some plutonium from the government as part of a con with Libyan terrorists in order to fuel his time machine, which is a modified De Lorean car. Marty sees his friend gunned down by the terrorists and, in trying to escape, accidentally transports himself to 1955. The spectacle of the past in this main sequence of the film depicts a 1950s America that is pristine and anodyne and yet the characters' actions, Marty's mother's early drinking and his father's ineptitude and cowardliness, indicate the origins of their ultimate fate. Marty finds the 1955 version of Doc Brown who then helps him plan his return. Unfortunately Marty's presence at the moment his parents get together undoes "history" and he jeopardizes the existence of his family altogether. The film at this point is able to conjoin the desire for Marty to return with the necessary task of rearranging history so that his father stands up to Biff the bully and takes charge of his relationship with his mother. The film culminates in a race against time, which ultimately results in Marty resolving his parents' relationship but having rearranged it so that the family he returns to has altered to become successful rather than coping. His father is a successful science fiction writer, his mother is healthy and slim, his brother wears a suit to the office, and his sister gets dates.

The film was received rapturously in terms of box office but critics were at best uncomfortable with the enjoyment they found. Derek Malcolm (1985), a British critic for the *Guardian*, wrote that it was "virtually impossible not to enjoy it in some way or another". However, Pauline Kael in the *New Yorker* found the film pandered to teenage tastes that "now dominate moviemaking" and that the film was "a fantasy about becoming mediocre i.e. successful" (Kael 1985: 57). The consumerist fantasy angle was picked up by other critics with *Time* magazine referring to it as another Spielberg-produced "fantasy adventure . . . designed to turn sentient adults into wonder-lusting children" (the film was a product of Spielberg's Amblin Entertainment). More scathingly, J. Hoberman called Marty "An American Oedipus – his reward: an improved standard of living for the entire family and a woman of his own".

A feature of this film is its play with history. Both Kael and Hoberman express their discontent with this in different ways; Kael wished "American moviemakers would stop using *Life* magazine for their images of America's past", while Hoberman referred to the "thoughtless racism" of the Chuck Berry joke. Both of these critiques demonstrate the unavoidable link between the Reaganesque precept that the solutions to the problems of the present lay in America's past. The film does offer an alternative reading, hinted at by Kael and Hoberman, that these visions of the imagined state of the nation are a symptom of a widely accepted idea that the USA suffered a trauma in the 1960s and 1970s that may have been unrecoverable. The resolutions of Marty's mother and sister are all to do with attractiveness and desirability, a comment of some kind on the effect of feminism in the 1960s, while the pristine *Life* magazine images have their *doppelgänger* effect in the 1980s. The joke is that the cinema that was, in the 1955 section, featuring *Cattle Queen of Montana* starring Reagan and Barbara Stanwyck had, by the 1980s, become an evangelical Assembly of Christ church, while the other cinema across the park (where a tramp has just been awoken by Marty's returning De Lorean) is now a porn theatre. The contrast between the religious Right and liberal relaxation of censorship anticipates the 1980s future with an uncanny accuracy. The America of the 1980s depicted in *Back to the Future* is a dystopic vision that, when probed, links contentment to consumption. The film's clever narration is not completely unaware of this, and of the fact that the humour and action only partly succeed in suppressing it.

References

Hoberman, J. (1985) Spielbergism and its discontents, *The Village Voice*, 9 July.
Kael, P. (1985) Review, *New Yorker*, 9 July.
Malcolm, D. (1985) In love with the future. *The Guardian*, 15 August.

Michael Hammond

Continued from page 272

20–23 million in the late 1970s and the 1980s (Finler 1988: 288). More importantly, the composition of the cinema audience changed. In 1983, 30–39-year-olds bought 18 per cent of all tickets purchased by persons over 11, up from 13 per cent in 1976; during the same period, the share of tickets bought by 16–29-year-olds declined from 62 per cent in 1976 to 55 per cent (Gertner 1985: 30A). On the one hand, there were simply more people in the 30–39 age group (which was largely made up of aging baby boomers), amounting to 18 per cent of the population over 11 as compared to 15 per cent in 1976; on the other hand, people in their thirties went to the cinema more often, partly, it can be assumed, to watch family adventure movies with their children.

Indeed, the birthrate was slowly rising again after 1975 as ever greater numbers of baby boomers were having children. The decade-long decline in the number of annual births bottomed out in 1975 (at 3.1 million), after which this number rose steadily once more, reaching 3.8 million in 1985 and peaking at 4.2 million in 1990, which was close to the post-war record in 1960 (Littman 1998: 11). The spending power of pre-teen children rose so dramatically during this period – from $2.8 billion in 1978 to $6.1 billion in 1989 – that one marketing expert went as far as declaring the 1980s "the decade of the child consumer" (McNeal 1992: 6, 32). In addition to spending their own money, pre-teen children influenced their parents' purchasing decisions, thus indirectly accounting for an estimated $130 billion of adult expenditure per year by the early 1990s, including 30 per cent of all movie ticket purchases and 25 per cent of all video rentals (McNeal 1992: 69).

Thus, when millions of baby boomers became parents and their children became consumers, they turned into a vast new audience for family entertainment (Allen 1999), and the many high-profile family adventure movies Hollywood produced in the wake of the *Star Wars* trilogy and *E.T.* signalled to those baby boomers and their children that family entertainment could be found at the cinema. At the same time, the Hollywood studios and their corporate parents pursued this family audience with other entertainment products and services, many of which were tied in with the release of family adventure movies – for example, a soundtrack album, a magazine cover story, a novelization, licensed toys, a new theme park ride, a spin-off television series and, most importantly, a videotape available for sale or rental (Hollywood's single most important source of income by the second half of the 1980s; Wasser 2001: 153).

The centrality of family adventure movies for the operations of today's media conglomerates is highlighted, first of all, by their continued dominance at the American box office. According to an inflation-adjusted chart (http://www.boxofficemojo.com/alltime/adjusted.htm, accessed June 2005), the 40 top-grossing films of the years 1984–2004 include the following family adventures:

- two further instalments of the *Star Wars* saga (1999 and 2002) and *Independence Day* (1993), which is, in key sequences, effectively a *Star Wars* ripoff;
- two *Indiana Jones* films (1984 and 1989);
- two *Jurassic Park* movies (1993 and 1997);
- four comic book adaptations (*Batman*, 1989; *Men in Black*, 1997; *Spider-Man*, 2002, and its 2004 sequel);
- six animated features by Disney (*Aladdin*, 1992; *The Lion King*, 1994; *Toy Story 2*, 1999; *Finding Nemo*, 2003) and Dream-Works (*Shrek*, 2001, and its 2004 sequel),

as well as a film inspired by a Disney theme park ride, *Pirates of the Caribbean: The Curse of the Black Pearl* (2003);

- six adaptations of classic and contemporary children's books (*Mrs. Doubtfire*, 1993; *How the Grinch Stole Christmas*, 2000; *Harry Potter and the Sorcerer's Stone*, 2001) and of books widely read by somewhat older children (the *Lord of the Rings* trilogy, 2001–3);
- two ghost stories (*Ghostbusters*, 1984, and *The Sixth Sense*, 1999), the second featuring a child, yet too intense for child audiences;
- a slapstick comedy with a child protagonist (*Home Alone*, 1990);
- two films about the historical experiences of those born in the 1950s and 1960s and their relationship to their parents or children (*Back to the Future*, 1985, and *Forrest Gump*, 1994);
- an epic romance, which, quite surprisingly, found a large child audience (*Titanic*, 1997);
- an adventure film about awe-inspiring natural phenomena which references *The Wizard of Oz* and begins with the heroine's childhood experiences (*Twister*, 1996).

Such family adventure movies together with traditional Disney animation also dominated video sales during this period (see the annual charts in *People* 2000: 110–12). An all-time video sales chart compiled in 1998 listed the following 15 best sellers: *Jurassic Park*, *Independence Day*, *Men in Black*, *E.T.*, *Forrest Gump* and *Batman* as well as Disney's *The Lion King*, *Snow White and the Seven Dwarfs* (1937), *Aladdin*, *Beauty and the Beast* (1991), *Toy Story* (1995), *Pocahontas* (1995), *Fantasia* (1940), *The Aristocats* (1970) and *One Hundred and One Dalmatians* (1961) (Jamgocyan 1998).

Since the late 1990s, the same patterns have been emerging among DVD sales.

Furthermore, family adventure films have been performing extremely well in foreign theatrical markets. The (non-adjusted) all-time chart (http://www.imdb.com/boxoffice/alltimegross?region=non-us, accessed June 2005) lists *Titanic*, the *Lord of the Rings* trilogy, three *Harry Potter* films, two *Jurassic Park* films, one *Star Wars* movie, *Independence Day*, two *Spider-Man* films, *Finding Nemo*, *The Lion King*, *Shrek 2*, *The Incredibles* and *The Sixth Sense* in the top 20.

The wholesale revenues that family adventure movies generate for their corporate owners from – in descending order of importance – worldwide DVD and video sales, foreign theatrical rentals, US rentals, product licensing, foreign TV sales and US TV sales can be enormous. Between 1999 and 2004, for example, ten films earned in excess of $1 billion (per film) for the Hollywood majors: two *Harry Potter* films and the *Lord of the Rings* trilogy (all Warner Bros), two *Star Wars* films (Fox), *Finding Nemo* and *Pirates of the Caribbean* (Disney), and *Spider-Man* (Columbia) (Epstein 2005: 237). Earlier members of this billion dollar club include *Titanic* (a Paramount-Fox co-production) and *Jurassic Park* (Universal). The billion dollar wholesale income of these films is, of course, only a fraction of the retail revenues they generated from cinema ticket sales, DVD and video sellthrough, DVD and video rentals, and the sale of licensed merchandise. If we also add the records and books, the fast-food meals and soft drinks that many of these films helped to sell, their centrality for the entertainment industry and for contemporary culture becomes even more apparent.

Conclusion

In the twenty-first century, Disney is no longer the most profitable American media company but it has retained its place among the international market leaders (Anon. 2004) and consolidated its status as one of the world's longest established and best-known brands (see Wasko et al. 2001). Moreover, Disney's operations since the 1950s have provided the other media conglomerates with an influential business model: the pursuit of an international family audience with a range of child-friendly products and services that are tightly integrated with each other and thus help each other's sales (see Kinder 1991; Lieberman 1997; Pecora 1998; Allen 1999; Tobin 2004; Lindstrom 2004; for a different take on Disney's influence on other corporations, see Bryman 2004).

Among other things, the success of Disney's business model has raised the spectre of a culturally homogenized globe on which, from an early age, the majority of children are exposed to, seduced by and absorbed into the fantasy worlds of *The Lion King*, *Star Wars*, *Harry Potter*, *Pokemon* and such like. One international study (Götz et al. 2005: 195) did indeed find "compelling evidence of the centrality of diverse media in children's fantasies", yet it concluded that "(c)ontrary to popular belief, children make sophisticated use of these mediated worlds" to suit their own circumstances, needs and purposes. For better or for worse, then, today's purveyors of family entertainment have – in the words of *National Geographic*'s 1963 article on Disney – "made a lasting impact on mankind" (De Roos 1963).

Acknowledgements

Unpaginated clippings on Disney and the Walt Disney Productions annual report for 1975 were examined in the "Walt Disney Productions" clippings files at the Performing Arts Research Library, New York Public Library at Lincoln Center. Archival research for this chapter was supported by the Arts and Humanities Research Board.

References

Allen, R.C. (1999) Home alone together: Hollywood and the "family film", in M. Stokes and R. Maltby (eds) *Identifying Hollywood's Audiences: Cultural Identity and the Movies*. London: BFI.

Anderson, C. (1994) *Hollywood TV: The Studio System in the Fifties*. Austin: University of Texas Press.

Anon. (1967) The end-plug's the thing for Disney TV programmes, *Newsday*, 15 August.

Anon. (1974) Anybody surprised? *Variety*, 28 August.

Anon. (1975) *Walt Disney Productions Annual Report 1975*.

Anon. (2004) *Variety*'s Global 50, *Variety*, 13 September: A5.

Barnouw, E. *et al.* (1997) *Conglomerates and the Media*. New York: The New Press.

Bryman, A. (2004) *The Disneyization of Society*. London: Sage.

Cohn, L. (1993) All-time film rental champs, *Variety*, 10 May: C76–108.

De Roos, R. (1963) The magic worlds of Walt Disney, *National Geographic*, (August): 159–

207, reprinted in E. Smoodin (1994) *Disney Discourse: Producing the Magic Kingdom*. New York: Routledge.

Elley, D. (2000) *The Variety Movie Guide 2000*. New York: Perigee.

Epstein, E.J. (2005) *The Big Picture: The New Logic of Money and Power in Hollywood*. New York: Random House.

Finler, J. (1988) *The Hollywood Story*. London: Octopus.

Gertner, R. (ed.) (1979) *International Motion Picture Almanac*. New York: Quigley.

Gertner, R. (ed.) (1985) *International Motion Picture Almanac*. New York: Quigley.

Gomery, D. (1994) Disney's business history: a reinterpretation, in E. Smoodin (1994) *Disney Discourse: Producing the Magic Kingdom*. New York: Routledge.

Götz, M., Lemish, D., Aidman, A. and Moon, H. (2005) *Media and the Make-Believe Worlds of Children: When Harry Potter Meets Pokemon in Disneyland*. Mahwah, NJ: Lawrence Erlbaum.

Hall, S. (2002) Tall revenue features: the genealogy of the modern blockbuster, in S. Neale (ed.) *Genre and Contemporary Hollywood*. London: BFI.

Harwood, Jim (1975) Advertisers sensitive to change in kiddies' purchasing power, *Daily Variety*, 20 February.

Jamgocyan, N. (1998) Big boat, small screen, *Screen International*, 26 June: 9.

Jowett, G. (1976) *Film: The Democratic Art*. Boston: Little, Brown.

Kinder, M. (1991) *Playing with Power in Movies, Television and Video Games: From Muppet-Babies to Teenage-Mutant-Ninja-Turtles*. Berkeley: University of California Press.

Klein, H.S. (2004) *A Population History of the United States*. Cambridge: Cambridge University Press.

Krämer, P. (1998) Would you take your child to see this film? The cultural and social work of the family-adventure movie, in S. Neale and M. Smith (eds) *Contemporary Hollywood Cinema*. London: Routledge.

Krämer, P. (2002) "The best Disney film Disney never made": children's films and the family audience in American cinema since the 1960s, in Steve Neale (ed.) *Genre and Contemporary Hollywood*. London: BFI.

Krämer, P. (2004) "It's aimed at kids – the kid in everybody": George Lucas, *Star Wars* and children's entertainment, in Y. Tasker (ed.) *Action and Adventure Cinema*. London: Routledge.

Krämer, P. (2005) *The New Hollywood: From Bonnie and Clyde to Star Wars*. London: Wallflower.

Lewis, J. (1972) Children, too have film rights, *Variety*, 5 January: 32.

Lieberman, D. (1997) Conglomerates, news, and children, in E. Barnouw et al. *Conglomerates and the Media*. New York: The New Press.

Lindstrom, M. (2004) *BRANDchild: Remarkable Insights into the Minds of Today's Global Kids and Their Relationship with Brands*. London: Kogan Page.

Littman, M.S. (1998) *A Statistical Portrait of the United States: Social Conditions and Trends*. Lanham, MD: Bernan.

Maltin, L. (1995) *The Disney Films*, 3rd edn. New York: Hyperion.

McBride, J. (1997) *Steven Spielberg: A Biography*. London: Faber & Faber.

McNeal, J.U. (1992) *Kids as Customers: A Handbook of Marketing to Children*. New York: Lexington Books.

Murphy, A.D. (1975) Audience demographics, film future, *Variety*, 20 August: 3.

Pecora, N.O. (1998) *The Business of Children's Entertainment*. New York: Guilford.

People (2000) *2001 People Entertainment Almanac*. New York: Cader Books.

Rose, B. (1982) From the outdoors to outer space: the motion picture industry in the 1970s, in M.T. Marsden, J.G. Nachbar and S.L. Grogg Jr. (eds) *Movies as Artifacts: Cultural Criticism of Popular Film*. Chicago: Nelson-Hall.

Schatz, T. (1993) The new Hollywood, in J. Collins, H. Radner and A. Preacher Collins (eds) *Film Theory Goes to the Movies*. New York: Routledge.

Schatz, T. (1997) The return of the Hollywood studio system, in E. Barnouw et al. *Conglomerates and the Media*. New York: The New Press.

Smoodin, E. (ed.) (1994) *Disney Discourse: Producing the Magic Kingdom*. New York: Routledge.

Steinberg, C.S. (1980) *Film Facts*. New York: Facts on File.

Tobin, J. (ed.) (2004) *Pikachu's Global Adventure: The Rise and Fall of Pokemon*. Durham, NC: Duke University Press.

Wasko, J. (2001) *Understanding Disney*. Oxford: Blackwell.

Wasko, J., Phillips, M. and Meehan, E.R. (eds) (2001) *Dazzled by Disney? The Global Disney Audiences Project*. London: Leicester University Press.

Wasser, F. (2001) *Veni, Vidi, Video: The Hollywood Empire and the VCR*. Austin: University of Texas Press.

Wattenberg, B.J. (1976) *The Statistical History of the United States*. New York: Basic Books.

Waugh, J.C. (1962) Trail blurred in film capital, *Christian Science Monitor*, 21 November.

Wolf, W. (1970) Poll of moviegoers uncorks surprises, *Entertainment World*, 27 January: 7.

THE VIETNAM WAR IN AMERICAN CINEMA

Susan Jeffords

Dennis Hopper in *Apocalypse Now*

THE VIETNAM WAR is the subject of some of the most popular films of the 1980s – among them films such as *First Blood* (1981), *Lethal Weapon* (1986), *Platoon* (1986), *Full Metal Jacket* (1987), *Good Morning, Vietnam* (1987), *Born on the Fourth of July* (1988), and *Casualties of War* (1989).[1] Not only did these films bring in some of the largest box office draws of the decade (and generate significant video sales both in the United States and abroad), but their screen credits boasted some of

Hollywood's finest directors – Stanley Kubrick, Oliver Stone, Brian De Palma – and most popular actors – Mel Gibson, Tom Cruise, Robin Williams, and Sylvester Stallone. Images from these films became part of the culture of the decade. From Ronald Reagan's quip at a press conference after the release of hostages in Lebanon – "Boy, I saw *Rambo* last night. Now I know what to do next time this happens" – to teenagers referencing *Platoon* for their understanding of what happened in the Vietnam War, these and other films like them helped to define the Vietnam War for a generation of Americans. In doing so, they also helped to define and structure our understandings about the United States and American culture as well.

Films about the Vietnam War did not appear just in the 1980s. Among the earliest and most influential films about war in Vietnam was *The Quiet American* (Mankiewicz, 1958), adapted from Graham Greene's allegorical tale about French, British, and American intervention in Vietnamese government affairs. Though the novel is devastatingly prophetic about the failures of American idealism to understand historically and socially different cultures, the Hollywood film ends up celebrating American innocence as a way to interact with the world. In the same year, the Hollywood adaptation of the Broadway musical hit, *South Pacific*, appeared on the screen. Richard Rodgers and Oscar Hammerstein's songs included lyrics that criticized the kind of overt racism that defined many aspects of the American War in Vietnam: "You've got to be taught to hate and fear/ You've got to be taught from year to year ... You've got to be taught to be afraid/ Of people whose eyes are oddly made/And people whose skin is a different shade −/ You've got to be carefully taught." Nonetheless, the film concludes by depicting a kind of happy paternalism that suggests that South-east Asians are in need of American care and guidance, an attitude that underscored much of the thinking about US military intervention in Vietnam.

Audiences in the 1960s saw one of the most influential and memorable films about the Vietnam War: John Wayne and Ray Kellog's 1968 adaptation of Robin Moore's novel, *The*

Green Berets. In a film that was made in close collaboration with the Pentagon, the war is drawn in stark terms of good and evil. The Viet Cong massacre innocent villagers, rape girls, and torture prisoners. In contrast, the honest and caring American soldiers give their lives to protect the Vietnamese right to democracy. In an echo of the ending of *South Pacific*, Col. Mike Kirby (played by John Wayne) says to a Vietnamese boy, "You're what this war is all about." The US Army often showed *The Green Berets* to soldiers when they first arrived in Vietnam, reinforcing a set of images about the war and the Vietnamese people to the American soldiers who would fight that war.[2] Numerous personal accounts from veterans of the war talk about their identification with heroic film characters, especially with John Wayne: "I had flash images of John Wayne films with myself as the hero"; "I was John Wayne in *Sands of Iwo Jima*".[3] For many Americans, *The Green Berets* typified the values and expectations that they had about the Vietnam War and how it would be fought.

For all of its heroic narrative and popularity, *The Green Berets* was the only major Hollywood production during this time that showed the war itself. Other films, largely "B" movies, focused instead on the returning veterans and depicted them as crazed and violent. Films such as *The Born Losers* (Tom Laughlin [T.C. Frank], 1967), *Angels from Hell* (Bruce Kessler, 1968), and *Chrome and Hot Leather* (Lee Frost, 1970) showed how Vietnam veterans brought home the war's violence to small towns (usually riding on motorcycles). Most Americans still gathered their information about the Vietnam War, not from Hollywood films, but from nightly news broadcasts. This was, after all, the first "television war", and one of America's most trusted newscasters, Walter

Cronkite, helped to interpret the war for American audiences.

However, in 1968, after the Tet offensive, Walter Cronkite shocked American audiences by declaring that "it seems now more certain than ever that the bloody experience of Vietnam is to end in a stalemate".[4] As Hollywood processed these changing sentiments about the war and the growing anti-war movement, new depictions of the Vietnam War began to appear. One of the most influential and memorable of these was Robert Altman's 1970 satire, *M*A*S*H*. Even though the film is set in a medical unit during the Korean War, audiences did not misunderstand the film's target – the war in Vietnam. The film paints an unflattering picture of a military bureaucracy that was focused more on regulations than on the people involved in the war, a system that treated the casualties of war as depersonalized bodies on operating tables. The film criticized the racism of the military[5] and questioned the reasons why anyone would be gung-ho about the war or the army that was fighting it. Following *M*A*S*H*, the 1970s witnessed a number of films that were overtly anti-war. Additional anti-war films appeared in the early 1970s, though they were not about the Vietnam War itself: *Johnny Got His Gun* (Dalton Trumbo, 1971) and *Slaughterhouse Five* (George Roy Hill, 1972).

However, as the Vietnam War reached its close, with the final US troops being withdrawn in 1973 and the fall of Saigon to North Vietnamese troops in 1975, only a few Hollywood films were made about the war. Of the few that reached any popularity, it was for their Vietnam veteran protagonists rather than for any depictions of the war itself. Among the most popular of these films were *Taxi Driver* (Martin Scorsese, 1971) and the series of *Billy Jack* films (Tom Laughlin [T.C.Frank], 1971/

1974/1977). Then, in 1978, some of the most powerful films about the Vietnam War were released, changing the way that American audiences thought about and understood the Vietnam War: *The Boys in Company C* (Sidney Furie), *Coming Home* (Hal Ashby), *Go Tell the Spartans* (Ted Post), *Who'll Stop the Rain?* (Karol Reisz), and one of the single most successful and influential films made about the Vietnam War, Michael Cimino's *The Deer Hunter*.

The film's star power alone would have brought it attention, with Robert de Niro, Meryl Streep, and Christopher Walken in leading roles. But what made *The Deer Hunter* so memorable for so many people was its riveting portrayal of the effect of the war on the lives of people who were involved in it, whether they were soldiers, wives, mothers, fathers, or neighbours. What *The Deer Hunter* showed more powerfully than any previous film was that there was no one in America who could escape the effects of this war, no matter what their political views might have been about it. The everyday aspects of people's lives – weddings, jobs, drinking with friends in a bar – were all changed effectively by the war, and it was clear that things could never go back to the way they had been before the war. In this, the film captured what may have been some of the truest sentiments expressed in any film about the war. *The Deer Hunter* contributed something else as well to the history of Hollywood's portrayal of the Vietnam War. It provided the first, and perhaps the single most memorable, image that viewers would carry with them as a "fact" about the war – the Russian-roulette P.O.W. scene. In the scene, American P.O.W.s are shown being forced to play Russian roulette while Vietnamese soldiers gamble over their lives. For many viewers, the scene is a dramatic metaphor for the war itself, as soldiers' lives were being taken by a random game of war that finally had no meaning. For other viewers, the Russian roulette game entered the pantheon of "facts" about the war, though debate continues as to whether any actual evidence for this exists.[6]

In considering the history of Hollywood representations of the Vietnam War, *The Deer Hunter* marks an important shift in the ways in which the war was represented in American culture. Along with the other films of 1978 – *Coming Home*, *The Boys in Company C*, and *Go Tell the Spartans* – *The Deer Hunter* portrays the Vietnam War as a bad war (though they are not uniform in their judgement as to whether it was a misjudged endeavour to begin with or whether the United States simply did not commit itself fully to winning). But most significantly, the film's focus on understanding the war and its effect on American culture was through the lives of individual soldiers who are shown themselves to have been the victims of this war as much as anyone else. This shift took representations of the war away from questions of political interest, foreign policy making, military strategies, imperialism, or government leadership and transformed them into questions of personal loss, pain, and suffering. It is a shift that was not only indicative of the way in which Americans were prepared to understand the loss in Vietnam but also served to shape future conversations about US military action.

Then, in 1979, Francis Ford Coppola released what many believe to be the quintessential film about the Vietnam War, *Apocalypse Now*. The film's plot – taken from Joseph Conrad's novel, *The Heart of Darkness* – centres around the renegade Col. Kurtz (played by Marlon Brando) who, realizing that the war is unwinnable as it is being fought by the American military, decides to fight the war in his own way with a group of Montangard tribesmen. Though effective, his methods are unacceptable to the American military, and they send an emissary to eliminate him, Captain Willard (Martin Sheen). On his route up-river to find Kurtz, Willard witnesses how the war is really being fought. From Army majors who select military targets based on the surfing possibilities of their beaches, to eerie night-fighting scenes lit by Christmas lights where no one is in command, to soldiers who massacre Vietnamese villagers but go to great lengths to protect a small puppy – this is Coppola's Vietnam War. Here there are no grand political schemes, no decisive victories, and no moral guidelines. There is only the force of individual will in search of meaning in the midst of chaos.

For a few years, Coppola's scathing vision of the "heart of darkness" of the Vietnam War seemed to overwhelm other visual attempts to depict the war, and it appeared as if *Apocalypse Now* would be the way that Hollywood films remembered the war. And then, in 1982, an unassuming production of a David Morrell novel changed not only the way audiences thought about the war but also the way that Hollywood thought about film production for the rest of decade. *First Blood*, which had somewhat of a sleeper opening, grossed $6.6 million in the first weekend (compare this to *E.T.: The Extra-Terrestrial*, for example, which grossed $12 million in its opening weekend in the same year, or to another Stallone film, *Rocky III*, which took in $16 million in its first weekend that year). Nor did the film ever do as well as other blockbusters that year (*An Officer and a Gentleman*, *Tootsie*, or *48 Hours*). Nonetheless, *First Blood* launched a film icon that became one of the most recognizable images in the 1980s – John Rambo –

and in so doing, this film and the sequels that followed it inaugurated a cultural shift in the ways in which American audiences thought about the Vietnam War and the men who fought in it.

First Blood (Ted Kotcheff) is the story of a Vietnam veteran, John Rambo, who is passing through the town of Hope, Oregon, when he is accosted by the town's sheriff, Will Teasle, who doesn't like Rambo's sloppy appearance. When Teasle arrests Rambo and has his deputies forcibly "clean him up", Rambo flashes back to a memory of being tortured by the Vietnamese and reacts violently. What ensues is an all-out battle between one soldier and an entire town's cadre of deputies and National Guardsmen. Rambo's skill as a soldier is such that his mentor, Col. Trautman, is able to assess the odds – a National Guard unit against a single soldier – as about fair. When Trautman explains that he has come to "rescue [the town] from Rambo", Teasle exclaims in disbelief, "Are you telling me that 200 of our men against your boy is a no-win situation for us?" Trautman's reply sums up much of the film's affective appeal for viewers: "You bring that many men, just remember one thing . . . A good supply of body bags." At the film's close, Col. Trautman escorts Rambo to a waiting police car against a background of an entire town in flames.

This is the affective appeal of *First Blood* and its sequels, *Rambo: First Blood, Part II* (George P. Cosmatos, 1985), and *Rambo III* (Peter McDonald, 1988). Like earlier films such as *The Deer Hunter*, *First Blood* shows Vietnam veterans as victims of a country that

Continued on page 286

Arnold Schwarzenegger

Following a successful career as a champion bodybuilder, Arnold Schwarzenegger crossed over into films in the 1970s. Credited as Arnold Strong, Schwarzenegger's extraordinary physique was on display in his debut role as Hercules in *Hercules in New York* (1970). Indeed, given that his voice was dubbed in this film, it seems that it was his physical attributes rather than acting skills that landed him this leading role. After a number of brief appearances throughout the 1970s, it was not until the 1980s that Schwarzenegger's film career really began in earnest. After taking a supporting role in the made-for-television film, *The Jayne Mansfield Story* (1980), Schwarzenegger's muscled body was once more the focus of attention in the subsequent "Conan" films (*Conan the Barbarian*, 1982, and *Conan the Destroyer*, 1984). But it was his appearance as the lethal cyborg in the blockbuster "sleeper hit", *The Terminator* (1984) that brought him global stardom and truly cemented his Hollywood career.

Although the female form has most commonly provided the focus for an inquiring "gaze" in Hollywood films (Mulvey 1975), the spectacular display of the muscled male body became somewhat ubiquitous in the 1980s blockbuster. For some film theorists the appearance of this muscled masculinity in films was linked with the rise of the neo-conservative politics of the period (see, for instance, Tasker 1993, and Jeffords 1994). The Schwarzenegger body becomes a heroic, nationalistic symbol allied with the Reagan and Bush administrations, a notion that is strengthened by Schwarzenegger's known affiliations with the Republican Party and his own political aspirations. Alternatively, the presentation of such a hyperbolic physique can be understood as a performance of masculinity clinging to residual notions of gender, and could even be read as a critique of the period's politics. The "fit" between fictional character and the Schwarzenegger star persona is further complicated in

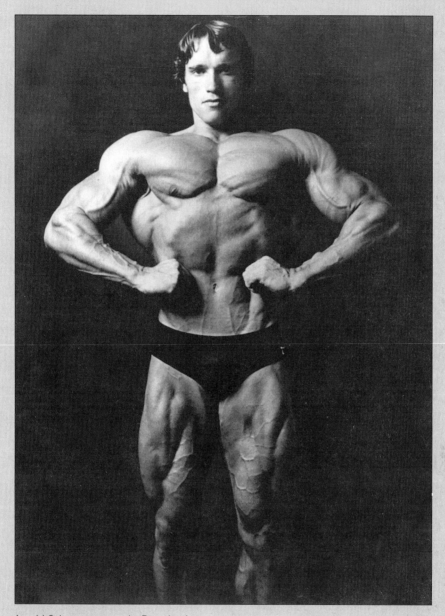

Arnold Schwarzenegger in *Pumping Iron*

considering the manifestly constructed nature of his body. While the Schwarzenegger body might remind audiences of his real-life achievements in the bodybuilding arena, the authenticity of his appearance remains questionable: these muscles are known to be consciously crafted and designed for display rather than formed as the "natural" outcome of a traditional sporting activity (see Richard Dyer's (1992) discussion of the unnatural construction of the bodybuilder in connection with this). Also, unlike some of his muscled contemporaries (Sylvester Stallone, Bruce Willis, Jean-Claude Van Damme), it is notable that Schwarzenegger's performances are remarkably inactive. Rather than presenting a picture of active masculinity, his bodily movements frequently appear considered, posed and held for inspection.

Aside from its big budget sequels (*Terminator 2: Judgment Day*, 1991; *Terminator 3: Rise of the Machines*, 2003), *The Terminator* was followed by a succession of science fiction and/ or action, star vehicles, in which Schwarzenegger invariably played a super-tough and resolute hero. However, alongside these films he has also undertaken central roles in a number of comedies designed for a broader, family audience (*Twins*, 1988; *Kindergarten Cop*, 1990; *Jingle All the Way*, 1996). Although frequently placed in a protective role that requires superior strength and tactical expertise, his characterization in these comedies generally parodies his action persona and works to offer up an image of Schwarzenegger that is more moderate, potentially appealing to a wide audience base.

References

Dyer, R. (1992) Don't look now: the male pin-up, in *Screen* (ed.), *The Sexual Subject: A Screen Reader on Sexuality*. London: Routledge, pp. 265–76.
Jeffords, S. (1994) *Hard Bodies: Hollywood Masculinity in the Reagan Era*. New Brunswick, NJ: Rutgers University Press.
Mulvey, L. (1975) Visual pleasure and narrative cinema, *Screen*, 13(3): 6–18.
Tasker, Y. (1993) *Spectacular Bodies: Gender, Genre and the Action Cinema*. London: Routledge.

Christine Cornea

Continued from page 284

has abandoned them in order to forget a bad war. As Rambo says, "Back there I could fly a gunship. I could drive a tank. I was in charge of million-dollar equipment. Back here I can't even hold a job washing cars!" What Rambo adds to this conversation is the idea that these veterans are men whose skills and commitments are much needed in American society and that any dismissal of them comes at great cost to the country. After all, as Rambo shows in all three films, he is a man who can get things done and who is willing to defend a just cause even when others have turned away. Pitted against a bureaucratic and weak government and an ineffective military, Rambo succeeds in achieving where others had failed, whether bringing back American P.O.W.s from Vietnam or defeating Soviet troops in Afghanistan.

Other popular films of the 1980s copied this theme of action-oriented, decisive, and heroic Vietnam veterans: Chuck Norris's *Missing in Action* series (1984, 1985, 1988), *Uncommon Valor* (Kotcheff, 1983), or *Heartbreak Ridge* (Clint Eastwood, 1986). These films reinforced a broader cultural effort to rethink the way that the Vietnam War was remembered. Rather than focusing on the political, economic, or military issues that underlay a philosophy that propelled the United States into this war, these films proposed that it was government bureaucracy, military sluggishness, or a national failure of will that brought about the loss of the Vietnam War. And caught in the web of these ineptitudes were the Vietnam veterans, who, according to these films, suffered twice: once, when asked to fight a war that wasn't winnable, and again when they came home and found they were blamed for the loss of the war. In contrast, these films – and messages coming from the Reagan White House as well – held up these soldiers as skilled, determined, and valuable, in fact, embodying just the values that the country most needed.

The *Rambo* films and their imitators ushered in a new way of thinking about both Vietnam veterans and war itself. These stories helped to re-establish America's lost faith in its soldiers and their abilities to fight a winnable war. Instead of thinking about soldiers as "baby-killers" and failures, these films taught American audiences to consider America's soldiers as heroic men of commitment and skill. Without the popular reassessments of soldiers that were portrayed in these films, it is doubtful whether the country would have been as willing to support new military interventions in Grenada, Nicaragua, Panama, or the Persian Gulf. Since then, Vietnam veterans appeared more frequently, both in Hollywood films (*Lethal Weapon*, *Universal Soldier*, *Top Gun*, *Die Hard*, *Under Siege*) and on television (*The A Team*, *Magnum, P.I.*, *Miami Vice* and *Hill Street Blues*, as well as *Tour of Duty* and *China Beach*, two television series devoted entirely to the Vietnam War). One of the most popular action comic books, *Predator*, has a Vietnam veteran as its main character. Much of the nation's popular understanding about the Vietnam War comes from these narratives, all of which paint a very different picture of the war and its causes from films of previous decades. As the Vietnam veterans themselves told us, films have a power to shape public thinking about wars. As Ron Kovic, author of *Born on the Fourth of July*, recalls: "I'll never forget Audie Murphy in *To Hell and Back* ... He was so brave I had chills running up and down my back, wishing it were me up there" (Kovic 1977: 54).

Because war stories are often told long after wars are over, it is important to always ask the question, "Why this film? Why now?" In asking those questions of Vietnam War films, we recognize that these films tell stories about the cultural moment in which they were produced as much as they say something about the Vietnam War itself. For example, in the 1970s and 1980s, a period when feminism had successfully challenged many of the traditional expectations and behaviours for men, films about war – the one milieu in which women still had limited roles – were one mechanism for re-establishing certain notions of masculinity and reworking the roles that men would play in relation to military service, still one of the key ways in which patriotism is defined in this country. Similarly, in a period when evidence of racial inequalities was readily available, the interracial bonding shown in combat units in Vietnam War films helped to create the image of a society in which these racial tensions had been resolved. Similar cultural debates about nationalism, economic divides, sexuality, attitudes towards technology, perceptions of government, and definitions of how we identify "friends" and "enemies" permeate these films, as they did the decades in which they were made.

Any summary of films made about the Vietnam War shows that there is no single story that is being told about this war and that films about the war reflect the cultural and social issues of their times rather than any fixed history of the war itself. Whether in support of the war – as in *The Green Berets*, or protesting against the war – as in *M*A*S*H*, or critiquing the national symbols that defined the war – as in *Apocalypse Now*, or praising the heroes who fought in the war – as in *Rambo 2*, films about the Vietnam War tell a variety of stories. Most importantly, these are not simply differing opinions about the war or stories told from different viewpoints; instead, these films are themselves about different cultural contexts that define this war and wars in general in different ways. Consequently, it is important to understand these films, not just for how they tell a story about the Vietnam War, but also for how they tell us stories about the cultures that produced them. Through these films, we can read a second history – that of the social, political, economic, and cultural issues that lay behind the films themselves and the audiences who loved them.

Notes

1   Many of the ideas in this chapter are contained in a presentation I made at a conference in Hanoi on Vietnam War films. That presentation was eventually published in Vietnamese in Lien and Auerbach (2001).

2   As the war wore on, soldiers often showed less enthusiasm for this film. As Gustav Hasford's (1980: 38) novel, *The Short Timers* puts it:

> The audience of Marines roared with laughter. This is the funniest movie we have seen in a long time … At the end of the movie, John Wayne walks off into the sunset with a spunky little orphan. The grunts laugh and threaten to pee all over themselves. The sun is setting in the China Sea – in the East –

which makes the end of the movie as accurate as the rest of it.

3   Quoted in Caputo (1977: 255) and Baker (1981: 23).

4   Broadcast February 27, 1968 over the CBS television network and quoted in Cohan (1983: 214).

5   At the same time, the film was deeply misogynist, depicting an overtly sexist medical and military establishment.

6   See, for example, the following web page devoted to *The Deer Hunter*: http://w3.gwis.com/~dml/tdh/.

References

Baker, M. (1981) *Nam*. New York: Berkley Books.

Caputo, P. (1977) *A Rumor of War*. New York: Ballantine.

Cohan, S. (ed.) (1983) *Vietnam: Anthology and Guide to a Television History*. New York: Alfred A. Knopf.

Hasford, G. (1980) *The Short Timers*. New York: Bantam.

Kovic, R. (1977) *Born on the Fourth of July*. New York: Pocket Books.

Lien, N. and Auerbach, J. (2001) Tiep Can Duong Dai Van Hoa My [*Contemporary Approaches to American Culture*]. Hanoi: Nha Xuat Ban Van Hoa.

THE 1980s AND AMERICAN DOCUMENTARY

Carl Plantinga

THE DOCUMENTARY FILM in the early twenty-first century holds a more significant place in American culture than ever before. Documentaries are enjoying unprecedented success in theatrical distribution, as is clearly evident in the box office numbers of *Fahrenheit 9/11* (2004), *Bowling for Columbine* (2002), *Winged Migration* (2003, Fig. 17 (*see plate section*)), *Super Size Me* (2004), *The Fog of War* (2003), and many others. Although *Fahrenheit 9/11* stands alone at over $119 million in theatrical receipts, 45 non-performance documentaries released since 1988 have cracked the $1 million mark (Box Office Mojo Web site at www.boxofficemojo.com/genres/chart/?id=documentary.htm, accessed 20 April 2005). Box office figures in themselves may tell us little about a film's significance. These documentaries, however, have stimulated national and international conversation, for example, about gun violence, the liabilities of fast food for human health, Bush policies on terrorism, and Robert McNamara's role in the Vietnam War.

Films and filmmakers of the 1980s played a vital role in developing this trend. Two of today's most renowned documentary film-makers, Michael Moore and Errol Morris, won both critical and commercial success with their first notable efforts, *Roger and Me* (1989) and *The Thin Blue Line* (1988). They and many others moved the documentary away from the conventions of direct cinema and of the sedate journalistic documentary, introducing new creative techniques and moving the documentary toward the realm of personal expression. The contention sowed by *Fahrenheit 9/11* is well known, but during the 1980s, too, the documentary was the site of hard-fought political struggle. In short, to understand the place of documentaries in American culture in the early twenty-first century, one would do well to examine the development of documentary filmmaking in the 1980s.

Documentaries and the culture wars

In the United States, the political tenor of the 1980s was dominated by the conservative, anti-communist policies of Ronald Reagan (1980–88). During this final decade of the Cold War came the collapse of communism in the Soviet Union and elsewhere and the fall of the Berlin Wall separating East and West Germany. The 1980s also brought American anti-communist military action in South and Central America and conservative political retrenchment within the United States. Although many documentaries of the time dealt with historical biographies and other topics unrelated to the decade's most controversial issues, the 1980s were also marked by a progressive movement in documentary filmmaking and by determined efforts of the Reagan Administration to counter that movement.

The makers of documentaries of the 1980s were a diverse lot compared to those working in the mainstream media. Many films were made by women and minorities and confronted issues of gender, ethnicity, sexuality, and American foreign and domestic policy, most often from a progressive standpoint. The decade witnessed dozens of films that critiqued covert American military action and foreign policy in South and Central America. For example, *When the Mountains Tremble* (1982), directed by Pamela Yates, Tom Sigel, and Peter Kinoy, critiques US support for a politically oppressive government in Guatemala. Many films also took race, gender, and sexuality as their subjects. *The Life and Times of Rosie the Riveter* (Connie Field, 1980) provides a history of the women who were asked to work in heavy industry during the Second World War, while Marlon Riggs' *Ethnic Notions* (1987) and *Tongues Untied* (1989) explore issues of race and sexuality in innovative ways. *The Times of Harvey Milk* (Robert Epstein and Richard Schmiechen, 1984) and *Common Threads: Stories from the Quilt* (1989) brilliantly highlight issues of violence against homosexuals and the alarming spread of AIDS, each winning an Oscar for best feature documentary in its respective year.

Funding has long been the most painful and difficult aspect of documentary filmmaking, and many filmmakers were forced to finance their films through many and varied sources. (One exception to this general rule is Ken Burns, who has often enjoyed the largesse of the General Motors Corporation for his historical documentaries such as *The Civil War*, 1990.) Many progressive documentaries were in part financed through government agencies, with grants from the National Endowment for the Humanities (NEH), the National Endowment for the Arts, the Corporation for Public Broadcasting, and/or state humanities councils.

The fact that many documentaries about social issues or foreign policy were government-funded and yet had a Left-wing perspective was not lost on Right-wing politicians. The Reagan Administration and Members of Congress worked against such films in various ways. North Carolina Republican Senator Jesse Helms objected to the airing of Marlon Riggs' *Tongues Untied* (1989) on the PBS documentary series *P.O.V.*, arguing that the film "blatantly promoted homosexuality as an acceptable lifestyle" (Day 1995: 326). Helms and others pushed for funding cuts for the NEA, which had partially financed the film. Republican attempts to cut funding to the NEH and NEA were intermittently successful, and managed to keep funding levels from increasing as the decade progressed, although production costs rose significantly.

The director of the NEH, William Bennett, also narrowed the definition of the humanities to exclude grants for social issue films, complaining that past projects of the NEH made it look like "a national organization for raising social consciousness" (*New York Times*, 10 June 1984: sec. 2). The NEH had funded such documentaries as *The Life and Times of Rosie the Riveter*, *The Good Fight* (Mary Dore, Noel Buckner, Sam Sills, 1983), and *Seeing Red* (Jim Klein and Julia Reichert, 1983), which sympathetically portray labourers, labour unions, and Leftist organizations. New guidelines for NEH funding under Bennett were announced in 1984, declaring ineligible projects thought to "advocate a particular programme of social action or change" (Stein 1984: sec 2).

Also under the Reagan Administration, the United States Information Agency (USIA) worked to deny "education" status to films it deemed propagandistic; such films were then subject to high import taxes overseas, which limited international distribution. After lawsuits were filed, various courts found the actions of the USIA to violate the First Amendment, but the USIA nonetheless managed to delay the export of many films critical of Reagan Administration policies (see Plantinga 2000: 382). The Reagan Administration attempted to block progressive filmmaking and especially government funding for such filmmaking, but it was only partially successful. For whatever reason, documentary filmmaking in the 1980s, when it leaned at all, leaned noticeably to the Left of the American political spectrum.

Documentaries in the cultural mainstream

The 1980s was a decade in which documentaries began to break into the mainstream. Several observers noted that by the mid to late 1980s, more documentary films were being shown in commercial theatres than ever before. The box-office success of a documentary is measured on a different scale than a fictional feature film, with a $500,000 box office gross being considered a major success. The breakthrough film appeared in 1976; Barbara Kopple's *Harlan County, U.S.A.*, a fascinating account of a dramatic miners strike in Appalachia, became the first independently made social documentary to gain widespread theatrical distribution. *The Atomic Cafe* followed with a gross of over $1 million in 1982. These films demonstrated that documentaries could appeal to broad audiences. In financial terms, the most successful nonperformance documentary of the decade was Michael Moore's breakthrough film, *Roger and Me* (1989), which earned $6.7 million, followed by *Koyaanisqatsi* (1983) at $3.2 million, *Imagine: John Lennon* (1988) at $2.2 million, *Hell's Angels Forever* (1983) at $2 million, *Streetwise* (1985) at $1.8 million, and *The Thin Blue Line* (1988) at $1.2 million (*Variety* 1991: 5–6).

No documentary filmmaker has enjoyed popular success to the degree that Michael Moore has. No director has brought more attention to the documentary, or has done more to convince the broader public that documentaries can be entertaining as well as informative. (This is not to assume that Moore's significance lies only in what he has done for documentary filmmaking.) Moore's penchant for political comedy and the "cinema of confrontation" were apparent in his first film, *Roger and Me*. Made on a miniscule budget, *Roger and Me* became one of the most popular and controversial films of the decade.

Roger and Me is enormously entertaining. Moore frames the documentary's narrative as an ironic quest, starring himself as an awkward and ultimately unsuccessful hero. Moore's sardonic wit is housed in an unwieldy body, making his determination to find and confront Roger Smith, then-C.E.O. of General Motors, all the more amusing as he lumbers his way into General Motors corporate headquarters or into the homes of unemployed autoworkers. The premise of the film is that General Motors has failed as a good corporate citizen of Flint, Michigan, its corporate headquarters, and indeed General Motors has failed America itself. By laying off auto-workers, closing factories, and opening new plants in Mexico where labour is cheap, it has devastated the city of Flint, leading to high unemployment, rising crime, and the slow death of the city. In telling the story, Moore peoples his film with colourful characters, including Deputy Sheriff Fred Ross (who evicts people from their homes), Rhoda Brit-ton (who sells rabbits for "pets or meat"), and various Flint officials who blithely trumpet the city's revitalization efforts (all of which are shown to fail miserably).

As could be expected, the automobile industry vigorously criticized Moore and *Roger and Me* after the film began to win attention, but the most intense controversy erupted when Harlan Jacobsen, then editor of *Film Comment*, pointed to several instances of apparent deception in the film (Jacobsen 1989: 16–26). In an interview and cover story for the magazine, Jacobsen accuses Moore of re-arranging the chronology of events for his film. Moore makes it appear as though an unem-ployed autoworker steals the cash register at a pizzeria while President Reagan is in the building, when in fact the register had been stolen a few days earlier. Moore makes it appear as though the massive layoffs in Flint occurred as a single event in 1987, when in fact they had been occurring in smaller numbers over a span of years. These are two of several instances in which Moore appears to have given false impressions of the order of events. To give *Roger and Me* the tidy and entertain-ing structure of a Hollywood movie, Moore presented events out of chronological order,

and this, according to Jacobsen, amounts to dishonesty.

Moore defended himself by saying that aside from trivial variations in chronology, his factual claims were accurate, and that he had been more interested in making a "movie" than a "documentary". And Moore's defenders were quick to point out that although some of the chronology may have been misrepresented, this does not weaken the film's basic argument. Criticism of Moore and his film continued, however. Richard Schickel of *Time*, for example, accused Moore of "imposing" a "fictional design that proves the predetermined point he wants to make" (Schickel 1990: 77). And Pauline Kael (1990: 91) took issue with Moore's brand of humour, arguing that the film ridicules the people it shows, and as Kael writes, "made me feel cheap for laughing". From the standpoint of documentary film-making, one could argue that *Roger and Me*, for all its strengths and weaknesses, was the most important documentary of the 1980s, not only for its effect in helping to bring docu-mentary into the mainstream but also for the widespread discussions it helped to raise about the ethics of documentary representation. Not only that, but it also introduced the world to a man who has become America's most infa-mous documentarian.

New styles and emerging filmmakers

The legacy of American direct cinema strongly affected documentary filmmaking in the United States in the 1960s and into the 1970s. Direct cinema and a similar French movement called *cinéma vérité* emerged in the late 1950s, when new filmmaking technologies allowed filmmakers enhanced mobility and unprece-dented spontaneity in filmmaking. Light-weight cameras and portable sound equipment enabled the recording of 16 mm images and synchronized sound with a crew of two persons moving independently, unattached by wires or cables. This new technology, together with the ethos of "authenticity" permeating youth culture, led to an aesthetic of "reality" that became a powerful motivation for documentary filmmakers. Filmmakers were to use the camera and sound equipment to record reality, and overt manipulations of the material, such as voiceover narration and non-diegetic music, were thought to add an authoritarian and artificial interpretation to an otherwise authentic and pristine recording of an event before the camera. The direct cinema filmmaker was to become a "fly on the wall", an impartial, passive, and objective observer.

In the 1980s, a few documentary filmmakers continued to work in the direct cinema style, most important among them Frederick Wiseman. Wiseman rejected the more extreme claims of direct cinema practitioners, and freely admitted that although his films avoid voiceovers, re-enactments, and other so-called manipulative techniques, they are subjective, what he calls cinematic "theories" of the institutions he explores. Wiseman continued to turn out such "voyages of discovery" (Grant 1992) in the 1980s, with films such as *Model* (1980), *The Store* (1983), *Racetrack* (1984), *Deaf* (1987), *Missile* (1988), and *Near Death* (1989).

Yet by far the greater number of documentary filmmakers rejected direct cinema and *cinéma vérité* methods of filmmaking. What follows is a description of the work of a few of these remarkable filmmakers.

Among the most celebrated documentary filmmakers of the 1980s, Errol Morris professed to admire Wiseman's films, but worked in a style that could hardly be further from Wiseman's. As Morris said,

I believe cinéma vérité set back documentary filmmaking twenty or thirty years … There's no reason why documentaries can't be as personal as fiction filmmaking and bear the imprint of those who made them. Truth isn't guaranteed by style or expression. It isn't guaranteed by anything. (Bates 1989: 17)

Most American documentary filmmakers of the 1980s worked in different stylistic idioms from direct cinema, typically using filmed interviews, archival footage, programme music, and even re-enactments and the staging of events. In *When the Mountains Tremble*, Pamela Yates re-enacts an angry meeting between the elected leader of Guatemala and the US ambassador to the country. Errol Morris used re-enactments and the staging of scenes to greatest effect, however. His celebrated *The Thin Blue Line* tells the story of the murder of a Texas patrolman and the ensuing criminal trial, strongly implying (proving, some might say) that the Texas courts tried and convicted the wrong man. Morris re-enacts the murder of the policeman from the perspectives of various witnesses, the re-enactments not being meant to represent the truth so much as subjective memories, and perhaps in some cases, lies. Morris takes this technique further in *A Brief History of Time* (1991), for which he had a set constructed to look like the office of the film's subject, disabled physicist, Stephen Hawking. The kind of truth to which Morris aspires has less to do with the outward appearance of the physical world than with human memory, ways of seeing, and frameworks of understanding.

Another emerging filmmaker of some note was Ross McElwee, whose film *Sherman's March* (1986) has since been canonized as an example of highly subjective, reflexive documentary. The film is as much about McElwee as anything, as the filmmaker records his own travels through the South, often directly speaking to the camera as he talks about his fears, reactions, plans, and feelings. McElwee is ostensibly to follow General Sherman's Civil War march of destruction through the South. The subtitle, *A Meditation on the Possibility of Romantic Love in the South During an Era of Nuclear Weapons Proliferation*, gives some idea of the other directions in which the film meanders. *Sherman's March* begins with a traditional voice-over narrator, giving historical details of Sherman's military campaign. But this nod to traditional historical documentary is soon overthrown for a more eclectic and idiosyncratic style, which is governed purely by the filmmaker's interests and obsessions.

The 1980s saw the emergence not only of more personal and subjective documentary filmmaking, but of what some have dubbed the "performative" documentary, a kind of filmmaking that lies in those fuzzy boundaries between fiction and nonfiction (Nichols 1994). A well-known American example of such a film is the aforementioned *Tongues Untied*, a funny and angry film that includes voiceover calls to the viewer in a kind of poetic chant, various sorts of posing for the camera, and a dance by the filmmaker, Marlon Riggs, all intermixed with traditional documentary footage of police brutality against black men at Howard Beach. The performative documentary, as the name implies, is structured as a kind of performance which incorporates traditional documentary elements within it.

Fashion photographer Bruce Webber brought an artful visual style and moody feel to his films *Broken Noses* (1987) and *Let's Get Lost* (with Nan Bush, 1988), both character studies. The latter, about troubled jazz trumpeter Chet

Baker, was nominated for an Academy Award, but *Broken Noses* is one of those forgotten gems that never received the attention it deserves. It tells the story of an energetic, kind-hearted professional boxer, Andy Minsker, and his boxing club for boys in Portland, Oregon. Both *Broken Noses* and *Let's Get Lost* use expressionistic black-and-white cinematography throughout (flash frames, quick fades in and out, artful compositions, expressionistic low-key lighting, moving lights and spots) and cool jazz scores by Chet Baker. Webber's films take us far from the realm of objective recording, and create a unique and expressive mood.

Other unconventional documentaries were produced by filmmakers working at the intersection of documentary and experimental film. Chief among these were Jill Godmilow and Trinh T. Minh-ha. Godmilow was denied an entry visa into Poland, where she had intended to make a film about the Solidarity movement. Her *Far From Poland* (1984) became a highly reflexive meditation not only on the movement she had hoped to explore but also on knowledge and representation themselves. The staged and re-enacted interviews, voiceovers over black, and reflexive questioning of the filmmaker-narrator, give the film a dense philosophical fabric. The Vietnamese-born American immigrant Trinh T. Minh-ha also worked at the fuzzy boundaries between documentary and experimental film, producing in the 1980s *Reassemblage* (1982), *Naked Spaces: Living is Round* (1985), and *Surname Viêt Given Name Nam* (1989). She is explicit in her rejection of conventional documentary truth and even meaning, using disruptive stylistic techniques to weave impressions, questionings, and complex associations, and leaving traditional documentary values such as coherence and clarity behind.

Let's Get Lost

Another notable documentarian is Les Blank, a Californian who has devoted his life to the making of films that joyfully celebrate American culture and its diverse influences. Among these films is *Sprout Wings and Fly* (1983), a tribute to Appalachian fiddler Tommy Jarrell; *In Heaven There is No Beer?* (1984), a rollicking journey through American polka music and dancing; *Gap-Toothed Women* (1987), described as a "valentine to women

born with a space between their teeth"; and *J'ai Été Au Bal/I Went to the Dance* (1989), a celebration of the Cajun and Zydeco music of Louisiana. Blank also produced one of the most fascinating studies of a film director ever made, *Burden of Dreams* (1982), which follows the messianic German director Werner Herzog as he slogs through the jungles of South America on location for the shooting of his *Fitzcarraldo* (1982). Blank avoids voiceover narrators, and many aspects of his style are observational. On the other hand, his unmistakable perspective – light-hearted, affectionate, and celebratory – emerges in his films through his choice of subject matter and through homespun titles and intertitles, staged "jokes", a camera that is eager to pick out odd and humorous bits of human behaviour, and amusing associations created through editing.

Converging into the mainstream: a conclusion

Convergence, the move toward the unification of the various media and technologies, is affecting the documentary as it has all modes and genres of the moving image media. The 1980s saw the development of small-format video and cable television. Video was used for surveillance, home videography, and community activism. Some documentary filmmakers used video for various preproduction tasks, for example, screen-testing potential interviewees. Nearly all feature documentaries, however, were still shot on 16 mm film; the digital revolution was still some years in the future.

In the area of distribution, however, the boundaries between film and television documentary began to blur seriously. As was previously shown, in the 1980s there was increased theatrical distribution for feature documentaries. Nonetheless, it was far more likely that a documentary film would be seen on public or cable television than in the theatres. The major commercial networks typically avoided feature-length documentaries, preferring short format "news magazines" such as CBS 60 Minutes. Public television became the site for many remarkable documentaries. The most prestigious documentary series on public television was Frontline, which produced regular feature documentaries of significant value. The genesis of a new PBS documentary series in 1988, P.O.V., provided a venue for ten to fifteen independently produced documentaries per year, and provided a significant opportunity to present films to the public. In 1988 and 1989, such films as Best Boy (Ira Wohl), Gates of Heaven (Errol Morris), Las Madres: The Mothers of Plaza del Mayo (Susana Muñoz and Lourdes Portillo), and Who Killed Vincent Chin? (Christine Choy and Renee Tajima) were all screened on P.O.V. The cable television network, Home Box Office (HBO), also began to produce and show feature documentaries, including Bill Couturie's Dear America: Letters Home from Vietnam (1987) and Common Threads: Stories from the Quilt.

Thus we can see that during the 1980s creative filmmakers emerged who produced significant works and pioneered many of the strategies and styles that have come to characterize the documentary film in the twenty-first century. These filmmakers also advanced discourse on the nature of the documentary while expanding its audience. The 1980s also brought the beginnings of trends toward media convergence and the distribution of feature documentaries in mainstream (and near mainstream) venues. P.O.V. and Frontline are still going strong at the time of this writing, and HBO has become a reliable venue for documentaries of quality and significance, its films having won several major awards. Moreover, it is not rare today to see documentaries reviewed and otherwise discussed in mainstream newspapers and magazines and on radio and television. This broad interest in documentary films is a comparatively new development and one which, we can hope, will lead to a healthier national discourse on a wide range of issues.

References

Bates, P. (1989) Truth not guaranteed: an interview with Errol Morris, *Cinéaste*, 17(1): 17.

Day, J. (1995) *The Vanishing Vision: The Inside Story of Public Television*. Berkeley: University of California Press.

Grant, B.K. (1992) *Voyages of Discovery: The Cinema of Frederick Wiseman*. Urbana: University of Illinois Press.

Jacobsen, H. (1989) Michael and me, *Film Comment*, (November–December): 16–26.

Kael, P. (1990) The currrent cinema, *The New Yorker*, 8 January.

Nichols, B. (1994) *Blurred Boundaries: Questions of Meaning in Contemporary Culture*. Bloomington: Indiana University Press, pp. 92–106.

Plantinga, C. (2000) American documentary in the 1980s, in S. Prince, *A New Pot of Gold: Hollywood Under the Electronic Rainbow, 1980–1989*. New York: Charles Scribner's Sons.

Schickel, R. (1990) Imposing on reality, *Time*, 8 January.

Stein, E. (1984) Leaner times for documentarians, *New York Times*, 10 June.

Variety (1991) 25 February, 5–6. Box office figures are through 1990.

MTV

On 1 August 1981, the MTV (Music Television) cable channel was launched by Warner Amex, using a format first conceived by former *Monkees* star Michael Nesmith. Two years later, the big-screen teen musical *Flashdance* (1983) hit box-office gold, thanks in part to music videos cut by director Adrian Lyne from film clips and performance footage, which ran extensively on MTV. Setting the template for tie-in successes such as *Footloose* (1984), *Purple Rain* (1984) and *Batman* (1989), *Flashdance* cemented a synergistic link between the aesthetics of pop promos and feature films. As Stephen Prince observes, "During the eighties, the majors targeted a core audience that could be reached simultaneously through film and pop music ... an audience that purchased huge amounts of recorded music and regularly watched MTV" (2000: 133).

Significantly, the first video aired on MTV was for The Buggles' hit, *Video Killed the Radio Star*. This sci fi, inflected fantasy was directed by Russell Mulcahy, one of several directors who would graduate from pop promos to feature film direction. Two money-spinning *Highlander* movies (1986 and 1991) were emblematic of the rapid-fire editing, flashy visuals and narrative flimsiness associated with the so-called "MTV aesthetic". Among Mulcahy's contemporaries were Steve Barron, whose *Billie Jean* video helped revitalize Michael Jackson's career, and whose feature credits include the international hit *Teenage Mutant Ninja Turtles* (1990); Julien Temple, whose long-form *Mantrap* (1983) and *Jazzin' for Blue Jean* (1984) promos resembled mini features, starring ABC and David Bowie respectively; and Tim Pope, The Cure's resident video director who graduated to the big screen with *The Crow: City of Angels* (1996). Yet it was *Top Gun* (1986), directed by advertising graduate Tony Scott, which came to define MTV's influence upon movie making, with its promo-inflected visuals, overly busy editing and pumping pop soundtrack bridging the gap between narrative cinema and modern musical video montage.

Locating the MTV aesthetic within the broader impact of television, E. Ann Kaplan (1987: 5) argues that "MTV produces a kind of decenteredness, often called 'postmodernist'." Dixon is more damning, claiming that: "An entire generation of viewers became visually hooked on the assaultive grabbing power of MTV's rapid-cutting, which thrusts new images – *any* image – at the viewer to prevent him/her from becoming even momentarily bored" (Dixon 2001: 360). This was a popular mantra, rehearsed throughout the 1980s by those who blamed the death of *auteur* cinema upon the rise of teenage audiences with short attention spans. Yet simultaneously, distinctive TV director Michael Mann was melding music and narrative in *Miami Vice* in a manner that would lay the groundwork for such acclaimed cinema classics as *Manhunter* (1986) and *Heat* (1995). According to Mann, who was at the forefront of a new wave of MTV-era American television:

> The intention in *Miami Vice* was to achieve the organic interaction of music and content. Sometimes an episode would be written around a song, as was the case with "Smuggler's Blues", where Glenn Frey wrote the song and it acted as a libretto for the episode ... As producer, I controlled the music selection with all the directors. (Romney and Wootton 1995: 140)

The influence of the "MTV aesthetic" matured in the 1990s, with the jumbled film-stocks and frenetic cross-cuttings of Oliver Stone's *JFK* (1991) and *Natural Born Killers* (1994) owing a clear debt to pop promos. In recent years, music video graduates such as Michel Gondry (*Eternal Sunshine of the Spotless Mind*, 2004) and Spike Jonze (*Being John Malkovich*, 1999; *Adaptation*, 2002) have laid to rest the once-accepted "truism" that the rise of pop-promo directors is synonymous with the triumph of style over content. Meanwhile, the MTV empire has launched MTV Films, whose varied production involvements have included Alexander Payne's *Election* (1999) and Jake Kasdan's *Orange County* (2002), alongside more low-brow fare like *Jackass* (2002) and the Adam Sandler comedy rehash, *The Longest Yard* (2005).

References

Dixon, W.W. (2001) Twenty-five reasons why it's all over, in J. Lewis (ed.), *The End of Cinema as We Know It: American Film in the Nineties*. New York: New York University Press, pp. 356–66.

Kaplan, E.A. (1987) *Rocking Around the Clock: Music Television, Postmodernism, and Consumer Culture*. London: Methuen.

Prince, S. (2000) *A New Pot of Gold: Hollywood Under the Electronic Rainbow, 1980–1989*. Berkeley: University of California Press.

Romney, J. and Wootton, A. (1995) *Celluloid Jukebox: Popular Music and the Movies Since the 50s*. London: BFI.

Mark Kermode

WOMEN IN RECENT US CINEMA

Linda Ruth Williams

THE POSITION OF women in the US film industry has shifted significantly since the 1960s, with the greatest period of change coming during the 1980s and 1990s. The ways in which women's filmmaking history has been understood also changed in this period. Women have been involved in all aspects of the filmmaking process since the birth of the medium. For Gwendolyn Foster, the question is not whether women have had the opportunity to contribute to the history of cinema, but why film historians have noticed so few of their contributions. Women's marginalization is twofold: after the 1920s they became rare breeds in the industry, but those who *were* working were also largely ignored by chroniclers (Foster 1999: xvi). Feminist criticism has done something to redress this since the 1970s, unearthing careers and significant work buried in film history. However, rich as this history is, it is also slight, compared with men's overwhelming shaping of the medium. Notable is Claire Johnston and others' work in the 1970s on Dorothy Arzner, and more recent analyses of Ida Lupino (Kuhn 1995; Donati 1996). Auteurist approaches have limited scope in studies of the studio era – Lupino and Arzner were the only female directors to develop significant bodies of work in classical Hollywood. Other filmmaking

professions fare better. There is, of course, a rich history of female stardom in the classical period, and Lizzie Franke's *Script Girls* shows how

> screenwriting has been one profession open to [women] throughout the history of Hollywood. (They've been allowed to be editors too, but sewing up films in a dark room under the judicious eyes of the director obviously limited their participation in the story-telling process . . .). (Franke 1994: 1)

Yet apart from these traditionally "feminine" areas (also including costume, make-up, and music), female involvement behind the camera was relatively limited from the coming of sound to the coming of feminism.

Things began to change in the late 1960s and 1970s, partly driven by the burgeoning women's movement, partly in response to its demands. Yet, as one collection of essays on (non-US) women's cinema notes, "as recently as the 1970s it seemed possible for a film festival to cover all aspects of women's filmmaking" (Levitin et al. 2003: 10). This is (thankfully) no longer the case; women's filmmaking is now far more prolific, particularly in independent production, while in Hollywood there are a few more female directors and far more women working in other areas of the industry. Ann Kaplan (2003: 16–22) reads women's film history in four phases: the first up to 1930 (the period of women pioneers); the second from 1930–60 (the period of "the Silencing of Women"); the third, from 1960–90, in which white women became more dominant in US and other national cinemas; the fourth, from 1990 onwards, in which a growing multiculturalism became evident in European and North American women's cinema. Of phase three she writes that women filmmakers "gained power from the 1970s/1980s sense of embattlement, of challenging an unjust patriarchal order and claiming what was due to women" (Kaplan 2003: 19), but she is also careful to point out that the landscape of North American filmmaking has most dramatically altered recently with the impact of work from independent and foreign filmmakers. It is argued in a number of studies that women from a wider range of social and racial groups have been able to foster filmmaking careers because this growth of independent cinema has facilitated better access to equipment and distribution. But this was also the time when women became far more prominent in Hollywood.

So who are the key figures who have contributed to this improvement since the 1960s? A common approach to an archeology of women in the phase of US film history known as the Hollywood Renaissance or the American New Wave (roughly 1967–75) mimicked the dominant auteurist models used for valuing male directors. Feminist histories of this period are predominantly director- and star-studies, yet this is at a time when female directors were still a rare breed. Christina Lane (2000: 13) writes in her important survey of women who have made the transition from independent to mainstream directing:

Before the 1970s, when access to commercial production opened up slightly, women had only two avenues for becoming Hollywood directors: as film actresses or as secretaries/production assistants who worked their way up through the ranks of the system. Only recently have women been hired as directors on the basis of their independent films.

Polly Platt, one of the most celebrated production designers of the period (*Targets*, 1969; *The Last Picture Show*, 1971; *Paper Moon*, 1973; *Pretty Baby*, 1978 – Platt also wrote the screenplay for *Terms of Endearment*, 1983) and now a successful producer (*Broadcast News* 1987; *The War of the Roses*, 1989; *The Evening Star*, 1996) never made the jump into directing (though Barbra Streisand at one point suggested they codirect *A Star is Born* (Abramowitz 2000: 101)). She has been rather critically overlooked by virtue of the fact that she worked at first largely on projects helmed by her (then) auteur-husband Peter Bogdanovich (some of the stories of "the women behind the male auteurs", including Platt's, are told in Abramowitz (2000) and in Biskind, 1998). Joan Tewkesbury and Carole Eastman's screenplays made phenomenal contributions to the American New Wave, yet the films developed from them (Tewkesbury's *Thieves Like Us*, 1974, and *Nashville*, 1975; Eastman's *Five Easy Pieces*, 1970) are more usually discussed as the genius-products of their auteur helmsmen (Robert Altman with the first two films; Bob Rafelson with *Five Easy Pieces*).

The move from screenwriting to directing has become more common for women in recent decades. In the 1970s, Elaine May made this move from an established position

Continued on page 302

Born in New York City in 1942, Barbra Streisand's remarkable career has spanned five decades from her Broadway debut in 1961 to her recent Hollywood turn in *Meet the Fockers* (2004). Streisand collects accolades like some people collect dust. She's gained Grammys and Emmys, Golden Globes and Oscars. She was the first female composer to win an Academy Award and the first female director-star to gain Best Director nominations for *Prince of Tides* (1991). Streisand is the most successful female recording artist ever, outsold only by Elvis. While her acting and singing career has been marked by extraordinary acclaim, Streisand's role as film director has not.

Streisand has directed three films: *Yentl* (1983), *Prince of Tides* (1991) and *The Mirror has Two Faces* (1996). It took her sixteen years to overcome studio opposition to make *Yentl*. In it Streisand plays a young Jewish woman in early twentieth-century Eastern Europe who disguises herself as a boy in order to study at yeshiva. This inherently controversial tale breaks various rules of gender and religious practice to provide an amusing, compelling and sometimes steamy story. It also breaks the rules of the musical: Streisand sings all the songs. Ambitious and skilful but, as some saw it, typically self-obsessed, *Yentl* made Streisand the first woman to direct, produce, co-write and star in a Hollywood film, but the Academy neither acknowledged nor rewarded this achievement.

Streisand's adaptation of Pat Conroy's best-selling novel of a man's, Tom Wilgo's, relationship with his suicidal sister's psychiatrist, represents her most accomplished piece. Well-crafted, intricate and often spell-binding *The Prince of Tides*, and especially Nick Nolte's performance as Tom, takes the cinematic romanticism it shares with *Yentl* and adds to it a psychological complexity absent from Streisand's other work. Her third film, however, veers in the opposite direction. *The Mirror Has Two Faces* trades in formulaic, nigh-on

Barbra Streisand in *Yentl*, which she wrote, directed, produced and starred in

reductive, comedy. In it, ugly duckling Rose – a familiar role for Streisand, indeed, a recognized Hollywood stereotype of Jewish women (see Erens 1984) – has a major make-over and wins the love of a previously unobtainable professor played by Jeff Bridges. Safe Streisand territory, the film is funny, self-deprecating, entertainment. The straight goy, I mean guy, who falls for her offsets her kvetching perfectly.

Yentl both built upon and cohered the key issues that make Streisand so interesting a star and so significant a contributor to, and figure within, American popular culture: her status as a (difficult) woman and as Jewish. As outspoken feminist and un-nose-jobbed Jew, these aspects of her identity, while infusing her film roles all the way from Fanny Brice through Rose Morgan to Roz Focker, seemed to set hurdles in her way. When a man acts, produces and directs he's called, according to Streisand, "a multitalented hyphenate. She's called vain and egotistical." Where her large gay following, left-wing sensibilities, and diva-ID, have oft associated her with issues of sexual liberalism, her star persona has resonated within Jewish Cultural Studies in her embodiment of gender, ethnic, and even queer, difference (see Boyarin et al. 2003 and Aaron 2000). Streisand's civic interests now feed into the television projects she works on as executive producer, her active role as Democrat supporter and, most strikingly, her political blog that dominates her Sony Star site.

References

Aaron, M. (2000) The queer Jew: from *Yid* to *Yentl* and back again, *Jewish History and Culture*, 3(1).

Boyarin, D., Itzkovitz, D. and Pellegrini, A. (eds) (2003) *Queer Theory and the Jewish Question* New York: Columbia University Press.

Erens, P. (1984) *The Jew in American Cinema*. Bloomington: Indiana University Press.

Michele Aaron

Continued from page 300

in a celebrated comedy double act with Mike Nichols (although some time after *he* had made the transition to Hollywood auteur status). May is one of the few women in a decade of male star-directors who achieved anything approaching auteur status, although this is more because of her reputation as, at first, "a classy genius [which] ensured that the red carpet rolled out in front of her" (Abramowitz 2000: 61) and, latterly, as a "difficult" player, precious about her work, repeatedly running over schedule. Quart (1988: 38) calls her "a figure of importance, both for the size of her talent and for her longevity". After the success of *A New Leaf* (1971) and *The Heartbreak Kid* (1972), stories of multiple takes, interminable improvisation, extensive re-edits, and attempts to remove her name, became legend. *Mikey and Nicky* (1976) is most associated with these production troubles, although it is also "the ultimate statement of a series of male buddy films that greeted the rise of feminism in the 1970s" (Quart 1988: 44). The financial disaster of *Ishtar* (1987), which May wrote, directed and composed music for, and which was one of the biggest failures of 1980s cinema, is also laid at her door ("failure", as Abramowitz (2000: 299) writes, or "even simple mediocrity, was a privilege afforded only men"). However she has continued to write (collaborating with Nichols again on *The Birdcage* 1996, and *Primary Colors*, 1998) and to work as a script doctor.

In the 1980s and 1990s more women took the route from writing to directing, including one of the most successful contemporary filmmakers, Nora Ephron. Ephron is mostly known for her seminal "chick flick" examinations of contemporary relationships and neuroses, developed through *When Harry Met Sally* (1989), which she wrote, and *Sleepless in Seattle* (1993) and *You've Got Mail* (1998), both of which she wrote and directed. She has also helmed other star-led projects marked by a light tone which belies their knowing cleverness, including *Mixed Nuts* (1994), *Michael* (1996), *Lucky Numbers* (2000), and *Bewitched* (2005). These are character comedies of manners and situation, but Ephron began her writing career in rather more serious terrain, penning the biopic of anti-nuclear activist *Silkwood* (1983), for which she received an Oscar nomination, and *Heartburn* (1986), adapted from her novel charting the painful break-up of her marriage to *Washington Post* writer Carl Bernstein. Other primarily screenwriting women with directorial credits include Kate Lanier, who helmed *Everybody Can Float* (1995) two years after writing the screenplay for *What's Love Got to Do with It*, and Caroline Thompson, who has specialized in children's cinema, and developed a special working relationship with Tim Burton cemented while writing and associate-producing *Edward Scissorhands*, which Burton directed in 1990. Thompson also co-wrote *The Nightmare Before Christmas* (1993) and *Corpse Bride* (2005), the first a project branded with Burton's possessive trademark, the second co-directed and co-produced by him. Other screenplay credits for Thompson include *Homeward Bound: The Incredible Journey* (1993) and *The Secret Garden* (1993), but she also directed as well as wrote two family films in the 1990s, *Black Beauty* (1994) and *Buddy*

(1997). If Thompson is, hitherto at least, generically consistent, a rather more diverse career trajectory is that of Leora Barish, who began with impeccable feminist credentials penning the screenplay for Susan Seidelman's *Desperately Seeking Susan* (1985), proceeding to co-write Chantal Ackerman's *Window Shopping* (1986), before helming her own *Venus Rising* in 1995. Her latest credit, however, is perhaps her most surprising, given this back catalogue: she has co-written the erotic thriller sequel, *Basic Instinct 2: Risk Addiction* (2006).

Women have increasingly infiltrated the mainstream through initial work in independent production, or else have preferred to keep the studios (and their controlling influence) at arm's length. Significant moves in independent women's cinema were made in the 1970s by Claudia Weill and Joan Micklin Silver. Weill made *Girlfriends* (1978) independently before moving on to the studio-backed *It's My Turn* (1980), and has since directed for television, while after the indie *Hester Street* (1975) Silver moved mainstream with *Head Over Heels* (1979), *Crossing Delancy* (1988) and *Loverboy* (1989). Connie Field also contributed significantly to developments in documentary filmmaking with *The Life and Times of Rosie the Riveter* (1980) and *Freedom on my Mind* (1994), as did Michelle Citron (*Daughter Rite* 1979). But producer Roger Corman also has a role in women filmmaker's development in the 1970s. Known primarily as an independent mogul-producer of low-budget films, he was also crucial in fostering talented individuals – names usually cited in this capacity are his illustrious graduates who spearheaded the New Wave: Jonathan Demme, Martin Scorsese, Jack Nicholson, Francis Ford Coppola. He has, however, also encouraged a number of

Continued on page 306

Rosanna Arquette and Madonna in *Desperately Seeking Susan*

A female-written, female-directed, female-produced and female-addressed film, arising out of a semi-independent production context, *Desperately Seeking Susan* raises key questions about gender and its relationship to representation, genre and authorship. Since its release the film has interested feminist critics and, as Christina Lane notes, it has been fêted "for its celebration of feminist themes around identification, desire and fantasy" (2000: 55). It was the second feature of director Susan Seidelman, whose name had become associated with both art-house and critical success since her first film *Smithereens* (1982). Its inclusion in the Cannes Film Festival (*Smithereens* was nominated for the Palme d'Or) made Seidelman the first female filmmaker to be in the competition. *Desperately Seeking Susan*, although more of a mainstream project, was still made for the low budget of $5 million. Its $27.5 million gross therefore brought significant returns to Orion Pictures, the "mini-major" under which the film was made. Its low budget may well have permitted the formation of a collaborative female team, and one in which personal interconnections shaped the material of the film. Lane (2000: 46–7) reports that screenwriter Leora Barish based the character of Roberta on her friend Rosanna Arquette, and that Seidelman's idea of casting Madonna as Susan impressed producers, Sarah Pilsbury and Midge Sanford, so much that they hired her to direct the film.

The narrative of the film, concerned as it is with the fascination of suburban housewife, Roberta (Rosanna Arquette) with the life and loves of independent single girl Susan (Madonna), is driven by female desire, identification and fantasy. In its exploration of these issues the film has some interesting continuities with the classical Hollywood "woman's film", while also, importantly, it reworks these concerns in a contemporary context. Roberta's fascination with Susan's romantic adventures becomes evident when she goes to the meeting place that Jim (Robert Loy) and Susan have arranged through their personal ads in order to observe what happens between them. In this Roberta can be compared with female characters in earlier women's films such as *Stella Dallas* (King Vidor, 1937); in her interest in romance and in her attention to fashion (particularly Susan's distinctive style, which she attempts to mimic). Roberta's character speaks to a feminist interest in the consumption of "feminine" popular cultures (see Modleski 1984; Radway 1984; LaPlace 1987 and Gaines 1990). Gaines in particular has noted the ability of costume to "tell the woman's story" in the classical Hollywood era, and Sarah Street undertakes a detailed discussion of the role of costume in *Desperately Seeking Susan*, arguing that costume both marks out Roberta and Susan as "different facets of the feminine" (Street 2001: 66), and functions centrally in Roberta's transformation (Street 2001: 71). Indeed, the film provides a potent example of the way that specific pieces of clothing can be invested with an array of meanings, and can act as narrative devices. Susan's individualized pyramid jacket signifies her unconventional personal style and her fluency in innovating her own "look". Here there are clear intertextual connections with Madonna's own iconographic literacy and her role in the construction, and reconstruction, of her polysemic star image; connections which, as Street (2001: 71) points out, are even more evident when the film is studied in retrospect. The jacket binds the two women together as Susan trades it for a pair of sequinned boots at a thrift store, and Roberta buys it. Susan's trading of looks shows her competence in putting together an always evolving and eclectic look, while Roberta's purchase of the (second-hand) jacket is part of her adventure and escape. As Charlotte Brunsdon (1997: 81) has argued, scenes in which female characters shop and try on clothes recur in "girls' films" in the 1980s and 1990s, signifying an historically specific shift to a post-feminist concept of female identity, influenced by notions of "performance, style and desire" that are "partly constructed through a relation to consumption" (Brunsdon 2001: 85). Brunsdon (2001: 86) cites *Desperately Seeking Susan* as an example of a film where "post-feminist women can try on identities and adopt them".

Roberta's possession of the jacket leads her to Susan via a locker key in the pocket, and it also transforms Roberta "into" Susan as she is mistaken for her ideal by a jewellery thief. Roberta's strong identification with Susan's character is explored by Jackie Stacey (1992) in her discussion of female spectatorship. Susan becomes part of Roberta's escapist journey away from her unhappy suburban marriage to the more unpredictable but exciting connections of the city. Stacey compares the film to *All About Eve* (Joseph L Mankiewicz, 1950), in which a young woman's obsession with an older theatrical star has a much more sinister cast. She argues that *Desperately Seeking Susan* foregrounds the difference and otherness between the characters, even as Roberta temporarily "becomes" Susan through her episode of amnesia and the coincidences of the plot (Stacey 1992: 256). Issues of female identity and identification are also discussed by Lucy Fischer. Arguing that typically the Hollywood woman's film dramatizes the heroine's choices between these "good" and "bad" roles, she understands Seidelman's film as both mobilizing this structure in opposing Roberta and Susan, but also significantly departing from it: "bad" girl Susan escapes censure at the close of the narrative and Roberta escapes from her stifling marriage. Fischer analyses the sequence in which Roberta watches classic woman's film *Rebecca* (Alfred Hitchcock, 1940), as an instance of the film's "dialogic" knowingness about its reworking of typical narrative structures.

However, *Desperately Seeking Susan* is not only engaged in a dialogue with the past of classical Hollywood. It is also conversant with the transatlantic influences of European auteurs of the New Wave. Laura Mulvey gives an account of the influence of Jacques Rivette's *Céline et Julie vont en bateau* (1974) on both Leora Barish's script and Seidelman's direction for *Desperately Seeking Susan*; indeed, Seidelman stated that Rivette's film was "a point of departure" for her (Mulvey 1998: 121). Mulvey's analysis reveals the common elements of the two films, in particular the theme of one woman's fascination with the life of another, and the way that both use ideas of magic and transformation to explore this fascination. As Mulvey argues, *Desperately Seeking Susan* remains a Hollywood film, albeit one that "belongs on the margins of Hollywood". This typifies the position of the film, as simultaneously connected to a tradition of art-house filmmaking and aware of the mainstream. It is literate in both popular feminine cultures, such as romance, and explores female sexual liberation through the more "edgy" punkish aesthetic embodied by Susan. It is this seeming ability to synthesize different perspectives that may have allowed the film to speak to different female viewers and to achieve its commercial and critical success. As Lane (2000: 47) suggests, "[the] historical context of the film helped to create a climate in which women in their thirties who had come of age during the second-wave feminist movement and teenage girls immersed in a nascent 'girl-culture' could converge at the movie theatre".

References

Brunsdon, C. (2001) *Screen Tastes: Soap Opera to Satellite Dishes*. London: Routledge.

Fischer, L. (1990) The desire to desire: *Desperately Seeking Susan*, in P. Lehman (ed.) *Close Viewings: An Anthology of New Film Criticism*. Tallahassee: University of Florida Press.

Gaines, J. (1990) Costume and narrative: how dress tells the woman's story, in J. Gaines and C. Herzog (eds) *Fabrications: Costume and the Female Body*. New York: Routledge.

Lane, C. (2000) *Feminist Hollywood: From Born in Flames to Point Break*. Detroit: Wayne State University Press.

LaPlace, M. (1987) Producing and consuming the woman's film: discursive struggle in *Now, Voyager*, in C. Gledhill (ed.) *Home is Where the Heart Is: Studies in Melodrama and the Woman's Film*. London: BFI.

Modleski, T. (1984) *Loving with a Vengeance: Mass-Produced Fantasies for Women*. London: Methuen.

Mulvey, L. (1998) New Wave interchanges: *Céline and Julie* and *Desperately Seeking Susan*, in G. Nowell-Smith and S. Ricci (eds) *Hollywood and Europe: Economics, Culture, National Identity, 1945–95*. London: BFI.

Radway, J. (1984) *Reading the Romance: Women, Patriarchy and Popular Literature*. London: University of North Carolina Press.

Stacey, J. (1992) Desperately seeking difference, reprinted in *The Sexual Subject: A Screen Reader in Sexuality*. London: Routledge.

Street, S. (2001) *Costume and Cinema: Dress Codes in Popular Film*. London: Wallflower Press.

Helen Hanson

Continued from page 303

women with flair, and as such has provided an alternative "off-Hollywood" route, which has gone some way towards compensating for the prevailing sexism of the mainstream industry. Three Corman graduates, helming some of the most distinctive "Cormanesque" titles which are also marked by feminist agendas, include Stephanie Rothman, Amy Holden Jones and Katt Shea. Rothman is known for her lively take on genre topics and for featuring women in active roles. She wrote and directed *The*

Student Nurses (1970) and *The Velvet Vampire* (1971) for Corman's New World Pictures, and did the same on *Terminal Island* (1973) and *Working Girls* (1974), among other projects, under the auspices of her production company, Dimension Pictures. Her small corpus of mostly exploitation films have consistently attracted critical attention but she never broke through into mainstream production. Rothman's career may bear out the feeling, described by Hollywood editor Anne Goursaud in a recent interview about the straight-to-video films she directed in the 1990s (Williams 2005: 409–416), that once painted with an exploitation brush, it is harder for women to move into bigger budget productions (as Corman's male protégés were able to do). Amy Holden Jones, however, *did* advance from the respected Corman-produced horror skit *The Slumber Party Massacre* (1982, with screenplay by feminist novelist Rita Mae Brown) and *Love Letters* (1984, starring Jamie Lee Curtis), to high-profile screenwriting contracts (*Mystic Pizza*, 1988; *Beethoven*, 1992; *Indecent Proposal*, 1993) and some more mainstream directorial credits (*Maid to Order*, 1987; *The Rich Man's Wife*, 1996). Katt Shea's career has followed a similar route, starting with *Stripped to Kill* (1987), *Dance of the Damned* (1988), *Stripped to Kill II* (1989) and *Streets* (1990) for Corman, before breaking into studio-backed productions with *Poison Ivy* (1992) and *The Rage: Carrie 2* (1999).

Shea's latter works have had bigger budgets and this move from the filmmaking fringes to the Hollywood establishment also characterizes the careers of Christina Lane's subjects, Martha Coolidge (from early documentary-style works such as *Old-Fashioned Woman*, 1974, to teen pics like *Valley Girls*, 1983 and melodramas like *Rambling Rose*, 1991, and *Angie*, 1993); Kathryn Bigelow (the nearest Hollywood has to a female auteur, with a distinctive action style); Lizzie Borden (from the seminal independent feminist films *Born in Flames*, 1983, and *Working Girls*, 1986, to the commercial erotic thriller *Love Crimes*, 1991); and Tamra Davis (from the exploitation remake *Guncrazy*, 1993, to the rap comedy *CB4*, 1993). Lane (2000) also explores the work of Darnell Martin, whose 1994 film, *I Like It Like That*, was actively marketed by Columbia as helmed by the "first African American woman to direct a major studio feature" (Lane 2000: 149). Martin received this with horror – the promotion effectively nullified the achievements of previous black filmmakers such as Leslie Harris (*Just Another Girl on the IRT*, 1992) or Euzhan Palcy (*A Dry White Season*, 1989). Other female directors have preferred to remain in the independent sector, including Allison Anders (who made some of the most interesting small films of the 1990s – *Gas Food Lodging*, 1992, *Mi vida loca*, 1993, *Grace of My Heart*, 1996); Julie Dash, whose celebrated *Daughters of the Dust* (1991) followed a respected corpus of films exploring the African-American experience; and Cheryl Dunye who described herself after the release of *The Watermelon Woman* (1997) as a maker of "independent independent film, not Hollywood independent film" (Donalson 2003: 197; Dunye's second feature, *My Baby's Daddy*, 2004, was, however, distributed by Miramax). Nancy Savoca has mainly directed films in the independent sector (*True Love*, 1989, won the Grand Jury Prize at the Sundance Film Festival; *The 24 Hour Woman*, 1999, premiered there), but also for studios (*Dogfight*, 1991 was backed by Warner Bros).

Another significant trend has been the moves of female stars, often frustrated with the limited roles they have been dealt, to establish

Continued on page 310

Sigourney Weaver has achieved what few female performers in Hollywood have, fostering a diverse acting career that promises to thrive into old age, consolidating her power as a screen player with production credits to her name, while refusing the typecasting of genre. Born Susan Weaver into a showbusiness family, and educated at Stanford and Yale, she is known as a multitalented patrician figure (partly on account of her Ivy League education, partly because she is impressively tall), noted for her thespian skills in a variety of roles on stage as well as on screen. She has played dramatic parts in films as diverse as *The Year of Living Dangerously* (1983), *Death and the Maiden* (1994), *Copycat* (1995) and *The Ice Storm* (1997), and has excelled in comedies such as *Ghostbusters* (1984), *Ghostbusters II* (1989), *Dave* (1993) and *Galaxy Quest* (1999). Perhaps most remarkably she won two Oscar nominations in the same year, for *Gorillas in the Mist* (1988), a biopic of conservationist Dian Fossey, and for *Working Girl* (1988), which allowed her to flex her performance muscles as an epoch-defining bitch boss.

Christine Geraghty argues that contemporary female stardom is more likely to be inflected by life factors than work factors, partly because women in Hollywood do not command the same career power as their male counterparts (movies rarely "open" on the basis of a woman's star name), and partly because fascination with private lives is far more acute in relation to women ("the common association in popular culture between women and the private sphere of personal relationships and domesticity fits with the emphasis, in the discourse of celebrity, on the private life and the leisure activity of the star", Geraghty 2000: 196). Weaver is a singular exception to this model, however. She is not obsessively secretive about her personal life but it is not the source of paparazzi fascination, as it is for younger stars with turbulent love lives. And not only is her name now synonymous with a cinematic franchise – the *Alien* series (*Alien*, 1979; *Aliens*, 1986; *Alien³*, 1992, *Alien: Resurrection*, 1997) – the franchise is also synonymous with *her*. A *Batman* film with an interchangeable male star playing the title role is to be expected; an *Alien* film without Weaver as Ellen Ripley seems unthinkable.

Ripley provides a fascinating core role for this diverse career. Appearing first in *Alien* as one of a band of employees on the spaceship *Nostromo* who battle the invading alien parasite of the title, Ripley is the only one to survive into the three sequels, becoming more central with each subsequent title. In *Alien³* she dies, sacrificing herself in order to obliterate the alien to whom she has become mother/host, but in *Alien: Resurrection* she reappears as a cloned woman-alien. Amy Taubin (1993: 96) writes that "one should not underestimate Sigourney Weaver's contribution to [*Alien³*'s] authorship", but this could perhaps be said of all the sequels, an effect of Weaver's production credit (in films three and four) as well as her hands-on shaping of the central role (she received an Oscar nomination for the role in *Aliens*). Across the series Weaver draws open the complexities of a character that is masculinized but resolutely female, tough but maternal, finally alien as much as human, emerging from hypersleep like Snow White but fighting like Rambo. Like her monstrous character in *Working Girl*, read as a backlash symptom, and, by Tasker (1998: 40–4) as a sign of new formations of class as well as sexual difference, Ripley has posed questions for feminists, as a fetishized mother/dominatrix figure as well as one of a breed of "new action heroines of the period" (O'Day 2004: 203). "Ripley demonstrated", writes Sherrie Inness, "that women did not have to look as though they stepped directly from a beauty parlor when they battled foes" (2004: 3), although this didn't stop Ridley Scott from featuring the actress as a woman-in-peril in her underwear in the first film of the series. For Barry Keith Grant (2004: 374) the question of whether Ripley, or Sarah Connor (Linda Hamilton) in the *Terminator* films (to which Ripley is frequently compared) "are progressive representations

Sigourney Weaver and Carrie Henn in *Aliens*

of women or merely contain them within a masculine sensibility has been a matter of considerable debate". Despite the fact that the *Alien* quartet is a rare foray into the genre, Weaver is frequently read by feminists or writers on contemporary cinema for her contribution to transformations in the iconography of women in action-adventure cinema in the 1980s and 1990s – see, for instance, Tasker's (1993) discussion of Ripley's "musculinity", Clover's (1992) analysis of her as a final girl, and Willis's (1997: 113) discussion of her "transformation of women's body language". Yet Geraghty (2000: 197) sees her stardom as distinct from the male "professional" star whose power comes from his close identification with a franchise: "Although she maintains a consistent star image as a strong woman, Weaver as an actress appears to refuse the restrictions of the professional category and hence the kind of stardom which the male action heroes have established."

It is said that Weaver, who appeared in *Alien* as a second-billed player, commanded a fee for *Alien: Resurrection* that was larger than the whole budget of the first *Alien* movie, and indeed her development of the franchise as co-producer has been central to its continued popularity, a regular element amidst significant production changes (the diverse styles of four different directors, varying narrative set-ups, and co-stars completely replaced with each new film). Only Weaver as Ripley and the omnipresent alien itself have remained consistent. Beyond this, Weaver is an astonishingly prolific actress, continuing to work, from the 1970s to the present, as a respected stage performer, alongside a film career that boasts nearly forty film roles.

References

Clover, C.J. (1992) *Men, Women and Chain Saws: Gender in the Modern Horror Film.* London: BFI.

Geraghty, C. (2000) Re-examining stardom: questions of texts, bodies and performance, in C. Gledhill and L. Williams (eds) *Reinventing Film Studies.* London: Arnold, pp. 183–201.

Grant, B.K. (2004) Man's favourite sport? The action films of Kathryn Bigelow, in Y. Tasker (ed.) *Action and Adventure Cinema.* London: Routledge, pp. 371–84.

Inness, S.A. (2004) Introduction: "Boxing gloves and bustiers": new images of tough women, in *Action Chicks: New Images of Tough Women in Popular Culture*, Basingstoke: Palgrave Macmillan, pp. 1–17.

O'Day, M. (2004) Beauty in motion: gender, spectacle and action babe cinema, in Y. Tasker (ed.) *Action and Adventure Cinema.* London: Routledge, pp. 201–18.

Tasker, Y. (1993) *Spectacular Bodies: Gender, Genre and the Action Cinema.* London: Routledge.

Tasker, Y (1998) *Working Girls: Gender and Sexuality in Popular Cinema.* London: Routledge.

Taubin, A. (1993) The "Alien" trilogy: from feminism to Aids, in P. Cook and P. Dodd (eds) *Women and Film: A Sight and Sound Reader.* London: Scarlet Press, pp. 93–100.

Willis, S. (1997) *High Contrast: Race and Gender in Contemporary Hollywood Film.* Durham, NC: Duke University Press.

Linda Ruth Williams

Continued from page 307

themselves as producers and, sometimes, directors. Diane Keaton, Barbra Streisand and Jodie Foster developed directing careers alongside their acting work in the 1980s and 1990s. Penny Marshall started as a performer (she was Laverne in the 1970s sit-com *Laverne and Shirley*) although she is now better known as the director of *Big* (1988), *A League of Their Own* (1992), and *Renaissance Man* (1994). In the 1970s, acting stars such as Streisand or Jane Fonda had enough industrial muscle to ensure that they could drive favoured projects forward, sometimes courtesy of their own production companies. Streisand's First Artists Production Company (founded with Sidney Poitier and Paul Newman in 1969) backed *A Star is Born* in 1976; Fonda's company IPC produced *Coming Home* (1978), both vehicles for the stars. These were mainstream movies but with – at least the producer/stars hoped – some radical credentials. Streisand saw her movie as "her feminist anthem, the tale of one woman's lonely struggle against a patriarchal society" (Abramowitz 2000: 100); Fonda describes *Coming Home* as "a way to help redefine masculinity" (Fonda 2005: 360). But this was a transitory time in female stardom; it is now far more usual for women to establish production companies (Sharon Stone's Chaos productions; Sandra Bullock's Fortis Films; Goldie Hawn's Hawn-Sylbert Movie Company; Jodie Foster's Egg Pictures).

This was also an important period for women moving into production from other lowlier studio roles or from success as agents.

Rachel Abramowitz (2000: xii) argues that even recently women worked in a depressing context, in

> an industry dominated not just by men but by the likes and dislikes of the young male consumer, and by a certain saber-rattling ethos of masculinity, in which women were relentlessly sexualized, their gender constantly accessed and reaccessed as a key component of their professional abilities.

But at least they are now *there*, making central decisions. In 1977, Julia Phillips became the first woman ever to win a Best Film Oscar for her production of *The Sting* (along with Michael Phillips and Tony Bill); Phillips' production credits later included *Taxi Driver* (1976) and *Close Encounters of the Third Kind* (1977), though she is perhaps best remembered for her infamous Hollywood exposé,

You'll Never Eat Lunch in This Town Again, which, as well as dishing mountains of dirt on her famous acquaintances, gives a lively insight into how women fared in the industry in the 1970s and 1980s. Landmark executive appointments which followed include Sherry Lansing's as President of Twentieth Century Fox in 1980 (making her the first female head of an established studio – Mary Pickford and Barbra Streisand had, of course, already headed-up studios they had themselves established), former über-agent Paula Weinstein's appointment as president of United Artists' motion picture division in 1981, and Dawn Steel's appointment as President of production at Paramount in 1984. Steel then moved on to the top job at Columbia, where she became "the first woman to oversee both the production and the marketing operations of a studio" (Sova 1998: 170). All three women were in

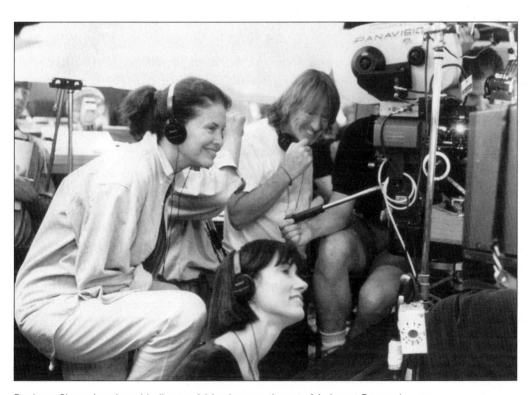

Producer Sherry Lansing with director Adrian Lyne on the set of *Indecent Proposal*

pole position to push forward some landmark products of New Hollywood: Steel was a pioneer in marketing tie-ins, while Lansing gained more freedom to develop favoured projects in later roles as an independent producer and then at Paramount – her films often feature strong female characters involved in popular-political or talking-point issues – *Fatal Attraction*, 1987; *The Accused*, 1988; *Indecent Proposal*, 1993. These executive success stories are not just the rare appointments of a few formidable and highly ambitious overachievers. Key executive roles were also taken on by Lucy Fisher (Zoetrope, then Warner Brothers) and Kathleen Kennedy (Amblin) and many more women took on the production of individual, often phenomenally successful projects during the 1980s and 1990s. In 1989, Lili Fini Zanuck (who had married into the Zanuck production dynasty) was the second woman to win a Best Picture Oscar for *Driving Miss Daisy*. Gale Ann Hurd is another Corman protégée who moved into bigger budgets with the *Terminator* series and other high-octane blockbusters (*Armageddon* 1998; *Hulk*, 2003).

The picture therefore looked far more positive for women at the end of the twentieth century. Women such as Kasi Lemmons and Troy Beyer, or Donna Deitch and Patricia Rozema, have energetically contributed to particular movements such as new black cinema and new queer cinema, discussed elsewhere in this book (see also Donalson 2003: 174-203). In an editorial overview for a special "Women Directors" edition of *Sight and Sound*, Leslie Felperin (1999: 10) wrote that

> things are basically getting better, albeit slowly. In the film industry, there are many more women producers, agents and

publicists than there ever used to be – perhaps because women are supposed to be better at "people management", a crucial skill for these jobs – and many more women screenwriters. The traditionally male-dominated technical fields such as cinematography, lighting and sound are slowly tipping towards a more even gender balance, while the proportion of women directors in the Director's Guild of America, though only 10 per cent, still represents an improvement over the 1985 level of 4 per cent.

In the 1990s screenwriting continues to be an attractive opening for women. Writers whose work deserves fuller analysis include Amanda Silver (*The Hand that Rocks the Cradle*, 1992; *Eye for an Eye*, 1996); Hilary Henkin (*Fatal Beauty*, 1987; *Romeo is Bleeding*, 1993; *Wag the Dog*, 1997); Barbara Benedek (*The Big Chill*, 1983; *Immediate Family*, 1989; *Sabrina*, 1995); Carol Sobieski (*Annie*, 1982, *Fried Green Tomatoes at the Whistlestop Café*, 1991; *Money for Nothing*, 1993); Becky Johnston (*The Prince of Tides*, 1991; *Seven Years in Tibet*, 1997); Lindy Laub (*For the Boys*, 1991; *They Come at Night*, 1998, which Laub also directed); June Roberts (*Mermaids*, 1990; *All the Queen's Men*, 2001), and Malia Scotch Marmo (*Hook*, 1991; *Madeline*, 1998). Some of these titles were also woman-directed or developed for stars' production companies (*For the Boys* for Bette Midler; *Mermaids* for Cher).

But such a diverse range of films raises the question of whether there is anything specifically female about these texts. Clearly any overview of women in US cinema in this period is bound to be selective, offering a survey of significant moments. The vast differences across and between films cited here demonstrate the diversity of projects which women have developed. When looking at

Fig. 11 (left): *Indiana Jones and the Temple of Doom*.

Fig. 12 (above): *Heaven's Gate*.

Fig. 13 (below): *Blade Runner*.

Action and landscape, past and future, 1980s-style.

Diverse views
in independent
production.

Fig. 14 (top): *Do the Right Thing.*

Fig. 15 (left): *Gloria.*

Fig. 16 (above): *Pink Flamingos.*

Documentary spectacle meets "in-your-face assault on the viewer".

Fig. 17 (top): *Winged Migration*.

Fig. 18 (bottom): *Armageddon*.

Neo-indies, smart movies and queer delights.

Fig. 19 (top): *Pulp Fiction*.

Fig. 20 (above): *The Incredibly True Adventure of Two Girls in Love*.

Fig. 21 (right): *American Beauty*.

some of the works of Kathryn Bigelow or Penny Marshall are we surprised that women should have taken on "boys subjects", or commanded such huge audiences? My students are sometimes amazed when they realize that the $100 million grossing *Wayne's World* was directed by a woman (Penelope Spheeris, who moved from documentary filmmaking and small titles like *The Decline of Western Civilization*, 1981, to the high-budget TV spinoff *The Beverly Hillbillies*, 1993). Nor do they think of *Look Who's Talking* (1989) and its sequel as "women's films", though director Amy Heckerling has also helmed more conventional chick-flick material (*Clueless*, 1995). The tricky question of how to approach the issue of women in cinema as a special case is similar to that raised when approaching new black cinema, and black filmmakers' relationships to the civil rights movement, racial labelling, and the movie industry. What is the difference between the labels "filmmaker" and "female filmmaker"? What burden do filmmakers bear when they become the representatives of their sex – and do men bear this burden in equal measures? Most female film directors want "to be seen as film-makers first and women film-makers second or not at all" (Felperin 1999: 10). For popular audiences, the most startling example of "feminist filmmaking" from the 1990s was not directed by a woman but a man, although it was written by Callie Khouri, who won an Oscar for her screenplay. *Thelma and Louise* (1991), according to Sharon Willis (1993: 120), "troubled borderlines that contemporary popular critical discourse continues to code as fragile: those between art and life, fantasy and agency, cinematic fiction and the life stories we tell ourselves". It also troubles notions about what men and women should be and do on screen, and behind the camera. Many films by

women have of course done this too, but whether they have been able consistently to achieve it for mass audiences is another question. And whether the greater involvement of women in the filmmaking process has radically transformed representations of screen gender remains an issue of fierce debate.

References

Abramowitz, R. (2000) *Is That a Gun in Your Pocket? Women's Experience of Power in Hollywood*. New York: Random House.

Biskind, P. (1998) *Easy Riders, Raging Bulls: How the Sex 'N' Drugs 'N' Rock 'N' Roll Generation Saved Hollywood*. London: Bloomsbury.

Donalson, M. (2003) And still they rise: black women directors, in *Black Directors in Hollywood*. Austin: University of Texas Press, pp. 174–203.

Donati, W. (1996) *Ida Lupino: A Biography*. Lexington: University of Kentucky Press.

Felperin, L. (1999) Editorial: chick flicks, *Sight and Sound*, (October): 10.

Fonda, J. (2005) *My Life So Far*. London: Ebury Press.

Foster, G.A. (1999) Foreword: women filmmakers, in *The St. James Women Filmmakers Encyclopedia: Women on the Other Side of the Camera*. Detroit: Visible Ink Press, pp. xiii–xviii.

Franke, L. (1994) *Script Girls: Women Screenwriters in Hollywood*,. London: BFI.

Kaplan, E.A. (2003) Women, film, resistance: changing paradigms, in J. Levitin, J. Plessis and V. Raoul (eds) *Women Filmmakers: Refocusing*. New York: Routledge, pp. 15–28.

Kuhn, A. (1995) *Queen of the "B"s: Ida Lupino Behind the Camera*. London: Flicks Books.

Lane, C. (2000) *Feminist Hollywood: From Born in Flames to Point Break*. Detroit: Wayne State University Press.

Levitin, J., Plessis, J. and Raoul, V. (eds) (2003) *Women Filmmakers: Refocusing*. New York: Routledge.

Quart, B.K. (1988) *Women Directors: The Emergence of a New Cinema*. New York: Praeger.

Sova, D.B. (1998) *Women in Hollywood: From Vamp to Studio Head*. New York: Fromm International.

Williams, L. R. (2005) *The Erotic Thriller in Contemporary Cinema*. Edinburgh: Edinburgh University Press and Bloomington: Indiana University Press.

Willis, S. (1993) Hardware and hardbodies, what do women want? A reading of *Thelma and Louise*, in J. Collins, H. Radner and A. Prencher Collins (eds), *Film Theory Goes to the Movies*. New York: Routledge, pp. 120–8.

1980–89	Rentals to date for year just ending
1980 *The Empire Strikes Back*	$120,000,000
1981 *Raiders of the Lost Ark*	$ 90,434,000
1982 *E.T.: The Extra-Terrestrial*	$187,000,000
1983 *Return of the Jedi*	$165,500,000
1984 *Ghostbusters*	$127,000,000
1985 *Back to the Future*	$ 94,000,000
1986 *Top Gun*	$ 82,000,000
1987 *Beverly Hills Cop II*	$ 80,857,776
1988 *Who Framed Roger Rabbit?*	$ 78,000,000
1989 *Batman*	$150,000,000

1980

Academy Awards
Best Picture: *Ordinary People* – Ronald L. Schwary
Best Director: Robert Redford – *Ordinary People*
Best Actor in a leading role: Robert de Niro – *Raging Bull*
Best Actor in a supporting role: Timothy Hutton – *Ordinary People*
Best Actress in a leading role: Sissy Spacek – *Coal Miner's Daughter*
Best Actress in a supporting role: Mary Steenburgen – *Melvin and Howard*
Cannes International Film Festival
Palme d'Or: *Kagemusha* – Akira Kurosawa and *All That Jazz* – Bob Fosse
Venice International Film Festival
Golden Lion: *Atlantic City* – Louis Malle and *Gloria* – John Cassavetes

1981

Academy Awards
Best Picture: *Chariots Of Fire* – David Puttnam
Best Director: Warren Beatty – *Reds*
Best Actor in a leading role: Henry Fonda – *On Golden Pond*
Best Actor in a supporting role: John Gielgud – *Arthur*
Best Actress in a leading role: Katharine Hepburn – *On Golden Pond*
Best Actress in a supporting role: Maureen Stapleton – *Reds*
Cannes International Film Festival
Palme d'Or: *Czlowiek Z Zelaza* – Andrzei Wadja
Venice International Film Festival
Golden Lion: *Die Bleierne Zeit* – Margarethe von Trotta

1982

Academy Awards
Best Picture: *Gandhi* – Richard Attenborough
Best Director: Richard Attenborough - *Gandhi*
Best Actor in a leading role: Ben Kingsley – *Gandhi*
Best Actor in a supporting role: Louis Gossett, Jr. – *An Officer and a Gentleman*
Best Actress in a leading role: Meryl Streep – *Sophie's Choice*
Best Actress in a supporting role: Jessica Lange – *Tootsie*
Cannes International Film Festival
Palme d'Or: *Missing* – Costa Gravas and *Yol* – Yilmaz Guney
Venice International Film Festival
Golden Lion: *Der Stand der Dinge* – Wim Wenders

1983

Academy Awards
Best Picture: *Terms of Endearment* – James L. Brooks
Best Director: James L. Brooks – *Terms of Endearment*
Best Actor in a leading role: Robert Duvall – *Tender Mercies*
Best Actor in a supporting role: Jack Nicholson – *Terms of Endearment*
Best Actress in a leading role: Shirley MacLaine – *Terms of Endearment*
Best Actress in a supporting role: Linda Hunt – *The Year of Living Dangerously*
Cannes International Film Festival
Palme d'Or: *Narayama-Bushi-Ko* – Shohei Imamura
Venice International Film Festival
Golden Lion: *Prénom Carmen* – Jean-Luc Godard

1984

Academy Awards
Best Picture: *Amadeus* – Saul Zaentz
Best Director: Milos Forman – *Amadeus*
Best Actor in a leading role: F. Murray Abraham – *Amadeus*
Best Actor in a supporting role: Haing S. Ngor – *The Killing Fields*
Best Actress in a leading role: Sally Field – *Places in the Heart*
Best Actress in a supporting role: Peggy Ashcroft – *A Passage to India*
Cannes International Film Festival
Palme d'Or: *Paris, Texas* – Wim Wenders
Venice International Film Festival
Golden Lion: *Rol Spokojnego Slonca* – Krzysztof Zanussi

1985

Academy Awards
Best Picture: *Out of Africa* – Sydney Pollack
Best Director: Sydney Pollack – *Out of Africa*
Best Actor in a leading role: William Hurt – *Kiss of the Spider Woman*
Best Actor in a supporting role: Don Ameche – *Cocoon*
Best Actress in a leading role: Geraldine Page – *The Trip to Bountiful*

Best Actress in a supporting role: Anjelica Huston – *Prizzi's Honor*
Sundance Film Festival
Grand Jury Prize Documentary: *Seventeen* – Joel DeMott and Jeff Kreined
Grand Jury Prize Dramatic: *Blood Simple* – Joel Cohen
Cannes International Film Festival
Palme d'Or: *Otac Na Sulzbenhom Putu* – Emir Kusturica
Venice International Film Festival
Golden Lion: *Sans toit ni loi* – Agnès Varda

1986

Academy Awards
Best Picture: *Platoon* – Arnold Kopelson
Best Director: Oliver Stone – *Platoon*
Best Actor in a leading role: Paul Newman – *The Color of Money*
Best Actor in a supporting role: Michael Caine – *Hannah and Her Sisters*
Best Actress in a leading role: Marlee Matlin – *Children of a Lesser God*
Best Actress in a supporting role: Dianne Wiest – *Hannah and Her Sisters*
Sundance Film Festival
Grand Jury Prize Documentary: *Private Conversations* – Christian Blackwood
Grand Jury Prize Dramatic: *Smooth Talk* – Joyce Chopra
Cannes International Film Festival
Palme d'Or: *The Mission* – Roland Joffé
Venice International Film Festival
Golden Lion: *Le rayon vert* – Eric Rohmer

1987

Academy Awards
Best Picture: *The Last Emperor* – Jeremy Thomas
Best Director: Bernardo Bertolucci – *The Last Emperor*
Best Actor in a leading role: Michael Douglas – *Wall Street*
Best Actor in a supporting role: Sean Connery – *The Untouchables*
Best Actress in a leading role: Cher – *Moonstruck*
Best Actress in a supporting role: Olympia Dukakis – *Moonstruck*
Sundance Film Festival
Grand Jury Prize Documentary: *Sherman's March* – Ross McElwee
Grand Jury Prize Dramatic: *Waiting for the Moon* – Jill Godmilow and *Trouble with Dick* –
Gary Walkow
Cannes International Film Festival
Palme d'Or: *Sous le soleil du Satan* – Maurice Pialat
Venice International Film Festival
Golden Lion: *Au revoir les enfants* – Louis Malle

1988

Academy Awards
Best Picture: *Rain Man* – Mark Johnson
Best Director: Barry Levinson – *Rain Man*
Best Actor in a leading role: Dustin Hoffman – *Rain Man*

Best Actor in a supporting role: Kevin Kline – *A Fish Called Wanda*
Best Actress in a leading role: Jodie Foster – *The Accused*
Best Actress in a supporting role: Geena Davis – *The Accidental Tourist*
Sundance Film Festival
Grand Jury Prize Documentary: *Beirut: The Last Home Movie* – Jennifer Fox
Grand Jury Prize Dramatic: *Heat and Sunlight* – Rob Nilsson
Cannes International Film Festival
Palme d'Or: *Pelle Erobreren* – Bille August
Venice International Film Festival
Golden Lion: *La leggenda del santo bevitore* – Ermanno Olmi

1989

Academy Awards
Best Picture: *Driving Miss Daisy* – Richard D. Zanuck, Lili Fini Zanuck
Best Director: Oliver Stone – *Born on the Fourth of July*
Best Actor in a leading role: Daniel Day-Lewis – *My Left Foot*
Best Actor in a supporting role: Denzel Washington – *Glory*
Best Actress in a leading role: Jessica Tandy – *Driving Miss Daisy*
Best Actress in a supporting role: Brenda Fricker – *My Left Foot*
Sundance Film Festival
Grand Jury Prize Documentary: *For All Mankind* – Al Reinert
Grand Jury Prize Dramatic: *True Love* – Nancy Savoca
Cannes International Film Festival
Palme d'Or: *sex, lies and videotape* – Steven Soderbergh
Venice International Film Festival
Golden Lion: *Beiqing shenghsi* – Hou Xiaoxian

SUGGESTED FURTHER READING

Abramowitz, R. (2000) *Is That a Gun in Your Pocket? Women's Experience of Power in Hollywood*. New York: Random House.

Anderegg, M. (ed.) (1991) *Inventing Vietnam: The War in Film and Television*. Philadelphia, PA: Temple University Press.

Corrigan, T. (1991) *A Cinema Without Walls: Movies and Culture After Vietnam*. New Brunswick, NJ: Rutgers University Press.

Fleming, C. (1998) *High Concept: Don Simpson and the Hollywood Culture of Excess*. London: Bloomsbury.

Hillier, J. (1993) *The New Hollywood*. London: Studio Vista.

Hillier, J. (2001) *American Independent Cinema*. London: BFI.

Jeffords, S. (1994) *Hard Bodies: Hollywood Masculinity in the Reagan Era*. New Brunswick, NJ: Rutgers University Press.

Kaplan, E.A. (1987) *Rocking Around the Clock: Music, Television, Postmodernism, and Consumer Culture*. London: Methuen.

King, G. (2002) *New Hollywood Cinema: An Introduction*. London: I.B. Tauris.

Lane, C. (2000) *Feminist Hollywood: From Born in Flames to Point Break*. Detroit: Wayne State University Press.

Lewis, J. (ed.) (1998) *The New American Cinema*. Durham, NC: Duke University Press.

Neale, S. (ed.) (2002) *Genre and Contemporary Hollywood*. London: BFI.

Pierson, J. (1996) *Spike, Mike, Slackers and Dykes: A Guided Tour across a Decade of Independent American Cinema*. London: Faber & Faber.

Prince, S. (2000) *A New Pot of Gold: Hollywood Under the Electronic Rainbow, 1980–1989*, vol. 10 of *History of the American Cinema*. Berkeley and London: University of California Press.

Stringer, J. (ed.) (2003) *Movie Blockbusters*. London: Routledge.

Tasker, Y. (1993) *Spectacular Bodies: Gender, Genre and the Action Cinema*. London: Routledge.

Wasko, J. (2001) *Understanding Disney*. Oxford: Blackwell.

QUESTIONS FOR DISCUSSION

This section contains brief background notes which are designed to guide students to some of the main issues that have been raised by the various articles on the 1980s. These are followed by some sample essay questions which both students and tutors may find useful in guiding class discussion as well as setting exercises.

Background Notes

As Stephen Prince points out, the Hollywood industry experienced considerable restructuring in the 1980s. The period saw the move away from the conglomeration of diverse companies that occurred in the late 1960s and 1970s toward mergers with multi-national communication companies like Time-Warner or the takeover of Fox by Rupert Murdoch's News Corporation. While non-US markets had always been important to the US motion picture industry, these markets grew in prominence as film became one of many products offered by the "oligarchy of global media giants". In addition, video, one of the perceived threats to the film industry in the 1970s, provided a welcome source of income as the home began to become the primary place where films were seen. By the mid-1980s the widespread dissemination of video had created a demand for product that helped to fuel a rise in independent, and at times more adventurous, filmmaking. Theatrical exhibition did not suffer, however, but became the platform upon which the sales of video versions were constructed. A popular film at the theatres generated video purchase and rentals. As this situation of increased demand developed, independent films found audiences that were smaller and more diverse than those for high-budget films. This is an important development in filmmaking that is often passed over in depictions of the 1980s Hollywood film as closely associated with the Cold War politics of Ronald Reagan.

Documentary filmmaking also benefited from the increased demand for product which provided an added source of finance and support just as the grants by the government were being curtailed. In the early part of the decade, funding sources, such as the National Endowment for the Arts and the Corporation for Public Broadcasting came under attack from the political Right, resulting in guidelines that prevented funding of any programme which advocated social change or action. Although this limited access to funds for documentary filmmakers, the changes in the industry and the demand for more product meant that documentary continued to be a vital form. Throughout the decade, documentary filmmakers were able to make inroads into the mainstream with films such as Michael Moore's *Roger and Me* (1989) or Earl Morris' *The Thin Blue Line* (1988) making healthy profits from theatrical distribution.

Questions

1 Many US films, both fiction and documentary, big-budget or independent were concerned with isues of national memory and identity. Writer and director Ethan Coen has said of the Coen brothers' work, "We grew up in America, and we tell American stories in American settings within American frames of reference. Perhaps our way of reflecting our system is more comprehensible to non-Americans because they already see the system as something alien" (*Joel and Ethan Coen*, ed. P. Korte and G. Seesslen, London: Titan Books, 1999, p. 172). Analyse two films in the light of this quotation *or* define an "American story" with reference to two films.

2 The 1980s is often cited as the period in which the action-spectacle cinema became a central genre in big-budget Hollywood production. Larry Gorss has said: "The genre we're living with today I date as commmencing in the Year of our Lord 1977, the year of *Star Wars* and *Close Encounters of the Third Kind*. For me these films mark a new moment in thinking successfully (and in newly marketable terms) about making visually spectacular cinema" (Big and Loud, in J. Arroyo (ed.), *Action/Spectacle: A Sight and Sound Reader*. London: BFI, 2000). Consider some of the most successful films of the 1980s and, identifying those which could be seen as heirs to the kind of cinema Gross is talking about, compare them with examples from the 1970s and/or the 1990s–present.

3 While it is clear that technological developments were most evident in the action-spectacle film, technological advances also aided smaller-budget films. How did changes in production technology impact on filmmaking practices in the 1980s?

4 The issue of gender politics in 1980s was often an explicit driving force in the narratives on both big-budget and smaller-budget independent films. Discuss two examples of Hollywood films made since 1980 which reflect or incorporate either the rise of feminism or the backlash against feminism, or choose two films which manage to explore both of these positions.

5 Peter Krämer notes that one of the important shifts in the industry during the 1970s was the adoption of "the Disney model" of family entertainment. Consider some non-Disney examples from the 1980s and discuss what constitutes the "family film".

6 Consider these two quotes:

> We have heard that a film's mode of production bears some relation to its mode of representation. Perhaps the many modes of financing independent films bear some relation to their meaning. (James Schamus, in To the rear of the back end: the economics of independent cinema, in S. Neale and M. Smith (eds), *Contemporary Hollywood Cinema*. London: Routledge, 1999, p. 91)

> *Stranger than Paradise* was both brilliant and attainable. The camera doesn't move for artistic reasons. Conveniently that made it much cheaper to make. When the budget drops, the profit potential rises. (John Pierson, *Spike, Mike, Slackers and Dykes: A Guided Tour Across a Decade of American Independent Cinema*. New York: Hyperion Books, 1996, p. 27)

Discuss the inter-relationship of production and aesthetics, constructing your argument around two case studies.

7   Independent cinema, as Jim Hillier has shown, covers a considerable range of styles of filmmaking as well as diverse modes of production. How might it be possible to define and differentiate such terms as cult cinema, underground cinema, art cinema, with reference to films from the 1980s?

8   Given the developments that led to the rise in independent productions, how might this account for the impact of the films of Spike Lee? A useful exercise would be to trace the funding methods Lee used for *She's Gotta Have It* (1986) and compare that with *School Daze* (1988) and *Do the Right Thing* (1989).

9   There has been some considerable discussion of the post-1960s period of Hollywood film-making as constituting a departure from the basic mode of storytelling of the classical studio era. Examples from 1980s independent US cinema can be brought to support this argument. Consider this David Lynch interview on the subject of point of view:

> Chris Rodley: I suppose what I'm asking is, where is the point of view in [*Eraserhead*]? At times it's hard to tell.
> David Lynch: That's good. I wouldn't even know what to say about that. Maybe if I wrote, I'd do it in the first person, third person … I don't know. It is what it is. (in Walter Donahoe (ed.) *Lynch on Lynch*, London: Faber and Faber, 2005, p. 72)

However, it is also possible to argue, as Kristin Thompson does, that those storytelling practices have not fundamentally changed. Referring to *The Godfather*, *Jaws* and *Star Wars*, she points out: "The ideal American film still centres around a well-structured carefully motivated series of events that the spectator can comprehend relatively easily" (*Storytelling in the New Hollywood*, Cambridge, MA: Harvard University Press, 1999, p. 8). Identify a few films, both "blockbusters" and independent films, and discuss them in relation to the way they construct character motivation, point of view and their clarity of storyline.

10 The 1980s saw considerable sophistication in marketing techniques for films and for the "spin-offs" they generated. Construct a case study of how one specific title was distributed and marketed to audiences in the 1980s.

the **90s** and beyond

NINETIES

INTRODUCTION

Cinema in the 1990s was curiously divided in its view of where it had come from and where it was going, Janus-faced in its simultaneous attempt to look forwards even as it couldn't help looking backwards. The 100th anniversary of the first public film screening took place in 1995, and cinema's centenary was celebrated at every turn, on every continent. Yet even as it indulged in nostalgia at its own short history, it was already almost unrecognizable as the form that glimmered on Parisian screens for a paying audience in December 1895. The exponential growth of video and DVD[1] underpinned the industry's increased reliance on sales to the "ancillary" market of home viewers, making the US film industry around the millennium on first glance unrecognizable as the child of Lumière. It is tempting to think of the primary characteristics of 1990s cinema in terms of what films had begun to look like, what filmmakers were now able to conjure up on the screen. If it is possible to think of such recent history in epochal terms, one might say its landmarks are Steven Spielberg/Industrial Light and Magic/Stan Winston's awesomely realistic dinosaurs in *Jurassic Park* (1993), or the marriage of Disney and Pixar, which produced the first full-length computer-animated film, *Toy Story* (1995), or the "bullet-time" of the Wachowski brothers' *Matrix* series. Or you might think of sequels and TV spin-offs, for this is the era that rehashed old staples and extended tried and tested ideas from small screen into the multiplex. Of the number one top grossing films for the years 1990 to 2000, five out of ten were sequels or prequels: *Terminator 2* (most lucrative film of 1991), *Home Alone 2* (ditto 1992), *Batman Forever* (1995), *Star Wars Episode 1: The Phantom Menace* (1999), *Mission Impossible 2* (2000). Add to this list the biggest grossing films of 1993, 1994, 1996, 1997 and 1998 (*Jurassic Park*, *The Lion King*, *Independence Day*, *Men in Black* and *Titanic* respectively), it is no wonder that the image of the decade is that of a Hollywood-dominated spectacle machine, making extravagant formulaic movies that play well in non-English-speaking foreign markets, at the expense of innovative development in character and storyline.

Whatever is said about the textual qualities of American cinema at the end of the century, the most significant characteristics of this moment are these: this was the period in which new (digital, virtual) media began most visibly to challenge, if not replace, old (cinematic, celluloid) media. It was also the era in which the home viewer (*not* the cinemagoer) became the primary audience, as the global film industry's exhibition and profit-focus shifted. From big screen to small, the 1990s was the decade in which for the first time more money was made from, and more movies were experienced in, the arena of the living room than that of the theatrical auditorium. This brave new world of lucrative video and DVD release means that now no film fails to make its money back, as long as you are willing to wait. *Last Action Hero* (1993), *Waterworld* and *Showgirls* (both 1995) may have been theatrical and critical disasters first time around, but producers could still be confident of an eventual return. Theatres still needed audiences of course, and new media technologies such as CGI helped to keep box office for multiplex spectacles buoyant. But by the second half of the 1990s a theatrical release was largely considered to be a "trailer" for the place where the real money is made, the aftersales of a movie on video and DVD, to be viewed in your living room at home. Living rooms of course also require entirely different viewing technologies. "Cinema" then no longer primarily means "going to the cinema", paying to visit a movie theatre and watch a film on the big screen at a time chosen by programmers. It means a range of experiences, celluloid and digital, theatrical and domestic, the projection of light through a film strip, but also via a cathode ray or a flat-screen PC monitor. So if you first saw *Scooby Doo* on TV and then enjoyed him blown up for the big screen, there's a good chance that distributors Warner Bros were planning for you to help him return to the living room when you later bring the movie home, packaged with all its ancillary materials. And what of that Scooby Doo talking toy, or Happy Meal, or logo-ed T-shirt, or screensaver? The "cinematic" also reaches out to a range of adjacent products, produced by the corporate giants who now own the old studio brand – books, toys, soundtrack CDs, video games, fashion. The film text then needs to be read as one element in an entertainment complex, perhaps just the inspiration for a range of products that really make the money. Film studies itself is only just waking up to this brave new world of synergistic diversity, which has expanded the terrain of scholarly enquiry way beyond analysis of films themselves.

The ornate film theatre of 1963 with which we started our discussion of the 1960s had, then, probably disappeared by the 1990s –

flattened and replaced by a block of apartments. Here inhabitants will have installed the latest home theatre system, technologically geared to mimicking the theatrical experience itself (this is, after all, the decade of great ironies; one can imagine an Amityville scenario that sees old-Hollywood-style horrors wreaked on the home viewer whose condo is built on the grave of a dead 1930s theatre). Such a state-of-the-art system might comprise perhaps a VCR player (by the late 1990s also a dying form), certainly a DVD player, Dolby surround sound, all connected to a widescreen television with cable and Internet access, giving the possibility of purchasing pay-per-view movies scheduled to one's leisure convenience. Or perhaps the consumer would have bypassed the TV set altogether, downloading movies and trailers onto a PC in a brave new world of virtual ownership and exchange. 1999's watershed movie, *The Blair Witch Project*, blazed its microbudgeted indie trail to world prominence by pioneering movie promotion on the Internet. These new cinematic conditions, vying between virtual and domestic spaces, mega-multiplexes and still-surviving art-houses, constitute the norm of our viewing moment. No doubt before long this description will require radical updating, as exhibition practices – the everyday ways in which we consume movies – continue to change.

It is interesting then that cinema's centenary was celebrated primarily in a festival of nostalgia of the "Hooray for Hollywood" kind. The retrospective flag waving was commonly augmented by list making which also looked forward to the new millennium, an event that foreshadowed the century's last decade. Both the American Film Institute and the British Film Institute, as well as numerous popular journals and newspapers across the planet, produced bespoke "100 greatest" charts, spanning either (in the case of the AFI list) "the first 100 years of American cinema (1896–1996)" or (in the case of the BFI list) British films made up to "the turn of the millennium".[2] Lists of this kind are a curious phenomenon, on the one hand tending to favour recent works that are fresh in the judges' minds, on the other hand engendering a certain canonical conservatism manifest in greater reverence for more established "classic" works (*Citizen Kane* regularly tops best movie lists). The BFI list is boldest in its inclusion of more recent movies, containing 16 titles released in the 1990s, many of which did respectably in US theatres and at the Academy Awards, and/or had US production backing and distribution. Most notably, Miramax – the indie distributor which became a giant in the 1990s, to be bought by Disney in 1993 and become one of the "big ten" Hollywood companies – promoted (sometimes to Oscar success) a number of 1990s titles in the BFI list, including *The English Patient* (1996), *Shakespeare in Love* (1998), *Brassed Off* (1996), *The Crying Game* (1992) and *Trainspotting* (1996). The AFI list is more historically cautious, containing only eight titles from the 1990s, all bar one (Spielberg's 1993 Holocaust melodrama *Schindler's List*, rated ninth in the chart) in the lower half (*The Silence of the Lambs*, 1991, at 65, *Forrest Gump*, 1994, at 71, *Dances with Wolves*, 1990, at 75, *Fargo*, 1996, at 84, *Goodfellas*, 1990, at 94, *Pulp Fiction*, 1994, at 95 and *Unforgiven*, 1992, at 98).

Inevitably this retrospective perspective promotes conventional choices as well as unfavourable comparisons between the greatness of "then" and the paucity of "now". It is the work of this section to temper this view by providing a sense of what was most significant and vibrant in the diverse forms of film work

produced in the United States since 1990. We would hope to augment the view of dominant Hollywood cinema which emerges from charts such as our Box Office earners list (p. 440 below) by emphasizing some of the new views taken in recent cinema, as well as newer ways of seeing. Barbara Klinger provides a crucial perspective on how viewing practices changed in the latter years of the century, while Geoff King looks at the sometimes outrageous forms that cinematic spectacle was able to take as technology led (and some would say undermined) narrative. The period has also been particularly marked for the diversity of production from minorities and those hitherto excluded by the conservatism of the established industry, particularly women, black and gay filmmakers. New opportunities for women began to open up most significantly in the 1980s, as discussed by Linda Ruth Williams and Helen Hanson above. Below Yvonne Tasker asks whether these shifts in opportunity behind the camera made any significant difference to the ways in which women have been represented on screen since the 1990s in action cinema, one of the decade's dominant genres. Michele Aaron discusses the movement now known as New Queer Cinema, crucial in bringing new talent to independent and, later, mainstream screens, and providing a broader view of what constitutes US culture today. Readers interested in the extraordinary flourishing of "indie" cinema since the 1980s will want to supplement their reading of Jim Hillier's chapter above with Aaron's work here, along with the essay below by Jeffrey Sconce on smart cinema. Michael Hammond also discusses the development of New Black Cinema from the late 1980s onwards, and the increasing involvement of black filmmakers in Hollywood as well as independent production. Also significant in this period, particularly since the release of Michael Moore's first film *Roger and Me* in 1989, was the renewal of popular interest in documentary filmmaking in the United States, reflected in Patricia Zimmermann's analysis of the movement recently. As Jim Hillier argued earlier, the 1990s saw the increasing effacement of the boundaries between the independent sector and mainstream Hollywood, and many of the movies discussed by these writers occupy a diffuse area of semi-indieness, being non-mainstream in spirit yet eventually finding themselves picked up by a mainstream distributor who ushers them into the multiplexes despite their sometime "fringe" subject matter.

Here, then, is a brief snapshot of this period's diversity. Take one year – 1992, for example. Perhaps not the most remarkable year in the decade as far as great cinematic leaps forward are concerned – we might be better off picking out the years of *Jurassic Park* (1993) or *Toy Story* (1995) or *Titanic* (1997) or *The Blair Witch Project* (1999) for moments of industry-transforming significance, or perhaps 1996, the year when DVDs were first launched onto the domestic market. There are, of course, many ways in which we could map out a skeletal cinematic history of this period – the tables of awards and statistics provided decade-by-decade throughout this book form one. Nevertheless, if 1992 was an "average" year, it was so only in the sense that the output of US cinema as a whole (if it can ever be said to exist as a "whole" – one of the founding questions of this book) was highly diverse, containing some remarkable cinematic ups and downs – there is little consistency to the late New Hollywood period. It featured, for instance, one of the most infamous shots of post-war cinema, when Sharon Stone uncrossed her legs and flashed her naked pudenda at consenting adult viewers in *Basic Instinct*. We might read this film's

wider significance for an understanding of this period in terms of its updating of *film noir* as neo-*noir*, or its startling contribution to the development of a new genre, the erotic thriller. We might also read it as an instance in the career of one of new Hollywood's most audacious émigré directors, Paul Verhoeven, who had already engaged in some striking revisions of US genre staples (*Robocop*, 1987; *Total Recall*, 1990). In 1990 the US film ratings board at the MPAA had introduced a new category to the roster of established brackets.[3] NC–17 (barring entry to a film to anyone under 17) was widely tipped as the classification that would do for serious 1990s filmmakers what the X category had done for the auteurs of *The Graduate*, *Easy Rider* or *Midnight Cowboy* in the late 1960s – allowing complex, nonpornographic topics to be dealt with in US cinema in an "adult" way. In fact, NC-17 proved just how conservative the United States had become by the 1990s: NC-17 films do not play well in the ostensibly family-friendly mall-culture of mainstream contemporary cinema, and because of their semi-adult nature, advertisers frequently won't promote them.[4] An NC–17 rating became the kiss of death to a movie, particularly after the disastrous release of Verhoeven's *Showgirls* in 1995.

Basic Instinct was released initially with an R rating, and is perhaps all the more significant for that, constituting one moment in contemporary cinema when the envelope of what was permissible on mainstream screens was visibly pushed a little further. But the film also evidences another 1990s innovation: the opportunity for filmmakers to return to their movies and produce "director's cut" versions for release on video or DVD, as Verhoeven did subsequently, delivering a far more explicit film text for home viewers (very occasionally this has also been done for a second theatrical release, as with Ridley Scott's 1992 *Blade Runner*). This neo-auteurial afterlife capitalized on the second-chance opportunity that the home viewer gives to a film. From the 1990s onwards, many theatrically released and cult movies were redrafted in a different form, and released with a plethora of extra features and apparatus appealing to the *cinéaste* and general film fan alike.[5]

If this gave directors some retrospective control over their work which they had lacked theatrically, it also showed that by the 1990s auteurs had been reincarnated as a fully fledged promotional device. Sometimes they had "final cut" (a phenomenon largely unheard of in the studio era). Usually their influence was mitigated by a complex of other powers: the vying control of the producers, the demands of agents, the responses of punters at test screenings – also a relatively recent practice used to predict the marketability of a film. What is meant by "director" had shifted by the 1990s. A number of figures who had established themselves as the *enfants terribles* of the Hollywood Renaissance, discussed as industry innovators in our sections on the 1960s and 1970s above, were established brand-name figureheads and industry leaders in late middle age: Spielberg continues to dominate the "A" list, with 13 films released under his direction between 1990 and 2005, and both of his Oscar wins coming in the 1990s.[6] Martin Scorsese's *Cape Fear* was released in most territories in 1992, one of a total of 10 films by the director between 1990 and 2005. Francis Ford Coppola directed *Dracula* in 1992, one of five films he has directed since 1990 (always a slow helmsman, he has become a more prolific producer lately). Brian De Palma released *Raising Cain* in 1992, one of seven films directed by him since 1990. The 1990s also saw 1970s director and latterly megaproducer George Lucas return to directing, with his three *Star Wars* prequels later in the decade. These are filmmakers whose work has spanned a vast breadth of post-war US history: Mike Nichols, lionized visionary of the Hollywood Renaissance (*Who's Afraid of Virginia Woolf?*, 1966; *The Graduate*, 1967) has moved from the 1970s veiled Vietnam satire, *Catch-22*, to the 1998 veiled Clinton satire, *Primary Colors*.

These releases helped to consolidate the auteur as a reliable means of commodifying style – a market icon rather than a receptacle of genius, as he had been incarnated three decades before. But some of these names are also still popularly perceived as bridging the mainstream Hollywood/independent cinema gap, or bringing an "indie" flavour to mass-market productions (numerous writers on the contemporary indie scene – Pierson (1995); Andrew (1998); Biskind (2005) – show the increasingly untenable distinction between independent and mainstream production after the 1980s). Robert Altman, for instance, released *The Player* in 1992, a dark skit on Hollywood that was a popular hit while also being promoted as a unique work bearing out individual perspective (Altman's name-brand guaranteeing some vestigial maverick vision). "Altman" thus becomes a marketing brand precisely because his films are perceived as delivering singular "quality" cinema, movies for thinking *cinéastes* that also manage to make it into the multiplexes and Blockbuster video. Altman has continued to work productively into his old age, directing 10 films between 1990 and 2005, as has another astonishingly prolific indie-mainstream figure, Woody Allen, who has continued to make one film in almost every year since *Annie Hall* in 1977 (in some years he has managed two, although quantity is not necessarily a guarantor of "quality" film-making – his output has been mixed).

These are established names, reliable players continuing to direct fairly mainstream films that will always attract interest and publicity. New arrivals on the scene and developing young talent helped to extend significant strands in end-of-century US cinema. Auteurism was and is also a prominent discourse in burgeoning "indie" production, with a range of hip young helmsmen (and increasingly women too) lending their names to the peculiar tone or style of their films. The bright young things of the late 1980s indie boom capitalized on their earliest successes with releases in 1992: Hal Hartley (*The Unbelievable Truth*, 1989, and *Trust*, 1990) released *Simple Men* that year; Jim Jarmusch followed his cult successes from the 1980s, which included *Stranger than Paradise* (1984) and *Down by Law* (1986), with his by then most mainstream film, *Night on Earth* (six more bigger-budgeted and increasingly star-led features have been released to date, including *Dead Man*, 1995, and *Broken Flowers*, 2005). Both the Coen Brothers and Steven Soderbergh released films in late 1991 that developed the promise of earlier work: Soderbergh's *Kafka* built on the success of his astonishing breakthrough title from 1989, *sex, lies and videotape*, which won the Palme d'Or in 1989, while Joel and Ethan Coen's *Barton Fink* marked perhaps a transitional moment in the journey from their low-budget origins (*Blood Simple* in 1984) to the starrier, $60 million *Intolerable Cruelty* (2003) – a movie fairly indistinguishable from "safe" studio fare. But perhaps the most spectacular entrance of 1992 was by Quentin Tarantino, whose *Reservoir Dogs*, lauded at its Sundance screening and picked up by Miramax, established him as a major talent. As Mark Kermode discusses below, Tarantino's edgy subject matter would always consign him to the fringes of Hollywood family viewing, but even on these terms he developed into one of the most important cinematic voices in the last decade of the century. And not for nothing was Miramax, the prototype indie giant, dubbed "the house that Quentin built"; independent cinema, as James Schamus (1998: 103) writes, quickly became during the 1990s "a victim of its own success, a success that has made the independent film game look more and more like a microcosm of the studio business". Miramax epitomizes this move, which saw genuinely independent producers and distributors becoming subsidiaries of major studios.

We are still, however, in the realms of the singular white male auteur figure, albeit sometimes alternatively funded and distributed. A number of young black directors also came to the fore during this period, particularly in the wake of Spike Lee's independent successes in the late 1980s. The early 1990s were an intense period for the vanguard of what came to be known as New Black Cinema, not least for Lee himself, who released his political biopic *Malcolm X* in 1992. Mario Van Peebles' *New Jack City* (1991),[7] John Singleton's *Boyz in the Hood*, (1991) and the Hughes brothers' *Menace II Society* (1993) were important urban/political trailblazers as well as being directorial debuts. Carl Franklin had been an established actor since the 1970s, and had – like many of his New Hollywood contemporaries – studied filmmaking at university before entering the industry, but his breakthrough film came also in 1992, with the Southern race-inflected road movie/thriller *One False Move*. But two of the most discussed films from this period were actually directed by women – Indian director Mira Nair's feature *Mississippi Masala*, and black US director Julie Dash's acclaimed historical essay *Daughters of the Dust* (both 1991). Indeed, since the 1980s there had been rather more opportunities for women to direct and produce, particularly in the independent sector – think of Allison Anders' Sundance success *Gas Food Lodging*, or Tamra Davis' neo-exploitation remake *Guncrazy*, or Katt Shea's teen pic/erotic thriller *Poison Ivy* (again, all 1992). The visions of a diverse range of US cinemas were then beginning to shift a little. Nevertheless these were small movies: Davis' cost $800,000, Shea's a rather more princely $3 million. Most audiences – especially those on a strict cinematic diet of *Basic Instinct* or *Home Alone 2* – didn't come near to these edgy little films. The popular view of "women's cinema" at the start of 1992 may for many viewers have begun and ended with Kathryn Bigelow's *Point Break*, Jodie Foster's *Little Man Tate*, or even Ridley Scott's *Thelma and Louise*, all released in the United States in 1991. Most of those who flocked to see *Wayne's World* in 1992 were entirely unaware that it was directed by a woman (Penelope Spheeris, who had been making movies since the 1960s); *A League of Their Own*'s female-helming (by Penny Marshall) was rather overshadowed by its co-star (Madonna). The same year also saw the quiet directorial debut – with *This is My Life* – of Nora Ephron, established writer of *Silkwood* (1983) and *When Harry Met Sally* (1989) who was to become one of recent cinema's most successful Hollywood women, subsequently helming *Sleepless in Seattle* (1993), *Michael* (1996) and *You've Got Mail* (1998).

These are perhaps evidence that character-led cinema was very much alive in the 1990s at most levels of production: the development of genres such as the rom com/chick flick, neo-noir, what Jeffrey Sconce calls (below) the smart film, and even the neo-Western, challenge the hegemony of the "Big and loud"

action film (Gross 1995: 6). Nevertheless, cinema was still largely a visceral medium, and in many ways the US industry remains buoyant because it continues to deliver standard kinetic thrills in large doses as well as more complex diverse products in smaller helpings. Perhaps 100 years on the rollercoaster attractions of a movie that can make you fear for your life, as audiences reportedly did when apprehending the spectacle of the Lumière brothers' *Train Arriving at the Station* in 1895, are not so different from the attractions of *Jurassic Park*. Cinematic spectacle still relies upon its ability to produce dramatic visceral changes in the audience, even if the adrenaline rush no longer propels you toward the exit.

However, this may now be predicated upon a different set of beliefs about movies, what they are and how they're made, as technology is demystified by the plethora of information available to even the most casual viewer in the Web era. While our bodies may manifest a similar responses to what Linda Williams (1991) calls "body genres", there may have been a shift in our ability to suspend disbelief. Since the 1970s CGI has usurped mechanical, on-set, special effects in the illusion-making process. By the 1990s, as Wheeler Winston Dixon (2001: 358) argues in his "Twenty-five reasons why it's all over", "We [the audience] no longer believe in images, since computer-generated images make any effect possible." Well, yes and no. Early audiences quickly became visual sophisticates, knowing the illusion of the image while wanting also to forget that illusion, all the better to enjoy the thrill of its make-believe. Just because the make-believe was, by the 1990s, more often constructed digitally than mechanically doesn't necessarily make the visual trickery of cinematic suspension of disbelief qualitatively different. But Winston Dixon is also making a further point about losing touch. "[R]eality", he writes "has lost out decisively, in favour of the utterly synthetic images of such blockbusters as *Titanic*."

Are we then looking forward to "a future cinema in which location shooting and live production might become obsolete" (Lewis 2001: 3)? Perhaps, but when was Hollywood *not* engaged in synthesizing images? And what of the other realities explored in US cinema since the 1990s, by the documentarists discussed below by Zimmermann, or the independent and other cinemas addressed both above and below by Hillier, Aaron and Sconce? Cinema since 1990 is not just film from *Jurassic Park* to *Titanic* (important as both movies were as milestones in the mainstream). It is also film from *Swoon* to *Happiness*, from *New Jack City* to *A Rage in Harlem*, from *Blue Steel* to *Baadasssss!* to *Bewitched*. Perhaps everything that has been said about the recent state of this art is contrarily true: US cinema is as cerebrally challenging as it is visceral, it can be both adult and infantile, politically engaged and entirely irresponsible. The continuing tradition of small-scale personal filmmaking anchored to the real has – at least so far – succeeded in sharing shelf space with the mega-monsters, if not always at the multiplex, then at least sometimes on your DVD player.

Notes

1   Digital versatile disk (sometimes known as digital video disk), the home-viewing success story of the century's last decade, which came to replace laserdisc as the digital form of choice.

2   See "AFI's 100 Years ... 100 Movies", at http://www.afi.com/tvevents/100years/ movies.aspx, and "The bfi 100" at http://www.bfi.org.uk/features/bfi100/. Each list is nation-specific, but not so century-encompassing as the explanatory rationale claims: the AFI list contains nothing before 1925, and the BFI list covers only the period from 1935 to 1999.

3   United States classification ratings as administered by the MPAA (Motion Picture Association of America) are as follows: G – general audiences; PG – parental guidance suggested; PG–13 – parents cautioned that material is inappropriate for children under 13; R – restricted – under-17s admitted only with a parent/guardian; NC–17 – no-one under 17 admitted. The UK classification categories (Uc, U, PG, 12A, 12, 15, 18 and R18) changed their definition in 2000. For further details, see the MPAA and BBFC (British Board of Film Classification) Websites, http://www.mpaa.org and http://www.bbfc.co.uk.

4   See Jon Lewis's "A quick look at censorship in the New Hollywood", particularly pp. 284–99, for a discussion of the foibles of NC-17 (Lewis 2000).

5   From the 1980s onwards back-catalogues of "classic" movies had also been steadily released for the home market on video; by the late-1990s these were getting the digital enhancement treatment and sometimes finding wider audiences than they had had on their original release.

6   For *Schindler's List* in 1993 and *Saving Private Ryan* in 1998.

7   As Melvin van Peebles' son, Mario was the next in line in a black cinematic dynasty.

References

Andrew, S. (1998) *Stranger than Paradise: Maverick Film-makes in Recent American Cinema*. London: Prion.

Biskind, P. (2005) *Down and Dirty Pictures: Miramax, Sundance and the Rise of Independent Film*. London: Bloomsbury.

Gross, L. (1995) Big and loud, *Sight and Sound*, 5(8): 6–10.

Kipnis, L. (1998) Film and changing technologies, in J. Hill, P. Church and S. Gibson (eds) *The Oxford Guide to Film Studies*. Oxford: Oxford University Press.

Lewis, J. (2000) *Hollywood v. Hard Core: How the Struggle over Censorship Saved the Modern Film Industry*. New York: New York University Press.

Lewis, J. (2001) The end of cinema as we know it and I feel . . ., in J. Lewis (ed.) *The End of Cinema As We Know It: American Film in the Nineties*. New York: New York University Press.

Pierson, J. (1995) *Spike, Mike, Slackers and Dykes: A Guided Tour Across a Decade of American Independent Cinema*. London: Faber.

Schamus, J. (1998) To the rear of the back end: the economics of independent cinema, in S. Neale and M. Smith (eds) *Contemporary Hollywood Cinema*. London: Routledge.

Williams, L. (1991) Film bodies: gender, genre and excess, *Film Quarterly*, 44(4): 2–13.

Winston Dixon, W. (2001) Twenty-five reasons why it's all over, in J. Lewis (ed.) *The End of Cinema as We Know It: American Film in the Nineties*. New York: New York University Press.

16 SPECTACLE AND NARRATIVE IN THE CONTEMPORARY BLOCKBUSTER

Geoff King

WHETHER THE IMAGINARY futurescapes and stellar technologies of science fiction or the teeming hordes and massive edifices of mythic fantasy, impressions of vast spectacle are central to many of the high-grossing blockbuster productions around which the fortunes of the Hollywood studios have primarily revolved in recent years. Think, for example, of the *Lord of the Rings* trilogy or the later instalments of the *Star Wars* cycle, box-office champions (and DVD box-set bonanzas) of the turn-of-the-millennium period. This dimension of the current blockbuster economy, with its visions aspiring to an evocation of something akin to the sublime, harks back directly to earlier traditions of spectacular cinema, examples such as biblical epics dating from the 1910s to the 1960s. There are also some key differences, however. Increasingly, the spectacular vistas of the 1990s and the early twenty-first century are the work of digital imaging technologies,

rather than the appearance of massed ranks of real performers or the construction of enormous sets (and, if painted backdrops were used in previous eras, their computer-generated equivalents are celebrated as considerably more "realistic", "seamless" or "convincing" in effect).

The current period is also one in which large-scale spectacle is situated less obviously than has often been the case in relation to the dominant sources of Hollywood's income. Spectacular vistas are one of the continuing sources of the appeal of the specifically theatrical/cinematic experience, as opposed to those of small screen media. That has been one of the specific attractions of spectacle to the industry since the decline in Hollywood's fortunes in the immediate post-war decades: spectacle as a way of tempting viewers back to the cinema, away from the comforts and conveniences of home viewing. Today, however, the picture is rather different. The bulk of Hollywood's revenue (approximately 75 per cent) comes from the small-screen incarnations of its products, on video, increasingly on DVD and in sales to various forms of television. Success in the cinema remains vitally important, establishing the value of films in subsequent channels of release, but what is the fate or role of large-scale spectacle on the small screen? It can still play an important role, perhaps increasingly so with the growing take-up of larger and wider screen televisions and the accompanying fidelity of DVD and its near-future successors. But other forms of spectacle also exist in contemporary Hollywood, which, it could be argued, function more effectively in the small-screen environment. The action film, particularly, but also in combination with other genres and subgenres, has witnessed the development of what can be termed an "impact aesthetic", based on strategies such as rapid editing and

unstable camerawork designed to create an impression of the subjective experience of being "inside" the action on-screen.

My aim here is to examine the different kinds of attractions and economies offered by these two forms of spectacle, sometimes used separately, sometimes in combination. Both, undoubtedly, have played an important role in the spectacular economy of recent mainstream Hollywood production. Whether or not spectacle of these varieties entirely dominates the contemporary blockbuster is another matter. A key question to be considered in this regard is the fate of narrative in this context. Has narrative been eclipsed or undermined by the emphasis on spectacle in recent Hollywood blockbuster and/or action formats, as has sometimes been suggested, or does it continue to provide a major source of orientation? Do the temptations of computer-generated

Continued on page 338

Hong Kong in Hollywood

The Hong Kong film industry has an extraordinarily productive heritage, which has long held a complex and symbiotic relationship with Hollywood. Benefiting in the 1930s and 1940s from the influx of several Shanghai production companies, which relocated to the comparative stability of this British colony, Hong Kong produced films shot in Mandarin and Cantonese and covered the full range of genres (comedies, costume dramas, action adventures, operas) for distribution in Asia, with a secondary market among the émigré communities of the West. "From the start", writes David Bordwell (2000: 18):

> Hong Kong film was indebted to America. In the silent era, several Chinese film-makers worked in Hollywood ... Hollywood films played in Hong Kong from the 1920s on, and *The Love Parade* (1929) and *Camille* (1937) were adapted into Cantonese plays and operas, which in turn were filmed. American production methods and lighting styles strongly influenced Cantonese cinema for decades after World War II. Whereas the Japanese studios encouraged experimentation, Hong Kong filmmakers stuck fairly closely to those guidelines for shot design and continuity editing first formulated in Hollywood.

Among the most productive Hong Kong movie-making dynasties from the 1930s onwards were the Shaw Brothers. Following the "old Hollywood" model of integrated production, distribution and exhibition, the Shaw Brothers became the region's most powerful movie-making force, alongside Motion Picture and General Investments Ltd (later the Cathay Film Company). In 1970, Raymond Chow and Leonard Ho (former Shaw Brothers executives) set up Golden Harvest and promptly scored an international hit with the Bruce Lee vehicle *The*

Spectacle and Narrative in the Contemporary Blockbuster   335

Big Boss (1971), thereby opening up a worldwide market for Hong Kong martial arts movies whose production costs were a fraction of comparable movies in Hollywood. Throughout the 1980s and 1990s the Hong Kong film industry continued to flourish, ranking second only to America in terms of worldwide film exports, while retaining a healthy share of its own domestic box office revenues. Not until 1997 (the year that sovereignty for the colony was returned to China, and that Hong Kong director Wong Kar-Wai won the best director prize at Cannes for *Happy Together*) did Hollywood productions account for more than 50 per cent of Hong Kong cinema ticket sales.

While much Hong Kong cinema had traditionally owed a thematic and structural debt to Hollywood, during the 1990s the dynamics of this cultural flow began to shift thanks to the increasing plagiarism-cum-homage of several high profile American directors (most notably Quentin Tarantino) who had been raised on Shaw Brothers and Golden Harvest imports. "[I]n what Uma Magal calls the 'reverse angle' of global cinema, Hollywood movies have been appropriating from Hong Kong", wrote Odham Stokes and Hoover at the end of this transitional decade.

> Directors show close-ups, made famous by the likes of John Woo and Ringo Lam, of speeding bullets, and stunt actors imitate the physical martial arts moves of Jackie Chan and Jet Li. Quentin Tarantino lifts the final segment of Lam's *City on Fire* (1987) for his own *Reservoir Dogs*, while Robert Rodriguez mimics the gunplay scenes of Woo's *The Killer* (1989) in *Desperado*. (Odham Stokes and Hoover 1999: 35)

Chuck Kleinhans (1998: 318) concurs, asserting that Rodriguez's low-budget debut feature (effectively a test-run for *Desperado*) "was picked up by US producers who thought *El Mariachi* seemed similar to the newly discovered films of Hong Kong director John Woo (who had influenced Tarantino and others)".

Famous for such elegiac action (or "heroic bloodshed") classics as *A Better Tomorrow* (1986), *Bullet in the Head* (1990) and *Hard-Boiled* (1991) (and hailed by his high-profile fans in the West as "God"), John Woo had worked his way up from script boy at Cathay Film before directing his first features in the mid-1970s. In the early 1990s he went to Hollywood to helm the English-language Jean-Claude Van Damme actioner *Hard Target* (1993). Although Universal reportedly surrounded Woo with a plethora of producers, and gave him a "body count quota" to rein in his more violent excesses, the film nevertheless retained Woo's personal stamp. "The central theme of religion and ethics binding characters together permeates *Hard Target*", writes Stephen Teo. "Lacking a complex hero (his star being Jean-Claude van Damme instead of Chow Yun-Fat), Woo plied his audience with neatly choreographed action sequences, but the film is a virtual textbook of classic Woo symbols for anyone who wants to discern them" (1997: 182). Stefan Hammond (2000: 197) agrees, arguing that, for all its concessions to Hollywood, "the film is like a John Woo primer for the uninitiated"; for Hammond the maestro's subsequent Hollywood ventures (most notably the identity-swap drama *Face/Off*, 1997) prove that "Woo got out of Hong Kong with his innocence intact" (Hammond 2000: 200). In the wake of Woo's success, other Hong Kong directors like Ronny Yu (*The Bride with White Hair*, 1993; *Phantom Lover*, 1995) were signed to direct Hollywood fare such as *Bride of Chucky* (1998), which breathed new life into a long dormant horror-comedy franchise. Woo, meanwhile, went on to helm the Tom Cruise action hit *Mission: Impossible II* (2000).

Woo's former leading man Chow Yun-Fat also rode the crest of this popular wave, skilfully parlaying the talents that had made him an Eastern legend and a salable Hollywood product.

The Killer

Woo served as executive producer on Antoine Fuqua's *The Replacement Killers* (1998), a formulaic actioner that rehashed the themes of Chow's Hong Kong successes. But it was a starring role opposite Jodie Foster in *Anna and the King* (1999) that proved Chow's versatile potential. More prominent still was actor/director Jackie Chan, heir to Bruce Lee's martial arts crown, who found mainstream success in knockabout Hollywood action comedies such as *Rush Hour* (1998) and *Around the World in 80 Days* (2004), both of which teamed him with an English-speaking comedian (Chris Rock and Steve Coogan respectively) who could handle the verbal high-kicks while Chan provided the physical humour. Chan had first worked in Hollywood in the early 1980s, with supporting roles in *Cannonball Run* (1980) and *Cannonball Run II* (1983) supplementing little-seen leads in *The Big Brawl* (1980) and *The Protector* (1985). Disillusioned with a lack of control over his American output, Chan went East. But the popularity of the Hong Kong hit *Police Story* (1985) and its sequels (which were wantonly plagiarized by Hollywood), and a US chart-topping hit with *Rumble in the Bronx* (1995), a Hong Kong production shot in Vancouver, prompted a return to America, where Chan finally cemented his reputation as a *bona fide* Hollywood star.

While Chan was finding his second wind in America, Tarantino was introducing the work of Hong Kong director Wong Kar-Wai to US audiences via his Rolling Thunder distribution label, which promoted *Chungking Express* (1994) to great critical acclaim. Tarantino would go on to pay explicit tribute to Hong Kong's Shaw Brothers in *Kill Bill vols. 1 and 2* (2004 and 2005) and to "present" the Hong Kong-China co-production of Zhang Yimou's *Hero* (2000) in the United States, where it became an unexpected box-office hit. Behind the scenes, martial arts director Yuen Woo-ping's distinctive work has memorably graced the Hollywood hits *The Matrix* (1999) and its two sequels, alongside Tarantino's *Kill Bill* movies. Yuen, who has long been a legend in Hong Kong, was also a key player in Taiwanese director Ang Lee's *Crouching Tiger, Hidden Dragon* (2000), the first of several Chinese-set period epics to find a home in US/UK multiplexes alongside Zhang's *Hero* (2002) and *House of Flying Daggers* (2004). Lee, who had proven his cross-cultural versatility by helming *Sense and Sensibility* (1995) in the United Kingdom and *The Ice Storm* (1997) in the United States, went on to direct the acclaimed revisionist American Westerns *Ride with the Devil* (1999) and *Brokeback Mountain* (2005) alongside the Hollywood comic-strip blockbuster *Hulk* (2003), his diverse endeavours further strengthening East–West filmmaking relations.

In recent years, a slew of English language remakes of Hong Kong hits have gone into production in Hollywood, thanks in part to the efforts of producers Roy Lee and Doug Davison. Through their Vertigo Entertainment organization, this entrepreneurial pair have brokered deals for films as diverse as *The Eye* (2002), a Hong Kong–Thailand co-production being remade in Hollywood by Japanese director Hideo Nakata, and *Infernal Affairs*, Andrew Lau and Alan Mak's hit Hong Kong crime series, which provides the basis for Martin Scorsese's *The Departed* (2006). In 2005, *House of Flying Daggers* star Ziyi Zhang led a cast which included Malaysian-born Hong Kong film legend Michelle Yeoh (best known to Western audiences through *Crouching Tiger, Hidden Dragon* and the Bond film *Tomorrow Never Dies*) and Gong Li (from *Raise the Red Lantern*) in the fêted Hollywood production *Memoirs of a Geisha*. With Hong Kong legend Stephen Chow's *Shaolin Soccer* (2001) and *Kung Fu Hustle* (2004) producing box-office dividends for American distributors in the United States, the cross-cultural interplay between Hollywood and Hong Kong continues to expand and diversify.

References

Bordwell, D. (2000) *Planet Hong Kong*. Cambridge, MA: Harvard University Press.

Hammond, S. (2000) *Hollywood East*. Chicago: Contemporary Books.

Kleinans, C. (1998) Independent features: hopes and dreams, in J. Lewis (ed.) *New American Cinema*. Durham, NC: Duke University Press, pp. 307–27.

Odham Stokes, L. and Hoover, M. (1999) *City on Fire: Hong Kong Cinema*. London: Verso.

Teo, S. (1997) *Hong Kong Cinema: The Extra Dimension*. London: BFI.

Mark Kermode

Continued from page 335

imagery (CGI), particularly, which enables almost any imagery to be realized on screen, lead filmmakers away from what some might see (according to particular value judgements) as the more "respectable" path of coherent or sustained narrative? Not really. Central elements associated with the "classical" variety of Hollywood narrative remain very much in evidence, if also combined, in some cases, with more episodic variants. But, first, back to spectacle itself.

Spectacle of the large-scale variety invites a particular mode of response from the viewer. We are invited to sit back and enjoy the sheer scale and impressive detail of the image, especially the apparently "seamless" manner with which digital artefacts are deployed, either alone or in combination with "real" live-action characters and settings. What exactly is involved here is quite complex. "Impressive spectacular realism" – as it might be termed – is a somewhat oxymoronic formulation. It combines spectacle that draws attention to itself *as* spectacle, something to be "wowed" by, with a "realism" (self-effacing, in that "the joints cannot be seen") usually understood as seeking to draw us into fictional world of the film. It can work either way; maybe both at the same time. How, for instance, might we be expected to respond to the spectacular cityscapes of *Star Wars: Episode II – Attack of the Clones* (2002) or *The Lord of the Rings: The Return of the King* (2003)?

Both clearly seem designed, at least in part, to draw admiration as impressive constructs. We are meant to be impressed by these as demonstrations of the spectacular capability of Hollywood cinema, whatever role they also play in the creation of an absorbing fantasy-fiction experience. We are meant to say "wow", either silently or aloud, at least some of the time. These kinds of visions (with their multichannel audio accompaniments, a dimension that merits separate analysis in its own right) function as an advertisement for what Hollywood can do, as was also the case with the breakthrough early 1990s digital special effects of *Terminator 2: Judgment Day* (1991) and *Jurassic Park* (1993). On one level, this is all about "production values" and the enshrinement of a form of cinema in which Hollywood, because of its superior financial resources, cannot be rivalled; a dynamic familiar from the history of the industry. In the contemporary global-scale moving-picture economy, Hollywood creates a territory on which it, alone, can compete (and the studio-distribution-corporate-parent structure is essentially an oligopoly; shared dominance rather than any real competition). Spectacle *as* spectacle is, thus, a matter of strongly market-driven aesthetics.

Spectacle of this kind invites an examination of its own qualities. What once might have been a search for flaws – obviously painted backgrounds or visible matt lines around photographically composited elements –

becomes, ideally, awe at their absence. This might involve entirely digital imagery such as the teeming skies above the city of Coruscant in *Attack of the Clones*, or blends of CGI and elements present in reality (pro-filmically) before the camera, as seems to be the case in the display of elements of Minas Tirith in *The Return of the King*. Part of the game for the viewer can be the attempt to work out which is which. *Can* we still see any of the joins? We might be convinced and "taken in", or perhaps remain more cynical and detached: is there something *too* synthetic, too lacking in analogue depth of tone and texture, about the all-digital construct, a criticism sometimes voiced of the last three productions in the *Star Wars* series?

What is involved here is a version of a dynamic that operates more generally in film viewing: a shift between the states of being "taken into" the fictional world and of remaining self-consciously aware of ourselves as watching a technically and technologically well-rendered construct. Spectacular vistas that make claims to the status of being "realistic" and "convincing" are not *just* intended, we can safely assume, to draw attention to their own qualities. Part of the dynamic is the familiar Hollywood sense of seeking to create an impression of immersion in the fictional world (an important issue when it comes to the subject of narrative, as considered below), in which case the quality of spectacular effects comes down to a question of the absence of obvious flaws as much as any notion of equivalence between representation and a real external referent. That we are capable of doing both at once, or of oscillating between the two states, has been suggested by some theorists of special effects (for example, LaValley 1985). In this sense, consideration of the experience of viewing major sequences of spectacle or special effects might illustrate the complex and multidimensional modality of the filmviewing experience more generally, rather than being something specific to a particular kind of cinema.

Spectacle in contemporary Hollywood is not just a matter of lofty vistas. It can take many forms. Taken at its widest or most literal, the term can, in fact, include rather a lot of the imagery offered by Hollywood and even some independent features. The figure of the star, for example, can be understood as operating at least partly in terms of spectacle, as can all sorts of "exotic" or larger-than-life imagery. The main focus of this essay, however, is on what might be understood as particularly *heightened* forms of spectacle. This includes a format that consolidated in the 1990s and early 2000s and can be seen as an alternative to the variety that invites the more contemplative gaze. This is spectacle that can be understood as offering a vicarious assault on the position of the viewer through strategies such as rapid editing, unstable camerawork and, in some cases, the propulsion of objects out towards the screen. The large-scale vista is often viewed from on high, either statically, or, more characteristically in contemporary Hollywood, via expansive wheeling, arcing or panning motions of the camera. The impact aesthetic, by contrast, is one that takes us "up close and personal", sometimes very much "down on the ground". The impression created is of a more subjective involvement in the action – and it is usually action sequences to which this treatment is given.

This is a style found particularly in the action cinema of the 1990s, the paradigmatic instance being the ubiquitous fireball/explosion sequence associated with myriad car chases, plane crashes or other sources of destructive impact. Rapidly cut montage sequences are often used to increase the percussive impression of the explosion, accompanied by rapidly shifting perspectives within the scene and juddering and/or handheld camerawork that simulates the impact on character or viewer. The fireball/explosion is not witnessed from a godlike position above. Its impact is created, instead, by a process of more overt and frenetic cinematic construction, a form that has roots in the cinema of Sergei Eisenstein's montage of attractions. From typical 1990s action features such as *The Rock* (1996) and *Con Air* (1997), strategies such as these have also been adopted in generic territories associated with the larger-scale forms of spectacle considered above. The science fiction/disaster hybrid *Armageddon* (1998, Fig. 18 (*see plate section*)) sees this approach taken to perhaps its limits, a film comprised largely of a succession of noisy, in-your-face assaults on the viewer. More telling, however, might be the use of a variant of this form of spectacle as the dominant aesthetic of *Gladiator* (2000), a Roman epic, the generic tradition of which is associated with the larger-scale variety of big-screen spectacle. In *Gladiator*, major action sequences are reduced at times to little more than a blur of hyperkinetic montage, whip pans and other camera-movement effects.

How might the use of this form of spectacle be explained, particularly its spread beyond the confines of the hyperbolic action film? A number of suggestions can be offered, including connections with small-screen media forms (King 2002). The kind of rapid editing and frenetic camera movement effects mobilized in the examples cited above draw at least partially on styles associated with TV advertising and music video, both of which have been increasingly prominent in recent decades within the wider culture and as sources of apprenticeship for aspiring film directors.

Russell Crowe in *Gladiator*

Formal devices of this kind are effective sources of spectacle on the small screen, where constant changes of image content are required (rather than large-scale imagery) if heightened visual impact is to be achieved within its limited confines (Ellis 1989). A direct link can be found in the careers of individual film-makers, figures such as Michael Bay, director of *The Rock* and *Armageddon*, and Ridley Scott, director of *Gladiator*, with backgrounds in advertising and/or music video. Styles associated with advertising and MTV might also be attractive to Hollywood as part of a more general effort to appeal to a generation of viewers for whom they have become a familiar part of the cultural background. Whether they have been used or promoted specifically because of the importance of small screen media to the wider Hollywood economy is much harder to assess. It is useful, where appropriate, to draw connections between specific aesthetics and the industrial context,

but many intervening variables occur, making any such conclusions largely speculative. An intensification based on faster cutting and more rapid camera movement, whether unsteady/handheld or smoother in nature, might be explained in action-oriented formats by a more general process of upping-the-ante required if equivalent doses of impact-attraction are to be sold to audiences that become familiarized to existing recipes. It is one thing to suggest, from the perspective of textual analysis, that the impact aesthetic *translates* to the small screen with relatively less loss than the large-scale form; quite another to assert that this can be seen as part of a conscious or deliberate industrially motivated strategy.

The large-scale vista also continues to thrive, as suggested by its use in major franchises such as the *Star Wars* and *Lord of the Rings* films. It has not shown any sign of being displaced by the high-impact aesthetic. The advent of CGI in the 1990s gave it a new lease of life, the limitless replicability of digital image components rendering simple the generation of a vast-teeming-horde variety of spectacle evident in numerous blockbusters of recent years. This is particularly evident in the epic battle scene, a familiar trope of the early 2000s: the hyperbolically massed hordes of drooling orcs in *The Lord of the Rings*, the regimented clone army of *Star Wars Episode II*, the vastly replicated expanse of Greek ships and the rival forces gathered outside the city walls of *Troy* (2004).

If *Armageddon* and *Gladiator* rely heavily on close-shot, jerky/blurry forms of visual impact, more typical of the current period is a greater balance between different forms of spectacle. *Troy*, for example, following *Gladiator* in a cycle of early 2000s classical epics, utilizes elements found in the films discussed earlier in this essay, but in less extreme forms. It has its large-scale vistas, as suggested above, but not quite on the scale of *The Lord of the Rings* films. A requirement for a degree of historical plausibility places limits on the magnitude of its imagery. Troy itself is rendered in a number of panoramic shots, for example, but its scope for "wow"-inducing spectacle is more constrained than the projections of entirely mythical fantasy. *Troy* also employs up-close impact effects in more proximate footage of battle. Some quick mini-pans and unsteady camerawork are used to heighten the concussive effect of combat. The camera moves somewhat arbitrarily: a pair of combatants will be held in frame and the camera will spasm, slightly, first to one side, then the other, not to follow the action but purely to fabricate a greater impression of impact. This is done quickly and in passing, however, rather than sustained as a central aesthetic principle. Elements of the style used in *Gladiator* are integrated rather more smoothly into the familiar, classical cinematic regime, in other words, as one element in the repertoire rather than a defining feature. Much the same is the case in the major battle set-pieces of *Return of the King*, in which the up-close "unsteady-cam" style is similarly combined with shots of larger scale. In the Crusades epic, *Kingdom of Heaven* (2005), Ridley Scott returns to the *Gladiator* aesthetic as an inscription of the intimate heat of combat, particularly the distinctive use of faster-than-usual shutter speeds that remove an element of motion-blur present in conventional cinematography. The result is a harsh strobing impression, a slightly stuttering quality of image, that adds to the impact effect, a device most notably employed in the opening beach-landing sequences of *Saving Private Ryan* (1998). This heightens a degree of disorientation created by close focus and rapid cutting inside the combat sequences of *Gladiator* and *Kingdom of Heaven*, an attempt to figure the chaos and terror of battle, the discomforting nature of which might explain why this element has been adopted less readily elsewhere.

Spectacle is a major selling point of the kinds of films discussed above. It may be the single most important factor. The ability to create spectacular images (translatable into box-office and subsequent media revenues) is, arguably, the driving force behind the decisions of major studios to either produce or back such features and to put behind them their enormous weight in global distribution and promotion. Spectacle is seen as of particular value, alongside stardom, in the overseas market, which has become increasingly important to Hollywood in recent decades, given its lesser dependence on issues of cultural or verbal translation. It is probably safe to say that a product such as the *Lord of the Rings* cycle only exists in the current Hollywood environment on the basis of its ability to deliver such qualities. None of this means, however, that narrative – the telling of stories, with their various dimensions – is of significantly less relevance to the films that result, contrary to the impression that is sometimes created by media commentators. All of the films considered above have strong narrative dimensions, generally quite in keeping with the "classical Hollywood narrative" recipe, as described most influentially by David Bordwell (1985). Our path through the onscreen events, however spectacular, is led by small groups of central characters, around which larger developments are articulated in sequences of clearly explained causes-and-effects. Thematic plot material is, as usual, paralleled by heterosexual romance, although this figures less centrally in *The Lord of the Rings*.

Spectacle is, in almost every instance, narratively situated. Spectacle does not exist in Hollywood features purely for its own sake (a situation closer to this extreme might be found in an IMAX production, shorter in length and more overtly designed to showcase a particular technology of exhibition, although even here some narrative dimension is usually likely to be found). We are returned at this point to the viewing dialectic considered earlier, between the pleasure of spectacle *as* spectacle and its role as a way of realizing the worlds in which particular narratives unfold. The latter dimension remains important. In *The Return of the King*, for example, the vast evil army that assembles outside Minas Tirith is impressive in its own spectacular right, without doubt, but a significant component of its impact lies in the resonance of the spectacle as part of a narrative *situation*, in this case as a threat to what the film presents as sources of "good" and of audience allegiance. The same goes for the spectacular clash of massed forces in *Troy*, even

if here our allegiances might be divided less clearly between figures on one side and the other. The point is that spectacle is rendered *meaningful* through context, and much of that context comes from narrative ingredients; from the "who" and "why" of the onscreen events; from character and plot.

How exactly this works can vary from one example to another. The *Star Wars* and *Lord of the Rings* cycles are somewhat unusual in the extent to which their events are situated in a single larger narrative arc. The last three *Star Wars* films are, of course, prequels, key events being established and *leading towards* others of which the viewer is likely already to be aware (the latter stages of *Revenge of the Sith*, 2005; prepare the principal ingredients of the first instalment). Elements of the overarching narrative frame are established at the start of each film, in the now-familiar credit-sequence crawl. Later instalments of *The Lord of the Rings* are more demanding of the viewer in broader narrative terms. The concluding episode, *The Return of the King*, makes few concessions to the viewer unfamiliar with the story so far, either from the first two films or the original Tolkein source. There is no opening credit exposition or any equivalent to the "previously on ..". formula used in contemporary American series/serial hybrid television. The viewer will soon become aware that the Hobbits Frodo and Sam are on some kind of "vital" mission, involving a ring with dangerous powers, but exactly what this involves is not spelled out. It is not until more than two hours into the film that Frodo states explicitly that the ring must be destroyed, and when Frodo and Sam begin to climb a volcano in Mordor; a good hour later, the viewer new to the franchise will still not have been informed that its crater is the only place where

Continued on page 347

Spectacle and Narrative in the Contemporary Blockbuster

Often considered a recent phenomenon, sequels and series have always been a fact of Hollywood. J. Hoberman has argued that New Hollywood is particularly dominated by "sequelitis", "a distinctive feature of Hollywood's output in the late 1970s and 1980s" (Neale 2000: 247, discussing Hoberman 1985). Thomas Schatz (1993: 21) sees the sequel and its ilk (the remake, reissue and series) as symptomatic of a "conservative turn", particularly in the mid-1970s, which "coincided with an upswing in defensive market tactics", while Timothy Corrigan has argued that they are "perhaps the strongest indicators of [a] wasting and evacuation of contemporary narrative" (Corrigan 1991: 167; see pp. 167–72 for Corrigan's wider critique of contemporary cinematic repetition, which is disputed by both Neale (2000: 256–7) and King (2003: 124)). However, Hollywood has long been involved in the production of serials and follow-up films that cash in on earlier successes. Neale (2000: 257) even argues that "serials, sequels and even 'remakes' predate the cinema". In the 1920s Douglas Fairbanks and Rudolph Valentino followed up *The Mark of Zorro* (1920) and *The Sheik* (1921) by playing *Don Q, Son of Zorro* (1925) and *Son of the Sheik* (1926). Well before the coinage of phrases like "sequel hook" and "franchise potential", the studios spun follow-ups from family ties (*Dracula's Daughter*, 1935; *The Return of Frank James*, 1941; *Son of Paleface*, 1953) or resurrections/returns/further adventures (*Tarzan and His Mate*, 1934; *The Saint Strikes Back*, 1939; *Return of the Cisco Kid*, 1939) and even scramblings of previously separate series (*The Gracie Allen Murder Case*, 1939; *Frankenstein Meets the Wolf Man*, 1943).

Series tended to be a low-budget staple, with long-lasting franchises in comedy (*Blondie*, *Mexican Spitfire*), horror (*The Mummy*, *Frankenstein*), crime (*Charlie Chan*, *Sherlock Holmes*), Western (*The Three Mesquiteers*, *Hopalong Cassidy*), medicine (*Dr Kildare*, *Dr Christian*) and homespun comedy-drama (*Andy Hardy*). It could be argued that most popular stars featured in series in that their vehicles presented them as essentially the same character from film to film, whether named as such in the case of Charlie Chaplin's Little Tramp or Mr Laurel and Mr Hardy, or whether they had differing character names, as in the various passing aliases adopted by Buster Keaton or Abbott and Costello. Bing Crosby and Bob Hope play different characters in the various 'Road to' movies, but they are always Bing and Bob. This is most obvious in comedy, but the same phenomenon obtains in other genres – the cowboy or adventure heroes played by John Wayne or the detective or cop heroes of Alan Ladd are mostly screen incarnations of "Duke Wayne" and "Alan Ladd" unless they step up in ambition to play roles that somehow exceed or even critique these established characters, as is the case with Wayne as Ethan Edwards in *The Searchers* (1956) or Ladd in and as *Shane* (1953).

Sequels tended to come after A-feature hits: *Four Daughters* (1938) was followed by *Four Wives* (1939) and *Four Mothers* (1941) and *Mrs Miniver* (1942) led to the less-well-remembered *The Miniver Story* (1950). It was established early, by the likes of *Son of Kong* (1933), that sequels would rarely live up to the critical or commercial success of originals, but there were occasions – like James Whale's *Bride of Frankenstein* (1935) – when a follow-up would be mounted with more care than an original, the perception of sequels as "a sure thing" meaning that studios were willing to countenance a more radical reading of the basic idea. However, Whale also tried the trick with a sequel to Universal's biggest prestige picture, *All Quiet on the Western Front* (1930), and came up, after a much-troubled shoot, with a career-derailing flop, *The Road Back* (1937).

In the classic Hollywood era, sequel titles tended to use "Son of" or "Rides Again" formats, but the numeric title seems to have been coined by Nigel Kneale in 1955 for the British TV serial *Quatermass II* (filmed in 1958 as *Quatermass 2*), although this didn't become

American industry standard until the 1970s. There still remains a subtle distinction between the more pompous "Part 2" (*The Godfather, Part 2*, 1974), the slightly aspirational Roman numeral 'II' (*The French Connection II*, 1975) and the plain-speaking "2" (*Jaws 2*, 1978). Though some numbered series have neared double figures (*Jason X*, 2002), it is notable that the longest-running franchises (*Tarzan, James Bond*) have avoided numerals, and other wannabes (*A Nightmare on Elm Street, Star Trek*) have progressed through various forms of numbering before abandoning them altogether – the actual titles of the *Elm Street* series show this subtle metamorphosis: *A Nightmare on Elm Street* (1984), *A Nightmare on Elm Street, Part 2: Freddy's Revenge* (1985), *A Nightmare on Elm Street 3: Dream Warriors* (1987), *A Nightmare on Elm Street 4: The Dream Master* (1988), *A Nightmare on Elm Street: The Dream Child* (1989), *Freddy's Dead: The Final Nightmare* (1991), *Wes Craven's New Nightmare* (1994).

The long-established problem of reviving a series after an entry appears to deliver closure, most notable with the destruction of the entire world at the finish of *Beneath the Planet of the Apes* (1970), is underlined by the tendency of franchise-holders to want to wind things up in style but then have second thoughts, so that *Friday the 13th: The Final Chapter* (1984) is inevitably followed by *Friday the 13th, Part V: A New Beginning* (1985). *Escape from the Planet of the Apes* (1971) uses time travel to get out of its plot-hole, while series followers became used to the trick, poached from chapterplays, of opening a sequel (*The Mummy's Tomb*, 1942; *Hell Up in Harlem*, 1973) with a re-edit of the finale of the previous film (*The Mummy's Hand*, 1940; *Black Caesar*, 1973) that reveals the hitherto unsuspected fact that characters we thought killed off weren't dead at all. Far simpler are those hero-dependent series that simply pick up heroes such as Tarzan, Sherlock Holmes, Batman or Indiana Jones a year or so later and bring on new villains to be bested and exotic locales to be visited (although one notices a tendency for arch-enemies like Professor Moriarty or Ernst Stavro Blofeld to survive falls from a great height or exploding volcano bases with some regularity). The invincibility of horror franchise characters like Freddy Krueger, Michael Myers or Jason Voorhees renders their later adventures somewhat redundant, as every climactic death (even the decapitation of Michael at the end of *Halloween H20: Twenty Years After*, 1998) is merely provisional, turning the overall "story" into an existentially meaningless succession of monotonous effects. Some writers have read this as part of the genre's postmodernism. Andrew Tudor argues that the incessant process of "sequelling" that has characterized horror features since the 1980s relies on an audience's genre understanding, particularly when series such as the *Scream* franchise (from 1996) are concerned:

> the process of "sequelling" ... has itself become a major convention of the genre, a phenomenon fully understood and, more important, expected and embraced by a generically competent horror audience. As a character observes in *Scream*, "these days you've got to have a sequel". (Tudor 2002: 106–7)

The first great series of the post-1960 era is only part American. The Bond cycle commenced with *Dr No* (1962) and was still running in 2006 with a new James Bond contracted in the form of Daniel Craig. This is a version of the "continuing hero" style of series, with each entry telling basically the same story as new villains, gadgets, allies and women are deployed, and a few scenes are replayed with knowing variations (Bond being briefed by M, flirting with Moneypenny, in a clinch on a boat with a girl) that offer the pleasures of familiarity but also a reward for paying attention. There are running jokes aimed at audiences who saw the earlier films, as with the gag at the expense of the shooting-the-

Die Hard 2: "How can the same shit happen to the same man twice?"

swordsman bit from *Raiders of the Lost Ark* (1981) in *Indiana Jones and the Temple of Doom* (1984). (The fact that the later film is a prequel means that the extra-textual wink as Harrison Ford confronts two swordsmen and reaches for his holster to find it empty makes no sense within the narrative of the film.) A variant on the continuing hero series is the recurring situation series, exemplified by the *Airport* films: there is a carry-over between films, in the person of airport crisis controller Joe Patroni (George Kennedy), but each instalment presents a different airport, different passengers and a different crisis. A crossbreed of the two strains comes in the *Die Hard* films, which have both a continuing hero (Bruce Willis's John McClane) and a recurring situation (one man alone against terrorists/criminals) and make some attempts at irony ("how can the same shit happen to the same man twice?" in *Die Hard 2*, 1990) and continuity (in *Die Hard with a Vengeance*, 1995, villain Jeremy Irons is out to avenge the death of his brother, villain Alan Rickman, at the end of *Die Hard* (1988)). The *Alien* cycle, polarized around Ripley (Sigourney Weaver) and the unnamed alien species, tries more radical genre shifts, from horror to war to action, but stays within this format of franchise, possibly keeping its options open in case the star should choose to depart.

Rarer is the "continuing saga" series, which tends to throw off fewer and bigger individual entries, exemplified by the *Planet of the Apes*, *Godfather* and *Star Wars* films. Here, we follow not individual heroes – though Vito and Michael Corleone are at the heart of the *Godfather*s just as Anakin and Luke Skywalker are the thread of *Star Wars* – but (as in a TV soap) families and, by extension, societies. In most series, the basic premise insists that the background stay the same, to the extent of recasting Tarzan or 007 when the original star becomes too old to play the ageless character, but in continuing sagas, we see Al Pacino's Michael at every stage of his life, from the fresh-faced ex-soldier introduced in *The Godfather*

(1972) to the old man who dies alone at the end of *The Godfather, Part III* (1990), and observe the constants of his character even as his situation in regards to his family or the larger worlds of organized crime, American capitalism and Roman Catholicism is ever-changing along with the larger course of history. Similarly, *Star Wars* takes place against the rise and fall of a galactic empire, and – quite radically for a franchise aimed at children – offers a villain who turns out once to have been a hero with the potential for heroism again, later looping back to show the monster as an innocent child, delivering as the apparently spirited heroic climax of *Star Wars Episode 1: The Phantom Menace* (1999) young Anakin rescuing his friends by becoming the wholesale killer later known as Darth Vader.

There are still instances of one-off sequels, though it is rare for a follow-up to allow completion (*Young Guns 2*, 1990, comes close) or even circularity (*The Color of Money*, 1986, which closes with the line that usually opens sequels: "I'm back"). If there have been no threequels following *Ghostbusters II* (1989), *Predator 2* (1990) or *Speed 2: Cruise Control* (1997) it is as likely to be down to disappointing box office, key participants unwilling to return or a general sense that the moment has passed, as it is to any actual conclusion of overall narrative. There remain artistic and entertainment grounds for the production of sequels, but – as ever – the key factor in their apparent dominance of summer release schedules is commercial.

References

Corrigan, T. (1991) *A Cinema Without Walls: Movies and Culture After Vietnam*. New Brunswick, NJ: Rutgers University Press.

Hoberman, J. (1985) Ten years that shook the world, *American Film*, 10(8): 34–59.

King, G. (2003) Spectacle, narrative, and the spectacular Hollywood blockbuster, in J. Stringer (ed.) *Movie Blockbusters*. London: Routledge.

Neale, S. (2000) *Genre and Hollywood*. London: Routledge.

Schatz, T. (1993) The new Hollywood, in J. Collins, H. Radner and A. Preacher Collins (eds) *Film Theory Goes to the Movies*. New York: Routledge.

Tudor, A. (2002) From paranoia to postmodernism? The horror movies in late modern society, in S. Neale (ed.) *Genre and Contemporary Hollywood*. London: BFI.

Kim Newman

Continued from page 343

the ring can be put beyond use (timings here are from the "special extended" edition). *Return of the King* is singularly lacking in the kind of narrative redundancy widely used, even within single features, to ensure that essential plot material is spelled out, repeated, and usually repeated once again. The cycle is structured very much as a serial, to be consumed in sequence and/or with the narrative support of knowledge from the source text.

Most spectacular Hollywood productions are designed to function more strongly on their own one-off terms, even in the case of franchise-sequels and spin-offs from other media such as comic books or videogames. In general, the Hollywood economy is one in which as few as possible barriers to viewer comprehension are sought, especially in the blockbuster production that seeks the maximum possible combination of audience constituencies. *Lord of the Rings* and the later

Star Wars films are exceptions to this rule, accounted for by industry assumptions about the size of audiences for whom the projects would be pre-sold on the basis of existing familiarity with their respective fictional universes.

One-off spectaculars or more conventional entries in franchised series also display no shortage of conventional narrative matter. *Troy* is a useful example to consider here, not so much despite but because of what might be considered its rather trite and superficially "Hollywood" narrative focus. "Inspired" by Homer's *Iliad* it might claim to be, but *Troy* evidences much narrative material that is entirely standard Hollywood fare. Whatever spectacle it offers is framed less by a clash between allied Greek forces and those of Troy than by what are presented as individualized character traits and relationships. Not even so much the wooing away from home of Helen (now "of Troy") (Diane Kruger) and the excuse that gives Agamemnon (Brian Cox) to lead an assault on the Trojans, the film revolves around a small number of characters who fit conventional Hollywood movie modes. Central is the figure of Achilles (Brad Pitt), clearly marked as the biggest star in this not-quite-Homeric firmament. Achilles is figured here in a manner familiar from many Hollywood productions: an heroic "outsider" character of prodigious abilities, acting on the basis of his own values, judgements, loves and loyalties, rather than those imposed by any authority. The way this plays might easily be dismissed as "typical Hollywood nonsense", which, on one level, it might well be. Nonsense or otherwise, however, this is normal, perhaps even paradigmatic, Hollywood narrative territory. *Troy* mixes its spectacle with large dollops of familiar/conventional melodrama and sentimentality, as

do all of the other examples included earlier in this discussion. They devote as much running time to this kind of material as they do to the mounting of spectacle; partly, perhaps, because it is considerably less expensive, but also because it remains a key part of the aesthetic infrastructure. Some might want to criticize the "quality" of *Troy*'s narrative on this level, which is fair enough, as far as it goes. A distinction needs to be made, however, between quality of narrative and the fact that narrative – of whatever "quality" – still remains a central plank of the film. Less-than-inspiring narrative, combined with spectacle, sometimes seems to lead to a misleading and rhetorical assertion that it is somehow the "reliance" on considerable elements of spectacle that is in some way responsible for narrative qualities that are in fact more widely found across Hollywood's output.

Spectacular films also continue, just as much as any others, to mobilize thematic narrative patterns. They lend themselves very easily to modes of narrative analysis that focus on qualities such as thematic oppositions structured into cultural texts. Science fiction blockbusters can in very many cases be read at one level as explorations of tensions between qualities such as "the human" and the impact of scientifically based technologies or rationalities. It hardly needs stating that the *Star Wars* and *Lord of the Rings* films are structured around variously characterized oppositions between "good" and "evil", light and dark sides. The spectacular blockbuster, like other Hollywood products, can often be read as implicitly offering attempts to reconcile thematic oppositions, as part of the pleasurable fantasy they offer to viewers (for more on this, see King 2000).

But do spectacular films, especially blockbusters, offer any examples of deviation from the "classical" narrative norm? The answer to this question depends on what, exactly, is meant by the notion of "classical" narrative. It is easy to exaggerate the extent to which most Hollywood features have ever been quite as coherently structured, with everything motivated and every loose end tied up, as is sometimes implied in Bordwell's model (see, for example, Cowie 1998). The "classical" formula is best seen as an ideal type or tendency, rather than something to which most, if any, films rigidly adhere. Some spectacular blockbusters have a distinctly episodic narrative structure that has been linked with the serial format of the 1930s and 1940s, especially examples such as the original *Star Wars* (1977) and *Raiders of the Lost Ark* (1981), each of which draws explicitly on the serial tradition. Even where this is the case, individual episodes are drawn into larger narrative arcs, as Warren Buckland (1998) suggests in a case study of *Raiders of the Lost Ark*, and as is also clearly the case in the later *Star Wars* films

Continued on page 352

Titanic

Titanic is the *Gone with the Wind* of the contemporary Hollywood period. Directed by James Cameron and grossing a record-breaking $1.2 billion in its first year, the film is a blueprint for the term "blockbuster". Garnering 11 Oscars including Best Director and Best Picture, *Titanic* managed to fold into its *experience* "something for everyone" (experience is a much more apt term than "spectacle/narrative" for this ultimate "event movie"). The *Titanic* "experience" included not only the film itself but also spinoffs that ranged from soundtrack CDs to the recreation of the Heart of the Ocean diamond by jewellers. The film relied upon the already existing *Titanic* cult of collectors and buffs, and at the same time sought to captivate the imagination of teen audiences. It is the future as P.T. Barnum could have seen it, but although it might point the way for Hollywood to come, it is also something of a cinematic cul-de-sac – a dead end. Its success, its spectacular largesse, its economy of character development and its astounding cost ($200 million) act as contradictory ingredients. The effect was something akin to sublime in that the profits were as awe-inspiring as the risk was terrifying.

A cautionary tale of hubris in the industrial age, *Titanic* is the contemporary Hollywood version of the story of the unsinkable ocean liner that went down on its maiden voyage. The contradictory nature of the film's success begins with director and writer James Cameron's choice of subject. This story had been done before, many times. It was filmed twice in the same year as the disaster, 1912, as *In Nacht und Eis* by the German-based Continental Film Company and *Saved from the Titanic* (Éclair), which told the true story of Éclair star Dorothy Gibson's escape from the sinking ship. It was subsequently filmed in Germany (*Atlantic*, 1929), Britain (*A Night to Remember*, 1958), and in Hollywood in 1953 as *Titanic*. In many respects Cameron's version was homage to these earlier films, particularly *A Night to Remember*. However, the subject had never guaranteed box office success and, in the case of *Raise the Titanic* (1980), was an unqualified disaster. The combination of such an attractive subject and Cameron's reputation for high-octane action cinema (*The Terminator*, 1984; *Aliens*, 1986; *Terminator 2: Judgment Day*, 1991; *True Lies*, 1994), and his proven ability to make phenomenal successes out of expensive projects, generated rich pre-release publicity. A major source of star gossip was his casting of Leonardo DiCaprio in the role of Jack, the film's male romantic lead. This was the subject of considerable Internet interest, particularly on teenage fan Web sites, following DiCaprio's recent success as Romeo in Baz Luhrmann's *Romeo + Juliet* (1996), a surprise hit with young female audiences.

The technological development on the film was a source of considerable prerelease "talk", as the industry's most advanced technical research and development groups such as Industrial Light and Magic were involved in developing digital effects specifically for the film. Cameron also had an established interest in the marine technology used in his filming of the actual wreck, which is featured at the beginning and end of the movie. This combination of "real" science with virtual technology culminates when, at the film's conclusion, the actual wreck transforms, or digitally morphs, into a shiny spectacle of the ship it was when it set sail from Southampton in April 1912. There was also the specially built set in Baja Mexico where a three-quarter-scale model of the liner was built with hydraulic lifts and other mechanics, which assisted in the reenactment of the sinking in a manner that is generally recognized as historically accurate. The authenticity of the ship's detail was a topic of considerable concern on Cameron's part, not only as an aesthetic but also because he recognized the detailed knowledge of *Titanic* buffs, who were a sector of the potential audience for the film. The production and financing were also an epic tale in their own right, with Paramount capping its original backing for the film at $60 million for the US domestic rights, while Fox agreed to back the rest of the film's costs for the international rights (almost always less than the US receipts on any given film). Fox, however, did not cap its investment, which grew to around $140 million. *Variety*'s Todd McCarthy (1997) in his pre-release review of the films wrote: "Paramount's $60 million investment for US rights on a $200 million-plus production has to be one of the bargain deals of the century. Whether Fox can come anywhere nearer to break-even in the rest of the world than the *Titanic* did to New York is another matter." As it stood, the $1.2 billion recouped in the first year justified the expense for Fox.

The pre-release talk around the film is also reminiscent of the type of ballyhoo that surrounded *Gone with the Wind* and the search for Scarlett in the late 1930s. And like that behemoth, the story – well known to most of the audience prior to seeing the film – was a romance cast against momentous historical events. In *Titanic* the story of the sinking is framed by a present-day memory as told by 102-year-old survivor Rose DeWitt Bukater (Gloria Stuart). The film opens with actual footage of the *Titanic* resting at the bottom of the Atlantic, as a professional treasure hunter Brock Lovett (Bill Paxton) searches for the Heart of the Ocean, the largest diamond in the world, believed to have been lost on the ship. All he uncovers is a sketch of a nude woman with the diamond around her neck. Rose claims to know something about the diamond, so Lovett brings her in and asks her to "go back to the *Titanic*". On seeing the sketch, she reveals that she is the woman in the picture. The story then braids a cross-class romance with the true story of the sinking of the liner, drawing considerable strength from its deft linkage between the romance as a tale of a young woman's spiritual liberation and the ship's demise as the result of rich men's blind and self-serving arrogance. The ship and the young Rose (Kate Winslet) are introduced in the first sequence of old Rose's memory. This opens with a majestic crane shot, after a crucial shot-reverse-shot of a little girl looking first at the ship and then at the car from which Rose will emerge. The camera ultimately comes to rest on Rose, revealing her to be rich and unimpressed with the ship's size. Travelling with her fiancé, the villainous Cal (Billy Zane), whom she does not love, her impending marriage is revealed as her mother's strategy to avoid financial disaster and social humiliation. This is undermined by Rose's affair with Jack Dawson, a poor American artist returning from Paris. The ship's topography is used as a metaphor for class boundaries, from Jack being entertained in first class for rescuing Rose from an attempted suicide, to Jack taking her down to a party in steerage where predominantly Irish immigrants are dancing and playing jigs. (The Irish immigrant theme resonated through the popularized Celtic themes deployed in James Horner's score, reflecting a wider trend in popular music.) Perhaps thankfully, the ship hits the iceberg just as Jack and Rose have consummated their love in the back seat of a car in the storage area.

Once the ship's demise begins, the film's pace accelerates, and Jack and Rose's relationship works as an effective, if traditional, device to bring a human dimension to the disaster. The cutting back and forth between the historically accurate events of the ship's sinking and the attempt by Jack to find Rose, then Rose's attempt to rescue Jack, belong to the cinema of D.W. Griffith. Suspense devices are woven into well-known accounts of the sinking, from the return of Captain Smith to his post, to the band playing *Nearer My God to Thee*, and the engineers staying at their posts in the bowels of the ship to keep the lights on for as long as possible. The effect is that the romance plot is literally surrounded by the detailed accuracy of the *mise en scène*, augmenting the appeal to a younger audience as well as *Titanic* buffs. This structure, which guides multiple levels of engagement along the same narrative axis, reaches its climax in the roller-coaster aesthetic of the final plunge into the icy waters from the broken stern of the ship, an event that one of Brock's assistants has described at the beginning of the film. The work of *Titanic* is first to *describe* what happened and then, via the affective aesthetic of both big and loud effects and melodramatic pathos, to show how it *felt*.

The comparisons with Hollywood epics such as *Gone with the Wind* and the technique of Griffith made above were reflected in the reception of the film. Even in popular critical response the film's status as "post modern artefact" was either hinted at or explicitly stated. As Matthew Bernstein has noted:

> Enthusiastic viewers ... might see Cameron's' traditional storyline as a rejection of the cult of postmodernist senselessly thrilling, contemporary action films to which Cameron had contributed ... [while] the films' detractors could find *Titanic*'s juxtaposition of an unsatisfactory storyline with the ship's sinking to be a vivid example of the film's lack of aesthetic coherence and an unwitting embodiment of Hollywood's post-modern aesthetic. (1999: 25)

Titanic's layered address offers a kind of productive ambiguity that the classical Hollywood style was most successful in delivering. By enabling multiple levels of engagement, the film provides various points of attraction, from the romance plot to the accuracy of the china at the dinner scene and the mixture of real historical figures with fictional ones. This formal and stylistic strategy worked to bring an uncommonly diverse range of audience demographic to the film.

References

Bernstein, M. (1999) "Floating triumphantly": the American critics on *Titanic*, in K.S. Sandler and G. Studlar (eds) *Titanic: Anatomy of a Blockbuster*. New Brunswick, NJ: Rutgers University Press.
McCarthy, T. (1997) Titanic, *Variety*, 3 November. http://www.variety.com/index.asp?layout=Variety100&reviewid=VE1117339997&content=jump&jump=review&category=1935&cs=1.
Sandler, K.S. and Studlar, G. (eds) (1999) *Titanic: Anatomy of a Blockbuster*. New Brunswick, NJ: Rutgers University Press.

Michael Hammond

Continued from page 349

ınd *The Lord of the Rings*. And, as Cowie suggests, episodic narrative is nothing new to the Hollywood even of the "Classical" era.

Spectacular Hollywood is usually a close blend of spectacular and narrative-oriented ingredients. Spectacle may rival narrative in some cases. It might exert a considerable pull of its own in the attention it claims on the eye and its self-advertisement of its own qualities, large-scale or more impact based. But it is deployed in a manner subject equally to the pull of narrative dynamics. There may be occasions when particularly heightened moments of spectacle seem to interrupt ongoing narrative development, to put narrative on hold, as it were, while some grand vista or explosive impact is given centre-stage. But it is equally likely that spectacle works to support narrative, even to enact key moments of narrative development. This has always been the case in the history of Hollywood, the particular mix variable according to the circumstances of specific conjunctures. Just as the coming of sound or colour might initially have drawn more attention to these dimensions in their own right, the advent and development of CGI during the 1990s and the early years of the 2000s put a particular emphasis on certain forms of spectacle – in this case, primarily, the large-scale vista. But Hollywood has a habit of integrating new developments into its familiar regimes, making them part of a wider repertoire rather than radical changes or exclusive sources of attraction. It is in the nature of Hollywood as big business to offer *blends* of different qualities, in order to appeal to wide constituencies. This might apply to both the mixture of spectacle and narrative and the combination of different forms of spectacle. The large-scale vista and the impact aesthetic can work together, in partnership, or each might be given greater emphasis in particular generic or other territories. A variable mix of the two certainly makes sense in a broader economic context in which Hollywood profits are founded on a combination of the appeals of the specifically cinematic, big-screen, and the domestic, small-screen, experiences.

References

Bordwell, D. (1985) The classical Hollywood style, 1917–60, in D. Bordwell, J. Staiger and K. Thompson (eds) *The Classical Hollywood Cinema: Film Style and Mode of Production to 1960*. London: Routledge.

Buckland, W. (1998) A close encounter with *Raiders of the Lost Ark*: notes on narrative aspects of the New Hollywood blockbuster, in S. Neale and M. Smith (eds) *Contemporary Hollywood Cinema*. London: Routledge.

Cowie, E. (1998) Storytelling: classical Hollywood cinema and classical narrative, in S. Neale and M. Smith (eds) *Contemporary Hollywood Cinema*. London: Routledge.

Ellis, J. (1989) *Visible Fictions: Cinema, Television, Video*, rev. edn. London: Routledge.

King, G. (2000) *Spectacular Narratives: Hollywood in the Age of the Blockbuster*. London: I.B. Tauris.

King, G. (2002) *New Hollywood Cinema: An Introduction*. London: I.B. Tauris.

LaValley, A.J. (1985) Traditions of trickery?: The role of special effects in the science fiction film, in G.E. Slusser and E.S. Rabkin (eds) *Shadows of the Magic Lamp: Fantasy and Science Fiction Film*. Carbondale: Southern Illinois University Press.

By 1946 the studio system, which had prevailed in the previous two decades, had become less stable. At the end of the decade not only did the studios experience a slow decline in audiences; they also began to lose their hold over talent. Stars such as Bette Davis, Ingrid Bergman, Humphrey Bogart and John Wayne completed contracts with studios and became more independent, signing shorter-term contracts and/or venturing into profit-sharing deals. As the entire Hollywood industry went into a decline, such deals became more risky and the star as producer disappeared, only to reemerge later in the 1950s. However, it was solid evidence of the ability of star power to attract funding for films. As the ground for film financing began to shift, the agent emerged as a central figure in putting together "package deals". The package system was not entirely new as MCA (Music Corporation of America), which had an agency wing, had been engaging in this type of work for radio since the 1930s. Lew Wasserman is credited as making MCA the most powerful talent agency in the 1950s, gaining profit-sharing deals for their stars, putting package deals together with television, and establishing a relationship with NBC. At the same time this development of a powerbase in the industry that covered television, film and radio attracted the attention of the Federal Trade Commission (Lev 2003: 144). Ultimately MCA merged with Universal but, in order to satisfy federal regulations on unfair business practices, divested its talent agency interests in 1962. By that time, however, the package unit system was in place as the most common means of producing Hollywood films.

Two agents, Freddie Fields and David Begelman, who had worked for Wasserman at MCA, formed their own talent agency, Creative Management Associates (CMA). Focusing on a small list of high-profile and income-generating clients, CMA had become a major player in the industry by the early 1970s. A merger with Marvin Josephson Associates, which included another smaller talent agency, International Famous Agency, resulted in the formation of International Creative Management (ICM). By the late 1970s ICM rivalled the long-established, and largest theatrical agency William Morris. At the same time (1975), five former Morris agents (Bill Haber, Ron Meyer, Rowland Perkins, Mike Rosenfield and Michael Ovitz) formed another agency, Creative Artists Agency (CAA). By 1979, there were therefore three major agencies in place in the industry, which would dominate the process of packaging film projects for the next two decades.

While the package unit system took hold and talent came under the control of agents, the studios had shifted to distributing and financing, and were no longer able to generate projects. Agents took on the role that production departments in the studio system had held, and looked for productive combinations of ideas and personnel, presenting them, *de facto*, to the studios with a considerable percentage of the deal. This also changed the way films were conceived because it meant that often the star and director would be set before a script was decided on. The advantage for agents in this system was that their clients would fill the major roles. Peter Biskind quotes Frank Yablans, chief of production at Paramount who called the system "backward": "The package was put together before the movie was ready to get made. So the script became the slave to the process, rather than the other way around. It was a lazy man's way of making movies" (Biskind 1998: 281). The system was not as inflexible as Yablans intimates, however, and particular personalities such as Stan Kamen at William Morris, Ovitz at CAA and Fields and Sue Mengers at ICM established reputations for their ability to put deals together that resulted in successful projects. They were also able to sidestep blame for unsuccessful projects, particularly in the case of Kamen, who represented Michael Cimino as he made the financially disastrous *Heaven's Gate*. Such was the value of their knowledge that they brokered major deals for the high-profile acquisitions and mergers of studios, particularly in the case of Ovitz with the MCA/Universal and

Matsushita deal in 1991. High-profile players such as Ovitz and Fields were only two of a number of agents who moved into production, with Ovitz heading Disney and Fields leading Orion (Prince 2000).

Throughout the history of Hollywood it has been the personality and drive of the individual agent that have distinguished the most successful agents and in turn those agents have been central to the success of the established firms. This was the case with the rise of the agent in the post-1960 period and continues to be the case at present although the power of the larger agents may be undergoing change. Much of the recent history of agencies has been characterized by the poaching of agents with important client rosters from each other as well as clients. This was begun as a response in the late 1980s to the creation of smaller agencies such as InterTalent Agency (ITA). Established in 1988 by Bill Block with former CAA agents Judy Hoffland and David Greenblatt, this company ran for four years until Block left to take up a senior position with ICM. Hoffland moved to United Talent Agency (UTA), which had been formed in 1991 through a merger of the Bauer Benedek Agency and Leading Artists. In the words of Hoffland, who compared the structure of the agency with the production company Castle Rock, UTA was "an elitist, smaller, and truly an alternative agency [with] a strong writer- and director-based business, our list of actors makes for a formidable force" (Eller 1992). The template of the agent as dealmaker and producer continued throughout the 1990s and was the preferred mode of operation by agencies large and small.

Agencies also continued to structure themselves along the same type of horizontally integrated models as the media conglomerates. Endeavor, another high-profile smaller firm that began with the defections of key figures from ICM in 1995, built up its personnel to represent clients across the entire range of media and publishing, making deals with Internet companies such as Salon.com to assist in content development of ideas generated initially for the Internet and to "guide them to mainstream outlets" (Salon.com Press release). In more recent years there have been growing signs that the powerful agent as dealmaker along the lines of Michael Ovitz may be changing. One significant development in the organization of the industry has affected the way that agents operate. As the deregulation of the industry has taken hold, entertainment conglomerates and vertically integrated companies such as Time Warner or Fox have combined film companies, television networks, music and Internet divisions. This combination has meant that projects are just as likely to originate within the company. This has not had an effect on established agents such as Ovitz who moved into production, although his tenure at Disney was not seen as a successful but is having an impact on both new and established agencies. In the face of these large conglomerates where script decisions and long-term planning of careers and projects are increasingly being made, agents in the late 1990s up to the present have found it harder to exercise the same kind of control over projects and hence have been less able to ensure the level of control and participation for their clients. By 2001, *Variety* columnist Claude Brodesser ended an article that outlined the animosity that had grown between agencies in Hollywood with a word of warning: "this internecine clash is happening at a time when there are fewer opportunities for a broader base of clients". With the perpetual reorganization of the industry, the role of agents, characterized as major powerbrokers in the post-1960 period, is undergoing yet another significant readjustment.

References

Anonymous (2000) Salon.com signs on with Endeavor for representation in cross-media and convergence development. Press release by Salon.com, 12 April. http://www.salon.com/press/releases/2000/04/12/endeavor/.

Biskind, P. (1998) *Easy Riders, Raging Bulls: How the Sex 'n' Drugs 'n' Rock'n'Roll Generation Saved Hollywood.* New York: Simon and Schuster.

Brodesser, C. (2001) Agency animus: tenpercenteries re-ignite H'wood turf wars, 30 May. http://www.variety.com/article/VR1117800338.

Eller, C. (1992) Ex-ITA exec cut deal to move to UTA, *Variety*, 14 October. http://www.variety.com/article/VR101392.

Lev, P. (2003) *The Fifties: Transforming the Screen, 1950–1959.* Vol. 7 of *History of the American Cinema.* New York: Charles Scribner's Sons.

Prince, S. (2000) The talent oligopoly, in *A New Pot of Gold: Hollywood Under the Electronic Rainbow, 1980–1989.* Berkeley: University of California Press.

Michael Hammond

17

WHAT IS CINEMA TODAY? HOME VIEWING, NEW TECHNOLOGIES AND DVD

Barbara Klinger

FROM EARLY TWENTIETH-CENTURY nickelodeons and motion picture palaces to contemporary multiplexes, cinema's status as a medium has always appeared to be inextricably intertwined with its highly visible public presence in movie theatres. Certainly, for most of the medium's history, movie theatres had represented the primary exhibition site and a significant source of revenue for Hollywood studios. Even when television developed into a popular post-theatrical venue for Hollywood's wares in the post-Second World War era, the film industry gained only one-tenth of its total income from sales of its titles to the major networks, leaving the movie theatre's economic primacy intact (Gomery 1988: 83). However, this state of affairs began to change dramatically in 1975

with the introduction of cable television and the VCR to the consumer market and their subsequent growth into indispensable parts of the US entertainment universe. By 1986, revenues from film exhibition on basic cable and video each outstripped the theatrical box office in the United States; by the early 1990s, each took in more than double the amount earned from the big screen (Wasko 1995: 3). With the combined force of the theatrical box office and ancillary venues, the major studios earned more money from their films in 1987 than in any previous year (Gomery 1988: 83). This economic turn of events inevitably had ramifications for the medium and its viewers. Although the motion picture theatre still acted as the first-run showcase of the Hollywood feature, the 1980s heralded significant transformations in the sheer presence of cinema in everyday life. As Douglas Gomery remarked, between network television, cable, and video, the North American public at this time enjoyed "the greatest access to feature films in the medium's history" (1988: 83).

Through a succession of technologies, formats, and systems designed to deliver motion pictures to home viewers through television or the computer, developments in the 1990s and early 2000s have only expanded and intensified this access. As new compression technologies allowed more information to be "squeezed" onto cable wires, cable has become an even greater "tube of plenty", offering subscribers hundreds of digital channels, including numerous movie channels, pay-per-view services (in which, from a menu of options and for a fee, subscribers select a film that is then transmitted to them for a one-time viewing), and video on demand (a more flexible means of renting movies and other media that offers a selection of hundreds of titles and the ability to manipulate them with VCR-like functions). The 1990s also saw the continuing success of video and the ascendancy of home theatre (an entertainment centre with a large-screen or projection TV, A-V receiver, multi-channel Dolby surround sound, and a cluster of five or more speakers), DVD (Digital Video Disk, also known as digital versatile disk), direct satellite systems, Internet streams of feature films and shorts, and other advances that affected motion picture exhibition in the home.

This proliferation of options has cemented the home's standing as the most significant viewing space today for cinema in the United States. Not only do more audiences view motion pictures at home than at the theatre, but developments in new entertainment technologies continue to target households as crucial sites for media consumption. As theatrical exhibition amounts to just one-quarter of Hollywood's global revenues, the home's priority as an exhibition venue extends to worldwide markets as well (Miller et al. 2001: 8). Yet, although industry historians have recognized the extraordinary economic importance of the "domesticated" film, its aesthetic and cultural significance has otherwise received little sustained theoretical and critical attention. Scholarship in film studies is largely preoccupied with cinema understood implicitly as a celluloid medium designed for theatrical projection. As it challenges cinema's analogical base, digital technology has caused some debate over cinema's fundamental identity. However, because this debate continues to focus on first-run theatrical exhibition – specifically the growth of digital production and fully digitized theatres – cinema's extensive existence outside of the multiplex in surrogate forms such as video and DVD has remained relatively unexplored.

Although there is a growing body of writing on watching movies at home (see Walkerdine 1989; Corrigan 1991; Gray 1992), the field requires a more fulsome critical and cultural study of this exhibition context and the versions of films and modes of viewing that characterize it. The film industry's post-theatrical distribution practices and a cadre of new technologies have made Hollywood films into a national pastime, leveraging for them a place in the daily routines and rituals of viewers that is central to understanding not only how the medium is presented and consumed within the household, but what cinema itself means to contemporary audiences.

I would argue that, like the public sphere, the home is distinguished by an array of film

Continued on page 363

The term neo-*noir* (or *après-noir*) came to prominence in the late 1970s and 1980s to describe a new cycle of films, usually crime thrillers, generically "knowing" in their quotation of the styles and themes of 1940s and 1950s *film noir*. Often strung around a suspense narrative, neo-*noir* films frequently feature hard-boiled voiceovers, *femmes* or *hommes fatales*, sometimes switchback plots, and are usually set in urban locales. This heady mix has been augmented by a postmodern reflection on what it means to update *noir* tropes in a way that is relevant to late twentieth-century Western culture. However, *film noir* made during the studio period was not initially an industry category but was rather a term first used by French critics to designate a new style of filmmaking perceived in a disparate range of different types of 1940s films. Neo-*noir*, on the other hand, was a highly self-aware form, developed by baby boom filmmakers who grew up watching classic *film noir* (often on television). Neo-*noir* thus developed as both a homage to a beloved genre and a marketing device. It has arguably made a clearer case for thinking of the problematic term *film noir* as a genre that is secure enough in its identity to form neo-*noir*'s antecedent and foundation. As Foster Hirsch (1999: 4) writes, "The films made 'after noir' may well constitute the strongest case for noir as a genre."

Andrew Spicer (2002: 130–74) divides neo-*noir* into modernist (before *Body Heat*, 1981) and postmodernist (1981 onwards), the first phase including titles from Sam Fuller and the 1960s TV series *The Fugitive* onwards. Roman Polanski's *Chinatown* (1975) has also been identified as a watershed release, although it is perhaps the most celebrated of a cluster of *noir*ish texts released in the 1970s. Directed by an émigré European (entirely appropriate given *noir*'s rich heritage as a genre in which émigré filmmakers flourished), *Chinatown* is a hard-boiled detective story set in the 1930s but with significant differences – the apparent *femme fatale* (Faye Dunaway) turns out to be a victim, or what Spicer (2002: 92–3) calls a "good-bad girl", and the plot twist deals with incest, something that, if it had covertly infiltrated classic *noir* texts, would have been subject to prevailing censorship conventions. The same goes for explicit sexuality. Following changes in classification practice at the MPAA in 1968, and developments in permissible filmmaking practices outlined in the first two parts of this book, it became possible for scriptwriters, producers and directors to take greater liberties with sexual and violent (sometimes sexually violent) material on US screens. Indeed, sex and violence remain the stock-in-trade of many neo-*noirs* and all erotic thrillers. In 1978, James Damico designated *noir*'s key narrative hallmark as being when the hero meets with a "non-innocent woman … to whom he is sexually and fatally attracted" (1996: 103). Usually, the scenario turns out more fatal for the woman. Key neo-*noir* titles from the mid-1970s onwards were also able to render explicit that which had been implicit in classic *noirs*; while *Looking for Mr Goodbar* (1977) gave the story of a woman liberated onto the singles-bar scene a *noir*ish twist and a murderous conclusion (mixed with a funky 1970s soundtrack), *Eyes of Laura Mars* (1978) is the story of a photographer of sado-masochistic fashion spreads (Dunaway again) who discovers she has an occult psychological connection with a serial murderer of glamorous models. Both mix *noir*-horror with women-in-peril scenarios. Made a little earlier (in 1971), *Klute*, the dark story of a prostitute (Jane Fonda), a detective (Donald Sutherland) and a serial killer featured prominently in the pathbreaking collection *Women in Film Noir* (Kaplan 1998) for its contemporary reinflection of the *femme fatale*. A number of neo-*noirs* revisit this old staple, making sense of the *femme fatale* in light of the second wave of feminism and postfeminist thinking – key neo-*femmes fatales* or postfeminist good-bad girl hybrids include Linda Fiorentino in *The Last Seduction* (1994), Madeleine Stowe in *China Moon* (1994) and Gina Gershon in *Black and White* (1998). Another sexual reinvention came – sensationally – with William Friedkin's *Cruising* (1980), which developed what was to become a narrative staple of the erotic thriller, that of a cop going undercover in unknown sexual territory in order to solve a murder. Crucially (though to the accompaniment of vociferous gay protest at the time) *Cruising* gave this trope a gay twist even as it invented it. It also prefigured later protests against gay representations in *Basic Instinct* (1992), and a subgenre of 1990s movies featuring "queer couples who kill" (Aaron 1999).

The cycle took on a self-reflexive momentum during the 1980s, including films as diverse as *Blue Velvet* (1986), *No Way Out* (1987) and *Black Widow* (1987), all of which seem to know exactly what generic game they are playing with every self-consciously "dark and deadly" shot, as they deal out perversion, complicity or sexual compromise in various doses (see discussion of these films in Grist 1994). Dennis Hopper has said that he deliberately set out to make *The Hot Spot* – a sexy tale of double-cross featuring a fall guy and a *femme fatale* (performed with relish by Virginia Madsen) – in homage to the *noirs* he had loved as a child. This is also true of films that were marketed as erotic thrillers: when making *Basic Instinct* (1992), Paul Verhoeven and his cinematographer Jan De Bont pondered on "how can we do a *film noir* that is basically a *film noir* of the nineties", developing an equally uneasy but hyper-illuminated visual style not characterized by "black shadows on the walls" but "effectively countering the film noir style by making '*film clair*'" (Williams 2005: 241).

Through the 1980s and 1990s neo-*noir* developed as a loose umbrella term describing a range of different types, cycles and subgenres (though this discussion is confined to its prominence in US cinema, neo-*noir* has also been identified in a wide range of other national cinemas). It has done particularly well as a form at moments of heightened paranoia, and, like *film noir*, can be interpreted as a revealing symptom or cultural sore spot that bears out underlying anxieties about sexuality, identity, moral boundaries. As Spicer (2002: 140–2) points out, "noirishness" was strongly evident in the 1970s conspiracy movies of the age of Watergate (Coppola's *The Conversation*, 1974, Alan J. Pakula's *The Parallax View*, 1974, and *All the President's Men*, 1976). The political ambivalence of the moment is also discernible in slippery auteur-*noirs* like Friedkin's *The French Connection* (1971) and Scorsese's *Taxi Driver* (1976), the latter boasting a screenplay by Paul Schrader, who went on to write Scorsese's masculinity-in-crisis-*noir* *Raging Bull* (1980), and direct the proto-erotic thriller *American Gigolo* (1980). *Noir* has long been a vehicle for cultural anxiety, and during the 1980s and 1990s the form was a conduit for worries about the so-called feminist backlash (*Fatal Attraction*, 1987; *Sea of Love*, 1989; see Faludi 1992: 140–70), the US failure in Vietnam, and AIDS. Foster Hirsch (1999: 9) interprets the mixture of eros and thanatos in which neo-*noir* trades as a morality tale – or paranoiac warning – about sexual practices: "the traditional link in noir narratives between sex and catastrophe is no longer merely symbolic or moralistic," he argues. "[E]rotic thrillers of the 1980s and 1990s are metaphors for the dangers of sex in the time of AIDS. A simmering offstage 'noise,' like World War II in 1940s noir, AIDS is a significant structuring absence" (Hirsch 1999: 188–9). Sexual catastrophe thus replaces the historical trauma (which underpinned 1940s *film noir*) as a key social anxiety which animates neo-*noir*'s edgy relationship to sex.

Some of the form's most familiar titles also played with contemporary generic boundaries, allowing a mixture of influences to pervade the *noir*ish template. In fact, it is hard to find a genre in the 1980s and 1990s that was not inflected by *noir* in some way. *Red Rock West* (directed by John Dahl, who also made *The Last Seduction*, 1994, one of the most critically acclaimed erotic thrillers) and James Foley's *After Dark, My Sweet* (1990) are loose neo-*noir* Westerns, substituting chiaroscuro lighting and monochrome film stock for desert overillumination and colour, all the better to expose the existential "darkness" of *femme fatale* and fallen anti-hero. Other neo-*noirs* rework the hard-boiled/private eye template, focusing more upon problem solving and violence than sexual spectacle – *The Long Goodbye* (1973), *Farewell My Lovely* (1975), *The Big Sleep* (1978), *Night and the City* (1992) – part of a long list of remakes of classic *noirs* which also includes the erotic *noir*, *The Postman Always Rings Twice* (1981). Some of the best respected, and biggest award-winning films of the period also exploited this newly fashionable format, twisting *policier* or gangster templates in *noir*ishly reflexive ways (*Blue Steel*, 1990; *Romeo is Bleeding*, 1993; *Bodily Harm*, 1995; *Heat*, 1995; *The Long Kiss Goodnight*, 1996; *Bound*, 1996; *Mulholland Falls*, 1996; *L.A. Confidential*, 1997; *Palmetto*, 1998; *Sin City*, 2005). Horror-*noir* hybrids became box office successes and international award winners (*Silence of the Lambs*, 1991; *Se7en*, 1995; *Manhunter*, 1986, and its remake *Red Dragon*, 2002). A number of new black cinema films also drew on *noir* motifs, including the Hughes Brothers' *Dead Presidents* and Carl Franklin's *One False Move* (1992). Franklin's innovative mid-1990s neo-*noir*, *Devil in a Blue Dress* (1995), starring Denzel Washington as detective Easy Rawlins, and based on a novel by Walter Mosley set in 1940s Los Angeles, and Bill Duke's earlier *Deep Cover* (1992), starring Laurence Fishburne as a policeman, were lauded for putting "the *noir* back into *film noir*" (Dargis 1996: 38); *Deep Cover* was read as an existential exploration that "casts Stevens [Fishburne] adrift in an infinity of mirrors, where almost every character he sees peers back as a distorted version of himself" (Harkness 1993: 28).

Neo-*noir* traces are also discernible in genres that may seem remote from the original *noir* template – Ridley Scott's science fiction classics *Alien* and *Blade Runner* are shot through with *noir*ishness (and the latter is also a sci-fi detective story complete with 1940s-style android *femme fatale*). Neo-*noir* also gave birth to the subgenre of female revenge narratives, including *Fatal Attraction* (1987), *Single White Female* (1992), *Poison Ivy* (1992), and various "killer nanny" horror hybrids (*The Hand that Rocks the Cradle*, 1992; *The Guardian*, 1990). All are arguably the cinematic descendants of Clint Eastwood's *Play Misty for Me*, a prototype female-psycho movie, which effectively mixed suspense and sex in its reforming of the *femme fatale* and her male victim (although – as in so many of these films – the woman still gets punished in the end). Despite this endemic sexism, the genre has proved attractive to women directors – as well as Kathryn Bigelow's films (all of which could be read as inflected by *noir* to various degrees), Lizzie Borden directed *Love Crimes* in 1992 and Sondra Locke directed *Impulse* in 1990, both undercover cop stories, while Donna Deitch's *Criminal Passion* (1994) features the genre staple of a female cop falling for the suspect. There have also been parody/comedy *noirs*, knowingly ticking off generic hallmarks (Carl Reiner's *noir* spoof *Dead Men Don't Wear Plaid*, 1982, and his erotic thriller spoof *Fatal Instinct*, 1993). Perhaps the moment at which a form can be parodied is the moment it becomes most securely established.

If *Body Heat* was, for Spicer, the prototype postmodern neo-*noir*, it also arguably established a related genre: the erotic thriller. The steamy story of insurance fraud (and something of a remake of the 1944 classic *Double Indemnity*, featuring a definitive *femme fatale* performance from Kathleen Turner), it was one of the first titles to be referred to as a neo-*noir* in publicity material, and – in its explicit sex scenes – arguably the first film to be called an erotic thriller. This term gained currency throughout the 1980s, although in many ways the neo-*noir* film and the erotic thriller are overlapping forms. Both take their cue from the thriller tropes of *noir*, both understand that much of *film noir* involved sexual subterfuge (criminal scenarios are often predicated on desire). The erotic thriller developed as a hybrid genre that drew on softcore pornography as much as it drew on *noir*, and made the most of more relaxed attitudes to sexual explicitness on mainstream screens in the 1980s and 1990s, although the critical and theatrical failure of Verhoeven's *Showgirls* (1995), and the later

Virginia Madsen, *The Hot Spot*'s consummate *femme fatale*

election of George W. Bush, signalled the onset of a new puritanism in Hollywood (Williams 2004: 18–20).

Nevertheless, the erotic thriller was hugely successful – Palmer (1994: 168) calls it "perhaps the most popular genre in the 1990s", both as a healthily budgeted theatrical form (*Body of Evidence*, 1993; *Jade*, 1995; *Wild Things*, 1998) and as a direct-to-video low-budget genre. This prolific "lower" end of the marketplace produced some phenomenally successful titles: Jag Mundhra's *Night Eyes* (1990) cost $1 million to make and made $30 million. Other titles, particularly those produced by Walter Gernert and Andrew Garroni under the successful independent direct-to-video production label Axis International, and those directed by "genre auteurs" such as Gregory Hippolyte (aka Greg Dark), Jim Wynorski or Fred Olen Ray, include *Carnal Crimes* (1991), *Sins of Desire* (1993) and *Mind Twister* (1994). More recently *Playboy* has produced some more overtly softcore thriller titles under its Eros label. These direct-to-video erotic thrillers deploy *noir* stylings and criminal narrative pretexts, and often feature strong heroines, though their prime market objective is to provide softcore spectacle for young male home viewers.

Both neo-*noirs* and erotic thrillers demonstrated that in an era characterized by expensive blockbusters it was possible to make engaging, sometimes highly profitable, movies on relatively small budgets (*Fatal Attraction* and *Basic Instinct* were among the most lucrative films of their years). Both genres are far more narrative- and character-dependent than they are effects-dominated, sometimes requiring only a basic framework of decent script, convincing performance and appropriate location to get off the box-office blocks. This has made these related genres particularly appealing to independent producers working on a shoestring. Of course, neo-*noirs* and erotic thrillers can still be expensive, A-list commodities – Joe Eszterhas became one of the most powerful figures in Hollywood in the early 1990s when he was paid unprecedented sums (between $3 million and $4.7 million) for his scripts (Eszterhas 2004: 11). Nor does star power come cheap – the fees of genre regulars like Michael Douglas or Sharon Stone, in the case of the erotic thriller, or Al Pacino, Russell Crowe or Robert de Niro, in the case of more recent neo-*noir* thrillers, are high, often constituting the most significant costing in the *noir* budget.

After the 1990s these genres became the preserve of direct-to-video directors on the one hand and brand-name auteurs on the other. *Noir*ishly-inflected erotic thrillers were released by some of the most respected names in cinema, following a tendency that had developed in the 1990s for auteur-figures to turn to pulp fiction or exploitation themes and give them a high-end, bigger budget gloss. Such films include Atom Egoyan's *Exotica* (1994) and *Where the Truth Lies* (2005), Donald Cammell's *Wild Side* (1995, recut in 2000), Abel Ferrara's *The Blackout* (1997), Stanley Kubrick's *Eyes Wide Shut* (2000), Chen Kaige's *Killing Me Softly* (2001), David Lynch's *Lost Highway* (1997) and *Mulholland Drive* (2001), Adrian Lyne's *Unfaithful* (2002), and Brian De Palma's *Femme Fatale* (2003). Here Egoyan, Ferrara, Lynch, Lyne and De Palma were building on a long history of auteur experimentation with dark eroticism. Perhaps the most celebrated – or notorious – of recent neo-*noirs* was Jane Campion's foray into erotic thriller territory with *In the Cut* (2003), which took vanilla rom-com star Meg Ryan and threw her (often without clothes) into a hostile urban milieu of sexual self-discovery and dodgy policemen. At the same time, some movies that were originally branded neo-*noirs* were rebranded as erotic thrillers for their later DVD release. As Williams (2005: 24) points out, *The Hot Spot*'s 2003 US DVD jacket blurb describes it as "a torrid erotic thriller", but the trailer originally advertised it as "Film Noir for the 90s". Marketing terms go in and out of vogue – something called an erotic thriller may sell better to someone wanting to view it at home, where seclusion facilitates private sexual spectacle. Clearly in cases such as *The Hot Spot* (plenty of crime *and* carnality), one man's neo-*noir* is another man's erotic thriller.

References

Aaron, M. (1999) 'Til death us do part: cinema's queer couples who kill, in M. Aaron (ed.) *The Body's Perilous Pleasures*. Edinburgh: Edinburgh University Press.

Andrews, D. (2006) *Soft in the Middle: The Contemporary Softcore Feature In Its Contexts*. Columbus: Ohio University Press.

Damico, J. (1996) Film noir: a modest proposal, in A. Silver and J. Ursini (eds) *Film Noir Reader*. New York: Limelight, pp. 95–105.

Dargis, M. (1996) Devil in a blue dress, *Sight and Sound*, (January): 38.

Eszterhas, J. (2004) *Hollywood Animal: A Memoir*. London: Hutchinson.

Faludi, S. (1992) *Backlash: The Undeclared War against Women*. London: Vintage.

Grist, L. (1994) Moving targets and black widows: film noir in modern Hollywood, in I. Cameron (ed.) *The Movie Book of Film Noir*. London: Studio Vista, pp. 267–85.

Harkness, J. (1993) Deep Cover, *Sight and Sound Film Review*, (February): 27–8.

Hirsch, F. (1999) *Detours and Lost Highways: A Map of Neo-Noir*. New York: Limelight.

Kaplan E.A. (ed.) (1998) *Women in Film Noir*, 2nd edn. London: BFI.

Palmer, R.B. (1994) *Hollywood's Dark Cinema: American Film Noir*. New York: Twayne.

Spicer, A. (2002) *Film Noir*. Harlow: Pearson Education.

Williams, L.R. (2004) No sex please we're American, *Sight and Sound*, (January): 18–20.

Williams, L.R. (2005) *The Erotic Thriller in Contemporary Cinema*. Edinburgh: Edinburgh University Press and Bloomington: Indiana University Press.

Linda Ruth Williams

Continued from page 357

cultures, each characterized by a set of aesthetics, evaluative criteria, and pleasures. As Tom Ryall writes of the public film culture (initially quoting Siegfried Kracauer), it is: "'an intermingling of ideas and institutions into recognisable formations' ... constituted by the ideologies of film that circulate and compete in a given historical period and the forms in which such ideologies are institution-alised". These cultures are shaped, for example, by the discourses of newspapers, magazines, and media companies, including film studios, particularly as they generate bodies of concepts that help define film during specific historical moments. Film cultures tend to coalesce into recognizable formations, but they are at the same time "complex non-monolithic" entities, comprised of practices and institutions that may support, oppose, or provide alternatives to each other. Whatever the configuration, as an "ensemble of practices" the film culture provides a "crucial determining framework for the production and consumption of films" (Ryall 1986: 2).

By linking the concept of film culture, normally associated with the public sphere, to the private sphere, I mean not only to suggest the applicability of the term to the circumstances of domestic viewing but to qualify any strict sense of the home's insularity. The home similarly involves institutions, practices, and ideologies that mingle to produce formations that exert pressure on how Hollywood films are viewed there. Examining home exhibition provides insight into the active intersection in domestic space of various social forces, media industry discourses and technologies, films, and the practices of viewers as they respond to movies. Despite their private setting, home film cultures do not operate in isolation from the larger culture. They are intimately connected to society, as it shapes tastes and conventions of movie watching, negotiates ideas about consumerism, and defines identities pertaining to family, gender, race, and class. Moreover, as home film cultures are acted upon, they in turn act back upon society, making any hard-and-fast divisions between private and public difficult to maintain. Yet, as we shall see, even with such intricate affiliations, home viewing has distinctive characteristics that enable it to be distinguished from its theatrical counterpart.

To pursue more concretely the concept of home film cultures – how they are constituted and how they activate dynamics of reception – I turn to the case of DVD, an entertainment technology that has swept the United States, dethroning video in the process. I begin by considering the market forces that have supported DVD's phenomenal growth. Then I suggest the role that its technological capabilities (as they have been promoted by media industries, among other social agents) have played in shaping the dynamics of household film consumption.

The DVD invasion

Introduced in 1997, the DVD is considered "the hottest selling consumer electronics product in history" and, alternately, "the most successful home entertainment device in history". By 2004, the number of US households owning at least one DVD player skyrocketed from 0 to 50 per cent, making DVD's penetration of the home faster than any previous entertainment technology, including television, VCRs, CDs, and home computers. As another sign of DVD's preeminence in the market, in the first few months of 2004, American consumers spent $1.78 billion at the box office and $4.8 billion on buying and renting DVDs and videos, with DVDs representing the lion's share of this figure. In addition, an increasing number of films (some of the first were 2001's *The Fast and Furious* and *Training Day*) generate more revenue from their DVD release than from their first-run theatrical appearances (Flynn 2002: C4; Lyman 2002: A1, A13; Nichols 2002a: B21; Waxman 2004: B1, B8).

In charting DVD's ascendancy, it is clear that quality issues joined with economics to play a powerful role. In terms of quality, the rivalry between video and DVD has echoed that between the LP and CD in the music business. In this face-off, a more cumbersome analogue-based platter, subject to scratches and other forms of deterioration, was displaced by a smaller, digitally based technology boasting higher quality reproductions and less susceptibility to degeneration. Similarly, video – called "crap vision" by director James Cameron – lacked the resolution and clarity of the DVD image, meaning that DVD was much better suited to deliver the superior sound and picture promised by home theatre systems. Further, from its inception, DVD equipment could also play CDs, allowing it both to capitalize on the CD's success and provide a device that could perform double entertainment duty. Along these same lines, DVD drives quickly became a fixture in multiple popular technologies associated with digital quality in the realm of personal use, from laptop and desktop computers to gaming systems, such as Sony PlayStation 2. Thus DVD was advantageously positioned to become an intimate and indispensable part of a high-tech universe of home and personal technologies.

The falling cost of DVD players, from approximately $600 to $700 in 1997 to under $200 by late 2001 and under $100 by 2004, has made the devices more affordable across a broader spectrum of the public, adding another underlying cause for the seeming omnipresence of this new technology. Economic considerations have also inspired Hollywood studios and video vendors to embrace DVD. By the end of the 1990s, motivated by the possibility of new and improved profits, the major studios were all involved in releasing recent films, as well as their libraries, on DVD. It costs just over $1 per disc to produce a DVD – far less than the manufacturing cost of a VHS. Moreover, because of their quality and lack of degeneration in replay, DVDs were even more strongly identified with the sell-through market than their predecessor, meaning more money for the studios and distributors. Whereas at the height of video's popularity, consumers bought approximately five videos a year, by 2002 they were buying at least 15 DVDs annually (Lyman 2002: A13 and Nichols 2002b: B25). Of the 10 million copies of *Harry Potter and the Sorcerer's Stone* (2001; aka *Harry Potter and the Philosopher's Stone*) sold from May to June in 2002, for instance, almost 60 per cent were DVDs, while *Lord of the Rings: Fellowship of the Ring* (2001) sold 5.2 to 6.5 million copies its first week in rerelease, with VHS comprising only 1 to 1.5 million of these sales (Lyman 2002: A13; Waxman 2004: B8).

Some video chains, such as Blockbuster, hesitated initially to offer numerous DVD titles, but mom-and-pop stores moved quickly into this market, chiefly because DVD proved to be more cost-effective. While a new film cost vendors approximately $18 on DVD, the same title ran for $35 on VHS. For smaller operations, lower prices enabled them to have more copies of a popular title on their shelves, thus making them more competitive with the chains. Such prices had obvious benefits for consumer sales, but the lower wholesale rates also meant that vendors of all kinds needed fewer rentals to make a profit. Further, while videos degenerated and became dirty through multiple rentals and were thus less useful when it came time to sell overstocks, the more durable DVDs could be sold easily after a few weeks of rental. By 2001, major video chains, such as Blockbuster and The Movie Gallery, had accepted the new format, featuring numerous DVD titles on their shelves. A year later, several major chain stores, including Borders Books and Music and Circuit City, announced that they would no longer carry prerecorded videocassettes, opting to sell only DVDs. Many commercial video vendors around the nation began relegating their video collections to increasingly dustier corners of their shops, while VCRs occupied increasingly smaller amounts of shelf space in the electronics sections of retail establishments now devoted to DVD players and other digital goods. Meanwhile, all-DVD Internet-based rental companies, such as Netflix, have sprung up and achieved great success with millions of subscribers.

Through the imprimatur of digital quality and economic incentives, DVD has thus suited the interests of electronics firms, Hollywood studios, video vendors, and consumers. With its prominent place in the market, DVD, not surprisingly, has begun to affect the way movies are watched in the home. As a relative of video in its playback capacities and concentration on Hollywood films, DVD raises similar issues about home film cultures while, because of its superior technical capabilities, further redefining how movies are offered to and experienced by home viewers.

DVD culture

Certainly home film cultures are characterized by the manner in which identity issues are constructed and acted out in the household. As empirical studies of television, the VCR, and other entertainment media have shown, family dynamics, gender, race, and class negotiate the way that any new medium will be deployed in domestic space.[1] Understanding that discussions of home film cultures must ultimately come to terms with such issues, these cultures can also be distinguished through other ensembles of practices. In what follows, I sketch some of the industrial and technological forces involved in the creation of DVD film culture, focusing on how these forces have contributed to and shaped the non-theatrical reception of films. Film cultures are comprised of overlapping and competing discourses; so my aim is not to produce a unified, coherent, or exhaustive account of this particular culture. Rather, I wish to identify some of its central features to engage the questions DVD raises for film theory, criticism, and history.

1. The techno-aesthetic

In some ways DVD offers the closest contemporary approximation of a public film culture of yore, when, in the post-Second World War era, cinephiles could partake freely of foreign films made by directors such as Fellini, Bergman, and Antonioni at their local art houses. Today, through services like Netflix, one can find art films and esoterica (such as Mario Bava's *Hercules in the Haunted World*, 1961) that would perhaps be most attractive to *cinéastes* and film buffs, allowing viewers access to cinema that provides an alternative to Hollywood and thus might be hard or impossible to find in the multiplex or on cable TV.

However, DVD has also inspired an aesthetic more directly beholden to its technical features. With its splashy presence in special effects films and in theatre sound systems, digital technology has become synonymous with quality sound and image reproduction. Along with the CD, home theatre, HDTV, and other developments, DVD is part of a home-based digital universe connected to a "high-tech" aesthetic that presumes the superiority of digital machines to their analogical counterparts and marvels over the advances of computer-age wizardry.

As part of a home theatre system, DVD, particularly widescreen DVD, appears capable of delivering cinema in a way that approximates the image and sound quality of the theatrical situation. In its ability to approach the cinematic experience, DVD begins to erode assumptions concerning the aesthetic debasement films are subject to in non-theatrical exhibition venues where they might be, for example, panned-and-scanned for cable broadcast. But more important, media industries, consumer magazines, and other sources sell DVD as one of the offspring of the so-called digital revolution, portraying it as an almost aristocratic medium. That is, the high-tech aesthetics propagated by these sources extend the label of aesthete to mainstream consumers: everyone can ascend to the level of audiophile or cinephile. As DVD is defined through an aesthetic based on technological knowledge, spectators who possess or pursue this knowledge become connoisseurs, while films are grasped through their ability to realize or disappoint the standards of digital excellence. So, for example, a reviewer assesses the DVD soundtrack for Brian De Palma's *Mission Impossible* (1996) as able to render, unlike the video version, the absolute quiet necessary for the vault sequence, while the glass breaking/deluge of water restaurant scene, by employing all of the surround sound speakers, realizes the full potential of the audio system. By contrast, the soundtrack for the Martin Lawrence comedy *Blue Streak* (1999), with its sound effects "thrown around wherever possible", is "loud, brash, and ultimately ... unappealing" (Total DVD 2000: 56–7).

Since the techno-aesthetic as purveyed by media industries attempts to shape viewing as a mode of privileged consumption and the film itself as a set of technological coordinates measured against expectations of digital quality, we might ask how the aristocratic mien attached to digital technologies constitutes home taste cultures that compete with, replace, or complement existing modes of media consumption. Further, since "domesticated" films have always existed in an inter-media environment by virtue of their exhibition via TV, DVD's placement in home theatre raises questions about cinema's relation to other media in the realm of reception. Questions for future research include:

- How is the film experience affected by associations with television and audio-technologies that have already established certain modes of viewing and listening?
- How have standards of theatrical cinema and the reputation of digital technology further affected or transformed these relations, as well as the manner in which home viewers watch films?

2. "Remote" viewing

As one of the most distinctive features of home media, the remote control represents a way of engaging movies impossible in a public cinema, where a film unspools continuously from a projector run by unseen hands or automated processes. With more precision than the VCR, the DVD remote allows significant manipulation of a film during viewing. In addition to fast-forward, rewind, step, and pause capabilities, the viewer can search a film by chapters, accurately pinpointing a target moment or scene.

A prevailing argument about this kind of flexibility in home viewing is that it gives viewers unprecedented power over media products, allowing them to circumvent the designs of the media industries and manipulate the narrative to their own ends (Cubitt 1991; Jenkins 1992). This kind of flexibility is evident, but the remote's impact on film consumption bears further scrutiny. Audience research conducted with university students shows that one potent use of the remote is to take viewers to a film's "high points".[2] That is, viewers fast-forward to or replay the funniest jokes in a comedy, the most romantic scenes in a romance, the most adrenaline-producing moments in an action film, or the musical numbers in a musical, locating scenes that deliver the essence of the film's generic identity. In this way, the remote facilitates a kind of intervention in the consumption of genre films, in which the film becomes the moments that crystallize its generic identity.

By allowing spectators to bypass the narrative, this intervention does not defy so much as confirm and extend film industry philosophies and practices. Home cinema plays a strategic role in the circulation of genre films, insofar as the use of the remote control foregrounds moments of essential generic spectacle, set pieces that fulfil the industry's and genre film's contract with the audience. The hypostatization of genre that occurs through this device helps promote the importance of spectacle over narrative, a long-standing hierarchy in Hollywood's credos of film production. While

viewers often attend films in theatres on the basis of generic expectations prompted by the industry's promotional apparatus and wait during the screening for moments of generic "pay off", DVD provides the opportunity to cut literally to the chase. Through the precision of the remote search features, viewers may forgo narrative elements that precede or follow an elaborate action scene, for example, to immerse themselves in the excitement and pleasures offered by definitive generic moments.[3] Thus, while the remote allows myriad ways of engaging with cinema that interfere with the inexorable linear flow spectators are subject to in theatres, it can also be deployed as a means of heightening and luxuriating in cinematic ideologies that are an intimate part of Hollywood's filmmaking ethos.

3. Special editions

Through ever-increasing numbers of ancillary channels, films are subject to multiple rereleases ... including special editions that contain a panoply of extras. These editions offer features that range from behind-the-scenes documentaries, trailers, and out-takes to commentary by directors, screenwriters, and actors. Video and laser disc were initially identified with the special edition, but it is now regarded as the province of DVD. In fact, DVD has made extras such an intimate and expected part of a film's reappearance that it would be hard, for example, for fans of *The Matrix* (1999) to imagine it without facts about how its digital special effects (especially "bullet time") or the choreography of its fight scenes by Hong Kong master Yuen Wo Ping were accomplished. Given DVD's economic power and the ability of its extra features to augment the film experience, some industry pundits contend that DVD has challenged the primacy of theatrical cinema, making a film's initial big-screen release, "little more than a preview trailer for the subsequent purchase of the DVD" (Lyman 2002: A13).

On the one hand, special editions stimulate intriguing questions about authenticity (particularly the "director's cut", an edition that claims to restore the filmmaker's original vision). If the DVD version supplies footage excised from the theatrical release because of studio interference or censorship, for example, is it more authentic than the "corrupted" big-screen version – especially if it realizes the director's intentions? Given the multiple versions of a film that may exist in such contested cases of release (such as Terry Gilliam's *Brazil*, 1985) or that may arise over time through restorations (such as Fritz Lang's *Metropolis*, 1927, and Hitchcock's *Vertigo*, 1958), how do we decide which is the "real" film? Reissues become more interesting for study as each new version becomes part of a film's life story that reveals the terms of its cultural revival and historical circulation.

On the other hand, DVDs have had a substantial effect on film culture in both private and public spheres, especially for younger audiences attracted both to blockbusters and technology. Viewers are increasingly aware of the director's intentions through "behind-the-scenes" information provided by the DVD's producers. By presenting data that help unlock a film's techniques and meaning, media industries enhance the importance of the director's words in shaping the film's significance and encourage viewers to consider themselves as members of a cognoscenti. As they provide audiences with access to apparently privileged information, media industries cultivate enthusiasts and, ideally, increased markets for their wares. In the process, DVD remobilizes discourses of authorship, foregrounds the magic of Hollywood and, once again, positions viewers as film experts. Add to these characteristics that DVD rivals the quality of celluloid pictorially and aurally, while generating discourses of authenticity and producing immediate intertexts (in the form of extras) that help shape interpretation, this technology represents an interesting area of friction for film theorists and critics who focus on cinema as a theatrical medium.

4. Alternative canons

Films that appear at the top of video/DVD rental and purchase charts are often blockbusters. The home market can echo theatrical patterns, expanding the domain of films that have seen massive success in the United States and abroad. However, an alternative canon of films – films that become particularly successful in video or DVD – has also emerged. As Douglas Gomery reports, for example, neither action blockbuster *Die Hard* (1988) nor critical favourite *Rain Man* (1988) was the top video rental in 1989; instead, it was the zany comedy *A Fish Called Wanda* (1988), a film that had seen only modest success at the box-office (Gomery 1992: 288). Similarly, *Austin Powers: International Man of Mystery* (1997) had a lacklustre big-screen debut, but gained such a substantial video audience that it generated sequels *Austin Powers: The Spy Who Shagged Me* (1999) and *Austin Powers in Goldmember* (2002). Films that have become surprise mega-hits on DVD include Mike Judge's satire *Office Space* (1999) and the Will Ferrell comedy *Old School* (2003).[4]

A Fish Called Wanda and *Office Space* are among a breed of films that attained a "cult"

Continued on page 372

As the first ever full-length, computer-generated, animated film, *Toy Story* (1995) was a landmark of cinema history, and one of the biggest box office successes of the 1990s. The product of the marriage of Pixar Animation Studios and Walt Disney Studios, both *Toy Story* and its critically acclaimed sequel *Toy Story 2* (1999) can be discussed on a number of levels, but are perhaps best read in terms of the industrial and the textual tales that they tell. In their Web-based mission statement Pixar state that their industrial framework is intimately interconnected with the kinds of films produced:

> Pixar's objective is to combine proprietary technology and world-class creative talent to develop computer-animated feature films with memorable characters and heart-warming stories that appeal to audiences of all ages. (http://corporate.pixar.com/pverview.cfm)

Film historians are right to read these films – as well as the other products of the Pixar/Disney alliance (*A Bug's Life*, 1998; *Monsters, Inc.*, 2001; *Finding Nemo*, 2003; *The Incredibles*, 2004 and the forthcoming *Cars*, 2006) – as marking a new phase in family entertainment, digital innovation – and profit opportunity.

Pixar Animation Studios originated as a hardware-development division of George Lucas's Lucasfilms Ltd but, on gaining its independence from Lucas's visual industry empire in 1986, it specialized in software animation and other systems, and the development of new creative projects. Pixar and Disney signed two agreements in the 1990s, the second (in 1997) sealing their collaboration on five movies, the last of which will be *Cars* in 2006. John Lasseter, one of Pixar's founding members and an executive vice-president, had worked as an animator for Disney before helming numerous award-winning early shorts, which put Pixar on the map in the late 1980s and early 1990s. He then went on to direct *Toy Story*, *Toy Story 2*, *A Bug's Life*, and *Cars*, and also receives executive producer credits on Hayao Miyazaki's pathbreaking Japanese animations *Spirited Away* (2001) and *Howl's Moving Castle* (2004). But it was *Toy Story* that broke the mould, garnering Lasseter a Special Achievement Academy Award. Where Disney's *Snow White and the Seven Dwarfs* showed that there was a market for full-length animated features in 1937, *Toy Story* showed that these could be digitally generated in a way which was both realistic and visually innovative, giving characters (and their backgrounds – the environments they inhabit) a kinetic three-dimensionality unattainable with traditional hand-drawn cel animation (which often feature moving characters against still, painted scenery). Paul Wells (1998: 180) calls Buzz and Woody, the "stars" of the various *Toy Story* outings, "neo-cartoon characters"; Lasseter's achievement is that he "combines the characteristics and comic structure of the cartoon form with the multiplicity of possibilities in the construction of material contexts made available by computer animation" (Wells 1998: 180).

All this, as reviewers of both films were quick to point out, would be nothing without some engagingly clever and affecting narratives. In the first film, Woody, a rather old-fashioned cowboy doll voiced by Tom Hanks, leads the assorted toys in Andy's bedroom, all of whom become animated when Andy isn't looking (as all children know, toys come alive at night). As Leslie Felperin (1996: 65) points out, toys have been the subject of animations since the 1898 stop-motion film *The Humpty Dumpty Circus*, but toys here also get into scrapes with which any human could identify. Andy gets a Buzz Lightyear Space Ranger for his birthday (voiced by Tim Allen), who threatens to supplant Woody as chief toy (he is equipped with more gadgets and buttons than the pull-string Woody), and who genuinely believes he is not a toy but a real astronaut (a delusion beautifully developed in *Toy Story 2*'s *Star Wars* skit). This identity confusion leads to some fascinating exchanges between Woody and Buzz, opening up

Toy Story

a more complex analysis of the existential state of toydom than a children's movie ever needs to, contributing to *Toy Story*'s popularity among adult audiences. When Buzz is kidnapped by the evil boy next door (Sid), Woody overcomes his feelings of jealousy, rescues Buzz, and, via a series of astonishing action-adventure sequences, the pair become partners, not rivals. Randy Newman's iconic song *You've Got a Friend in Me* seals *Toy Story*'s generic identity as an animated buddy movie.

Toy Story 2, widely lauded (like *The Godfather Part 2*) as one of the few sequels that turn out even better than the original (and *Toy Story* was a hard act to beat), is a rather more complex tale, pulling off an amazing combination of intellectual and emotional intricacy, fast-paced narrative thrills and spills, and visual bravado. In its bid to please both parents and their children, it manages to be clever in a postmodern, adult-friendly way, yet still searingly touching. The knowing nods to adult culture do not make it any less of a children's film, and certainly don't hold back the action. Again the story is about – as Paul Wells (2003: 99) puts it – "toys resisting their own obsolescence"; Kim Newman likens them to *Blade Runner*'s replicants, as they confront the difficult idea that they are "only 'alive' so long as they can retain the attention of their quixotic owners" (Newman 2000: 57). In *Toy Story 2* it is Woody who is kidnapped, by a man (voiced by Wayne Knight) who recognizes his value as a collector's item rather than a plaything. It transpires that Woody is a rare vintage toy, famous star of *Woody's Roundup*, a 1950s TV show, and part of a gang comprising of Jessie the Cowgirl (Joan Cusack), Stinky Pete the Prospector (Kelsey Grammer) and Bullseye, the faithful horse. The avaricious collector plans to make a profit selling the four of them as a set to a Japanese toy museum. Woody both resists and is drawn to the notion: "This is effectively a choice between the temporary pleasures of being loved, played with and ultimately abandoned by a child – a story heart-rendingly played out through Jessie's song, 'When you

[she] loved me' – and the immortality of preservation without use" (Wells 2003: 100). Of course, Woody makes the right choice emotionally, aided by his friends from Andy's room who – led by Buzz – come to rescue him. In yet another virtuoso climactic sequence, Woody escapes the plane to Japan, Stinky Pete – who actively *wanted* to become a museum piece – is palmed off on a little girl at the baggage collection (making him finally face up to his fate as a toy), and Woody takes Bullseye and Jessie with him to become new and loved members of Andy's room. But Pixar films are never over until they're over. In what has come to be a house trademark, fictional "out-takes" from the supposed live action filming of the movie play across the end credits, featuring Buzz, Woody *et al.* (and – in *Monsters, Inc.* – Mike and Sully) out of character, appearing as the "stars" or jobbing actors that they are, fluffing their lines and playing on-set practical jokes. This entertainingly surreal postmodern wraparound undercuts any schmaltz the film's sentiment may have promoted but also belies the vast amount of work that went into each film frame on a complex project like a Pixar movie (*Toy Story* was four years in the making; longer, if you count the development of the script and the technology upon which it relies).

Both *Toy Story* and *Toy Story 2* have been hugely successful, spawning a range of ancillary products (toys as well as videos and DVDs), plus the spin-off TV and direct-to-video series *Buzz Lightyear of Star Command* (2000, made for video, TV and in game form; *Toy Story 2* was itself originally destined to be a direct-to-video film). Pixar's Web site makes useful reading for anyone interested in recent US cinema at its most outrageously financially successful, listing as it does the numerous broken records notched up by its titles (for example, new records for opening weekend figures coming with each new feature film; *Finding Nemo* as the eighth highest grossing film of all time and, in 2004, the top-selling DVD of all time). It also underlines the synergistic truth of all merchandise movies in the contemporary period: "Such revenues are derived from marketing campaigns surrounding the theatrical release of the animated film, which, in turn, drive demand for home videos, television, toys, and other film-related merchandise." The *Toy Story* franchise missed no opportunities in this area, and Buzz, Woody and related products continue to sell well. Here again the industrial and the textual must be read together, since the sophisticated postmodern awareness of the marketplace displayed in particular by the script of *Toy Story 2* has meant that its toy "stars" also seem to "know" their function in the toyshop. As Tour Guide Barbie says when she takes Hamm, Mr Potato Head and Slinky through the Buzz Lightyear aisle on their navigation of the toystore, "Back in 1995" (the year of *Toy Story*'s release) "short-sighted retailers did not order enough toys to meet demand" (referring to a real marketplace phenomenon that followed the understocking of Buzz Lightyears in real toyshops). This is not the only nudge at the toy industry: Newman (2000: 57) argues that the fact that Barbie is represented here as particularly airheaded is Pixar's revenge against Mattel, who refused to license her to appear in the first *Toy Story* but let her have a cameo in *Toy Story 2* because they recognized the first film's success. Of course, however much they may joke about toy stores, the producers also know that they have here a product ready-made to walk from the screen into the store and then past the checkout into a child's bedroom. When Woody flops back into toy mode as Andy enters the room in the movies he looks just like the "real" Woody toy a child may own, reinforcing the notion that he just *might* come alive when you're not looking. Woody and Buzz toys also speak with the voices of the actors who play them, reinforcing the way in which toys here seem to cross the line between character, star and product (an area explored by Wells 2003). The proposed narrative of *Toy Story 3*, slated for release in 2008, revolves around the product recall of a faulty Buzz to his Taiwan factory, promising to develop this canny awareness of marketplace foibles.

References

Felperin, L. (1996) Toy Story, *Sight and Sound*, (March): 65–6.
Newman, K. (2000) Toy Story 2, *Sight and Sound*, (March): 56–7.
Wells, P. (1998) *Understanding Animation*. London: Routledge.
Wells, P. (2003) To affinity and beyond: Woody, Buzz and the new authenticity, in T. Austin and M. Barker *Contemporary Hollywood Stardom*. London: Arnold, pp. 90–104.

Linda Ruth Williams

Continued from page 368

status in ancillary circulation, demonstrating that home taste cultures can stray from blockbuster hegemony. This does not mean that such occurrences necessarily undermine business as usual. Studios have produced and distributed many of these films; their success in whatever venue becomes a means of further lining the industry's coffers and generating revenue that feeds its blockbuster habit. As the examples of the original *Austin Powers* and the more recent *The Bourne Identity* (2002) suggest, ancillary success may directly affect production, leading to the creation of a sequel or a franchise. The fact that home and public film cultures are intertwined economically suggests that the taste cultures produced within each sphere likewise have the capacity to interact and influence one another. While this reciprocity must be acknowledged, it remains important to reckon with the proliferation of film canons that exist in popular culture, not only as they exist beyond academe's ivory towers, but, at least for a period of time, as they demonstrate that box office figures and the audience's penchant for big-screen blockbusters tell only part of the story.

5. Film collecting

Once the domain of a specialized cadre of devoted *cinéastes* who acquired films on 16 mm, video and DVD have witnessed the democratizing of this activity, now shared by millions of film buffs and "regular" moviegoers alike. Contemporary film collecting has been stimulated by the success of the studios' "sell-through" strategy (that is, their decision to offer titles for sale in the home market in the $20 rather than the $100 range). According to Robert C. Allen, "Between 1983 and 1992, the number of feature films priced for sell-through increased at an average annual rate of 52 per cent, from 59 million copies to 264 million." Beginning in 1992, the sell-through market for video surpassed the theatrical take. In 1996, domestic box-office revenue totalled $5.9 billion, while consumers rented $8.7 billion worth of videos and bought $7.6 billion pre-recorded tapes (Allen 1999: 11 and Komiya and Litman 1990: 41).

With prices averaging around $20, DVD has been especially groomed for "sell-through", while its superiority to video has enhanced its appeal to collectors. Industry figures that reveal the titles of best-selling DVDs – typically children's films and/or blockbusters – suggest that the tastes of the major audiences for these films, respectively, families and young men, are centrally involved in the circulation of films in the home. However, home film collecting raises other considerations as well. Most films crossing the threshold of a personal library will enter into a system of classification. Far from being completely idiosyncratic, such systems are influenced by multiple sources, from video and DVD vendors and the media industries to academe. As James Clifford notes of personal collections in general, "The collection and preservation of an authentic domain of identity cannot be natural or innocent ... inclusions in all collections reflect wider cultural rules – of rational taxonomy, of gender, of aesthetics" (1993: 52–3). Any kind of collecting – stamps, war souvenirs, art, books, toys, etc. – is affected at the very least by notions of value, systems of classification, and other frameworks utilized by larger cultural provinces and institutions. Thus, a home collector might arrange films by period, genre, nation, director, studio, or actor, demonstrating familiarity with procedures of arrangement employed by other institutions, again indicating the pervasive presence of the public in the private.

Collecting strategies also bear on the worth and meaning a film has for its home audiences (Tashiro 1997: 11–18 and Dinsmore 1998: 315–26). A collector's selection of particular artefacts may be shaped by the perceived value those artefacts have acquired as classics, rarities, and other marketable categories. Moreover, through the accompanying background materials it furnishes, the collector's edition (e.g., the "definitive" version of *The Wizard of Oz*, 1939) provides the sense of authenticity and history so important to establishing an archival object's worth. The impact of this contextualization is also revealing in the case of the reissue of older films: these films must be transformed in some way to suit contemporary consumers. To produce the necessary makeover, collectors editions engage in historical revisionism, reframing the social contexts in which older films once circulated, redefining their meanings, and, in many cases,

digitally remastering their image and sound. Hence, through procedures of selection and classification and strategies of updating old films, the enterprise of collecting represents yet another part of home film culture that muscularly animates film meaning and significance.

6. Repetition

Although younger viewers return ritually to see blockbusters on the big screen, repeated viewing is a cornerstone of movie playback in the home. Public and private film cultures are connected in this regard, yet home film culture's almost synonymous relationship with repetition, coupled with its audience's ability to view a title again at any time, raises the issue of how this dynamic influences and transforms the movie experience in a particularly striking way.

Committed repetition (stemming from a strong desire to view a specific title multiple times) allows the film to become an intimate part of the viewer's daily life and a fixture of his or her emotional landscape. In this regard, among its other effects, repetition produces an inevitable relationship with nostalgia. Like the re-encounters more familiarly associated with popular songs (or, in literary circles, with Proust's madeleine), seeing a film again triggers a flood of impressions from the past that illuminate moments from one's history with unexpected vividness. As certain repeated films enter the personal register, they provide landmarks within autobiographies, points of orientation to the past and the present, engendering a kind of time travel. Small screen films thus attain a significant relation to memory and hence to memory studies. As Annette Kuhn argues,

Memory work presents new possibilities for enriching our understanding not only of how films work as texts, but also of how we use films and other images and representations to make our selves, how we construct our own histories through memory, even how we position ourselves within wider, more public, histories. (1995: 39)

Within the framework of memory and nostalgia, home cinema provides an opportunity to investigate film's relationship to subjectivity and history, enlarging our sense of film's affective and ideological operations in daily life.

The repetition of certain film titles also has ramifications for group identity. Repetition often takes on a ritual function, confirming a group's solidarity, while demonstrating its difference from other, perhaps more mainstream, taste cultures. A recent instance of this is the popularity among US African-American rappers of Brian De Palma's Cuban gangster epic, *Scarface* (1983). Lambasted by many critics in its first run, the film found new life in ancillary exhibition: its display of the excessive luxuries available in American life to racial minorities, as well as its depiction of graphic violence and drug use, gave it cult status.[5] This example suggests that looking at a film or films canonized by certain social groups as especially repeatable provides another view of how influential taste hierarchies are established in the home. Further, as it occurs through social dynamics unforeseeable by the film's producer, the ritual embrace of a title in its post-theatrical life vividly shows that what happens outside of the motion picture theatre is key to a robust understanding of a film's cultural and ideological significance.

Conclusion

We should view the aspects of DVD film culture that I have examined as part of a complex chemistry of factors bearing on domestic viewing. This culture helps comprise, but does not exhaust, what David Morley refers to as the "social architecture" of the viewing experience in the home – that is, the impact that multiple contexts within the household have on how media are consumed (1995: 170–1). However, by entertaining, even in a preliminary way, the impact that media industries, technological capabilities, and viewing strategies related to DVD have on the reception of films in the home, we can see that the domestic environment elicits forceful reconstitutions of film meaning, while it continues to articulate cinema's cultural role and relationship to viewers beyond the big screen. As cinema exceeds the four walls of the theatre, it attains its most encompassing presence in everyday life, a presence essential to understanding its definition and future as a medium.

Notes

1   Television studies has been the site of the richest work on the impact that family relationships and/or gender have on viewing. Some of the canonical works on this subject include Ang (1985); Morley (1986); Morley (1992, especially pp. 221–69), and Silverstone and Hirsch (1992).

2   This finding comes from surveys that I conducted in 2000 with 350 university students about their film-viewing habits at home, particularly in relation to their use of home entertainment technologies.

3   The remote may also be used in other ways to affect movie consumption. Survey results suggested that as film purists in the home insist on watching a feature film from start to finish without the interference of the remote, they may deploy

theatrical standards of viewing. To such viewers, the remote in these circumstances is anathema, a concession to distracted modes of viewing associated with TV.

4 As of early 2004, *Office Space*, which had taken in only $10 million at the box office, has earned an additional $40 million on DVD, and *Old School* took in $73 million theatrically and gained another $143.5 million on DVD (Waxman 2004: B8).

5 This reading of *Scarface* can be found in the Def Jam documentary, *Origins of a Hip-Hop Classic*, available on the 2003 DVD twentieth anniversary edition of the film.

References

Allen, R.C. (1999) Home alone together, in M. Stokes and R. Maltby (eds) *Identifying Hollywood Audiences*. London: BFI.

Ang, I. (1985) *Watching Dallas: Soap Opera and the Melodramatic Imagination*. London: Methuen.

Clifford, J. (1993) On collecting art and culture, in S. During (ed.) *The Cultural Studies Reader*. London: Routledge.

Corrigan, T. (1991) *A Cinema Without Walls: Movies and Culture After Vietnam*. New Brunswick, NJ: Rutgers University Press.

Cubitt, S. (1991) *Timeshift: On Video Culture*. London: Routledge.

Dinsmore, U. (1998) Chaos, order, and plastic boxes: the significance of videotapes for the people who collect them, in C. Geraghty and D. Lusted (eds) *The Television Studies Book*. New York: St. Martin's Press.

Flynn, L.J. (2002) One man's two challenges, *New York Times*, 3 June.

Gomery, D. (1988) Hollywood's hold on the new television technologies, *Screen*, 29(2): 82–9.

Gomery, D. (1992) *Shared Pleasures: A History of Movie Presentation in the United States*. Madison: University of Wisconsin Press.

Gray, A. (1992) *Video Playtime: The Gendering of a Leisure Technology*. London: Routledge.

Jenkins, H. (1992) *Textual Poachers: Television Fans and Participatory Culture*. London: Routledge.

Komiya, M. and Litman, B. (1990) The economics of the prerecorded videocassette industry in J.R. Dobrow (ed.) *Social and Cultural Aspects of VCR Use*. Hillsdale, NJ: Lawrence Erlbaum Associates.

Kuhn, A. (1995) *Family Secrets: Acts of Memory and Imagination*. London: Verso.

Lyman, R. (2002) Revolt in the den: DVD. Has the VCR headed to the attic?, *New York Times*, 26 August.

Miller, T., Govil, N., McMurria, J. and Maxwell, R. (2001) *Global Hollywood*. London: BFI.

Morley, D. (1986) *Family Television: Cultural Power and Domestic Leisure*. New York and London: Routledge.

Morley, D. (1992) *Television Audiences and Cultural Studies*. New York: Routledge.

Morley, D. (1995) Television: not so much a visual medium, more a visible object, in C. Jenks (ed.) *Visual Culture*. London: Routledge.

Nichols, P.M. (2002a) A first take on "Ring", Part 2, *New York Times*, 29 August.

Nichols, P.M. (2002b) DVD has begun to take over, *New York Times*, 28 June.

Ryall, T. (1986) *Alfred Hitchcock and the British Cinema*. Urbana: University of Illinois Press.

Silverstone, R. and Hirsch, E. (1992) *Consuming Technologies: Media and Information in Domestic Space*. London and New York: Routledge.

Tashiro, C. (1997) The contradictions of video collecting, *Film Quarterly*, 50(2): 11–18.

Total DVD (2000) Reviews of *Mission Impossible* and *Blue Streak*, (September): 56–7.

Walkerdine, V. (1989) Video replays: families, films, and fantasy, in V. Burgin, C. Kaplan, and J. Donald (eds) *Formations of Fantasy*. London: Routledge.

Wasko, J. (1995) *Hollywood in the Information Age: Beyond the Silver Screen*. Austin: University of Texas Press.

Waxman, S. (2004) Studios rush to cash in on DVD boom, *New York Times*, 20 April.

Tom Hanks

Tom Hanks has made a career out of being an ordinary American guy in often extraordinary circumstances. From the humorous sufferings of a single man in his twenties in *Splash* (1984) to the recently widowed single father in *Sleepless in Seattle* (1993) or the AIDS-stricken character in *Philadelphia* (1993), Hanks has made a virtue of giving the appearance of playing himself in each film. Born in 1956 in Concord, California, Hanks' childhood was marked by persistent moving as his father, a chef, changed jobs regularly. In his early school years Hanks was the new kid at school almost every six months, a condition that he claims trained him for acting. At Chabot Junior College in Hayward, California, he began to study acting seriously, and opted for community theatre while at California State University Sacramento after failing to be cast in college productions. He left college to work in the Great Lakes Shakespeare Company in Cleveland and then later went to New York where he had some limited success in theatre. His first break came in landing a leading role in the ABC situation comedy, *Bosom Buddies* (1980–2). The premise was two advertising executives who solve their problem of finding an apartment in New York by opting to dress in drag in order to live in a women-only building. While the series lasted only two years Hanks attracted the attention of Ron Howard who would later direct him in his first hit, *Splash*. Hanks' relationships with first Howard and later Penny Marshall (*Big*, 1988) were important in launching his career and providing a firm ground for his congenial star persona. Howard and Marshall, schooled in the comic nostalgia represented by the long-running television series *Happy Days* (1974–84) and *Laverne and Shirley* (1976–83), understood and were attracted by the elements in Hanks' comic abilities, which enhanced their films, and these movies in turn benefited the young actor. Those roles were not in themselves overt references to a better time in the way that *Happy Days* was, but they did place a flawed but decent character in the distinctly American city of New York. The return of a nice guy to the streets of the city in romantic comedy, whether in the guise of a guy who can't say "I love you" (*Splash*) or as a 12-year-old in the body of a man (*Big*), drew upon a resilient genre of the kind Cary Grant and James Stewart found comfortable. In both films Hanks' childish nature and comic style were central to his innocence and markedly different from the previous denizens of Gotham played by Robert de Niro, Dustin Hoffman or Harvey Keitel in the late 1960s and 1970s.

By the early 1990s Hanks had two more successes, with *Joe Versus the Volcano* (1990) and *A League of their Own* (1992), and one well-documented disaster, *Bonfire of the Vanities* (1992). He then appeared in the AIDS drama *Philadelphia* (1993), for which he won his first

Academy Award. The film drew criticism for its sexless portrayal of a gay man, and its consistent compromises directed at an assumed heterosexual audience, but it was generally recognized that Hanks' portrayal was understated and drew effectively on his established affable persona to draw the sympathy of conservative mainstream Hollywood audiences.

Hanks' star persona blurs the line between character and actor and person in a manner that rivals that of the stars of the classic period. Like those of certain studio-era stars, his films tend to present a window into the nature of his character as a person. In *Turner and Hooch*, a film that is not usually called up in accounts of his Oscar-winning career, he plays a detective who is not so much hard-boiled as a soft touch, and it is that self-reflecting, slightly vulnerable will-bend-but-won't-break aspect that suggests he is more human than stellar. Such qualities are a recipe for stardom of the kind that Hollywood reserves, in its own self-generating history, for the true immortals, and most of these tend to come from the pre-1960s studio period. Yet Hanks is clearly of his generation of baby boomers. He is not, however, representative of that generation's taste in their teenage years, when they were the audience for rebels and outcasts in the 1960s and 1970s. Rather he embodies, in his mannerisms and his choice of material, the kind of conservative sensibility of that generation just as they began to have kids themselves. He is often called the modern-day James Stewart, which is to say that he is likeable, seems to walk effortlessly through his roles, and at the end delivers to the audience a character with a common vulnerability and sense of decency that they recognize (or hope to recognize) in themselves.

This relationship with the boomer generation was nowhere more apparent than in his portrayal as the idiot savant in Robert Zemeckis' *Forrest Gump* (1994), which literally replayed the post-Second World War traumas of the 1960s and 1970s. Hanks said of the phenomenal success of the film, "We've all been through a lot. And we're really tired. But there is a kind of communal thing: if we handled that we can handle anything that's going to come our way" (Gristwood 1994). The film placed Hanks' character in actual footage from landmark media moments in US history, from a meeting with John F. Kennedy, the arrival of the first black students, Vivian Malone Jones and James Hood, at the University of Alabama in 1963, to an appearance on the Dick Cavett show with John Lennon. Its box-office gross at $329 million was almost five times the $77 million of *Philadelphia*.

It was perhaps inevitable that Hanks would work with Steven Spielberg, whose concerns during the 1990s were also centred on relating the "hurts of history" – *Schindler's List* (1993) and *Amistad* (1997). He cast Hanks in his war film *Saving Private Ryan*, in 1998, as the war-weary Lt. John Miller who just wants to do his job and go home. Spielberg stated that Hanks was his only choice: "Tom, you know, represents . . . the best in all of us. Young people look at him as their father, and older people look at him as their squad leader, their Captain Miller" (CNN transcript). The film was the first of a series of collaborations with Spielberg which culminated in *Terminal* (2004), in which Hanks portrayed an East European man exiled from his country but refused entrance to the United States, and so forced to live permanently in an airport. The actor has also been active as a producer with over 28 projects, both film and television, to his credit, including *Polar Express* (2004), *Castaway* (2000), *My Big Fat Greek Wedding* (2004) and the critically lauded TV series, *Band of Brothers* (2001). His role as a "player" in Hollywood has been quietly run, and he seems to have been able to keep his private life largely private. Deliberately or not, his insistence on the separation of his public and personal lives has worked to reinforce his long-standing "regular guy" persona on screen.

References

Anonymous (2005) CNN people in the News. Broadcast 26 February.
  http://edition.cnn.com/TRANSCRIPTS/0502/26/pitn.01.html.
Gristwood, S. (1994) Hollywood's Mr Nice, *Evening Standard*, 29 September.

Michael Hammond

AMERICAN DOCUMENTARY FILM IN THE 1990s

Patricia R. Zimmermann

THE DECADE OF the 1990s can be periodized as beginning in 1988–9 with the massive mergers in the entertainment industry with the Time/Warner mega merger and ending with the terrorist attacks on the World Trade Center in 2001. By the 1990s, independent documentary encompassed a wide and diverse range of styles, including archivally based works, direct cinema, experimentations with form, stylistic hybrids, activist and collective practices, and anti-copyright interventions.

Documentary also embraced and explored diversity not only in terms of topics dealing with race, ethnicity and national identity, but with a significant expansion of diverse producers and directors. During the 1990s, documentary expressed and cracked open cultural difference and also engaged the wider world, ravaged by civil wars, AIDS, and military aggression. It also mobilized a multiplicity of technologies, from 16 mm, to camcorder, to DV, to digital compositing. By the end of the period, documentary was beginning to migrate to the Internet, adopting open source models for sharing materials generated across the globe and adapting to the possibilities of streaming short works.

In the context of massive cutbacks in news, public affairs, and documentary units at the commercial networks, independent documentary gained prominence as a site for investigative muckraking, personal expression of identities, formal innovation, and political discourse. In this decade, documentary institutions flourished, supporting a range of documentary forms and catapulting documentary into festivals, seminars, commercial cable, art cinemas, and scholarly conferences. In the context of transnational media mergers, moves away from investigative reporting and the push to infotainment on the commercial networks, *P.O.V.* and *Frontline* on public television emerged as the premiere showcases for muckraking documentary, showing some of the most politically significant work of the period. The nonprofit distribution sector supported a range of specialty documentary practices, particularly in the educational film market, aimed at universities and colleges. This established a visible presence for documentary as a teaching tool and important part of film exhibition.

The formation of ITVS and its impact on documentary

American independent documentary emerged as a corollary to radical political movements in the late 1960s and 1970s such as the anti-Vietnam War movement, feminism, and civil rights. The films produced in this earlier period were designed to give voice to the disenfranchised, make visible the invisible, critique power, create consciousness, and mobilize political action. They were, for the most part, opposed to the dominant media and conventional American ideologies, and circulated within various political movements as organizing tools.

However, throughout the 1970s, independents became increasingly organized, demanding greater access to public television, cable, grants and film festivals through such organizations as the Association of Independent Film and Video Makers (AIVF), formed in 1973. Drawing on communitarian principles and activist organizing, AIVF became a major voice in advocacy for independent producers. For a decade, beginning in the late 1970s, AIVF, community activists and independent producers lobbied Congress to ensure that diverse and independent voices not usually seen on commercial television would be served by public television. In 1988, after several rounds of hearings where independent documentary producers testified, the US Congress passed legislation that mandated that the Corporation for Public Broadcasting negotiate with independent producers. This legislation established the Independent Television Service (ITVS), which began distributing approximately $6 million to independent producers in 1991. As a major funder of documentary in the United States, ITVS is required to "engage creative risks" and "advance issues and represent points of view not usually seen on public or commercial television". In addition, it is required to address "the needs of underserved and underrepresented audiences". To this end, it often partners with the Minority Consortia, which include African Americans, Native Americans, Latinos, Asian Americans and Pacific Islanders.

As an institution supporting American independent film, ITVS has had an enormous impact on long-form documentary in the United States. It has supplied a range of strategic planning and promotional services for the films they support, helping to market the films in a very dense market with many media outlets, and maintaining an extensive website with links to distributors, broadcast dates, and additional information on the films.

Many of the long-form documentaries screened at the Sundance Film Festival, Full Frame Documentary Film Festival, and other prominent festivals have received funding through ITVS. Major festival and art cinema circuit films that have been funded, launched and promoted by ITVS include Alan Berliner's *Nobody's Business*, Lourdes Portillo's *The Devil Never Sleeps* (1994) and her *Senorita Extraviada, Missing Young Women* (2001), Judith Helfand's *A Healthy Baby Girl* (1996), Marlon Rigg's *Black Is … Black Ain't* (1995), Tony Buba's *Struggles in Steel: A Story of African American Steelworkers* (1996), Whitney Dow and Marco Williams' *Two Towns of Jasper* (2002), Deann Borshay Liem's *First Person Plural* (2000), Renee Tajima-Pena's *My America: Or Honk If You Love Buddha* (1997) (Zimmermann 2000).

A landmark ITVS-funded film of the mid-1990s, Carma Hinton and Richard Gordon's *The Gate of Heavenly Peace* (1996), chronicled the student demonstrations of Tiananmen Square in Beijing in June of 1989. Funded with grants from the National Endowment for the Humanities, the Ford Foundation, Rockefeller and other institutions, this 3-hour epic documentary interviewed 20 students, workers, teachers, and scholars involved in the pro-democracy movement in China, boldly mining its political and social complexities, fissures and controversies. Carma Hinton, daughter of famed China scholar Will Hinton, was raised in China and speaks Chinese as her first language, sustaining complex and intimate interviews that go far beyond a recounting of events and move into political analyses of strategy and ideologies. The filmmakers amassed over 400 hours of archival footage of the pro-democracy movement in Tiananmen Square, including a variety of amateur camcorder footage.

When the film premiered at the 1995 New York Film Festival, it catalysed international controversy from both the Chinese government and the Chinese exile dissident movement – neither of whom agreed with the depiction of events and ideas in the film. The Chinese government prevented feature filmmaker Zhang Yimou from attending the festival. This epic, sprawling and complex film was recut to two hours for public television broadcast. In 1998, President Bill Clinton screened *The Gate of Heavenly Peace* as part of his briefing for his trip to China.

The Gate of Heavenly Peace also created a pathbreaking, extensive companion website (www.tsquare.tv), which provided transcripts of the film, links to debates in the English and Chinese-speaking press, historical context, more interviews, and additional essays. The site is not simply an advertising adjunct for the film but expands the discourse of the film to include the international debates and deep historical context, one of the first of its kind for a major feature-length documentary.

Organizations supporting documentary

Massive defunding of media arts at the federal and state levels changed the nonprofit arts infrastructure that had developed in the United States during the 1970s and 1980s, spurring political organization, increased professionalization of the media arts field, and hybrid projects spanning the profit/nonprofit sectors. Galvanized by Republicans and the Christian Right, the culture wars attacked documentary and experimental media with charges of misuse of public funds for work exploring radical anti-American politics and sexuality.

A pivotal case underscoring these debates about publicly funded culture centred around Jesse Helms' attack on Marlon Riggs' (1989) experimental documentary on black gay men and AIDS, *Tongues Untied*, for sexually explicit images – one of the most vociferous and significant battles of the culture wars. Helms accused Riggs of using public funds to produce homosexual pornography, and used the film to argue that arts and culture should not receive public funding. The film had been funded with a $5000 regional regrant from the National Endowment for the Arts. Further, some public television station managers refused to broadcast the film, citing "offensive language" and affronts to "community standards" (http://www.current.org/prog/prog114g.html).

These culture wars had conflicting effects on documentary practice. Federal and state funding for media arts declined significantly, especially in the area of infrastructure support for institutions and centres as well as funding for individual artists, but these same controversies brought documentary, always a marginal genre, to national attention as a democratic public sphere. Some public funders cut grants to media arts by more than 50 per cent. Although by no means compensating for these dramatic losses in public funding, a range of other forward-thinking private foundations worked to stimulate cutting-edge, innovative long-form documentary production, such as the Jerome Foundation, the Open Society Institute and Soros Foundation, John D. and Catherine T. MacArthur Foundation, the Thomas Phillips Johnson and Jane Moore Johnson Foundation, the Andy Warhol Foundation for the Visual Arts, the Park Foundation, and the Rockefeller Foundation.

Despite almost continuous attacks from the Christian Right and neoconservatives, American public television in the 1990s functioned as both an incubator and a national showcase for independently produced documentary. Launched in 1988, *P.O.V.*, public television's showcase for challenging work by independent producers, represents one of the major broadcast presences for independent documentary. It has 12–14 shows per year, and has provided a significant launching pad for American long-form documentary, featuring such films as Peter Adair's *Absolutely Positive* (1991) exploring AIDS; Mark Kitchell's *Berkeley in the 60s* (1991) on the anti-Vietnam War movement; Julie Gustafson's *Casting the First Stone*, on the struggles over abortion rights; Anne Lewis Johnson's *Fast Food Women* (1992), Susana Munoz and Lourdes Portillo's *Las Madres: The Mothers of the Plaza de Mayo* (1988), and Christine Choy and Renee Tajima's *Who Killed Vincent Chin?* (1989) on a racially motivated murder in Detroit.[1] Started in 1983 at WGBH in Boston, *Frontline* emerged as one of the only programmes in the broadcast landscape to engage with major social and political issues such as the war in Iraq, the genocide in Rwanda, military affairs, the environment and politics.

Other nonprofit organizations with long histories in the independent documentary world mobilized to feature documentary and provide much-needed forums for discussion of the form and advocacy. The Association of Independent Film and Videomakers (AIVF), which had formed in the early 1970s out of oppositional independent filmmakers, emerged in a prominent role during the culture wars, defending filmmakers and engaging in intensive lobbying. Their national magazine, *The Independent*, featured many stories on documentary production, financing, distribution and exhibition. Started in 1955 by his widow Frances, the Robert Flaherty Film Seminars in the 1990s presented programmes that explored the connections between experimental film and documentary within a more international matrix.

The National Association of Media Arts and Culture (NAMAC), founded in 1980 by various media arts centres, rose to prominence during this period as a major national voice for the increasingly heterogeneous media arts field, which ranged from public television long-form producers to cable access to museums to media arts collectives.[2] It had a major impact on the field of media arts through its exploration of the impact of new technologies, its advancement of professionalization of administration of the field, and its ability to open up conversation between different sectors and layers of the nonprofit media arts field. On a more scholarly vector, the Visible Evidence Conferences on Documentary commenced in 1993, moving to different venues across the United States and abroad and promoting a rigorous theoretical and historical investigation of documentary.

In the 1990s, the lines between nonprofit and for-profit documentary blurred, not only with the success of some white male

Paris is Burning

filmmakers (Errol Morris, Michael Moore) in crossing over from educational to theatrical exhibition, but with funding and festivals. HBO/Cinemax developed a strong profile for funding edgy documentary, with several academy awards and nominations in both feature and short documentary. Filmmakers who had established national reputations in direct cinema in the 1970s and 1980s aligned with HBO: Jon Alpert, Albert Maysles, Barbara Kopple. HBO broadcast important films on topics that PBS would not touch: for example, breast cancer (*Rachel's Daughters*, 1997) and the rapes during the Bosnian War (*Calling the Ghosts*, 1996) (Dempsey 1997; Ault 2000; Chen 2000).

In the context of its embrace of independent features, the Sundance Film Festival became a major force in advancing American independent documentary. The imprimatur of a Sundance screening greatly aided filmmakers in securing commercial or nonprofit distribution and more extensive exhibition. Many of the documentary films screened at Sundance had garnered funding from ITVS, HBO, the National Endowment for the Arts, and the Rockefeller Foundation, illustrating the strong interconnections between these organizations. Major American documentary films as varied in style and politics as Michael Moore's *Roger and Me* (1989), Tami Gold and Kelly Anderson's *Out at Work* (1996), Jennie Livingston's *Paris is Burning* (1990), Ross McElwee's *Six O'Clock News* (1996), Trinh T.

Minh-ha's *Shoot for the Contents* (1991), and Peter Friedman, Tom Joslin and Mark Massi's *Silverlake Life: The View from Here* (1993) all screened in the documentary division at Sundance.

During the 1990s, the nonprofit distribution sector gained a foothold in American universities and among curators and programmers as independent, noncorporate work moved out of its marginalized, oppositional stance into a major current in media arts that represented significant innovations in form, content, approach and argument. These distributors for the most part were founded in the midst of political movements in the late 1960s and 1970s, maturing as organizations that promoted independent media with pointed outreach to specific target audiences, mostly in film festivals, libraries and universities.

Often overlooked in most conventional histories of documentary, these independent nonprofit distributors form the baseline infrastructure supporting these diverse media practices, connecting the works with audiences. The major distributors include Women Make Movies, National Association of Asian Telecommunications, California Newsreel, Third World Newsreel, First Run/Icarus Films, Video Data Bank and Electronic Arts Intermix.

Experimental form meets documentary content

In the 1990s, the genre divides between experimental work exploring formal elements such as framing, composition, editing, light and structure within a non-narrative framework and documentary work engaging issues and the complexities of human interactions as an investigation, deconstruction and argument

blurred. These hybrid forms problematized the modes of address of both experimental and documentary, activating the cinematic as a liminal zone for inquiry into form and function (MacDonald 2001).[3]

A group of filmmakers arising from feminist politics, with its insistence on linking the personal and political, and from the move in the 1980s documentary away from interviews illustrated with compilation footage, began to make films that investigated personal life and deployed formal experimentation as an analytical metacommunication. A pathbreaking feminist filmmaker exploring the threshold between experimental and documentary, Su Friedrich's *Ties that Bind* (1984), about her mother's life in Nazi Germany, represents a landmark film that shifted documentary practice into more psychic terrains. *Sink or Swim* (1990) mines her relationship with her father, and *Hide and Seek* (1996) journeys into her childhood and lesbianism. Alan Berliner, a filmmaker known for his work with home movies and archival footage in *A Family Album* (1986), employed structural film form to explore his father in *Nobody's Business* (1996), and his grandfather in *Intimate Stranger* (1991). Sadie Benning's pixelvision diaries of her anguished yet funny lesbian adolescence combined personal exploration with extreme close-ups and grainy, canted imagery in works such as *A Place Called Lovely*, *Welcome to Normal* and *Jollies* (1989–90). And long-time underground filmmaker George Kuchar's *Weather Diaries* (1990–5) connect weather to his own body.

A contemplative hybrid mode also developed in the 1990s, expanding tenets of structural film with an interest in place, location, landscape and history. James Benning's *Deseret* (1995) and *North on Evers* (1992), *Four Corners* (1997) and *El Valley Centro* (2000) work as meditations on the links between land and its invisible histories. Peter Hutton explores the Hudson River through abstract, painterly and highly structured compositions in *Study of a River* (1996) and *Time and Tide* (2000). Leighton Pierce's work mines the micro-landscapes of the intimate objects arrayed in daily life in such works as *Red Shovel* (1992), *Fifty Feet of String* (1995) and *The Back Steps* (2001). Naomi Uman's *Leche* (1998) probes a Mexican dairy farm with compositions and editing that evoke its daily rhythms.

The compilation documentary film movements of the 1970s and 1980s deployed archival footage as evidence, but in the 1990s footage filmmakers transformed these images into interrogations of visual ideologies, conceptual grids and resonant cultural iconographies. This move was partly a materialist response to the virtualization of the image by the digital and partly within the context of an expansion of interest in the marginal archive as a cultural repository to be unpacked, deconstructed, revamped.

Expanding from earlier experimental filmmakers like Bruce Connor and Joseph Cornell, filmmakers scavenged images from a range of sources beyond traditional archives, including instructional, educational, health, amateur, cult, popular culture and other marginalized cinematic practices. Most of these films abandoned the talking heads interview, which had anchored compilation films in discourse, and privileged the image itself as a site for interrogation through montage and manipulation. Notable filmmakers include Phil Solomon (*Twilight Psalm 11: Walking Distance*, 1999), Martin Arnold (*Alone: Life Wastes Andy Hardy*, 1998), Jay Rosenblatt (*The Smell of Burning Ants*, 1994; *Human Remains*, 1998), Naomi Uman (*Removed*, 1999), Abigail Childs (*Is This What You Were Born For?*

1989), Craig Baldwin (*Tribulation 99: Alien Anomalies Under America*, 1999), Jennifer Reeves (*The Girl's Nervy*, 1995; *Fear of Blushing*, 2001) and Bill Morrison (*The Film of Her*, 1996; *Decasia*, 2001).

Documentary spectacles

In the 1990s, documentary also entered more commercial exhibition arenas through an embrace of surreality, humour and spectacle. Feature-length documentaries from makers such as Errol Morris and Michael Moore had theatrical runs, as well as a variety of films about nature that featured elaborate musical scores (*Powaqqatsi*, 1988; *Microscosmos*, 1996; *Baraka*, 1992; *Winged Migration*, 2001, Fig. 17 (*see plate section*)).

One of the most significant developments in the commercialization of documentary spectacle was IMAX, the large screen immersive exhibition featured in museums and specialty venues. Premiered at Expo 70 in Japan, by the 1990s, IMAX was a permanent feature of the film exhibition landscape, offering a spectatorial experience saturated with auditory, sensory and visual excess, contrasting with the small screens of video and DVD in the home. With an image spanning 72 feet by 52 feet, IMAX films offered increased resolution from its 70 mm film run sideways through special cameras, lending itself to nature as awe-inspiring spectacle. *Everest* (1998), chronicling a group attempting to reach the summit of mountain, was the top-grossing IMAX film of all time. Other spectacle documentaries included *Cirque du Soleil: The Journey of Man* (2000), *Antarctica* (1991) and *Space Station 3D* (2002) (Stern 1997; Olson 1998a, 1998b).

New technologies and political activism

New technologies such as cable access, satellite, camcorders, DV, digital compositing and the Internet offered new ways for activists and collectives to mobilize documentary for social and political change. The new technologies provided not only cheaper tools, increasing access to production for women, people of colour and sexual minorities, but also presented new possibilities for distribution and exhibition beyond film festivals and theatrical exhibition.

Founded in 1981, Paper Tiger Television is a video collective that produces 30-minute shows that offer "a critical understanding of the communications industry". The programmes are broadcast on cable access television, a public service provision required of cable companies, but increasingly endangered. The programmes adopt a low-tech, handmade style and a critique of current events in the United States and around the globe that is adept at responding quickly to events. They often feature prominent public intellectuals like Noam Chomsky, Herb Schiller, Amy Goodman, and others analysing media representations and politics. The programmes also frequently feature footage shot by activists around the globe, often on camcorder or DV. In the 1990s, Paper Tiger Television produced a wide range of works on significant topics ignored or marginalized by the mainstream big media. *The Gulf Crisis TV Project* (1990) consisted of four 30-minute shows on the first Gulf War. *NAFTA: A Three Way Tie for Last* (1993) probed economic and trade relations between Mexico, Canada and the United States. *Media Machete: The Chiapas Media Project* (1998) looked at the Zapatista uprising in Chiapas. In collaboration with Big Noise Films and the Independent Media Center,

Paper Tiger produced one of the only noncorporate media representations of the massive protests against the WTO meeting, *Showdown in Seattle* (1999), a five-part series.

An outgrowth of Paper Tiger, Deep Dish Satellite was founded in 1988. It uses satellite technology to create "a progressive television network" that can be downlinked all across the globe. It links local cable access producers and activists with a national and international network of cable television stations and individual satellite dish owners. Two important projects, which included multiple programmes culled from across the country, include *Behind Censorship: The Assault on Civil Liberties* (1991) and *Sick and Tired of Being Sick and Tired* (1994).

Consumer-grade portable technologies such as the camcorder and digital video shed their amateur status and helped to create a more diverse documentary landscape. Ellen Spiro's *Diana's Hair Ego: AIDS Info Upfront* (1989), Gregg Bordowitz's *Fast Trip, Long Drop* (1991), *Testing the Limits' Voices from the Front* (1992) and Robert Hilferty's *Stop the Church* (1990) helped to define AIDS activist mediamaking. *Take Over* (Pamela Yates and Peter Kinoy, 1992) gave camcorders to the homeless as they reclaimed HUD housing in six different cities in a major political action. *A.K.A. Don Bonus* (1995) was shot on a camcorder by highschool senior, Sokly Ny, a Cambodian immigrant to San Francisco, in collaboration with professional filmmaker Spencer Nakasako. The Not Channel Zero Collective zeroed in on institutionalized racism with works such as *The Nation Erupts* (1992), on the Rodney King riots in Los Angeles, and *X 1/2: The Legacy of Malcolm X* (1993).

Marshalling digital compositing technologies, media artists began to change the indexicality and referentiality of the documentary image through layering, morphing, computer animation and other forms of image manipulation, creating complex visual landscapes that opened up political discourse to a more polyvocal style. *Obsessive Becoming* (Daniel Reeves, 1995) unpacked the relationship between war and masculinity with archival footage, home movies, digital compositing and morphing. *First World Order* (Philip Mallory Jones, 1994) used morphing to make visual connections between indigenous peoples around the globe. *Zapatista* (Big Noise Films, 1998), about the Chiapas uprisings and Subcommante Marcos in Mexico, and *This is What Democracy Looks Like* (Big Noise Films, 2000), about the 1999 anti-WTO Seattle protests, combine activist DV footage, digital compositing, and multiple-layered DJ soundtracks to create a new form of political cinema.

Pirates and the anti-copyright movement

As the decade collided into the new millennium, a major aesthetic and political battle loomed for documentary: copyright. As the transnational entertainment industry shifted aggressively from production into global distribution across a range of technologies and media platforms, intellectual property became its most lucrative and risk-free real estate after theme parks. However, the declining costs of new technologies like DV and the advance of digitalization and networked communications countered this intensification and centralization of corporate capital with lossless, easy reproduction of images and sounds.

A dizzying, dense collage manifesto for anti-copyright and fair use, Craig Baldwin's *Sonic Outlaws* (1995) charts the Negativland/ U2 lawsuit, a landmark case for media artists working in appropriated sound and image. Negativland, the audio collage art collective

formed in 1980, had sampled part of a U2 track and mixed it with an outtake of Casey Kasem saying some malapropisms. They lost the suit on copyright infringement, but emerged as major voices in the fair use/anticopyright battles of the decade. Creating a compelling argument against copyright, *Sonic Outlaws* investigates copyright infringement, found sound, culture jamming, and fair use through pirated and archival materials as well as interviews with media pirates such as the Barbie Liberation Organization, Tape Beatles, and Emergency Broadcast Network.

Confronted with enormous cutbacks to the arts, media artists armed themselves with digital technologies and pirated images and sounds in open warfare to protect an increasingly diminished public domain and fair use. A wide range of artists working in a multiplicity of styles pirated images to launch counteroffensives against the entertainment industry, nationalism, psychic imaginaries, and conservative politics. Drawing on long traditions of collage, and emboldened by cut and mix techniques from hip hop, documentary artists as diverse as Les Leveque (*4 Vertigo*, 2000), Alex Rivera (*Why Cybraceros*, 1995), Kathy High (*I Need Your Full Cooperation*, 1989), Dee Halleck (*Gringo in Mananaland*, 1995), and Brian Springer (*Spin*, 1995) pirated imagery to deconstruct Hollywood, labour, women's health, Latin America and the presidential political race (Zimmermann 2000).

With the World Trade Center attacks and the ensuing war on terror and war in Iraq, media piracy accelerated in remix projects that spanned analogue and digital such as the Guerilla News Network, www.indymedia.org, Konscious.com, and ITVS's A 9.11 Moment. Many of these projects were based on open source models, and used streaming technologies for downloads on the Internet. Media piracy intensified as a way to interrogate nationalism and as a means to open up a closed-down public sphere during one of the worst news blackouts in US history.

Notes

1   For additional background and information on programmes, see http://www.pbs.org/pov/
2   For more information on NAMAC, see http://www.namac.org
3   I am indebted to Scott MacDonald for his extensive conversations to share his deep insights with me regarding the blurring between experimental and documentary styles and modes of address in the 1990s. For more extensive interviews and analysis, see MacDonald (2001) and (2005).

References

Ault, S. (2000) Docu Festival to honor HBO's Nevins, *Variety*, 29 March.

Chen, A. (2000) Org to fete Kopple, HBO, *Variety*, 28 June.

Dempsey, J. (1997) Lee's HBO doc to screen, *Variety*, 7 February.

MacDonald, S. (2001) *The Garden in the Machine: A Field Guide to Independent Films about Place*. Berkeley: University of California Press.

MacDonald, S. (2005) *A Critical Cinema 4*. Berkeley: University of California Press.

Olson, E. (1998a) Mandalay inks deal with IMAX, *Variety*, 28 May.

Olson, E. (1998b) Nova teams up for two Antarctic dox, *Variety*, 25 November.

Stern, C. (1997) IMAX docu for space station, *Variety*, 21 May.

Zimmermann, P.R. (2000) *States of Emergency: Documentaries, Wars, Democracies*. Minneapolis: University of Minnesota Press.

NEW BLACK CINEMA

Michael Hammond

In the late 1980s and early 1990s films produced and/or directed by black filmmakers were making significant in-roads into major Hollywood production. This period is usually cited as starting in the mid-1980s with Spike Lee's *She's Gotta Have It* (1986), reaching a particular peak with the "ghetto action films" of the early 1990s and is continuing, as much of the directing, producing, technical and acting talent that began in the independent sector has made the move to major studio productions. The success of Spike Lee's *Do the Right Thing* (1989, Fig. 14 (*see plate section*)) grabbed the attention of the majors in a more or less permanent way which opened the door to better financing for films by black filmmakers. However, there are considerable caveats to this narrative. For example, it was clear that while the "gangsta" content of the "hood" cycle of the 1990s suggested that Hollywood was tapping into black audiences as a significant market, criticism arose that many of these films were replaying the African-American experience primarily through crime and the dystopic conditions of the ghetto. Another caveat is in terms of its origins. This development of a New Black Cinema did not simply begin with Lee but owes its existence to two contingent factors, which arose in the late 1970s and early 1980s. The first was the rise of

black independent cinema as the result of the creation of filmmaking cultures outside of the Hollywood mainstream. The second was the continuing residue of the blaxploitation films from the 1970s, which had initially demonstrated to the majors the profit potential of films for black urban audiences. The first represents a commitment to the development of an alternative aesthetic to mainstream white Hollywood, and the second, an association with exploitation production strategies and by implication an apparently less politically motivated but no less distinct aesthetic development. Both of these represent the considerable complexity and overlap in the debates concerning the rise of a new black American cinema in the last two decades of the twentieth century.

An important and necessary antecedent to this was the rise of independent cinema generally, of which black independent cinema was a central part. Craig Watkins has pointed to the fact that "The black independent movement developed its most definitive features in the 1970s" at the same time that the changes in the exhibition sector from the rise of multiplexes to the growth of cable television, home video and pay-per-view television resulted in more effective means of targeting niche markets. Further, increased availability of filmmaking equipment and technology alongside changes in film financing (where "The independent filmmaker collects capital through a variety of alternative means: art grants, foundations, bank loans, private investors, and local fund-raising efforts") meant that artistic decisions were less prone to corporate interference (Watkins 1998: 86–7). This resulted in "the bulk of African-American filmmaking operat[ing] mainly on the independent circuit" (Watkins 1998: 96).

Black independent cinema in the 1970s and early 1980s was distinct in its development of a particular sensibility as "a collective group engaged in a historically specific episode of cultural struggle" (Watkins 1998: 98). On the West Coast this was represented by university-based black filmmaking groups such as the "LA rebellion" at UCLA and, on the East Coast, through the Black Filmmakers Foundation (BFF). Rather than a purely university-based collective, the BFF assisted the development and training of aspiring black filmmakers by building a filmmaking culture, albeit often through universities, driven by the

Continued on page 392

The Hughes Brothers

While Spike Lee, John Singleton, and even Mario Van Peebles have been afforded greater attention in both the popular press and academic studies, perhaps the most exciting talents to emerge from the "New Black Cinema" of the 1980s and 1990s were the Hughes brothers, Allen and Albert. Having cut their teeth on short films and pop videos, the twins made their first feature, *Menace II Society* (1993), at the age of 20, and promptly scooped the MTV Best Picture award. Since then, their cinematic output has been far from prolific (they have a meagre three features, and a controversial documentary, *American Pimp* (1999) to their credit so far), yet the Hughes' distinctive combination of confrontational themes, hip soundtracks, and vibrant visuals bespeak bold, unruly talent. "The Hughes brothers exhibit a comprehension of the power of the image", writes Donaldson (2003: 156) "and they do not hesitate to place an image, regardless of its graphic display, in the faces of the viewers ... [They] serve up a commercial style that examines the experiences of African American males whose spirit and potential are nullified by an indifferent society."

From the grim urban American violence of *Menace II Society* (which cost $3.5 million and grossed close to $30 million) to the Anglo-Gothic sensibilities of *From Hell* (2001) (a box-office disappointment despite a popular graphic novel source and the star power of Johnny Depp), the Hughes' canon has often been dismissed as a pop-promo-inflected triumph of style over substance. Kleinhans (2002: 66) charges them with having "exploited 'in the hood' and rap/hip hop sensibilities and themes to gain box office success", while Andrew categorizes their debut as an "over-emphatically stylish" (1998: 342). Reviewing *From Hell* in the British Film Institute journal *Sight and Sound*, Richards (2002: 45) finds little to praise other than its confirmation that the Brothers are "formidable visual stylists". Yet the bravura breadth and scope of *Dead Presidents* (1995), an epic American fable on a par with Scorsese's *Goodfellas*, defies such critical indifference. Spanning the turbulent years from 1968 to 1973, *Dead Presidents* charts an alternative cultural history through the trials of Anthony Curtis (Larenz Tate) who graduates from sparky teenager to desperate gangster via a horrifying stint in Vietnam. Aided by a superbly chosen jukebox soundtrack, and boasting a terrific central performance by Tate, the movie skips nimbly between enthralling nostalgia, appalling horror (the brief battlefield scenes rival the traumatic imagery of *Apocalypse Now*), and tense drama. The heist sequence, with black men savagely camouflaged in white face, is unforgettably daring; of it Ed Guerrero (1998: 340) writes, "If *Dead Presidents* is canonized

Allen and Albert Hughes on the set of *Menace II Society*

for nothing else, it will be for the brilliantly imagined image of black bandits in whiteface stealing the government's worn-out, about-to-be-burned money, or for the close-up shots of the faces on that money burning in the film's opening credit sequence." Blending pertinent political observation with an engrossing personal narrative, *Dead Presidents* remains one of the most underrated movies of the 1990s. Guerrero (1998: 341) concedes that although the film's panoramic narrative may alienate some viewers, its sheer scope proves that 'the Hughes brothers are willing to experiment with form, to push the material beyond normative boundaries of what would have routinely been edited down by the dominant film industry to an apolitical, adventure-cape flick". Although their output remains erratic, the Hughes remain "two of the most important black directors who excel by Hollywood standards, while maintaining their ethnic edge" (Donaldson 2003: 156).

References

Andrew, G. (1998) *Stranger than Paradise: Maverick Film-makers in Recent American Cinema*. London: Prion.

Donaldson, M. (2003) *Black Directors in Hollywood*. Austin: University of Texas Press.

Guerrero, E. (1998) A circus of dreams and lies: the black film wave at middle age, in J. Lewis (ed.) *The New American Cinema*. Durham, NC: Duke University Press, pp. 328–52.

Kleinhans, C. (2002) Charles Burnett, in Y. Tasker (ed.) *Fifty Contemporary Filmmakers*. London: Routledge, pp. 65–73.

Richards, A. (2002) From Hell, *Sight and Sound*, (March): 45.

Mark Kermode

Continued from page 390

political commitment to "redress the institutional disenfranchisement of black filmmakers and audiences" (Watkins 1998: 97).

The rise of independent cinema saw a commensurate dissatisfaction with the purely formalist practices of the *avant-garde* generally, or more accurately, incorporated non-classical stylistic devices and non-linear narrative constructions. This was particularly true of developments of certain filmmakers on both coasts, who utilized various "oppositional" techniques within narrative forms as a means of representing the black experience of white-dominated American culture and history more lyrically and forcefully. The work of black filmmakers such as Bill Gunn (*Ganja and Hess*, 1973), Haile Gerima (*Bush Mama*, 1973, *Ashes and Embers*, 1982, *Sankofa*, 1993), Charles Burnett (*Killer of Sheep*, 1977), Julie Dash (*Illusions*, 1982, *Daughters of the Dust*, 1991), and Spike Lee (*She's Gotta Have It*, 1986) demonstrate this. Manthia Diawara points to the "symbolic, reflexive and expressive styles" of these films as they construct narrative space as an alternative to the classical construction of "hierarchical disposition of objects on the screen". They "use spatial narration as a way of revealing and linking Black spaces that have been separated and suppressed by White times, as a means of validating Black culture … of cultural restoration [and] a way for Black filmmakers to reconstruct Black history" (Diawara 1993: 11–13).

Spike Lee's filmmaking aesthetic should be seen within these important precursors in terms of the developing aesthetic of formally transgressive devices and techniques as a means of representing the experience of being Black in ways which both challenge the assumptions and effects of mainstream

narrative cinema and at the same time connect with audiences. Lee's importance to New Black Cinema lies partly in his further development of techniques established by Burnett, Gerima, Dash and others. However, he has been particularly inventive in his strategies for film funding and in his understanding that public promotion of his challenge to Hollywood industry perceptions of both black filmmakers and black audiences would feed into the widespread fascination with black culture among young white audiences. His film funding strategies often deploy multi-sourcing techniques, such as with *She's Gotta Have It* where he received some grants but more importantly was able to attract a number of small private investors, plus his own acquisition of credit to complete the film. He has also been able to use his cannily constructed public persona as a high profile media personality to his advantage. For instance, he used the press to publicly criticize Warner Bros for racism when they balked at providing financing to finish *Malcolm X* (1992), which had run over budget. "Lee charged that despite his track record of critically and commercially successful films, studios continued to treat him unfairly by restricting him to low budget productions" (Watkins 1998: 128). Lee's resourcefulness was again demonstrated when he managed to gain finance to complete the film "by making personal appeals to wealthy black entertainers" (Watkins 1998: 129). In addition to gaining funding for his films, Lee has also been instrumental in promoting his films through linking them and his own political concerns about issues of race with commercial culture's fascination with black culture. While he has been criticized for his tie-ins and media endorsements, he has been able to utilize "a peculiar mix of black cultural resistance and identity politics" which underscores his "public image as a controversial filmmaker to carve out a market niche and attract media publicity" (Watkins 1998: 134). While Lee has generally been restricted to lower budgets, his reputation and use of the media in this way have enabled him to retain a degree of control over his films.

Lee's aesthetic offers one example that Manthia Diawara attributes as a feature of the "Black expressive style" in New Black Cinema, which utilizes space as its primary ground for engagement with mainstream Hollywood cinema. However, Lee has demonstrated a commitment to playing this out within the realms of popular cinema. He negotiates tensions within the African-American social world in ways that are accessible and recognizable to black audiences. This offers a more nuanced alternative to a strategy of deploying inversions of racial stereotypes, which has the effect both of lending undue space to the stereotype and in the process denying that space to develop more relevant and realistic characterizations and situations, which will engage audiences. In the process this produces more complex characters and at the same time exposes fissures and tensions within the social worlds he constructs. He resists closure, such as the end of *Do the Right Thing* where the audience is given two quotes, one from Martin Luther King, the other by Malcolm X, that seem diametrically opposed. This attention to form and commitment to challenging themes has had the effect of providing Lee with an "indie-art" filmmaker's status while attracting respectable audiences, a combination that seems to place him alongside other modern-day auteurs with some industry clout like Martin Scorsese, Jane Campion or David Cronenberg.

Lee's position in the New Black Cinema, while important, does not represent the entire movement, although his relationship with both the independent world and the Hollywood majors is somewhat unique. By far the most interest from majors was generated by the second category of New Black Cinema that Manthia Diawara identifies as those concerned with time, possessing linear narratives and cinematic realism. A high profile example of this is the "ghetto action film cycle". Citing John Singleton's *Boyz in the Hood* (1991), Ernest R. Dickerson's *Juice* (1992), Matty Rich's *Straight out of Brooklyn* (1991) and Bill Duke's *Deep Cover* (1992), she contrasts these narratives' use of time with the emphasis on space and more elliptical temporal structures in the films of Julie Dash, Spike Lee and others. In these films "narrative time coincides with the development of the lives of the characters in the films. These films produce an effect of realism by creating an overlap between the rite of passage into manhood and the narrative time of the story" (Diawara 1993: 20). These narrative structures fit easily into the classical paradigm with goal-oriented protagonists, plausible cause–effect relations and the suppression of temporal and spatial relations in favour of the development of plot. However, these films also take as their setting the urban ghetto and in this sense the construction of this socially and culturally loaded space provides the films with both realism and an avenue of connection not only with young black audiences but also exploits white youth's fascination with black urban culture. These films, while criticized as simply reproducing broad stereotypical assumptions about the nihilistic and violent existence of black youth, can also be seen to offer subtle critiques of the social and political power imbalances that the urban ghetto represents. Referring to a "ghettocentric imagination" as a structuring

Continued on page 396

In 1986, John Singleton was a senior in High School and had already attracted the attention of the Film School at the University of Southern California, well known for its links to the feature filmmaking business in Hollywood. In that same year Spike Lee was experiencing success with his first feature *She's Gotta Have It*. This would have a considerable effect on black filmmakers throughout the country and Singleton was no exception. Lionized as a *wunderkind* director after the success of his first feature *Boyz in the Hood* (1991), one of the first of the gangster action cycle films, he did not forget this influence: "If it wasn't for him [Lee], I wouldn't be making movies" (*The Voice* 1991: 11). Five years before that film, however, Singleton's time at USC was productive in that he won three writing awards as an undergraduate and was signed by the Creative Artists Agency. His style of filmmaking owes little to the type of independent aesthetic that characterized the LA Rebellion and later NYU graduate Lee. Instead his narrative style is more closely aligned with mainstream Hollywood. In *Boyz in the Hood* Singleton was able to find a way of incorporating aspects of the gangster film and melodrama in rendering young black men's limited choices and dangerous solutions. Its realistic depiction not only of gang violence but also family relationships and formation offered a more nuanced view of the African-American ghetto experience in South Central Los Angeles. This view has been praised for its attempt to counter dominant representations of that experience through realism, and also criticized for neglecting to do the same for the domestic experience, instead opting for a more conservative set of solutions. The relationship at the core of *Boyz* lies between the main character Tre Styles and his father Furious, who helps to guide him through the life-threatening experience of growing up in the ghetto. Singleton's remark in his interview with *The Voice* that "African-American men have to take more responsibility for raising their children, especially their boys" coincided with conservative media representations of African-American family life. This has attracted criticism for its gender politics which restates the "pathology paradigm", and its tendency to "reinforce popular interpretation of black familial life" (Watkins 1998: 225). While this is a valid criticism of a number of the ghetto action cycle films (e.g. *Menace II Society* [Hughes Brothers, 1993], *Juice* [Ernest Dickerson, 1992], *New Jack City* [Mario Van Peebles, 1991], *Straight out of Brooklyn* [Matty Rich, 1991]), what marks Singleton's film is its account of positive relationships, and its intelligent analysis of the underlying causes of the conditions which poorer African Americans endure. By offering an alternative to the prevailing two-dimensional image of the violent behaviour of young black males in the popular press and media at the time (which to a large extent continues), the film's overall impact touched a chord with audiences. Arguably even the critiques of the film's representation of familial relationships opened the way for a more detailed debate. All this, and it was a significant hit with mainstream audiences.

The success and treatment of the subject matter of *Boyz in the Hood* helped it to transcend the label of exploitation, however, and it was nominated for two Academy Awards, Best Screenplay and Best Director, as well as being well received at the Cannes Film Festival. Singleton's next two films were critical disappointments although perhaps laudably they did not attempt to capitalize on the ghetto action cycle that *Boyz* had helped to initiate. He returned to form with *Rosewood* (1997), a true story about the burning of a predominately black town in Florida by whites in 1923. In 2000, he stepped in to direct *Shaft*, a mainstream big budget Hollywood remake of the 1971 classic. It was an attempt to exploit the interest in blaxploitation films kindled by Quentin Tarantino's *Jackie Brown* (1997). The film was a financial success if not a critical one, and assured Singleton's status as a mainstream director. His work since then has been divided between directing and producing live and animated features and he has also moved into video game production. His most recent

Tyra Ferrell in *Boyz in the Hood*

feature, *Four Brothers* (2005), has repeated the box office success of *Shaft*. Singleton's material consistently works through themes associated with African-American issues through mainstream narrative and generic frameworks, and by incorporating hip hop culture and sensibilities by using well-known rap stars such as Ice Cube, the late Tupac Shakur (*Poetic Justice*, 1993), Busta Rhymes (*Higher Learning*, 1995) and Andre Benjamin aka Andre 3000 of Outkast (*Four Brothers*, 2005). This has allowed him to continue to connect with young audiences, both black and white, and has secured his position as writer/director/producer in mainstream popular media.

References

Collins, P.H. (1991) *Black Feminist Thought: Knowledge, Consciousness, and the Politics of Empowerment*. New York: Routledge.

Diawara, M. (1993) Black American cinema: the new realism, in Manthia Diawara (ed). *Black American Cinema*. London: Routledge, pp. 3–25.

Jackson, S. (2005) Fast and furious, *BFM*, Nov/Dec, 8(33): 17–18.

Sloan, L. (1991) The Voice interview, John Singleton, *The Voice*, 10 September, 11–12.

Watkins, C. (1998) *Representing: Hip Hop Culture and the Production of Black Cinema*. Chicago and London: University of Chicago Press.

Michael Hammond

Continued from page 393

principle in these films, Watkins defines this as "The expressive culture of black youth [which] loosely organises a world-view that cultivates varying ways of interpreting, representing, and understanding the changing social, economic, and political contours of ghetto dislocation" (1998: 197–8). Albert and Allen Hughes demonstrate one of the advantages of utilizing this in their 1993 film *Menace II Society*, where they are able to give voice to how black youth see the world and their place within it. Through the use of voice-over of the main character Caine, they are able to articulate "the frustrations and disappointments of poor black youth. The spectator is invited to make sense of the social and economic transitions that reshape postindustrial ghetto life from Caine's point of view" (Watkins 1998: 203). Having said that, these films do not escape the critique that they continue to pathologize ghetto violence and black male youth behaviour through gender relations. *Menace II Society*, *Straight out of Brooklyn* and *Boyz in the Hood*, through their assumption of the necessity of the strong father figure and depiction of loveless home lives, are open to the charge that they reinforce the conservative view that the breakdown or non-existence of family life is the root cause of violent behaviour and poverty. While not offering a defence of this, Craig Watkins points to the fact that New Black Cinema has been a privileged site of cultural production which has been able to "animate a broad range of discourses that circulate in the African American community" (Watkins 1998: 230). This has had the effect of extending discourse to a much wider audience range that incorporates not only white American youth but also youth culture globally.

Having its roots in exploitation cinema meant that the "gangster action cycle" therefore offered both opportunities and limitations. It had the regressive effect of cementing the Hollywood industry's expectations of new projects into the narrow realm of ghetto-based pictures. While the early development of the New Black Cinema centred around a collective aim of exploring African-American experiences, the success of many of those associated with New Black Cinema has led them to explore subject matter and themes that are not necessarily associated with or obviously related to those earlier concerns. Spike Lee's more recent films have not been able to command the kind of budgets he raised for *Malcolm X* but he continues to work within popular genres while attempting to weave into them relevant political and social themes including those that cross racial boundaries such as *Summer of Sam* (1999) and *25th Hour* (2002). The Hughes Brothers have made some notable attempts to move beyond the genre, particularly with *From Hell* (2001), an inventive adaptation of the Alan Moore and Eddie Campbell graphic novel of the Jack the Ripper murders. This underscores the cabalistic behaviour of freemasonry with a sensibility, or "accent", that comes from a clear visual understanding of what white conspiring men with dark intent might look like. Julie Dash has continued to work in television and film, most recently with the award-winning *The Rosa Parks Story* (2003).

Critic Nelson George has recently pointed to the long-lasting effect hip hop has had on American culture as well as the film industry. It is of course a phenomenon in popular music and fashion whose attitude, accents and rhythms have been adopted and adapted globally. George points to the "flava" that hip hop has exerted on mainstream Hollywood cinema in films as diverse as *The Woodsman*, which co-stars Mos Def, and *8 Mile*, white rapper Eminem's vehicle, directed by Curtis Hanson. It is not hard to recognize the impact hip hop culture has had on the industry at multiple levels from producing stars such as Fresh Prince, aka Will Smith, as top flight bankable Hollywood fare, to A-list directors such as Antoine Fuqua (*Training Day*, 2001) or F. Gary Gray (*Be Cool*, 2005), with their start as hip hop music video directors. Finally, George notes in a tone of optimism that while the Hollywood industry continues to be a difficult, if nigh impossible arena for black filmmakers, technology, in the form of the digital video camera, is making filmmaking as accessible as the 808 computerized music-making machine made creating records (2005: 11–12). Such an impact could signal a new chapter in the circulation of images of African-American experience through black expressive cultures that push at the boundaries and limitations that the media industry has imposed throughout its history and right up to the present day.

References

Diawara, M. (1993) Black American cinema: the new realism, in Manthia Diawara, *Black American Cinema*. London: Routledge, pp. 3–25.

George, N. (2005) Boyz in the Wood, in "Blackworld", supplement publication in *Sight and Sound*, May, 8–12.

Reid, M.A. (2005), Haile Gerima "Sacred Shield of Culture", in Christine Holmlund and Justin Wyatt (eds) *Contemporary American Independent Film*. London: Routledge, pp. 141–54.

Watkins, C. (1998) *Representing: Hip Hop Culture and the Production of Black Cinema*. Chicago: University of Chicago Press.

NEW QUEER CINEMA

Michele Aaron

NEW QUEER CINEMA is the name attached to a wave of queer films that gained critical acclaim on the festival circuit in the early 1990s. Coined, and largely chronicled, by film theorist B. Ruby Rich, New Queer Cinema, or NQC as I will refer to it, represented the exciting prospect that lesbian and gay images and filmmakers had turned a corner. No longer burdened by the approval-seeking sackcloth of positive imagery, or the obscurity of marginal production, films could be both radical and popular, stylish and economically viable.

The wave, or movement, consisted of the surprise hits of Sundance 1991 and 1992 – *Paris is Burning* (Jennie Livingston, 1990), *Poison* (Todd Haynes, 1991), and *Swoon* (Tom Kalin, 1992) – and many other films. The larger crop is generally noted to include

Poison

Tongues Untied (Marlon Riggs, 1990), *My Own Private Idaho* (Gus van Sant, 1991), *Young Soul Rebels* (Isaac Julien, 1991), *R.S.V.P* (Laurie Lynd, 1991), *Edward II* (Derek Jarman, 1991), *Khush* (Pratibha Parmar, 1991), *The Hour and Times* (Christopher Munch, 1992) and *The Living End* (Gregg Araki, 1992) as well as work by filmmakers Sadie Benning, Cecilia Dougherty, Su Friedrich, John Greyson and Monica Treut. The films, as Rich pointed out, had few aesthetic or narrative strategies in common, but what they seemed to share was an attitude. She found them "irreverent" and "energetic", and, according to J. Hoberman, their protagonists were "proudly assertive" (Hoberman 1992: 31; Rich 1992: 32). Indeed, what binds the group together is, I feel, best described as defiance. This defiance can be thought of as operating on several levels, all of which serve to illuminate the characteristics of NQC.

Firstly, despite the fast rules of acceptable subjects dictated by Western popular culture, these films give voice to the marginalized, not simply in terms of focusing on the lesbian and gay community, but on the subgroups contained within it. For example, both *Tongues Untied* and *Young Soul Rebels* explore black gay male experience (the latter also offering the rarity of the interracial couple). *My Own Private Idaho* has male prostitutes for protagonists. The documentary *Paris is Burning* attends to the gay and transsexual Hispanic and Latino youth of the New York drag ball scene.

Secondly, the films are unapologetic about their characters' faults or, rather, crimes: they eschew positive imagery. *Swoon*, *Poison* and *The Living End* beautify the criminal and (homo)eroticize violence. The gay male couples at the centre of *Swoon* and *The Living End* revel in their murderous relationships.

Kalin's highly stylized cinematography and use of black-and-white turn the film's unseemly events into an exquisite period piece. In a central scene, a high angle tableau of the courtroom is cross-cut with footage from the original trial. As an "alienist" describes the pair's pathology from the stand, a bed upon which they frolic, floppy-haired and embraced, fills the space in front. Araki, on the other hand, poses his main characters as West Coast-cool, well-groomed despite being on the road, "hot" but preoccupied. Meanwhile, Haynes borrows heavily from Jean Genet's *Un chant d'amour* (1950), especially its aesthetic and erotic charge, in imparting one inmate's sexual obsession for another in the dark vaults and unshaven terrain of a men's prison.

Thirdly, the films defy the sanctity of the past, especially the homophobic past. *Edward II*, *The Hours and Times* and *Swoon* all revisit historical relationships and firmly instate the overlooked homosexual content. *Edward II* tells of King Edward's homosexual relationship with Galveston. *The Hours and Times* develops the erotic dynamic between John Lennon and Brian Epstein. *Swoon* retells the Leopold and Loeb murder case, and, most importantly, Hitchcock's rendition of it in *Rope*, but with the homosexuality of the murderers fully restored.

Fourthly, the films frequently defy cinematic convention in terms of form, content and genre. The shorts of Sadie Benning, shot on a Fisher Price Pixel Vision, employ all manner of textual innovation to provide ragged, experimental but no less confident pieces. John Greyson's *Zero Patience* offers the unlikely pairing of AIDS and the musical (a combination which later would find remarkable international success in the Broadway hit, *Rent*). Indeed, Greyson has been distinguished for his dislocation of traditional film practices.

Jules Pidduck (2002: 270) sees him as "reappropriating mainstream media" through his use "of split screens and embedded images". Like other new queer artists he also reappropriates mainstream genres and formats (feature length rather than just shorts) and, ultimately, distribution/exhibition channels. New Queer Cinema also incorporates a defiance of the sanctity of mainstream cinema history. Just in case one misses Kalin's swipe at Hitchcock, *Swoon* restages a scene right out of *Rear Window* with Jeff and Lisa's romantic dialogue taking place between the male lovers. Haynes, in firmly identifying with the outlaw filmmaking of Genet, grounds New Queer Cinema in, well, Old Queer Cinema – the uncompromising work of Genet, Fassbinder, Warhol, Sayles – rather than in the mainstream gains in gay representation. The lack of respect for the governing codes of, for example, form or content, linearity or coherence, indeed, for Hollywood itself, has much in common with postmodernism. In fact, it was in terms of postmodernism, as "Homo Pomo",

that Rich (1992: 32) first described NQC.

Finally, the films in many ways defy death. The joyful murderers of *Swoon* and *The Living End* resist its sobering effect. But the key way in which death is defied is in terms of AIDS. Death is defied as the life-sentence passed by the disease: the HIV+ leads of *The Living End* instead find the "time-bomb" to be totally liberating. It is even defied as final: in *Zero Patience* the first victim of AIDS comes back to life.

It is not simply that a sense of defiance characterizes these films, but that it marks them as queer. Indeed, "queer" and its critical and cultural ascendancy are the crucial context for understanding the emergence and evolution of NQC, and it is to this that I now turn.

Queerly there

Queer, a derogatory term levelled at the non-hetero seeming, was reappropriated in the late 1980s and early 1990s by its victims as a

Continued on page 403

The Silence of the Lambs

An award-winning genre piece, *The Silence of the Lambs* stands as an early 1990s marker of the mainstreaming of horror. With strong dramatic performances and striking imagery, the film succeeded for contemporary critics and audiences both as horror (it was promoted as the scariest film of the year) and as drama. *The Silence of the Lambs* drew from and spoke to strong levels of media interest in the figure of the serial killer, as well as drawing on popular knowledge of profiling and forensics (practices outlined in true crime magazines, fiction and programming). Adapted from a best-selling novel by Thomas Harris (originally published in 1988), *The Silence of the Lambs* features two contrasting white male serial killers who are systematically played off against each other. Hannibal Lecter (Anthony Hopkins) is urbane, insightful and incarcerated; as both psychiatrist and cannibal, Lecter's power and violence centre on the mouth. Jame Gumb/"Buffalo Bill" (Ted Levine), by contrast, is mobile yet inarticulate; his pursuit of a succession of large women whom he starves and skins involves a different kind of assault on the body.

Together Lecter and Bill are suggestive of different aspects of a popular fascination with the male serial killer. On the one hand, Lecter as killer is presented as a superior intellect, one who does not regard himself as governed by society's rules, and who cannot be assessed by the "standard tests". He is, in other words, exceptional. Lecter's monstrous ability to get inside people's heads, to exploit their fears and anxieties, as well as his crude capability for

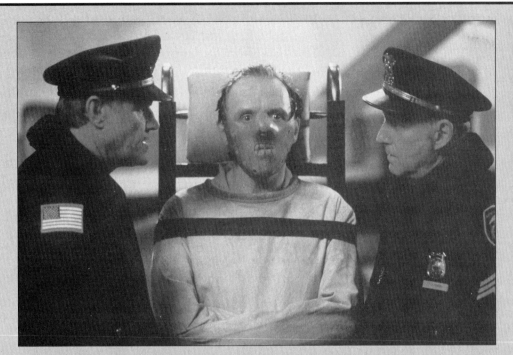

The Silence of the Lambs

violence – something reserved until his gruesome escape in the latter part of the film – renders him a figure of both fear and authority, an ambivalent status that certainly caused concern among some of the film's contemporary commentators. Indeed, Lecter is literally an authority within the narrative as the FBI consult him in an attempt to profile/track Buffalo Bill. Bill/Gumb's asocial status is of a very different kind to Lecter's. His failure to communicate effectively and his evidently perverse desire to craft a woman suit from the hides of his female victims, mark Gumb as both voiceless monster and sexually ambiguous predator. Indeed, that Gumb was at least potentially readable as "gay", and *Silence* itself as homophobic, was another cause of controversy on the film's release.

For media studies scholars the film's foregrounding of a female investigator, in the figure of trainee FBI agent Clarice Starling (Jodie Foster) made *The Silence of the Lambs* an object of some interest. While, as Linda Mizejewski notes, female investigators are familiar figures in both fiction and latterly television, within the cinema she remains an unusual presence, only rarely occupying a leading role. If the critical and commercial success of *The Silence of the Lambs* suggested that this paucity of cinematic female investigators might change, this was not ultimately to be realized. Foster's Starling was an acknowledged reference point for the characterization of Dana Scully (Gillian Anderson) in Fox's television hit *The X-Files* (1993–2002); female investigators and/or profilers also appear in films such as *Kiss the Girls* (1997), *The Bone Collector* (1999), *Murder By Numbers* (2002), *Taking Lives* (2004), *Twisted* (2004), yet these remain exceptions in cinematic terms. Moreover, the fact that Starling is characterized in terms of her intellect and ambition, rather than glamour or sexual availability, and that she nonetheless remains a figure of empathy and integrity, is within the Hollywood cinema, remarkable. Considering the emphasis placed on both Starling's rookie status and her uncertain, troubled identity (her tentative class mobility; the extent to which she is haunted by her father's death), *The Silence of the Lambs* can be more-or-less explicitly read as a personal and professional rite of passage narrative. In the opening sequence Starling runs alone, training her body; the film's conclusion features her graduation as an FBI agent. Her successful maturation serves to underline the perversity of Gumb/Bill's doomed attempts at transformation suggested by the imagery of butterflies within the film. The metaphor of transformation suggested by the cocoons Bill inserts into his victim's throats, is already somewhat ambivalent: Bill's cocoons of choice are not those of butterflies but rare moths, bugs associated with decay as much as spectacular transformation. As this suggests, Gumb/Bill remains a rather one-dimensional monster.

The Silence of the Lambs arguably achieved its mainstream success through the hybridization of two familiar story types: horror and the detective or police procedural. Both Lecter and Starling are mediating figures in this generic hybridization. Indeed, whatever his transgressions, Gumb lacks the complexity of characterization possessed by Lecter and Starling by virtue of their association with different Hollywood genres. Lecter is both monstrous killer and articulate profiler, straddling horror and investigative fictions. Starling, for her part, is characterized not only as novice investigator, but also as the ''final girl'' described by Carol Clover as a founding character type of the slasher film, and even as a (justly) paranoid victim/heroine of the female gothic. In this context Starling's quest to find Bill before he slays Catherine Martin (he holds his victims captive for three days before killing them) is also a journey of self-discovery; her experiences, empathy for Bill's victims and Lecter's invasive questioning lead to the revival of long-buried memories of loss and of the desire to succeed. Starling's quest, both personal and professional, leads her to an intense series of exchanges with Lecter who professes himself intrigued by the young trainee. Their relationship, or at least the exchanges of views and information between them, is central to the film, punctuating the more active/conventional police search for the killer; given the intensity of their connection, the difference in their ages and the Hollywood cinema's insistence of framing adventurous women in the shadow of their fathers, it is perhaps not surprising that many critics read these scenes as suggestive of a romantic, erotic or paternal relationship between the two. Whatever one makes of such accounts, it is clear that Starling's striving is presented as intimately connected with the need to come to terms with the past. Though there are analogies between Starling and Bill in their troubled identities and quest for personal change, Starling's characterization is far more complex. Drawing on character types associated with a series of genres, Starling combines rational investigator, intuitive profiler and victim/heroine; a representative of law enforcement who does not yet possess the authority to which she aspires, Starling is both inside and outside the FBI, just as The Silence of the Lambs is inside and outside both horror and the police procedural.

References

Clover, C.J. (1992) *Men, Women and Chain Saws: Gender in the Modern Horror Film*. London: BFI.

Mizejewski, L. (2004) *Hardboiled and High Heeled: The Woman Detective in Popular Culture*. New York: Routledge.

Seltzer, M. (1998) *Serial Killers: Death and Life in America's Wound Culture*. London: Routledge.

Tasker, Y. (2002) *The Silence of the Lambs*. London: BFI.

Yvonne Tasker

Continued from page 400

defiant means of empowerment, echoing black activists' use of "nigger" in the 1960s. Relieving the burden of the titular expansion of L-G-B-T (lesbian, gay, bisexual and transgender), queer's most basic function is as an umbrella term or catch-all for uniting various forms of non-straight sexual identity. But it means much more than this. Queer represents the resistance to, primarily, the normative codes of gender and sexual expression – that masculine men sleep with feminine women – but also to the restrictive potential of gay and lesbian sexuality – that only men sleep with men, and women sleep with women. In this way, queer, as a critical concept, encompasses the non-fixity of gender expression and the non-fixity of both straight and gay sexuality. As Richard Dyer (2002: 4) rightly reminds us, the contemporary formulation of queer functions in sharp contrast to its past, it signifies a fluidity of identity where, historically, queer represented an "exclusive and fixed sexuality". To be queer now, then, means to be untethered from "conventional" codes of behaviour. At its most expansive and utopian, queer contests (hetero- and homo-) normality.

As a theoretically lucrative "oppositional stance" (Meyer 1994: 3) and the latest trajectory of gender theory, queer gained in academic currency throughout the 1990s, fuelled by the cultural marketplace. Indeed, *Paris is Burning* was a prime example in Judith Butler's *Bodies That Matter* (a work central to the academic ascendancy of queer). As a cultural trend – coming to characterize the so-called queer 1990s – queerness represents the flirtation with non-fixity embodied in the mainstream by "lesbian chic" and films like *The Object of My Affection* (Nicholas Hytner, 1998) and, alternatively, by "dykes-fuck-fellas" storylines found in lesbian erotica and staged in the NQC film *Go Fish* (Rose Troche, 1994).[1] The queer figure *par excellence* was the transsexual, and the decade saw the publication of work on the subject by the "community's" quasi leaders, Kate Bornstein and Leslie Feinberg.[2] It would also see the use of Del La Grace Volcano's transgendered images in an episode of *Sex in the City* and climax in the major success of *Boys Don't Cry*, which told Brandon Teena/Teena Brandon's short life-story, in 1999.

In order to understand NQC fully, one must understand "queer" as critical intervention, cultural product and political strategy (and NQC as an art-full manifestation of the overlap between the three). Queer represented the reappropriation of the power of the antagonistic, homophobic society, through reclaiming the term of abuse but also through a new approach to "gay" politics: a taking on of the institution, rather than a fearful, assimilated, complicity. Direct action, as practised by Queer Nation, ACT UP and Outrage, was the key strategy of queer politics in the late 1980s and early 1990s, with AIDS accelerating its urgency. The sense of defiance characterizing NQC is the obvious product of this political exigency and practice:

> For many members of a generation coming to political consciousness haunted by AIDS but collectively strengthened by AIDS activism, *queer* has become an attractive and oppositional self-label that acknowledges a new cultural context for politics, criticism, reception-consumption, and production. (Creekmur and Doty 1995: 6)

Many of NQC's practitioners, Kalin and Greyson most obviously, are firmly located within this activist background. In fact, NQC cannot be removed from the context of the AIDS epidemic. While *Paris is Burning* is, ostensibly, about the issues of race, queerness and poverty in the 1980s/1990s, AIDS nevertheless lurks in the background. José Arroyo has claimed that AIDS is the absent centre of two of the foundational new queer films, *Edward II* and *My Own Private Idaho* (1993: 70–96). Monica Pearl (1999: 210–25) identified it as the subtext of two mainstream genres of contemporary cinema: the sex thriller and the "reincarnation film". Both Kalin and Haynes have concluded that AIDS is, actually, what their films were all about (see Saunders 1998: 134; and Lim 2002: 43).

Douglas Crimp (1993: 315), using AIDS activist history to comprehend queerness, sees ACT UP members as the archetypal queers for they were characterized by "identification *across* identities": a straight woman fought for a gay male friend's treatment, a white lesbian pursued health access for black HIV-infected mothers. This is what made AIDS activism necessarily queer. Of course, "identification across identities" is, fundamentally, what happens in cinema, as the spectator aligns himself or herself with someone else on screen. NQC, then, marks the emphasis upon and success of this "cross-identification", as, say, the gay or, more significantly, the straight spectator's identification with the queer villain who is so unlike "him" self. Cross-identification is, also, as I will suggest below, central to popular cinema's altered stake in queer spectatorship.

It must be remembered that queer's defiance is levelled at mainstream homophobic society *but also* at the "tasteful and tolerated" gay culture that cohabits with it (Smyth 1992: 48). In fact, the new queer artists or "queercore" of the early 1990s, as Dennis Cooper refers to them, were defined as much, if not more, by their opposition to gay culture as to straight (Cooper 1996: 296; Smyth 1992). It is no surprise then that NQC would have a

particularly fraught relationship with the mainstream – after all, popular success undermines oppositionality – and would find many of its strongest critics within the gay community. Indeed, my exposition of the films' commonalities glosses over several of the charges levelled at the categorization and celebration of NQC. Most immediate is the issue of the movement's roll-call. As was often pointed out, NQC, in its earliest formulation, was a boys' own story. The female delegates and those of colour were added in haste and retrospectively (see Parmar 1992: 35; Taubin 1992: 37). Indeed, the narrowness of queer's application has been an ongoing issue among its proponents. Queer is not just about gender and sexuality, but the restrictiveness of the rules governing them and their intersection with other aspects of identity. To be really queerly is to apprehend "the complexity of what actually happens 'between' the contingent spaces where each variable [race, class, gender] intersects with the others" (Mercer 1991: 193). Secondly, the embracing of negative stereotypes and, in particular, the enduring centrality of the queer villain continues to torment. As Michael Saunders points out, such characters embody queer defiance and anti-assimilationism, for many, their radical status is always to be tempered if not upstaged by their overwhelming ability to confirm and perpetuate the homophobic stereotypes of the majority.[3] That said, the argument is not so simply polarized within the films themselves. Indeed, one must evaluate the difference between the more apparent politics of *Swoon* and the seeming gratuity of *The Living End* . . . or just resist the call to judge them altogether. As Ellie Hansen (1999: 11) notes,

Every film with a queer theme, no matter what the sexuality of its director or the origin of its funding, is still embattled in a highly moralistic debate over the correctness of its politics, as though art were to be valued only as sexual propaganda.

New Queer Cinema is, of course, a contested category. It is contested for its exclusivity (and tokenistic inclusivity). It is contested for its unwarranted optimism: in heralding a minor revolution when a few films do not a movement make; in promoting queer villainy while homophobic violence rages; and in suggesting a queer-friendliness of mass culture when the majority, as Harry Benshoff argues, remain unaltered.[4] The category is contested also for the US-centricity of its films and theory. Perhaps the most irreparable of charges against NQC is that the promise indicated by the films of the early 1990s was never fully realized. Despite that initial furore on the Indie scene, and the dramatic increase in the production of, and audience for, queer films during the 1990s, a new *and enduring* sector of popular radical work failed to materialize (Rich 1993: 85). In many ways this is hardly surprising, for how can a marriage between the popular and the radical be sustained when such an association erodes the very meaning of each? By the end of the decade, NQC had, as Rich argued, journeyed from "radical impulse to niche market" with its range of fairly innocuous and mostly unremarkable films targeting a narrow, rather than all-inclusive, new queer market (Rich 2000: 23). These films included *Clare of the Moon* (Nicole Conn, 1992), *Bar Girls* (Marita Giovanni, 1994), *Jeffrey* (Christopher Ashley, 1995), *The Incredibly True Adventures of Two Girls in Love* (Maria Maggenti, 1995, Fig. 20 (*see plate section*)), *Gazon Maudit* (Josephine Balasko, 1995), *Thin Ice* (Fiona Cunningham-Reid, 1995), *When Night is Falling* (Patricia Rozema, 1995), *Hollow Reed* (Angela Pope, 1997), *Losing Chase* (Kevin Bacon, 1996), *The Watermelon Woman* (Cheryl Dunye, 1996), *Kiss Me Guido* (Tony Vitale, 1997), *Everything Relative* (Sharon Pollack, 1997), *All Over Me* (Alex Sichel, 1997), *High Art* (Lisa Cholodenko, 1998), *Fucking Amål/Show Me Love* (Lukas Moodysson, 1998) and *But I'm a Cheerleader* (Jamie Babbit, 2000). *Swoon* and *Poison* stand almost alone in terms of critical attention garnered by the New Queer films. Indeed, it is not until *Boys Don't Cry* that queerness could claim such a spotlight again, but for some the Academy's praise, if not the film itself, reeked of mainstream recuperation.[5] Cynically put, NQC kick-started Hollywood's awareness of a queerer audience (a combination of the "pink profit" zone and the general public's current interests) and its appropriation and dilution of queer matters. Albeit "gaysploitation", queer work and queer themes found financial support and the careers of Haynes and Araki were launched (Lim 2002: 39). Ultimately, however, there was little more than superficial change.

That said, there is evidence to suggest that NQC triggered significant cultural and critical (and small-p political) gains. Its real impact, and value, are not to be measured by the quantity or quirkiness of potential members, but by the queerer culture it ushered in. As Rich (2002: 43) asked of NQC ten years on: "Did it disappear, or is it everywhere?"

Queerly cultured

The upside of Hollywood's appropriation of the new queer potential was the acceptability of queer themes and queer characters in the mainstream. (Mainstream in terms of exhibition and distribution, if not production: for this was also a period when the polarity of the

Independent and Hollywood sectors was fraying.) No longer consigned to the sole role of gay neighbor (who meets untimely death), 1990s Hollywood's homosexuals lived varied and accomplished lives. Not sad young men but sane, sexy stars (see *My Best Friend's Wedding*, *In and Out*): not merely manly but hot and feisty women (see *Basic Instinct*, *Bound*). Stereotypes were revised rather than rejected. *As Good as it Gets* (James L Brooks, 1997), for example, offers the "gay man next door", but the character is soon shown to be far more stable than the film's protagonist whose homophobia becomes one of his and the narrative's learning curves. According to *In and Out* (Frank Oz, 1997), the shorthand signs for male homosexuality − a love of show tunes and overgesticulation − are alive and well in Kevin Kline's gay man but accompanied by macho-incarnate Magnum (Tom Sellick). There were what might be called "queer experiment" films − those where characters explore their sexuality, such as *Chasing Amy* (Kevin Smith, 1997), *The Object of My Affection* and *The Next Best Thing* (John Schlesinger, 2000). All of these, however, offer the explorations of a gay character and it is not until *Kissing Jessica Stein* (Charles Herman-Wurmfeld, 2002) that we receive "straight" protagonists (or, rather, a "straight" audience) secure enough in themselves to enjoy a short spell of sexual reorientation.

The legacy of NQC is evident also in the surge of non-Hollywood films in 1994/5 about lesbian couples who kill. This art-house group clearly testifies to the currency and exploitation of the queerer text. *Fun* (Rafael Zelinski, US/Canada 1994), *Sister my Sister* (Nancy Meckler, UK 1994), *La Cérémonie* (Claude Chabrol, Fr/Ger. 1995), *Butterfly Kiss* (Michael Winterbottom, UK 1994) and *Heavenly Creatures* (Peter Jackson, NZ 1994) raised the same kinds of questions as NQC (primarily the rejection of positive images) and offered similarly innovative, stylish narratives and compelling, if corrupt, characters. Although embraced and lambasted by queer critics (as is the norm), the group confirms that queer films are not the sole provenance of queer filmmakers. And hopefully, by return, this suggests that "straight" films are not the sole provenance of "straight" filmmakers. This erosion of the essentialism of the creative process has been noted by Rich (2000: 24) who, looking beyond the directors, attributes the triumphs of straight actors playing gay to the "runaway success of the New Queer Cinema works". Likewise, in Rupert Everett's recent successes, *An Ideal Husband* and *The Importance of Being Earnest* (Oliver Parker I, 1999 and 2002), we find the out/queer actor enjoying "straight" roles (although how straight and comedic Wildean characters can be is questionable).

The queering of contemporary Western culture is not about the products alone, but about their theorization. Dovetailing with the emergence and evolution of NQC was the proliferation of queer film theory. This can be thought of as operating on three related levels. Firstly, as the critical exploration of queer imagery and directors: in other words, the wave of films provided a focus for those cinema scholars among the expanding audience. Secondly, as a rereading and reclaiming of classical texts: a retrospective queering of film history. Thirdly, as a discussion of queer spectatorship: what these queer texts reveal about the spectator's experience of cinema.

Alongside the ever-increasing body of critical work on the films of NQC and on the queerer mainstream that followed, theorists have pursued the movement's impact upon non-Anglo-American and non-narrative filmmaking. Broadening the category, and challenging our understanding, of NQC, attention has turned to queer film within, for example, European, Antipodean, Third and experimental contexts (see Jennings, Pidduck and Hok-Sze Leung, in Aaron 2004). Perhaps the most noted scholarly contributions exist, not surprisingly, within the realm of revising cinema history. For example, Patricia White's 1999 book *Uninvited* and Alexander Doty's *Flaming Classics* in 2000 both queered classical Hollywood, by which I mean they revealed queer themes and characters within a range of conventional texts. Indebted to the lesbian and gay film history (of Richard Dyer, Vito Russo, etc.), these studies are, instead, queer. While they similarly uncover gay or lesbian encodings or decodings (that is, the intervention of the films' creators or audiences), they question narrative cinema's normative rather than heterosexual economy. Such studies are, inevitably, about spectatorship, about how the general spectator is "invited to make lesbian inferences" (White 1999) or to adopt "reception positions that can be considered 'queer' in some way, regardless of a person's declared sexual and gender allegiances" (Doty 1993: xi). But this queer spectatorship is not the sole domain of the classical period or the subtext-rich narrative.

Founded upon the spectator's alignment or identification with or gravitation towards a "character-not-you", narrative cinema itself depends upon establishing empathy, alliances and desire along lines not restricted to normative patterns of attraction. Cinema, as I implied above, is rooted in queer processes. Not only has NQC helped generate this kind of thinking, it has encouraged mainstream culture to harness cinema's queer potential. This is not another way of describing Hollywood's flirtation with queer imagery but, instead, represents a shift from the disavowal

to the avowal, the open affirmation, of queer implications. No longer does popular culture have to seem to render queer configurations safe – through, for example, humour, homophobia or other memos of heterosexuality, and, especially, closure. In the remarkably popular *Boys Don't Cry*, the queerness of Brandon's girlfriend (and the spectator by implication) is indulged rather than repressed, as time and time again the narrative constructs her complicity in "his disguise" as a man. Popular culture no longer *has to* disavow queerness, but, of course, it still does – for to keep queerness at bay, safely restricted in its influence, ensures the impact of its interventions and, more than this, sustains the status quo. And, after all, such things underline mainstream entertainment. What is crucial to remember is that disavowal is a defensive mechanism; queerness must only appear to be quelled. This, perhaps, is the lesson of NQC: it must be contested so that it can endure, it must remain marginal so that it can flirt effectively with the centre. While the films and the directors stopped "stealing" the show at Sundance a long time ago, edgy, inspiring, acclaimed but still defiant films – like *By Hook or By Crook* (Silas Howard and Harry Dodge, 2001), or *L.I.E.* (Michael Cuesta, 2001) – just keep on coming.

Notes

1 See Budge and Hamer (1994). See also the short fiction of Pat Califia and Thomas (1993: 91–104).
2 See Bornstein (1994) and Feinberg (1996), and the *Sex in the City* series, one episode featuring the work of Del La Grace Volcano.
3 For discussions of the "monsters'" charms, see Benshoff (1997) and Saunders (1998: 19). For the debate on homophobia and

queer villains, see Holmlund (1994); Pidduck (1995: 64–72); Griggers (1995: 162–76); Aaron (1999: 67–84) and Smelik (2004: 68–79).

4 The 1990s saw the brutal murders of, for example, Mathew Shepard and Brandon Teena. See also Benshoff (2004: 172–86).

5 See the debate on *Boys Don't Cry* in *Screen*, 2001, vol. 42, parts 1–3.

References

Aaron, M. (1999) 'Til death us do part: cinema's queer couples who kill, in M. Aaron (ed.) *The Body's Perilous Pleasures*. Edinburgh: Edinburgh University Press.

Arroyo, J. (1993) Death desire and identity: the political unconscious of "New Queer Cinema", in J. Bristow and A.R. Wilson (eds) *Activating Theory: Lesbian, Gay, Bisexual Politics*. London: Lawrence and Wishart.

Benshoff, H. (1997) *Monsters in the Closet: Homosexuality and the Horror Film*. Manchester: Manchester University Press.

Benshoff, H. (2004) Reception of a queer mainstream film, in M. Aaron (ed.) *New Queer Cinema: A Critical Reader*. Edinburgh: Edinburgh University Press.

Bornstein, K. (1994) *Gender Outlaw: On Men, Women and the Rest of Us*. New York: Routledge.

Budge, B., and Hamer, D. (eds) (1994) *The Good, the Bad, and the Gorgeous: Popular Culture's Romance with Lesbianism*. London: Pandora.

Butler, J. (1993) *Bodies That Matter: On the Discursive Limits of "Sex"*. New York: Routledge.

Cooper, D. (1992) Queercore, *Village Voice*, 30 June.

Cooper, D. (1996) Queercore, in D. Morton (ed.) *The Material Queer: A Les B-Gay Cultural Studies Reader*. Boulder, CO: Westview Press.

Creekmur, C.K. and Doty, A. (1995) Introduction, in *Out in Culture: Gay, Lesbian, and Queer Essays on Popular Culture*. London: Cassell.

Crimp, D. (1993) Right on, girlfriend! In Michael Warner (ed.) *Fear of a Queer Planet: Queer Politics and Social Theory*. Minneapolis: University of Minnesota.

Doty, A. (1993) *Making Things Perfectly Queer: Interpreting Mass Culture*. Minneapolis: University of Minnesota Press.

Doty, A. (2000) *Flaming Classics: Queering the Film Canon*. London: Routledge.

Dyer, R. (2002) *The Culture of Queers*. London: Routledge.

Feinberg, L. (1996) *Transgender Warriors: Making History from Joan of Arc to Ru Paul*. Boston: Beacon Press.

Griggers, C. (1995) Phantom and reel projections: lesbians and the (serial) killing-machine, in J. Halberstam and I. Livingston (eds) *Posthuman Bodies*. Bloomington: Indiana University Press.

Hansen, E. (ed.) (1999) *Out Takes: Essays on Queer Theory and Film*. Durham, NC: Duke University Press.

Hoberman, J. (1992) Out and Inner Mongolia, *Premiere*, October.

Hok-Sze Leung, H. (2004) New Queer Cinema and Third Cinema, in M. Aaron (ed.) *New Queer Cinema: A Critical Reader*. Edinburgh: Edinburgh University Press.

Holmlund, C. (1994) A decade of deadly dolls: Hollywood and the woman killer, in H. Birch (ed.) *Moving Targets: Women, Murder and Representation*. Berkeley: University of California Press.

Jennings, R. and Lominé, L. (2004) Nationality and New Queer Cinema: Australian film, in M. Aaron (ed.) *New Queer Cinema: A Critical Reader*. Edinburgh: Edinburgh University Press.

Lim, D. (2002) The reckless moment: two pioneers of the New Queer Cinema look back on a short-lived sensation, *Village Voice*, 26 March.

Mercer, K. (1991) Skin head sex thing, in Bad Object Choices (eds) *How Do I Look?* Seattle: Bay Press.

Meyer, M. (1994) Introduction: reclaiming the discourse of camp, in M. Meyer (ed.) *The Politics and Poetics of Camp*. London: Routledge.

Parmar, P. (1992) Queer questions, *Sight and Sound*, (September): 35.

Pearl, M. (1999) Symptoms of AIDS in contemporary film: mortal anxiety in an age of sexual panic, in M. Aaron (ed.) *The Body's Perilous Pleasures: Dangerous Desires and Contemporary Culture*. Edinburgh: Edinburgh University Press.

Pidduck, J. (1995) The Hollywood fatal femme: (Dis)figuring feminism, family, irony, violence, *Cineaction*, 38 (Fall): 64–72.

Pidduck, J. (2002) After 1980: margins and mainstreams, in R. Dyer (ed), *Now You See It*, 2nd edn. London: Routledge.

Pidduck, J. (2004) New Queer Cinema and experimental video, in M. Aaron (ed.) *New Queer Cinema: A Critical Reader*. Edinburgh: Edinburgh University Press.

Rich, B.R. (1992) New Queer Cinema, *Sight and Sound*, 2: 5.

Rich, B.R. (1993) Reflections on a queer screen, *GLQ*, 1(1): 83–91.

Rich, B.R. (2000) Queer and present danger, *Sight and Sound*, (March).

Rich, B.R. (2002) Vision quest: searching for diamonds in the rough, *Village Voice*, 26 March.

Saunders, M.W. (1998) *Imps of the Perverse: Gay Monsters in Film*. Wesport, CT: Praeger.

Smelik, A. (2004) Art cinema and murderous lesbians, in M. Aaron (ed.) *New Queer Cinema: A Critical Reader*. Edinburgh: Edinburgh University Press.

Smyth, C. (1992) *Lesbians Talk Queer Notions*. London: Scarlet Press.

Taubin, A. (1992) Beyond the sons of Scorsese, *Sight and Sound*, (September).

Thomas, T. (1993) Me and the boys, in S. Bright (ed.) *The Best American Erotica 1993*. New York: Macmillan.

White, P. (1999) *Uninvited: Classical Hollywood Cinema and Lesbian Representability*. Bloomington: Indiana University Press.

21
FANTASIZING GENDER AND RACE: WOMEN IN CONTEMPORARY US ACTION CINEMA

Yvonne Tasker

THIS CHAPTER EXPLORES gendered representation in selected examples of US action and adventure cinema since the mid-1990s. Although there is much to be said about men and masculinity in the genre, my essay focuses on the cultural significance of the action heroine. Briefly, towards the end of the 1990s a discernible shift takes place in the embodiment of the woman in Hollywood action, a shift that I characterize in terms of the emergence of a "postfeminist action heroine". I'm not arguing that this figure replaces some pre-existing *feminist* action heroine, although for many critics the functioning of action as a site of gender trouble is one of the factors that has rendered it so compelling. Instead I'm using the term postfeminist to signal ways in which the construction of contemporary action-oriented female protagonists draws on wider discourses of gender currently operating in US culture. For my purposes, postfeminism can be understood as a form of popularized feminism, by which I mean the incorporation of (a) assumptions about female economic and legal equality into the political/cultural mainstream, and (b) the evident anxiety that stems from an assumption that such changes have taken place. Popular feminism, needless to say, constitutes a partial and particular understanding of feminism as an agenda already achieved. It attempts to articulate and even speak for the figure of the independent woman while negotiating cultural anxieties that independence or, particularly relevant for this discussion of the action heroine, agency might render women unfeminine, allow them to usurp male authority, or even to reject men (and by extension heterosexuality) altogether. Postfeminist culture speaks gender within the terms of both liberation and celebration, on one hand, regression and backlash, on the other. Similarly, contemporary action and adventure cinema celebrates the physicality and capacity for violence embodied in the (typically lithe) body of the action heroine, while reassuring audiences as to her sexual desirability/availability. A more fearful evocation of the physically capable woman as masculine, mannish or lesbian also persists within contemporary visual culture, whether in the form of villains or noble but ultimately doomed supporting characters. Here I seek to map what is at stake in these developments and to consider some of the ways in which the action heroine remains a figure of relevance for feminism.

At a rudimentary level the action heroine is interesting for feminism to the extent that she troubles mainstream cinema's routine configuration of women in terms of tropes such as passivity, hysteria, monstrous maternity or sexualized threat. Thus the fact that female protagonists in action might be accorded even limited amounts of narrative agency represents something of a departure from the norms of Hollywood representation as theorized by pathbreaking works of feminist scholarship in the 1970s and early 1980s.[1] Like the *femme fatale* of film *noir*, the action heroine can be understood as a complex and ambivalent response to feminism, a figure articulating both female desire and patriarchal anxiety.[2] The action heroine is reminiscent of the *femme fatale* in another fashion too: the extent to which she responds to feminism, to questions of female agency and self-determination, without being clearly legible as either feminist or anti-feminist. Indeed, it is precisely the

erasure of feminist *politics* from the cinematic representation of female strength (and weakness) that accounts for the uncertainty expressed by many feminist scholars in the face of "new" configurations of agency such as that embodied by the action heroine. It is in line with this observation that I frame my discussion of the action heroine in this chapter in terms of a postfeminist culture.

The late 1990s emergence of the action heroine as a figure associated primarily with glamour and sexuality seems to be both backward- and forward-looking, with the high-profile cinematic reworking of *Charlie's Angels* (2000) an indicative example. The original show (ABC, 1976–81) was a successful example of the "jiggle genre", a variant of the crime format that Linda Mizejewski (2004) locates as one successful strategy deployed by network television to counteract increasing levels of concerns over violent imagery. As Mizejewski notes, however, despite its emphasis on the female body as sexual spectacle, with multiple costume changes, eroticized undercover work and so on, the show was extremely successful in attracting female viewers. Indeed, she describes its characteristic combination of feminism and anti-feminism in a way that is more than familiar from contemporary film and television texts.[3] Television has provided an important precedent for more recent Hollywood imaginings of the action heroine/active female protagonist with the critical and commercial success of a diverse range of shows including *The X-Files* (Fox, 1993–2002), *Xena: Warrior Princess* (1995–2001), *Buffy the Vampire Slayer* (WB/UPN 1997–2003), *Dark Angel* (Fox, 2000–2), and latterly *Alias* (ABC, 2001–).[4]

Another important generic context for the kinds of violent spectacle showcased in recent

Continued on page 413

Jodie Foster, consummate child star turned accomplished Oscar-winning actress and respected director, is an important figure and contemporary cinematic phenomenon, excelling on both sides of the camera. She was a prolific child performer, and had won her two Best Actress Awards before she was 30, for playing Sarah Tobias in *The Accused* and Clarice Starling in *The Silence of the Lambs*. Her star brand is almost uniquely work focused, despite being augmented by a few scandal events such as her unwitting role in a presidential assassination attempt (John Hinckley gunned down Ronald Reagan and three of his aides in 1981, in order to impress Foster after seeing her in *Taxi Driver*), and an attempted "outing" (Staiger 1993: 142). More Hepburn than Garbo, it is reserve rather than reclusiveness that seems to characterize this private persona. If she has tried to live an uncomplicated and ultra-private life, she has embraced a cluster of contradictions in her work. Child roles in dozens of commercials and TV series traded on her white Californian looks. At an unnervingly early age she played youth at its most disturbingly adult, notably as Iris, the 12-year-old prostitute of *Taxi Driver*, and Tallulah, the pocket-sized speakeasy broad in Alan Parker's bizarre gangster movie for kids, *Bugsy Malone*. These 1976 roles were preceded by a streetwise child-drunk in *Alice Doesn't Live Here Anymore* (1975) and followed by a child murderer in *The Little Girl Who Lives Down the Lane* (1977). For each fallen angel there is a feisty apple-pie Disney favourite, often hoodlums-with-a-heart; Foster was popular with the studio from her first film appearance at the age of 10 in *Napoleon and Samantha* (1972), with Michael Douglas, through *One Little Indian* and *Tom Sawyer* in 1973, to *Candleshoe* and *Freaky Friday*, both in 1977. The latter saw mother and daughter change bodies one Friday 13th, enabling the 15-year-old Jodie to play both adolescent daughter *and* middle-aged mother.

As an alumnus of Yale University and, before that, of the elite bilingual *Le Lycée Français de Los Angeles* (which equipped her to translate for Scorsese at Cannes when promoting *Taxi Driver*), Foster developed a persona marked by intelligence rather than objectification. Even the sexualized roles that marked her work as a young adult (from *Foxes* to *Catchfire* (a.k.a. *Backtrack*)) present femininity divided by dark desires rather than erotic availability. Her actorly filmography betrays a surprisingly mixed bag of roles: child performances shaped by unsettling maturity; feisty "women on the edge" roles in the 1980s; post-Clarice Starling leading ladies who singlehandedly carry major mainstream productions (*Contact*, *Anna and the King*, *Panic Room*). Another more sexually precocious Foster convincingly partnered some unlikely leading men in the 1990s. She was a luminous romantic match for Richard Gere in *Sommersby*, a flirtatious poker-playing foil to Mel Gibson's *Maverick*, and a coquettish whore in Woody Allen's *Shadows and Fog*. This intellectual patrician figure has an ambivalent relationship to both class and "classiness", driven by liberal sensibilities and a penchant for playing working-class women, waitresses living in trailer parks; even Clarice, it is said in *The Silence of the Lambs*, is "not more than one generation away from poor white trash". Dede Tate and Sarah Tobias in particular are reminiscent of nineteenth-century views of working-class women infantilized by class and gender. And though their struggles are partly presented as problems of gender – Sarah's need to validate her experience of rape; Dede's singular mothering dilemmas – it is interesting that Foster's feminist choices are often underpinned by a class agenda. In *The Accused*, *Little Man Tate* and *Nell*, her underclass figures are pitted against ambitious, enfranchised middle-class women who offer a different style of professional mothering (Kelly McGillis's lawyer, Dianne Wiest's educationalist, Natasha Richardson's psychologist respectively). For such a fiercely articulate actress, Foster's screen feats of mumbled and humble inarticulacy are mesmerizing; B. Ruby Rich (1993: 52) has called her acting style the "extraordinary

ordinary"; Tasker (2002: 25) writes that it is "Starling/Foster's spectacular brand of ordinariness" that *The Silence of the Lambs* showcases. Universally respected as an actor, Foster has two respected directorial outings under her belt. *Little Man Tate* and *Home for the Holidays* are quirky comedy-dramas, supplementing her image as a "serious" thespian. She also at one time helmed her own production company, Egg Pictures, backed first by Orion and then by PolyGram (Krämer 2003: 208).

Foster gives us complex incarnations of women who grasp the symbolic order with both hands as they strive to wield public power, but who remain implicated in the mire of family, emotion, memory, however disinterested their professionalism. Social power for Clarice the FBI agent, Anna the teacher and Ellie the astronomer is achieved without disavowing the fractures of female psychic life. Yet for a strong woman whose self-control and image control are legendary, surprisingly often the beautiful contradictions that divide her screen face are driven by a masochistic aesthetic. She may announce herself to be a feminist humanist (as she did to a cheering audience at Yale in 1998), but her heroines are seldom paeans to liberated politics or political correctness. Instead they are marked by a recognition that women rarely slip into the social niche of authority without the barbs of sexuality sticking. Perhaps men don't either; but that is not Foster's concern.

References

Krämer, P. (2003) "A woman in a male-dominated world": Jodie Foster, stardom and 90s Hollywood, in T. Austin and M. Barker (eds) *Contemporary Hollywood Stardom*. London: Arnold, pp. 201–14.

Rich, B.R. (1993) Never a victim: Jodie Foster, a new kind of female hero, in P. Cook and P. Dodd (eds) *Women and Film: A Sight and Sound Reader*. London: Scarlet Press, pp. 50–61.

Staiger, J. (1993) Taboos and totems: cultural meanings of *The Silence of the Lambs*, in J. Collins, H. Radner and A. Preacher Collins (eds) *Film Theory Goes to the Movies*. New York: Routledge, pp. 142–54.

Tasker, Y. (2002) *The Silence of the Lambs*. London: BFI.

Linda Ruth Williams

Continued from page 411
action and adventure films has to do with the influence of Hong Kong filmmaking and the resulting emphasis on a combination of special effects, martial arts, athleticism and wirework. In a series of high-profile US releases, spectacular action sequences that stage the celebratory performance of an already-achieved female athleticism and physical power serve as a driving aesthetic element. With both male and female bodies fantasized as doing/being/becoming the "impossible", suspension of disbelief functions differently in relation to discourses of gender if not, or not as emphatically, in relation to race and class (a point to which I return below). The commercial success and cultural impact of two films in particular – *The Matrix* (1999) and *Crouching Tiger, Hidden Dragon* (2000) – can be taken as indicative. These transnational productions exemplify, albeit in rather different ways, the interaction of Asian and Hollywood cinemas and the different sources upon which they, in turn, draw. As Leon Hunt notes, "The interface between martial arts games and films seems to be a three-way dialogue and not

simply dependent on blurring East/West binaries – Hollywood ('blockbuster' spectacle, CGI, *The Matrix*), Japan (*animé*, Manga) and Hong Kong (action aesthetics, kung fu films and stars)" (2003: 184). The "downloading" of martial arts skills for the Hollywood cinema suggests an appropriative relationship rather than dialogue, however. In related fashion the enactment of racial hierarchies in *Kill Bill: Vol 1* (2003) and *Vol 2* (2004) – in which a blonde, white woman defeats African-American, Asian and white antagonists in sequence – indicates the perpetuation of stereotypes within the film's playful generic mix. The racial and gendered ambivalence of the action heroine also comes to the fore in critical discussion of *Crouching Tiger, Hidden Dragon*, whether in terms of its feminist potential (Chan 2004) or concerns as to its "inauthenticity" in terms of Asian martial arts traditions (perspectives that are addressed by Klein 2004: 20).

Female action stars (if one can speak of such figures) of the 1980s and early 1990s negotiated a perceptible tension between the kind of body considered suitable for glamorous display (whether on the red carpet or in photo shoots) and that geared up for action. It is in this context that feminist critics have commented on the androgynous, even masculine appearance of certain iconic female figures in films such as *Alien* (1979) and the rather later *Blue Steel* (1990). The 1990s saw a high level of feminist engagement with action and other body genres, with questions of female agency centralized. Although critics disagreed on how best to make sense of her, the cinematic/televisual action heroine had become firmly established as an iconic figure of embodied female agency by the mid-1990s. Feminist commentary on key 1980s and 1990s blockbuster texts, such as the *Alien* films (the second in the series, *Aliens* [1986] in

particular) and *Terminator 2* (1991), explored the significance of female masculinity in producing images of women invested with physical and/or narrative agency. By the end of the decade, however, Hollywood had settled on a rather different version of the action heroine, and indeed the action cinema. Two examples will serve to signal the different strategies through which the action heroine was embodied in the US cinema of the early mid-1990s as against more recent manifestations. Firstly, consider the appearance of former model Kristanna Loken as the relentless cyborg enemy in the long-delayed *Terminator 3* (2003). While Linda Hamilton's muscled-up maternal vigilante in James Cameron's *Terminator 2* had become a reference point for feminist debate,[5] the fetishistic and fearful T-X (or "Terminatrix") was firmly located within a sexualized regime of representation in which female agency is both disturbing and eroticized. The conventional science-fiction tropes of alien/human, bio/machine are mediated through a familiar star discourse of white male obsolescence (the aging Schwarzenegger's declining facility for action),[6] a CGI anti-tech paranoia and woman as monstrous other. Secondly, contrast the very different articulations of the female action figure as embodied by Demi Moore in 1997's *G.I. Jane* and her comeback role as "fallen" angel Madison Lee in *Charlie's Angels: Full Throttle* (also 2003).[7] In the former film an emphasis on muscles and work (the labour of soldiering) situates Moore as mannish female soldier, while in the latter her sexy yet powerful body is a source of cinematic spectacle (and tabloid speculation). Her age may render her villainous in *Charlie's Angels: Full Throttle*, yet martial arts and wirework also render her breathtakingly (if somewhat campy) spectacular.[8] That the final showdown between Lee/Moore and the film's legitimate angels (played by Drew Barrymore, Cameron Diaz and Lucy Liu) takes place on the stage of a deserted theatre underlines the spectacular presentation of fighting women for our pleasure, albeit articulated in the knowing tone that characterizes the film as a whole (reassuring us, in effect, that it is all in fun). In all four films the body is worked on, figured as a site of control and discipline as well as mutability through the diverse practices of working out, cosmetic surgery, stuntwork and CGI.

In an essay entitled "Beauty in motion", Marc O'Day (2004) refers to the trend epitomized by films such as *Charlie's Angels* as an emergent "action babe cinema", a phrase he uses to summarize the cinematic and televisual interest in young, fighting women whose function as sexual spectacle is packaged together with an onscreen display of martial skills

Continued on page 419

Unforgiven

The Western after 1960 became distinctly downbeat. A mainstay of production in the classical period, production of Westerns from 1960 dropped to almost 10 per cent of the number produced in the 1950s (Buscombe 2004: 8). Throughout the ensuing decades it became subject to consistent pronouncements of its death and from apparent confirmation of that demise through parodic treatments such as *Blazing Saddles* or attempts to revive it as a star vehicle (i.e *Maverick* or *Young Guns*) with little regard for the genre. The late films of John Ford, those of Sam Peckinpah, Don Siegel and the Spaghetti westerns of Sergio Leone and later Clint Eastwood were notable exceptions. These examples developed the possibilities for critical examinations of masculinity, violence, America's colonial past and the myth of individualism the genre had always explored but in its many versions rarely expressed. *Unforgiven* inherited this tradition and in its working through of those themes entered unexpectedly into the pantheon of that earlier tradition and sealed Clint Eastwood's place alongside those directors who through their understanding of the genre shaped and changed it.

Unforgiven won four Oscars in 1993, including best picture and, for Eastwood, best director. The David Webb Peoples script was written in 1976 and Eastwood acquired it in 1985, apparently waiting until he was old enough to play the role. It tells the story of a reformed and widowed gunfighter and killer who picks up his old ways one more time to earn badly needed money for himself and his two small children. The film drew on the resonance of Eastwood's earlier characters with audiences. Like Siegel's *The Shootist* (1976), which featured an aging and dying gunfighter played by John Wayne (who had cancer at the time), there was a sense that this would be the last time that Eastwood would take to the saddle and the six-gun. *Unforgiven* is dedicated to "Sergio and Don", as a nod not only to their influence on Eastwood but also to the characters that they helped to create. *Unforgiven* stands out in that it takes the theme of melancholy not as a nostalgia for a lost age, nor for the genre itself. Rather it casts aside any sense that the story of the West or the way it has been told was noble. In its place is a stark portrait of an unmerciful world created by the violence that guns bring and that a misplaced sense of justice validates.

The film begins with the sound of a lone guitar overlaying a widescreen sunset and the silhouette of a man digging a grave which set the rhythm of this piece. The simple meandering melody and the movement of the solitary figure are as slow and inexorable as the turning of the earth and the fate of killers. But this world will not play out as ordered, for no one in this film is in control of their destiny, the only destiny is the grave, the only retribution is hollow and no one is absolved. The scene fades and the next scene begins with

Women in Contemporary US Action Cinema **415**

Unforgiven

a long shot of a town, Big Whiskey, Wyoming. In this scene Delilah (Anna Thompson), a prostitute, has her face slashed by a cowboy because she laughed at the size of his penis. The Sheriff, Little Bill Daggett (Gene Hackman) is called and, instead of hanging the cowboys, he makes them pay Skinny, the owner of the bordello, a string of ponies as compensation for his investment in Delilah, in Daggett's words, his "property". The prostitutes, led by Strawberry Alice (Frances Fisher), decide to pool their money and offer a bounty of $1000 on the heads of the cowboys.

The figure in the opening, it is revealed, is William Munny, a pig farmer. He and his children live in a weathered shack that appears to be on the verge of collapse. The homestead, a staple of the genre, is here tenuous and impermanent; a camera shot from outside one door reveals the dark inside, with a view to the open door on the other side. Unlike the warmth of the cabin from which John Ford's famous last shot of *The Searchers* frames the departure of Ethan (John Wayne), this cabin is cold and transient. Munny's farming skills are just as inept, the pigs are sick and he falls in the mud trying to round them up. He is confronted by a young man on a horse who calls himself the Schofield Kid and brags about the number of men he has killed. The Kid wants to know if he is William Munny, who his uncle has told him was "as cold as the snow and don't have no weak nerve nor fear". He asks him to go with him to kill the cowboys and collect the bounty, embellishing the story of the cut-up prostitute. Munny says no, as he has given up those old ways, and the Kid leaves. Munny has second thoughts and goes after the Kid and on his way picks up his friend Ned (Morgan Freeman) who had been his partner in the old days and is now living peacefully as a farmer with his wife Sally Two Trees (Cherrilene Cardinal). The film never registers in the dialogue that Ned is black and Sally is Native American. Instead, the resonance of those tragic histories are imbedded in the iconic image of Sally, resigned as she looks on the fatal folly of her husband and his friend and, later on, in the death of Ned by whipping at the hands of Little Bill. As they ride north to Big Whiskey another gunfighter arrives by train, English Bob (Richard Harris) who brags about the superiority of the British monarchy, a sure sign of trouble. He has in tow W.W. Beauchamp (Saul Rubinek) who writes pulp novels about the romance of the West and gunfighters, another form of story embellishment and myth-making.

Not long after the arrival in Big Whiskey (where the carrying of firearms is not allowed), English Bob is confronted and sadistically beaten in the street by Little Bill, himself seeking a quieter life than the violent one he seems to have lived. Bill's threat to whip the cowboys at the beginning of the film signals his sadistic nature but his savage beating of English Bob, underscored by dramatic low tones in the music, serve notice to the audience that Will, Ned and the Kid have a formidable adversary. Little Bill justifies this as a warning to other bounty hunters. In *All on Accounta Pullin' a Trigger* (Hogrewe 2002), the documentary made for the 10th Anniversary DVD release, Gene Hackman says that Eastwood asked him to look at Los Angeles police chief Daryl Gates who believed strongly in law and order, when preparing for the role. He was head of the LAPD during the Rodney King beating and the Los Angeles riots. Little Bill has a desire for order which he will maintain at all costs, his sense of justice tied up with a skewed morality. Bill doesn't see the cutting up of Delilah as a crime because, as Strawberry Alice points out, they're whores. The film ultimately leads to a confrontation between William Munny and Little Bill, not only because the genre demands it, but because they are so similar in their desire to leave their violent pasts behind. Bill's sense of justice and unwavering belief that violence limits violence drive the film's central conflict.

The first time William Munny and Little Bill meet is in the saloon and bordello. While Ned and the Kid are upstairs, Little Bill beats Munny for carrying a revolver and makes him crawl out of the saloon on his belly like a snake. The hissing rain and Munny's feverish dreams of the Angel o' Death, who has "snake eyes", underpin the indelible stain that killing has imprinted on Munny and Bill. Munny is taken to a hideout set up by the women while he recovers. He is nursed by Delilah. After he recovers, he joins Ned and the Kid as they stalk the two cowboys. Ned shoots the horse from under one of the cowboys while he is working but realizes that he can no longer kill. Munny takes the Spencer rifle from Ned and kills the cowboy. Afterwards Ned leaves Munny and the Kid to kill the other cowboy, the one who actually cut Delilah, and sets out for home. The Kid kills the second cowboy and as they are waiting for one of the girls to deliver the money under a tree outside the town, the Kid reveals that he has never killed anyone before and with each drink of whiskey he realizes what he has done. In the words of Edward Buscombe, the scene is "perhaps the greatest he [Eastwood] has ever done" (2004: 65). As the Kid comes to the terrible realization that he has killed a man, one of the women comes to give them the money and tells Munny that a posse of cowboys caught Ned and that Little Bill has whipped him to death. As Munny reaches for the whiskey we are reminded that he attributed his murderous past to drunkenness. He turns into the killer of the past and will avenge Ned.

The last scene of the film appears to undo all of its meditations on violence, on masculinity, on perverse applications of law and the questionable virtues upon which the myth of the gunfighter and indeed the Western itself rests. Munny walks into the saloon accompanied by the reptilian hissing of the rain outside, taking Little Bill and the posse by surprise. He kills Skinny, the obsequious and brutal proprietor of the whorehouse, and then Little Bill in a gunfight. He becomes the Angel o' Death. Standing over Little Bill he responds to Bill's plea "I don't deserve this, to die like this. I was building a house." Munny's response interprets Little Bill's own sense of justice: "Deserve's got nothing to do with it", he says, and kills him.

Unforgiven

Unforgiven is arguably a "revisionist" Western, a term which is usually applied to reflective Westerns which revise the assumptions and myths that are central to the Western. Virtually all of these are post-1960 although revision in its other sense can mean a revision of history, and can be applied to many reactionary Westerns throughout the history of the genre. *Unforgiven* operates uniquely within the reset boundaries brought by feminism, the unbelievability of any less than critical account of the manifest destiny ideology of American imperialism and the camp associations which unmask the facade of masculinity of partners on the range. It does this by providing as its impetus the injustice and misuse of patriarchal power by the law and unscrupulous capitalists. Strawberry Alice and the other girls seek justice and revenge for Delilah. The hero still, however, operates as the reluctant gunfighter, in the tradition of *Shane* (1953) and *High Noon* (1952). William Munny's attempt to "walk the line" offers no absolution, as it is Munny who kills the first cowboy, who was only guilty by association. The irony that closes the film is that it is not for money that he kills Little Bill, it is personal, it is for Ned. One cannot help but recognize though that the death by whipping of Ned and the cutting up of Delilah both resonate with the historical injustice that are the basis of the revisionist Western. As he leaves the town in the pouring rain, he says that they had "better bury Ned right, [and] better not cut up or otherwise harm no whores". His vengeance is for the two characters, a black man and a woman. And in a chilling frame with the American flag in the background to the right he says, "Or I'll come back and kill everyone of you sons o' bitches". Such an ambiguity is both unexpected but also within the classical Hollywood tradition of providing a range of probable readings. One can imagine both "red" conservative audiences and "blue" liberal audiences finding satisfaction here.

References

Buscombe, E. (2004) *Unforgiven*. London: BFI.
Grist, L. (1996) Unforgiven, in Ian Cameron and Douglas Pye (eds) *The Movie Book of the Western*. London: Studio Vista.
Hogrewe, J. (2002) *All on Accounta Pullin' a Trigger*, documentary made for 10th Anniversary DVD release of *Unforgiven*.
Kitses, J. (2004) *Horizons West: Directing the Western from John Ford to Clint Eastwood*. London: BFI.
Plantinga, C. (1998) Spectacles of death: Clint Eastwood and violence in *Unforgiven*, *Cinema Journal* 37(2), Winter.
Slotkin, R. (1992) *Gunfighter Nation: The Myth of the Frontier in Twentieth Century America*. New York: Athenium.
Thumin, J. (1995) "Maybe he's tough but he sure can't build a house": masculinity and in/competence in *Unforgiven*, in Pat Kirkham and Janet Thumin, (eds) *Me Jane*. London: Lawrence and Wishart, reprinted in Jim Kitses and Gregg Rickman (eds) (1998) *The Western Reader*. New York: Limelight Editions.
Tompkins, J. (1992) *West of Everything: The Inner Life of Westerns*. London: Oxford University Press.

Michael Hammond

Continued from page 415

in an evocation of sexy female empowerment. O'Day details the ways in which publicity materials surrounding certain female stars emphasize both their sexual desirability (and implicitly their availability) and the authenticity of their physical performance. Thus reference to a rigorous programme of training has become a staple feature, with promotional materials assuring us that various female performers acquired familiarity with weaponry and martial arts (Uma Thurman is described as a "fighting machine" in a promotional feature for *Kill Bill*, for instance, while Daryl Hannah demonstrated her moves on talk shows). The payoff in ideological and visual terms is that martial arts involves both strength and grace, "beauty in motion" as O'Day puts it, expressed in the form of the disciplined (female) body. O'Day's examples include *Charlie's Angels, Lara Croft: Tomb Raider* (2001), *Crouching Tiger, Hidden Dragon, X-Men* (2000), *Resident Evil* (2002) and *Final Fantasy* (2001), indicating an ethnically and racially diverse group of female stars united by their extratextual construction as "babes", with profiles in men's magazines featuring suggestive illustrations and interviews.

The contradictory terms of fantasy and authenticity are thus put into play here at a variety of levels. The reinvigorated US action of the late 1990s involved a combination of CGI and Hong Kong-style wirework, producing action spectacle through tropes of authenticity (an emphasis on the training programmes undertaken by performers) and the fantastic (elaborately choreographed sequences in which bodies seem to perform beyond their capabilities). The Hollywood cinema's typical articulation of the action heroine as sexual spectacle can thus be understood as part of a more generalized move

Carrie-Anne Moss in *The Matrix*

towards fetishized action. This is not to suggest that Carrie-Anne Moss as Trinity in *The Matrix, The Matrix Reloaded* (2003) and *The Matrix Revolutions* (2003), or the trio of Diaz, Liu and Barrymore in *Charlie's Angels* and *Charlie's Angels: Full Throttle*, are any more or less figures of patriarchal fantasy than Linda Hamilton in the first two *Terminator* films or Sigourney Weaver in the *Alien* cycle. That the latter titles more evidently figure female agency through muscularity and weaponry, rather than the sexy bodies endowed with high levels of martial arts skills showcased in the former, relates to a range of factors of which gender is only one.

As I have already indicated, much feminist scholarship relating to action has concerned itself with the gendering of agency. In keeping with what remains to a large extent a tradition of scholarship informed by psychoanalysis, the action heroine has been read as masculinized – a disturbing and potentially disruptive evocation of the woman who takes action – and as a reassuring sexual spectacle whose connotations of availability undercut her agency. I have argued elsewhere that the "masculine" qualities necessary for the action heroine to function in a male world are inscribed on her muscular body, a process that codes her in terms of "musculinity" (Tasker 1993: 149). Possessing conventionally masculine attributes yet clearly biologically female, the action heroine troubles gendered systems of representation. Paradoxically, however, she also works to reaffirm gendered hierarchies to the extent that her agency is rarely simply reported, as it were; instead the fabric of the film works to contextualize her presence through narrative and visual devices that, in a variety of ways, serve to explain her. That she is never entirely explained away, however, feeds the ambivalence (and interest) of this figure for feminism. In their flaunting of both action as explicitly staged and the female body as spectacular attraction, it is difficult to engage with the US action films that I'm discussing here in the established terms of feminist analysis. They are knowing, self-conscious and adopt a celebratory attitude towards femininity. In this way they seem to deflect criticism in advance, incorporating and forestalling a certain stern response. That this response is typically imagined as "feminist" within popular discourse functions of course to associate feminism with a repressive, anti-pleasure position, a generational rebuke to the older woman (and possibly the maternal position that she signifies) that is both acknowledged and disavowed in the significantly youthful articulation of female bodily empowerment.[9]

The high-profile cinematic adaptation of popular game avatar Lara Croft suggests a Hollywood cinema taking inspiration from new media forms. And yet, both in the conventions adopted in that film and a variety of other adventure narratives, contemporary Hollywood clearly looks to the past. In the recent revamping of a colonial adventure tradition exemplified by the successful cycle of *Mummy* films, multiracial casting and capable action heroines seem designed to excuse the casual racism of the genre.[10] *The Mummy* (1999) features Rachel Weisz as Evelyn Carnahan, a librarian with a passion for knowledge and books (rather than power or treasure, the preoccupation of most of the film's male characters) and a desire to prove her scholarly worth in the field. With English and Egyptian parentage, Evelyn is explicitly marked as a border-crossing figure, her gender transgressions contextualized by her ethnicity. In order to prove herself, Evelyn, accompanied by her comically inept, cowardly but basically good-hearted brother Jonathan (John Hannah) and American romantic hero Rick O'Connell (Brendan Fraser), sets out to locate the ancient city of Harmunaptra. The object of their desire is a book, which is coincidentally made of precious materials and thus serves as an enticement for those seeking both knowledge and wealth. Early on in their travels the party lose all their clothes and equipment, a familiar adventure trope that forces the group to fall back on their own initiative and even their own labour. It also justifies Evelyn's costuming in explicitly eroticized Eastern garb; to Rick, who has been busy securing camels, Evelyn's new appearance secures her desirability. With her black dress, beaded diaphanous veil, bare head and long abundant hair, Evelyn's "eastern" appearance alludes to her transgressive exoticism while her downcast eyes suggest feminine submissiveness, Evelyn's

Continued on page 422

Authorship criticism has frequently focused upon filmmakers who can be seen to work both within and outside the conventions of popular genre cinema. As a filmmaker strongly associated with an innovative approach to genre, it is not surprising that Kathryn Bigelow should have attracted interest despite a relatively small number of feature credits. Moreover, her atypical career profile as a female director, particularly one associated with body genres (horror, action, thrillers, science fiction and so on) has also generated interest from feminist critics. The title of a 2003 anthology, *The Cinema of Kathryn Bigelow: Hollywood Transgressor* is perhaps indicative. Although her status as Hollywood insider/outsider has been a staple feature of academic commentary, the commercial success of *Near Dark* (1987) and particularly *Point Break* (1991) have not been matched by Bigelow's more recent features, *Strange Days* (1995), *The Weight of Water* (2000) and *K-19: The Widowmaker* (2002).

Although Bigelow's first low-budget feature, *The Loveless* (1982), co-directed with Monty Montgomery, certainly generated interest, it was her *noir*-horror-Western *Near Dark* (1987) that attracted wider attention to the filmmaker's interest in combining generic elements. *Near Dark* features elements of grim comedy, but its generic interplay is not straightforwardly parodic in the familiar fashion of 1990s horror. Instead, both the Western setting and neo-*noir* aesthetic of this vampire tale render a form of horror typically associated with old Europe into an uncanny vision of the US heartland. The eerie, stylish *Blue Steel* (1990), in which Jamie Lee Curtis's rookie New York cop confronts a serial killer sexually obsessed with her, has developed a reputation as a complex, ambivalent hybrid of thriller and woman's picture, suggesting that Bigelow's facility with genre might allow her to bend the rules of gendered representation.

The range of genres across which Bigelow has worked tends to mitigate against the concerns of conventional authorship criticism in terms of establishing thematic congruities

Strange Days

Kathryn Bigelow

Women in Contemporary US Action Cinema 421

or characteristic visual/stylistic elements. Critics have sought such continuity in the figure of an accelerated visual spectacle (the point of view sequences in *Strange Days*, for instance) and in the idea of Bigelow as a filmmaker who works with genre (and, for some, with gender) in productive ways. In this context it may not be surprising that it is *Strange Days* that, although commercially disappointing, has attracted most academic (and indeed popular) interest. Deploying a neo-*noir*, near-future Los Angeles setting, *Strange Days* maps a science fiction tale onto a racially tense urban context. Loser-hero Lenny (Ralph Fiennes) is matched by the more-than-capable Mace (Angela Bassett), the friend he both exploits and depends on as his shady dealings in "clips" (illegal recordings of extreme or erotic experiences) draw him into a complex plot of double dealing, secrecy and corruption. The film's stunning visuals, provocative themes and somewhat unsatisfactory plotting epitomize the virtues and limits of Bigelow's filmmaking more generally. The complexities of spectatorship, long a theme of film scholarship, are here drawn out in a fashion that is by turn crude, touching and thought-provoking. In short, *Strange Days* speculates in an intensely visual/visceral form, on the power of images, the possibilities of genre, and the pleasures and dangers of spectatorship. It thus exemplifies the concerns with gender, vision and power that feature so strongly within Bigelow's film work, and which have made her a source of fascination for many scholars of popular cinema.

References

Jermyn, D. and Redmond, S. (2003) *The Cinema of Kathryn Bigelow: Hollywood Transgressor*. London: Wallflower.

Lane, C. (2000) *Feminist Hollywood: From "Born in Flames" to "Point Break"*. Detroit: Wayne State University Press.

Tasker, Y. (1999) Bigger than life, *Sight and Sound*; 9(5): 12–15.

Yvonne Tasker

Continued from page 420

availability is highlighted by both her direct eye contact with Rick and the contrast posed by the more conventionally veiled Arab women who surround her. Evelyn's troublesome presence (she is described early on as a "catastrophe") culminates in her reckless reading from an ancient book ("no harm ever came from reading a book"), in the process raising the mummified remains of Imhotep (Arnold Vosloo) and unleashing a series of (biblical) plagues. *The Mummy Returns* (2001), set in 1933, has the O'Connells (now married with a young son, Alex) once again tackle Imhotep. Evelyn's intense visions of ancient times reiterate her Anglo-Egyptian heritage;

these visions are subsequently revealed to be memories of Evelyn's past life as Nefertiri, the Pharaoh's daughter. O'Connell meanwhile, who bears an ancient tattoo (acquired, he informs us, in a Cairo orphanage) is revealed to be linked to the all-male Medjai, "descendants of Pharoh's sacred bodyguards".

With their Anglo-American alliance firmly in charge of "native" characters, both loyal and treacherous, *The Mummy* and *The Mummy Returns* enact a pastiche of classic Hollywood's familiar ethnic and racial hierarchies. Significantly for the purposes of this chapter, we can note that in line with her lineage *The Mummy Returns* invests Evelyn not only with secret knowledge but martial abilities; a setpiece sequence has Nefertiri/Evelyn and Anck-Su-Namun (Patricia Valasquez) battling it out for a royal audience of ancients. Although she is defeated by Anck-Su-Namun in ancient times and in the present, Evelyn ultimately defeats her rival in a contemporary restaging of their combat (although only after her own son has brought her back from the dead), going on to rescue husband Rick. Weisz's librarian displays a feisty spirit that is perhaps rebellious in the context of the interwar period in which the films are set yet remains comfortable for a contemporary audience. The third film in the cycle, *The Scorpion King* (2002), is a prequel, set in ancient times, spinning off from a character featuring in *The Mummy Returns*. The main female character is the explicitly eroticized sorceress played by Kelly Hu, although a variety of fighting women, played by actors of different races, also appear in the film. The star of the show is wrestler "The Rock" (Dwayne Johnson) paired with enemy turned ally Balthazar (Michael Clarke Duncan) in a throwback to an earlier cycle of muscle movies. Although the element of physical spectacle is most pronounced in *The Scorpion King*, all three films deploy exoticized ancient settings that allow for the display of scantily clad female (and male) bodies. Fighting women thus function as one element of the "exotic" spectacle. The casual racism and misogyny of the *Mummy* films are embedded within a context that is so explicitly "parodic" that criticism seems forestalled – "Self-reflexivity has become the order of the day in commercial cinema," writes Christopher Sharrett (2001: 320). Even so, I would want to draw attention to the fetishistic imagery (racial and sexual) deployed in such films, to consider the ways in which it serves to disavow what is simultaneously asserted.

The attention of feminist scholars has tended to focus on gender and the action heroine, but the extent to which both race and ethnicity are important elements within the genre's articulation of the action heroine has not received as much sustained attention. This is perhaps particularly surprising given that action is a fantasy/fantastic space that has long allowed room, albeit limited, for non-white and non-Anglo performers who are frequently relegated to the margins of Hollywood production. Paying attention to the significance of race and ethnicity within US action traditions, as Mary Beltrán (2004: 187) notes, "problematizes previous scholarship" in the area. Such scholarship has typically framed images of the action heroine in terms of an active/passive binary in which the female body is either available as a site of sexual spectacle or a site of (some "masculine") agency. Yet discourses of race, gender and sexuality inform each other in complex fashion. Thus Beltrán (2004: 187) writes that because "Latina stars typically have been constructed as flamboyant, excessive bodies in both film roles and star publicity", we might productively direct our attention to "the interplay of this racialized star function and of the aesthetics and politics of the Hollywood action hero". That the reconfiguration of the action heroine in big-budget productions occurs in a period also characterized by the greater visibility of African American, Latino and Asian performers within the genre is not to my mind insignificant. Indeed, as I hope to foreground in my analysis here, these elements interact in complex fashion.

In the early 1990s I suggested that while "racial and gendered discourses are not interchangeable, they are interlocked in their sexualisation of relations of power. The troubling body is fetishised and thus, provisionally, made safe" (Tasker 1993: 32). This characteristic double structure (by which the anxieties provoked by the troubling body are both given expression and made safe) remains discernible in the mutually reinforcing discourses of gender and race at work in contemporary action. We see, for example the normalizing (in Hollywood terms) of the action heroine through her inscription as a figure of glamorous desirability, and the more-or-less explicit invitation to read images of fighting women as in some way "feminist". Or we might consider the way in which traditions of black action cinema speak to a racialized experience of oppression that is written on and through the body; black action can be read as both a recuperative fantasy of the black body and a site for the physical expression of anger, whether politicized or not.[11] Equally, however, although action/adventure functions as an important site for African-American, Asian and other non-white/Anglo performers – as in *The Matrix* films, for instance – in its most high-profile examples the genre reiterates Hollywood's racial hierarchies through which white/Anglo men (and occasionally women) are seen to be in charge.

In the remainder of this chapter I focus on two different variants of women in action (although there are certainly others that could be considered). The first concerns the glamorous, fetishized figure of the woman in action, as exemplified by *Charlie's Angels*. I place this figure firmly within the context of postfeminist culture, suggesting that we view the sexualized action heroine as a particular mediation of female agency. The second explores texts in which the enhanced physicality of the action heroine is understood in some way as a response to her social position as a woman. Both variants call attention to the erasure (and occasional acknowledgement) of political perspectives on the female body as

sexed, gendered, raced and classed in contemporary US action.

With its playful tone, combination of action, comedy and sexual display, *Charlie's Angels* and *Charlie's Angels: Full Throttle* epitomize the big-budget version of the first variant. Openly raiding Hong Kong cinema for its fight choreography, *Charlie's Angels* presents its sexy female protagonists as girlish women skilled in martial arts. Like the *Lara Croft* and *Mummy* films, *Charlie's Angels* present smart, fit (and typically affluent) young women who are either in search of adventure or who happen to lead adventurous and glamorous lives. These women are typically free from responsibilities; depicted as forceful figures, their presentation as sexual spectacle is seemingly a choice, one that we are encouraged to read as empowering (this is quite explicit in the comic action scenario of *Miss Congeniality* (2000) in which Sandra Bullock's Gracie Hart discovers herself while undercover as a contestant at a beauty pageant). *Charlie's Angels: Full Throttle* alludes to feminist-inflected themes of sisterhood in the bonds of loyalty and friendship between the angels, though Alex and Dylan's fears that Natalie may marry boyfriend Pete and thus leave them behind makes clear the traditionalist logic that marriage and career are not compatible for women. A subtext concerning male violence within relationships is also invoked through Dylan's backstory and her evident fear (overcome, of course) of former boyfriend Seamus O'Grady. Yet these female characters essentially live the contextless (precisely fantastic/fantasized) lives of the postfeminist action heroine in which class and racial distinctions are presented as superficial differences of style. In *Full Throttle* Alex's father is played by white, British comic John Cleese; her mother is neither mentioned nor pictured, rendering

Alex's Asian ethnicity an unremarkable marker of difference. The narrative erasure of Liu's Asianness (even as her on-screen presence as the most prominent contemporary female Asian American star defies that erasure) recalls Beltrán's comment on the strategic "racelessness" deployed in recent examples of Hollywood action. Of the couple at the heart of *Romeo Must Die* (2000), African American Trish (Aaliyah) and Asian Han (Jet Li), she writes:

> Ultimately, the duo survives by embracing 'racelessness,' ethnic identities that are achieved through the consumption and sharing of music, fashion and cultural forms such as martial arts, rather than by accepting their former ethnic community allegiances and in-group prejudices. (Beltrán 2005: 59)

What is at stake here is the erasure not so much of difference, but of any political dimension to such difference. There are evident analogies here between the articulation of, say, the martial arts as a "raceless" commodity available to all and the post-feminist rhetoric of choice (premised on affluence, privilege and youth), which is so literally embodied in the mobile figure of the action heroine.

The eroticized action heroine does not only appear in comic scenarios such as *Charlie's Angels*. By way of contrast we might consider the figure of Trinity/Carrie-Anne Moss in *The Matrix* films. It is worth noting that it is Trinity's spectacular abilities and physical presence that introduce viewers to the world of the matrix in the first film's opening sequence. Surrounded by hapless male police officers ("I think we can handle one little girl"), fetishistically clad in her shiny black skin-tight costume, slicked back hair and shades (part superhero, part action heroine), Trinity overwhelms her opponents through her martial abilities; she is seen briefly poised in space before delivering a brutal yet graceful kick, a moment that registers an (as yet unexplained) ability to defy the logic of space and time. Though it is Neo (Keanu Reeves) who is firmly established in narrative terms as "The One", *The Matrix Reloaded* likewise begins with a crowd-pleasing sequence of Trinity in action (subsequently revealed as Neo's dream/vision/fantasy). Trinity may be presented in the familiar fetishistic terms of the comic book (as are the other film characters such as Jada Pinkett Smith's Niobe) but this fantasy self is also counterpointed with her grungy Zion persona, a contrast that serves as the film's own commentary on fantasy and authenticity, on the lure of illusion, the glamour of action and the possibilities of the "real".

A few action scenarios posit violence or physicality as a response to an experience of oppression located in contemporary US society (in contrast to, say, the ancient world tyrant against whom Mathayus struggles in *The Scorpion King* or the machine-dominated world of *The Matrix*). In films such as *Set It Off* (1996) and *Enough* (2002) active/action women are situated within a context in which they lack choices, experiencing clear limits on their physical or social mobility. The former advertises itself as an action-packed gangster movie but the latter is generically more easily framed as a woman's picture such that the promotional tagging of Jennifer Lopez's central character, Slim, as "a new kind of action hero" seems out of keeping with the tone of the film. Both films involve the action heroine in a more explicitly politicized understanding of the limits experienced by women. Hollywood, however, deals with the issues posed by social and cultural hierarchies in a typically fantastic manner; within this schema both action and violence hold a privileged place, and the underdog who (literally) fights back is valorized in populist terms, a dynamic evident in both these examples.

Set It Off follows four African-American, working-class women who, lacking the fantasized mobility that characterizes so many action narratives, opt to rob banks. That this "choice" is made in relation to an experience of low-wage labour, sexual exploitation and racial prejudice is made explicit. In the opening sequence, Frankie (Vivica A. Fox) is a horrified bystander when the bank at which she works is robbed. Her acquaintance with one of the perpetrators makes Frankie a suspect figure, and despite her exemplary work record she is dismissed; her subsequent anger – and inside knowledge – fuel the women's move into crime. Without references, Frankie joins the other women who work as cleaners, their unseen labour servicing the opulent interiors inhabited by wealthy whites. Both Stony (Jada Pinkett) and timid single mother Tisean (Kimberly Elise) are represented as nurturing figures whose transition into criminality is triggered by grief and care (the police shooting of Stony's beloved brother, in whom she has invested her ambitions for the future; Tisean's inability to pay for a sitter for her young son during working hours). Cleo's (Queen Latifah) pleasure in criminality is, by contrast, "explained" through little more than her lesbianism and her coding as a masculine presence within the film. In contrast to the fantasies of agency and physical mobility discussed above, the limits placed on the movements of black women are foregrounded within *Set It Off*, with the group's move into criminality framed through racial and gendered discourse. As Kimberly Springer has shown, these discourses are also at work in the narrative fate of the characters, with Stony the sole survivor escaping with the cash and the most violent death reserved for Cleo, "a woman who transgressed gender, race, and heterosexual norms, unrepentantly" (Springer 2001: 193).

The limits that result from class and racial hierarchies are foregrounded in *Set It Off*, but *Enough*'s Slim enacts the sort of social mobility through heterosexual union (from service work to wife) which banker Keith (Blair Underwood) offers to Stony. Waitress Slim's marriage to wealthy WASP Mitch (Billy Campbell) removes her from the support network offered by her coworkers at the restaurant, making her vulnerable to her husband's increasingly violent behaviour. Though she attempts to flee, the law offers no respite and Slim ultimately trains herself as a fighter in order to confront her tormentor head on. Here again, the woman's physical mobility is subject to limits: Slim is constantly moving, but her movement is compelled and she is unable to find safety. Her transformation through martial arts training enables Slim to assert control of the body, to make a stand. As we have seen, contemporary action draws on tropes of "authenticity" and "fantasy" in somewhat paradoxical fashion; these tropes are also importantly shaped by discourses of gender and race (fantasies of authenticity are, it goes without saying, central to Western culture's figuring of race and ethnicity). Beltrán understands this when she writes of Karen Sisco/Jennifer Lopez's construction as calm and capable in *Out of Sight* (1996) that her "Latin ethnicity and thus association with 'urban' street smarts arguably makes this construction more believable" (Beltrán 2004: 193). *Enough* similarly draws on associations of Latina toughness while leaving Slim's ethnicity unspecified. However, although it features an action heroine, and centres on questions of female agency, *Enough* is not an action film. Indeed, the film's indebtedness to a rape revenge tradition in which victimized women fight back should already be clear.[12] The feminist-informed tradition of rape revenge (in which women's experience of sexual violence is acknowledged and healed) also prefigures the choice-led rhetoric associated with postfeminism, evident in Lopez's description of physical training as a means of "empowering yourself".

I have suggested in this chapter that even as the figure of the active/action woman is made safe through a variety of strategies, she is also imagined and given space through that imagining. Like the *femme fatale*, then, the action heroine is rendered a representable figure of female agency through codes that are evidently patriarchal and typically misogynist. While the action heroine responds to feminism, she is not a figure that can be clearly read as either feminist or anti-feminist. It is no surprise that the two films discussed here that most explicitly engage with women who lack choices (women typically elided from postfeminist culture's optimistic rendition of achievement and opportunity) foreground tropes of race and class. Suspension of disbelief within action is, after all, predicated on a set of cultural assumptions as to what different bodies are capable of, just as all body genres (action, horror) involve an assertion of (and rationale for) which bodies matter.

Notes

1   For a useful summary of feminist critical perspectives in this period and subsequently, see Thornham (1997).

2   The 1978 publication of E. Ann Kaplan's well-known anthology of essays, *Women in Film Noir* (London: BFI) signals the early importance of the *femme fatale* for feminist scholarship.

3   For a further discussion of the original show's relationship to feminism, see Gough-Yates (2001).

4   See also syndicated shows like *Relic Hunter* (1999–2002), starring Tia Carerra as a Lara Croft-style archaeologist, or the Pamela Anderson vehicle *VIP* (1998–2002) in which she heads up a firm of sexy female bodyguards. For feminist perspectives on some of these shows, see Helford (2000).

5   See, for instance, Tasker (1993) and Willis (1997).

6   For a useful discussion of stardom and white male aging, see the discussion of Clint Eastwood in Holmlund (2002).

7   For a useful discussion of Moore's star persona in action, see Williams (2004).

8   In terms of the equation between female aging and villainy, we might also consider Sharon Stone's character in *Catwoman* (2004). The film's somewhat tortuous plot thematizes age through a sinister product that seems to defy the aging process while producing monstrous results (including in Stone's case, immense physical strength) for the women who employ it.

9   Of course, Laura Mulvey's pathbreaking 1975 essay "Visual pleasure and narrative cinema" did indeed call for a scepticism towards the pleasures offered to female spectators by Hollywood cinema.

10   Beltrán (2005) comments on the casting of multiracial actors including Keanu Reeves, Vin Diesel and The Rock.

11   I am indebted here to Amy Ongiri's formulation of "spectacular blackness" as part of her paper "'Kill them with karate': *Black Belt* and the irrecuperable wounded black male body" presented at Martial Arts/Global Flows, Duke University, 2005.

12 The attempts to frame the film as a credible commentary on the experience of domestic violence are also somewhat compromised by the magical figure of Slim's wealthy estranged father who (eventually) provides her with material support and access to both a personal trainer and the high-tech equipment she needs to confront her husband in his domestic space in the climatic fight between the two.

References

Beltrán, M. (2004) Más macha: the new Latina action hero, in Y. Tasker (ed.) *Action and Adventure Cinema*. London: Routledge.

Beltrán, M. (2005) The new Hollywood race-lessness: only the fast, furious, (and multiracial) will survive, *Cinema Journal*, 44(2): 50–67.

Chan, K. (2004) The global return of the *Wu Xia Pian* (Chinese sword-fighting movie): *Ang Lee's Crouching Tiger, Hidden Dragon*, *Cinema Journal*, 43(4): 3–17.

Gough-Yates, A. (2001) Angels in chains? Feminism, femininity and consumer culture in *Charlie's Angels*, in B. Osgerby and A. Gough-Yates (eds) *Action TV: Tough Guys, Smooth Operators and Foxy Chicks*. London: Routledge.

Helford, E.R. (2000) *Fantasy Girls: Gender in the New Universe of Science Fiction and Fantasy Television*. Oxford: Rowman and Littlefield.

Holmlund, C. (2002) *Impossible Bodies: Femininity and Masculinity at the Movies*. New York: Routledge.

Hunt, L. (2003) *Kung Fu Cult Masters: From Bruce Lee to Crouching Tiger*. London: Wallflower.

Klein, C. (2004) *Crouching Tiger, Hidden Dragon*: a diasporic reading, *Cinema Journal*, 43(4): 18–42.

Mizejewski, L. (2004) *Hardboiled and High Heeled: The Woman Detective in Popular Culture*. New York: Routledge.

O'Day, M. (2004) Beauty in motion: gender, spectacle and action babe cinema, in Y. Tasker (ed.) *Action and Adventure Cinema*. London: Routledge.

Sharrett, C. (2001) End of story: the collapse of myth in postmodern narrative film, in J. Lewis (ed.) *The End of Cinema as We Know it: American Film in the Nineties*. New York: New York University Press.

Springer, K. (2001) Waiting to set it off: African American women and the Sapphire fixation, in M. McCaughey and N. King (eds) *Reel Knockouts: Violent Women in the Movies*. Austin: University of Texas Press.

Tasker, Y. (1993) *Spectacular Bodies: Gender, Genre and the Action Cinema*. London: Routledge.

Thornham, S. (1997) *Passionate Detachments: An Introduction to Feminist Film Theory*. London: Edward Arnold.

Williams, L.R. (2004) Ready for action: *G.I. Jane*, Demi Moore's body and the female combat movie, in Y. Tasker (ed.) *Action and Adventure Cinema*. London: Routledge.

Willis, S. (1997) *Race and Gender in Contemporary Hollywood Film*. Durham, NC: Duke University Press.

SMART CINEMA

Jeffrey Sconce

A **TOPIC OF** often contentious artistic and political debate, *smart cinema* describes a mode of cinematic practice that emerged among a new generation of post-baby boomer filmmakers during the 1990s. Relying heavily on irony, black humour, fatalism, relativism, and occasional nihilism, this cinema became a particularly active battleground in a larger moral debate over the place of cynicism, irony, postmodernism, secular humanism, and cultural relativism in contemporary popular culture. In a 1998 editorial for the *Los Angeles Times*, for example, Kenneth Turan bemoaned what he described as an onslaught of "pointlessly and simplistically grim films", complaining that a new generation of misguided filmmakers had created a cinematic ethos where "the lust for the grim precludes the good". That same week *L.A. Weekly* film critic Manohla Dargis coined the phrase, "the new nihilism". Dargis observed:

> It doesn't seem too sensational to suggest that right now in this country we are being inundated with a cinema of hate, a cinema that encourages our sadism, our scorn and, worst of all, our total disinterest toward the world, other human beings, and just maybe ourselves.

This cinema had and has many variations: the arch-emotional nihilism of Todd Solondz in *Storytelling* (2001), *Happiness* (1998), and *Welcome to the Dollhouse* (1995), and of Neil LaBute in *Your Friends and Neighbors* (1998) and *In the Company of Men* (1997); Alexander Payne's "blank" political satires *Election* (1999) and *Citizen Ruth* (1996); Hal Hartley's postmodern screwball comedies *The Unbelievable Truth* (1990), *Trust* (1991), and *Henry Fool* (1998); post-*Pulp Fiction* black comedies of violence such as *Very Bad Things* (1998), *Go* (1999), *Two Days in the Valley* (1996); Wes Anderson's bittersweet *Bottle Rocket* (1994), *Rushmore* (1998), and *The Royal Tenenbaums* (2001); P.T. Anderson's operatic odes to the San Fernando valley *Magnolia* (1998) and *Boogie Nights* (1997); the "cold" melodramas of *The Ice Storm* (1997), *The Sweet Hereafter* (1997), and *Safe* (1995); and the "matter-of-fact" surrealism of *Being John Malkovich* (1999) and *Donnie Darko* (2001). In 1991, Richard Linklater's docudrama of hipster anomie, *Slacker*, not only captured aspects of this sensibility through its desultory formal structure, but served as well as a veritable ethnographic record of the emerging collegiate/bohemian subculture of irony that would so dominate popular taste in 1990s culture.

Taken together, these admittedly disparate and yet often ideologically sympathetic films suggest an interesting shift in the strategies of "art cinema", here defined as movies marketed in explicit counter-distinction to mainstream Hollywood fare as "smarter", "artier", and more "independent" (however questionable and manufactured such distinctions might actually be). Always a vague and contentious "genre", the art film in the 1990s became an even more untidy category than in decades past, especially as it extended certain European

Donnie Darko

art-house traditions while also morphing into the more postmodern playground of "indie" cinema. Though the films listed above vary greatly in terms of their conditions of production and financing, marketers, critics, and audiences almost invariably placed them as a "smart" cinema in symbolic opposition to the imaginary mass-cult monster of mainstream, commercial, Hollywood cinema (perhaps best epitomized by the "dumb" films of Jerry Bruckheimer, Michael Bay, and James Cameron). Not quite "art" films in the sober Bergmanesque art house tradition, nor "Hollywood" films in the sense of 1200-screen saturation bombing campaigns, nor "independent" films according to the DIY outsider credo, "smart" films nevertheless share an aura of "intelligence" (or at least ironic distance) that distinguished them (and their audiences) from the perceived "dross" (and "rabble") of the mainstream multiplex.

To the extent that this smart cinema has a core set of practices and principles, this foundation is primarily a function of sensibility and tone. Previous forms of art cinema concentrated on formal experimentation with film style and narrative structure as a means of critiquing the codes of "bourgeois realism" and/or "bourgeois society", but smart cinema for the most part re-embraced classical narrative strategies, instead experimenting with irony and disengaged tone as a means of critiquing mainstream taste and culture. Any attempt to delineate the "sensibility" should begin by acknowledging that a larger panic over ironic culture seems to have been particularly important (and maybe even entirely confined) to the United States. Symbolically unified by Patrick Buchanan's incendiary "culture war" speech at the 1992 Republican Convention, conservative commentators quickly gravitated toward "irony" as a convenient label to describe a particular form of pop culture and by extension, its relativistic audience. Beyond the "moral relativism" of Solondz and LaBute so despised by Turan, for example, the 1990s also saw the more mainstream popularity on American television of *Beavis and Butthead, Seinfeld*, and *The Simpsons*, each a series that provoked civic custodians to bemoan a loss of "common" cultural and moral values. With distant roots in Popism, irony remained a cultural dominant in the gallery and the literary salon as well, while sarcasm, "air quotes", and the knowing consumption of kitsch became increasingly popularized practices.

One of the most pronounced battle lines in the war over "irony" was generational. Often, critics pinned the nation's move toward an ironic sensibility on the so-called "Generation-X", a demographic category as unstable as the trope of irony itself. The term derives from Douglas Coupland's (1991) much-discussed novel of the same name, the story of smart, highly educated men and women, born in the 1960s and 1970s, who missed out on the postwar US gravy train of unlimited economic growth and opportunity enjoyed by the baby boomers who preceded them. Distrustful of the hippie past, dismayed by the yuppie present, and disillusioned with a bumpy future, so the narrative goes, a bitter Gen-X retreated into ironic disengagement as a means of non-participatory co-existence with boomers and their domination of the cultural and political landscape. In addition to his detailed taxonomy of Gen-X types, Coupland captured this generation's strange mix of pop delight and disaffection by describing forms of "slumming" popular with this demographic, modes of ironic cultural consumption where bowling, Cool Whip, and platform shoes become, not so much things to enjoy in their own right, but experiences in quotation marks. Thus did a "camp" sensibility – the ironic and

aestheticized view of the world famously described by Susan Sontag (2001) in the early 1960s – migrate beyond its previous confines in gay subculture and the New York intelligentsia to inform an entire "generation's" engagement of mass culture. As the decade wore on, X-er irony became not just a strategy of consumption and cohabitation, but also a mode of cultural production, especially as younger talent moved into creative positions in the entertainment industry. Many articles on the irony epidemic, for example, focused on the immense influence of the Gen-X television writers produced by the *Harvard Lampoon*, one of the nation's oldest collegiate satirical papers. Coverage of a new generation of film directors, meanwhile, often emphasized their troubled relationship to the consecrating functions of "film school", a scene increasingly identified with the aesthetics of the movie brats and their boomer audience. Self-taught *enfant terrible*, Quentin Tarantino, whose film education consisted of working in a video store, became alternately the hero or villain of this trend. While one would not want to equate the ironic sensibility of the 1990s wholly with age, it is interesting that so many of the directors at the heart of "smart" cinema debate were born as late-boomers or within Gen-X proper (Solondz – 1959; Hartley – 1960; Haynes – 1961; LaBute – 1961; Payne – 1961; Tarantino – 1963; P.T. Anderson – 1970, Wes Anderson – 1970).

Born of these wars over taste, age, and attitude, smart cinema presents dark comedies and disturbing dramas that often showcase such disaffection and ironic distance. As with any group of directors/writers working within a set of period filmmaking practices, American smart cinema should be seen as a shared set of stylistic, narrative, and thematic elements deployed in differing configurations by individual films. These elements include: (1) the cultivation of "blank" style and incongruous narration; (2) a fascination with "synchronicity" as a principle of narrative organization; (3) a related thematic interest in random fate; (4) a focus on the white middle-class family as a crucible of miscommunication and emotional dysfunction; (5) a recurring interest in the politics of taste, consumerism, and identity. These elements do not necessarily appear in all of the films at the core of the irony/nihilism debates, but they do circulate with enough frequency to suggest widespread diffusion in smart cinema directors. Nor should it be imagined that those films that *do* trade in these elements necessarily subscribe to a uniform textual politics or worldview. There is, for example, a significant difference between Solondz's treatment of a middle-class husband's suburban meltdown in *Happiness* and its treatment in that film's more palatable and institutionally honoured *doppelgänger*, *American Beauty* (1999, Fig. 21 (*see plate section*)).

The centrepiece of the 1990s smart film might best be termed "blank" style. Blankness, in this context, does not refer to "invisibility" (as frequently discussed in relation to classical Hollywood editing), but can be described as an attempt to convey a film's story, no matter how sensationalistic, disturbing, or bizarre, with a sense of *dampened affect*. Of course, there is no such thing as truly "blank" style or narration – only a set of strategies employed to signify the idea of "blankness". Each is antiseptic in its own way, but films like *Crash* (1996), *Happiness*, *Safe*, *The Ice Storm*, and *Your Friends and Neighbors* are in fact highly stylized, their sense of authorial effacement and blank presentation achieved not through a feigned *vérité* but

Continued on page 434

Quentin Tarantino

A collision of talent, narcissism, and media over-exposure led Quentin Tarantino to become "the most visible new American film-maker to have emerged during the 1990s" (White 2002: 338). After famously serving his apprenticeship as video store clerk (his dodgy TV acting career, and directorial debut *My Best Friend's Birthday* are less well rehearsed (Clarkson 1995)), Tarantino wrote, directed and starred in *Reservoir Dogs* (1992), a wittily verbose crime caper owing a debt to Ringo Lam's *City on Fire* (1987). Boosted by a toe-tapping 1970s soundtrack and a notorious ear-slicing set piece (former gore-maestro Wes Craven controversially walked out of a screening), *Reservoir Dogs* became a Sundance Film Festival sensation. Picked up by Miramax, the film had muted box office impact in the United States, but scored international success, which helped make a celebrity of its creator. Tarantino's unfilmed script back catalogue (*True Romance, Natural Born Killers, From Dusk Till Dawn*) soon began to litter cinemas under other directors. A plethora of product ensued, spawning the adjective "Tarantino-esque" to describe an emergent blend of wisecracking, violently self-reflexive movies, a "byword for both pop-culture reference and popular post modern cinema" (Woods 2000: 5).

Tarantino's second feature as writer/director/star was the Cannes Palme d'Or and Oscar winner *Pulp Fiction* (1994), a bravura melting pot of hard-boiled stories that, like its predecessor, spawned a bestselling soundtrack CD mixing pop tracks with quotable dialogue riffs. Yet the sense that Tarantino was spreading his talents too thinly came to a head with the disastrous *Four Rooms* (1995), a portmanteau quartet that did little credit to any of its contributing directors (Tarantino, Robert Rodriguez, Allison Anders, Alexandre Rockwell). Having apparently exhausted critical goodwill with cameos in forgettable fare such as *Sleep with Me* (1994), *Destiny Turns on the Radio* (1995) and *Girl 6* (1996), Tarantino found his feet

Reservoir Dogs

with *Jackie Brown* (1997), an adaptation of Elmore Leonard's *Rum Punch*, which remains his most mature and accomplished movie to date. Starring blaxploitation legend Pam Grier – best known for roles in *Coffy* (1973) and *Foxy Brown* (1974) – with strong support from Robert Forster, Samuel L. Jackson and Robert de Niro, *Jackie Brown* eschewed the sometimes vacuous Tarantino-esque aesthetics of yore, allowing its thriller narrative to unfurl at an engrossing and engaging pace. Apparently, this was not what fans wanted; a poor box-office response (less than $40 million in the United States, compared with *Pulp Fiction*'s $107 million) marked *Jackie Brown* as a commercial disappointment. A long period of silence followed, during which reports of a forthcoming war movie (the as yet unrealized *Inglorious Bastards*) were rife. Finally, in 2003, Tarantino returned as writer/director of *Kill Bill: Vol 1*, a splashy sensationalist tribute to the Shaw Brothers' kung fu movies which ran so over-length that producers agreed to split the film into two separate movies. Along with *Kill Bill: Vol 2* (2004), this blood-spurting romp helped place Tarantino back on box-office form, its success being matched by the graphic novel adaptation *Sin City* (2005), on which Tarantino received a "guest director" credit.

References

Clarkson, W. (1995) *Quentin Tarantino: Shooting from the Hip.* London: Piatkus.
White, G. (2002) Quentin Tarantino, in Y. Tasker (ed.) *Fifty Contemporary Filmmakers.* London: Routledge, pp. 338–346.
Woods, P. (2000) *Quentin Tarantino: The Film Geek Files.* London: Plexus.

Mark Kermode

Continued from page 432

through a series of stylistic choices mobilized to signify dispassion, disengagement, and disinterest. Often, this stylistic strategy manifests itself in most basic form through framing and editing patterns. Surveying these films, one cannot help but be struck by the frequent (even dominant) use of long shots, static composition, and sparse cutting. Vibrant editing and camera movement, so pivotal in 1970s American art cinema, would seem to have been usurped in 1990s smart cinema by a preference for static *mise en scène* and longer shot lengths. The impact of many of these films depends, in the end, on the complex formal challenge of rendering the uncomfortable and unspeakable with such acute blandness, giving these films a "matter-of-fact" quality to them that no doubt leads to their common indictment as "nihilistic".

Another operative principle in "blank" narration, found in practitioners of irony across the ages, is the tactical use of incongruity. While some films employ a tableau style to render the extreme, unpleasant and sensationalistic in terms of "world-weary" disinterest (itself a form of incongruity), others create "blankness" through a more radical juxtaposition of mismatched (i.e. ironic) form and content. The opening moments of 1999's *Election*, for example, begin with duelling voiceovers from high-school teacher Jim McAllister (Matthew Broderick) and his annoyingly ambitious student, Tracey Flick (Reese Witherspoon). Images of classrooms, football fields, and pep rallies – accompanied by the voices of McAllister's earnest idealism and Flick's youthful naiveté – suggest the film will play as a pedestrian teen comedy, evoking in large part the well-known coming-of-age films directed by John Hughes in the 1980s. But then, almost as a *non sequitur*, narrator

McAllister adds as an afterthought, "Oh yes, there's one more thing you should know about Tracey Flick." We then cut to a close-up of McAllister's fellow high-school teacher, Dave Novotny (Mark Harelik), as he excitedly says of Tracey, "Her pussy gets so wet you wouldn't believe it." Suddenly, the safe boundaries of a typical Hughes comedy have been punctured by this leering admission of sexual harassment and statutory rape. As a result of this sudden juxtaposition, the calculatedly banal voiceovers and opening generic cues become increasingly ironic for the rest of the film, so much so that, by film's end, voiceover and image are often in direct conflict.

Whether cultivated through strategies of disengagement or disjunction, "blank" style in and of itself does not create "tone". When critics attack these films as ironic, cynical, fatalistic, or even nihilistic, they are responding to a tone produced by this style's application to larger narrational and thematic structures. In particular, the diagnosis of nihilistic fatalism seems closely related to larger issues of narrative causality. David Bordwell's (1987) discussion of narrative strategies in the European art film of the 1950s and 1960s is useful here as a point of comparison. As opposed to Hollywood's emphasis on linearity, character causality, and a three-act structure leading toward a pronounced deadline, characters in "classic" art cinema, Bordwell argues, are typically without clear-cut narrative goals, wandering as passive observers through a certain social milieu in a series of seemingly unconnected episodes (Bordwell 1987: 207). In both cases formal structure and textual politics are closely interwoven. Just as the classical Hollywood cinema posits a rational agent in control of his own destiny, "the art film's thematic crux, its attempt to pronounce judgments upon modern life and la condition humaine", argues Bordwell, "depends on its formal organization" (1987: 208).

Certainly related to earlier art film strategies, smart cinema also offers significant departures from this European-derived paradigm. As we might expect, historical changes in art, cinema, and the culture that nurtures art cinema itself have led to a different conception of *la condition humaine* as well as the "formal organization" one might employ to capture this elusive state of being. Perhaps the most significant change in narrative causality involves the increasing prevalence of multiprotagonist stories and episodic story structure. Although certainly not true of all contemporary smart cinema, many of these films (especially the "dramas") do favour a rotating series of interlocking episodes, centring not on a central unifying character's dynamic action (as in the classical Hollywood cinema) or relatively passive observations (as in previous art cinema), but instead on a series of seemingly random events befalling a loosely related set of characters. (In this respect, the most influential model for contemporary art narration may well come from Robert Altman, and in particular, Altman's move toward highly episodic multiprotagonist dramas like *Nashville* (1975) and *A Wedding* (1978). Altman himself returned with a "smart" film in 1993 with *Short Cuts*.) This shift to ensemble protagonists and episodic structure, in turn, when coupled with "blank" style and narration creates a formal organization ideally suited to the more postmodern (and one might say postBoomer) *la condition humaine* so central to these films. The favoured narrative structure is no longer the passive observer of an absurd world who eventually experiences some form of epiphany, but rather a range of characters subjected to increasing despair and/or humiliation captured in a rotating series of interlocking scenes in which some endure while others are crushed. The operatic finale to the second act of Paul Thomas Anderson's *Magnolia* is most explicit in this regard, as characters unrelated in the diegesis join together to sing a shared cross-cutting coda of their individual loneliness, suffering, and alienation.

This shift from the Modernist protagonist's search for meaning to the postmodern ensemble "fucked by fate" can also be discerned in the centrality of coincidence and synchronicity as an organizing principle in contemporary smart cinema. Classical Hollywood narration, of course, most frequently sought to avoid excessive coincidence, deeming it an easy and ultimately unrealistic plot device that viewers would find suspect (Bordwell et al. 1985: 13). In many respects, this mix of irony and synchronicity evokes the fiction of Kurt Vonnegut, an author who has been a perennial favourite of disaffected youth for many decades, and who has no doubt been widely read by many of the filmmakers and viewers in the Gen-X marketplace. Vonnegut's brand of irony, of course, often collided the grand and the trivial in bittersweet comedies about the illusion of free will, and just as often revelled in an almost mystical veneration of coincidence and synchronicity.

Paradoxically, in recent cinema, unrealistic coincidences have morphed into the new realism of synchronicity, an overarching belief in the fundamentally random and yet strangely meaningful structure of reality (even if that "meaning" is total absurdity). For example, with its prologue of a suicidal man accidentally shot through the heart while jumping from a building, *Magnolia* begins by explicitly meditating on the role of coincidence and synchronicity in modern life. The final destruction of *Election*'s Jim McAllister derives from a seemingly inconsequential moment in the film's opening credits when he unknowingly misses a trashcan while throwing away a sandwich, an injustice witnessed by the school's bitter janitor. *American Beauty*'s Lester Burnham (Kevin Spacey) dies from a rather strange episode of homophobic synchronicity. The narrative achronology of *Pulp Fiction*, the mirrored repetition of the "gallery scene" in *Your Friends and Neighbors*, and the simultaneous global taxi rides of *Night on Earth* (1991) each draw attention to the synchronicities of their characters in time and space. *Mystery Train* (1989) and *Run Lola Run* (1998) use a tripartite structure to foreground the fates of synchronicity as a formal and thematic strategy, while *Donnie Darko* (2001) uses a time-loop strategy to ponder the synchronicity of the universe. The entire narrative design of *Slacker*, finally, foregrounds this fascination with synchronicity as its main organizing principle.

The move to an episodic cast rather than a lone protagonist presents a shift in emphasis from "coincidence" to "synchronicity", that is, the narrative (and philosophical) investment in the "accident" yields to a narrative (and philosophical) belief in a logic of the random. Though these films can follow different trajectories (many find redemption in *Magnolia* while in *Happiness* everyone attains complete emotional annihilation), this shared structure in passive synchronicity suggests that the contemporary smart cinema protagonist has become, in many cases, even more listless than his or her European ancestors. More acted upon than acting, these contemporary protagonists are often prisoners of emotional abuse, sterile environments, or even just fate itself, walking embodiments of that famed postmodern bumpersticker, "shit happens!" Buses crash into lakes. Jet engines fall from the

sky. Children die from downed power lines. The suspense, such that there is, comes from seeing just how much shit any one character can endure and how clever the universe (or filmmaker) can be in meting out its interconnected twists of fate.

Moving beyond the more general formal aspects of style and narrative organization, many of these films also share a number of recurring story elements and thematic concerns. Two themes seem particularly central to 1990s smart cinema: interpersonal alienation within the white middle class (usually focused on the family) and alienation within contemporary consumer culture. While earlier modes of art cinema often explored the nebulous condition of "alienation" in more abstract metaphysical or philosophical terms, American smart cinema favours a limited investigation of anomie within the more narrow constraints of suburban family life, urban courtship, and consumer identity. To the extent that these films have an explicit political agenda, it lies in the familiar theme that repression and miscommunication make the white middle class particularly ill suited for either relationships or marriage. So ubiquitous is this theme that it has led to a number of "stock" shots in smart cinema: the "awkward couple" shot (a strained "couple" shot in tableau form separated by blank space); the "awkward coupling" shot (a camera placed directly over the bed recording passionless sex); and in "family" films, the "awkward dining" shot (long shots of maladjusted families trapped in their dining rooms).

More interesting than this explicit agenda to dissect the white middle class as a crucible of emotional dysfunction, many of these films also engage, either explicitly or at the margins, in a more subtle critique of the politics of identity within consumer culture. This interest takes many forms, from playful derision of various "taste cultures" to more complex considerations of the links between identity and consumerism. Midway through Anderson's *Boogie Nights*, for example, pornstars Dirk Diggler (Mark Wahlberg) and Reed Rothchild (John C. Reilly) decide to try their hand at rock-n-roll, and in a prolonged scene of uncomfortable derision, we watch as the two earnestly work at writing incredibly banal songs, all the time wearing the most ludicrous of 1980s rock-n-roll fashions. In Stephen Frears' *High Fidelity* (2000), meanwhile, record store owner and rock connoisseur Rob Gordon (John Cusak) is horrified to learn that his girlfriend is leaving him for a new-age baby boomer who listens to that latest facile trend, "world music". For Gordon, the issue of proper "taste" is ultimately more painful than the pangs of sexual jealousy. In a mass murder fantasy in *Happiness*, psychiatrist/sniper Bill Maplewood arrives for his date with infamy wearing a pastel plaid shirt, pressed khakis, and brown loafers, a less-than-subtle joke about the L.L. Bean-ality of evil. An early crisis point in *Safe* involves the colour of a new couch. In *Ghost World*, the ever-meta Enid (Thora Birch) is upset when local hipsters at a 'zine store mistake her knowing quotation of a "classic 1977 punk rock outfit" with a naïve exercise in démodé cool. *Being John Malkovich* and *Fight Club* (1999), finally, employ strategies of narrative fragmentation to explore issues of consumerism and identity, the first as a comedy and the second as an action/drama.

In a culture where "Gen-X" in particular apparently has an intuitive understanding of the "commodity fetish" and Baudrillard's (1996) "system of objects", it is not surprising that the cinema itself should take up these questions in rather self-conscious and even didactic fashion. Beyond the rather tiresome portraits of suburban dysfunction lies a more interesting impatience with semiotic naiveté, and with it, either direct or indirect meditations on the workings of habitus and identity. From the perspective of traditional Leftist politics, smart cinema seems to advocate irresponsible resignation to the horrors of life under advanced capitalism and an attendant disregard for the traditional villains of racism, sexism, and class division. From the Right, these films seem to advance an irresponsible worldview where truth and morality are no longer of concern. From within the prism of irony, however, many of these films suggest the futility of pure politics or absolute morality, concentrating instead on the prison-house of habitus and the politics of postmodern paralysis. As the fixation on quotation, distance, and consumer taste suggests, one thing this sensibility cannot abide is an inability to understand how one's tastes, gestures, and actions "read" in the larger cultural field. How does one act in a world where all is gesture? How does one tell stories in a world where all aesthetic and political strategies are ultimately tired and predictable? Why would one expose oneself to the ridicule of being caught in a series of modernist cinematic clichés?

Conclusion

By the time hijacked planes destroyed the World Trade Center on September 11, 2001, it was clear that "irony" had become an extremely charged code word masking a number of larger social, cultural, and aesthetic divisions stewing over the previous ten, 20, maybe even 30 years. So bitter was this conflict, apparently, that many pundits exploited "9/11" as an opportunity to take yet another shot at the perceived decadence of an overly ironic culture. "There's going to be a seismic change", predicted *Vanity Fair's* Graydon Carter in the days following the disaster. "I think it's the end of the age of irony. Things that were considered fringe and frivolous are going to disappear" (Beers 2001).

Irony didn't disappear, of course, but many of the directors most closely associated with a smart cinema aesthetic have nevertheless gradually changed the tone and structure of their work (although I certainly do not want to suggest such changes were in direct response to either 9/11 or critics of this type of cinema). Solondz's 2005 film *Palindromes*, for example, saw the director pursuing an even more essayistic style, in this case revelling quite earnestly in the ideological contradictions inherent on both sides of the abortion debate. Even as the film rather directly confronts each side's dogmatic self-delusion, however, much of the film retains Solondz's established strategy of presenting his characters in terms of sharply drawn caricatures of lifestyle and consumption (in this case, Right-wing religious zealots versus selfish liberal yuppies). While Wes Anderson's *The Life Aquatic with Steve Zissou* (2004) is wholly in keeping with his work from the 1990s, Alexander Payne's *About Schmidt* (2002) and *Sideways* (2004) have seen the director temper the arch irony of his earlier films to embrace a more naturalistic comic style (and, in turn, several Academy Award nominations). Todd Haynes, meanwhile, continued to explore the politics of "blankness" in his rather bloodless homage to Douglas Sirk, *Far From Heaven* (2002). While Sirk's reputation among cinephiles has been a function of his perceived "excesses" in narration and *mise en scène*, Hayne's encounter with Sirkian material was a classic exercise in "dampened affect" and highly reminiscent of his earlier work in *Safe*. The emphasis on multiple protagonists and the mysteries of synchronicity continues in Paul Haggis' *Crash* (2004), which, like *Magnolia* before it, rather fatalistically follows the intertwined fates of several characters in Los Angeles. In *Elephant* (2004) and *Last Days* (2005), finally, Gus van Sant elicits the prevailing tone of smart cinema – perhaps even nostalgically – by directly addressing issues of youthful alienation and anomie in the 1990s through barely disguised treatments of the Columbine massacre and the suicide of rock star Kurt Cobain.

Like any "group style" or thematic centre that comes to dominate a period of filmmaking, the formal, tonal, and moral qualities of "smart cinema" will no doubt continue to circulate, especially among those filmmakers most closely associated with the cultural moment of late-boomer and Gen-X politics. As a style that at least implicitly always defined itself in opposition to the perceived acceleration and superficiality of Hollywood cinema, much depends as well on how thoroughly "mainstream" cinema integrates this sensibility in its own product. And, because the "smart film" was, in its heyday, so closely tied to age, history, and generational experience, its influence will no doubt continue to dissipate as the next generation (the "millennials" or "Gen-Y", as they have been called) moves into prominence in the film industry. Described by many as more conservative and less cynical than the generation that preceded them, perhaps their ascendancy in the cultural marketplace will eventually bring an end to the corrosive irony, black humour, and synchronistic fatalism so lamented by cultural conservatives. Even if this is the case, however, the ongoing competition between older critics and younger producers practically ensures that the cinema will continue to figure prominently in generational struggles over culture, no matter what form the actual conflicts and films end up taking.

References

Baudrillard, J. (1996) *The System of Objects.* Trans. James Benedict. London: Verso.

Beers, D. (2001) *Irony is dead! Long live irony!* http://www.salon.com/mwt/feature/2001/09/25/irony_lives/

Bordwell, D. (1987) *Narration in the Fiction Film.* Madison: University of Wisconsin Press.

Bordwell, D., Staiger, J. and Thompson, K. (1985) *The Classical Hollywood Cinema: Film Style and Mode of Production to 1960.* New York: Columbia University Press.

Bourdieu, P. (1993) *The Field of Cultural Production.* New York: Columbia University Press.

Coupland, D. (1991) *Generation X: Tales for an Accelerated Culture.* New York: St. Martin's Press.

Dargis, M. (1998) Whatever: the new nihilism, *LA Weekly*, 26 November.

Frank, T. (1998) *The Conquest of Cool: Business Culture, Counterculture, and the Rise of Hip Consumerism.* Chicago: University of Chicago Press.

Rudnick, P. and Andersen, K. (1989) The irony epidemic, *Spy*, March.

Schamus, J. (2001) A rant, in Lewis, J. (ed.) *The End of Cinema as We Know It.* New York: New York University Press.

Sontag, S. (2001) Notes on camp. *Against Interpretation: And Other Essays.* New York: Picador.

Turan, K. (1998) Fade to pitch black, *Los Angeles Times*, 22 November.

Wallace, D.F. (1998) E unibus pluram: television and U.S. fiction, in *A Supposedly Fun Thing I'll Never Do Again.* New York: Little, Brown and Co.

1990–2000	Rentals to date for year just ending
1990 Ghost	$94,000,000
1991 Terminator 2	$112,000,000
1992 Home Alone 2: Lost in New York	$102,000,000

From 1993*	Domestic box office gross for year just ending
1993 Jurassic Park	$337,832,005
1994 The Lion King	$298,879,911
1995 Batman Forever	$184,031,112
1996 Independence Day	$306,155,579
1997 Men in Black	$250,004,561
1998 Titanic	$488,200,000
1999 Star Wars Episode 1: The Phantom Menace	$430,443,350
2000 Mission Impossible 2	$215,400,000

* From 1993 Variety tracked the top box office performers in the calendar year. From 1993 the Anniversary Editions have included a list of the top 125–200 titles and their domestic box office grosses.

1990

Academy Awards
Best picture: *Dances with Wolves* – Jim Wilson and Kevin Costner
Best director: Kevin Costner – *Dances with Wolves*
Best actor in a leading role: Jeremy Irons – *Reversal of Fortune*
Best actor in a supporting role: Joe Pesci – *Goodfellas*
Best actress in a leading role: Kathy Bates – *Misery*
Best actress in a supporting role: Whoopi Goldberg – *Ghost*
Sundance Film Festival
Grand Jury Prize Documentary: *H-2 Worker* – Stephanie Black and *Water and Power* – Pat O'Neill
Grand Jury Prize Dramatic: *Chameleon Street* – Wendell B. Harris, Jr.
Cannes International Film Festival
Palme d'Or: *Wild at Heart* – David Lynch
Venice International Film Festival
Golden Lion: *Rosencrantz and Guildenstern are Dead* – Tom Stoppard

1991

Academy Awards
Best picture: *The Silence of the Lambs* – Edward Saxon, Kenneth Utt and Ron Bozman
Best director: Jonathan Demme – *The Silence of the Lambs*
Best actor in a leading role: Anthony Hopkins – *The Silence of the Lambs*
Best actor in a supporting role: Jack Palance – *City Slickers*
Best actress in a leading role: Jodie Foster – *The Silence of the Lambs*

Best actress in a supporting role: Mercedes Ruehl – *The Fisher King*
Sundance Film Festival
Grand Jury Prize Documentary: *American Dream* – Barbara Kopple and *Paris Is Burning* – Jennie Livingston
Grand Jury Prize Dramatic: *Poison* – Todd Haynes
Cannes International Film Festival
Palme d'Or: *Barton Fink* – Joel Coen
Venice International Film Festival
Golden Lion: *Urga* – Nikita Mikhalkov

1992

Academy Awards
Best picture: *Unforgiven* – Clint Eastwood
Best director: Clint Eastwood – *Unforgiven*
Best actor in a leading role: Al Pacino – *Scent of a Woman*
Best actor in a supporting role: Gene Hackman – *Unforgiven*
Best actress in a leading role: Emma Thompson – *Howard's End*
Best actress in a supporting role: Marisa Tomei – *My Cousin Vinny*
Sundance Film Festival
Grand Jury Prize Documentary: *A Brief History of Time* – Errol Morris and *Finding Christa* – Camille Bishops and James Hatch
Grand Jury Prize Dramatic: *In the Soup* - Alexandre Rockwell
Cannes International Film Festival
Palme d'Or: *Den Goda Viljan* – Bille August
Venice International Film Festival
Golden Lion: *Qui Ju da guansi* - Zhang Yimou

1993

Academy Awards
Best picture: *Schindler's List* – Steven Spielberg, Gerald R. Molen and Branko Lustig
Best director: Steven Spielberg – *Schindler's List*
Best actor in a leading role: Tom Hanks – *Philadelphia*
Best actor in a supporting role: Tommy Lee Jones – *The Fugitive*
Best actress in a leading role: Holly Hunter – *The Piano*
Best actress in a supporting role: Anna Paquin – *The Piano*
Sundance Film Festival
Grand Jury Prize Documentary: *Children of Fate: Life and Death in a Sicilian Family* – Andrew Young and Susan Todd, and *Silverlake Life: The View From Here* – Tom Joslin and Peter Friedman
Grand Jury Prize Dramatic: *Ruby in Paradise* – Victor Nunez, and *Public Access* – Bryan Singer
Cannes International Film Festival
Palme d'Or: *The Piano* – Jane Campion, and *Bawang Bieji* – Chen Kaige
Venice International Film Festival
Golden Lion: *Short Cuts* – Robert Altman, and *Trois couleurs Bleu* – Krzysztof Kieslowski

1994

Academy Awards
Best picture: *Forrest Gump* – Wendy Finerman, Steve Tisch and Steve Starkey
Best director: Robert Zemeckis – *Forrest Gump*
Best actor in a leading role: Tom Hanks – *Forrest Gump*
Best actor in a supporting role: Martin Landau – *Ed Wood*
Best actress in a leading role: Jessica Lange – *Blue Sky*
Best actress in a supporting role: Dianne Wiest – *Bullets over Broadway*
Sundance Film Festival
Grand Jury Prize Documentary: *Freedom on My Mind* – Connie Field and Marilyn Mulford
Grand Jury Prize Dramatic: *What Happened Was...* – Tom Noonan
Cannes International Film Festival
Palme d'Or: *Pulp Fiction* – Quentin Tarantino
Venice International Film Festival
Golden Lion: *Before the Rain* – Milcho Manchevski and *Aiqing wansui – Vive l'amour* – Tsai Ming-liang

1995

Academy Awards
Best picture: *Braveheart* – Mel Gibson, Alan Ladd, Jr. and Bruce Davey
Best director: Mel Gibson – *Braveheart*
Best actor in a leading role: Nicolas Cage – *Leaving Las Vegas*
Best actor in a supporting role: Kevin Spacey – *The Usual Suspects*
Best actress in a leading role: Susan Sarandon – *Dead Man Walking*
Best actress in a supporting role: Mira Sorvino – *Mighty Aphrodite*
Sundance Film Festival
Grand Jury Prize Documentary: *Crumb* – Terry Zwigoff
Grand Jury Prize Dramatic: *The Brothers Mcmullen* – Edward Burns
Cannes International Film Festival
Palme d'Or: *Underground* – Emir Kusturica
Venice International Film Festival
Golden Lion: *Cyclo* – Tran Ahn Hung

1996

Academy Awards
Best picture: *The English Patient* – Saul Zaentz
Best director: Anthony Minghella – *The English Patient*
Best actor in a leading role: Geoffrey Rush – *Shine*
Best actor in a supporting role: Cuba Gooding, Jr. – *Jerry Maguire*
Best actress in a leading role: Frances McDormand – *Fargo*
Best actress in a supporting role: Juliette Binoche – *The English Patient*
Sundance Film Festival
Grand Jury Prize Documentary: *Troublesome Creek: A Midwestern* – Jeanne Jordan and Steven Ascher
Grand Jury Prize Dramatic: *Welcome to the Dollhouse* – Todd Solondz

Cannes International Film Festival
Palme d'Or: *Secrets and Lies* – Mike Leigh
Venice International Film Festival
Golden Lion: *Michael Collins* – Neil Jordan

1997

Academy Awards
Best picture: *Titanic* – James Cameron and Jon Landau
Best director: James Cameron – *Titanic*
Best actor in a leading role: Jack Nicholson – *As Good As It Gets*
Best actor in a supporting role: Robin Williams – *Good Will Hunting*
Best actress in a leading role: Helen Hunt – *As Good As It Gets*
Best actress in a supporting role: Kim Basinger – *L.A. Confidential*
Sundance Film Festival
Grand Jury Prize Documentary: *Girls Like Us* – Jane Wagner and Tina DiFeliciantonio
Grand Jury Prize Dramatic: *Sunday* – Jonathan Nossiter
Cannes International Film Festival
Palme d'Or: *Unagi* – Shohei Imamura and *Ta'm e Guilass* – Abbas Kiarostami
Venice International Film Festival
Golden Lion: *Hana-bi* – Takeshi Kitano

1998

Academy Awards
Best picture: *Shakespeare in Love* – David Parfitt, Donna Gigliotti, Harvey Weinstein, Edward Zwick and Marc Norman
Best director: Steven Spielberg – *Saving Private Ryan*
Best actor in a leading role: Roberto Benigni – *Life Is Beautiful*
Best actor in a supporting role: James Coburn – *Affliction*
Best actress in a leading role: Gwyneth Paltrow – *Shakespeare in Love*
Best actress in a supporting role: Judi Dench – *Shakespeare in Love*
Sundance Film Festival
Grand Jury Prize Documentary: *The Farm* – Jonathan Stack and Liz Garbus, and *Frathouse* – Todd Phillips and Andrew Gurland
Grand Jury Prize Dramatic: *Slam* – Marc Levin
Cannes International Film Festival
Palme d'Or: *Mia Eoniotita Ke Mia Mera* – Theo Angelopoulos
Venice International Film Festival
Golden Lion: *Così ridevano* – Gianni Amelio

1999

Academy Awards
Best picture: *American Beauty* – Bruce Cohen and Dan Jinks
Best director: Sam Mendes – *American Beauty*
Best actor in a leading role: Kevin Spacey – *American Beauty*
Best actor in a supporting role: Michael Caine – *The Cider House Rules*
Best actress in a leading role: Hilary Swank – *Boys Don't Cry*
Best actress in a supporting role: Angelina Jolie – *Girl, Interrupted*

Sundance Film Festival
Grand Jury Prize Documentary: *American Movie* – Chris Smith
Grand Jury Prize Dramatic: *Three Seasons* – Tony Bui
Cannes International Film Festival
Palme d'Or: *Rosetta* – Jean Pierre and Luc Dardenne
Venice International Film Festival
Golden Lion: *Not One Less* – Zhang Yimou

2000

Academy Awards
Best picture: *Gladiator* – Douglas Wick, David Franzoni and Branko Lustig
Best director: Steven Soderbergh – *Traffic*
Best actor in a leading role: Russell Crowe – *Gladiator*
Best actor in a supporting role: Benicio Del Toro – *Traffic*
Best actress in a leading role: Julia Roberts – *Erin Brockovich*
Best actress in a supporting role: Marcia Gay Harden – *Pollock*
Sundance Film Festival
Grand Jury Prize Documentary: *Long Night's Journey Into Day* – Frances Reid and Deborah Hoffman
Grand Jury Prize Dramatic: *Girlfight* directed by Karyn Kusama, and *You Can Count On Me* – Kenneth Lonegran
Cannes International Film Festival
Palme d'Or: *Dancer in the Dark* – Lars von Trier
Venice International Film Festival
Golden Lion: *Dayereh* – Jafar Panahi

2001

Academy Awards
Best picture: *A Beautiful Mind* – Brian Grazer and Ron Howard
Best director: Ron Howard – *A Beautiful Mind*
Best actor in a leading role: Denzel Washington – *Training Day*
Best actor in a supporting role: Jim Broadbent – *Iris*
Best actress in a leading role: Halle Berry – *Monster's Ball*
Best actress in a supporting role: Jennifer Connelly – *A Beautiful Mind*
Sundance Film Festival
Grand Jury Prize Documentary: *Southern Comfort* – Kate Davis
Grand Jury Prize Dramatic: *The Believer* – Henry Bean
Cannes International Film Festival
Palme d'Or: *The Son's Room (La Stanza del Figlio)* – Nanni Moretti
Venice International Film Festival
Golden Lion: *Monsoon Wedding* – Mira Nair

2002

Academy Awards
Best picture: *Chicago* – Martin Richards
Best director: Roman Polanski – *The Pianist*
Best actor in a leading role: Adrien Brody – *The Pianist*

Best actor in a supporting role: Chris Cooper– *Adaptation*
Best actress in a leading role: Nicole Kidman – *The Hours*
Best actress in a supporting role: Catherine Zeta-Jones – *Chicago*
Sundance Film Festival
Grand Jury Prize Documentary: *Daughter from Danang* – Gail Dolgin and Vincente Franco
Grand Jury Prize Dramatic: *Personal Velocity* – Rebecca Miller
Cannes International Film Festival
Palme d'Or: *The Pianist* – Roman Polanski
Venice International Film Festival
Golden Lion: *The Magdalene Sisters* – Peter Mullan

2003

Academy Awards
Best picture: *The Lord of the Rings: The Return of the King* – Barrie M. Osborne, Peter Jackson and Fran Walsh
Best director: Peter Jackson – *The Lord of the Rings: The Return of the King*
Best actor in a leading role: Sean Penn – *Mystic River*
Best actor in a supporting role: Tim Robbins – *Mystic River*
Best actress in a leading role: Charlize Theron – *Monster*
Best actress in a supporting role: Renée Zellweger – *Cold Mountain*
Sundance Film Festival
Grand Jury Prize Documentary: *Capturing the Friedmans* – Andrew Jarecki
Grand Jury Prize Dramatic: *American Splendor* – Shari Springer Berman and Robert Pulcini
Cannes International Film Festival
Palme d'Or: *Elephant* – Gus Van Sant
Venice International Film Festival
Golden Lion: *Vozvrašcenje* – Andrej Zvjagintsev

2004

Academy Awards
Best picture: *Million Dollar Baby* – Clint Eastwood, Albert S. Ruddy, Tom Rosenberg
Best director: Clint Eastwood – *Million Dollar Baby*
Best actor in a leading role: Jamie Foxx – *Ray*
Best actor in a supporting role: Morgan Freeman – *Million Dollar Baby*
Best actress in a leading role: Hilary Swank – *Million Dollar Baby*
Best actress in a supporting role: Cate Blanchett – *The Aviator*
Sundance Film Festival
Grand Jury Prize Documentary: *DiG!* – Ondi Timoner
Grand Jury Prize Dramatic: *Primer* – Shane Carruth
Cannes International Film Festival
Palme d'Or: *Fahrenheit 9/11* – Michael Moore
Venice International Film Festival
Golden Lion: *The Return* – Andrei Zvyagintsev

SUGGESTED FURTHER READING

Aaron, M. (ed.) (2004) *New Queer Cinema: A Critical Reader*. Edinburgh: Edinburgh University Press.

Andrew, G. (1998) *Stranger Than Paradise: Maverick Film-Makers in Recent American Cinema*. London: Prion.

Arroyo, J. (ed.) (2000) *Action/Spectacle: A Sight and Sound Reader*. London: BFI.

Biskind, P. (2005) *Down and Dirty Pictures*. London: Bloomsbury.

Collins, J., Radner, H. and Collins, A.P. (eds) (1993) *Film Theory Goes to the Movies*. New York: Routledge.

Donalson, M. (2003) *Black Directors in Hollywood*. Austin: University of Texas Press.

Guerrero, E. (1998) A circus of dreams and lies: the black film wave at middle age, in Jon Lewis (ed.) *The New American Cinema*. Durham, NC: Duke University Press, pp. 328–52.

Hirsch, F. (1999) *Detours and Lost Highways: A Map of Neo-Noir*. New York: Limelight.

Holmlund, C. and Wyatt, J. (eds) (2005) *Contemporary American Independent Film*. London: Routledge.

King, G. (2000) *Spectacular Narratives: Hollywood in the Age of the Blockbuster*. London: I.B. Tauris.

Levatin, J., Plessis, J. and Raoul V. (eds) (2003) *Women Filmmakers: Refocusing*. New York: Routledge.

Lewis, J. (ed.) (2001) *The End of Cinema as We Know It: American Film in the Nineties*. New York: New York University Press.

Lott, T. (1998) Hollywood and independent black cinema, in S. Neale and M. Smith (eds) *Contemporary Hollywood Cinema*. London: Routledge.

Neale, S. and Smith, M. (eds) (1998) *Contemporary Hollywood Cinema*. London: Routledge.

Tasker, Y. (1998) *Working Girls: Gender and Sexuality in Popular Cinema*. London: Routledge.

Tasker, Y. (ed.) (2002) *Fifty Contemporary Filmmakers*. London: Routledge.

Tasker, Y. (ed.) (2004) *Action and Adventure Cinema*. London: Routledge.

Wasko, J. (1995). *Hollywood in the Information Age: Beyond the Silver Screen*. Austin: University of Texas Press.

Wells, P. (1998) *Understanding Animation*. London: Routledge.

Willis, S. (1997) *High Contrast: Race and Gender in Contemporary Hollywood Film*. Durham, NC: Duke University Press.

Wyatt, J. (1994) *High Concept: Movies and Marketing in Hollywood*. Austin: University of Texas Press.

QUESTIONS FOR DISCUSSION

This section contains brief background notes which are designed to guide students to some of the main issues that have been raised by the various articles on the 1990s and beyond. These are followed by some sample essay questions which both students and tutors may find useful in guiding class discussion as well as setting exercises.

Background Notes

The way in which you might encounter a film had increased significantly in the early 1990s. The home viewing format of video as well as subscription-based cable and satellite channels were just as likely to be the form that you saw a movie in as the theatre. As in the 1980s the theatre continued to hold a central place in launching films but the subsequent releases on video and on cable/satellite were the most dependable revenue streams for the major studios. Such revenue streams both justified and made it possible for studios and film financers to meet the increasing cost of making a feature film. Justin Wyatt's notion that green-light decisions on mainstream high-budget material depended upon "high-concept", that is, an easily grasped idea around which a film could be marketed, usually around a single visual image, continued with mega-budget films such as the *Jurassic Park* franchise (1993, 1997, 2001), *Independence Day* (1996) or *Titanic* (1997). However, at the same time filmmaking on smaller budgets continued as independent filmmakers and companies were able, through the increased revenue streams, to make sustainable profits and, in the case of Miramax, able to achieve "major" status, following its merger with Disney in 1993.

Independent filmmaking continued to be a means for new filmmakers to draw the attention of the majors and therefore gain access to bigger budgets. This was particularly evident in the shift from independent to mainstream made by a number of black filmmakers. Spike Lee's film *Do the Right Thing* (1989) had secured his position with the majors although his struggle with Warner Brothers over completing *Malcolm X* (1992) showed that the major studios were reluctant to support material that was politically contentious and not fully exploitable across other related popular culture industries. Instead, black filmmakers such as the Hughes brothers or John Singleton, through initiating the ghetto-action film cycle with *Menace II Society* and *Boyz in the Hood* respectively, were able to tap into the widespread popularity of African-American popular music and culture. Films which could generate appeal, and therefore profits, across media in this way fit squarely into the preferred business model of the industry. This did not, however, preclude independent filmmakers from finding niche audiences through developing sub-genres or modes such as New Queer Cinema or what Jeffrey Sconce has called "smart cinema" or the surprisingly vital, profit-generating trend in documentary. All of these benefited from the proliferation of "delivery systems" ranging from video, cable and satellite television to the Internet, and their attendant revenue streams which made it possible to target specific audiences with specific taste preferences.

In the 1990s technological developments increased the accessibility of new digital production technology and the Internet, the most significant development in home communications technology since television, continues to exert a major impact in the early twenty-first century. These technologies have contributed to the convergence of capabilities, perhaps most obviously in the home computer which is capable of downloading films, playing soundtracks and DVDs as well as creating or altering audio-visual moving images. These convergences have resulted in struggles for intellectual property as the global entertainment industry sought to curtail the widespread reproduction of films, programmes, music and other media forms. These conflicts over copyright and fair use continue up to the present day.

Questions

1   One consistent theme in popular media discussions of the Hollywood blockbuster has been the prevalence of special effects, often described as being detrimental to the narrative. Geoff King in his article above asks what the "fate of narrative" is in this form which seems dominated by spectacle. Discuss the role of spectacle in the storytelling process of a film which could be called a "blockbuster (i.e. *Jurassic Park*, *Terminator 2: Judgment Day*, *Independence Day*). How did changes in production technology impact on this type of high-budget filmmaking practices in the 1990s?

2   Michele Aaron suggests that the loosely connected group of films that have come to be called New Queer Cinema share an "attitude". They give voice to marginalized groups, resist simplistic, "positive" representations of those groups, defy the homophobic past and rework cinematic conventions. The term "queer" has also been reappropriated to mean being free from conventional codes of behaviour, a meaning which expands beyond sexuality and contests accepted notions of normality. One way of exploring this would be to compare some of the films that have come to be categorized as "queer" such as *Swoon* (Tom Kalin, 1992) or *Tongues Untied* (Marlon Riggs, 1990) with more mainstream films such as *Philadephia* (Jonathan Demme, 1993), *Boys Don't Cry* (1999) or *Brokeback Mountain* (Ang Lee, 2005). Following that comparison with mainstream films, discuss the impact on this "queer" sensibility on mainstream cinema more generally. Trace the work of a director of your choice as an exponent of New Queer Cinema such as Todd Haynes, Jennie Livingston, Laurie Lynd or Gus Van Sant.

3   Justin Wyatt points to the "high-concept" method which places marketing as the driving force behind creative decision-making in mainstream Hollywood films. Using a high-profile film, construct a case study of how one specific title was distributed and marketed to audiences in the period 1990-2005. As a counterbalance to the marketing in the US, research the marketing of the film for a country other than the USA.

4 Yvonne Tasker argues that "Popular feminisms ... constitute a partial and particular understanding of feminism as an agenda already achieved". In the 1990s the action heroine emerged in various guises which seemed to call upon or echo that assumption in various contradictory ways. Take some films with strong women characters from the 1990s and discuss their relevance with Tasker's definition of "postfeminism". For example, discuss *Thelma and Louise* (Ridley Scott, 1992) as either a buddy movie or a road movie or compare the forms of violence and authority represented by the characters of Clarice Starling (Jodie Foster) in *The Silence of the Lambs*, Megan Turner (Jamie Lee Curtis) in *Blue Steel*, Marge Gunderson (Frances McDormand) in *Fargo*, Trinity in *The Matrix* (or another film of your choice).

5 Given that women played more active roles in action cinema in the 1990s, it may be useful to consider how femininity functions as a source of visual fascination (focusing particularly on *mise en scène*, narrative, cinematography) in these films. How does this extend to other genres? Following that, choose a set of films, either within a genre or production cycle, and discuss how masculinity figures as the central spectacle.

6 Using one or two films by a particular director, discuss the use of a stylistic element (e.g. music, cinematography, *mise en scène*) in relation to the formal norms of classical Hollywood cinema.

7 Does a truly independent American cinema exist? Discuss with close reference to two or three films and their production/exhibition context. You might want to look at the history of Miramax as an example.

8 The New Black Cinema seems to have two intersecting points of origin, the first in independent cinema with the films of Spike Lee, Julie Dash or Marlon Riggs and the second in "exploitation" with films by the Hughes brothers, Matty Rich or John Singleton. Tommy L. Lott has noted: "notions of contemporary black cinema that rely on too rigid a dichotomy between independent and studio films are unable to accommodate recent developments in the film industry" ("Hollywood and independent black cinema", in S. Neale and M. Smith (eds) *Contemporary Hollywood Cinema*, 1998, p. 211). Discuss this statement, using at least two films to illustrate your argument.

9 Arguably there was a strand of nostalgia for classical Hollywood and for 1950s America that was central to the "New Hollywood" of Spielberg/Lucas and their acolytes such as Robert Zemeckis. Such nostalgia was also critically explored and undermined by filmmakers such as David Lynch in the 1980s. This nostalgia extended to a revitalization and/or updating of classic genres such as *film noir* or the gangster film. Analyze how one or two films work with the narrative and stylistic conventions of a specific genre which was revisited in the period 1990-2005 (e.g. neo-*noir*, the disaster movie, the gangster film). Discuss one or two of these films in terms of one or two of the following: postmodernism; pastiche; nostalgia.

10 Analyze the ways in which one key "issue of difference" (e.g. sexual, racial, age) is set up in the narrative or by the visual style of two films of your choice from the period. Is it useful to

discuss the work of mainstream directors in terms of their gender or racial group or sexual identification?

11 Stars continued to be a necessary risk-reducing factor in filmmaking. The role of the star in the package unit system was vital in securing funding and in many cases stars set up their own production companies. Trace the career of a star of your choice. What does this reveal about the way that films are made? How are choices for projects influenced by the developing star persona? What role does the circulating media play in developing that persona? To what extent does the star have control over the circulation of their image and what steps are available to take in achieving that? Gathering articles from newspapers, fan magazines and the tabloid press, choose a star who has had difficulty with the press and examine how the story played out and how that might have affected their subsequent choice of projects.

GLOSSARY

ancillary markets: In film industry terms, this means markets for income generation beyond the initial theatrical release. These usually mean the markets for the rental and sale of the film in video and DVD versions, sale to television networks for broadcast but also product tie-ins ranging from video games and toys to novelizations, comic book adaptations and clothing.

auteur: A much debated term in film studies but in its strictest sense refers to the director or in a few cases, the producer, seen as the "author" of the film. Used as an evaluative term to distinguish directors of "quality" or of singular "vision".

baby boomers: Refers to the generation of people born between 1946 and 1964. This was referred to as a "boom" because of the rise in birth rates following the Second World War.

Betamax: The first home-viewing and recording video tape system designed by Sony. Introduced in 1975, the Betamax system vied with the competing VHS system by Matsushita for dominance of the market. By 1985, however, VHS had become the dominant format.

blimped cameras: Blimps refer to sound dampening devices on film cameras developed for filming with sychronized sound.

blockbuster: Usually refers to a big-budget film which has made exceedingly high profits. The term is also used to refer to films which have inordinately high production costs which require above-average success to make a profit. "Block" usually means the profit margin of a film.

B movie: B movie originally referred to low budget films made in the 1930s and 1940s by the major studios and by the small "poverty row" production companies such as Monogram and Republic. They got their name from accompanying the major studios higher-budget "A" features on double bills. In the 1950s and 1960s companies such as American International Pictures combined low-budget production with sensational subject matter. In the process the B movie became a short-hand expression for a kitsch and/or camp aesthetic adopted by *avant-garde* and underground filmmakers of the 1960s, e.g. Jack Smith, Andy Warhol and Kenneth Anger, and in the 1980s and 1990s with independent filmmakers such as John Waters and Quentin Tarantino. The tradition of low-budget exploitation filmmaking continued through the 1970s and with the "direct-to-video" film.

CGI: An acronym for "computer-generated imagery", CGI in film production refers to the use of 3D computer graphics to create or contribute to special effects.

cinéma vérité: See *direct cinema*.

conglomeration: term used to refer to the wave of corporate take-overs or mergers of major Hollywood studios in the 1960s and early 1970s. Music Corporation of America took over Universal in 1962; Gulf & Western took over Paramount in 1966; Transamerica took over United Artists in 1967; Warner

Brothers first merged with television distribution company Seven Arts which was taken over by Kinney National Services in 1969; and the leisure tycoon Kirk Kerkorian took over MGM in 1970. Only Disney and Twentieth Century Fox were unaffected, although both adopted similar practices of diversification.

direct cinema: Documentary filmmaking technique which records an event as it occurs. This was developed in the 1950s and 1960s from the availability of portable hand-held 16mm cameras and sync-sound recording equipment. It is also referred to as *cinéma vérité* or "cinema truth".

direct to video: Films which do not receive a theatrical release but are distributed on video and/or DVD formats.

DVD: Acronym which means "digital versatile disc" or it sometimes refers to "digital video disk". A digital format playback system that has become the standard system for home viewing in the early twenty-first century.

exploitation cinema: A term referring to films, often low-budget, which use ("exploit") sensational subject matter and themes, usually involving sex and violence, to generate controversy and to reach (also "exploiting") particular sectors of the film audience.

Hollywood studio system: Refers to the period in the history of American cinema which roughly dates from 1920 to 1960 when five major companies (Loews [MGM], RKO, Twentieth Century Fox, Warner Brothers, Paramount) – "the big five" – and three "little" companies (Universal, Columbia and United Artists) effectively dominated the commercial film industry in the United States and by and large most "foreign" markets. Production was centred in studios in Southern California and

was characterized by a type of mass production where the labour of producing a film was divided in order to maximize production efficiency.

horizontal integration: The practice of a company from one aspect of an industry combining with another company from the same sector. This is exemplified in the trend in the 1980s and 1990s where major studios partnered with other production companies which resulted in the large global media conglomerates of Time-Warner or the ownership of Columbia Pictures Entertainment by the Sony Corporation.

Motion Picture Association of America (MPAA): The American film industry's primary trade association. It was originally set up in 1922 as the Motion Picture Producers and Distributors of America (MPPDA) in order to establish agreed standards of practice for the industry and to act as a public relations body dealing with other public institutions including the US Federal and State governments. In 1940 the MPDAA's name was changed to the MPAA.

MPAA Ratings System: A ratings system meant as a guide to the suitability of the films for particular audiences exhibited in the United States. One of the most important functions of the MPDAA (see *Motion Picture Association of America*) was the regulation of film content and this was made explicit in the establishment of the Production Code in 1930 which was a set of guidelines the studios agreed to follow. However, in 1966 due to pressure from court rulings on specific films, the new head of the MPAA Jack Valenti established a ratings system to replace the Production Code. The original categories were "G" for general audiences, "M" for mature audiences, "R" for restricted audiences (with no minors admitted without being accompanied by an adult), and "X" where no one under 17 was allowed admission. These remained unchanged until 1984 when "M" was partitioned into two ratings: "PG" (parental guidance) and "PG13". The latter indicated a higher intensity of potentially objectionable content than PG but not enough to warrant an "R" rating. PG13 encouraged parents to monitor the viewing for children aged 13 and under. The "X" rating, unlike the original "G", "M" and "R" ratings, was not copyrighted and consequently any unrated film could self-supply the X category. By the 1970s "X" had become associated with explicitly pornographic films. Finally, in 1990, the rating of NC17 was invented and copyrighted in an attempt to create a respectable (i.e. non-pornographic) category of films for adults.

multiplex: Refers to a cinema exhibition complex which houses a multiple number of theatres. This trend arose in the 1960s as it accompanied the development of shopping malls and became widespread by the 1980s and 1990s.

package unit system: A term used to describe the system of film production which brings together the necessary components (script, personnel, equipment, etc.) as a "package" for the production of one film. This differs from studio-based systems in which these components were owned by or held under long-term contract with a studio to produce a number of films.

"Paramount Decrees"/anti-trust legislation: The Supreme Court decision of 1948 which ruled that the major studios were in violation of the Sherman Anti-trust Act by restraining free trade in the exhibition sector. It required studios to divest, that is sell off or place under a separate ownership, the majority of their exhibition holdings (i.e. theatres) (see *vertical integration*).

platform release: The technique of releasing a film in a few select areas, usually major cities that are recognized as "cultural centres", where it is hoped the film will have appeal. If the film gathers good reviews and good "word of mouth", this is seen as a "platform" upon which to build an audience for it in the wider market.

Portapak: A lightweight video camera and recorder combination introduced by Sony in 1967. This made video production widely available and had a significant impact on the production practices and aesthetics of documentary film and video making.

production cycle: Typically a group of films with similar subject matter often produced around the same time or following a particularly successful film of that type. For example, the number of films set during the Vietnam War that were produced after the success of *Platoon* (1986) such as *Hamburger Hill* (1987), *Good Morning, Vietnam* (1987), *Full Metal Jacket* (1987), *In Country* (1989), *84 Charlie Mopic* (1989). This is distinguished from genre in that it tends to refer to a finite period of time in which the films are produced and released.

revenue stream: A steady flow of income from a particular source. For example, until the 1950s the primary revenue stream for the Hollywood film industry has been box office receipts. In the late 1950s, as the studios were experiencing ever decreasing attendance figures, the sale of their back catalogue of films to television networks became another source of income. Similarly with the advent of video in the early 1980s and later DVD playback systems, the sale and rental of films in these formats became added sources of income. Revenue streams are not limited to these examples and can be any dependable source of income for a company.

road-show release: The practice of releasing normally big budget pictures in a few prestige theatres in large cities with the surrounding publicity of a legitimate theatre production. Higher ticket prices for bookable seats accompanied the employment of musical overtures and intermissions. These engagements could run over a period months, or even over a year. While this practice dates back to the early 1920s, it became a preferred method by the industry in the 1950s. These were linked with wide-screen and big-screen technologies and for a time, until the mid-1960s, generated high rates of return.

runaway productions: Term used for films financed by US production companies but filmed on location outside the United States.

saturation booking: Technique of releasing a film in a large number of theatres nationwide and/or worldwide in order to take advantage of pre-release publicity and recoup initial investment in the first few weeks of release.

sync sound: Refers to filming with sound recording equipment that is linked to the camera and synchronizes the sound with the moving image.

synergy: The combination of separate elements which is greater than the sum of its individual parts. The term has come to be used in the film industry to describe the combination of film production with related products or services in ways which are mutually beneficial. A high profile example is Disney's practice of surrounding its film products with subsidiary products ranging from television spin-offs to toys to theme parks. Mergers of companies which have related products or services such as media conglomerates like Time-Warner are often cited as having "synergy".

vertical integration: Refers to the process where a company owns or controls all of the phases in the production and distribution of its product. The term is most often applied to the *Hollywood studio system* from the 1920s to 1948 when the "big five" (Loews [MGM], RKO, Twentieth Century Fox, Warner Brothers, Paramount) were "vertically integrated" in that they owned and controlled the production and distribution of their films and owned their own nationwide theatre chains while the "little three" (Universal, Columbia and United Artists) primarily owned only production and distribution of their product. In 1948, the practice was found to be in violation of antitrust laws by the US Supreme Court. Under this ruling the major studios were forced to sell the majority of their theatre holdings. However, another form of vertical integration persisted in the 1960s and 1970s through mergers with companies that had substantial holdings in news and broadcast media. In the 1980s the practice of owning theatres returned primarily because of the wording of the original 1948 Supreme Court decree, which was a ruling on trade practices rather than specifically forbidding ownership of theatres by the majors.

VHS: Acronym for Video Home System which was launched by Matsushita in 1976 and became the dominant video playback system for home viewing until superseded by DVD in the late 1990s and early twenty-first century.

BIBLIOGRAPHY

Aaron, M. (1999a) 'Till Death Us Do Part: Cinema's Queer Couples Who Kill, in M. Aaron (ed.) *The Body's Perilous Pleasures*. Edinburgh: Edinburgh University Press.

—— (ed.) (1999b) *The Body's Perilous Pleasures*. Edinburgh: Edinburgh University Press.

—— (2000) The Queer Jew: From *Yid* to *Yentl* and Back Again, *Jewish History and Culture*, Summer *3*(1).

—— (ed.) (2004) *New Queer Cinema: A Critical Reader*. Edinburgh: Edinburgh University Press.

Abramowitz, R. (2000) *Is That a Gun in your Pocket? Women's Experience of Power in Hollywood*. New York: Random House.

Agan, P. (1975) *Clint Eastwood: The Man Behind the Myth*. New York: Pyramid Books.

Allen, R.C. (1999) Home Alone Together: Hollywood and the "Family Film", in M. Stokes and R. Maltby (eds) *Identifying Hollywood's Audiences: Cultural Identity and the Movies*. London: BFI.

Altman, R. (1999a) *Film/Genre*. London: BFI.

—— (1999b) The American Film Musical as Dual-Focus Narrative in *The American Film Musical*. Bloomington: Indiana University Press, pp. 16–27.

Anderson, C. (1994) *Hollywood TV: The Studio System in the Fifties*. Austin: University of Texas Press.

Andrew, D. (1993) The Unauthorized Auteur Today, in J. Collins, H. Radner, and A.P. Collins (eds) *Film Theory Goes to the Movies*, New York: Routledge, pp. 77–85.

Andrew, G. (1998) *Stranger Than Paradise: Maverick Film-Makers in Recent American Cinema*. London: Prion.

Andrews, D. (2006) *Soft in the Middle: The Contemporary Softcore Feature in Its Context*. Athens, OH: Ohio University Press.

Ang, I. (1986) *Watching Dallas: Soap Opera and the Melodramatic Imagination*. London and New York: Methuen.

Anon. (1961) Change in Policy Decided on at Fox, *New York Times*, 8 May.

Anon. (1963a) *Cleo*'s 13 Million Dollar Advance, *Kine. Weekly*, 4 April.

Anon. (1963b) Fox to Make Six Road Show Films, *Kine. Weekly*, 17 October.

Anon. (1965a) World-wide Advertising Campaign for Fox's Road Show Films, *Kine. Weekly*, 14 January.

Anon. (1965b) *Sound of Music* Set to Become All-time Winner, *Kine. Weekly*, 16 December.

Anon. (1966) Fox Roadshows in $20m Fox US TV Deal, *Kine. Weekly*, 6 October.

Anon. (1967a) Fox Income Reaches All-time High, *Kine. Weekly*, 1 April.

Anon. (1967b) The End-Plug's the Thing for Disney TV Programmes, *Newsday*, 15 August.

Anon. (1968) 20th-Fox's Record 6-Month Profit; Cost Cut Outpaces Income Drop, *Variety*, 4 September.

Anon. (1969) It Was Our Battle of Britain, *Kine. Weekly*, 3 July.

Anon. (1970a) Zanuck on Cassettes: "4–5 Years after Theatres", *Kine. Weekly*, 5 September.

Anon. (1970b) 20th Century-Fox Shake-up Prepares for Expansion, *Kine. Weekly*, 6 September.

Anon. (1970c) 20th-Fox Losses, but Profits Soon, *Kine. Weekly*, 19 September.

Anon. (1971a) Richard Zanuck and David Brown out of Fox, *Kine. Weekly,* 2 January.

Anon. (1971b) Fox Forecasts Profit in First Quarter, *Kine. Weekly,* 20 March.

Anon. (1971c) Zanuck Quits the Chair at Fox, *Kine. Weekly,* 22 May.

Anon. (1972a) Fight "Black Exploitation" in Pix, *Variety,* 16 August.

Anon. (1972b) Radical American Film?: A Questionnaire. *Cinéaste,* 5.4: 14–20.

Anon. (1974) Anybody Surprised? *Variety,* 28 August.

Anon. (1990) The current cinema, *The New Yorker,* 8 January, 91.

Arroyo, J. (1993) Death Desire and Identity: The Political Unconscious of New Queer Cinema, in J. Bristow and A.R. Wilson (eds), *Activating Theory: Lesbian, Gay, Bisexual Politics.* London: Lawrence and Wishart, pp. 70–96.

—— (ed.) (2000) *Action/Spectacle Cinema.* London: BFI.

The Art that Matters: A Look at Today's Film Scene by the Under-Thirties (1969) *Saturday Review,* 52(27): 7–21.

Auster, A. and Quart, L. (1984) American Cinema of the Sixties, *Cineaste,* 13(2): 4–12.

Ayer, D, Bates, R.E and Herman, P.J. (1982) Self-Censorship in the Movie Industry: A Historical Perspective on Law and Social Change, in G. Kindem (ed.) *The American Movie Industry: The Business of Motion Pictures.* Carbondale: Southern Illinois University Press, pp. 215–50.

Bach, R. (1986) *Final Cut: Dreams and Disaster in the Making of Heaven's Gate,* London: Faber & Faber.

Bachman, G. (1961) The Frontiers of Realist Cinema: The Work of Ricky Leacock, *Film Culture,* (Summer): 19–23.

Balio, T. (1976) *United Artists: The Company Built by the Stars.* Madison: University of Wisconsin Press.

—— (ed.) (1985) *The American Movie Industry,* 2nd edn. Madison: University of Wisconsin Press.

—— (1987) *United Artists: The Company That Changed the Film Industry.* Madison: University of Wisconsin Press.

—— (ed.) (1990) *Hollywood in the Age of Television.* Boston: Unwin Hyman.

—— (2002) Hollywood Production Trends in the Era of Globalisation, 1990–99, in S. Neale (ed.) *Genre and Contemporary Hollywood.* London: BFI.

Barnes, S. (1993) *Greenwich Village 1963: Avant-garde Performance and the Effervescent Body.* London: Duke University Press.

Barnouw, E. (1993) *Documentary: A History of the Non-fiction Film.* New York and Oxford: Oxford University Press.

—— et al. (eds) (1997) *Conglomerates and the Media.* New York: The New Press.

Barsam, R. (1973) *Non-Fiction Film.* New York: E.P. Dutton.

Bart, P. (1990) *Fade Out: The Calamitous Final Days of MGM.* New York: William Morrow.

Barthel, J. (1966) Biggest Money-Making Movie of All Time – How Come? *The New York Times,* 20 November.

Bates, P. (1989) Truth Not Guaranteed: An Interview with Errol Morris. *Cinéaste,* 17(1): 17.

Battcock, G. (ed.) (1967) *The New American Cinema: A Critical Anthology.* New York: Dutton.

Baudrillard, J. (1996) *The System of Objects,* trans. J. Benedict. London: Verso.

Beaupré, L. (1967) One-third Film Public: Negro; Columbia and UA Pitch for Biz. *Variety,* 29 November.

—— (1986) How to Distribute a Film, in P.

Kerr (ed.) *The Hollywood Film Industry*. London: Routledge & Kegan Paul/BFI.

Beers, D. (2001) Irony is Dead! Long Live Irony! From http://www.salon.com/mwt/feature/2001/09/25/irony_lives/ (accessed 25 September 2001).

Bellour, R. (1986) Psychosis, Neurosis, Perversion, in M. Deutelbaum and L. Poague (eds), *A Hitchcock Reader*. Aimes: Iowa State University Press. (Original article published 1979 in *Camera Obscura*, 3–4.)

Belton, J. (1992) *Widescreen Cinema*. Cambridge, MA: Harvard University Press.

—— (1994) *American Cinema/American Culture*. New York: McGraw-Hill, Inc.

Beltrán, M. (2004) Más Macha: The New Latina Action Hero, in Y. Tasker (ed.) *Action and Adventure Cinema*. London: Routledge, pp. 186–200.

—— (2005) The New Hollywood Raceless-ness: Only the Fast, Furious, (and Multi-racial) Will Survive, *Cinema Journal*, 44(2): 50–67.

Bennett, L. (1971) The Emancipation Orgasm: Sweetback in Wonderland, *Ebony*, 26: September, 106–16.

Benshoff, H. (1997) *Monsters in the Closet: Homosexuality and the Horror Film*. Manchester: Manchester University Press.

—— (2000) Blaxploitation Horror Films: Generic Reappropriation or Reinscription? *Cinema Journal* 39(2): 31–50.

—— (2003) The Closet 2000: Receiving Mr. Ripley, in M. Aaron (ed.) *New Queer Cinema*. Edinburgh: Edinburgh University Press.

Berman, M. (1982) *All That is Solid Melts into Air: The Experience of Modernity*. New York: Verso.

Bernstein, M. (1986) Fritz Lang Incorporated, *The Velvet Light Trap*.

—— (1993) Hollywood's Semi-Independent Production, *Cinema Journal* 32(2).

—— (1999) "Floating Triumphantly": The American Critics on *Titanic*, in K.S. Sandler and G. Studlar (eds) *Titanic: Anatomy of a Blockbuster*. New Brunswick, New Jersey and London: Rutgers University Press, pp. 14–28.

Betz, M. (2003) Art, Exploitation, Under-ground, in M. Jancovich, A.L. Reboll, J. Stringer and A. Willis (eds) *Defining Cult Movies: The Cultural Politics of Oppositional Tastes*. Manchester: Manchester University Press, pp. 202–22.

Biskind, P. (1975a) Subpoenaed Over a Movie on Radicals, *The New York Times*, 5 June, p. 27.

—— (1975b) Does the US Have the Right to Subpoena a Film in Progress?, *The New York Times*, 22 June, 19, 26.

—— (1983) *Seeing Is Believing: How Holly-wood Taught Us to Stop Worrying and Love the '50s*. London: Pluto Press.

—— (1998) *Easy Riders, Raging Bulls: How the Sex 'n' Drugs 'n' Rock 'n' Roll Generation Saved Hollywood*. London: Bloomsbury.

—— (2005) *Down and Dirty Pictures*. London: Bloomsbury.

Biskind, P. and Weiss, M.N. (1975) The Weather Underground: Take One, *Rolling Stone* 6 November: 36–43, 78–88.

Blue, J. (1965) One Man's Truth: An Inter-view with Richard Leacock, *Film Comment*, 3(2).

Bogle, D. (1973) *Toms, Coons, Mulattoes, Mammies, and Bucks: An Interpretive History of Blacks in American Films*. New York: Bantam Books.

Bondanella, P. (1995) *Italian Cinema: From Neorealism to the Present*. New York: Continuum Books.

Bordwell, D. (1987) *Narration in the Fiction Film*. Madison: University of Wisconsin Press.

—— (1991) *Making Meaning: Inference and Rhetoric in the Interpretation of Cinema*. Cambridge, MA: Harvard University Press.

—— (2000) *Planet Hong Kong*. Cambridge, MA: Harvard University Press.

Bordwell, D., Staiger, J. and Thompson, K. (1985) *The Classical Hollywood Cinema: Film Style and Mode of Production to 1960*. London: Routledge.

Bordwell, D. and Thompson, K. (2003) *Film Art: An Introduction*. London: McGraw-Hill.

Bornstein, K. (1994) *Gender Outlaw: On Men, Women and the Rest of Us*. New York and London: Routledge.

Boss, P. (1986) Vile Bodies and Bad Medicine, *Screen* 27, Jan/Feb.: 14–24.

Bourdieu, P. (1993) *The Field of Cultural Production*. New York: Columbia University Press.

Boyarin, D., Itzkovitz, D. and Pellegrini, A. (eds) (2003) *Queer Theory and the Jewish Question*. New York: Columbia University Press.

Boyd, T. (1997) *Am I Black Enough for You? Popular Culture from the 'Hood and Beyond*. Bloomington: Indiana University Press.

Boyle, D. (1997) *Subject to Change: Guerrilla Television Revisited*. New York: Oxford University Press.

Brody, J.D. (1999) The Returns of Cleopatra Jones, *Signs*, 28(1), 91–121.

Brooks, X. (2003) Special Relationship: Why Is Miramax so Willing to Give Tarantino $55m and Carte Blanche for His New Movie? *The Guardian Review*, 18 July.

Brown, G. (1995) *Movie Time*. New York: Macmillan.

Bruck, C. (2003) *When Hollywood Had a King: The Reign of Lew Wasserman, Who Leveraged Talent into Power and Influence*. New York: Random House.

Brunsdon, C. (1997) *Screen Tastes: Soap Opera to Satellite Dishes*. London and New York: Routledge

Bruzzi, S. (1997) *Undressing Cinema: Clothing and Identity in the Movies*. London: Routledge.

Bryman, A. (2004) *The Disneyization of Society*. London: Sage.

Buckland, W. (1998) A Close Encounter with *Raiders of the Lost Ark*: Notes on Narrative Aspects of the New Hollywood Blockbuster, in S. Neale and M. Smith (eds) *Contemporary Hollywood Cinema*. London: Routledge.

—— (2003) The Role of the Auteur in the Age of the Blockbuster, in J. Stringer (ed.) *Movie Blockbusters*. London and New York: Routledge.

Budge, B. and Hamer, D. (eds) (1994) *The Good, the Bad, and the Gorgeous: Popular Culture's Romance with Lesbianism*. London: Pandora.

Bukatman, S. (1997) *Blade Runner*, BFI Modern Classics series, London: BFI.

Buscombe, E. (2004) *Unforgiven*, BFI Modern Classics series, London: BFI.

Carr, R.E. and Hayes, R.M. (1988) *Wide Screen Movies: A History and Filmography of Wide-Gauge Filmmaking*. Jefferson, North Carolina and London: McFarland.

Carroll, N. (1983) From Real to Reel: Entangled in the Nonfiction Film, in *Philosophical Exchange*. Brockport, NY: SUNY Brockport.

Carson, C. (1981) *In Struggle: SNCC and the Black Awakening of the 1960s*. Cambridge, MA: Harvard University Press.

Cassavetes, J. (1960) What's Wrong with Hollywood? *Film Culture*, 19.

Chan, K. (2004) The Global Return of the *Wu Xia Pian* (Chinese Sword-Fighting Movie): Ang Lee's *Crouching Tiger, Hidden Dragon*, *Cinema Journal*, 43(4), 3–17.

Charity, T. (1994) Santa Claws, *Time Out*, 23–30 November, 22–3.

Chion, M. (1999) *The Voice in the Cinema* (ed., trans. C. Gorbman). New York: Columbia University Press.

Christie, I. and Dodd, P. (1996) *Spellbound: Art and Film*. London: Hayward Gallery and BFI.

Clagett, T.D. (1990) *William Friedkin: Films of Aberration, Obsession and Reality*. North Carolina: McFarland.

Clarkson, W. (1995) *Quentin Tarantino: Shooting from the Hip*. London: Piatkus.

Clifford, J. (1993) On Collecting Art and Culture, in S. During (ed.) *The Cultural Studies Reader*. London: Routledge, pp. 52–3.

Clover, C. (1992) *Men, Women and Chain Saws: Gender in the Modern Horror Film*. London: BFI.

Coate, M. (2003) The Original First-Week Engagements of *Star Wars*. http://www.in70mm.com/news/2003/star_wars/star_wars_1977.htm#Trivia%20(US%20and%20Canada%20release, (accessed 24 June 2003).

Cocks, J. (1971) Peckinpah: Primitive Horror, *Time*, 98(20), December, 85–7.

Cohan, S. and Hark, I.R. (eds) (1997) *The Road Movie Book*. London and New York: Routledge.

Cohen, M.S. (1973) The Corporate Style of BBS: Seven Intricate Pieces, *Take One*, 3(12), 19–22.

Cohn, L. (1993) All-Time Film Rental Champs, *Variety*, 10 May, C76–108.

Collins, P.H. (1991) *Black Feminist Thought: Knowledge, Consciousness, and the Politics of Empowerment*. New York: Routledge.

Conant, M. (1978) *Antitrust in the Motion Picture Industry*. New York: Arno.

Conner, B. (1999) *2000BC: The Bruce Conner Story, Part 2*. Minneapolis: Walker Art Center.

Cook, D.A. (1998) Auteur Cinema and the "Film Generation" in 1970s Hollywood, in J. Lewis (ed.) *The New American Cinema*. Durham, NC: Duke University Press, pp. 11–37.

—— (2000) *Lost Illusions: American Cinema in the Shadow of Watergate and Vietnam, 1970–1979*. Vol. 9 of *History of the American Cinema*. New York: Scribner's.

Cook, P. and Bernink, M. (eds) (1999) *The Cinema Book*, 2nd edn. London: BFI.

Cooper, D. (1996) Queercore, in D. Morton (ed.) *The Material Queer: A LesBiGay Cultural Studies Reader*. Boulder, CO: Westview Press.

Corman, R., with Jerome, J. (1998) *How I Made a Hundred Movies in Hollywood and Never Lost a Dime*. New York: Da Capo Press.

Corrigan, T. (1991) *A Cinema Without Walls: Movies and Culture After Vietnam*. New Brunswick, NJ: Rutgers University Press.

—— (1998) Auteurs and the New Hollywood, in J. Lewis (ed.) *The New American Cinema*. Durham, NC: Duke University Press, pp. 38–63.

Costello, D.P. (1972) From Counter-Culture to Anti-Culture, *Commonweal*, 46(16), 14 July, 383–6.

Coupland, D. (1991) *Generation X: Tales for an Accelerated Culture*. New York: St. Martin's Press.

Cowie, E. (1998) Storytelling: Classical Hollywood Cinema and Classical Narrative, in S. Neale and M. Smith (eds)

Contemporary Hollywood Cinema. London: Routledge.

Creekmur, C.K. and Doty, A. (1996) Introduction, in *Out in Culture: Gay, Lesbian, and Queer Essays on Popular Culture*. London: Cassell.

Crimp, D. (1993) Right On, Girlfriend!, in M. Warner (ed.) *Fear of a Queer Planet: Queer Politics and Social Theory*. Minneapolis: University of Minnesota.

Cripps, T. (1990) *Sweet Sweetback's Baadasssss Song* and the Changing Politics of Genre Film, in P. Lehman (ed.) *Close Viewings: An Anthology of New Film Criticism*. Tallahassee: Florida State University Press, pp. 238–61.

Cubitt, S. (1991) *Timeshift: On Video Culture*. London and New York: Routledge.

Custen, G.F. (1997) *20th Century's Fox: Darryl F. Zanuck and the Culture of Hollywood*. New York: Basic Books.

Dale, M. (1997) *The Movie Game: The Film Business in Britain, Europe and America*. London: Cassell.

Damico, J. (2004) Film Noir: A Modest Proposal, in A. Silver and J. Ursini (eds) *Film Noir Reader*. London: Limelight Editions, pp. 95–105.

Dargis, M. (1996) Devil in a Blue Dress, *Sight and Sound*, January, 38.

—— (1998) Whatever: The New Nihilism, *LA Weekly*, 26 November.

Davis, A. (1983) *Women, Race, Class*. New York: Vintage.

—— (1998) Afro Images: Politics, Fashion, and Nostalgia, in M. Guillory and R. Green (eds) *Soul: Black Power, Politics, and Pleasure*. New York: New York University Press, pp. 23–31.

Day, J. (1995) *The Vanishing Vision: The Inside Story of Public Television*. Berkeley and Los Angeles: University of California Press.

Denby, D. (1972) Violence Enshrined, *Atlantic Monthly*, 229, 118–22.

—— (1973) Men Without Women, Women Without Men, *Harper's*, September, 247, 51–4.

De Roos, R. (1963) The Magic Worlds of Walt Disney, *National Geographic*, August, 159–207. Reprinted in E. Smoodin (ed.) (1994) *Disney Discourse: Producing the Magic Kingdom*. New York: Routledge.

DeVany, A. (2004) *Hollywood Economics: How Extreme Uncertainty Shapes the Film Industry*. New York: Routledge.

Diawara, M. (1993) Black American Cinema; The New Realism, in M. Diawara (ed.) *Black American Cinema*. London: Routledge, pp. 3–25.

Dick, B.F. (ed.) (1992) *Columbia Pictures: Portrait of a Studio*. Lexington: University Press of Kentucky.

—— (1997) *City of Dreams: The Making and Remaking of Universal Pictures*. Lexington: University Press of Kentucky.

—— (2001) *Engulfed: The Death of Paramount Pictures and the Birth of Corporate Hollywood*. Lexington: University Press of Kentucky.

Diehl, D. (1970) The Simenon of Cinema, *Show*, May, 1(5), 26–30, 86–7.

Dinsmore, U. (1998) Chaos, Order, and Plastic Boxes: The Significance of Videotapes for the People Who Collect Them, in C. Geraghty and D. Lusted (eds) *The Television Studies Book*. New York: St. Martin's Press Inc., pp. 315–26.

Dixon, W.W. (2001) Twenty-Five Reasons Why It's All Over, in J. Lewis (ed.) *The End of Cinema as We Know It: American Film in the Nineties*. New York: New York University Press, pp. 356–66.

Doherty, T. (1988) *Teenagers and Teenpics: The Juvenilization of American Movies in the*

1950s. Boston and London: Unwin Hyman.

Dohrn, B., Ayers, B., Jones, J. and Sojourn, C. (1974) *Prairie Fire: The Politics of Revolutionary Anti-Imperialism*. New York and San Francisco: Communications Co.

Donalson, M. (2003) *Black Directors in Hollywood*. Austin: University of Texas Press.

Donati, W. (1996) *Ida Lupino: A Biography*. Lexington: University of Kentucky Press.

Dougan, A. (1997) *Martin Scorsese*. London: Orion.

Doty, A. (1993) *Making Things Perfectly Queer: Interpreting Mass Culture*. Minneapolis: University of Minnesota Press.

—— (2000) *Flaming Classics: Queering the Film Canon*. London: Routledge.

Durgnat, R. (2002) *A Long Hard Look at "Psycho"*. London: BFI.

Dyer, R. (1978) American Cinema in the '70s: *The Towering Inferno*, *Movie*, 21, 30–3.

—— (1992a) Don't Look Now: The Male Pin-Up, in M. Merck (ed.) *The Sexual Subject: A Screen Reader on Sexuality*. London: Routledge, pp. 265–76.

—— (1992b) Entertainment and Utopia, in R. Dyer *Only Entertainment*. London and New York: Routledge, pp. 17–34.

—— (1998) *Stars*, 2nd edn. London: BFI.

—— (2002) *The Culture of Queers*. London: Routledge.

Eames, J.D. (1982) *The MGM Story*. London: Octopus Books.

Ebert, R. (1980) *Heaven's Gate*, *Chicago Sun-Times*, 26 November, 14.

Edmundson, M. (1997) *Nightmare on Main Street: Angels, Sadomasochism, and the Culture of Gothic*. Cambridge, MA: Harvard University Press.

Elley, D. (2000) *The Variety Movie Guide 2000*. New York: Perigee.

Ellis, J. (1989) *Visible Fictions: Cinema, Television, Video*, 2nd edn. London: Routledge.

Elsaesser, T. (1975) The Pathos of Failure: American Films in the 70s – Notes on the Unmotivated Hero, *Monogram*, 6, 13–19.

—— (1985) Tales of Sound and Fury: Observations on the Family Melodrama, in B. Nichols (ed.) *Movies and Methods*, Vol. II. Berkeley: University of California Press, pp. 165–89.

Engelhardt, T. (1995) *The End of Victory Culture: Cold War America and the Disillusioning of a Generation*. New York: Basic Books.

Epstein, E.J. (2005) *The Big Picture: The New Logic of Money and Power in Hollywood*. New York: Random House.

Erens, P. (1984) *The Jew in American Cinema*. Bloomington: Indiana University Press.

Erlick, A. (1970) Which Way Is Up? (Editorial), *International Motion Picture Exhibitor*, 20 May, 1.

Eszterhas, J. (2004) *Hollywood Animal: A Memoir*. London: Hutchinson.

Esterow, M. (1964) *Cleopatra* Termed "Success", *New York Times*, 27 March.

Evans, R. (1994) *The Kid Stays in the Picture*. New York: Hyperion.

Faludi, S. (1992) *Backlash: The Undeclared War against Women*. London: Vintage.

Farber, D. (ed.) (1994) *The Sixties: From Memory to History*. Chapel Hill: University of North Carolina Press.

Farber, M. (1971) *Negative Space*. New York: Praeger.

Farber, S. (1969) End of the Road? *Film Quarterly*, Winter, 23(3), 3–16.

Feinberg, L. (1996) *Transgender Warriors: Making History from Joan of Arc to Ru Paul*. Boston: Beacon Press.

Felperin, L. (1996) *Toy Story*, in *Sight and Sound* in *Sight and Sound Film Review*

Volume, January 1996 to December 1996, London: BFI, pp. 65–6.

—— (1999) Editorial: Chick Flicks, *Sight and Sound*, October, 10.

Feuer, J. (1993) *The Hollywood Musical*. London: The Macmillan Press Ltd.

Figgis, M. (2000) Low Budget, High Fidelity, *The Guardian Review*, 25 February.

Finler, J. (1988) *The Hollywood Story*. London: Octopus.

—— (2003) *The Hollywood Story*, 3rd edn. London: Wallflower.

Fischer, L. (1990) The Desire to Desire: *Desperately Seeking Susan*, in P. Lehman (ed.) *Close Viewings: An Anthology of New Film Criticism*. Tallahassee: University of Florida Press.

Fleming, C. (1998) *High Concept: Don Simpson and the Hollywood Culture of Excess*. London: Bloomsbury.

Flynn, L.J. (2002) One Man's 2 Challenges. *New York Times*, C4, 3 June.

Fonda, J. (2005) *My Life So Far*. London: Ebury Press.

Foster, G.A. (1999) Foreword: Women Filmmakers, in *The St. James Women Filmmakers Encyclopedia: Women on the Other Side of the Camera*. Detroit: Visible Ink Press, pp. xiii–xviii.

Frank, T. (1998) *The Conquest of Cool: Business Culture, Counterculture, and the Rise of Hip Consumerism*. Chicago: University of Chicago Press.

Frederick, R.B. (1976) Terror-Joy of *Jaws*: $102,650,000. *Variety*, 8, 7 January.

French, P. (2005) *Westerns: Aspects of a Movie Genre, and Westerns Revisited*. Manchester: Carcanet.

Friedman, L.D. (1991) *Unspeakable Images: Ethnicity and the American Cinema*. Urbana: University of Illinois Press.

Friedman, L.D. and Notbohm, B. (eds) (2000) *Steven Spielberg: Interviews*. Jackson: University Press of Mississippi.

Friedman, L.S. (1997) *The Cinema of Martin Scorsese*. London: Roundhouse Publishing.

Fuchs, C.J. (1991) "All the Animals Come Out at Night": Vietnam Meets *Noir* in *Taxi Driver*, in M. Anderegg (ed.) *Inventing Vietnam: The War in Film and Television*. Philadelphia, PA: Temple University Press, pp. 33–55.

Gaines, J. (1990) Costume and Narrative: How Dress Tells the Woman's Story, in J. Gaines and C. Herzog (eds) *Fabrications: Costume and the Female Body*. New York and London: Routledge.

Gallafent, E. (1994) *Clint Eastwood: Actor and Director*. London: Studio Vista.

Gelmis, J. (1970) *The Film Director as Superstar*. Harmondsworth: Penguin.

George, N. (1994) *Blackface: Reflections on African-Americans and the Movies*. New York: HarperCollins.

—— (2005) Boyz in the Wood, in "Blackworld", supplement publication in *Sight and Sound*, May, 8–12.

Geraghty, C. (2000) Re-examining Stardom: Questions of Texts, Bodies and Performance, in C. Gledhill and L. Williams (eds) *Reinventing Film Studies*. London: Arnold, pp. 183–201.

Gertner, R. (ed.) (1979, 1985) *International Motion Picture Almanac*. New York: Quigley.

Gidal, P. (1977) *Structural Film Anthology*. London: British Film Institute.

Gilbey, R. (2003a) Younger and Wiser, *The Observer Review*, 23 February.

—— (2003b) Gerry, *Sight and Sound*, 10 October.

Gilliatt, P. (1969) The Current Cinema: Into the Eye of the Storm, *New Yorker*, 19 July, 70.

Gitlin, T. (1987) *The Sixties: Years of Hope, Days of Rage.* New York: Bantam.

Gledhill, C. (1978a) *Klute* 1: A Contemporary Film Noir and Feminist Criticism, in E.A. Kaplan (ed.) *Women and Film Noir.* London: BFI, pp. 6–21.

—— (1978b) *Klute* 2: Feminism and *Klute*, in E.A. Kaplan (ed.) *Women and Film Noir*, London: BFI, pp. 112–28.

Gomery, D. (1988) Hollywood's Hold on the New Television Technologies, *Screen,* Spring, 29(2), 83.

—— (1992) *Shared Pleasures: A History of Movie Presentation in the United States.* Madison: University of Wisconsin Press.

—— (1994) Disney's Business History: A Reinterpretation, in E. Smoodin (ed.) *Disney Discourse: Producing the Magic Kingdom.* New York: Routledge.

—— (1998) Hollywood Corporate Business Practice and Periodising Contemporary Film History, in S. Neale and M. Smith (eds) *Contemporary Hollywood Cinema.* London: BFI.

—— (2005) *The Hollywood Studio System: A History*, 2nd edn. London: BFI.

Goodwin, M. (1972,) Tooling up for Armageddon, *Take One*, June, 3(4), 6–7.

Gordon, A. (1989) Science-Fiction and Fantasy Film Criticism: The Case of Lucas and Spielberg, *Journal of the Fantastic in the Arts*, 2(2), 81–94.

Götz, M., Lemish, D., Aidman, A. and Moon, H. (2005) *Media and the Make-Believe Worlds of Children: When Harry Potter Meets Pokemon in Disneyland.* Mahwah, NJ: Lawrence Erlbaum.

Gough-Yates, A. (2001) Angels in Chains? Feminism, Femininity and Consumer Culture in *Charlie's Angels,* in B. Osgerby and A. Gough-Yates (eds) *Action TV: Tough Guys, Smooth Operators and Foxy Chicks.* London: Routledge, pp. 83–99.

Gould, O. (1969) Anatomy of a Murder. *Brighton Film Review*, 15, 5.

Graham, D. (1987) Western Movies Since 1960, in J.G. Taylor and C.J. Lyon (eds) *A Literary History of the American West.* Fort Worth: Texas Christian University Press, pp. 1256–61.

Graham, P. (1964) Cinema-Vérité in France, *Film Quarterly,* Summer.

Grant, B.K. (ed.) (1986) *Film Genre Reader.* Austin: University of Texas Press.

—— (1992) *Voyages of Discovery: The Cinema of Frederick Wiseman.* Urbana and Chicago: University of Illinois Press.

—— (2004) Man's Favourite Sport? The Action Films of Kathryn Bigelow, in Y. Tasker (ed.) *Action and Adventure Cinema.* London: Routledge, pp. 371–84.

Gray, A. (1992) *Video Playtime: The Gendering of a Leisure Technology.* London and New York: Routledge.

Gray, H. (1995) *Watching Race: Television and the Struggle for Blackness.* Minneapolis: University of Minnesota Press.

Greene, E. (1996) *Planet of the Apes as American Myth: Race and Politics in the Films and Television Series.* Jefferson, NC: McFarland and Co.

Grist, L. (1994) Moving Targets and Black Widows: Film Noir in Modern Hollywood, in I. Cameron (ed.) *The Movie Book of Film Noir.* London: Studio Vista, pp. 267–85.

—— (1996) *Unforgiven*, in I. Cameron and D. Pye (eds) *The Movie Book of the Western.* London: Studio Vista.

—— (2000) *The Films of Martin Scorsese, 1963–1977: Authorship and Context.* Basingstoke: Palgrave Macmillan.

Gristwood, S. (1994) Hollywood's Mr Nice, *Evening Standard*, 29 September, 29.

Gross, L. (2000) Big and Loud, in J. Arroyo (ed.) *Action/Spectacle: A Sight and Sound Reader*. London: BFI, pp. 3–8.

Grundmann, R. (2003) *Andy Warhol's Blow Job*. Philadelphia, PA: Temple University Press.

Guback, T. (1985) Hollywood's International Market, in T. Balio (ed.) *The American Film Industry*. Madison: University of Wisconsin Press, pp. 387–409.

Guerrero, E. (1993) *Framing Blackness: The African American Image in Film*. Philadelphia, PA: Temple University Press.

—— (1998) A Circus of Dreams and Lies: The Black Film Wave at Middle Age, in J. Lewis (ed.) *The New American Cinema*. Durham, NC: Duke University Press, pp. 328–52.

—— (2002) *Do the Right Thing*. BFI Modern Classic, London: BFI.

Gussow, M. (1970) Studio System Passé – Film Forges Ahead, *New York Times*, 27 May.

—— (1972) The Baadasssss Success of Melvin Van Peebles, *New York Times*, 20 August.

Gustafson, R. (1985) What's Happening to Our Pix Biz?: From Warner Bros. to Warner Comunications, Inc., in T. Balio (ed.) *The American Film Industry*. Madison: University of Wisconsin Press, pp. 574–86.

Hagopian, K. (1997) Declarations of Independence: A History of Cagney Productions. *The Velvet Light Trap*, 22.

Halberstadt, I. (1976) Interview with Fred Wiseman, in R. Barsam (ed.) *Non-Fiction Film: Theory & Criticism*. New York: E.P. Dutton, pp. 310–14.

Haleff, M. (1964) The Maysles Brothers and Direct Cinema, *Film Comment*, 2(2).

Hall, Stuart (1981) Notes on Deconstructing "the Popular", in R. Samuel (ed.) *People's History and Socialist Theory*. London: Routledge and Kegan Paul, pp. 227–40.

Hall, S. (2000) Hard Ticket Giants: Hollywood Blockbusters in the Widescreen Era. Unpublished doctoral dissertation, University of East Anglia.

—— (2002) Tall Revenue Features: The Genealogy of the Modern Blockbuster, in S. Neale (ed.) *Genre and Contemporary Hollywood*. London: British Film Institute.

Hammond, M. (1993) The Historical and Hysterical: Melodrama, War and *Dead Poets Society*, in P. Kirkham and J. Thumim (eds) *You Tarzan: Masculinity, Movies and Men*. London: Lawrence and Wishart, pp. 53–64.

—— (2002) Some Smothering Dreams: The Combat Film in Contemporary Hollywood, in S. Neale (ed.) *Genre and Contemporary Hollywood*. London: BFI.

—— (2004) *Saving Private Ryan*'s Special Affect, in Y. Tasker (ed.) *The Action and Adventure Cinema*. London: Routledge.

Hammond, M. and Mazdon, L. (eds) (2005) *The Contemporary Television Series*. Edinburgh: Edinburgh University Press.

Hammond, S. (2000) *Hollywood East*. Chicago: Contemporary Books.

Hanhardt, J. (1976) The Medium Viewed: The American Avant-Garde Film, in *A History of the American Avant-Garde Cinema*. New York: American Film Association.

Hankin, K. (2002) *The Girls in the Black Room: Looking at the Lesbian Bar*. Minneapolis: University of Minnesota Press.

Hansen, E. (ed.) (1999) *Out Takes: Essays on Queer Theory and Film*. Durham, NC: Duke University Press.

Hartmann, J. (1994) The Trope of Blaxploitation in Critical Responses to Sweetback, *Film History*, 6, 382–404.

Harvey, D. (1990) *The Condition of Post-modernity: An Enquiry into the Origins of Cultural Change*. New Malden, MA and Oxford: Blackwell Publishing.

Harwood, J. (1975) Advertisers Sensitive to Change in Kiddies' Purchasing Power, *Daily Variety*, 20 February.

Haskell, M. (1971) Three Documentaries, in L. Jacobs (ed.) *The Documentary Tradition: From Nanook to Woodstock*. New York: Hopkinson and Blake.

Hawkins, J. (2000) *Cutting Edge: Art-horror and the Horrific Avant-garde*. Minneapolis: University of Minnesota Press.

Helford, E.R. (ed.) (2000) *Fantasy Girls: Gender in the New Universe of Science Fiction and Fantasy Television*. Lanham MD: Rowman and Littlefield Publishers.

Hershberger, M. (2005) *Jane Fonda's War: A Political Biography of an Antiwar Icon*. New York: The New Press.

Hess, J. (1975) Feds Harass Film Crew, *Jump Cut*, 7 Aug.–Sept.: 23-5.

Hill, J. and Gibson, P.C. (1998) *The Oxford Guide to Film Studies*. Oxford: Oxford University Press.

Hill-Collins, P. (1991) *Black Feminist Thought: Knowledge, Consciousness, and the Politics of Empowerment*. New York: Routledge.

Hillier, J. (1993) *The New Hollywood*. London: Studio Vista.

—— (2001) *American Independent Cinema*. London: British Film Institute.

Hirsch, F. (1999) *Detours and Lost Highways: A Map of Neo-Noir*. New York: Limelight.

Hobbs, F. and Stoops, N. (2002) US Census Bureau, "Census 2000 Special Reports, Series CNSR-4", *Demographic Trends in the 20th Century*. Washington, DC: US Government Printing Office: 30.

Hoberman, J. (1985a) Spielbergism and Its Discontents, *The Village Voice*, 9 July, 48–9.

—— (1985b) Ten Years that Shook the World, *American Film*, 10(8), 34–59.

—— (1992) Out and Inner Mongolia, *Premiere*, October, 31.

—— (2001) *On Jack Smith's Flaming Creatures and Other Secret Flix of Cinemaroc*. New York: Granary Books.

—— (2003a) *The Dream Life: Movies, Media and the Mythology of the Sixties*. New York: New Press.

—— (2003b) *The Magic Hour: Film at the Fin de Siècle*. Philadelphia, PA: Temple University Press, pp. 33–5.

Hollinger, H. (1982) Production Control Changes Marked 1981, *Variety*, 13 January, 1.

Holmlund, C. (2002) *Impossible Bodies: Femininity and Masculinity at the Movies*. New York: Routledge.

Holzer, H.M. and Holzer, E. (2002) *Aid and Comfort: Jane Fonda in North Vietnam*. New York: McFarland.

hooks, b. (1990) *Yearning: Race, Gender, and Cultural Politics*. Boston: South End Press.

Horak, J.C. (ed.) (1995) *Lovers of Cinema: The First American Film Avant-Garde 1919–1945*. Madison: University of Wisconsin.

Hughes, D. (2001) *The Complete Lynch*. London: Virgin.

Hugo, C. (1980–81) American Cinema in the '70s: The Economic Background, *Movie*, Winter/Spring, 27/28, 47.

Hunt, L. (2003) *Kung Fu Cult Masters: From Bruce Lee to Crouching Tiger*. London: Wallflower.

Inness, S.A. (2004) *Action Chicks: New Images of Tough Women in Popular Culture*. Basingstoke: Palgrave Macmillan, pp. 1–17.

Jacobs, D. (1977) *Hollywood Renaissance: Altman, Cassavetes, Coppola, Mazursky,*

Scorsese and Others. South Brunswick and New York: A.S. Barnes and Co.

Jacobson, H. (1989) Michael and Me, *Film Comment*, November–December, 16–26.

Jaffe, P. (1965) Editing Cinema Vérité, *Film Comment*, Summer, 3(3).

James, D. (1987) Chained to Devilpictures: Cinema and Black Liberation in the Sixties, in M. Davis, M. Marable, F. Pfeil, M. Sprinker (eds) *The Year Left 2: An American Socialist Yearbook*. London: Verso.

—— (1989) *Allegories of Cinema: American Film in the Sixties*. Princeton, NJ: Princeton University Press.

—— (ed.) (1992) *To Free the Cinema: Jonas Mekas and the New York Underground*. Princeton, NJ: Princeton University Press.

—— (1995) *That's Blaxploitation: Roots of the Baadasssss 'Tude*. New York: St Martin's Press.

Jameson, F. (1988) Periodizing the 60s. in S. Sayres, A. Stephanson, S. Aronowitz and F. Jameson (eds) *The 60s Without Apology*. Minneapolis: University of Minnesota Press, pp. 178–209.

—— (1993) *Postmodernism, or the Cultural Logic of Late Capitalism*. New York and London: Verso.

Jamgocyan, N. (1998) Big Boat, Small Screen. *Screen International*, 26 June, 9.

Jeffords, S. (1994) *Hard Bodies: Hollywood Masculinity in the Reagan Era*. New Brunswick, NJ: Rutgers University Press.

Jenkins, H. (1992) *Textual Poachers: Television Fans and Participatory Culture*. London and New York: Routledge.

Jermyn, D. and Redmond, S. (2003) *The Cinema of Kathryn Bigelow: Hollywood Transgressor*. London: Wallflower.

Johnston, C. (1973) Women's Cinema as Counter-Cinema, in C. Johnston (ed.) *Notes on Women's Cinema*. London: Society for Education in Film and Television.

Johnston, S. (1988) Chance of a Ghost, *The Independent*, 28 July, 13.

—— (1999) The Flashback Kid, *Sight and Sound*, 9(11).

Jones, K. (2005) Hail the Conquering Hero, *Film Comment*, May/June 2005, archived at http://www.filmlinc.com/fcm/5-6-2005/Sarris.htm (accessed 6 June, 2005).

Jowett, G. (1976) *Film: The Democratic Art*. New York: Little, Brown, and Co.

Kael, P. (1970) Review of *Tora! Tora! Tora! New Yorker*, 3 October.

—— (1972a) Saint Cop, *New Yorker*, 15 January, 78–82.

—— (1972b) Review, *New Yorker*, 47, 29 January, 83.

—— (1973) *Deeper into Movies*. London: Calder and Boyars.

—— (1985) Review, *New Yorker*, 9 July, 37–8.

Kaplan, E.A. (1978) *Women in Film Noir*. London: BFI.

—— (1987) *Rocking Around the Clock: Music, Television, Postmodernism, and Consumer Culture*. London: Methuen.

—— (2003) Women, Film, Resistance: Changing Paradigms, in J. Levatin, J. Plessis and V. Raoul (eds) *Women Filmmakers: Refocusing*. New York: Routledge, pp. 15–28.

Kaufman, A. (2002) *Steven Soderbergh: Interviews*. Jackson, MI: University Press of Mississippi.

Kauffmann, S. (1975) *Living Images*. New York: Harper and Row.

Kawin, B.F. (1986) Children of the Light, in B.K. Grant, *Film Genre Reader*. Austin: University of Texas Press, pp. 236–57.

Keane, S. (2001) *Disaster Movies: Cinema of Catastrophe*. London: Wallflower Press.

Kerman, J.B. (ed.) (2003) *Retrofitting Blade Runner: Issues in Ridley Scott's Blade Runner* and Philip K. Dick's "Do Androids Dream of Electric Sheep?" Bowling Green, OH: Bowling Green University Popular Press.

Kermode, M. (1995) Twisting the Knife, in J. Romney and A. Wootton (eds) *Celluloid Jukebox: Pop Music and the Movies since the 50s*. London: BFI, pp. 8–19.

—— (1997) *The Exorcist*. London: BFI.

Keyser, L. (1981) *Hollywood in the Seventies*. New York and London: A.S. Barnes/ Tantivy Press.

Kifner, J. (1977) Weather Underground Splits Up Over Plan to Come into the Open, *The New York Times*, 18 January, 12.

Kinder, M. (1991) *Playing with Power in Movies, Television and Video Games: From Muppet-Babies to Teenage-Mutant-Ninja-Turtles*. Berkeley: University of California Press.

King, G. (2000) *Spectacular Narratives: Hollywood in the Age of the Blockbuster*. London: I.B. Tauris.

—— (2002) *New Hollywood Cinema: An Introduction*. London: I.B. Tauris.

—— (2003) Spectacle, Narrative, and the Spectacular Hollywood Blockbuster, in J. Stringer (ed.) *Movie Blockbusters*. London: Routledge, pp. 114–27.

King, N. (2004) The Last Good Time We Ever Had: Remembering the New Hollywood Cinema, in T. Elsaesser, A. Horwath, and N. King (eds) *The Last Great American Picture Show: New Hollywood Cinema in the 1970s*. Amsterdam: Amsterdam University Press, pp. 19–20.

Kipnis, L. (1998) Film and Changing Technologies, in J. Hill and P.C. Gibson (eds) *The Oxford Guide to Film Studies*. Oxford: Oxford University Press.

Kitses, J. (2004) *Horizons West: Directing the Western from John Ford to Clint Eastwood*. London: BFI.

Klein, C. (2004) *Crouching Tiger, Hidden Dragon*: A Diasphoric Reading, *Cinema Journal*. 43(4), 18–42.

Klein, H.S. (2004) *A Population History of the United States*. Cambridge: Cambridge University Press.

Kleinans, C. (1998) Independent Features: Hopes and Dreams, in J. Lewis (ed.) *New American Cinema*. Durham, NC: Duke University Press, pp. 307–27.

—— (2002) Charles Burnett, in Y. Tasker (ed.) *Fifty Contemporary Filmmakers*. London: Routledge, pp. 65–73.

Klinger, B. (1994) *Melodrama and Meaning: History, Culture and the Films of Douglas Sirk*. Bloomington and Indianapolis: Indian University Press.

—— (1997) The Road to Dystopia: Landscaping the Nation in *Easy Rider*, in S. Cohan and I.R. Hark (eds) *The Road Movie Book*. London and New York: Routledge, pp. 179–203.

Koch, S. (1991) *Stargazer: Andy Warhol's World and His Films*, revised and updated, 3rd edn. New York: Marion Boyars.

Kolker, R. (1988) *A Cinema of Loneliness*, 2nd edn. New York and Oxford: Oxford University Press.

Komiya, M. and Litman, B. (1990) The Economics of the Prerecorded Videocassette Industry, in J. R. Dobrow (ed.) *Social and Cultural Aspects of VCR Use*. Hillsdale, NJ: Lawrence Erlbaum Associates, Publishers.

Krämer, P. (1997) The Lure of the Big Picture: Film, Television and Hollywood, in J. Hill and M. McLoone (eds) *Big Picture, Small Screen: The Relations Between Film and Television*. Luton: John Libbey.

—— (1998a) Post-Classical Hollywood, in J. Hill and P. Church (eds) *The Oxford Guide to Film Studies*. Oxford and New York: Oxford University Press, pp. 289–309.

—— (1998b) Would You Take Your Child to See This Film? The Cultural and Social Work of the Family-Adventure Movie, in S. Neale and M. Smith (eds) *Contemporary Hollywood Cinema*. London: Routledge, pp. 294–311.

—— (2002a) "The Best Disney Film Disney Never Made": Children's Films and the Family Audience in American Cinema Since the 1960s, in S. Neale (ed.) *Genre and Contemporary Hollywood*. London: BFI.

—— (2002b) Spielberg, in Y. Tasker (ed.) *Fifty Contemporary Filmmakers*. London: Routledge, pp. 319–28.

—— (2003) "A Woman in a Male-Dominated World": Jodie Foster, Stardom and 90s Hollywood, in T. Austin and M. Barker (eds) *Contemporary Hollywood Stardom*. London: Arnold, pp. 201–14.

—— (2004) "It's Aimed at Kids – the Kid in Everybody": George Lucas, *Star Wars* and Children's Entertainment, in Y. Tasker (ed.) *Action and Adventure Cinema*. London: Routledge.

—— (2005) *The New Hollywood: From Bonnie and Clyde to Star Wars*. London: Wallflower.

Kramer, R. (1968–69) "Newsreel" [collected statements], *Film Quarterly* 20(2) Winter, 44.

Kuhn, A. (1995a) *Family Secrets: Acts of Memory and Imagination*. London: Verso.

—— (1995b) *Queen of the "B's: Ida Lupino Behind the Camera*. London: Flicks Books.

Labarthe, A. and Marcorelles, L. (1963) Entretien avec Robert Drew et Richard Leacock. *Cahiers du Cinéma*, February, (24), 140.

Laderman, D. (2002) *Driving Visions: Exploring the Road Movie*. Austin: University of Texas Press.

Lalanne, J-M. (2003) Gus Van Sant: Localisation Zero, *Cahiers du Cinéma*, 577.

Lane, C. (2000) *Feminist Hollywood: From Born in Flames to Point Break*. Detroit: Wayne State University Press.

LaPlace, M. (1987) Producing and Consuming the Woman's Film: Discursive Struggle in *Now, Voyager*, in C. Gledhill (ed.) *Home is Where the Heart Is: Studies in Melodrama and the Woman's Film*. London: BFI.

LaValley, A. J. (1985) Traditions of Trickery?: The Role of Special Effects in the Science Fiction Film, in G.E. Slusser and E.S. Rabkin (eds) *Shadows of the Magic Lamp: Fantasy and Science Fiction Film*. Carbondale: Southern Illinois University Press.

Leab, D. (1976) *From Sambo to Superspade: The Black Experience in Motion Pictures*. Boston: Houghton Mifflin.

Leffingwell, E., Kismaric, E.C. and Heiferman, M. (eds) (1997) *Jack Smith: Flaming Creatures: His Amazing Life and Times*. London: Serpent's Tail.

Le Grice, M. (1976) *Abstract Film and Beyond*. London: Studio Vista.

Leong, I., Sell, M. and Thomas, K. (1997) Mad Love, Mobile Homes, and Dysfunctional Dicks: On the Road with *Bonnie and Clyde*, in S. Cohan and I.R. Hark (eds) *The Road Movie Book*. London and New York: Routledge, pp. 70–89.

Lev, P. (1993) *The Euro-American Cinema*. Austin: University of Texas Press.

—— (2000) *American Films of the '70s: Conflicting Visions*. Austin: University of Texas Press.

—— (2003) *The Fifties: Transforming the Screen, 1950–1959*, vol. 7 of *History of the American Cinema*. New York: Charles Scribner's and Sons.

Levatin, J., Plessis, J. and Raoul, V. (eds)

(2003) *Women Filmmakers: Refocusing*. New York: Routledge.

Levin, G.R. (1971) *Documentary Explorations*. Garden City, NY: Anchor Press.

Levy, A. (1967) Will Big Budgets Spoil Roger Corman? *Status/Diplomat*, March, 46–52.

Lewis, J. (1972) Children Too Have Film Rights, *Variety*, 32, 6 January.

Lewis, J. (2000) *Hollywood V. Hardcore: How the Struggle Over Censorship Created the Modern Film Industry*. New York: New York University Press.

—— (ed.) (2001), *The End of Cinema As We Know It: American Film in the Nineties*. New York: New York University Press.

Lieberman, D. (1997) Conglomerates, News, and Children, in E. Barnouw et al., *Conglomerates and the Media*. New York: The New Press.

Lim, D. (2002) The Reckless Moment: Two Pioneers of the New Queer Cinema Look Back on a Short-Lived Sensation, *Village Voice*, 26 March, 43.

Lindstrom, M. (2004) *BRANDchild: Remarkable Insights Into the Minds of Today's Global Kids and Their Relationship with Brands*. London: Kogan Page.

Linnett, R. (1985) As American As You Are: Jim Jarmusch and "Stranger than Paradise", *Cinéaste* 14(1).

Lipsitz, G. (1998) Genre Anxiety and Racial Representation in 1970s Cinema, in N. Browne (ed.) *Refiguring American Film Genres, History, and Theory*. Berkeley: University of California Press.

Littman, M.S. (1998) *A Statistical Portrait of the United States: Social Conditions and Trends*. Lanham, MD: Bernan.

Livingstone, P. (1966) "Dim Little Flick" Becomes a World-Beater, *Kine. Weekly*, 17 December.

Lobban, G. (1995) Coming in 70mm: Is There a Future for 70mm Theatrical Prints?, *Cinema Technology*, April.

Lott, T. (1998) Hollywood and Independent Black Cinema, in S. Neale and M. Smith (eds) *Contemporary Hollywood Cinema*. London: Routledge, pp. 211–28.

Lyman, R. (2002) Revolt in the Den: DVD. Has the VCR Headed to the Attic? *New York Times*, 26 August, A1, A13.

Lyne, W. (2000) No Accident: From Black Power to Black Box Office, *African American Review*, 34(1), 39–59.

MacDonald, J.F. (1993) *Blacks and White TV: Afro-Americans in Television Since 1948*. Chicago: Nelson-Hall.

MacDonald, S. (2001) *The Garden in the Machine: A Field Guide to Independent Films about Place*. Berkeley: University of California Press.

—— (2002) *Cinema 16: Documents Toward a History of the Film Society*. Philadelphia, PA: Temple University Press.

—— (2005) *A Critical Cinema: Interview With Independent Filmmakers: No. 4*. Berkeley: University of California Press.

Malcolm, D. (1985) In Love with the Future, *The Guardian*, 15 August.

Maltby, R. (1995) *Hollywood Cinema*. Oxford: Blackwell.

—— (1996) "A Brief Romantic Interlude": Dick and Jane Go to 3½ Seconds of the Classical Hollywood Cinema, in D. Bordwell and N. Carroll (eds) *Post-Theory: Reconstructing Film Studies*. Madison: University of Wisconsin Press.

—— (1998) "Nobody Knows Everything",: Post Classical Histriographies and Consolidated Entertainment, in S. Neale and M. Smith (eds) *Contemporary Hollywood Cinema*. London: BFI.

Maltin, L. (1995) *The Disney Films*, 3rd edn. New York: Hyperion.

Mamber, S. (1974) *Cinéma Vérité in America.* Cambridge, MA: MIT Press.

Marcorelles, L. (1963) L'expérience Leacock. trans. J. Hillier, *Cahiers du Cinéma,* February (22): 144.

Marcus, G. (1977) *Mystery Train: Images of America in the Rock'N'Roll Music.* New York: Omnibus Press.

Marsden, M.T. and Nachbar, J. (1987) The Modern Popular Western: Radio, Television, Film, and Print, in Western Literature Association's *A Literary History of the American West.* Fort Worth: Texas Christian University Press, pp. 1263–82.

Martinez, G., Martinez, D. and Chavez, A. (eds) (1998) *What It Is … What It Was! The Black Film Explosion of the '70s in Words and Pictures.* New York: Hyperion.

Massey, A. and Hammond, M. (1999) "But It Was True! How Can You Laugh?" The Reception of *Titanic* in Britain and Southampton, in K. Sandler and G. Studlar (eds) *Titanic: Anatomy of a Blockbuster.* New Brunswick, NJ: Rutgers University Press, 39–64.

Matthews, T.D. (1994) *Censored.* London: Chatto and Windus.

Matusow, A.J. (1984) *The Unnravelling of America: A History of Liberalism in the 1960s.* New York: Harper and Row

McBride, J. (1997) *Steven Spielberg: A Biography.* London: Faber and Faber.

McCall, N. (1995) *Makes Me Wanna Holler: A Young Black Man in America.* New York: Vintage.

McCarthy, T. (1997) Titanic, *Variety,* 3 Nov., archived at http://www.variety.com/index.-asp?layout=Variety100&reviewid= VE1117339997&content=jump&jump= review&category= 1935&cs=1, (accessed 4 November, 2005).

McNary, D. (2004) Comics No Longer King: Cable Bulldozes Once Lucrative Stand-up Genre, 4 Jan., http://www.variety.com/index.asp? (accessed 7 November, 2005).

McNeal, J.U. (1992) *Kids as Customers: A Handbook of Marketing to Children.* New York: Lexington Books.

McWilliams, D. (1970) Frederick Wiseman, *Film Quarterly,* 24(1)

Medovoi, L. (1998) Theorizing Historicity, or the Many Meanings of *Blacula, Screen,* 39(1), 1–21.

Mekas, J. (1972) *Movie Journal: The Rise of the New American Cinema, 1959–71.* New York: Macmillan.

Mellencamp, P. (2001) The Zen of Masculinity – Rituals of Heroism in *The Matrix,* in J. Lewis (ed.) *The End of Cinema as We Know it: American Film in the Nineties.* New York: New York University Press, pp. 83–94.

Mercer, K. (1991) Skin Head Sex Thing: Racial Difference and the Homoerotic Imaginary, in Bad Object-Choices (ed.) *How Do I Look?: Queer Film and Video.* Seattle: Bay Press.

—— (1994) *Welcome to the Jungle: New Positions in Black Cultural Studies.* New York: Routledge.

Meyer, M. (1994) Introduction: Reclaiming the Discourse of Camp, in M. Meyer (ed.) *The Politics and Poetics of Camp.* London: Routledge.

Michelson, A. (1966) The Radical Inspiration, in P.A. Sitney (ed.) *Film Culture: An Anthology.* London: Secker and Warburg, pp. 404–21.

—— (1976) Toward Snow, in P. Gidal (ed.) *Structural Film Anthology.* London: BFI, pp. 38–44.

Miller, T., Nitin, G., McMurria, J. and Maxwell, R. (2001) *Global Hollywood.* London: BFI.

Mizejewski, L. (1992) *Divine Decadence: Fascism, Female Spectacle and the Makings of Sally Bowles*. Princeton, NJ: Princeton University Press.

—— (2004) *Hardboiled and High Heeled: The Woman Detective in Popular Culture*. New York: Routledge.

Modleski, T. (1984) *Loving with a Vengeance: Mass-Produced Fantasies for Women*. London: Methuen.

—— (1988) *The Women Who Knew Too Much: Alfred Hitchcock and Feminist Theory*. New York and London: Routledge.

Monaco, J. (1979) *American Film Now: The People, the Power, the Money, the Movies*. New York: New American Library.

Monaco, P. (2003) *The Sixties, 1960–1969*, vol. 8 of *History of American Cinema*. Berkeley and London: University of California Press.

Morley, D. (1986) *Family Television: Cultural Power and Domestic Leisure*. New York and London: Routledge.

—— (1992) *Television Audiences and Cultural Studies*. New York and London: Routledge.

—— (1995) Television: Not So Much a Visual Medium, More a Visible Object, in C. Jenks (ed.) *Visual Culture*. London and New York: Routledge, pp. 170-1.

Morris, M. (2001) What a Lucky Soderbergh, *The Observer Review*, 7 January.

Mulvey, L. (1975) Visual Pleasure in Narrative Cinema, *Screen*, 13(3), 6–18.

—— (1998) New Wave Interchanges: *Céline and Julie* and *Desperately Seeking Susan*, in G. Nowell-Smith and S. Ricci (eds) *Hollywood and Europe: Economics, Culture, National Identity 1945–95*. London: BFI.

Murphy, A.D. (1975) Audience Demographics, Film Future, *Variety*, 20 August, 3.

Neal, L. (1969) Beware of the Tar Baby, *New York Times*, 3 August.

Neal, M.A. (2002) *Soul Babies: Black Popular Culture and the Post-soul Aesthetic*. New York: Routledge.

Neale, S. (2000) *Genre and Hollywood*. London and New York: Routledge.

—— (ed.) (2002) *Genre and Contemporary Hollywood*, London: BFI.

Neale, S. and Smith, M. (1998) *Contemporary Hollywood Cinema*, London: Routledge.

Newman, K. (1996) Introduction, in K. Newman (ed.) *The BFI Companion to Horror*. London: BFI, pp. 11–16

—— (2000) "*Toy Story 2*", *Sight and Sound*, March, 56–7.

Newsweek (1970) The New Movies, *Newsweek*, 76(7), 42–54.

Newton, H. (1971), "He Won't Bleed Me": A Revolutionary Analysis of *Sweet Sweetback's Baadasssss Song*, *Black Panther* 6, A–L, 19 June.

Nichols, B. (1972) Newsreel: Film and Revolution, unpublished master's thesis, University of California, Los Angeles.

—— (1980) *Newsreel: Documentary Filmmaking on the American Left*. New York: Arno Press.

—— (1981) *Ideology and the Image*. Bloomington: University of Indiana Press.

—— (1983) The Voice of Documentary, *Film Quarterly* 36(3), Spring: 17–30.

—— (1994) *Blurred Boundaries: Questions of Meaning in Contemporary Culture*. Bloomington: Indiana University Press.

Nichols, P.M. (2002) DVD Has Begun to Take Over, *New York Times*, 28 June, B25.

—— (2003) A First Take on "Ring", Part 2. *New York Times*, 3 September, B21.

Nochimson, M.P. (1997) *The Passion of David Lynch*. Austin: University of Texas Press.

Nyce, B. (2004) *Scorsese Up Close: A Study of the Films.* London: Scarecrow Press.

Nystrom, D. (2004) Hard Hats and Movie Brats: Auteurism and the Class Politics of the New Hollywood, *Cinema Journal*, 3(3): 18–41.

O'Connell, P.J. (1992) *Robert Drew and the Development of Cinéma Vérité in America.* Carbondale: Southern Illinois University Press.

O'Day, M. (2004) Beauty in Motion: Gender Spectacle and Action Babe Cinema, in Y. Tasker (ed.) *Action and Adventure Cinema.* London: Routledge, pp. 201–18.

Odham Stokes, L. and Hoover, M. (1997) *City on Fire: Hong Kong Cinema.* London: Verso.

Ongiri, A. (2005) Kill Them with Karate: Black Belt and the Irrecuperable Wounded Black Male Body. Paper presented at Martial Arts/Global Flows Conference, Duke University, 11–12 February.

O'Pray, M. (ed.) (1989) *Andy Warhol: Film Factory.* London: BFI.

—— (2003) *Avant-Garde Film: Forms, Themes and Passions.* London: Wallflower Press.

Ottoson, R.L. (1985) *AIP: A Filmography.* New York: Garland Publishing Inc.

Palmer, R.B. (1994) *Hollywood's Dark Cinema: American Film Noir.* New York: Twayne.

Parmar, P. (1992) Queer Questions, *Sight and Sound*, September: 35.

Patterson, L. (1975) *Black Films and Film-makers.* New York: Dodd, Mead and Co.

Paul, S. (1999) *The Seventies Now.* Durham, NC: Duke University Press.

Paul, W. (1994) *Laughing Screaming: Modern Hollywood Horror and Comedy*, New York: Columbia University Press.

Pearl, M. (1999) Symptoms of AIDS in Contemporary Film: Mortal Anxiety in an Age of Sexual Panic, in M. Aaron (ed.) *The Body's Perilous Pleasures.* Edinburgh: Edinburgh University Press, pp. 210–25.

Pearson, R. and Uricchio, W. (1991) *The Many Lives of the Batman: Critical Approaches to a Superhero and His Media.* London: Routledge.

Pecora, N.O. (1998) *The Business of Children's Entertainment.* New York: Guilford.

People (2000) *2001 People Entertainment Almanac.* New York: Cader Books.

Perkins, T. (1991) The Politics of Jane Fonda, in C. Gledhill (ed.) *Stardom: Industry of Desire.* London: Routledge, pp. 237–50.

Phillips, J.D. (1982) Film Conglomerate Blockbusters: International Appeal and Product Homogenization, in G. Kindem (ed.) *The American Movie Industry: The Business of Motion Pictures.* Edwardsville and Carbondale: Southern Illinois University Press, pp. 327–39.

Pidduck, J. (1995) The Hollywood Fatal Femme: (Dis)Figuring Feminism, Family, Irony, Violence, *Cineaction* 38, 64–72.

—— (2002) After 1980: Margins and Mainstreams, in R. Dyer (ed.) *Now You See It*, 2nd edn. London: Routledge.

Pierson, J. (1996) *Spike, Mike, Slackers and Dykes: A Guided Tour across a Decade of Independent American Cinema.* London: Faber and Faber.

Pinedo, I.C. (1997) *Recreational Terror: Women and the Pleasures of Horror Film Viewing.* New York: State University of New York Press.

Pirie, D. (ed.) (1981) *Anatomy of the Movies.* London: Winward.

Plantinga, C. (1998) Spectacles of Death: Clint Eastwood and Violence in *Unforgiven*, *Cinema Journal*, 37(2), Winter, 65–83.

—— (2000) American Documentary in the 1980s, in S. Prince (ed.) *A New Pot of Gold:*

Hollywood Under the Electronic Rainbow, 1980–1989. New York: Charles Scribner's Sons.

Polan, D. (2001) The Confusions of Warren Beatty, in *The End of Cinema as We Know It: American Film in the Nineties.* New York: New York University Press, pp. 141–9.

Poussaint, A. (1974) Blaxploitation Movies: Cheap Thrills that Degrade Blacks, *Psychology Today,* 7, 22–31.

Prawer, S.S. (1980) *Caligari's Children: The Film as Tale of Terror.* New York: Da Capo Press.

Prince, S. (1998) *Savage Cinema: Sam Peckinpah and the Rise of Ultraviolent Movies.* London: Athlone Press.

—— (2000) *A New Pot of Gold: Hollywood Under the Electronic Rainbow, 1980–1989.* Berkeley: University of California Press.

Pulver, A. (2000) Indie Reservation, *The Guardian Review,* 31 March.

Pye, M. and Myles, L. (1979) *The Movie Brats: How the Film Generation Took Over Hollywood.* New York: Holt, Rinehart, and Winston.

Quart, B.K. (1988) *Women Directors: The Emergence of a New Cinema.* New York: Praeger.

Quinn, E. (2001) "Pimpin' Ain't Easy": Work, Play, and "Lifestylization" of the Black Pimp Figure in Early 1970s America, in B. Ward (ed.) *Media, Culture and the Modern American Freedom Struggle.* Gainesville: University Press of Florida.

—— (2005) *Nuthin' but a "G" Thang: The Culture and Commerce of Gangsta Rap.* New York: Columbia University Press.

Radway, J. (1984) *Reading the Romance: Women, Patriarchy and Popular Literature.* London: University of North Carolina Press.

Randall, R.S. (1985) Censorship from *The Miracle* to *Deep Throat,* in T. Balio (ed.) *The American Film Industry.* Madison: University of Wisconsin Press, pp. 432–57.

Ray, R.B. (1985) *A Certain Tendency of the Hollywood Cinema, 1930–1980.* Princeton, NJ: Princeton University Press.

Rayner, J. (2000) The Cult Film, Roger Corman and *The Cars That Ate Paris,* in X. Mendik and G. Harper, *Unruly Pleasures: The Cult Film and its Critics.* Guildford: FAB Press, pp. 223–33.

Rebello, S. (1998) *Alfred Hitchcock and the Making of Psycho.* London: Marion Boyars.

Rees, A.L. (1999) *A History of Experimental Film and Video.* London: BFI.

—— (2001) Working Both Sides of the Street: Film and Art in Michael Snow, in *Michael Snow: Almost Cover to Cover Catalogue.* Bristol: Black Dog Publishing.

Reid, M. (1988) The Black Action Film: The End of the Patiently Enduring Black Hero, *Film History,* 2(1), 23–36.

Reid, M.A. (2005) Haile Gerima "Sacred Shield of Culture", in C. Holmlund and J. Wyatt (eds) *Contemporary American Independent Film.* London: Routledge, pp. 141–54.

Reiner, R. (1981) Keystone to Kojak: the Hollywood Cop, in P. Davies and B. Neve (eds) *Cinema, Politics, and Society in America.* Manchester: Manchester University Press, pp. 195–220.

Renan, S. (1967) *The Underground Film: An Introduction to Its Development in America.* London: Studio Vista.

Renov, M. (1987) Newsreel Old and New – Towards an Historical Profile, *Film Quarterly* 41(1) Fall.

Research Department of Security Pacific National Bank (1974) The Motion Picture Industry in California: A Special Report,

Journal of the Producers' Guild of America,
March 7.

Reynaud, B. (2003) Les producteurs indépendents en difficulté: Stratégies de survie
des "indies", *Cahiers du Cinéma*, March:
577.

Rhines, J. (1996) *Black Film/White Money.*
New Brunswick, NJ: Rutgers University
Press.

Rich, B.R. (1992) New Queer Cinema, *Sight
and Sound*, 2(5), 32.

—— (1993a) Never a Victim: Jodie Foster, a
New Kind of Female Hero, in P. Cook and
P. Dodd (eds) *Women and Film: A Sight and
Sound Reader.* London: Scarlet Press, pp.
50–61.

—— (1993b) Reflections on a Queer Screen,
GLQ: A Journal of Lesbian and Gay Studies,
1(1).

—— (2000) Queer and Present Danger, *Sight
and Sound*, March, 23.

—— (2002) Vision Quest: Searching for
Diamonds in the Rough, *Village Voice*, 26
March, 43.

Richards, A. (2002) From Hell, *Sight and
Sound*, March, 45.

Riley, C. (1972) Shaft Can Do Everything, I
Can Do Nothing, *New York Times*, 14
August.

Robinson, C. (1998) Blaxploitation and the
Misrepresentation of Liberation, *Race and
Class*, 40(1), 1–12.

Roddick, N. (1980) Only the Stars Survive:
Disaster Movies in the Seventies, in D.
Bradby, L. James and B. Sharratt (eds)
*Performance and Politics in Popular Drama:
Aspects of Popular Entertainment in
Theatre, Film and Television 1800–1976.*
Cambridge: Cambridge University Press.

Rodley, C. (ed.) 1997 *Lynch on Lynch.*
London: Faber and Faber.

Rodowick, D.N. (1984) The Enemy Within:

The Economy of Violence in *The Hills
Have Eyes*, in B. K. Grant (ed.) *Planks of
Reason: Essays on the Horror Film.* Metu-
chen, N.J. and London: The Scarecrow
Press, pp. 321–30.

Romney, J. (1995) Access All Areas: The Real
Space of Rock Documentary, in J. Romney
and A. Wootton (eds) *Celluloid Jukebox: Pop
Music and the Movies since the 50s.* London:
BFI, pp. 82–93.

Romney, J. and Wootton, A. (1995) *Celluloid
Jukebox: Popular Music and the Movies Since
the 50s.* London: BFI.

Rose, B. (1982) From the Outdoors to Outer
Space: The Motion Picture Industry in the
1970s, in M. T. Marsden, J. G. Nachbar
and S. L. Grogg Jr. (eds) *Movies as Artifacts:
Cultural Criticism of Popular Film.* Chicago:
Nelson-Hall.

Rosen, M. (1973) *Popcorn Venus: Women,
Movies and the American Dream.* New York:
Coward, McCann and Geoghegan.

Rosenthal, A. (1971) *The New Documentary in
Action.* Berkeley: University of California
Press.

Rothman, W. (1982) *Hitchcock – The
Murderous Gaze.* Cambridge, MA: Harvard
University Press.

—— (2000) Looking Back and Turning
Inward: American Documentary Films of
the Seventies, in D.A. Cook (ed.) *Lost
Illusions: American Cinema in the Shadow of
Watergate and Vietnam, 1970–1979*, vol. 9
of *History of the American Cinema.* New
York: Charles Scribner's Sons.

Rowe, C. (1982) Myth and Symbolism in the
Work of Kenneth Anger, in *The Baudelairean Cinema: A Trend within the American Avant-garde.* Ann Arbor, MI: UMI
Research Press, pp. 71–86.

Rubel, D. (1994) Blackboard Jungle, in

Marshall Crenshaw (ed.) *Hollywood Rock.* London: Plexus.

Rudnick, P. and Andersen, K. (1989) The Irony Epidemic. *Spy*, March: 94.

Ryall, T. (1986) *Alfred Hitchcock and the British Cinema.* Urbana: University of Illinois Press.

Ryan, D. and Kellner, J. (1988) *Camera Politica: The Politics and Ideology of Contemporary Hollywood Film.* Bloomington: Indiana University Press.

Salt, B. (1992) *Film Style and Technology: History and Analysis.* London: Starword Books.

Sandler, K. S. and Studlar, G. (eds) (1999) *Titanic: Anatomy of a Blockbuster.* New Brunswick, NJ: Rutgers University Press.

Sarris, A. (1962/3) Notes on the *auteur theory* in 1962, *Film Culture.* 27, winter, 1–8, reprinted in P. Adams Sitney (ed.) (1970) *Film Culture Reader.* New York: Praeger Publishers, pp. 121–35.

—— (1968) *The American Cinema: Directors and Directions, 1929–1968.* New York: Dutton.

—— (1978) After *The Graduate, American Film,* 3 (9), 32–7.

—— (ed.) (1997) *The St. James Women Filmmakers Encyclopedia: Women on the Other Side of the Camera.* Detroit: Visible Ink Press.

Saunders, M.W. (1998) *Imps of the Perverse: Gay Monsters in Film.* Westport; CT: Praeger.

Sayre, N. (1996) *Sixties Going on Seventies,* New Brunswick: Rutgers University Press.

Schaefer, E. (1999) *Bold! Daring! Shocking! True! A History of Exploitation Films, 1919–59.* Durham, NC: Duke University Press.

Schamus, J. (1998) To the Rear of the Back End: The Economics of Independent Cinema, in S. Neale and M. Smith (eds) *Contemporary Hollywood Cinema.* London and New York: Routledge.

—— (2001) A Rant, in J. Lewis (ed.), *The End of Cinema as We Know It: American Film in the Nineties.* New York: NYU Press, pp. 253–260.

Schatz, T. (1983) *Old Hollywood/New Hollywood: Ritual, Art and Industry.* Studies in Cinema, no. 15. Ann Arbor, MI: UMI Research Press.

—— (1988) *The Genius of the System: Hollywood Filmmaking in the Studio Era.* New York: Pantheon.

—— (1993) The New Hollywood, in J. Collins, H. Radner and A.P. Collins (eds) *Film Theory Goes to the Movies.* New York: Routledge.

—— (1997) The Return of the Hollywood Studio System, in E. Barnouw et al. (eds) *Conglomerates and the Media.* New York: The New Press.

Schindler, C. (1996) *Hollywood in Crisis: Cinema and American Society, 1929–1939.* London: Routledge.

Schneider, S.J. (2004) The Essential Evil in/of *Eraserhead* (or, Lynch to the Contrary), in E. Sheen and A. Davison (eds) *The Cinema of David Lynch: American Dreams, Nightmare Visions.* London: Wallflower, pp. 5–18.

Sconce, J. (1993) Spectacles of Death: Identification, Reflexivity, and Contemporary Horror, in J. Collins, H. Radner, and A.P. Collins (eds) *Film Theory Goes to the Movies.* New York and London: Routledge, pp. 103–19.

Scorsese, M. and Wilson, H.M. (1997) *A Personal Journey with Martin Scorsese through American Movies.* London: Faber.

Segaloff, N. (1990) *Hurricane Billy: The Stormy Life and Films of William Friedkin.* New York: William Morrow and Co.

Seltzer, M. (1998) *Serial Killers: Death and Life in America's Wound Culture*. London: Routledge.

Sergeant, J. (ed.) (1997) *Naked Lens: Beat Cinema*. London: Creation Books.

Shamberg, M. and Raindance Corporation (1971) Meta-Manual, in *Guerrilla Television*. New York: Holt, Rinehart, and Winston.

Sharrett, C. (2001) End of Story: The Collapse of Myth in Postmodern Narrative Film, in J. Lewis (ed.) *The End of Cinema as We Know It: American Film in the Nineties*. New York: New York University Press, pp. 319–31.

Shiel, M. (2003a) A Nostalgia for Modernity: New York, Los Angeles, and American Cinema in the 1970s, in M. Shiel and T. Fitzmaurice (eds), *Screening the City*. London and New York: Verso, pp. 160–79.

—— (2003b) Why Call Them "Cult Movies"? American Independent Filmmaking and the Counterculture in the 1960s, *Scope Online Journal of Film Studies*, Institute of Film Studies, University of Nottingham, www.nottingham.ac.uk/film/journal/index.htm (accessed 12 May, 2005).

Shipman, D. (1966) The All-Conquering Governess, *Films and Filming*, August.

Silet, C.L.P (ed.) (2002) *The Films of Steven Spielberg*. London: Scarecrow.

Silver, A. and Ursini, J. (eds) (1996) *Film Noir Reader*. New York: Limelight.

Silverman, S. (1988) *The Fox That Got Away: The Last Days of the Zanuck Dynasty at Twentieth Century-Fox*. Secaucus, New Jersey: Lyle Stuart.

Silverstone, R. and Hirsch, E. (1992) *Consuming Technologies: Media and Information in Domestic Space*. London and New York: Routledge.

Sitney P.A. (1971) *Film Culture: An Anthology*. London: Secker and Warburg.

—— (2000) *Visionary Film: The American Avant-Garde 1943–1978*. 3rd edn. London: Oxford University Press.

Sklar, R. (1975) *Movie-Made America: A Cultural History of American Movies*. New York: Chappell and Co.

—— (1988) When Looks Could Kill: American Cinema of the Sixties. *Cineaste*, 16(1–2), 50–3.

—— (1999) The Lost Audience: 1950s Spectatorship and Historical Reception Studies, in M. Stokes and R. Maltby (eds) *Identifying Hollywood's Audiences: Cultural Identity and the Movies*. London: BFI.

Sloan, L. (1991) The Voice Interview, John Singleton, *The Voice*, 10 September, 11–12.

Sloane, L. (1969) A New Zanuck Looks at a New Century, *New York Times*, 19 October.

Slotkin, R. (1992) *Gunfighter Nation: The Myth of the Frontier in Twentieth-Century America*. New York: Atheneum.

Smelik, A. (2003) Ceremonial Killings: "New Queer Art Cinema and its Murderous Girls in Love, in M. Aaron (ed.) *New Queer Cinema: A Critical Reader*. Edinburgh: Edinburgh University Press.

Smith, P.S. (1986) *Andy Warhol's Art and Films*. Ann Arbor, MI: UMI Research Press.

Smoodin, E. (ed.) (1994) *Disney Discourse: Producing the Magic Kingdom*. New York: Routledge.

Smyth, C. (1992) *Lesbians Talk Queer Notions*. London: Scarlet Press.

Sontag, S. (2001) *Against Interpretation and Other Essays*. London: Vintage.

Sova, D.B. (1998) *Women in Hollywood: From Vamp to Studio Head*. New York: Fromm International.

Spicer, A. (2002) *Film Noir*. Harlow: Pearson Education.

Spoto, D. (1983) *The Life of Alfred Hitchcock: The Dark Side of Genius*. London: Collins.

Springer, K. (2001) Waiting to Set It Off: African American Women and the Sapphire Fixation, in M. McCaughey and N. King (eds) *Reel Knockouts: Violent Women in the Movies*. Austin: University of Texas Press, pp. 172–99.

Stacey, J. (1992) Desperately Seeking Difference, in Screen Editorial Collective (eds) *The Sexual Subject: A Screen Reader in Sexuality*. London: Routledge. (Original article published Winter 1987 in *Screen*, 28(1), 48–61).

Staiger, J. (1993) Taboos and Totems: Cultural Meanings of *The Silence of the Lambs*, in J. Collins, H. Radner and A.P. Collins (eds) *Film Theory Goes to the Movies*. New York: Routledge, pp. 142–54.

—— (2003) Authorship Approaches, in D.A. Gerstner and J. Staiger (eds) *Authorship and Film*. New York: Routledge, pp. 27–57.

Stanfield, P. (2004) Walking the Streets: Black Gangsters and the "Abandoned City" in the 1970s Blaxploitation Cycle, in L. Grieveson, E. Sonnet, and P. Stanfield (eds) *Mob Culture: Essays on the American Gangster Film*. New Brunswick, NJ: Rutgers University Press.

Stein, E. (1984) Leaner Times for Documentarians, *New York Times*, Sec. 2, 10 June.

Steinberg, C.S. (1980) *Film Facts*. New York: Facts on File.

—— (1982) *Reel Facts: The Movie Book of Records*. New York: Vintage.

Stoddart, H. (1995) Auteurism and Film Authorship, in J. Hollows and M. Jancovich (eds) *Approaches to Popular Film*.
Manchester: Manchester University Press, pp. 37–58.

—— (2003) The Auteur Theory Revisited, in V. W. Wexman (ed.) *Film and Authorship*. New Brunswick, NJ: Rutgers University Press, pp. 21–9.

Stokes, M. and Maltby, R. (eds) (1999) *Identifying Hollywood's Audiences: Cultural Identity and the Movies*. London: BFI.

Stoney, G. (1978) "We've Never Had It So Good": Observations on the American Social Documentary, *Sightlines*, Fall.

—— (1983/4) The Future of the Documentary, *Sightlines*, Fall/Winter.

Street, S. (2001) *Costume and Cinema: Dress Codes in Popular Film*. London and New York: Wallflower Press.

Suarez, J. (1996) *Bike Boys, Drag Queens and Superstars: Avant-Garde , Mass Culture, and Gay Identities in the 1960s Underground Cinema*. Bloomington: Indiana University Press.

Sweeney, L. (1970) The Movie Business is Alive and Well and Living in San Francisco, *Show*, 1(4), 34–7, 82.

Tarratt, M. (1986) Monsters from the Id, in B.K. Grant (ed.) *Film Genre Reader*. Austin: University of Texas Press, pp. 258–77.

Tashiro, C. (1997) The Contradictions of Video Collecting, *Film Quarterly*, 50(2), 11–18.

Tasker, Y. (1993) *Spectacular Bodies: Gender, Genre and the Action Cinema*. London: Routledge.

—— (1998) *Working Girls: Gender and Sexuality in Popular Cinema*, London: Routledge.

—— (1999) Bigger than Life, *Sight and Sound*. 9(5), 12–15.

—— (2002) *The Silence of the Lambs*, BFI Modern Classics, London: BFI.

Taubin, A. (1992) Beyond the Sons of Scorsese, *Sight and Sound*, September, 37.

—— (1993) The "Alien" Trilogy: From Feminism to AIDS, in P. Cook and P. Dodd (eds) *Women and Film: A Sight and Sound Reader*. London: Scarlet Press, pp. 93–100.

—— (1999) God's Lonely Man, *Sight and Sound*, April, 17–19.

Taylor, C. (1971) Focus on Al Maysles, in L. Jacobs (ed.) *The Documentary Tradition: From Nanook to Woodstock*. New York: Hopkinson and Blake.

Taylor, P. (1999) *Steven Spielberg*. London: Batsford.

Teo, S. (1997) *Hong Kong Cinema: The Extra Dimension*. London: BFI.

Thompson, B. (1995) Pop and Film: The Charisma Crossover, in J. Romney and A. Wootton (eds) *Celluloid Jukebox: Popular Music and the Movies since the 1950s*. London: BFI.

Thompson, K. (1999) *Storytelling in the New Hollywood: Understanding Classical Narrative Technique*. Cambridge, MA: Harvard University Press.

—— (2002) *Storytelling in Film and Television*. Cambridge, MA: Harvard University Press.

Thomson, D. (1992) *Showman: The Life of David O. Selznick*. New York: Knopf.

—— (1996) *Rosebud: The Story of Orson Welles*. London: Little, Brown and Company.

—— (2004a) *The New Biographical Dictionary of Film*. London: Little, Brown and Company.

—— (2004b) *The Whole Equation*. London: Little, Brown and Company.

Thornham, S. (1997) *Passionate Detachments: An Introduction to Feminist Film Theory*. London: Edward Arnold.

Thumin, J. (1995), "Maybe He's Tough But He Sure Can't Build A House": Masculinity and In/Competence in *Unforgiven*, in P. Kirkham and J. Thumin (eds) *Me Jane*. London: Lawrence and Wishart, reprinted in J. Kitses and G. Rickman (eds) (1998) *The Western Reader*. New York: Limelight Editions.

Tobin, J. (ed.) (2004) *Pikachu's Global Adventure: The Rise and Fall of Pokemon*. Durham, NC: Duke University Press.

Tompkins, J. (1992) *West of Everything: The Inner Life of Westerns*. London: Oxford University Press.

The Top Grossing Movies of All Time at the USA Box Office. *Internet Movie Database. http://us.imdb.com/Charts/usatopmovies* (accessed May 2003).

Trecker, J.L. (1972) Sex, Marriage, and the Movies, *Take One*, 3(5), 12–15.

Trilling, D. (1970) *Easy Rider* and its Critics, *Atlantic Monthly*, September 226(3), 0–5.

Tudor, A. (2002) From Paranoia to Postmodernism? The Horror Movies in Late Modern Society, in Steve Neale (ed.) *Genre and Contemporary Hollywood*. London: BFI, pp. 105–16.

Turan, K. (1998) Fade to Pitch Black, *Los Angeles Times*, 22 November.

Tyler, P. (1974) *Underground Film: A Critical Inquiry*. Harmondsworth: Penguin Books.

United States Census Bureau (2000) *Statistical Abstract of the United States*. www.census.gov. (Accessed 1 August 2005).

Van Deburg, W. (1992) *New Day in Babylon: The Black Power Movement and American Culture, 1965–1975*. Chicago: University of Chicago Press.

—— (1997) *Black Camelot: African–American Culture Heroes in Their Times, 1960–1980*. Chicago: University of Chicago Press.

Van Peebles, M. (1996) *The Making of Sweet Sweetback's Baadasssss Song*. Edinburgh: Payback Press.

Variety's Global 50 (2004) *Variety*, 13 September, 5.

Vogel, A. (1972) [untitled review]. *The Village Voice*, 3 February, 73.

Wagstaff, C. (1992) A Forkful of Westerns: Industry, Audiences, and the Italian Western, in R. Dyer and G. Vincendeau (eds) *Popular European Cinema*. London: Routledge, pp. 245–62.

Wakefield, D. (1969) The War at Home, *Atlantic Monthly*, 224(4), 119–24.

Walkerdine, V. (1989) Video Replays: Families, Films, and Fantasy, in V. Burgin, J. Donald and C. Kaplan (eds), *Formations of Fantasy*. London: Routledge, pp. 167–99.

Wallace, D.F. (1998) E Unibus Pluram: Television and US Fiction, in *A Supposedly Fun Thing I'll Never Do Again*. New York: Little Brown and Company.

Walt Disney Productions (1975) *Walt Disney Productions Annual Report 1975*.

Ward, R. (1976) Black films, white profits. *Black Scholar*, 7(8), 13–24.

Washington, M. and Berlowitz, M. (1975) Swat "Superfly": Blaxploitation Films and High School Youth, *Jump Cut*, 23–4.

Wasko, J. (1982) *Movies and Money: Financing the American Film Industry*. Norwood, New Jersey: Ablex.

—— (1995) *Hollywood in the Information Age: Beyond the Silver Screen*. Austin: University of Texas Press.

—— (2001) *Understanding Disney*. Oxford: Blackwell.

Wasko, J., Phillips, M. and Meehan, E.R. (eds) (2001) *Dazzled by Disney? The Global Disney Audiences Project*. London: Leicester University Press.

Wasser, F. (2001) *Veni, Vidi, Video: The Hollywood Empire and the VCR*. Austin: University of Texas Press.

Watkins, S.C. (1998) *Representing: Hip Hop Culture and the Production of Black Cinema*. Chicago: University of Chicago Press.

Wattenberg, B. J. (1976) *The Statistical History of the United States*. New York: Basic Books.

Waugh, J.C. (1962) Trail Blurred in Film Capital, *Christian Science Monitor*, 21 November.

Waugh, T. (1985) Beyond *vérité*: Emile de Antonio and the New Documentary of the 1970s, in B. Nichols (ed.), *Movies and Methods*, Vol. 2. Berkeley and London: University of California Press, pp. 233–57.

Waxman, S. (2004) Studios Rush to Cash in on DVD Boom, *New York Times*, 20 April, B1, B8.

Weis, E. (1982) *The Silent Scream: Alfred Hitchcock's Sound Track*. London and Toronto: Associated University Presses.

Wells, P. (1998) *Understanding Animation*. London: Routledge.

—— (2003) To Affinity and Beyond: Woody, Buzz and the New Authenticity, in T. Austin and M. Barker (eds) *Contemporary Hollywood Stardom*. London: Arnold, pp. 90–104.

White, G. (2002) Quentin Tarantino, in Y. Tasker (ed.) *Fifty Contemporary Film-makers*. London: Routledge, pp. 338–46.

White, P. (1999) *Uninvited: Classical Hollywood Cinema and Lesbian Representability*. Bloomington: Indiana University Press.

White, T.H. (1975) *Breach of Faith: The Fall of Richard Nixon*. New York: Atheneum Publishers.

Williams, L. (1983) When the Woman Looks, in M. A. Doane, P. Mellencamp and L. Williams (eds) *Re-Vision: Essays in Feminist Film Criticism*. Frederick, MD: University Publications of America.

—— (1991) Film Bodies: Gender, Genre and Excess, *Film Quarterly*, 44, 4, Summer, 2–13.

—— (1994) Learning to Scream, *Sight and Sound*, December, 14–17.

—— (2000) Discipline and Fun: *Psycho* and Postmodern Cinema, in C. Gledhill and L. Williams (eds) *Reinventing Film Studies*. London: Arnold.

Williams, L. R. (1999) The Inside-Out of Masculinity: David Cronenberg's Visceral Pleasures, in M. Aaron (ed.) *The Body's Perilous Pleasures: Dangerous Desire and Contemporary Culture*. Edinburgh: Edinburgh University Press, pp. 30–48.

—— (2002) Mother Courage, *Sight and Sound*, May, 12–14.

—— (2004a) Ready for Action: *G.I. Jane*, Demi Moore's Body and the Female Combat Movie, in Y. Tasker (ed.) *Action and Adventure Cinema*. London: Routledge, pp. 169–86.

—— (2004b) No Sex Please We're American, *Sight and Sound*, January, 18–20.

—— (2005) *The Erotic Thriller in Contemporary Cinema*. Edinburgh: Edinburgh University Press.

Williams, T. (2003) *The Cinema of George A. Romero: Knight of the Living Dead*. London: Wallflower Press.

Willis S. (1993) Hardware and Hardbodies, What Do Women Want?: A Reading of *Thelma and Louise*, in J. Collins, H. Radner and A. P. Collins (eds) *Film Theory Goes to the Movies*. New York: Routledge, pp. 120–8.

—— (1997) *High Contrast: Race and Gender in Contemporary Hollywood Film*. Durham, NC: Duke University Press.

Winant, H. (2001) *The World is a Ghetto: Race and Democracy Since World War II*. New York: Basic Books.

Winston, B. (1996) *Technologies of Seeing: Photography, Cinematography and Television*. London: BFI.

Wlodarz, J. (2004,) Beyond the Black Macho: Queer Blaxploitation, *Velvet Light Trap*, 53, 10–25.

Wolf, R. (1997) *Andy Warhol, Poetry, and Gossip in the 1960s*. London: University of Chicago Press.

Wolf, W. (1970) Poll of Moviegoers Uncorks Surprises, *Entertainment World*, 27 January, 7.

Wollen, P. (1989a) The Two Avant-Gardes, in M. O'Pray (ed.) *Andy Warhol: Film Factory*. London: BFI.

—— (1989b) Raiding the Ice Box, in M. O'Pray (ed.) *Andy Warhol: Film Factory*. London: BFI.

Wood, M. (1975) *America in the Movies, or, "Santa Maria, It Had Slipped My Mind!"*. London: Secker and Warburg.

Wood, R. (1986) *Hollywood from Vietnam to Reagan*. New York: Columbia University Press.

—— (1989) *Hitchcock's Films Revisited*. New York: Columbia University Press.

Woods, P.A. (1997) *Weirdsville USA: The Obsessive Universe of David Lynch*. London: Plexus.

—— (2000) *Quentin Tarantino: The Film Geek Files*. London: Plexus.

Wu, H.H. (2003) "Trading in Horror, Cult and Matricide": Peter Jackson's Phenomenal Bad Taste and New Zealand Fantasies of Inter/National Cinematic Success, in M. Jancovich, A. L. Reboll, J. Stringer and A. Wallis (eds) *Defining Cult Movies: The Cultural Politics of Oppositional Taste*. Manchester: Manchester University Press, pp. 84–108.

Wyatt, J. (1994) *High Concept: Movies and Marketing in Hollywood*. Austin: University of Texas Press.

—— (1998a) From Roadshowing to Saturation Release in J. Lewis (ed.) *The New

Hollywood. Durham, NC: Duke University Press.

—— (1998b) The Formation of the "Major Independent", in S. Neale and M. Smith (eds) *Contemporary Hollywood Cinema.* London: Routledge, pp. 74–90.

Yacowar, M. (1986) The Bug in the Rug: Notes on the Disaster Genre, in B.K. Grant (ed.) *Film Genre Reader.* Austin: University of Texas Press.

—— (1993) *The Films of Paul Morrissey.* Cambridge and New York: Cambridge University Press.

Youngblood, G. (1970) *Expanded Cinema.* New York: Dutton.

Zanuck, D.F. (1966) World Markets Justify the Big Risk, *Kine. Weekly* Supplement, 29 September.

Zimmermann, P. (2000) *States of Emergency: Documentaries, Wars, Democracies.* Minneapolis: University of Minnesota Press.

FILMOGRAPHY

(All films are US productions unless otherwise indicated.)

8 Mile (Curtis Hanson, 2002)

55 Days at Peking (Nicholas Ray, 1963)

84 Charlie MoPic (Patrick Duncan, 1989)

1776 (Peter H. Hunt, 1972)

1941 (Steven Spielberg, 1979)

2001: A Space Odyssey (Stanley Kubrick, 1968)

20000 Leagues Under the Sea (Richard Fleischer, 1954)

About Schmidt (Alexander Payne, 2002)

Absent-Minded Professor, The (Robert Stevenson, 1961)

Abyss, The (James Cameron, 1989)

Accidental Tourist, The (Lawrence Kasdan, 1988)

Accused, The (Jonathan Kaplan, 1988)

Adaptation (Spike Jonze, 2002)

Addiction, The (Abel Ferrara, 1995)

Affliction (Paul Schrader, 1997)

Agony and the Ecstasy, The (Carol Reed, 1965)

Aiqing wansui / Vive l'amour (Tsai Ming-liang, Central Taiwan, 1994)

Airplane! (Jim Abrahams, 1980)

Airport (George Seaton, 1970)

Airport 1975 (Jack Smight, 1974)

Airport '77 (Jerry Jameson, 1977)

Aladdin (John Musker, 1992)

Albero Degli Zoccoli, L'/The Tree Of Wooden Clogs (Ermanno Olmi, Italy, 1978)

Alice Doesn't Live Here Anymore (Martin Scorsese, 1974)

Alice's Restaurant (Arthur Penn, 1969)

Alien (Ridley Scott, 1979)

Aliens (James Cameron, 1986)

All Over Me (Alex Sichel, 1996)

All Quiet on the Western Front (Lewis Milestone, 1930)

All That Jazz (Bob Fosse, 1979)

All the President's Men (Alan J. Pakula, 1976)

All the Vermeers in New York (Jon Jost, 1992)

Always (Steven Spielberg, 1989)

Amadeus (Milos Forman, Company, 1984)

Amarcord (Federico Fellini, Italy, 1973)

American Beauty (Sam Mendes, 1999)

American Dream (Barbara Kopple 1990)

American Graffiti (George Lucas, 1973)

American Movie (Chris Smith, 1999)

American Splendor (Shari Springer Berman and Robert Pulcini, 2003)

American Tail, An (Don Bluth, 1987)

American Werewolf in London, An (John Landis, 1981)

Amistad (Steven Spielberg, 1997)

Anatomy of a Murder (Otto Preminger, 1959)

Andromeda Strain, The (Robert Wise, 1971)

Angels Hard As They Come (Joe Viola, 1971)

Annie Hall (Woody Allen, 1977)

Apartment, The (Billy Wilder, 1960)

Apocalypse Now (Francis Ford Coppola, 1979)

Apollo 13 (Ron Howard, 1995)

Aristocats, The (Wolfgang Reitherman, 1970)

Armageddon (Michael Bay, 1998)

Arthur (Steve Gordon, 1981)

Artificial Intelligence, A.I. (Steven Spielberg, 2001)

As Good as it Gets (James L. Brooks, 1997)

Atlantic City, USA. (Louis Malle, Elie Kfouri, 1980)

Au revoir les enfants/Goodbye, children (Louis Malle, 1987)

Austin Powers: International Man of Mystery (Jay Roach, 1997)

Austin Powers: The Spy Who Shagged Me (Jay Roach, 1999)

Austin Powers in Goldmember (Jay Roach, 2002)

Ba Wang Bie Ji (Chen Kaige, Hong Kong/China, 1993)

Back to the Future (Robert Zemeckis, 1985)

Back to the Future Part II (Robert Zemeckis, 1989)

Back to the Future Part III (Robert Zemeckis, Inc., 1990)

Badlands (Terrence Malick, 1973)

Bad Lieutenant (Abel Ferrara, 1992)

Bad News Bears, The (Michael Ritchie, 1976)

Baisers volés/Stolen Kisses (François Truffaut, France, 1968)

Balcony, The (Joseph Strick, 1963)

Ballad of Cable Hogue, The (Sam Peckinpah, 1970)

Ballad of Little Jo, The (Maggie Greenwald, 1993)

Ballad of Naramaya, The/Narayama-Bushi-Ko (Shohei Imamura, Japan, 1983)

Bananas (Woody Allen, 1971)

Barbarella (Roger Vadim, Dino De Laurentiis, 1968)

Barcelona (Whit Stillman, 1994)

Barefoot in the Park (Gene Saks, 1967)

Bar Girls (Marita Giovanni, 1994)

Barton Fink (Joel Coen, 1991)

Basic Instinct (Paul Verhoeven, 1992)

Bat 21 (Peter Markle, 1988)

Batman (Tim Burton, 1989)

Batman and Robin (Joel Schumacher, 1997)

Batman Forever (Joel Schumacher, 1995)

Batman Returns (Tim Burton, 1992)

Battle Beyond the Stars (Jimmy Teru Murakami, 1980)

Battle of Algiers, The/La battaglia di Algeri (Gillo Pontecorvo, Italy/Algeria, 1966)

Battle of Orgreave, The (Mike Figgis, 2002)

Battlestar Galactica (Richard Colla, 1978)

Beach Party (William Asher, 1963)

Beautiful Mind, A (Ron Howard, 2001)

Beauty and the Beast (Gary Trousdale, 1991)

Bedknobs and Broomsticks (Robert Stevenson, 1971)

Before the Rain (Milcho Manchevski, 1994)

Beguiled, The (Don Siegel, 1970)

Being John Malkovich (Spike Jonze, 1999)

Being There (Hal Ashby, 1979)

Believer, The (Henry Bean, 2001)

Belle de jour (Luis Buñuel, France/Italy, 1967)

Beneath the Planet of the Apes (Ted Post, 1969)

Ben-Hur (William Wyler, 1959)

Best Years of Our Lives, The (William Wyler, 1946)

Beverly Hills Cop (Martin Brest, 1984)

Beverly Hills Cop II (Tony Scott, 1987)

Beverly Hills Cop III (John Landis, 1994)

Beyond the Poseidon Adventure (Irwin Allen, 1979)

Bible: In the Beginning..., The/La Bibbia (John Huston, Dino De Laurentiis Italy/US, 1966)

Big Bad Mama (Steve Carver, 1974)

Big Bus, The (James Frawley, 1976)

Big Chill, The (Lawrence Kasdan, 1983)

Big Doll House, The (Jack Hill, 1971)

Big Jake (George Sherman, 1971)

Big Trouble (John Cassavetes, 1985)

Billy Jack (Tom Laughlin, 1971)

Birdman of Alcatraz, The (John Frankenheimer, 1962)

Birds, The (Alfred Hitchcock, 1963)

Black Belt Jones (Robert Clouse, 1973)

Black Caesar (Larry Cohen, 1973)

Black Hawk Down (Ridley Scott, 2001)

Black Hole, The (Gary Nelson, 1979)

Black Stallion, The (Carroll Ballard, 1979)

Blackboard Jungle (Richard Brooks, 1955)

Blackenstein (William A. Levey, 1973)

Blacula (William Crain, 1972)

Blade (Stephen Norrington, 1998)

Blade II (Guillermo del Toro, 2002)

Blade Runner (Ridley Scott, 1982)

Blade Trinity (David S. Goyer, 1998)

Blair Witch Project, The (Daniel Myrick, 1999)

Blazing Saddles (Mel Brooks, 1974)

Bleierne Zeit, Die/The German Sisters (Margarethe von Trotta, German Federal Republic, 1981)

Blood Feast (Herschell Gordon Lewis, 1963)

Blood Simple (Joel Cohen, 1983)

Bloody Mama (Roger Corman, 1970)

Blow Up (Michelangelo Antonioni, GB/Italy, 1966)

Blue Max, The (John Guillermin, 1966)

Blue Sky (Tony Richardson, 1994)

Blue Steel (Kathryn Bigelow, 1990)

Blue Streak (Les Mayfield, 1999)

Blue Velvet (David Lynch, 1986)

Blues Brothers, The (John Landis, 1980)

Bob and Carol and Ted and Alice (Paul Mazursky, 1969)

Bonnie and Clyde (Arthur Penn, 1967)

Boogie Nights (Paul Thomas Anderson, 1997)

Born in Flames (Lizzie Borden, 1983)

Born on the Fourth of July (Oliver Stone, 1989)

Bottle Rocket (Wes Anderson, 1996)

Bound (Andy Wachowski, 1996)

Bourne Identity, The (Doug Liman, 2002)

Boxcar Bertha (Martin Scorsese, 1972)

Boy and His Dog, A (L.Q. Jones, 1975)

Boys Don't Cry (Kimberly Peirce, 1999)

Bram Stoker's Dracula (Francis Ford Coppola, 1992)

Braveheart (Mel Gibson, 1995)

Brazil (Terry Gilliam, GB, 1985)

Breezy (Clint Eastwood, 1973)

Bride of Frankenstein (James Whale, 1935)

Bridge on the River Kwai, The (David Lean, 1957)

Bridge Too Far, A (Richard Attenborough, 1977)

Brief History of Time, A (Errol Morris, GB/USA, 1991)

Bring Me the Head of Alfredo Garcia (Sam Peckinpah, 1974)

Brink's Job, The (William Friedkin, 1978)

Brother of the Wind (Dick Robinson, 1972)

Brothers Mcmullen, The (Edward Burns, 1995)

Browning Version, The (Mike Figgis, 1994)

Buck Rogers in the 25th Century (Daniel Haller, 1979)

Bucket of Blood, A (Roger Corman, 1959)

Buffalo Bill and the Indians or Sitting Bull's History Lesson (Robert Altman, 1976)

Bullets over Broadway (Woody Allen, 1994)

Bullitt (Peter Yates, 1968)

But I'm a Cheerleader (Jamie Babbit, 1999)

Butch Cassidy and the Sundance Kid (George Roy Hill, 1969)

Butterfield 8 (Daniel Mann, 1960)

Butterflies Are Free (Milton Katselas, 1972)

Butterfly Kiss (Michael Winterbottom, UK 1994)

By Hook or By Crook (Silas Howard and Harry Dodge, 2001)

Cabaret (Bob Fosse, 1972)

Cactus Flower (Gene Saks, 1969)

Caged Heat (Jonathan Demme, 1974)

California Split (Robert Altman, 1974)

California Suite (Herbert Ross, 1978)

Camelot (Joshua Logan, 1967)

Candidate, The (Michael Ritchie, 1972)

Capturing the Friedmans (Andrew Jarecki, 2003)

Car Wash (Michael Schulz. 1976)

Cardinal, The (Otto Preminger, 1963)

Carnal Knowledge (Mike Nichols, 1971)

Carnival of Souls (Herk Harvey, 1964)

Carousel (Henry King, 1956)

Carpetbaggers, The (Edward Dmytryk, 1964)

Carrie (Brian De Palma, 1976)

Cat Ballou (Eliot Silverstein, 1965)

Cat on a Hot Tin Roof (Richard Brooks, 1958)

Catch Me If You Can (Steven Spielberg, 2003)

Catch-22 (Mike Nichols, 1970)

Catwoman (Pitof, Warner Bros. 2004)

Céline et Julie vont en bateau/Celine and Julie go Boating (Jacques Rivette, France, 1974)

Cérémonie, La (Claude Chabrol, France/Ger 1995)

Chameleon Street (Wendell Harris, 1989)

Chant d'Amour, Un (Jean Genet, France, 1950)

Chariots of Fire (Hugh Hudson, UK, 1981)

Charlie's Angels (McG, 2000)

Charlie's Angels: Full Throttle (McG, 2003)

Charly (Ralph Nelson, 1968)

Chase, The (Arthur Penn, 1966)

Chasing Amy (Kevin Smith, 1997)

Chelsea Girls (Andy Warhol, 1966)

Chelsea Walls (Ethan Hawke, 2001)

Chicago (Rob Marshall, 2002)

Child is Waiting, A (John Cassavetes, 1963)

Children of a Lesser God (Randa Haines, 1986)

Children of Fate: Life and Death in A Sicilian Family (Susan Todd and Andrew Young, 1993)

Chilly Scenes of Winter/Head Over Heels (Joan Micklin, 1979)

Chinatown (Roman Polanski, 1974)

Chisum (Andrew V. MacLagen, 1970)

Chitty Chitty Bang Bang (Ken Hughes, 1968)

Choose Me (Alan Rudolph, 1984)

Chronique des Années de Braise (Mohammed Lakdha-Hamina, Algeria, 1975)

Cider House Rules, The (Lasse Hallström, 1999)

Citizen Ruth (Alexander Payne, 1996)

City of Hope (John Sayles, 1991)

City of Sadness, A/Beiqing Chengshi (Hou Hsiao-hsien, Taiwan, 1989)

City Slickers (Ron Underwood, 1991)

Clare of the Moon (Nicole Conn, 1992)

Classe Operaia Va in Paradiso, La (Elio Petri, Italy, 1971)

Cleopatra (Twentieth Century-Fox, 1963)

Cleopatra Jones (Jack Starrett, 1973)

Clerks (Kevin Smith, 1994)

Clockwork Orange, A (Stanley Kubrick, 1971)

Close Encounters of the Third Kind (Steven Spielberg, 1977)

Close to Eden/Urga (Nikita Mikhalkov, France/ USSR, 1991)

Coal Miner's Daughter (Michael Apted, 1980)

Cocoon (Ron Howard, 1985)

Coffy (Jack Hill, 1973)

Cold Creek Manor (Mike Figgis, 2003)

Cold Mountain (Anthony Minghella, 2003)

Color of Money, The (Martin Scorsese, 1986)

Color Purple, The (Steven Spielberg, 1985)

Colors (Dennis Hopper, 1988)

Coma (Michael Crichton, 1978)

Coming Home (Hal Ashby, 1978)

Con Air (Simon West, 1997)

Conan the Barbarian (John Milius, 1982)

Conan the Destroyer (Richard Fleischer, 1984)

Concorde: Airport '79, The (David Lowell Rich, 1979)

Connection, The (Shirley Clarke, 1962)

Contact (Robert Zemeckis, 1997)

Conversation, The (Francis Ford Coppola, 1976)

Coogan's Bluff (Don Siegel, 1968)

Cool Hand Luke (Stewart Rosenberg, 1967)

Cool World, The (Shirley Clarke, 1963)

Così ridevano (Gianni Amelio, Italy, 1998)

Cotton Comes to Harlem (Ossie Davis, 1970)

Count Yorga, Vampire (Bob Kelljan, 1970)

Country (Richard Pearce, 1984)

Cowboys, The (Warner Bros, 1972)

Crash (David Cronenberg, 1996)

Crash (Paul Haggis, 2004)

Cries and Whispers (Ingmar Bergman, 1974)

Cronaca Familiare (Valerio Zurlini, Fr./Italy, 1962)

Crouching Tiger, Hidden Dragon (Ang Lee, 2000)

Crumb (Terry Zwigoff, 1994)

Cyclo (Tran Ahn Hung, Vietnam/Fr./Hong Kong, 1995)

Czlowiek Z Zelaza/Man of Iron (Andrzei Wadja, Poland, 1981)

Dances with Wolves (Kevin Costner, 1989)

Daniel (Sidney Lumet, 1983)

Dark Crystal, The (Jim Henson, Frank Oz, Gary Kurtz, 1983)

Dark Star (John Carpenter, 1974)

Darling (John Schlesinger, 1965)

Daughter from Danang (Gail Dolgin and Vincente Franco, 2002)

Daughters of the Dust (Julie Dash, 1992)

Dawn of the Dead (George Romero, 1979)

Day Mars Invaded Earth, The (Maury Dexter, 1962)

Day of the Dead (George Romero, 1985)

Day the Earth Stood Still, The (Robert Wise, 1951)

Day the World Ended, The (Roger Corman, 1956)

Dayereh (Jafar Panahi, Iran, Switzerland, Italy, 2000)

Daytrippers, The (Greg Motolla, 1996)

Dead (John Huston, 1987)

Dead Man (Jim Jarmusch, 1995)

Dead Man Walking (Tim Robbins, 1995)

Dead Ringers (David Cronenberg, 1988)

Deadly Blessing (Wes Craven, 1981)

Death Race 2000 (Paul Bartel, 1975)

Death Wish (Michael Winner, 1974)

Deep Throat (Gerard Damiano, 1972)

Deer Hunter, The (Michael Cimino, 1977)

Deliverance (John Boorman, 1972)

Dementia 13 (Francis Ford Coppola, 1962)

Den Goda Viljan/Good Intentions (Bille August, Sweden, 1992)

Deserto Rosso (Michelangelo Antonioni, 1964)

Desperately Seeking Susan (Susan Seidelman, 1985)

Destination Inner Space (Francis D. Lyon, 1967)

Destination Moon (Irving Pichel, 1950)

Detective, The (Gordon Douglas, 1968)

Devil in Miss Jones, The (Gerard Damiano, 1973)

Diaboliques, Les (Henri George Clouzot, France, 1954)

Dial M for Murder (Alfred Hitchcock, 1954)

Diamonds are Forever (Guy Hamilton, UK, 1971)

Die Artisten in der Zirkuskuppel: ratlos (Alexander Kluge, W. Germany, 1968)

Die Blechtrommel (Völker Schlondorff, W. Ger./Fr./Poland/Yugo., 1979)

Die Hard (John McTiernan, 1988)

Die Hard 2 (Renny Harlin, 1990)

Die Hard with a Vengeance (John McTiernan, 1995)

Dim Sum (Wayne Wang, 1985)

Dirty Dancing (Emile Ardolino, 1987)

Dirty Dozen, The (Robert Aldrich, 1967)

Dirty Harry (Don Siegel, 1971)

Do Not Disturb (Ralph Levy, 1965)

Do the Right Thing (Spike Lee, 1989)

Doctor Dolittle (Richard Fleischer, 1967)

Doctor Zhivago (David Lean, 1965)

Dog Day Afternoon (Sidney Lumet, 1975)

Dolce Vita, La (Federico Fellini, Italy, 1960)

Dolemite (D'Urville Martin, 1975)

Don't Look Down (Larry Shaw, [TV] 1998)

Donnie Darko (Richard Kelly, 2001)

Down By Law (Jim Jarmusch, 1986)

Dr. Black, Mr. Hyde (William Crain, 1976)

Dr No (Terence Young, UK/USA, 1962)

Dr Strangelove (Stanley Kubrick, 1964)

Dressed to Kill (Brian De Palma, 1980)

Drive, He Said (Jack Nicholson, 1971)

Driving Miss Daisy (Bruce Beresford, 1989)

Drugstore Cowboy (Gus Van Sant, 1989)

Duel (Steven Spielberg, 1971, made-for-TV movie, with European theatrical release in 1972/3, and US theatrical release in 1983)

Duel in the Sun (King Vidor, 1946)

Earthquake (Mark Robson, 1974)

Easy Rider (Dennis Hopper, 1969)

Eat, Drink, Man, Woman (Ang Lee, 1994)

Ed Wood (Tim Burton, 1994)

Edward II (Derek Jarman, 1991)

El Cid (Anthony Mann, 1961)

El Dorado (Howard Hawks, 1967)

El Norte (Gregory Nava, 1984)

Election (Alexander Payne, 1999)

Electra Glide in Blue (James William Guercio, 1973)

Elephant (Gus Van Sant, 2003)

Elmer Gantry (Richard Brooks, 1960)

Emmanuelle (Just Jaeckin, France, 1974)

Empire of the Sun (Steven Spielberg, 1987)

Empire Strikes Back, The (George Lucas, 1980)

English Patient, The (Anthony Minghella, 1996)

Enough (Michael Apted, 2002)

Enter the Dragon (Warner, 1973)

Eraserhead (David Lynch, 1977)

Erin Brockovich (Steven Soderbergh, 2000)

Escape from New York (John Carpenter, 1981)

Escape from the Planet of the Apes (Don Taylor, 1971)

E.T. – The Extraterrestrial (Steven Spielberg, 1982)

Every Which Way But Loose (James Fargo, 1978)

Everybody Says I Love You (Woody Allen, 1996)

Everything Relative (Sharon Pollack, 1997)

Everything You Always Wanted to Know About Sex (Woody Allen, 1972)

Evil Dead, The (Sam Raimi, 1982)

Evita (Alan Parker, 1996)

Excalibur (John Boorman, 1981)

Exodus (Otto Preminger, 1960)

Exorcist, The (William Friedkin, 1973)

Faces (John Cassavetes, 1968)

Faculty, The (Robert Rodriguez, 1998)

Fahrenheit 9/11 (Michael Moore, 2004)

Fail Safe (Sidney Lumet, 1964)

Fall of the House of Usher, The (Roger Corman, 1960)

Fall of the Roman Empire, The (Anthony Mann, 1964)

Fallen (Gregory Hoblit, 1997)

Fantasia (James Algar and Samuel Armstrong, 1940)

Far From Heaven (Todd Haynes, 2002)

Fargo (Joel Coen, 1996)

Farm, The (Jonathan Stack and Liz Garbus, 1998)

Fast and Furious, The (Rob Cohen, 2001)

Festen (Thomas Vinterberg, Denmark, 1998)

Fiddler on the Roof (Norman Jewison, 1971)

Fight Club (David Fincher, 1999)

Final Fantasy (Hironobu Sakaguchi, 2001)

Finding Forrester (Gus Van Sant, 2000)

Finding Nemo (Andrew Stanton and Lee Unkridge, 2003)

First Blood (Ted Kotcheff, 1982)

First Men in the Moon, The (Nathan Juran, 1964)

First Name Carmen/Prénom Carmen (Jean-Luc Godard, France, 1983)

Fish Called Wanda, A (Charles Crichton, USA/GB, 1988)

Fisher King, The (Terry Gilliam, 1991)

Fistful of Dollars, A (Sergio Leone, 1964)

Fists of Fury (Wei Lo, Hong Kong, 1971)

Fitzcarraldo (Werner Herzog, 1982)

Five Easy Pieces (Bob Rafelson, 1970)

Flashdance (Adrian Lyne, 1983)

Flash Gordon (Frederick Stefani, 1936)

Flash Gordon (Mike Hodges, 1980 remake)

Flesh (Paul Morrissey, 1968)

Fly, The (David Cronenberg, 1986)

Footloose (Herbert Ross, 1984)

For a Few Dollars More (Sergio Leone, 1964)

For All Mankind (Al Reinert, 1989)

Forbidden Planet (Fred M. Wilcox, 1956)

Forrest Gump (Robert Zemeckis, 1994)

Fortune Cookie, The (Billy Wilder, 1966)

Four Daughters (Michael Curtiz, 1938)

Four Horsemen of the Apocalypse, The (Vincente Minnelli, 1962)

Four Mothers (William Keighley, 1941)

Four Wives (Michael Curtiz, 1939)

Foxy Brown (Jack Hill, 1974)

Frankenstein Meets the Wolf Man (Roy William Neill, 1943)

Frankenstein Unbound (Roger Corman, 1989)

Frathouse (Todd Phillips and Andrew Gurland, 1998)

Freddy's Dead: The Final Nightmare (Rachel Talalay, 1991)

Freedom on My Mind (Connie Field and Marilyn Mulford, 1994)

French Connection, The (William Friedkin, 1971)

French Connection II, The (John Frankenheimer, 1975)

Friday the 13th (Sean S. Cunningham, 1980)

Friday the 13th: The Final Chapter (Joseph Zito, 1984)

Friday the 13th, Part V: A New Beginning (Danny Steinmann, 1985)

Fucking Åmal/Show Me Love (Lukas Moodysson, 1998)

Fugitive, The (Andrew Davis, 1993)

Full Frontal (Steven Soderbergh, 2002)

Fun (Rafael Zelinski, US/Canada, 1994)

Funny Girl (William Wyler, 1968)

Funny Lady (Herbert Ross, 1975)

Further Adventures of the Wilderness Family, The (Frank Zuniga, 1977)

Fuses (Carolee Schneeman, 1967)

Gandhi (Richard Attenborough, US/India/ GB, 1982)

Gardens of Stone (Francis Ford Coppola, 1987)

Gas Food Lodging (Allison Anders, 1992)

Gas-s-s-s! (Roger Corman, 1971)

Gazon Maudit (Josephine Balasko, 1995)

German Sisters, The/Die Bleierne Zeit (Margarethe von Trotta, German Federal Republic, 1981)

Gerry (Gus Van Sant, 2001)

Getaway, The (Sam Peckinpah, 1972)

Getting Straight (Richard Rush, 1970)

Ghost (Jerry Zucker, 1990)

Ghostbusters (Ivan Reitman, 1984)

Ghostbusters II (Ivan Reitman, 1989)

Ghost Dog: Way of the Samurai (Jim Jarmusch, 1999)

Ghost World (Terry Zwigoff, 2001)

Ghosts of Mars (John Carpenter, 2001)

G.I. Jane (Ridley Scott, 1997)

Girl, Interrupted (James Mangold, 1999)

Girlfight (Karyn Kusama, 2000)

Girls Like Us (Jane Wagner and Tina DiFeliciantonio, 1997)

Gladiator (Ridley Scott, 2000)

Glass Shield, The (Charles Burnett, 1995)

Glen and Randa (Jim McBride, 1971)

Gloria (John Cassavetes, 1980)

Glory (Edward Zwick, 1989)

Go (Doug Liman, 1999)

Go Fish (Rose Troche, 1994)

Go Tell the Spartans (Ted Post, 1978)

Go-Between, The (Joseph Losey, 1970)

Godfather, The (Francis Ford Coppola, 1972)

Godfather, Part II, The (Francis Ford Coppola, 1974)

Gone with the Wind (Victor Fleming, 1939)

Good Fellas (Martin Scorsese, 1990)

Good Intentions/Den Goda Viljan (Bille August, Sweden, 1992)

Good Morning, Vietnam (Barry Levinson, 1987)

Good Will Hunting (Gus Van Sant, 1997)

Good, the Bad, and the Ugly, The (Sergio Leone, 1966)

Goodbye, Children/Au revoir les enfants (Louis Malle, France/FDR, 1987)

Goodbye Girl, The (Herbert Ross, 1977)

Goodbye Mr Chips (Herbert Ross, 1969)

Goonies, The (Richard Donner, 1985)

Gosford Park (Robert Altman, 2001)

Gracie Allen Murder Case, The (Alfred E. Green, 1939)

Graduate, The (Mike Nichols, 1967)

Grapes of Wrath, The (John Ford, 1940)

Gray's Anatomy (Steven Soderbergh, 1996)

Grease (Randal Kleiser, Paramount, 1978)

Grease 2 (Patricia Birch, 1982)

Great Race, The (Blake Edwards, 1965)

Great Texas Dynamite Chase, The (Michael Pressman, 1976)

Greatest Story Ever Told, The (George Stevens, 1965)

Green Berets, The (Ray Kellogg and John Wayne, 1968)

Green Ray, The/Le rayon vert (Eric Rohmer, France, 1986)

Greetings (Brian De Palma, 1968)

Gremlins (Joe Dante, 1984)

Guess Who's Coming to Dinner (Stanley Kramer, 1967)

Guns of Navarone, The (J. Lee Thompson, 1961)

H-2 Worker (Stephanie Black, 1990)

Habit (Larry Fessenden, 1997)

Hair (Milos Forman, 1979)

Halloween (John Carpenter, 1978)

Halloween H20: Twenty Years After (Steve Miner, 1998)

Hamburger Hill (John Irvin, 1987)

Hana-bi (Takeshi Kitano, Japan, 1997)

Hang 'em High (Clint Eastwood, 1967)

Hannah and Her Sisters (Woody Allen, 1986)

Hannibal (Ridley Scott, 2001)

Hanoi Hilton, The (Lionel Chetwynd, 1987)

Happiest Millionaire, The (Norman Tokar, 1967)

Happiness (Todd Solondz, 1998)

Harry and Tonto (Paul Mazursky, 1974)

Harry Potter and the Sorcerer's Stone (Chris Columbus, 2001)

Hatari! (Hiward Hawks, 1962)

Haunted Palace, The (Roger Corman, 1963)

Hawaii (George Roy Hill, 1966)

Head (Bob Rafelson, 1968)

Hearts and Minds (Peter Davis, BBS, 1974)

Heat (Paul Morrissey, 1973)

Heat and Sunlight (Rob Nilsson, 1987)

Heaven's Gate (Michael Cimino, 1980)

Heavenly Creatures (Peter Jackson, NZ, 1994)

Hell Up in Harlem (Larry Cohen, 1973)

Hell's Angels on Wheels (Richard Rush, 1967)

Hello, Dolly! (Gene Kelly, 1969)

Hemingway's Adventures of a Young Man (Martin Ritt, 1962)

Henry . . . Portrait of a Serial Killer (John McNaughton, 1988)

Henry Fool (Hal Hartley, 1998)

Herbie Rides Again (Robert Stevenson, 1974)

Hercules/Le Fatiche di Ercole (Pietro Francesci, Italy/Spain, 1958)

Hercules in New York (Arthur Allan Siedelman, 1970)

Hercules in the Haunted World (Mario Bava, 1961)

Hercules Unchained (Pietro Francisci, 1959)

Hi, Mom! (Brian De Palma, 1970)

High and the Mighty, The (William A. Wellman, 1954)

High Art (Lisa Cholodenko, 1998)

High Fidelity (Stephen Frears, 2000)

High Noon (Fred Zinneman, 1952)

High Plains Drifter (Clint Eastwood, 1973)

Hills Have Eyes, The (Wes Craven, 1978)

Hired Hand, The (Peter Fonda, 1971)

Hireling, The (Alan Bridges, 1973)

Hollow Reed (Angela Pope, 1997)

Hollywood Boulevard (Joe Dante, 1976)

Hombre (Martin Ritt, 1967)

Home Alone (Chris Columbus, 1990)

Home Alone 2: Lost in New York (Chris Columbus, 1992)

Home from the Hill (Vincente Minnelli, 1960)

Homicidal (William Castle, 1960)

Hook (Steven Spielberg, 1991)

Hotel (Richard Quine, 1967)

Hotel (Mike Figgis, 2001)

Hour and Times, The (Christopher Munch, 1992)

Hours, The (Stephen Daldry, 2002)

House of Dark Shadows (Dan Curtis, 1970)

How the Grinch Stole Christmas (Ron Howard, 2000)

How the West Was Won (John Ford and Henry Hathaway, 1962)

Howards End (James Ivory, GB/Japan, 1992)

Howling, The (Joe Dante, 1981)

Hud (Martin Ritt, 1963)

Hulk (Ang Lee, 2003)

Hurricane, The (John Ford, 1937)

Husbands (John Cassavetes, 1970),

Hustler, The (Robert Rossen, 1961)

I Am Curious: Yellow (Vilgot Sjöman, Sweden, 1969)

I Know What You Did Last Summer (Jim Gillespie, 1997)

I Love You, Alice B. Toklas (Hy Averback, 1968)

Ice Station Zebra (John Sturges, 1968)

Ice Storm, The (Ang Lee, 1997)

Ideal Husband, An (Oliver Parker, 1999)

If (Lindsay Anderson, 1968)

Il Caso Matei (Francesco Rosi, Italy, 1972)

Il Gattopardo (Luchino Visconti, Italy/ FR, 1963)

Images (Robert Altman, 1972)

Importance of Being Earnest, The (Oliver Parker, 2002)

In and Out (Frank Oz, 1997)

In Cold Blood (Richard Brooks, 1967)

In Old Chicago (Henry King, 1937)

In Search of Noah's Ark (James L. Conway, 1976)

In the Bedroom (Todd Field, 2001)

In the Company of Men (Neil LaBute, 1997)

In the Heat of the Night (Norman Jewison, 1967)

In the Soup (Alexandre Rockwell, 1992)

Incredibles, The (Brad Bird, 2004)

Incredibly True Adventures of Two Girls in Love, The (Maria Maggenti, 1995)

Independence Day (Roland Emmerich, 1996)

Indiana Jones and the Last Crusade (Steven Spielberg, 1989)

Indiana Jones and the Temple of Doom (Steven Spielberg, 1984)

Internal Affairs (Mike Figgis, 1990)

Interview with a Vampire (Neil Jordan, 1994)

Intruder, The (Roger Corman, 1961)

Invasion of the Body Snatchers (Philip Kaufman, 1978, Abel Ferrara, 1993)

Invasion USA. (Joseph Zito, 1985)

Invocation of My Demon Brother (Kenneth Anger, 1969)

Iris (Richard Eyre, UK/USA, 2001)

Iron Eagle (Sidney J. Furie, 1986)

It Conquered the World (Roger Corman, 1956)

It's Alive (Larry Cohen, 1975)

Ivanovo Detstvo (Andrej Tarkovskij, 1962)

Jason and the Argonauts (Don Chaffey, 1963)

Jason X (James Isaac, 2001)

Jaws (Steven Spielberg, 1975)

Jaws 2 (Jeannot Szwarc, 1978)

Jayne Mansfield Story, The (Dick Lowry, 1980)

Jeffrey (Christopher Ashley, 1995)

Jeremiah Johnson (Sydney Pollack, 1972)

Jerk, The (Carl Reiner, 1979)

Jerry Maguire (Cameron Crowe, 1996)

Jesus Christ Superstar (Norman Jewison, 1973)

Jingle All the Way (Brian Levant, 1996)

Joe (John G. Avildsen, 1970)

Joe Kidd (John Sturges, 1972)

Judgement at Nuremberg (Stanley Kremer, 1961)

Julia (Fred Zinnemann, 1977)

Jungle Book, The (Wolfgang Reithermann, 1967)

Junior Bonner (Sam Peckinpah, 1972)

Jurassic Park (Steven Spielberg, 1993)

Jurassic Park: The Lost World (Steven Spielberg, 1997)

K-19: The Widowmaker (Kathryn Bigelow, 2002)

Kafka (Steven Soderbergh, 1991)

Kagemusha/Shadow of the Samurai (Akira Kurosawa, Japan, 1980)

Khush (Pratibha Parmar, 1991)

Kids (Larry Clark, 1995)

Kill Bill: Vol 1 (Quentin Tarantino, 2003)

Kill Bill: Vol 2 (Quentin Tarantino, 2004)

Killer of Sheep (Charles Burnett, 1977)

Kill-Off, The (Maggie Greenwald, 1990)

Kindergarten Cop (Ivan Reitman, 1990)

King and I, The (Walter Lang, 1956)

King Kong (John Guillermin, 1976)

King of Marvin Gardens, The (Bob Rafelson, 1972)

King of New York (Abel Ferrara, 1990)

King of the Hill (Steven Soderbergh, 1993)

Kingdom of Heaven (Ridley Scott, 2005)

Kiss Me Guido (Tony Vitale, 1997)

Kiss of the Spider Woman (Hector Babenco, Brazil/USA, 1985)

Kissing Jessica Stein (Charles Herman-Wurmfeld, 2002)

Klute (Alan J. Pakula, 1971)

Knack ... And How to Get It, The (Richard Lester, 1965)

Krakatoa, East of Java (Bernard L. Kowalski, 1969)

Kramer vs. Kramer (Robert Benton, 1979)

Krull (Peter Yates, 1983)

Kustom Kar Kommandos (Kenneth Anger, 1966)

Labyrinth (Jim Henson, 1986)

L.A. Confidential (Curtis Hanson, 1997)

Lady Sings the Blues (Sidney J. Furie, 1972)

Lara Croft: Tomb Raider (Simon West, 2001)

Last Chants for a Slow Dance (Jon Jost, 1977)

Last Days (Gus Van Sant, 2005)

Last Detail, The (Hal Ashby, 1973)

Last Emperor, The (Bernardo Bertolucci, China/Italy, 1987)

Last House on the Left, The (Wes Craven, 1972)

Last Movie, The (Dennis Hopper, 1971)

Last Picture Show, The (Peter Bogdanovich, 1971)

Last Seduction, The (John Dahl, 1994)

Last Tango in Paris (Bernardo Bertolucci, Italy/France, 1973)

Last Temptation of Christ, The (Martin Scorsese, 1988)

Last Year in Marienbad/L'année dernière à Marienbad (Alain Resnais, France/Italy, 1961)

Latino (Haskell Wexler, 1985)

Lawrence of Arabia (David Lean, 1962)

Leaving Las Vegas (Mike Figgis, 1995)

Legend (Ridley Scott, 1985)

Legend of the Holy Drinker, The/La leggenda del santo bevitore (Ermanno Olmi, Italy/France, 1988)

Let's Do It Again (Sidney Poitier, 1975)

L.I.E. (Michael Cuesta, 2001)

Liebestraum (Mike Figgis, 1991)

Life and Times of Grizzly Adams, The (Richard Freidenberg, 1974)

Life Aquatic with Steve Zissou, The (Wes Anderson, 2004)

Life Is Beautiful (Roberto Benigni, Italy, 1997)

Lilies of the Field (Ralph Nelson, 1963)

Limey, The (Steven Soderbergh, 1999)

Lion in Winter, The (Anthony Harvey, 1968)

Lion King, The (Roger Allers and Rob Minkoff, 1994)

Little Big Man (Arthur Penn, National General, 1970)

Little Caesar (Mervyn LeRoy, 1931)

Little Mermaid, The (Ron Clements and John Musker, 1989)

Little Night Music, A (Harold Prince, 1977)

Little Nikita (Richard Benjamin, 1988)

Little Shop of Horrors, The (Roger Corman, 1960)

Living End, The (Gregg Araki, 1992)

Logan's Run (Michael Anderson, 1976)

Lolita (Stanley Kubrick, 1962)

Lonely Are the Brave (David Miller, 1962)

Long Goodbye, The (Robert Altman, 1973)

Long Night's Journey into Day (Frances Reid and Deborah Hoffman, 2000)

Longest Day, The (Ken Annakin and Andrew Marton, 1962)

Lord of the Rings: Fellowship of the Ring, The (Peter Jackson, 2001)

Lord of the Rings: The Return of the King, The (Peter Jackson, 2003)

Losing Chase (Kevin Bacon, 1996)

Loss of Sexual Innocence, The (Mike Figgis, 1999)

Lost Horizon (Charles Jarrott, 1973)

Love Bug, The (Robert Stevenson, 1969)

Love Story (Arthur Hiller, 1970)

Love Streams (John Cassavetes, 1983)

Loveless, The (Kathryn Bigelow and Monty Montgomery, 1982)

Lucifer Rising (Kenneth Anger, 1973)

Ma nuit chez Maud/My Night at Maud's (Eric Rohmer, France, 1969)

Mack, The (Michael Campus, 1973)

Madigan (Don Siegel, 1968)

Magdalene Sisters, The (Peter Mullan, 2002)

Magnolia (P.T. Anderson, 1999)

Magnum Force (Ted Post, 1973)

Mala Noche (Gus Van Sant, 1986)

Mame (Gene Saks, 1974)

Man and a Woman, A/Une Homme et Une Femme (Claude Lelouch, France, 1966)

Man Called Horse, A (Elliot Silverstein, 1970)

Man for All Seasons, A (Fred Zinnemann, 1966)

Man of Iron/Czlowiek Z Zelaza (Andrzei Wadja, Poland, 1981)

Man of La Mancha (Arthur Hiller, 1972)

Man Who Fell to Earth, The (Nicolas Roeg, 1976)

Man Who Knew Too Much, The (Alfred Hitchcock, 1956)

Man Who Shot Liberty Valance, The (John Ford, 1962)

Man Who Wasn't There, The (Joel Coen, 2001)

Manchurian Candidate, The (John Frankenheimer, 1961)

Manhunter (Michael Mann, 1986)

Mani Sulla Città, Le (Francesco Rosi, FRANCE/Italy, 1963)

Mark of Zorro, The (Fred Niblo, 1920)

Marnie (Alfred Hitchcock, 1964)

Mars Attacks! (Tim Burton, 1996)

Martin (George Romero, 1978)

Mary Poppins (Robert Stevenson, 1964)

M*A*S*H (Robert Altman, 1971)

Masque of the Red Death (Roger Corman, 1964)

Matewan (John Sayles, 1987)

Matrix, The (Andy and Larry Wachowski, 1999)

Matrix Reloaded, The (Andy and Larry Wachowski, 2003)

Matrix Revolutions, The (Andy and Larry Wachowski, 2003)

McCabe and Mrs Miller (Robert Altman, 1971)

Mean Machine, The (Robert Aldrich, 1974)

Mean Streets (Martin Scorsese, 1973)

Medium Cool (Haskell Wexler, 1969)

Meet the Fockers (Jay Roach, 2004)

Melvin and Howard (Jonathan Demme, 1980)

Men in Black (Barry Sonnenfeld, 1997)

Men with Guns (John Sayles, 1997)

Metropolis (Fritz Lang, 1927)

Metropolitan (Whit Stillman, 1990)

Mi Vida Loca (Allison Anders, 1994)

Mia Eoniotita Ke Mia Mera (Theo Angelopoulos, France/Italy/Greece, 1998)

Michael Collins (Neil Jordan, 1996)

Mickey One (Arthur Penn, 1965)

Midnight Cowboy (John Schlesinger, 1969)

Midway (Jack Smight, 1976)

Mighty Aphrodite (Woody Allen, 1995)

Miniver Story, The (H.C. Potter, 1950)

Minnie and Moskowitz (John Cassavetes, 1971)

Minority Report (Steven Spielberg, 2002)

Miracle Worker, The (Arthur Penn, 1962)

Mirror has Two Faces, The (Barbra Streisand, 1996)

Misery (Rob Reiner, 1990)

Misfits, The (John Huston, 1961)

Mishima (Paul Schrader, 1985)

Miss Congeniality (Donald Petrie, 2000)

Miss Julie (Mike Figgis, 1999)

Missing (Costa-Gavras, 1981)

Mission, The (Roland Joffé, 1986)

Mission Impossible (Brian De Palma, 1996)

Mission Impossible 2 (John Woo, 2000)

Mission to Mars (Brian De Palma, 2000)

Missouri Breaks, The (Arthur Penn, 1976)

Monster (Patty Jenkins, 2003)

Monster's Ball (Marc Forster, 2001)

Moonraker (Lewis Gilbert, 1979)

Monsoon Wedding (Mira Nair, 2001)

Moonstruck (Norman Jewison, 1987)

Moulin Rouge (Baz Luhrmann, 2001)

Mr Death (Errol Morris, 1999)

Mr Jones (Mike Figgis, 1993)

Mrs. Doubtfire (Chris Columbus, 1993)

Mrs Miniver (William Wyler, 1942)

Mummy, The (Stephen Sommers, 1999)

Mummy Returns, The (Stephen Sommers, 2001)

Mummy's Hand, The (Christy Cabanne, 1940)

Mummy's Tomb, The (Harold Young, 1942)

Murder on the Orient Express (Sidney Lumet, 1974)

My Best Friend's Wedding (P.J. Hogan, 1997)

My Brother's Wedding (Charles Burnett, 1983)

My Cousin Vinny (Jonathan Lynn, 1992)

My Fair Lady (George Cukor, 1964)

My Left Foot (Jim Sheridan, GB/Ireland, 1989)

My Own Private Idaho (Gus Van Sant, 1991)

Mystery Train (Jim Jarmusch, 1989)

Mystic River (Clint Eastwood, 2003)

Naked Kiss, The (Samuel Fuller, 1964)

Narayama-Bushi-Ko/The Ballad of Naramaya (Shohei Imamura, Japan, 1983)

Nashville (Robert Altman, 1975)

National Lampoon's Animal House (John Landis, 1978)

Near Dark (Kathryn Bigelow, 1987)

Network (Sidney Lumet, 1976)

New Nightmare (Wes Craven, 1994)

New York, New York (Martin Scorsese, 1977)

Next Best Thing, The (John Schlesinger, 2000)

Nicholas and Alexandra (Franklin J. Schaffner, 1971)

Night Moves (Arthur Penn, 1975)

Night of the Living Dead (George A. Romero, 1968)

Night on Earth (Jim Jarmusch, 1991)

Nightmare on Elm Street, A (Wes Craven, 1984)

Nightmare on Elm Street, Part 2: Freddy's Revenge, A (Jack Scholder, 1985)

Nightmare on Elm Street 3: Dream Warriors, A (Chuck Russell, 1987)

Nightmare on Elm Street 4: The Dream Master, A (Renny Harlin, 1988)

Nightmare on Elm Street: The Dream Child, A (Stephen Hopkins, 1989)

No Highway in the Sky (Henry Koster, 1951)

No Way Out (Roger Donaldson,1987)

Norma Rae (Martin Ritt, 1979)

North by Northwest (Alfred Hitchcock, 1959)

Not One Less (Zhang Yimou, China, 1999)

Nothing But a Man (Michael Roemer 1964)

Now, Voyager (Irving Rapper, 1942)

O Pagador de Promessas (Anselmo Duarte, Brazil/ Portugal, 1962)

Object of my Affection, The (Nicholas Hytner, 1998)

Ocean's Eleven (Steven Soderbergh, 2002)

Office Space (Mike Judge, 1999)

Officer and a Gentleman, An (Taylor Hackford, 1981)

Old School (Todd Phillips, 2003)

Oliver! (Carol Reed, 1968)

Omega Man (Boris Sagal, 1971)

Omen, The (Richard Donner, 1976)

On a Clear Day You Can See Forever (Vincente Minnelli, 1970)

On Golden Pond (Mark Rydell, 1981)

On the Beach (Stanley Kramer, 1959)

On the Waterfront (Elia Kazan, 1953)

One Flew Over the Cuckoo's Nest (Milos Forman, 1975)

One from the Heart (Francis Ford Coppola, 1982)

One Hundred and One Dalmations (Clyde Geronomi and Hamilton Luske, 1961)

One Night Stand (Mike Figgis, 1997)

Ordinary People (Robert Redford, 1980)

Otac Na Sulzbenom Putu/When Father Was Away on Business (Emir Kusturica, Yugoslavia, 1984)

Other Side of the Mountain, The (Larry Peerce, 1975)

Our Man Flint (Daniel Mann, 1966)

Out of Sight (Steven Soderbergh, 1998)

Outlaw Josey Wales, The (Clint Eastwood, 1976)

Out-of-Towners, The (Arthur Hiller,1970)

Padre Padrone (Vittorio Taviani, Italy, 1977)

Paint Your Wagon (Joshua Logan, 1969)

Pale Rider (Clint Eastwood, 1985)

Palindromes (Todd Solondz, 2004)

Paper Chase, The (James Bridges, 1973)

Paper Moon (Peter Bogdanovich, 1973)

Papillon (Franklin J. Schaffner, 1973)

Parallax View, The (Alan J. Pakula, 1974)

Parapluies du Cherbourg, Les (Jacques Demy, France/W. Germany, 1964)

Parent Trap, The (David Swift, 1961)

Paris Is Burning (Jennie Livingston, US/GB, 1990)

Paris, Texas (Wim Wenders, 1984)

Passage du Rhin, Le (André Cayatt, IT/FR/ W. Germany, 1960)

Passion Fish (John Sayles, 1992)

Pat Garrett and Billy the Kid (Sam Peckinpah, 1973)

Patch of Blue, A (Gy Green, 1965)

Patton (Franklin J. Schaffner, 1970)

Pawnbroker, The (Sidney Lumet, 1964)

Peeping Tom (Michael Powell, GB, 1960)

Peggy Sue Got Married (Francis Ford Coppola, 1986)

Pelle Erobreren/Pelle the Conqueror (Bille August, Denmark/Sweden, 1987)

People Under the Stairs, The (Wes Craven, 1991)

Personal Velocity: Three Portraits (Rebecca Miller, 2002)

Phantom Menace, Star Wars Episode 1, The (George Lucas, 1999)

Phase IV (Saul Bass, 1975)

Philadelphia (Jonathan Demme, 1993)

Pianist, The (Roman Polanski, 2002)

Piano, The (Jane Campion, Australia/France, 1993)

Piranha (Joe Dante, 1978)

Pirates of the Caribbean: The Curse of the Black Pearl (Gore Verbinski, 2003)

Places in the Heart (Robert Benton, 1984)

Planet of the Apes (Franklin J. Schaffner, 1968)

Planet of the Apes (Tim Burton, 2001)

Platoon (Oliver Stone, 1986)

Play Misty for Me (Clint Eastwood, 1971)

Plaza Suite (Arthur Hiller, 1971)

Pleasantville (Gary Ross, 1998)

Pocahontas (Mike Gabriel and Eric Goldberg, 1995)

Point Break (Kathryn Bigelow, 1991)

Poison (Todd Haynes, 1991)

Pokemon (Michael Haigney and Kunihiko Yuhama, 1999)

Pollock (Ed Harris, 2000)

Portrait of Jason (Shirley Clarke, 1967)

Poseidon Adventure, The (Ronald Neame, 1972)

Predator 2 (Stephen Hopkins, 1990)

Premature Burial, The (Roger Corman, 1962)

Prime of Miss Jean Brodie, The (Ronald Neame, 1969)

Prince of Tides (Barbra Streisand, 1991)

Prisoner of Second Avenue, The (Melvin Frank, 1975)

Private Conversation (Christian Blackwood, 1985)

Prizzi's Honor (John Huston, 1985)

Psycho (Alfred Hitchcock, 1960)

Psycho (Gus Van Sant, 1998)

Psych-Out (Richard Rush, 1968)

Public Enemy, The (William A. Wellman, 1931)

Pulp Fiction (Quentin Tarantino, 1994)

Quiju da guansi/The Story of Qui Ju (Zhang Yimou, China/Hong Kong, 1992)

Rachel, Rachel (Paul Newman, 1968)

Raging Bull (Martin Scorsese, 1980)

Ragtime (Milos Forman, 1981)

Raiders of the Lost Ark (Steven Spielberg, 1981)

Rain Man (Barry Levinson, 1988)

Rain People, The (Francis Ford Coppola, 1969)

Rains Came, The (Clarence Brown, 1939)

Raise the Titanic (Jerry Jameson, 1980)

Rambo III (Peter MacDonald, 1988)

Raven, The (Roger Corman, 1963)

Re-Animator (Stuart Gordon, 1985)

Rear Window (Alfred Hitchcock, 1954)

Rebecca (Alfred Hitchcock, 1940)

Rebel Rousers (Martin B Cohen, 1967, released 1970)

Rebel Without a Cause (Nicholas Ray, 1955)

Red Dawn (John Milius, 1984)

Red Planet (Anthony Hoffman, 2000)

Red Rock West (John Dahl, 1994)

Reds (Warren Beatty, 1981)

Report (Bruce Conner, 1963–67)

Reservoir Dogs (Quentin Tarantino, 1992)

Resident Evil (Paul W.S. Anderson, 2002)

Return of Frank James, The (Fritz Lang, 1940)

Return of the Cisco Kid (Herbert I. Leeds, 1939)

Return of the Jedi (George Lucas, 1983)

Return of the Pink Panther, The (Blake Edwards, 1975)

Return of the Secaucus Seven, The (John Sayles, 1980)

Revenge of the Sith (George Lucas, 2005)

Reversal of Fortune (Barbet Schroeder, 1990)

Ride the High Country (Sam Peckinpah, 1962)

Right Stuff, The (Phillip Kaufman, 1983)

Risky Business (Paul Brickman, 1983)

River, The (Mark Rydell, 1984)

River's Edge (Tim Hunter, 1986)

Road, The/Yol (Serif Gören, Switzerland, 1982)

Road Back, The (James Whale, 1937)

Robin Hood (Wolfgang Reitherman, 1973)

RoboCop (Paul Verhoeven, 1987)

Rock, The (Michael Bay, 1996)

Rocky (John G. Avildsen, 1976)

Rocky II (Sylvester Stallone, 1979)

Rocky IV (Sylvester Stallone, 1985)

Rocky Horror Picture Show, The (Jim Sharman, 1975)

Rok Spokojnego Slonca/The Year of the Quiet Sun (Krzysztof Zanussi, Poland/USA/GFR, 1984)

Rollerball (Norman Jewison, 1976)

Rollercoaster (James Goldstone, 1977)

Romeo and Juliet (Franco Zeffirelli, 1968)

Romeo Must Die (Andrzej Bartkowiak, 2000)

Romero (John Duigan, 1989)

Rooster Cogburn (Stuart Millar, 1975)

Rope (Alfred Hitchcock, 1948)

Rosemary's Baby (Roman Polanski, 1968)

Rosencrantz and Guildenstern Are Dead (Tom Stoppard, 1990)

Rosetta (Jean Pierre and Luc Dardenne, 1999)

Royal Tenenbaums, The (Wes Anderson, 2001)

R.S.V.P (Laurie Lynd, 1991)

Ruby in Paradise (Victor Nunez, 1993)

Run Lola Run (Tom Tykwer, 1998)

Running on Empty (Sidney Lumet, 1988)

Rushmore (Wes Anderson, 1998)

Ryan's Daughter (David Lean, 1970)

Safe (Todd Haynes, 1995)

Safe Place, A (Henry Jaglom, 1971)

Saint Strikes Back, The (John Farrow, 1939)

Salt of the Earth (Herbert J. Biberman, 1954)

Salvador (Oliver Stone, 1986)

San Francisco (W.S. Van Dyke, 1936)

Sand Pebbles, The (Robert Wise, 1966)

Sandpiper, The (Vincente Minnelli, 1965)

Sans toit ni loi/Vagabond (Agnès Varda, France, 1985)

Saturday Night Fever (John Badham, 1977)

Savage Eye, The (Joseph Strick, Ben Maddow and Sidney Meyers, 1959)

Savage Innocents, The (Nicholas Ray, 1959)

Savage Seven, The (Richard Rush, 1968)

Save the Tiger (John G. Avildsen, 1973)

Saving Private Ryan (Steven Spielberg, 1998)

Scarecrow (Jerry Schatzberg, 1973)

Scarface (Brian De Palma, 1983)

Scent of a Woman (Martin Brest, 1992)

Schindler's List (Steven Spielberg, 1993)

Schizopolis (Steven Soderbergh, 1996)

Scorpion King, The (Chuck Russell, 2002)

Scream (Wes Craven, 1996)

Searchers, The (John Ford, 1956)

Secret Invasion, The (Roger Corman, 1964)

Secretary (Steven Shainberg, 2002)

Secrets and Lies (Mike Leigh, France/UK, 1996)

Serpico (Sidney Lumet, 1973)

Set It Off (F. Gary Gray, 1996)

Se7en (David Fincher, 1995)

sex, lies and videotape (Steven Soderbergh, 1989)

Sexual Freedom in Denmark (M.C. Von Hellen, Denmark, 1972)

Shadow of the Samurai/Kagemusha (Akira Kurosawa, Japan, 1980)

Shadows (John Cassavetes, 1959)

Shaft (Gordon Parks, 1971)

Shaft's Big Score (Gordon Parks, 1972)

Shakespeare in Love (John Madden, 1998)

Shampoo (Hal Ashby, 1975)

Shane (George Stevens, 1953)

She's Gotta Have It (Spike Lee, 1986)

Sheik, The (George Melford, 1921)

Sherman's March (Ross McElwee, 1985)

Shine (Scott Hicks, 1996)

Shining, The (Stanley Kubrick, 1980)

Shivers (David Cronenberg, 1976)

Shock Corridor (Samuel Fuller, 1963)

Shocker (Wes Craven, 1989)

Shooting, The (Monte Hellman, 1965)

Shootist, The (Don Siegel, 1976)

Short Cuts (Robert Altman, 1993)

Shot in the Dark, A (Blake Edwards, 1964)

Shrek (Andrew Adamson and Vicky Jenson, 2001)

Shrek 2 (Andrew Adamsom and Kelly Asbury, 2004)

Sideways (Alexander Payne, 2004)

Signore e Signori (Pietro Germi, Italy/ France, 1965)

Silence of the Lambs, The (Jonathan Demme, 1991)

Silent Running (Douglas Trumbull, 1972)

Silverlake Life: The View From Here (Thomas H. Joslin and Peter Friedman, 1993)

Simple Men (Hal Hartley, 1992)

Sister my Sister (Nancy Meckler, UK, 1994)

Sisters (Brian De Palma, 1973)

Sixth Sense, The (M. Night Shyamalan, 1999)

Skyjacked (John Guillermin, 1972)

Slacker (Richard Linklater, 1991)

Slam (Marc Levin, 1998)

Slamdance (Wayne Wang, 1987)

Slaughterhouse-Five (George Roy Hill, 1972)

Sleeper (Woody Allen, 1973)

Slow Moves (Jon Jost, 1983)

Smithereens (Susan Seidelman, 1982)

Smokey and the Bandit (Hal Needham, 1977)

Smooth Talk (Joyce Chopra, 1985)

Snow White and the Seven Dwarfs (Disney, 1937)

Solaris (Steven Soderbergh, 2002)

Soldier Blue (Ralph Nelson, 1970)

Son of Flubber (Robert Stevenson, 1963)

Son of Kong (Ernest B. Schoedsack, 1933)

Son of Paleface (Frank Tashlin, 1952)

Son of the Sheik (George Fitzmaurice, 1926)

Son's Room, The /La Stanza del Figlio (Nanni Moretti, Italy/France, 2001)

Sophie's Choice (Alan J. Pakula, 1982)

Sorcerer/Wages of Fear (William Friedkin, 1977)

Sorority Girl (Roger Corman, 1957)

Sound of Music, The (Robert Wise, 1965)

Sounder (Martin Ritt, 1972)

Sous le Soleil de Satan/Under Satan's Sun (Maurice Pialat, France, 1987)

South Pacific (Joshua Logan, 1958)

Southern Comfort (Kate Davis, 2001)

Soylent Green (Richard Fleischer, 1973)

Spartacus (Stanley Kubrick, 1960)

Speed (Jan de Bont, 1994)

Speed 2: Cruise Control (Jan de Bont, 1997)

Spider-Man (Sam Raimi, 2002)

Spider-Man 2 (Sam Raimi, 2004)

Splash (Ron Howard, 1984)

Splendor in the Grass (Elia Kazan, 1961)

Spook Who Sat By the Door, The (Ivan Dixon, 1973)

St Valentine's Day Massacre, The (Roger Corman, 1967)

Stagecoach (John Ford, 1939)

Star! (Robert Wise, 1968)

Star is Born, A (Frank Pierson, 1976)

Star Trek: The Motion Picture (Robert Wise, 1979)

Star Trek II: The Wrath of Khan (Nicholas Meyer, 1982)

Star Wars (George Lucas, 1977)

Star Wars Episode 1: The Phantom Menace (George Lucas, 1999)

Star Wars Episode II: Attack of the Clones (George Lucas, 2002)

State Fair (José Ferrer, 1962)

State of Things, The/Der Stand der Dinge (Wim Wenders, USA/Portugal/FDR, 1982)

Stella Dallas (King Vidor, 1937)

Stepfather, The (Joseph Ruben, 1986)

Sting, The (George Roy Hill, 1972)

Stolen Kisses/Baisers volés (François Truffaut, France, 1968)

Story of Adèle H, The (François Truffaut, France, 1975)

Story of Qui Ju, The/Quiju da guansi (Zhang Yimou, China/Hong Kong, 1992)

Story of Ruth, The (Henry Koster, 1960)

Storytelling (Todd Solondz, 2001)

Strange Days (Kathryn Bigelow, 1995)

Stranger Than Paradise (Jim Jarmusch, 1984)

Straw Dogs (Sam Peckinpah, 1971)

Strawberry Statement, The (Stuart Hagmann, 1970)

Student Nurses, The (Stephanie Rothman, 1970)

Subject Was Roses, The (Ulu Grosbard, 1968)

Sugarland Express, The (Steven Spielberg, 1974)

Summer of '42 (Robert Mulligan, 1971)

Sunday (Jonathan Nossiter, 1997)

Sunshine Boys, The (Herbert Ross, 1975)

Super Fly (Gordon Parks Jr., 1972)

Superman (Richard Donner, 1978)

Superman II (Richard Lester, 1980)

Sure Fire (Jon Jost, 1990)

Suture (Scott McGehee and David Siegel, 1993)

Swarm, The (Irwin Allen, 1978)

Sweet Bird of Youth (Richard Brooks, 1962)

Sweet Charity (Bob Fosse, 1968)

Sweet Hereafter, The (Atom Egoyan, 1997)

Sweet Sweetback's Baadasssss Song (Melvin Van Peebles, 1971)

Swoon (Tom Kalin, 1992)

Sword in the Stone, The (Wolfgang Reitherman, 1963)

Ta'm e Guilass (Abbas Kiarostami, France/ Iran, 1997)

Tape (Richard Linklater, 2001)

Targets (Peter Bogdanovich, 1967)

Tarzan and His Mate (Cedric Gibbons, 1934)

Taxi Driver (Martin Scorsese, 1976)

Teaching Mrs Tingle (Kevin Williamson, 1999)

Teenage Mutant Ninja Turtles (Steve Barron, 1990)

Tell Them Willie Boy Is Here (Abraham Polonsky, 1969)

Tender is the Night (Henry King, 1962)

Tender Mercies (Bruce Beresford, 1982)

Terminal Man, The (Mike Hodges, 1973)

Terminator, The (James Cameron, 1984)

Terminator 2: Judgment Day (James Cameron, 1999)

Terminator 3: Rise of the Machines (Jonathan Mostow, 2003)

Terms of Endearment (James L. Brooks, 1983)

Texas Chain Saw Massacre, The (Tobe Hooper, 1974)

That Darn Cat (Robert Stevenson, 1965)

That's Entertainment (Jack Haley Jr., 1974)

They Shoot Horses Don't They? (Sydney Pollack, 1969)

Thieves Like Us (Robert Altman, 1974)

Thin Blue Line, The (Errol Morris, 1988)

Thin Ice (Fiona Cunningham-Reid, 1995)

Thing, The (John Carpenter, 1982)

Thing from Another World, The (Christian Nyby, 1951)

Thirteen (Catherine Hardwicke, 2003)

Thomas Crown Affair, The (Norman Jewison, 1968)

Thoroughly Modern Millie (George Roy Hill, 1967)

Those Magnificent Men in Their Flying Machines (Ken Annakin, 1965)

Thousand Clowns, A (Fred Coe, 1965)

Three Colours Blue/Trois couleurs Bleu (Krzysztof Kieslowski, France/ Switzerland/ Poland, 1993)

Three Days of the Condor (Sydney Pollack, 1975)

Three Seasons (Tony Bui, 1999)

Thunderball (Terence Young, 1965)

Thunderbolt and Lightfoot (Michael Cimino, 1974)

THX1138 (George Lucas, 1971)

Timecode (Mike Figgis, 2000)

Titanic (James Cameron, 1997)

Titus (Julie Taymor, 1999)

TNT Jackson (Cirio H. Santiago, 1974)

To Catch a Thief (Alfred Hitchcock, 1955)

To Kill a Mockingbird (Robert Mulligan, 1963)

To Sir with Love (James Clavell, 1967)

To Sleep with Anger (Charles Burnett, 1990)

Tom Jones (Tony Richardson, 1963)

Tomb of Ligeia, The (Roger Corman, 1964)

Too Late Blues (John Cassavetes, 1961)

Tootsie (Sydney Pollack, 1982)

Top Gun (Tony Scott, 1986)

Topkapi (Jules Dassin, 1964)

Tora! Tora! Tora! (Richard Fleischer and Kinji Fukasaku, 1970)

Total Recall (Paul Verhoeven, 1990)

Touch of Class, A (Melvin Frank, 1973)

Towering Inferno, The (John Guillermin and Irwin Allen, 1974)

Toxic Avenger, The (Michael Herz and Lloyd Kaufman, 1985)

Toy Story (John Lasseter, 1995)

Toy Story 2 (John Lasseter and Ash Brannon, 1999)

Traffic (Steven Soderbergh, 2000)

Training Day (Antoine Fuqua, 2001)

Trapp Family, The (Lee Kresel and Wolfgang Liebeneiner, W. Germany, 1960)

Trash (Paul Morrissey, 1970)

Tree of Wooden Clogs, The/L'Albero Degli Zoccoli (Ermanno Olmi, Italy, 1978)

Trip, The (Roger Corman, 1967)

Trip to Bountiful, The (Peter Masterson, 1985)

Tristana (Luis Buñuel, 1970)

Trouble in Mind (Alan Rudolph, 1986)

Trouble with Dick (Gary Walkow, 1987)

Trouble with Harry, The (Alfred Hitchcock, 1955)

Troublesome Creek: A Midwestern (Jeanne Jordan and Steven Ascher, 1995)

Troy (Wolfgang Petersen, 2004)

True Grit (Henry Hathaway, 1969)

True Love (Nancy Savoca, 1989)

Trust (Hal Hartley, 1991)

Twelve Angry Men (Sidney Lumet, 1957)

Twilight Zone – The Movie (Joe Dante and John Landis, 1983)

Twins (Ivan Reitman, 1988)

Twister (Jan de Bont, 1996)

Two Days in the Valley (John Herzfeld, 1996)

Two-Lane Blacktop (Monte Hellman, 1971)

Two Mules for Sister Sara (Clint Eastwood, 1971)

Two Weeks in Another Town (Vincente Minnelli, 1962)

Ulzana's Raid (Robert Aldrich, 1972)

Unagi (Shohei Imamura, Japan, 1997)

Unbelievable Truth, The (Hal Hartley, 1990)

Undead, The (Roger Corman, 1959)

Under Fire (Roger Spottiswoode, 1983)

Underground (Emir Kusturica, 1995)

Underneath, The (Steven Soderbergh, 1995)

Une Aussi Longue Absence (Henri Colpi, France/Italy, 1961)

Unforgiven (Clint Eastwood, 1992)

Untouchables, The (Brian De Palma, 1987)

Urga/ Close to Eden (Nikita Mikhalkov, France/USSR, 1991)

Usual Suspects, The (Bryan Singer, 1995)

Vagabond /Sans toit ni loi (Agnès Varda, France, 1985)

Vaghe stelle dell'Orsa (Luchino Visconti, Italy, 1965)

Valley of the Dolls (Mark Robson, 1967)

Vanishing Point (Richard C. Sarafian, 1971)

Velvet Vampire, The (Stephanie Rothman, 1971)

Vertigo (Alfred Hitchcock, 1958)

Very Bad Things (Peter Berg, 1998)

Videodrome (David Cronenberg, 1983)

V.I.Ps, The (Anthony Asquith, 1963)

Viridiana (Luis Bunuel, 1961)

Vive l'amour/Aiqing wansui (Tsai Ming-liang, Taiwan, 1994)

Von Richtofen and Brown (Roger Corman, 1970)

Von Ryan's Express (Mark Robson, 1965)

Voyage to the Bottom of the Sea (Irwin Allen, 1961)

Vozvraščenje (Andrej Zvjagintsev, 2003)

Waking Life (Richard Linklater, 2001)

Wall Street (Oliver Stone, 1987)

Water and Power (Pat O'Neill, 1989)

Watermelon Woman, The (Cheryl Dunye, 1996)

Way of the Dragon, The (Bruce Lee, 1972)

Way We Were, The (Sydney Pollack, 1973)

We Were Soldiers (Randall Wallace, 2002)

Wedding, A (Robert Altman, 1978)

Wedding Banquet, The (Ang Lee, 1993)

Weight of Water, The (Kathryn Bigelow, 2000)

Welcome to the Dollhouse (Todd Solondz, 1995)

West Side Story (Robert Wise, 1961)

Westworld (Michael Crichton, 1973)

Whatever Happened to Baby Jane? (Robert Aldrich Hammer, 1962)

What Happened Was... (Tom Noonan, 1994)

What's New, Pussycat? (Clive Donner, 1965)

What's Up, Doc? (Peter Bogdanovich, 1972)

When Father Was Away on Business/Otac Na Sulzbenom Putu (Emir Kusturica, Yugoslavia, 1984)

When Night is Falling (Patricia Rozema, 1995)

When Time Ran Out... (James Goldstone, 1980)

Where Eagles Dare (Brian G. Hutton, 1968)

Who Framed Roger Rabbit? (Robert Zemeckis, 1988)

Who's Afraid of Virginia Woolf? (Mike Nichols, 1966)

Who's That Knocking at My Door? (Martin Scorsese, 1968)

Wild Angels, The (Roger Corman, 1966)

Wild at Heart (David Lynch, 1990)

Wild Bunch, The (Sam Peckinpah, 1969)

Wild in the Streets (Barry Shear, 1968)

Wilderness Family, The (Stewart Raffill, 1975)

Willie Dynamite (Gilbert Moses, 1974)

Willow (Ron Howard, 1988)

Wiz, The (Sidney Lumet, 1978)

Wizard of Oz, The (Victor Fleming, 1939)

Woman Under the Influence, A (John Cassavetes, 1974)

Women in Cages (Gerardo de Leon, 1971)

Women in Love (Ken Russell, 1969)

Woodstock (Michael Wadleigh, 1970)

Working Girl (Mike Nichols, 1988)

Working Girls (Lizzie Borden, 1987)

X – The Man With X-Ray Eyes (Roger Corman, 1963)

X-Men (Bryan Singer, 2000)

Year of Living Dangerously, The (Peter Weir, 1982)

Year of the Quiet Sun, The/Rok Spokojnego Slonca (Krzysztof Zanussi/USA/GFR, 1984)

Yentl (Barbra Streisand, 1983)

Yol/The Road (Serif Gören, Switzerland, 1982)

You Can Count On Me (Kenneth Lonegran, 2000)

Young Frankenstein (Mel Brooks, 1974)

Young Guns 2 (Geoff Murphy, 1990)

Young Soul Rebels (Isaac Julien, 1991)

Your Friends and Neighbors (Neil LaBute, 1998)

Z (Costa Gavras, France/Algeria, 1969)

Zabriskie Point (Michelangelo Antonioni, 1970)

Zero Patience (John Greyson, 1993)

Zorba the Greek (Michael Cacoyannis, 1964)

Documentary Films

4 Vertigo (Les Leveque, 2000)

A.K.A. Don Bonus (Sokly Ny and Spencer Nakasako, 1995)

ABC anthology title: Close-Up

Absolutely Positive (Peter Adair, 1991)

All My Babies (George C. Stoney, 1953)

Alone: Life Wastes Andy Hardy (Martin Arnold, 1998)

Antarctica (John Weiley, 1991)

Atomic Café, The (Jayne Loader and Kevin Rafferty, 1982)

Back Steps, The (Leighton Pierce, 2001)

Baraka (Ron Fricke, 1992)

Basic Training (Fred Wiseman, 1971)

Behind Censorship: The Assault on Civil Liberties (Deep Dish Satellite, 1991)

Beirut: the Last Home Movie (Jennifer Fox, 1987)

Berkeley in the 60s (Mark Kitchell, 1991)

Best Boy (Ira Wohl, 1979)

Black Is ... Black Ain't (Marlon Riggs, 1995)

Bowling for Columbine (Michael Moore, 2002)

Broken Noses (Bruce Webber, 1987)

Burden of Dreams (Les Blank, 1982)

Calling the Ghosts (Mandy Jacobson and Karmen Jelincic, 1996)

CBS Reports: Harvest of Shame (November 1960)

CBS Reports: Hunger in America (Charles Kurault, 1968)

Chair, The (Robert Drew, 1962)

Chiefs (Leacock, 1969)

Chronique d'un été (Morin and Rouch, France, 1960)

Cirque du Soleil: The Journey of Man (Keith Melton, 2000)

Civil War, The (Ken Burns, 1990)

Columbia Revolt (Uncredited, 1968)

Common Threads: Stories from the Quilt (Rob Epstein and Jeffrey Friedman, 1989)

Deaf (Fred Wiseman, 1987)

Dear America: Letters Home From Vietnam (Bill Couturie, 1987)

Decasia (Bill Morrison, 2001)

Deseret (James Benning, 1995)

Devil Never Sleeps, The (Lourdes Portillo, 1994)

Diana's Hair Ego: AIDS Info Upfront (Ellen Spiro, 1989)

Don't Look Back (Donn Pennebaker, 1967)

El Pueblo Se Levanta (Uncredited, 1971)

El Valley Centro (James Benning, 2000)

Ethnic Notions (Marlon Riggs, 1987)

Everest (David Breashears and Stephen Judson, 1998)

Fahrenheit 9/11 (Michael Moore, 2004)

Family Album, A (Alan Berliner, 1986)

Far From Poland (Jill Godmilow, 1984)

Fast Food Women (Anne Lewis Johnson, 1992)

Fast Trip, Long Drop (Gregg Bordowitz, 1991)

Fear of Blushing (Jennifer Reeves, 2001)

Fifty Feet of String (Leighton Pierce, 1995)

Film of Her, The (Bill Morrison, 1996)

Finding Christa (Camille Billops and James Hatch 1991)

First World Order (Philip Mallory Jones, 1994)

Fog of War, The (Errol Morris, 2003)

Four Corners (James Benning, 1997)

Frontline (TV, Michale Kirk, Katerina Monemvassitis, Ofra Bikel, 1983-present)

Gap-Toothed Women (Les Blank, 1987)

Gate of Heavenly Peace, The (Carma Hinton and Richard Gordon, 1996)

Gates of Heaven (Errol Morris, 1980)

Gimme Shelter (Albert Maysles and David Maysles, 1970)

Girl's Nervy, The (Jennifer Reeves, 1995)

Good Fight, The (Mary Dore, Noel Buckner, Sam Sills, 1983)

Grey Gardens (Ellen Hovde, Albert Maysles, 1976)

Gringo in Mananaland (Dee Halleck, 1995)

Gulf Crisis TV Project, The (Paper Tiger Television, 1990)

Happy Mothers Day (Leacock, ABC, 1962)

Harlan County, USA. (Barbara Kopple, 1976)

Healthy Baby Girl, A (Judith Helfand, 1996)

Hell's Angels Forever (Richard Chase and Leon Gast, 1983)

Hide and Seek (Su Friedrich, 1996)

High School (Frederick Wiseman, 1968)

Human Remains (Jay Rosenblatt, 1998)

I Need Your Full Cooperation (Kathy High, 1989)

Imagine: John Lennon (Andrew Solt, 1988)

In Heaven There is No Beer? (Les Blank, 1984)

In the Year of the Pig (Emile de Antonio, 1969)

Intimate Stranger (Alan Berliner, 1991)

Is This What You Were Born For? (Abigail Childs, 1989)

J'ai Été Au Bal/I Went to the Dance (Les Blank, 1989)

Jollies (Sadie Benning, 1989–1990)

Koyaanisqatsi (Godfrey Reggio, 1983)

Las Madres: The Mothers of the Plaza De Mayo (Susana Munoz and Lourdes Portillo, 1988)

Law and Order (Frederick Wiseman, 1969)

Leche (Naomi Uman, 1998)

Les Raquetteurs/Snowshoes (Michel Brault, Canada, 1958)

Let's Get Lost (Bruce Webber and Nan Bush, 1988)

Life and Times of Rosie the Riveter, The (Connie Field, 1980)

Lonely Boy (Roman Kroiter and Wolf Koenig, 1962)

Louisiana Story (Robert J. Flaherty, 1948)

March of Time (newsreel series, 1935–1951)

Married Couple, A (Allen King, 1969)

Media Machete: The Chiapas Media Project Media (Paper Tiger Television, 1998)

Meet Marlon Brando (David and Albert Maysles, 1966)

Microscosmos (Claude Nuridsany and Marie Pérennou, FRANCE/IT/Switzerland, 1996)

Missile (Frederick Wiseman, 1988)

Missing Young Women (Lourdes Portillo, Mexico, 2001)

Model (Frederick Wiseman, 1980)

Monterey Pop (D.A. Pennebaker, 1968)

My America: Or Honk If You Love Buddha (Renee Tajima-Pena, 1997)

NAFTA: A Three Way Tie for Last (Paper Tiger Television, 1993)

Naked Spaces: Living is Round (Trinh T. Minh-ha, 1985)

Nation Erupts, The (Not Channel Zero Collective, 1992)

Near Death (Fred Wiseman, 1989)

Nobody's Business (Alan Berliner, 1996)

North on Evers (James Benning, 1992)

Nuer, The (Robert Gardner, 1970)

Obsessive Becoming (Daniel Reeves, 1995)

On the Pole (screened by CBS)

Out at Work (Tami Gold and Kelly Anderson, 1996)

Paris is Burning (Jennie Livingston, 1990)

Place Called Lovely, A (Sadie Benning, 1989–1990)

Powaqqatsi (Godfrey Reggio, 1988)

Primary (Robert Drew, 1960)

Public Access (Bryan Singer, 1993)

Racetrack (Fred Wiseman, 1984)

Rachel's Daughters (Allie Light and Irving Saraf, 1997)

Reassemblage (Trinh T. Minh-ha, 1982)

Red Shovel (Leighton Pierce, 1992)

Removed (Naomi Uman, 1999)

Roger and Me (Michael Moore, 1989)

Salesman (Al Maysles, 1968)

Salesman (David and Albert Maysles, 1969)

San Francisco State: On Strike (1969)

See It Now (Don Hewitt, CBS Documentary series, 1951–58)

Seeing Red (Jim Klein and Julia Reichert, 1983)

Senorita Extraviada (Lourdes Portillo, 2001)

Seventeen (Joel DeMott and Jeff Kreines, 1983)

Sherman's March: A Meditation on the Possibility of Romantic Love in the South During an Era of Nuclear Weapons Proliferation (Ross McElwee, 1986)

Shoot for the Contents (Trinh T. Minh-ha, 1991)

Showdown in Seattle (Paper Tiger Television, 1999)

Sick and Tired of Being Sick and Tired (Deep Dish Satellite, 1994)

Silverlake Life: The View from Here (Peter Friedman, Tom Joslin and Mark Massi, 1993)

Sink or Swim (Su Friedrich, 1990)

Six O'Clock News (Ross McElwee, 1996)

Smell of Burning Ants, The (Jay Rosenblatt, 1994)

Sonic Outlaws (Craig Baldwin, 1995)

Space Station 3D (Toni Myers, 2002)

Spin (Brian Springer, 1995)

Sprout Wings and Fly (Les Blank, 1983)

Stop the Church (Robert Hilferty, 1990)

Store, The (Fred Wiseman, 1983)

Streetwise (Martin Bell, 1984)

Struggles in Steel: A Story of African American Steelworkers (Tony Buba, 1996); *Two Towns of Jasper* (Whitney Dow and Marco Williams, 2002); *First Person Plural* (Deann Borshay Liem, 2000)

Study of a River (Peter Hutton, 1996)

Super Size Me (Morgan Spurlock, 2004)

Surname Viêt Given Name Nam (Trinh T. Minh-ha, 1989)

Take Over (Pamela Yates and Peter Kinoy, 1992)

Teach Our Children (Adam Jones, 1980)

Testing the Limits' Voices from the Front (Sandra Elgear and Robyn Hutt, 1992)

Thin Blue Line, The (Erroll Morris, 1988)

This is What Democracy Looks Like (Big Noise Films, 2000)

Ties that Bind (Su Friedrich, 1984)

Time and Tide (Peter Hutton, 2000)

Times of Harvey Milk, The (Robert Epstein and Richard Schmiechen, 1984)

Titicut Follies (Fred Wiseman, 1967)

Toby and the Tall Corn (Willard Van Dyke 1954 – TV)

Tongues Untied (Marlon Riggs, 1989)

Tribulation 99: Alien Anomalies Under America (Craig Baldwin, 1999)

Twilight Psalm 11: Walking Distance (Phil Solomon, 1999)

Victory at Sea (Henry Salamon, NBC, 1952)

Waiting for the Moon (Jill Godmilow, 1987)

Weather Diaries (George Kuchar, 1990–1995)

Welcome to Normal (Sadie Benning, 1989–1990)

What's Happening: The Beatles in the USA (Albert and David Maysles, 1964)

When the Mountains Tremble (Pamela Yates, Tom Sigel, and Peter Kinoy, 1983)

Who Killed Vincent Chin? (Christine Choy and Renee Tajima, 1989)

Why Cybraceros (Alex Rivera, 1995)

Wife Swap (Martin Fuller and Sam Maynard, 2003-)

Winged Migration (Jacques Perrin and Jacques Cluzaud, 2001)

Women's Film, The (Louise Alaimo and Judy Smith, 1971)

X 1/2.: The Legacy of Malcolm X (Not Channel Zero Collective, 1993)

Yanki No! (Robert Drew, 1960)

Zapatista (Big Noise Films, 1998)

Television

Alfred Hitchcock Presents (Revue Studios, 1955–62)

Alias (Touchstone Television/Bad Robot, J.J. Abrams, 2001-present)

Amazing Stories (Amblin Entertainment/ Universal TV, Steven Spielberg, 1985–1997)

Animaniacs (Amblin Entertainment/Warner Bros Television et al., Steven Spielberg, 1993–98)

Band of Brothers (Dreamworks Television/ HBO/BBC et al., Steven Ambrose/Tom Hanks/Steven Spielberg, 2001)

Beavis and Butthead (MTV Animation, Mike Judge/Yvette Kaplan, 1993–97)

Buffy the Vampire Slayer (WB/UPN, Joss Whedon, 1997–2003)

CBS 60 Minutes (CBS, Don Hewitt, 1968-present)

Charlie's Angels (Spelling/Goldberg, Ivan Goff/Ben Roberts, 1976–1981)

Dallas (Lorimar Television, David Jacobs, 1978–91)

Dark Angel (20th Century Fox Television, James Cameron/Charles H. Eglee, 2000–2002)

ER (Amblin Entertainment/John Wells Productions, Michael Crichton, 1994-present)

P.O.V. (PBS, Marc Weiss, 1988-present)

Quatermass II (BBC, Nigel Kneale, 1955)

Seinfeld (Castle Rock Entertainment/West Shapiro, Larry David/Jerry Seinfeld, 1990-98)

Simpsons, The (20th Century Fox Television, Matt Groenig, 1989-present)

Star Trek (Desilu Productions et al., Gene Roddenberry, 1966–69)

Taken (Dreamworks Televsion, Leslie Bohem/ Steven Spielberg, 2002)

X-Files, The (Fox, Chris Carter, 1993- 2002)

Xena: Warrior Princess (MCA Television Entertainment Inc./Renaissance Pictures et al., John Schulian/Robert G. Tapert, 1995– 2001)

INDEX

Page numbers for figures have *f*, those for tables have *t*. Where Illustrations in the plate section are referred to in the text the page number has *p*.

Blacula (film), 136, 146, 194
Blade Runner (film), 232*p*, 240*p*, 329, 360
Blank, Les, 295
The Black Hole (film), 175, 231, 272
The Blackout (film), 362
The Black Stallion (film), 132
The Blair Witch Project (film), 137, 326, 328
blaxploitation, 184–98
'blaxploitation' movies, 147–9, 184–98, 389
Blazing Saddles (film), 146, 179*f*, 195, 269, 415
blimped camera for sound dampening, 451
Bloch, Robert, 134
Block, Bill, 354
blockbuster movies:
    defined, 451
    part of the industry, 240–1, 244–5
    (1960's), 45–6
    (1970s), 164–81
    spectacle and narrative (1990's), 334–55
Blonde Cobra (film), 65
Blood Feast (film), 134
Blood Simple (film), 136, 330
Bloody Mama (film), 21
Blow-Up (film), 34, 69, 82
Blue, J., 84
Blue Steel (film), 332, 360, 414, 421
Blue Velvet (film), 136, 212, 226, 235, 359
The Blue Max (film), 47
The Blues Brothers (film), 164
B movie, defined, 451
Bob and Carol and Ted and Alice (film), 19, 19*f*
Bodies That Matter (Butler), 403
Bodily Harm (film), 360
Body Chemistry (film), 22
Body Double (film), 225
Body Heat (film), 225, 360
Body of Evidence (film), 361
Bogart, Humphrey, 353
Bogdanovich, Peter, 20, 22, 35, 134, 150, 300
Bogdanovitch, Mitch, 77
Bogle, D, 185

Bondanella, P., 29
Bonfire of the Vanities (film), 376
Bonnie and Clyde (film), 6*p*, 7, 8, 14*p*, 15, 16, 24, 34, 92, 96, 97, 99, 104, 125, 133, 147, 252
Boogie Nights (film), 429, 437
Boorman, John, 92, 120, 232
Borden, Lizzie, 248, 254, 307, 360
Bordowitz, Greg, 386
Bordwell, David, xxi, 29, 106, 120, 250, 335, 343, 349, 434, 435
Born in Flames (film), 307
Born on the Fourth of July (film), 160, 237, 280, 287
Bornstein, Kate, 403
The Born Losers (film), 281
Bosom Buddies (TV), 376
Boss, Pete, 33
Bottin, Rob, 135
Bottle Rocket (film), 429
Bound (film), 360, 406
The Bourne Identity (film), 372
Bowie, David, 82, 297
Bowling for Columbine (film), 289
Boxcar Bertha (film), 22, 133
Box Office Champs (Kay), xxi
box office figures:
    (1960-2004), xix
    (1960's), 108
    (1970's), 213
    (1980's), 315
    (1990's), 440
A Boy and His Dog (film), 231
Boyarin, Daniel, 302
Boyd, Stephen, 41
Boyd, T., 195
Boyle, D., 203
Boys Don't Cry (film), 261, 262, 403, 405, 407
The Boys in Company C (film), 282, 283
Boyz in the Hood (film), 330, 393, 394, 396
Braindead (film), 33
Brakhage, Stan, 64, 70, 252
Branagh, Kenneth, 55
Brando, Marlon, 150, 283
Brandon, Teena, 403
Brassed Off (film), 327
Brault, Michel, 77

Brayne, Bill, 83
Brazil (film), 368
Breezy (film), 132
A Bridge Too Far (film), 164
A Brief History of Time (film), 248, 293
Bride of Chucky (film), 336
Bride of Frankenstein (film), 344
Bridges, Jeff, 302
Bring Me the Head of Alfredo Garcia (film), 105, 147
The Bride with White Hair (film), 336
The Bridge on the River Kwai (film), 57, 100
The Brink's Job (film), 180
British Film Institute *see* BFI (British Film Institute)
Broadcast News (film), 300
Brodesser, Claude, 354
Brody, J.D., 193
Brokaw, Frances Seymour, 161
Brokeback Mountain (film), 338
Broken Flowers (film), 330
Broken Noses (film), 294
Bronston, Samuel, 51
Brooks, James L., 406
Brooks, Mel, 176, 212
Brooks, Richard, 80, 119
Brooks, Xan, 255, 256
The Browning Version (film), 260
Brother of the Wind (film), 270
Brown, David, 49
Brown, James, 194
Brown, Rita Mae, 307
Bruckheimer, Jerry, 238, 430
Bruiser (film), 32
Brunsdon, Charlotte, 305
Bruzzi, S., 193
Bryman, A., 276
Buba, Tony, 380
A Bucket of Blood (film), 21
Bucklland, Warren, 256
Buckner, Noel, 291
Buck Rogers in the 25th Century (film), 175
Buddy (film), 303
Buddy Holly Story (film), 81
Buena Vista, 258, 266
Buffalo Bill and the Indians (film), 105
Buffy the Vampire Slayer (film), 411

PUBLISHER'S ACKNOWLEDGEMENTS

The authors and the publisher would like to thank the following for their help in supplying and granting permission to use the following images:

Cover images

Do the Right Thing, courtesy of The Kobal Collection
Jaws, courtesy of The Kobal Collection
Blue Steel, courtesy of The Kobal Collection
Easy Rider, courtesy of The Kobal Collection
Kill Bill, courtesy of The Kobal Collection

Title page

Batman, courtesy of The Kobal Collection

1960s Section

Easy Rider, courtesy of The Kobal Collection
Badlands, courtesy of The Kobal Collection
Bob & Carol & Ted & Alice, courtesy of The Kobal Collection
Roger Corman, courtesy of The Kobal Collection
The Sound of Music, courtesy of The Kobal Collection
Night of the Living Dead, courtesy of Aquariuscollection
Cleopatra, courtesy of The Kobal Collection
*M*A*S*H*, courtesy of Aquariuscollection
Cabaret, courtesy of Aquariuscollection
Chelsea Girls, courtesy of The Kobal Collection
Don't Look Back, courtesy of The Kobal Collection
Woodstock, courtesy of Aquariuscollection
101 Dalmatians, courtesy of Aquariuscollection
Psycho, courtesy of The Kobal Collection
Reds, courtesy of Aquariuscollection

1970s Section

Jaws, courtesy of The Kobal Collection
Catch-22, courtesy of The Kobal Collection
The Towering Inferno, courtesy of The Kobal Collection
Carrie, courtesy of The Kobal Collection
Dirty Harry, courtesy of The Kobal Collection
One Flew Over the Cuckoo's Nest, courtesy of The Kobal Collection
Taxi Driver, courtesy of The Kobal Collection
Klute, courtesy of The Kobal Collection
Steven Spielberg and E.T., courtesy of The Kobal Collection
Star Wars, courtesy of The Kobal Collection
Blazing Saddles, courtesy of The Kobal Collection
The Exorcist, courtesy of The Kobal Collection
Sweet Sweetback, courtesy of Aquariuscollection
Eraserhead, courtesy of The Kobal Collection

1980s Section

Top Gun, courtesy of Aquariuscollection
Robocop, courtesy of The Kobal Collection
Pee Wee's Big Adventure, courtesy of The Kobal Collection
Matewan, courtesy of The Kobal Collection
Back to the Future, courtesy of The Kobal Collection
Apocalypse Now, courtesy of The Kobal Collection
Pumping Iron, courtesy of The Kobal Collection
Let's Get Lost, courtesy of The Kobal Collection
Yentl, courtesy of The Kobal Collection
Desperately Seeking Susan, courtesy of Aquariuscollection
Aliens, courtesy of Aquariuscollection
Producer Sherry Lansing with director Adrian Lyne on the set of *Indecent Proposal*, courtesy of The Kobal Collection

1990s Section

Jurassic Park, courtesy of Aquariuscollection
The Killer, courtesy of The Kobal Collection
Gladiator, courtesy of The Kobal Collection
Die Hard 2, courtesy of The Kobal Collection
Virginia Madsen, *The Hot Spot*'s **consummate** *femme fatale*, courtesy of The Kobal Collection
Toy Story, courtesy of Aquariuscollection
Paris is Burning, courtesy of The Kobal Collection

Allen and Albert Hughes on the set of *Menace II Society*, courtesy of Aquariuscollection
Boyz in the Hood, courtesy of The Kobal Collection
Poison, courtesy of The Kobal Collection
The Silence of the Lambs, courtesy of The Kobal Collection
Unforgiven, courtesy of The Kobal Collection
The Matrix, courtesy of Aquariuscollection
Strange Days, courtesy of The Kobal Collection
Donnie Darko, courtesy of The Kobal Collection
Reservoir Dogs, courtesy of The Kobal Collection

Colour Plates Section

1960s

Mary Poppins, courtesy of Aquariuscollection
Bonnie and Clyde, courtesy of The Kobal Collection
Hello Dolly!, courtesy of The Kobal Collection
West Side Story, courtesy of Aquariuscollection

1970s

The Exorcist, courtesy of Aquariuscollection
The Godfather Part II, courtesy of The Kobal Collection
American Graffiti, courtesy of The Kobal Collection
Grease, courtesy of The Kobal Collection
Alien, courtesy of The Kobal Collection
Sleeper, courtesy of The Kobal Collection

1980s

Indiana Jones and the Temple of Doom, courtesy of The Kobal Collection
Heaven's Gate, courtesy of The Kobal Collection
Blade Runner, courtesy of The Kobal Collection
Do the Right Thing, courtesy of The Kobal Collection
Gloria, courtesy of The Kobal Collection
Pink Flamingos, courtesy of The Kobal Collection

1990s

Winged Migration, courtesy of The Kobal Collection
Armageddon, courtesy of The Kobal Collection
Pulp Fiction, courtesy of The Kobal Collection

The Incredibly True Adventure of Two Girls in Love, courtesy of The Kobal Collection
American Beauty, courtesy of The Kobal Collection

Notes
A version of 'New Queer Cinema' appeared as the Introduction in Michele Aaron (ed.) *New Queer Cinema: A Critical Reader* (Edinburgh: Edinburgh University Press, 2004).
'Smart Films' is an updated version of an article which first appeared in *Screen* 43:4 (2002).